ΠΟΤΑΜΙΚΟΝ

Sinews of Acheloios

A Comprehensive Catalog of the Bronze Coinage of the Man-Faced Bull, with Essays on Origin and Identity

Written and edited by

Nicholas J. Molinari

and

Nicola Sisci

Archaeopress Archaeology

ARCHAEOPRESS PUBLISHING LTD
Gordon House
276 Banbury Road
Oxford OX2 7ED

www.archaeopress.com

ISBN 978 1 78491 401 1
ISBN 978 1 78491 402 8 (e-Pdf)

Cover illustration: Bronze litra of Herbessos, c. 338 to 336 BC, depicting Acheloios Herbessos as a man-faced bull (Image courtesy of Classical Numismatic Group, Inc., Lancaster, PA and London, England; Background image features a segment of the Black Sea, courtesy of NASA).

This book is available direct from Archaeopress or from our website www.archaeopress.com

Printed and bound in Great Britain by Marston Book Services Ltd, Oxfordshire

...τῶν λαμπρῶν πηκτῶν τε ἓν γένος ὑδάτων χαλκὸς συσταθεὶς γέγονεν

...this particular kind of the bright and solid waters, being compounded thus, is termed ‘bronze.’

Plato, *Timaeus*, 59c (W.R.M. Lamb translation)

Contents

Preface

Originally, the primary goal of *Potamikon* was to catalog every known variety of ancient bronze coinage featuring a man-faced bull. But it quickly became much more than a catalog of coins, particularly when we could not find a clear answer as to the identity of the man-faced bull. So we did some investigating, and as the layers unraveled and more and more interesting things emerged, we soon found ourselves peering down a very deep rabbit hole. It turned out that, in order to really understand the identity of the man-faced bull, we'd also have to investigate the origin of the iconography. Against our better judgment, and prompted by the enthusiasm of some early contributors (especially David Macdonald and Shannon Glasheen Brock), we decided to jump in, and the book became an investigation into the origin and identity of the man-faced bull, as well as a catalog of coins. This seems fitting, since now the factual data of the catalog is balanced by the theoretical essays of the text. Ultimately, the outpouring of support from an older generation of scholars has been tremendous, and the quality of this book is to a great extent the result of the assistance of others. But the controversial suggestions in this book are all our own (as are any mistakes), and the inclusion of the names of various scholars that we thank at the end of the preface does not indicate that they accept or endorse the content of this book.

Part I of the book examines the origin and identity of the man-faced bull. It will help if we conceptualize this part of the project by borrowing a metaphor employed by Descartes (and later Heidegger): The roots of the man-faced bull tradition, deeply embedded in the human psyche, are in Old European culture, c. 5th Millennium BC. The tiniest tendrils of these roots reach back much deeper into the mixanthropic cave art of Paleolithic times, tens of thousands of years earlier. The trunk of the tree, emerging from the roots, is in the Near-East and also Cyprus. Here the iconography and surrounding mythology are appropriated for a number of uses over thousands of years, each adding a new ring to the tree. At the top of the trunks we have the branches: to India, Egypt, Anatolia, and the western Mediterranean areas of Sicily, Sardinia, and Italy. Each of these branches in turn separates into further branches (like the Hittites, Etruscans, Oscans, Greeks, and others), some of which we follow very closely in Part II of this book. The bronze coinage of the man-faced bull, which this book catalogs, is only a very small part of a truly massive tree.

Part II of the book contains the catalog, which is arranged geographically, then alphabetically, then chronologically. We begin with Sicily and then move to Italy, followed by Akarnania, and then finally we cover the remaining issues, all of which are east of Magna Graecia. Since bronze coinage of the man-faced bull appeared first in Sicily, we decided to start there and then move north and then east. Catalog entries provide denomination, dating, a picture of the coin, obverse and reverse description, weight and diameter (when available), and additional references. Occasionally, a picture or line drawing was not available, and in such cases we digitally modified illustrations that originally appeared in Goltzius' *Sicilia et Magna Graecia, sive, Historiae vrbivm et popvlorvm Graeciae ex antiqvis nomismatibvs* (1644), or similar works. When citing a coin from this book in a section other than its own, we use the following format: The 16th coin listed in the catalog would be listed as MSP I, 16, an abbreviation of 'Molinari Sisci Potamikon, Vol. 1, No. 16'. Most other notes and references throughout the document are in accordance with the *Chicago Manual of Style*, 15th Edition.

The appendix offers the following: First, Curtis Clay's translation of Joseph Eckhel's '*De tauro cum facie humana*,' which he very generously produced for the Potamikon Project. Second, we include Dr. Lloyd W. Taylor's essay on the Indian humped man-faced bull appearing on rare Seleukid bronzes. We end with an extensive bibliography of the sources consulted during the research and writing of this book and general index that includes numismatic devices.

In closing, we would like to thank the following individuals for their contributions to the Potamikon Project:

Shannon Glasheen Brock, Alberto Campana, David MacDonald, N. Keith Rutter, Marina Taliercio-Mensitieri, Rabun Taylor, Vincenzo La Rosa, Massimo Cultraro, Curtis Clay, Alessandro Calciati, Hans-Peter Isler, Angela Rosciano, Frank Hole, Luigi Graziano, Maria Caccamo Caltabiano, Lloyd Taylor, Orazio La Delfa, Alan Walker, Renate M. van Dijk, Andrew Burnett, Andrew McCabe, David Sear, Oliver Hoover, Klaus Vondrovec, M.H. Crawford, Suzanne Frey-Kupper, Maurizio Riguzzi, Brian Kritt, Michel Amandry, J.M. Kenoyer, Jean Donohoe, Massimiliano Bertelli, J.D. Bateson, Richard Abdy, Paolo Nebiolo, Enrico Giovannelli, Alessandro Di Ludovico, Giorgia Gargano, Giacomo Benati, Davide Nadali, Pietro Maria Militello, Luca Girella, Mario Nassa, Maurizia Lucchino, Larissa Bonfante, Francesco Camia, Enrico Giannitrapani, Evangeline Markou, Noemi Ghetti, Andrew Shapland, Chrysanthi Gallou, Anita Crispino, Madame Zerkane of the BnF, Bruno Lambert, John Gomer, August Oberti, Joseph Sermarini and our friends on the Forvm Classical Numismatic Discussion Board, specifically: Peter Hope, Hans-Joachim Hoeft, John Francisco, Martin Rowe, Michael Davis, Mark Fox, Shawn Caza, Jay Grande, Patricia Lawrence, Andreas

Reich, Barry Murphy, Lars Rutten, and Pekka Kemppinen, the Massachusetts Library System Resource Sharing Team, especially Jenn Del Cegno, the Resource Sharing Team of the National Library in Turin, especially Franco Bergamasco, Luisa Szauber, Maria Panucci, Monica Vivolo, Gabriella Ghiano, and Antonella Minotillo, our friends on Lamoneta, the Dallas Museum of Art, the Town of Milford, Massachusetts and the faculty and students of Milford High School, especially Daniel Nelson, Eamon Cunningham, Ben Liberto, and Michael A. Molinari. And, finally, a special thanks to our publisher: Archaeopress of Oxford, and especially David Davison and Rajka Makjanic, for seeing the importance of our book and assisting us throughout its production.

We would also like to thank the following numismatic firms and museums, all of whom allowed use of images, and without whom we would have no book: Classical Numismatic Group, and especially Dale Tatro and Travis Markel; Numismatik Lanz; Numismatica Ars Classica; Gitbud & Naumann and Numismatik Naumann; HD Rauch; Munzen & Medaillen (GmbH); Fritz Rudolf Künker; ArtCoins Roma; AH Baldwin and Sons; Dix Noonan Webb; Auctiones; Gerhard Hirsch Nachfolger; Forvm Ancient Coins; Jean Elsen & ses fils; London Ancient Coins; Nomos AG; Roma Numismatics; Spink and Son; Bibliothèque nationale de France, département des Monnaies, médailles et antiques; the Trustees of the British Museum and the British Museum Department of Coins and Medals.

This book is dedicated to Kate and Pamela, two incredibly patient and supportive women who allowed us to spend many hours fixated on man-faced bulls, when we should have been fixated on them.

Nicholas Molinari & Nicola Sisci

Why the Man-Faced Bull?: A Philosophical Introduction

When the 2004 Indian Ocean Tsunami killed 228,000 people on the coast of Indonesia and the surrounding area, people were reminded of the power of nature, particularly water.[1] Within one day, an entire region was fundamentally changed: entire communities were utterly destroyed, the infrastructure suffered billions of dollars worth of damage, and, perhaps worst of all, families that had existed there for many generations were swept away without a trace. Such experiences are a brutal reminder of the overwhelming power of nature to take away life at a moment's notice, leaving in its wake a brief experience of stark reality.

But there is another, more pleasant side to the coin. Nature gives just as it takes away. Approximately 350,000 people are born each day across the globe.[2] The population is now over seven billion. And that is just human beings. Billions of examples of new life sprout up every instant, from the tiniest single-celled organisms to the largest sea creatures; life is emerging all around us. And who is to say what lies outside of the known universe? Just recently scientists using data from the Kepler telescope estimated that 8.8 billion potentially habitable planets exist in the galaxy.[3] Such numbers are essentially unfathomable, but the point is that nature is literally bursting with life.

Ancient humans faced wild nature on a daily basis, and they were much more actively engaged participants in its unfolding than we are today. They didn't have much of a choice. If not seeking food, they were making sure not to become food. They sought shelter when the gods were angry and rejoiced when they were generous. Humans had to work the earth, or scour it, in order to sustain life. But there was always more to human experience than instinctual responses to external stimuli. It was never just eating, sleeping, and procreating. Human beings paid tribute to the principles of life. They made fertility idols and sketched imitations of nature on the walls of caves. They held festivals that celebrated nature's benefits and participated in somber ceremonies in recognition that it can all be taken away. But ultimately, as part of nature, human beings represent its consciousness. Human experience is the self-reflecting principle of nature in the same way that individual consciousness is the self-reflecting element of the human body, and this has been evident since the very first examples of prehistoric art.

So, at the outset of this work, we ask ourselves: Why the man-faced bull? Why did the ancients find a bull with a human face so appealing? What is it about this iconography that is significant, both to ancient people and to human beings today?

The man-faced bull's significance is grounded in the fact that it best captures the intimate strife at the heart of the relation of nature and man.[4] It is an image that captures two essential things: on the one hand, it represents the wild and unpredictable, though fertile and life-giving qualities of nature as depicted through the bull. Ultimately, the bull represents relentless, bare nature. On the other hand, the addition of a human face captures the intelligibility projected upon nature that man executes as a fundamental part of his existence. Mankind offers to nature a level of consciousness and in doing so, we are able to exert ourselves upon it in the same fashion that it exerts itself upon us: Relentlessly, in a dynamic interplay of reciprocal exertion. The image of a bull with a man's face conveys this basic characteristic that exists between nature and man, and for the authors of this work, no image in the ancient or modern world does a better job.

This book, in a sense, is a tribute to ancient man and his devotion to the man-faced bull. But it is also a tribute to the man-faced bull himself, and to what he represents. Of all the ancient gods it is the man-faced bull that is closest to us. He is not some distant figure making decisions about our fate, or some detached principle of cause and effect. He represents us and our surroundings, and the sacredness of both as one magnificent phenomenon.[5] Apparently, some of the ancient Greeks recognized the particular significance of this image, too, as we see in **Fig.1**, which depicts the Greek pantheon surrounding our beloved man-faced bull, whose head sits on an altar.[6] And in Plato's *Phaedrus*, in which we get a glimpse of Plato's over-arching view of man in relation to the cos-

[1] USGS, 'Magnitude 9.1 – Off the West Coast of Northern Sumatra,' in *U.S. Geological Survey* (U.S. Department of the Interior, 2005).
[2] World Health Organization, '50 Facts: Global health situation and trends 1955-2025,' in *World Health Report* (1998).
[3] C. Moskowitz, 'Kepler Telescope Finds Plethora of Earth-Size Planets,' in *Scientific American* (November 2013).

[4] See below, pg. 24-5 for an examination of Empedocles of Akragas and his association with the man-faced bull. Empedocles believed two underlying forces governed nature, Love and Strife, and he is the only ancient Greek author to mention the man-faced bull in descriptive terms, as βουγενῆ ἀνδρόπρωρα (Fr. 61, Aelian *Nat. anim.* XVI, 29).
[5] As Jacques Cauvin observes, 'an animal species can be integrated into the bestiary of symbolism of a culture only in so far as, in some manner, the culture recognizes something of itself in the animal and projects on to it some subliminal dimension of its collective psychology' (J. Cauvin, *The Birth of the Gods and the Origins of Agriculture*, translated by Trevor Watkins (Cambridge UP, 2000), 123).
[6] Greek, c. 370 BC, Pergamon Museum, Berlin.

mos, the dialogue takes place in the most appropriate of places, a shrine to Acheloios[7] on the banks of a river.[8]

Ultimately, it is our belief that the man-faced bull is much more than a clever depiction of a river-god. On coinage alone the image is remarkably widespread, and the meanings attached to this image, as we will soon see, are varied yet thoroughly interwoven.[9] Sometimes he appears in tombs, deep underground, mediating between two worlds. Sometimes he appears on coinage, triumphantly standing while being crowned by nymphs. In some traditions, he is said to be a protector of children, while in others, he is a fearsome creature subdued by the might of Herakles. Whatever the custom, since his beginning some 7,000 years ago in Neolithic agricultural communities, he has been worshiped by millions of people for thousands of years. But in the end, he is always intimately related to water, and as water he is part of us.[10] For the man-faced bull is the god of water and as such, as Thales[11] attested, the originating, underlying, and final principle of all things.

---

[7] There are many different orthographic representations for Acheloios. Throughout this text we will use 'Acheloios,' as it is closest to Homer and Hesiod's Ἀχελώϊος, whereas 'Achelous' is the Latin version of Ἀχελῷος, a later term employed by Plato, Apollodorus, Euripides, Herodotus, Thucydides, Plutarch, Pausanias, and others.

[8] Plato, and H.N. Fowler, *Plato: Phaedrus* (Cambridge, MA: Harvard University Press, 2001), 230c.

[9] Rabun Taylor puts it best: 'Water- particularly in its earthbound, chthonic manifestations- carries powerful intimations of fertility and increase. The same element can be a force of death and destruction. Its symbolism is interesting precisely because it is binary. Water is life and death. It nurtures and it kills; it strengthens and it enfeebles' (R. Taylor, 'River Raptures: Containment and Control of Water in Greek and Roman Constructions of Identity,' in *The Nature and Function of Water, Baths, Bathing, and Hygiene from Antiquity through the Renaissance*, edited by Cynthia Kosso and Anne Scott (Leiden: Brill, 2009), 21-22).

[10] About 60% of the average human body is composed of water.

[11] Thales of Miletus (c. 7th century BC) posited the notion that everything existing in the world comes from water, the governing origin of nature: 'Θαλῆς μὲν ὁ τῆς τοιαύτης ἀρχηγὸς φιλοσοφίας ὕδωρ φησὶν εἶναι› (H. Diels, and W. Kranz, *Die Fragmente der Vorsokratiker* (Berlin: Weidmann, 1952), 11 A 12=Aristotle, *Metaphysics* 983b). Artistotle uses ὕδωρ, not Ἀχελώϊος, but the entire account is very much second-hand, relying on Aristotles' assumption that Thales' philosophy involved the dynamics of moisture, ὑγρός. L. Posteraro saw the origins of this philosophy already appearing in Homeric epic, in which many heroes of the Trojan War are sons of rivers, and, upon dying, return to the rivers (L. Posteraro, 'Origine di Alife. Simbolismo delle sue tradizioni e della sua moneta,' in *R.I.N.* (1916), 318).

Part I:

Concerning the Origin and Identity of the Man-Faced Bull

Section One

On the Origin of Man-Faced Bull Iconography

Introduction

In order to have a meaningful discussion on the identity of the man-faced bull in Magna Graecia and the surrounding area, it is first necessary to investigate its appearance throughout history. The image of the man-faced bull was in use for well over 5,000 years, and spanned an enormous geographical area: on Greek coinage alone it covers nearly 2 million square kilometers, and nearly double that if one includes the rare issues from Ai Khanoum, on the eastern edge of modern Pakistan.[1] Despite the incredibly vast area and time period covered, there appears to be a central theme, water, and a single point of origination, Old Europe. The goal of this chapter is to shed light on the iconography as it shifted throughout time from one culture to the next and in doing so, perhaps we can begin to unravel the underlying thread that binds together all these manifestations. The intercultural processes that link one area to the next are admittedly highly complex and often difficult to define, as one faces pathways that do not appear along a single line but, rather, are the result of a series of segments that are to be read, interpreted, and reassembled by the investigator. Nonetheless, this chapter does demonstrate that the figure of the man-faced bull has characteristics to which many different cultures can relate. Moreover, although the addition of a human head to an animal is a common component of ancient religious iconography, we suggest this particular iconography was absorbed, adapted, and modified from one culture to the next as it made its way around the ancient world.

Ultimately, in Part I of this book we suggest that the origin and development of man-faced bull iconography involved two primary waves of diffusion in the ancient world: a first wave of diffusion during the Bronze Age that produced a fertile background upon which a second wave of diffusion was superimposed in the course of the first centuries of the 1st millennium BC, primarily during the orientalizing and archaic periods. While the first wave of diffusion begins in Old Europe and spreads outward through Anatolia and into Cyprus, Italy, and the Near East, the second wave is primarily from East to West. Although the man-faced bull himself appears only twice in Bronze Age Sicily, water cults and the imagery of the bull are widespread in the area, and archaeological evidence attests to eastern elements influencing the area from a very early date (4th millennium BC), providing some additional evidence to support the notion of a common origin of the man-faced bull tradition.[2] Thus, while consistent cultural continuity for man-faced bull iconography is not fully demonstrated in this work, we do exhibit some important indicators that lay the groundwork for its later establishment.

Chapter I: Paleolithic Art-Iron Age

Paleolithic Art[3]

Our story begins very early indeed, and not even in Magna Graecia or with man-faced bulls, but instead on the banks of a river in Paleolithic Europe, where a curious depiction of a bison man appears in Chauvet Cave of southern France, dating to about 30,000 BC (**Fig. 2**). A pubic triangle stands before the Bison man, and above the two appears the forepart of a lion. The entire scene is depicted on a 'phallic-like protuberance' at the very end of the End Chamber of the cave, a spot set apart from the rest of the art and reinforcing the scene's significance for Paleolithic visitors.[4] The protuberance is surrounded by walls covered with a fascinating array of animal depictions, and bones from various species are scattered about. The ceilings and floors are covered with millions of calcite crystallizations and stalagmite and stalactite emerge all around. Nearby there is an altar with a bear skull placed on top. A small natural pool that might have served some ritual function appears in one of the inner chambers. The entire phenomenon of Chauvet Cave is indeed magical, and an appropriate place for the emergence of what might be the man-faced bull's earliest ancestor.[5] In his film, Werner Herzog goes so far as to

---

1 The northernmost appearance is Istros. The southernmost appearance is Kyrene (North Africa). Technically, the easternmost appearance is Ai Khanoum (eastern Pakistan), but the square kilometers were calculated using Cilicia, because there are no other issues between Cilicia and the rare examples from Ai Khanoum, some 2,000 miles east. The westernmost appearance is Arse (eastern Spain).

2 There is also genetic evidence that indicates that inhabitants of modern Tuscany who share DNA with ancient Etruscans emigrated from somewhere outside of the Italian peninsula (S. Ghirotto, et al., 'Origins and Evolution of the Etruscans' mtDNA,' in *PLoS ONE* 8(2): e55519 (2013), 4). In fact, this group shares DNA with modern Anatolians, indicating both groups have a distant relation, possibly in the area of Old Europe and the Black Sea, dating to c. 7,600 BC, just before the emergence of the man-faced bull. The date would be 5,000 BC if one assumes complete isolation of the modern Tuscan and Anatolian populations after the split, which is unrealistic. 7,600 years ago is suggested by the authors as more likely. Ibid., 4-6.

3 Paleolithic Europe is the subject of this section, but other anthropomorphic and zoomorphic iconographies appear in cave art in the Indus Valley during the Upper Paleolithic period. See J.M. Kenoyer, 'Master of Animals and Animal Masters in the Iconography of the Indus Tradition,' in *The Master of Animals in Old World Iconography*, edited by D. B. Counts and B. Arnold (Budapest, 2010), 39.

4 For an overview of the archaeological site, see: J. Clottes, *Return To Chauvet Cave, Excavating the Birthplace of Art: The First Full Report* (London: Thames & Hudson, 2003).

5 For a visual trip through Chauvet Cave, see W. Herzog, 'The Cave of Forgotten Dreams,' Documentary Film (North Hollywood: Creative Differences, 2011).

suggest this very place is where man gained his spirit.[6] And it is here with our very first bull man where one can identify elements that, quite remarkably, will consistently reappear with the man-faced bull in various cultures all the way through to the Greek world some 29,500 years later: caves and the subterranean world,[7] the notion of fertility and reproduction, bucrania and other skulls (presumably) used in apotropaic ritual, the positioning of an antagonistic lion above, and, most importantly, water,[8] as the underlying element of the entire enterprise.[9]

Over the next 10,000 to 20,000 years man-bull hybrids begin to appear in several places in southern Europe: on a cave painting at le Gabillou, France, dated 19,000 to 16,000 BC;[10] a bull man from Cueva de la Pileta, Spain, dated to c. 13,000 BC; another at Caverne des Espélugues, Southern France.[11] There are additional examples of bull and bison men from the surrounding area, all from about the same time period. The 'sorcerer' identified by Henri Breuil in Trois-Frères, Ariège, France, is somewhat similar in appearance to a man-faced bull, insofar as it has a human-like face, but the figure's horns are more moose-like.[12] There is another bull-man from the same cave, this one surrounded by a herd of animals and playing a flute (an early indication of the taming of animals?).[13] Another example, from la Pasiega, c. 16,000 to 14,000 BC, appears to be an ithyphallic man-bull and has the general appearance of an apotropaic deity (**Fig. 3**).[14] Finally, what appears to be a man-faced bison appears at Niaux, Ariège, France, dating to c. 17,000 to 12,000 BC,[15] and is apparently the closest iconographic relative to the man-faced bull from Paleolithic times (**Fig 4**). Due to the layered nature of cave art absolute identification is impossible, since the image appears to be drawn over another. [16] However, even if the design was not intentional, the image of a bearded man's face would have been as obvious to Paleolithic observers as it is to us today.

This man-bull combination of Paleolithic art and its obvious association with fertility, combined with the likely notions of the repulsion of evil and the taming of animals, is similar to the later man-faced bull traditions of other cultures. The iconography itself and its fixed location indicate a very primitive recognition of the special relationship of nature and man, and also demonstrate the self-reflective nature of our early ancestors. Therefore, while these are not man-faced bulls and did not immediately precede them, they do represent a visual recognition of the interplay of nature and man, a recognition later articulated in the man-faced bull tradition which probably evolved, at least to some extent, from these early bull men of Paleolithic art.

Cattle Cults

An important social phenomenon marks the transition from Paleolithic bull-men to true man-faced bulls, and that is the emergence of 'cattle cults' and the domestication of cattle throughout the Old World,[17] including Anatolia,[18] the Fertile Crescent,[19] Europe,[20] India,[21] and Cyprus.[22] The domestication of cattle is said to have occurred first in the Near East, c. 8,000 to 10,000 BC,[23] although evidence of a separate domestication for the *Bos indicus* around the same time is strong.[24] Most domestic cattle, with few exceptions, stem from *Bos primigenius namadicus*, which had a range covering almost the entire Old World.[25]

[6] Ibid.

[7] Raybun Taylor (personal correspondence, Summer 2015) points out that caves naturally preserve such works, and that many other iconographies at Chauvet probably have nothing to do with their being drawn on cave walls. This is a fair criticism, but we decided not to omit mention of this because the bison man occupies such a fundamental position in the cave, painted on a central protuberance. Thus, in our view, it is *his* cave.

[8] The river outside Chauvet, flowing through Pont d'Arc, is an important landmark. As we will see in the Greek world, the man-faced bull will appear in many places alongside rivers. While one cannot directly tie the bison man of Chauvet to these fluvial elements, they are worth mentioning, especially since he appears to be the central figure of the cave.

[9] This is not to say there was cultural continuity from this bison man to the first man-faced bulls, but perhaps this is evidence of a natural psychological pairing of these accompanying features.

[10] According to O. Fuentes, this figure resembles Pan but has a bull's head, and appears to be playing a flute. See O. Fuentes, 'The depiction of the individual in prehistory: human representations in Magdalenian societies,' in *Antiquity*, Vol. 87, No. 228 (2013), 985-1000.

[11] M. Gimbutas, *The Language of the Goddess* (California: UP, 1974), 176-178, figs. 275-276.

[12] N.K. Sandars, *Prehistoric Art in Europe* (London: Penguin, 1968), fig. 73.

[13] Ibid.,fig. 74.

[14] La Pasiega, Anthropomorph, c. 16000 to 14000 BC, in M. Gimbutas, *Language of the Goddess*, 176-178, figs. 275-276.

[15] Painted man-faced (?) bison from Niaux, Ariège, France. N.K. Sandars, *Prehistoric Art in Europe*, fig. 57.

[16] It is worth noting, however, that in the Near East there are many man-faced bison appearing contemporaneously with man-faced bulls.

[17] D. Wengrow, 'Rethinking 'Cattle Cults' in Early Egypt: Towards a Prehistoric Perspective on the Narmer Palette,' in *Cambridge Archaeological Journal*, 11:1 (2001), 91.

[18] D. Perkins, Jr., 'Fauna of Çatal Hüyük: Evidence for Early Cattle Domestication in Anatolia,' in *Science*, New Series, Vol. 164, No. 3876 (1969), 177-179.

[19] Cf. H. Frankfort, *The Birth of Civilization in the Near East* (Bloomington: Indiana University Press, 1951).

[20] Cf. I. Hodder, *The Domestication of Europe* (Oxford: Blackwell, 1990).

[21] R. T. Loftus, et al., 'Evidence for Two Independent Domestications of Cattle,' in *Proceedings of the National Academy of Sciences of the United States of America*, Vol. 91, No. 7 (1994), 2757-2761.

[22] Cf. V. Karageorghis, *The Coroplastic Art of Ancient Cyprus* (Nicosia: A.G. Leventis Foundation, 1991).

[23] H. Epstein, *The Origin of the Domestic Animals of Africa*, Vol. 1 (New York: Africana Publishing Corp., 1971).

[24] R. Loftus, 'Evidence for Two Independent Domestications of Cattle,' 2757-2761. For an argument that African cattle did not necessarily come from the Near East, as traditionally thought, see: W.P. McHugh, 'Cattle Pastoralism in Africa—A Model for Interpreting Archaeological Evidence from the Eastern Sahara Desert,' in *Arctic Anthropology*, Vol. 11, Supplement: Festschrift Issue in Honor of Chester S. Chard (1974), 236-244.

[25] W.J.A. Payne, *Cattle Genetic Resources*, edited by C.G. Hickman (Amsterdam: Elsevier, 1991), 51-72. *Bos taurus* have been found at Mohenjo-Daro and Harappa sites c. 2250 BC.

Nearly coinciding with this domestication of cattle was the emergence of said 'cattle cults,' and evidence of the pervasive use of bucrania for various religious practices abounds in the following sections. Cattle quickly became an integral part of the day-to-day lives of people, both practically and spiritually.[26] In most cases such cattle cults were probably intimately related to water, too. In the modern world, it takes approximately 816,000 gallons of water to raise and sustain one cow throughout its life.[27] Perhaps it was less in ancient times, but the modern figures are still revealing for our purposes: an abundance of water is absolutely essential to the lives of cattle, and so the water-bull association has roots as old as the domestication of cattle itself, since only a constant source of water, likely a river, could sustain a herd.[28]

In his essay, David Wengrow argues the term 'cult' understates the significance of the early incorporation of cattle into the daily existence of man, suggesting instead a 'pervasive investment of human values in cattle... that seems likely to have been woven into the political and economic, as well as spiritual, aspects of social life.'[29] Cattle were used in place of human sacrifices;[30] as a medium of exchange, including compensation for crimes;[31] and as a means of transferring family status from one generation to the next.[32] His arguments concern mostly Pre-Dynastic Egypt, where cattle cults were migratory, but they can probably be extended without difficulty to the entire Old World, since such early groups of humans operated in very similar ways regardless of location. In fact, the very first agricultural communities, the Khamian sites in the Levant, which date 10,000 to 9500 BC, employed the iconography of the woman and bull, particularly at Mureybet in the north,[33] where bull skulls and other parts are found used in ritual practices.

The pervasive importance of cattle and their incorporation into human experience helps set the stage for our analysis of the emergence of man-faced bull iconography. Although the debate about a strictly agricultural or religious origin is open,[34] and it was probably an interplay of both, the domestication of cattle in general represents, on one level, a domestication of humans, for it was not until the incorporation of cattle into the daily lives of people that the need for farming came to the forefront,[35] and with it, civilization's emergence. It should be no surprise then that the first man-faced bulls appear in Neolithic times, at the dawn of human civilization.

Neolithic Art

It is in Old Europe that the first true man-faced bulls appear, thousands of years before the motif would be adopted into the culture of the Greek world and much earlier than previously suggested.[36] The very first of these, a man-faced bull from Fafos II at Kosovo Mitrovica, has (intentionally?) broken horns and an M inscribed on its chest, indicating that the figure is a fluvial deity.[37] Another important specimen, **Fig. 5**, from Karanovo VI culture, second half of the 5th millennium BC,[38] is an ithyphallic man-faced bull.[39] The object is a vessel that contained white paste, its head acting as the cap. It was found at Goljam Izvor, in Bulgaria, just west of the Black Sea, during regular excavations in 1931. Interestingly, on it, too, the left horn appears to be broken. Another nearly identical piece also has a slightly broken horn.[40] The broken horn is very likely an intentional feature of these artifacts; in fact, there is similar evidence throughout Neolithic times. Milos Spasic reports many bovine figurines with 'intentionally broken horns' found in Vinča culture sites from the early 5th millennium BC.[41]

[26] Cf. J. Cauvin, *The Birth of Gods and the Origins of Agriculture*.

[27] Sean McNaughton, Jason Lee, Jane Vessels, Mollie Bates, and Rebecca Hale, 'Hidden Water,' in *National Geographic*, April 2010 Supplement (Washington D.C.: National Geographic Partners, 2010), citing the work of A.Y. Hoekstra and A.K. Chapagain, *Globalization of Water*, Water Footprint Network, University of Twente, Netherlands, waterfootprint.org.

[28] For the importance of water to Neolithic peoples, see M. Johnson, 'Water, animals and agricultural technology: a study of settlement patterns and economic change in Neolithic southern Greece,' in *Oxford Journal of Archaeology* 15, 3 (1996), 267-95.

[29] D. Wengrow, 'Rethinking 'Cattle Cults' in Early Egypt,' 98.

[30] G. Lienhardt, *Divinity and Experience: The Religion of Dinka* (Oxford: Clarendon Press, 1961).

[31] D. Wengrow, 'Rethinking 'Cattle Cults' in Early Egypt,' 93.

[32] Ibid.

[33] J. Cauvin, *The Birth of Gods and the Origins of Agriculture*, 23-28. At Mureybet, bull skulls, horns, and shoulder-blades have been found buried in benches and, later, walls, from 10,000 BC.

[34] For a good overview, see E. Isaac, 'On the Domestication of Cattle' in *Science*, New Series, Vol. 137, No. 3525 (1962), 195-204.

[35] F. Hassan, 'The Predynastic Egypt,' in *Journal of World Prehistory*, Vol. 2 (1988), 136-85. See also W. Wetterstrom, 'Foraging and farming in Egypt: the transition from hunting and gathering to horticulture in the Nile Valley,' in *The Archaeology of Africa: Food, Metals and Towns*, edited by T. Shaw et al., One World Archaeology Series, 20 (London: Routledge, 1993), 165-226.

[36] H.P. Isler suggests but does not prove a connection between the Greek Acheloios and the Near Eastern man-faced bull in H.P.Isler, *Acheloos: Eine Monographie* (Bern, 1970), 92ff.

[37] M. Gimbutas, *The Goddesses and Gods of Old Europe*, fig. 237, dating 5000 to 4500 BC. Broken horns described in M. Gimbutas, *The Language of the Goddess*, 180. The 'M' symbol, or chevron, and its relation to water is discussed in ibid, 20. G. Semerano agrees with the fluvial connotation corresponding to the pre-historic M (G. Semerano, *L'infinito. Un Equivoco Millenario. Le antiche civiltà del vicino oriente e le origini del pensiero greco* (Milano: Mondadori, 2001), 14). M. Maric discusses the importance of water insofar as it relates to the sites Neolithic people (Vinča) chose to inhabit, claiming it provided abundance and protection, but also could be dangerous, indicating a clear understanding of the binary nature of water among the first people to employ man-faced bull iconography : 'Encircled in water, these sites were fully dependent on its dynamics and occasional perils caused by annual or seasonal flooding. On the other hand, such a vivid environment formed and shaped by water provided a bounty of goods, resources, and experiences that helped sustain these sites for hundreds of years' (M. Maric, 'Encircled in Water: Modelling watercourses of the late Neolithic- early Copper Age Vinča culture sites in the Danube region (c. 5300-4500 BC),' in *Quaternary International* XXX (2014), 9).

[38] DeLay Veselinov Dilov, Regional History Museum in Razgrad, personal correspondence with authors.

[39] The figure might have very small stylized wings, but it is uncertain.

[40] T. Ivanov, 'Two Religious Courts of Razgrad,' in *Art*, 9-10 (1981), 72.

[41] 'Almost all the figurines I have had the chance to see have broken horn tips, which in many cases certainly was not the result of clumsiness

This characteristic is strongly reminiscent of the much later figurative representations of the myth of Acheloios, whose horn was broken off by Herakles and became the cornucopia, a symbol of abundance and fertility, but also representative of the taming of rivers in general.[42] In addition, there is evidence from Vinča sites that drainage waterways situated around settlements operated as defensive barriers against rival groups, providing the first ever association between a culture employing man-faced bull iconography and the use of waterways as a defensive tool, which becomes, in terms of general apotropaic associations, a hallmark of the man-faced bull tradition in other geographic locations.[43]

Another Old European man-faced bull also comes from Karanovo VI, displayed in the Kardzhali Regional Historical Museum,[44] and another is from Karanovo V,[45] now in the Regional History Museum of Stara Zagora. Marina Gimbutas, in *The Gods and Goddesses of Old Europe,* lists some additional man-faced bulls or bulls with 'human masks':[46] a crouching man-faced bull from Gumelniţa;[47] a bull with human eyes from Sitagroi, Macedonia;[48] and another man-faced bull from Valač, this one also with the fluvial 'M,' but appearing on its forehead.[49] All of these pieces further confirm that the man-faced bull was an iconographic model fairly often represented in prehistoric art. Finally, a piece described by Gimbutas as a 'female death goddess,' is probably another man-faced bull head **(Fig.6a)**.[50] Its death connotation also should be noted, as it is the first of many funerary associations with the man-faced bull.

Spasic reports some bucrania made of clay, 'resembling the heads of hybrid human/animal and anthropomorphic representations,'[51] from excavations at Vinča culture sites dated to the early 5th millennium BC.[52] Bucrania themselves appear over a large geographical area, from the Near East to Central Europe, and they are often found in archaeological contexts related to Neolithic and Chalcolithic agro-pastoral communities[53] and later in Bronze Age contexts widespread from Asia to Western Europe, including Cyprus and North Africa. Such artifacts have been interpreted by scholars as either religious symbols associated with deities, or as totems representing the group of people using them; or even as objects linked to funerary rites revealing a belief in the afterlife.[54] The widespread use of the bucrania symbol in the prehistoric world is 'a profound and intimate display of the complex relationship between man and beast.'[55] Bucrania were made either in clay or by casting a real bovine skull in clay. In the context of Vinča culture those made entirely of clay were introduced later than those made from real skulls, and 'became more hybrid, resembling a similar representational shift in anthropomorphic imagery.'[56] Bucrania were often placed inside houses and meant to bless inhabitants with fertility, or buried within the walls of buildings. They were even hung on the outer walls of buildings, meant to protect inhabitants.[57] Many bucrania have been found in house foundation deposits, pits, and burials.[58] Other scholars have pointed out how Mesopotamian bucrania represented fertility.[59] Evidence of the use of horns[60]

and/or careless handling by Vinča people and such fragmentation is not the result of post-depositional effects. [...]the practice of breaking the horns of bull figurines is undoubtedly closely connected with social practice, ideology and various other social agents in Vinča culture. Thus the fragments could have operated as a part of a broader idea or concept of humanity/animality' (M. Spasic, 'Cattle to settle – bull to rule: on bovine iconography among Late Neolithic Vinča culture communities,' in *Documenta Praehistorica XXXIX* (2012), 302).

42 The symbolic meaning of fertility and sexuality in relation to the broken horn is very ancient, evidence of such associations dating to c. 25,000 BC. For example, the cave sculpture known as 'Laussel Venus' found in 1911 at Marquay in Dordogne, France (today stored in the Musée D'Aquitane in Bordeaux). It is one of the earliest known relief sculptures of human art, depicting a voluptuous female figure, whose left arm draws attention to her large abdomen and vulva, and in her right arm she holds a bison horn, incised with 13 lines, possibly symbolizing 13 moons and 13 menstrual cycles in one year. See J.R. Roberts, *History of the World* (New York: Penguin, 1976); A. Marshack, *The Roots of Civilization* (Mount Kisco (NY): Moyer Bell Ltd, 1991), 335. For a recent association of horns with fertility in the ancient Near East, see J.G. Frazer, *Adonis Attis Osiris: Studies in the History of Oriental Religion* (La Vergne: Kessinger, 2003) 123.

43 M. Maric, 'Encircled in Water: Modelling watercourses of the late Neolithic- early Copper Age Vinča culture sites in the Danube region (c. 5300-4500 BC),' 5-7. In some cases (e.g. Bajbuk), the settlements were 'flanked on two sides' by the water of the rivers, indicative of the dual apotropaic man-faced bulls we will see in the Near East, where they operate as apotropaic deities (ibid., 9).

44 A. Raduncheva, 'Eneolithic craft-manufacturing center of the Sedlare villiage of Kardzhali,' in *Yearbook of the National Archaeological Museum*, X (1997), 162-175, fig. 4.

45 P. Kaltchev, *Neolithic Dwelling of Stara Zagora.* Exposition Catalog, (Stara Zagora: Regionalen istoricheski muzeĭ, 2005), 50.

46 M. Gimbutas, in *The Language of the Goddess*, re-attributes some of these figures as goats or 'centaurs,' but the earlier identification seems to better reflect the iconography and related mythology.

47 c. 4500 BC. M. Gimbutas, *The Goddesses and Gods of Old Europe, 6500-3500 BC, Myths and Cult Images* (Berkeley: University of California, 1982), fig. 240.

48 c. 4500 BC. Ibid., fig. 241.

49 c. 4500 to 4000 BC. Ibid, fig. 238.

50 From M. Gimbutas, *The Living Goddess* (Oakland: University of California Press, 2001), 23, fig. 14a.

51 M. Spasic, 'Cattle to settle – bull to rule,' 301.

52 Ibid., 299, fig. 3 (Gomolava); 300, fig.6.1; 301, fig.7 (Jakovo); 303, fig. 11.3 (Stubline).

53 M. Spasic, 'Cattle to settle – bull to rule,' 297-8.

54 R. M. van Dijk, 'The Motif of the Bull in the Ancient Near East: An Iconographic Study,' Unpublished MA Thesis (University of South Africa, 2011), 11-38.

55 Ibid., 38.

56 M. Spasic, 'Cattle to settle – bull to rule,' 305.

57 See R.M. van Dijk, 'The Motif of the Bull,' 17, for the Early Bronze Age site of Alacahoyuk in Anatolia.

58 M. Spasic, 'Cattle to settle – bull to rule,' 298; N. Russel, *Social Zooarchaeology: Humans and Animals in Prehistory* (Cambridge University Press, 2012).

59 J. Mellaart, *Earliest Civilizations of the Near East* (New York: McGraw-Hill, 1965), 124. See also R.M. van Dijk, 'The Motif of the Bull,' 18, for the meaning of bucrania found in ancient burials as apotropaic devices providing protection to the deceased in African late Paleolithic sites; and see ibid., 25, for the same meaning in First Dynastic Period Egypt.

60 E. Alba, 'L'Ipogeo della Nurra,' in *L'Ipogeismo nel Mediterraneo: origini, sviluppo, quadri culturali: atti del Congresso internazionale, 23-28 maggio 1994, Università degli studi di Sassari, Facoltà di Lettere e filosofia, Istituto di Antichità, arte e discipline etnodemologiche e Dipartimento di Scienze umanistiche e dell'antichità*, Vol. 2 (Sassari, 2000), 761-778.

and bull protomes[61] to decorate burials is widespread in Neolithic, Chalcolithic, and Bronze Age Sardinia: E. Alba reports 34 burials in which horns and protomes are interpreted as representations of a male bull-deity acting as protector of graves and symbol of regenerative power, partner of a Mother-goddess whose statuettes are often associated with graves.[62] An interesting aspect of the use of sculpted bull heads in Sardinian prehistoric graves lies in their association with false doors carved into walls, in which case the accompanying bull represents a liminal deity: guardian of the door between the world of the living and the dead.[63] The same theme of the false door, either carved or painted in red, appears in many orientalizing and archaic Etruscan tombs.[64] The false doors in funerary contexts are known even in Egypt by the end of the fourth to the second half of the 2nd millennium BC.[65] Evidence also exists of bull-shaped wooden coffins used since prehistoric times until the Iron Age in Maiorca.[66] At the other end of the Mediterranean Sea, in prehistoric Cyprus (discussed in depth in the next chapter), bucrania were used as masks by priests during religious rituals, as attested by figurines found in archaeological excavations. Also in Cyprus one finds evidence of bucrania used to decorate places of religious significance.[67] It is remarkable when comparing all of the aforementioned evidence with the usual find spots of Etruscan man-faced bull heads and masks, used as apotropaic antefixes in temples, or those found in burials.[68] A further interesting point of connection concerns archaeological evidence for 3rd millennium BC Mesopotamian man-faced bull heads with apotropaic 'door guardian' functions, discussed in depth below.[69]

All of these examples of man-faced bulls combined with the parallel use of (sometimes) anthropomorphic bucrania suggest that the man-faced bull was a cultic image of Old Europe well-rooted in early agrarian societies,[70] and that this figure exhibited fluvial, apotropaic, chthonic, and liminal characteristics. Moreover, if the man-faced bull of Old Europe was part of the overall cultural scheme of the time, then it seems plausible that some elements of it would have persisted in later civilizations. When considering the later associations of the man-faced bull with water, fertility, the repulsion of evil, and death, this will become clearer. Ultimately, it seems that in these early examples of man-faced bulls there is a tribute to the interplay of nature and man in early agrarian society that would later emerge in the civilizations of the Near East, India, Egypt, Cyprus, and, eventually, the Greek world.[71]

The Near East and Levant

The iconography of the man-faced bull probably migrated from Old Europe to the Near East during the 'Ubaid' period,[72] when the first large scale water works

[61] G. Tanda, *Arte preistorica in Sardegna. Le figurazioni taurine scolpite dell'Algherese nel quadro delle rappresentazioni figurate degli ipogei sardi a 'domus de janas'* (Sassari, 1977); P. Basoli, and A. Foschi Nieddu, 'La Tomba delle Protomi Taurine in località Montalé (Sassari),' in *RSP*, XL (1988).

[62] E. Alba, 'L'Ipogeo della Nurra,' 766. For pottery with bull protomes in relief found in Sardinian prehistoric graves, see G. Ugas 'Strutture insediative seminterrate e ipogeismo sepolcrale nella Sardegna Preistorica,' in *L'Ipogeismo nel Mediterraneo*, 890.

[63] G. Bacco, 'La necropoli ipogeica di Campumajore-Busachi (OR),' in *L'Ipogeismo nel Mediterraneo*, 973; G. Meloni 'Le domus de janas del Logudoro-Mejlogu,' in *L'Ipogeismo nel Mediterraneo*, 796.

[64] F.J.Tritsch, 'False Doors on Tombs,' in *JHS*, 63 (1943), 113-5; M. Cristofani, 'Storia dell'arte e acculturazione: le pitture tombali arcaichedi Tarquinia,' in *Prospettiva* (1976), 2-10; R.A. Staccioli, 'Le finte porte dipinte nelle tombe arcaiche etrusche,' in *Quad Chieti*, 1 (1980), 1-17; J.R. Jannot, 'Sur les fausses portes étrusques,' in *Latomus*, 43, 2 (1984), 273-83; A. Naso, *Architetture dipinte: decorazioni parietali non figurate nelle tombe a camera dell'Etruria meridionale : VII-V sec. a.C.* (Rome:Bretschneider, 1996). Annalisa Tasso marks a correlation between these findings in the West and the symbol of the false door in Eastern Mediterranean funerary art, which depicts the symbol of a snake near the false door, representing both an apotropaic power and, coming from the underground, a chthonic deity. A. Tasso, *Pylai aidao: un percorso iconografico e letterario sulla diffusione del tema delle Porte dell'Ade da oriente a occidente* (Oxford: Archaeopress, 2013).

[65] E. Bresciani, *Grande enciclopedia illustrata dell'antico Egitto* (De Agostini, 2005).

[66] G. Pons, 'Sarcòfagos tauromorfos en la Protohistòria Mallorquina,' in *Rev. de Arqueologia*, 83 (Madrid, 1988), 32-9; H. Gornés, 'Ipogei del Talaiotico finale: analisi e interpretazione della necropoli di Cales Coves, Minorca,' in *L'Ipogeismo nel Mediterraneo*, 20 (2000), 559.

[67] R.M. van Dijk, 'The Motif of the Bull,' 36.

[68] For the use of man-faced bull masks as antefixes in places of worship and in tombs in the Etruscan and Greek worlds, see Chapter 4.

[69] F.A.M. Wiggermann, *Mesopotamian Protective Spirits: The Ritual Texts* (Groningen: STYX & PP Publications, 1992), 176, citing M.R. Behm-Blancke, *Das Tierbild in der Altmesopotamischen Rundplastik.* Baghdader Forschungen, Band 1 (Mainz, 1979), 51.

[70] For the hypothesis concerning prehistoric cults related to bull imagery, see: M. Rice, *The Power of the Bull* (London, 1998). See also J. Cauvin, *The Birth of the Gods and the Origins of Agriculture*.

[71] For a study concerning anthropocentrism on Neolithic artifacts, see G. Naumov, 'Neolithic anthropocentrism: the principles of imagery and symbolic manifestation of corporeality in the Balkans,' in *Documenta Praehistorica XXXVII* (2010), 227-238.

[72] There is reasonable evidence to support contact between these areas during this time period. For an overview of Near Eastern (Ubaid) and southern European (Old European) influences in Anatolia throughout the Chalcolithic and Bronze Age, see S.R. Steadman and G. McMahon, *The Oxford Handbook of Ancient Anatolia: (10,000-323 BCE)* (Oxford: University Press, 2011), 159-66. It is worthwhile to quote them: 'In general, it can be said that by the early fifth millennium B.C.E., the whole of Anatolia has seen a change of character. One of the most notable innovations is a shared set of features in the pottery repertoire (both shapes and decoration), which establish a *koiné* that encompasses most of Anatolia but reaches far into the northern Aegean and the southern Balkans. At the same time, however, pottery traits...testify to the continuity of older traditions,' (ibid. 160), which were strongly influenced by the Near East, 'Despite the general eastern influences, there exists a distinctive type of figurine which connects the area to the southern Balkans'(ibid., 164). For earlier Neolithic influence of the Near East on southern Europe, see especially R. King and P.A. Underhill, 'Congruent Distribution of Neolithic Painted Pottery and Ceramic Figurines with Y-chromosome Lineages,' in *Antiquity* 76 (2002), 707-14, which argues that Near Eastern people migrated into southern Europe and spread pottery styles. However, it is certainly reasonable to suggest reciprocal influence from Old Europe to the Near East. See also, R.A. Carter and G. Philip, 'Deconstructing the Ubaid,' in *Beyond the Ubaid: Transformation and Integration in the Late Prehistoric Societies of the Middle East*, edited by R.A. Carter and G. Philip (Chicago: The Oriental Institute of the University of Chicago, 2010), 7. For evidence of long-distance trade within the 'Ubaid Horizon', see G.J. Stein, 'Local Identities and Interaction Spheres: Modeling Regional Variation in the Ubaid Horizon,' in *Beyond the Ubaid: Transformation and Integration in the Late Prehistoric Societies of the Middle East*, 29, which specifically mentions obsidian from eastern Anatolia appearing in southern Mesopotamia,

appear in the Mesopotamian lowlands.[73] These are characterized by man-made channels that allow water to flow to otherwise non-arable land, and also help control flooding and drain excess water from swampy areas. The archaeological evidence shows that along these channels arose settlements, and that this was the first step towards the flowering of urban Mesopotamia, thanks to the widespread availability of fresh surface waters.[74] Ultimately, access to fresh water allowed an increase in agriculture, the introduction of the plow, and consequently an increase in welfare (nourishment supplementation) and resources (increase in craft production, and the start of mass production of ceramics), from which emerged a new economic and political organization, oriented towards centralized political and cultural activities.[75] Given all this, it should be no surprise that the man-faced bull reemerges under these circumstances, as a fluvial god, on two seals from the late Ubaid period **(Fig. 6b and 6c).** [76]

In general, its appearance in this region is less straightforward than in Old Europe, for the people of the ancient Near East and Levant had a very rich mythology full of theriomorphic creatures.[77] In fact, the bull as an object of religious worship in the region dates back to c. 10,000 BC.[78] Two essential problems confront us in the Near East. On the one hand, many different creatures combine human and bovine features and have an accompanying mythology similar to the man-faced bull of the Greek world. On the other hand, actual man-faced bulls appear to be used to represent various mythological figures.[79] To confuse things further, there is the later appearance of the winged man-headed bull, the Assyrian gateway guardian which seemingly found its own way onto Greek coinage; and Gugalanna, another winged man-headed bull who is the notorious combatant of Gilgamesh. Moreover, other man-faced bulls and composite man-bull figures appear in nearby Anatolia and the Levant on cylinder seals.[80] Overall, five major themes are covered in this section, all of which are intimately related to one another and the later Greek and western Mediterranean tradition of man-faced bulls and Acheloios:[81] the bull-man and the mythology of Kusarikku and Tiamat; the appearance of regular, mostly unidentified man-faced bulls; the winged man-headed bull; Gugalanna, the so-called 'Bull of Heaven;' and finally, an analysis of Asallúhi, the god of rivers who carries the epithet 'princely bison,' and may very well be the closest link to the Greek and Etruscan traditions of Acheloios.

The Bull-Man, Kusarikku, and Tiamat

In ancient Mesopotamia, starting in the Early Dynastic Period, the repertoire of Sumerian glyptic art begins to be crowded with mythological beings which modern scholars refer to as 'bull-men,'[82] and such bull-men are called Gud-Alim[83] (Sumerian) or Kusarikku[84] (Akkadian).

---

and mace-heads coming from northern Iran (It is interesting to note a military item coming from the general area Kramer identified as a potential Sumerian origination point, whom he claimed were northern mercenaries that eventually took control of southern Mesopotamia, as discussed in note 76). Stein adds further interesting observations, 'Although fragmentary, the available evidence indicates the existence of a complex web of inter-regional exchange whose individual strands crisscrossed and linked the various regions in the Ubaid horizon' (ibid.). In reference to a standardization of burial practices in the 5th millennium, including the northern regions of Syria, Hole suggests 'this implies that there was a strongly held and widely shared set of beliefs and practices throughout the Ubaid world and even beyond' (F. Hole, 'Symbols of Religion and Social Organization at Susa,' in *The Hilly Flanks and Beyond: Essays on the Prehistory of Southwestern Asia Presented to Robert J. Braidwood*, edited by T.C. Young, P.E.L. Smith, and P. Mortensen (Chicago: The Oriental Institute, 1983), 176).

[73] M. Liverani, *Antico Oriente. Storia società economia* (Bari: Laterza, 2011) 76-79.

[74] Ibid.

[75] Ibid. Traces of influence from Ubaid culture, emerging from archaeological evidence of pottery, are known for Syria, Anatolia, the Euphrates Valley, Iran, and Oman (M. Liverani, *Antico Oriente. Storia società economia*, 81).

[76] For discussion of the seals, see F. Hole, 'A Monumental Failure: the Collapse of Susa,' in *Beyond the Ubaid: Transformation and Integration in the Late Prehistoric Societies of the Middle East*, 236, fig. k and l . For a concise outline of our theory of the diffusion of the iconography, see below, p. 97ff. Kramer was the first to argue that the Sumerians were not native to Mesopotamia, but were an invading force from the north, possibly originating in Tanscaucasia or Transcaspia. His argument is based on literary evidence, in which he explains the Sumerian Heroic Age by comparing it to the Greek, Indian, and Teutonic versions. Ultimately, he argues that mercenaries occupying the outlying rural areas were employed in southern Mesopotamia and eventually overcame those political systems and took power (S. Kramer, 'New Light on the Early History of the Ancient Near East,' in *American Journal of Archaeology* (1948), 158-160). It is interesting that mercenary use and multiculturalism are at the forefront of Kramer's description, just they will be for our discussion of the diffusion of the iconography during the Iron Age and Orientalizing period into the Greek world (see Chapter 2). The latest Old European man-faced bull is from Valač culture, which might date as late as 4000 BC, whereas the first man-faced bulls of the Near East, from Susa, might date as early as 3750 BC. If we rely on a piece from Christie's, 'Mesopotamian Limestone Amulet,' attributed as Late Uruk-Jemdet Nasr Period, c. 3300 to 2900 BC, we have another early example of a man-faced bull in Near Eastern art. Christie's Sale 1734, Antiquities, Lot 45. December, 2006.

[77] Cf. J. Black and A. Green, *Gods and Demons and Symbols of Ancient Mesopotamia* (Texas: UP, 1992).

[78] J. Cauvin, *The Birth of the Gods and the Origins of Agriculture*, 29.

[79] Such figures probably had differentiated identities in the 3rd millennium, as they often appear together in the same contest scene. For example, see the seal impression from the Acropolis of Susa dated mid 3rd millennium BC (R.M. van Dijk, 'The Motif of the Bull,' 71, fig. 6) in which we have a bull-man, a man-headed bull and a 'minotaur,' though the last is an anachronistic naming. Still, the different figures might be derived from a common ancestral prototype, as suggested by F.A.M. Wiggermann, *Mesopotamian Protective Spirits*, 174.

[80] In Anatolia, the iconography of the bull for religious purposes dates to at least 10,000 BC. In fact, a monumental relief sculpture at Çatalhöyük depicts the woman goddess giving birth to the bull. J. Cauvin, *The Birth of the Gods and the Origins of Agriculture*, 29.

[81] In this section we will often use 'Acheloios' in place of 'man-faced bull,' leaving aside the issues of identity considered in the next section.

[82] L. Romano, 'La corona del dio. Note sull'iconografia divina nel Protodinastico,' in *Vicino Oriente XIV Annuario del Dipartimento di Scienze Storiche Archeologiche e Antropologiche dell'Antichità - Sezione Vicino Oriente* (Rome, 2008), 41.

[83] R.M. van Dijk, 'The Motif of the Bull,' 68. F.A.M. Wiggermann, *Mesopotamian Protective Spirits*, 175, reports other forms attested on ancient ritual texts: *GUD.ALIM, GUD.DUMU.AN.NA, GUD.DUMU. dUTU*. The variant *GUD.ALIM* is mostly used to denote the active ithyphallic bison-man. In Ebla, *ALIM* is related to Akkadian *LÛ* (bull). Feminine variants for the name are also attested.

[84] R.M. van Dijk, 'The Motif of the Bull,' 68. For an excellent study of Mesopotamian textual sources for Gud-Alim/Kusarikku, see:

Both mythological figures are generally thought to take on the guise of a man-faced bull or man-faced bison,[85] and as such many of the attributes of Kusarikku the bull-man are thought to carry over to the mythology of the man-faced bull. Unfortunately, the line between the two is unclear, and it is difficult to distinguish which texts naming Kusarriku refer to him as a bull-man, and which refer to him as a man-faced bull. The so-called bull-men usually have the lower body of a bison or bull and the upper body of a human, with a bearded man's face and bovine ears and horns (**Fig. 7**).[86] The first iconographic examples of this creature are in Mesopotamia in the Early Dynastic Period I.[87] Some scholars speculate that the iconography may have originated in Elam,[88] and it is commonly seen in the art of the ancient Sumerian city Girsu, c. 2500 to 2300 BC.[89] Bull-men are still found in the art of the Achaemenid Period, some two millennia later.[90]

On Mesopotamian, Syrian, and Levantine seals, clay plaques, and bas-reliefs, bull-men are often represented in pairs, or even triplicate.[91] They are usually depicted on cylinder seals in 'contest scenes,' engaged in battles with heroes or other beasts, usually lions.[92] Lambert reports an Anatolian seal with the representation of a bull-man with streams of water springing from his body.[93] M. Rice[94] suggests that the bull-man was meant to express man's dominance and control over wild nature.[95] R.M. van Dijk[96] points out how bull-men, although malevolent in the epic visual representations, were more commonly seen as protective beings in ritual texts.[97]

Kusarikku, specifically, appears on ancient Mesopotamian inscriptions concerning ritual practices as a door-keeping apotropaic entity, a symbol inclusive of divine benevolence and prosperity as a so-called 'deputy of life,' indicating the figure's liminal properties.[98] This beneficent and protective function is also made clear by the presence of bull-men among the Lamas goddesses, on the facade of molded bricks of the temple of the Elamite sun-god Inshushinak, built at the end of the 3rd millennium at Susa.[99] The doorkeeping aspect indicates some relation to the later man-faced bull and winged man-faced bull traditions.

There is also archaeological and textual evidence of Kusarikku amulets made of clay, buried in house foundations during building rituals in ancient Mesopotamia (Kusarikku as a bull man, specifically).[100] During such rituals the exorcist buried figures of Kusarikku and other apotropaic beings at several points throughout the house to prevent it from being invaded by evil. As reported by Wiggermann, these buried clay figures have been found in excavations, and the importance of these finds lies in linking textual descriptions with the iconography (This evidence also suggests a connection with the aforementioned Neolithic rituals). In Mesopotamian ritual texts there are clear instructions concerning the nature and material with which these figurines had to be made: with a specific clay from a sacred pit, as ordained for the 'creatures

F.A.M. Wiggermann, *Mesopotamian Protective Spirits*, 176. The scholar reports examples of Kusarikku in a Mesopotamian god list.

85 J. Black and A. Green, *Gods, Demons and Symbols of Ancient Mesopotamia,* 51; A. Green, 'Ancient Mesopotamian Religious Iconography,' in *Civilizations of the Ancient Near East*, edited by J.M. Sasson (Peabody: Hendrickson Publishers, 2000) 1837-1855. See also, D.P. Hansen, 'The Reclining Human-Faced Bison Sculpture from Area SS,' in *Excavations at Tell Brak, Vol. 2: Nagar in the third millennium BC,* 261. Some scholars even argue that the Neo-Assyrian winged man-faced bulls can be identified with the Kusarikku defeated by the god Ninurta in the ancient texts (A. Annus, *The God Ninurta: in the Mythology and Royal Ideology of Ancient Mesopotamia* (Helsinki: Neo-Assyrian Text Corpus Project, 2002), 117). To give substance to his hypothesis the scholar analyzed the details of two particular representations of winged man-faced bulls, suggesting a merging of this figure with the fish-*apkallu* (See below for an analysis).

86 The human face is bearded in most cases, but some examples of early, beardless Near Eastern heads of bull-men are known on seals and sculptures, see: E. Evershed, et al., *Larousse Encyclopedia of Prehistoric and Ancient Art* (London, 1962), 64, fig.78; Faraj Basmachi, *Treasures of the Iraq Museum* (Baghdad: Ministry of Information, 1975), Pl.80; R. L. Zettler and L. Horne, *Treasures from the Royal Tombs of Ur* (Philadelphia: University of Pensylvania Museum of Archaeology Press, 1998), fig.40.

87 L. Romano, 'La corona del dio,' 41.

88 R.M. van Dijk, 'The Motif of the Bull,' 68.

89 In particular, the archaeological site of Telloh, excavated by by E. de Sarzec (1877 to 1900) and A. Parrot (1931 to 1933). Cf. E. de Sarzec, *Découvertes en Chaldéée. Publié par les soins de L. Heuzey. Avec le concours de A. Amiaud et F. Thureau-Dangin* (Paris: E. Leroux, 1884-1912).

90 J. Black and A. Green, *Gods, Demons and Symbols of Ancient Mesopotamia,* 49; R.M. van Dijk, 'The Motif of the Bull,' 243.

91 In archaic and classical Etruria the apotropaic mask of the man-faced bull is often depicted in multiples.

92 There is a seal with a contest scene in which a bull-man is involved, which shows an inscription identifying its owner as a royal servant having the role of 'cupbearer.' J. Oates and D. Oates, 'Archaeological Reconstruction and Historical Commentary,' in *Excavations at Tell Brak, Vol. 2*, 385.The first contest scenes on Mesopotamian seals date back to the late 4th millennium. D. Collon, *First Impressions. Cylinder Seals in the Ancient Near East* (London: British Museum Press, 1987). F.A.M. Wiggermann, *Mesopotamian Protective Spirits*, 177, rejects the modern scholarly tradition identifying the hero with Gilgamesh and the bull-man with Enkidu.

93 W.G. Lambert, 'Trees, Snakes and Gods in Ancient Syria and Anatolia,' in *Bulletin of the School of Oriental and African Studies*, 48-3 (London, 1985), 448. Also reported in R.M.van Dijk, 'The Motif of the Bull,' 70. Lambert believes that the Anatolian representation of the bull-man springing water from his body suggests the merging of the Bull-Man and Lahmu, a Near Eastern river deity. We do not fully agree with Lambert's speculations, although they are plausible. It is much more likely a merging of the bull-man with the water-god Enki (Ea in Akkadian culture). For iconography of Enki with water springing from his body on Mesopotamian cylinder seals of the mid 3rd millennium BC, see: S. Johnston, *Religions of the Ancient World: A Guide* (Cambridge: Belknap Press of Harvard University Press, 2004), 606, fig.9.c. For a visual representation of Enki connected to fluvial and chthonic connotations of man-faced bulls, see **Fig. 11**.

94 M. Rice, *The Power of the Bull,* 272.

95 R.M. van Dijk, 'The Motif of the Bull,' 68.

96 Ibid., 72.

97 This same ambivalence is exhibited in representations of the Greek Acheloios: a violent creature fighting with Herakles in the mythological narratives, but also a protective apotropaic being.

98 F.A.M. Wiggermann, *Mesopotamian Protective Spirits*, 86.

99 R.M. van Dijk, 'The Motif of the Bull,' 249.

100 See F.A.M. Wiggermann, *Mesopotamian Protective Spirits*, in particular Text IV (purification of a new house) and Text V (building ritual, lines 9-23).

of Apsu.'[101] In fact, clay figurines of Kusarikku with inscriptions reading 'go out death, enter life,' have been found in archaeological contexts as well.[102] Many clay plaques showing depictions of Kusarikku as a bull-man have also been discovered in Mesopotamian graves and temples. The plaques were placed within to protect the inhabitants from evil, similar to earlier practices involving bucrania.[103] According to van Dijk, such plaques, functioning as votive and apotropaic objects, were mass produced in open moulds and probably sold near temples.[104] This evidence demonstrates the importance of Kusarikku as an apotropaic figure for the common people of Mesopotamia.[105]

A common attribute of Kusarikku on Mesopotamian visual representations is the *banduddû,*[106] a bucket held by him containing water that was used in purification and healing rituals. This evidence demonstrates a clear connection with the later Greek Acheloios, and the rituals of lustratio linked to his cult. According to Wiggermann, 'in rituals the *banduddû* was filled with water, the exorcist imitates Marduk, who, on the advice of Ea, takes water from the 'mouth of the twin rivers,' casts his spell over it, and sprinkles it over the sick man.'[107]

Kusarikku is also closely related to Tiamat and early Mesopotamian creation myths. In Mesopotamian textual sources dating to the end of the 2nd millennium BC Kusarikku is mentioned among the other creatures created by Tiamat[108] to battle Marduk.[109] In his essay on Ocean and Acheloios, G.B. D'Alessio[110] highlights the relation of Acheloios to Kusarikku and also Tiamat, and makes a very convincing connection between the myths of Acheloios and earlier Near Eastern mythology (both in relation to cosmogony and the labors of Herakles).[111] To briefly summarize: In terms of cosmogony, it is literally from Tiamat that the Tigris and Euphrates are created, and D'Alessio connects this with the notion that, in the Greek tradition, the waterways of the world are essentially sinews of Acheloios.[112] In terms of the labors of Herakles, Tiamat's horns are broken off in a battle with Marduk, much as in the battle of Acheloios and Herakles, in which Herakles breaks off Acheloios' horn.[113] Unfortunately, no iconographic evidence exists and only literary sources can be used to make comparisons. As reported by D'Alessio, Tiamat is not usually an object of Mesopotamian art and so it is

[101] Ibid, 50. In *Enuma Elis*, Tiamat has a husband, called Apsu, described as the subterranean source of sweet water from which rivers are born. Later he will be identified as the abode of Enki (F.A.M. Wiggermann, 'Mythological Foundations of Nature,' in *Natural Phenomena: Their Meaning, Depiction and Description in the Ancient Near East*, edited by D.W.J. Meijer (Amsterdam: North Holland, 1992), 279-304, 283). In the earliest stages of Mesopotamian cosmogony Apsu was intended more as a cosmic structure than a personified deity, as the foundation of the 'Holy Mound,' also called 'Mountain of the Spring,' a procreative cosmic locality (ibid., 285). The Near Eastern man-faced bulls are linked to this myth, as they often appear on cylinder seals represented with forelegs on a mound. For examples, see: F.A.M. Wiggermann, 'Scenes from the Shadow Side,' in *Mesopotamian Poetic Language: Sumerian and Akkadian: Proceedings of the Groningen Group for the Study of Mesopotamian Literature*, edited by M.E. Vogelzang and H.L.J. Vanstiphout (Groningen: Styx, 1996), fig.7-8. There is also a wall painting from the Amorite Palace at Mari, stored at the Louvre, object AO 19825. In addition, there is a depiction in which the man-faced bull appears near a mound from which springs the Tree of Life (S. Johnston, *Religions of the Ancient World,* 601). In the later stages of Mesopotamian cosmogony the modern universe is founded, and it covers the Holy Mound, which sinks away into the depths and becomes a retreat for underworld gods (F.A.M. Wiggermann, 'Mythological Foundations of Nature,' 286). Clearly, all these entangled symbolisms related to the figure of the Near Eastern man-faced bulls (water, fertility, liminal-chthonic, etc.) are strongly reminiscent of the symbolic meanings that will later be related to the figure of Acheloios in the Greek world. A further link is the Mesopotamian seals with man-faced bulls and mounds, from the Mesopotamian texts of the 3rd millennium (F.A.M. Wiggermann, 'Mythological Foundations of Nature,' 286). After the modern cosmos is founded and the Holy Mound goes down in the Underworld, another cosmic entity arises, the 'Foot Hills,' called by Ninurta to prevent the waters from flooding Sumer (ibid.). Once again in this myth there is a potential prototype of another symbolic meaning related to the Greek Acheloios: water control of rivers (For this symbolic meaning related to the figure of the Greek man-faced bull, see H. Di Giuseppe, 'Acheloo e le acque deviate,' in *I riti del costruire nelle acque violate, Atti del convegno internazionale*, edited by H. Di Giuseppe and M. Serlorenzi (Rome, 2010), 69-90). Finally, it is worth recalling that in the ancient world for thousands of years the mound had a funerary purpose.

[102] F.A.M. Wiggermann, *Mesopotamian Protective Spirits*, 51.

[103] J. Black and A. Green, *Gods, Demons and Symbols of Ancient Mesopotamia,* 49.

[104] R.M. van Dijk, 'The Motif of the Bull,' 248-9.

[105] For an example, see ibid., 248, fig. 9.

[106] The *bandudû* is also an attribute of the fish-*apkallu*, which we will discuss in the sub-paragraph on winged man-headed bulls.

[107] F.A.M. Wiggermann, *Mesopotamian Protective Spirits,* 66.

[108] Kusarikku belongs to a group of apotropaic beings called 'the core of Tiamat's army' (F.A.M. Wiggermann, *Mesopotamian Protective Spirits,* 50), or also, 'those of the water of the river,' or, 'those that repel the evil ones, of Ea and Marduk,' (ibid., 164).

[109] J. Bottéro, 'Antiquités assyro-babyloniennes,' in École pratique des hautes études. 4e section, Sciences historiques et philologiques (Annuaire, 1976) 89; J. Bottéro, 'Les noms de Marduk, l'écriture et la 'logique' en Mésopotamie ancienne,' in *Essays on the Ancient Near East in Memory of Jacob Joel Finkelstein*, edited by M. de Jong Ellis (Hamden (CT): Published for the Academy by Archon Books, 1977), 112.

[110] G.B. D'Alessio, 'Textual Fluctuations and Cosmic Streams: Ocean and Acheloios,' in *The Journal of Hellenic Studies*, Vol. 124 (2004), 16-37.

[111] The Greek Herakles (and even more so his Phoenician counterpart, Melqart) are also deities with solar connotations, and so there is a connection in the Greek myths between the man-faced bull and a solar deity. The same connection existed in the Mesopotamian myths of Gud-alim, Kusarikku and the lamassu, as all those figures were related to Shamash, the Akkadian Sun God (A. Green, 'Ancient Mesopotamian Religious Iconography,' 1867 and 1848; J. Aruz and R. Wallenfels, *Art of the First Cities: the Third Millennium B.C. from the Mediterranean to the Indus* (New York: Metropolitan Museum of Art, 2003), 440. The same connection emerges from textual sources. In fact, the form *GUD.DUMU.dUTU* (F.A.M. Wiggermann, *Mesopotamian Protective Spirits,* xi, 176), related to logograms used to denote Kusarikku (see e.g. line 16 of Text IV, 'Purification of a new house,' reported in ibid, 122), points to a relation of the bull-man with the Sumerian Sun God Utu (the Akkadian Shamash). The same relation pertains to the man-faced bull: the apotropaic *SAG-ALIM* ('the head of the man-faced bull/bison') is described in ancient texts as the 'emblem of Utu,' and a mace head with a carved man-faced bull/bison head dated to the Early Dynastic IIIa period was dedicated to Utu (for both evidence and related bibliography see ibid, 176 note 10).

[112] G.B. D'Alessio, 'Textual Fluctuations and Cosmic Streams: Ocean and Acheloios,' 25.

[113] Ibid.

unknown what she actually looked like, apart from having horns and a tail. Kusarikku, however, is often depicted in art as a bull man, man-faced bull, or man-faced bison, as mentioned above.[114] In fact, Kusarikku as a bull-man was depicted in Anatolia until the 8th century BC, as demonstrated by the Herald's wall reliefs stored at the Museum of Anatolian Civilization of Ankara.[115] In any event, as D'Alessio points out, it is Ninurta, often said to be the inspiration for Herakles, who killed Kusarikku in the sea (*tâmit*).[116] Thus, while there is no direct Kusarikku- Acheloios or Tiamat- Acheloios relation, some of the earlier mythology was clearly incorporated into the latter.

Man-faced bulls

There are regular man-faced bulls in Near Eastern culture, too.[117] Although many scholars state that the first Mesopotamian man-faced bulls appeared during the Early Dynastic Period II,[118] published evidence exists of this motif depicted on seals from Ur dated to the Early Dynastic Period I,[119] suggesting that the man-faced bull, in addition to the bull-man, was already embedded in Mesopotamian culture at a very early date. In fact, man-faced bulls seem to appear on the aforementioned seals from Susa (**Fig. 6b and 6c**), dated to the late Ubaid period (mid 4th millennium BC). These man-faced bulls are distinguished by the headdresses they wear that appear on much later winged man-headed bulls of the late Bronze Age and Iron Age. In fact, on **Fig. 6b** the topmost figure has three vertical dashes above him that might represent wings. On **Fig. 6c** there are three horizontal lines that probably represent water gushing from the figure's mouth, which reemerges on later man-faced bull renditions. The identification of these creatures as man-faced bulls rather than regular bulls rests on the headdresses and flat faces, which do not exhibit bovine snouts. In fact, the topmost figure on **Fig. 6b** appears to have a dash indicating a nose and another to indicate a beard. Ultimately, given the contemporaneous waterworks[120] in the area it is reasonable to suggest they are man-faced bulls with distinct fluvial connotations.

The iconography evidently became more popular during the following periods for unknown reasons. In fact, there are many man-faced bulls in Mesopotamian art from the late Early Dynastic Period II[121] up until the Akkadian period.[122] There are also representations of man-faced bulls outside of Mesopotamian lands, in Syria and later in Anatolia, where they are often involved in a contest scene and, much like the bull-man, depicted as opponents of heroes[123] or subdued by lions from above.[124] Another common representation is the man-faced bull with his foreleg raised onto a mound (**Fig. 8**).[125]

There are additional examples of man-faced bulls in Mesopotamian Early Dynastic glyptic art[126] and sculpture. The style can differ considerably[127] depending on the location of finds, but the evidence is consistent with a ritual function for such objects.[128] The famous

[114] J. Black and A. Green, *Gods, Demons and Symbols of Ancient Mesopotamia*, 51.

[115] The relief was found at the ruins of the ancient city of Karkemish, on the frontier between Turkey and Syria

[116] G.B. D'Alessio, 'Textual Fluctuations and Cosmic Streams: Ocean and Acheloios,'26.

[117] For examples of man-faced bulls on Mesopotamian glyptic art of the Early Dynastic Period, see H. Frankfort, *Cylinder Seals. A Documentary Essay on the Art and Religion of the Ancient Near East* (London, 1939), Pl.XIX. There are many other archaeological and textual examples confirming how the man-faced bulls, and other composite man-bull representations, 'acted as protective figures by people of all social standing across the ancient Near East, from the Prehistoric period until the time of the Persian Empire' (R.M. van Dijk, 'The Motif of the Bull,' 243).

[118] See L. Romano, 'La corona del dio,' and related bibliography.

[119] L. Legrain and L. Woolley, *Archaic seal-impressions* (London: Oxford University Press, 1936) 498; Pierre Amiet, *La glyptique mésopotamienne archäique* (Paris: Éditions du Centre national de la recherche scientifique, 1961), 748 and 1260; G. Eisen, *Ancient Oriental Seals and Other Seals, with a Description of the Collection of Mrs. William H. Moore* (Chicago, 1940), Pl.III.17; R.M. van Dijk, 'The Motif of the Bull,' 245-246.

[120] See note 72 above.

[121] L. Romano, 'La corona del dio,' 42.

[122] R.M. van Dijk, 'The Motif of the Bull,' 70.

[123] Such representations were probably among the sources of artistic inspiration for later Greek depictions of the mythological combat between Acheloios and Herakles wearing lion's skin.

[124] There was undoubtedly an important symbolic significance for this imagery, as the lion vs. bull combat is depicted very frequently over a time span of two millennia, and it appears in important Near Eastern locations such as near the throne room at Persepolis (R.M. van Dijk, 'The Motif of the Bull,' 74-6). Such combat, among other meanings, probably had an astral significance related to fertility, and one even sees the lion above the bison-man at Chauvet.

[125] Cylinder Seal, Early Dynastic Period, 2600 to 2400 BC (BMC ME 22962). Note, also, that the man-faced bulls are attacked by the lion-headed bird, Anzu, and are defended by a human and a bull man.

[126] For the earliest depictions of man-faced bulls on Early Dynastic Period glyptic art, see H. Frankfort, *More sculpture from the Diyala region* (Chicago: University Press, 1943), Pl.19. For a later Akkadian example of a lapis-lazuli amulet shaped in the form of man-faced bull, see **Fig. 10**. See also, Polish-Syria Expedition to Tell Arbid, 'Akkadian and Post-Akkadian Periods' on *Sector S- Step Trench* (Polish Centre of Mediterranean Archaeology, University of Warsaw, 2013), available at http://www.tellarbid.uw[dot]edu.pl/sectors/s/.

[127] One can see the man-faced bull represented in a recumbent posture, with head turned to left or right, or also in frontal posture. A common feature in 3rd and 2nd millennium sculptures is the detail of the forelegs folded beneath the body, signifying that the beast is reclining. The same feature will be adopted by the Greeks to depict Acheloios. Interestingly, there are even representations of the protomes of Mesopotamian man-faced bulls, which becomes very popular in later Greek examples. For an example dated to the Early Dynastic Period II described as a human-faced bison resting on bended knees, see H. Frankfort, *More sculpture from the Diyala region*, Pl.49, defined as perhaps forming an attachment for furniture. See also, D.P.Hansen, 'The Reclining Human-faced Bison Sculpture from Area SS,' 260.

[128] For other significant examples, see: Double vase in the shape of a man-faced bull, dated to the Early Dynastic Period III (Louvre Museum. Ale Richelieu. Rez-de-chaussée – Section 01c. Element 32, Vitrine 7); Lamp in the shape of a human-headed bull, stored at the British Museum (R.M. van Dijk, 'The Motif of the Bull,' 246, fig.4); Arm-rest in the shape of a human-headed bull from Khafajeh, stored at The University of Pennsylvania Museum (H. Frankfort, *The Art and Architecture of the Ancient Orient* (New Haven: Yale University Press, 1996), 59, fig.61); Pouring vessel in the shape of a human-headed bull, stored at the University of Pennsylvania Museum (J. Aruz and R.Wallenfels, *Art of the First Cities*, no. 69). An identical object dated to the Early Dynastic Period III is described as a 'Lampe,' and

limestone statue of a man-faced bull found in 1990 at Tell Brak in north-eastern Syria comes from the excavations of a building dating to the Akkadian Period, but scholars guess it may date considerably earlier,[129] likely to the Protodynastic period, and some elements of the iconography are even reminiscent of the Protoliterate Period.[130] According to Hansen[131] such pieces might have been set beside a doorway associated with a temple or shrine.[132]

The so-called Great Lyre of Ur, dated to the Early Dynastic Period II, c. 2650 BC, depicts two man-faced bulls surrounding a man (**Fig. 9**).[133] The University of Pennsylvania Museum describes the scene as a representation of royal control over nature, and the entire panel from which it comes represents various scenes of funerary rites.[134] Aruz and Wallenfel also recognized a funerary meaning in the scene, and the man surrounded by the two man-faced bulls could portray the deceased ruler, for whom the harp was buried as part of the grave goods.[135] Wiggermann supposed the same meaning, pointing out how the depicted scene has a strong symbolic meaning related to the Mesopotamian imagery of the 'Other Side,' the name used by the author to define the Mesopotamian world of the dead.[136] Thus there is an early, distinct chthonic association for the man-faced bulls of the Near East.

An additional chthonic, liminal association for the man-faced bull is seen in post-Akkadian burial practices of the ancient Near East (**Fig. 10**).[137] At Tell Arbid a lapis lazuli man-faced bull of Akkadian style was found in the grave of a child. Perplexed archaeologists suggest that the child was buried with a treasured family heirloom that survived many generations.[138] Burial with a child might also indicate a connection with the Greek man-faced bull who was closely associated, as a river god, with the protection of youth.[139] One ancient textual source supports this hypothesis, a clay tablet dated to the 18th century BC, classified by Farber as an 'incantation to pacify a baby,' in other words a lullaby, in which the bull-man is named.[140]

There are even artifacts that suggest statuettes of man-faced bulls were used as foot rests by rulers.[141] In Near Eastern theogonies and cosmogonies the dead gods remain as divine elements of the contemporary world. Remarkably, Mesopotamian religion lacks a clearly articulated underworld of the dead, but there were deities belonging to a group of chthonic gods concerned with growth and decay, and they ruled the 'Big Heart,' which, according to Johnston, was 'the ground underfoot where dead bodies decompose' and 'the souls of the dead travel through the desert to a cosmic river in the west.'[142] These foot rests might indicate recognition of this characteristic of the man-faced bull in the Near East.

An additional chthonic association for the Near Eastern man-faced bull, and one also shared with Acheloios, is the phenomenon of Mesopotamian man-faced bulls wearing horned headdresses, sometimes adorned with multiple pairs of horns.[143] The same style adornment is worn by other gods and goddesses,[144] as a mark of divinity dating

published in A. Caubet and M. Bernus-Taylor, *The Louvre* (London: Scala Books, 1991), 22. For additional examples of pouring vessels from the Royal Cemetery at Ur, see D.P.Hansen, 'The Reclining Human-Faced Bison Sculpture from Area SS,' 260.

129 D. Oates and J. Oates, 'Excavations at Tell Brak 1990-91,' in *Iraq*, 53 (1991), 127-45, Pl. 26-7; O. Rouault, M. G. Masetti-Rouault, and A. Abou-Assaf, *L'Eufrate e il tempo le civiltà* del *medio Eufrate e della Gezira siriana* (Milano: Electa, 1993), 293; D.P.Hansen, 'The Reclining Human-faced Bison Sculpture from Area SS,' 257-63.

130 D.P. Hansen, 'The Reclining Human-faced Bison Sculpture from Area SS,' 259; D. Oates and J. Oates, 'Excavations at Tell Brak 1990-91,' 296.

131 D.P. Hansen, 'The Reclining Human-faced Bison Sculpture from Area SS,' 257.

132 For other examples of man-faced bulls from Syrian sites, dated from the Early Dynastic Period to the Akkadian Periods, see: A. Parrot, *Le Temple d'Ishtar* (Paris: Mission Archeologique de Mari, 1956), Pl.VIII (amulet); P. Matthiae, 'Masterpieces of Early and Old Syrian art: discoveries of the 1988 Ebla excavations in a historical perspective,' in *Proceedings of the British Academy*, LXXV (1989), 25-56, Pl.III, IV, VI (limestone inlays); H. Weiss, *Ebla to Damascus: Art and Archaeology of Ancient Syria: an Exhibition from the Directorate-General of Antiquities and Museums, Syrian Arab Republic* (Washington, D.C.: Smithsonian Institution Traveling Exhibition Service, 1985), 177 (steatite and gold amulet); D. Oates et al., *Excavations at Tell Brak,* 295-9, fig.317 (shell amulet); D.M. Matthews, *The Early Glyptic of Tell Brak: Cylinder Seals of Third Millennium Syria* (Fribourg: University Press, 1997) , no. 284, no.287, and no.316 (seal).

133 The University of Pennsylvania Museum, as published in C. J. Du Ry, *Art of the Ancient Near and Middle East* (New York: Harry N. Abrams, 1970), 55.

134 Museum Exhibit: Iraq's Ancient Past: Rediscovering Ur's Royal Cemetery. University of Pennsylvania Museum of Archaeology and Anthropology, 2013. See specifically the webpage dedicated to the Great Lyre of Ur: http://www.penn.museum/sites/iraq/?page_id=58

135 J. Aruz and R. Wallenfels, *Art of the First Cities,* 106.

136 F.A.M. Wiggermann, 'Scenes from the Shadow Side,' 217.

137 Polish-Syria Expedition to Tell Arbid. 'Akkadian and Post-Akkadian Periods' on *Sector S- Step Trench.*

138 Ibid.

139 J. Larson, *Greek Nymphs: Myth, Cult, Lore*. (Oxford: UP, 2001), 98.

140 'O baby who dwelt in the dark, - Out you came and saw the daylight. / Why do you cry? why do you [wail?] - And why did you not cry before you were born? / You've roused the house god, the bull-man has woken: - 'Who was it roused me? Who was it made me jump?' / 'The baby roused you! The baby made you jump!' – 'Like a drinker of wine, like one born in a tavern: -- Let slumber befall it!" (W. Farber, 'Zur älteren akkadischen Beschwörungsliteratur,' in *ZA*, 71 (Berlin 1981), 62. We also want to point out the liminal features of this text in which the bull-man is named: the baby going from dark (the antenatal existence) to daylight and the invocation to make the baby fall asleep. Another interesting element is the final allusion to the wine drinker, in which we could perhaps see a link to the later connotations of human-faced bovines from other geographic areas, like Hathor in Egypt (discussed below).

141 For an example and related bibliography, see I. Claire's writing at the Louvre site: http://www.louvre.fr/en/oeuvre-notices/recumbent-bull-mans-head

142 S. I. Johnston, *Religions of the Ancient World: A Guide* (Cambridge (MA): Belknap Press of Harvard University Press, 2004), 398.

143 L. Romano, 'La corona del dio, ' 41-57.

144 Many of these gods' headdresses on sculptures dated to the Early Dynastic Period show a bull's head carved between the horns, indicating that the horns worn by the god are related to the symbolic value of the bull (R. M. van Dijk, 'The Motif of the Bull,' 138).

back to the Early Dynastic Period in Mesopotamia, and also later in Anatolia, Cyprus,[145] and the Levant.[146] Such horned headdresses are often trimmed with vegetation.[147] The detail of vegetation coupled with horns suggests the symbolic role of fertility related to these gods.[148] It seems likely that these iconographic representations served as the basis for later Greek mythological narratives of Acheloios and the construction of the following important detail, related by Ovid and concerning the loss of Acheloios' horn in the battle with Herakles: 'He concealed his loss with willow leaves or reeds and rushes worn upon his head.'[149] Moreover, there is archaeological evidence showing vegetation emerging from Acheloios' forehead, just as described in the ancient textual sources.[150]

Compelling evidence exists for a fluvial association with the Near Eastern regular man-faced bull (in addition to the aforementioned seals from Susa). A Syrian cylinder seal published in a drawing by Ward, originally published by Lajard, depicts a figure seated on a throne which is sustained by two man-faced bulls (**Fig. 11**).[151] Two water streams spring from the top of the heads of the man-faced bulls, and the seated figure seems to collect that water in an ampulla of sorts. This piece is a good example of the early journey of the man-faced bull from Mesopotamia to the Syrian coast of the Mediterranean Sea, and this is likely the first attested visual evidence of a fluvial connotation for the man-faced bull in Near Eastern art. The cult practice of ablutions with holy water is attested in the prehistoric Near East since 4500 BC,[152] and since 3500 BC evidence exists of a Mesopotamian god of water called Enki (Akkadian Ea) who was worshipped at a 'national religious center,'[153] and has been identified as the figure on this seal seated above the man-faced bulls.[154] Enki was also believed to be involved in determining fate,[155] and was associated with the roots of plants.[156] On Akkadian texts he is addressed as 'Lord of the Deep,' and on later Assyrian texts the clay pit from which exorcists made statuettes of Kusarikku was sacred to him.[157] All of this reinforces the similarities of Near Eastern man-faced bull mythology and that of the Greek Acheloios: water, divination, fertility, and subterranean connotations.

Many other later examples of regular man-faced bull sculptures dating to Ur III exist.[158] They often wear a horned headdress, a common Near Eastern attribute for divine beings. These man-faced bulls occasionally have holes in their backs for removable offering bowls. R.M. van Dijk argues that this suggests a ritual function, in which worshippers asking for protection made offerings to the deity.[159] Man-faced bulls will continue to be depicted in Near Eastern visual art until the Achaemenid Period.[160]

Winged Man-Headed Bulls

Initially, when the very first winged man-headed[161] bulls of the Near East were uncovered, it was naturally assumed they were the inspiration for the man-faced bull

145 Representations of horned caps on bronze figurines were very popular in Cyprus during Bronze Age. There is a striking resemblance between Levantine and Cypriot horned deities and bronze figurines made in Sardinia during the Bronze Age. See below, pg 36ff.

146 R.M. van Dijk, 'The Motif of the Bull,' 130.

147 D. Collon, 'Clothing and Grooming in Ancient Western Asia,' in *Civilizations of the Ancient Near East* (New York: Scribner, 1995), 507.

148 R.M. van Dijk, 'The Motif of the Bull,' 132.

149 Ovid, and A. D. Melville, *Metamorphoses* (Oxford: UP, 1986), 9.99-100.

150 A kernos dated to the 5th century BC, found at Lavinio, has been attributed to ancient Italic populations of Latium. Today the kernos is stored at the Archaeological Museum of Pomezia.

151 W. H. Ward, *The seal cylinders of western Asia* (Washington: Carnegie, 1910), 321, fig.1024; F. Lajard, *Introduction a l'étude du culte public et des mystères de Mithra en Orient et en Occident. Volume 2* (Paris: Imprimerie Royale, 1847), Pl. XXXII, no.7. Neither scholar gives a precise date or location for the seal. Lajard defined the piece as 'Babylonian,' whereas Ward states that the seal 'is rather Syrian or Hittite than Babylonian, although the influence is chiefly from Babylonia.' (W. H. Ward, *The seal cylinders of western Asia*, 321). The Syrian attribution of this seal is more likely than Hittite, as there exists no convincing comparison in Hittite seals (cf. D.G. Hogart, *Hittite Seals, with particular reference to the Ashmolean Collection* (Oxford: 1920). There are clear comparisons with the seated figure holding the ampulla associated with ankh and star in field, seen on Syrian seals dated from 1800 to 1720 BC, from the Marcopolic Collection (cf. B. Teissier, *Ancient Near Eastern Cylinder Seals from the Marcopolic Collection* (Berkeley: 1984) no.456 and no.508-9). Interestingly, we will see the same cultic associations, in which the man-faced bull exhibits celestial and life-renewing characteristics much later, when the man-faced bull is paired with the ankh on the archaic coinage of Cyprus, and with star or sun symbols on the later Campanian coinage.

152 S. I. Johnston, *Religions of the Ancient World: A Guide*, 396.

153 Ibid.

154 Ibid., 606 and fig.9.c.

155 F.A.M. Wiggermann, 'Mythological Foundations of Nature,' 212ff, 6b.

156 M. Krebernik, *Die Beschwörungen aus Fara und Ebla: Untersuchungen zur altesten keilschriftlichen Beschworungsliteratur* (Olms, 1984), 228ff.

157 See F.A.M. Wiggermann, *Mesopotamian Protective Spirits*, Text I, line 152: *Sep lemutti Ma bit ameli parasu*, 'to block the entry of the evil in someone's house.'

158 For some examples, see: B. André-Salvini, 'Art of the First Cities : The Third Millenium B.C. from the Mediterranean to the Indus,' Exposition (New York: The Metropolitan Museum of Art, 2003); A. Caubet, *Exposition des quatre grandes civilisations mondiales: La Mésopotamie entre le Tigre et l'Euphrate. Exposition itinérante, Setagaya, Musée d'art de Setagaya, 5 août 2000-3 décembre 2000, Fukuoka, Musée d'art asiatique de Fukuokua, 16 décembre 2000- 4 mars 2001* (Tokyo: NKH, 2000), no. 120; A. Parrot, *Tello, vingt campagnes de fouilles (1877- 1933)* (Paris: Albin Michel, 1948); A. Spycket, *La statuaire du Proche-Orient ancien* (Leyde: Brill 1981); Louvre Museum, Ale Richelieu, Room 2, Case 4. Object no. AO 2752. A miniature serpentine sculpture dates to c. 2100 BC, which is stored at the California Museum of Art. This specimen is quite interesting for the connotation of fertility and eroticism, as the bull's erected phallus is visible on the underside of the sculpture. The ithyphallic representation will be a very common feature for the later Etrurian and Greek man-faced bulls.

159 R.M. van Dijk, 'The Motif of the Bull,' 247.

160 R.M. van Dijk, 'The Motif of the Bull,' 243.

161 Unlike true man-faced bulls, most Assyrian figures have a human neck protruding from a bovine body, with bovine ears and horns. We therefore use 'winged man-headed bull,' to describe the creature. There are some Greek representations of Acheloios as a (sometimes winged) man-headed bull, and on some coinage (Iaitas and Laos, for example) a man-headed bull appears.

of the Greek world.[162] They are called Lamassu, Sēdu or Aladlammû. [163] The winged man-headed bull is generally manifested in the form of a colossal statue and seen in pairs at the entrances of buildings and rooms,[164] and acts primarily as an apotropaic deity.[165] In Mesopotamian religion wings were a symbol associated with exorcists, and in the ancient sources the protective deities are sometimes invoked as 'the winged one.' In fact, modern scholars have linked winged Mesopotamian figures, including the winged man-headed bull, to Christian cherubs, and there may therefore be some association of 'Nike' flying above the Greek man-faced bull as an integral link in this chain.[166] Winged man-headed bulls themselves appeared in the Near East around 1800 BC (earliest estimate) and lasted for over one thousand years.[167] According to Roaf, the Neo-Assyrian winged man-headed bull could have developed from the Early Dynastic Mesopotamian recumbent man-faced bulls.[168] Some scholars,[169] in reference specifically to Neo-Assyrian palaces, identified the winged man-headed bull and all other Near Eastern man-faced bulls with Sēdu, the evil demon of personified disease named on Mesopotamian ritual texts.[170] This identification has not been confirmed by archaeological evidence and it seems, at first glance, to be counterintuitive to recognize an evil demon of disease as an apotropaic device protecting palaces and purifying houses and their inhabitants. And as one can see in the ritual text reported by Wiggermann, the name Sēdu is coupled with that of Lamassu, in a context in which they are both described by the ancient source as spirits of good.[171] Thus, the only conceivable way for this association to have any merit is if one considers it in relation to medicinal practices in which 'the hair of the dog' notion is employed, i.e. it takes an element of that which causes illness to eliminate illness (iconographically, this is similar to the use of gargoyles). This binary aspect is related to water, too, and finds many parallels in the later Greek traditions.[172]

Beyond the apotropaic functions, at least two extant examples of the winged man-headed bull suggest he is some kind of water deity (not including the late Ubaid seal from Susa). The first case is a rare instance in which the winged man-headed bull is not portrayed in colossal statue form: The famous relief from Sargon II's palace at Khorsabad, today displayed at the Louvre,[173] which shows a winged man-headed bull depicted as part of a larger scene with an Assyrian fleet. Here the creature is on water.[174] This scene was once thought to depict an attack on a maritime stronghold[175] or the construction of a city or palace.[176] Another hypothesis concerns the Assyrian military expedition to Cyprus across the Mediterranean Sea, recorded in the annals of Sargon II.[177] However, the most commonly accepted interpretation is that of the Assyrian military expedition to the area of modern Lebanon, along the Phoenician coast, to obtain cedar wood intended for Sargon's palace.[178] It is also important to note that Sennacherib, Sargon II's son, accomplished some remarkable feats in the realm of water control and

[162] G.B. D'Alessio, 'Textual Fluctuations and Cosmic Streams,' 16-37.

[163] There is no general agreement amongst scholars as to the names of these figures. J. Black and A. Green, *Gods, Demons and Symbols of Ancient Mesopotamia*, 115, suggest lamassus was Akkadian for Sumerian Lama, a female figure generally taking on a human form, with male names Alad (Akkadian Sēdu). They claim that the winged man-faced bull is probably Aladlammu, the female form being Apsasu.

[164] The use of winged man-headed bulls as gateway guardians for palaces, temples and cities was very common during the Neo-Assyrian Period, in particular.

[165] There is agreement among scholars on the function of winged man-headed bulls as gateway guardians for Neo-Assyrian palaces. An inscription on two panels between the hind legs of the winged man-headed bull stored at the Louvre Museum (from Door K of the palace of Sargon II at Dur Sharrukin, present-day Khorsabad) praises the ruler by rehearsing his virtues, and calls down a curse on whomever should seek to harm the edifice. For textual evidence related to the protective function for colossal statues, see translated inscriptions in: R.F. Harper, 'Transliteration and Translation of Cylinder A of the Esarhaddon Inscriptions,' in *Hebraica*, 4/2 (1888), 115-7. The name Lamassu, used in litanies to invoke protective spirits, is also attested on Assyrian textual sources, see *Sep lemutti Ma bit ameli parasu*, 'to block the entry of the enemy in someone's house,' lines 123, reported as Text I in F.A.M. Wiggermann, *Mesopotamian Protective Spirits*. This protective function is strikingly similar to the earlier Kusarikku in Mesopotamian culture

[166] See S. Dalley, 'The Influence of Mesopotamia upon Israel and the Bible,' in *The Legacy of Mesopotamia*, edited by S. Dalley (Oxford: Oxford University Press, 1998), 57-83.

[167] Cf. V. Danrey, 'Winged Human-Headed Bulls of Nineveh: Genesis of an Iconographic Motif,' in *Iraq*, Vol. 66 (London, 2004), 133-9.

[168] M. Roaf, *Cultural Atlas of Mesopotamia and the Ancient Near East* (New York, 1996), 87; R.M. van Dijk, 'The Motif of the Bull,' 249.

[169] J. Reade, 'Assyrian Architectural Decoration: Techniques and Subject-Matter,' in *Baghdader Mitteilungen* (Berlin, 1979), 17ff.

[170] See F.A.M. Wiggermann, *Mesopotamian Protective Spirits*, 95.

[171] 'you shall write 'who repels the evil constables' and on his left 'who causes to enter the *sēdu* of good and the *lamassu* of good' — you shall make,' and 'To block the entry of the enemy in someone's house,' lines 122-3, from F.A.M. Wiggermann, *Mesopotamian Protective Spirits*, 11.

[172] R. Taylor, 'River Raptures: Containment and Control of Water in Greek and Roman Constructions of Identity,' in *The Nature and Function of Water, Baths, Bathing and Hygiene from Antiquity through Renaissance*, edited by C. Kosso and A. Scott (Leiden: Brill, 2009) 21-22. For the notion of pollution and consecration in the Greek world, especially in relation to water, see ibid., 31-36. He quotes Carol Dougherty: 'The Greeks conceptualize defilement as the inversion of a positive religious value; it still carries religious force. Blood and dust can bring pollution, but they can also consecrate' (C. Dougherty, 'It's Murder to Found a Colony,' in *Cultural Poetics in Archaic Greece: Cult, Performance, Politics*; edited by Carol Dougherty and Leslie Kurke (New York, 1993), 186).

[173] Dated 713 to 706 BC, object no. AO19889.

[174] M.A. Atac, *The Mythology of Kingship in Neo-Assyrian Art* (Cambridge: University Press, 2010), fig. 122; R.M. van Dijk, 'The Motif of the Bull,' 252, fig. 12-13.

[175] Possibly the siege of Pelusium by Sennacherib or the taking of Ashdod by Sargon.

[176] E. Fontan, 'La Frise du Transport du Bois, Décor du Palais de Sargon II à Khorsabad,' in *Cedrus Libani, Archaelogy and History in Lebanon*, Vol. 14, edited by C. Doumet-Serhal (London, 2001), 58-63. See also the Louvre's website for AO19889: http://www.louvre.fr/en/oeuvre-notices/frieze-transportation-timber

[177] P. Albenda, *A Mediterranean Seascape from Khorsabad* (Malibu: Undena Publications, 1983), 1-17; E. Ascalone, *Mesopotamia* (Milan: Electa, 2005), 236; R.M. van Dijk, 'The Motif of the Bull,' 252.

[178] E. Fontan, 'La Frise du Transport du Bois, Décor du Palais de Sargon II à Khorsabad,' 58-63: 'The timber was loaded on ships that sailed north along the Phoenician coast, skirting Tyre then Ruad; it was no doubt unloaded at the mouth of the Orontes River. From there the timber could be transported to Assyria by river.'

regulation: he built 150 km of water related works,[179] invented the sluice gate,[180] constructed the earliest known example of an above ground aqueduct,[181] and may even have developed the predecessor to the Archimedean water screw.[182] Despite all his accomplishments with water regulation, eventually he may have been crushed to death by a winged man-headed bull which his own son allegedly toppled onto him![183]

The second piece suggesting a fluvial connotation is the colossal statue from the main entrance of the throne room of Ashurnasirpal II's Northwest Palace at Nimrud (**Fig. 12**).[184] This winged man-headed bull wears a headdress shaped like a fish's head, and his belly is covered with what appears to be fish scales. Annus, on the basis of such evidence, articulated a hypothesis concerning the gateway guardian figures identified with Kusarikku.[185] For this particular iconography he makes a comparison to the earliest Near Eastern images of fish-*apkallu*[186] wearing clothes shaped like the body of a fish,[187] in which the fish's headdress is worn in the exact same fashion as the Ashurnasirpal winged man-headed bull. Fish-*apkallu* have been identified by scholars as protective deities linked to water cults, and also primeval sages born in streams[188] who share the wisdom of Enki. All of this evidence suggests a merging of the symbolism of these figures with the Ashurnasirpal winged man-headed bull as manifested visually in the fish head headdress and scales.[189]

Gugalanna: The Bull of Heaven

Another identity for the Near Eastern winged man-headed bull is Gugalanna, also known as 'The Great Bull of Heaven,' a mythological monster linked to the Sumerian *Epic of Gilgamesh* (**Fig. 13**). Since the late 2nd millennium BC Gugalanna has been depicted as a winged man-faced bull but is clearly differentiated from the other winged man-headed bulls in the accompanying iconography and literature of the time.[190]

It is impossible to ignore the elements of assimilation between the killing of Gugalanna by Gilgamesh and the defeat of Acheloios by Herakles. In both cases the result is related to the fertility of the land. In the case of Gilgamesh and Gugalanna[191] such fertility is symbolized with the end of the drought and the return of the abundant harvest.[192] Moreover, in the earlier Sumerian poem *Bilgames and the Bull of Heaven*, the predecessor to the later *Epic of Gilgamesh*, after the hero has defeated the creature he dismembers it and dedicates the horns to Inanna in her temple.[193] And in the later Babylonian *Epic of Gilgamesh*, Tablet VI, the horns are described as 'thirty minas of lapis lazuli in a solid block [...] six kor of oil the capacity of both,' a clear indication of abundance.[194] Likewise, in the case of Herakles and his battle with Acheloios, fertility is linked to the horn that he snatches from Acheloios' head, which then becomes the cornucopia, a now universal symbol of fertility and abundance. Aside from mythological similarities, there are artistic parallels in which both cultures represent the antagonist with a figure that merges human and bovine parts. In particular, it is striking to observe the posture of Gugalanna and Acheloios, with distinct kneeling forelegs,[195] as they are subdued by the heroes who grasp their horns.

---

179 Cf. K. Radner, 'Nineveh, Assyria's capital in the 7th century BC,' in *Knowledge and Power in the Neo-Assyrian Empire* (United Kingdom: Higher Education Academy, 2011).

180 T. Jakobsen, 'The Water Supplies of Nineveh,' in *Sennacherib's Aqueduct at Jerwan*, edited by T. Jacobsen and Seton Lloyd (Chicago: University Press, 1934), 41.

181 S. Lloyd, 'Architectural Description of the Aqueduct,' in *Sennacherib's Aqueduct at Jerwan* (Chicago, 1935), 6-18.

182 See S. Dalley and J. P. Oleson 'Sennacherib, Archimedes, and the Water Screw: The Context of Invention in the Ancient World,' in *Technology and Culture*, Volume 44, Number 1 (2003), 1-26.

183 S. Dalley, *Esther's Revenge at Susa: from Sennacherib to Ahasuerus* (Oxford: University Press, 2008) 64–66.

184 'the room which the king would want to protect the most' (R.M. van Dijk, 'The Motif of the Bull,' 255).

185 Ibid., 254, after A. Annus, *The God Ninurta: in the Mythology and Royal Ideology of Ancient Mesopotamia* (Helsinki: Neo-Assyrian Text Corpus Project, 2002), 117.

186 Fish-*apkallu* are Near Eastern figures somewhat similar to Greek nymphs, but male. Cf. G. Whittaker, 'Milking the Udder of Heaven: A Note on Mesopotamian and Indo-Iranian Religious Imagery,' in *From Daēnā to Dīn. Religion, Kultur und Sprache in der iranischen Welt: Festschrift für Philip Kreyenbroek zum 60. Geburtstag*, edited by C. Allison, A. Joisten-Pruschke and A. Wendtland (Wiesbaden: Harrassowitz, 2009), 130.

187 F.A.M. Wiggermann, *Mesopotamian Protective Spirits*, 76.

188 J. Black and A. Green, *Gods and Demons and Symbols of Ancient Mesopotamia*, 82-83, 163-4. A common attribute of Fish-*apkallu* is the *banduddû*, shared in common with Kusarikku in early Mesopotamian visual art, as mentioned above.

189 R.M. van Dijk, 'The Motif of the Bull,' 255.

190 For an example dated to the late 2nd Millennium BC, see F.A.M. Wiggermann, *Mesopotamian Protective Spirits*, 176, note 10. For later evidence see R.M. van Dijk, 'The Motif of the Bull,' 212, fig.11-2; J. Aruz and R. Wallenfels, *Art of the First Cities*, 483, fig.114 (Chalcedony cylinder seal impression); D. Collon, *First Impressions*, no. 858 (Seal of *Qerub-dini-ili*).

191 In the Babylonian *Epic of Gilgamesh* the Bull of Heaven is a monster triggered by Ishtar for revenge against Gilgamesh, who declined to marry the goddess. The Bull of Heaven rages on 'Heart,' devastating the land around Uruk and killing hundreds of men (R.M. van Dijk, 'The Motif of the Bull,' 211). There is a relation with Acheloios who, as a river deity, possesses the power to devastate lands and destroy men (by floods). A further relation between the two mythological episodes is possibly shown by some visual representations: van Dijk published the picture of a terracotta plaque showing the slaying of the Bull of Heaven, photographed by the author at the Vorderasiatische Museum (R.M. van Dijk, 'The Motif of the Bull,' 212, fig.10). On the plaque Gilgamesh is portrayed grasping a horn and hitting the bull with a club, a typical attribute of the late Greek Herakles.

192 The spring equinox at the time of the Sumerians coincided with the presence in the horizon of the constellation Taurus.

193 'from flasks made of its horns Inanna in Eanna did pour sweet oil' (R.M. van Dijk, 'The Motif of the Bull,' 34 and 211-2).

194 Ibid.

195 Addressing this posture Rabun Taylor made the observation that on Neapolitan coinage the man-faced bull, who appears to be swimming on many varieties, is actually 'kneeling in assent to being sacrificed' (Personal correspondence, Spring, 2015). This is tied in with the notion of loss and gain as they are symbolized in the cornucopia, discussed in depth in the Greek section.

Asallúhi

Asallúhi (also Asarlúhi)[196] is the son of the god of subterranean waters,[197] Enki, who appeared on the aforementioned cylinder seal collecting water from the heads of two man-faced bulls.[198] In Sumerian texts, he is said to be a god of healing[199] and magical knowledge.[200] He is also recognized as a liminal figure in medical practices, mediating between his father, Enki, and the patient,[201] and in some cases he absorbs many of the qualities of his father.[202] In one text he is even described as, 'the supervisor of the purification priests of *E-abzu* (Apsu).' Furthermore, he is the god of the 'river of ordeal' and, most importantly, referred to as both the 'princely bison' and 'light of the gods.'[203]

Although the iconography of Asallúhi is unknown to modern commentators, the 'princely bison' epithet, *alim nun-na*, suggests a possible connection to the man-faced bull tradition, and may even be related to the earlier name *gud-alim*, which was presented as a potential Sumerian counterpart to the Akkadian Kusarikku, often thought to be depicted as a man-faced bull. In fact, Whittaker goes so far as to connect the etymology of Asallúhi to the Indo-European tradition via Kusarikku, which many suggest is not an original Akkadian name.[204] Moreover, in a hymn to Asallúhi, we have a clear description of him that connects his bovine and fluvial aspects: 'Son endowed with a broad understanding, whose movement is that of an animal with large horns in the reed-beds; Asarlúhi, mighty deluge determining great fates, unleashed and knowing no course whatsoever!'[205] Thus, perhaps the man-faced bulls beneath Enki are representations of Asallúhi, a god of the subterranean waters 'that rises to the surface of the earth in springs and marshes, ultimately flowing as rivers.'[206] The princely river god manifested as a bison would suggest this, and according to Pausanias,[207] Homer refers to Acheloios with the 'prince' epithet. Moreover, in a text describing ritual purifications, the purified water is referred to specifically as 'the son of his god,' wherein the god referenced is Enki.[208]

Additional evidence exits which demonstrates Asallúhi is the closest ancestor to Acheloios. For instance, during ritual practices priests would shout, 'I am Asallúhi,' possibly indicating the use of masks wherein the priest 'becomes' the god, a distinct trait of ritual practices for Acheloios.[209] Moreover, Asallúhi, like Acheloios, might have been used as a civic emblem for cities: 'Kuara, the beloved city which you have chosen in your heart, lives in joy because of you.'[210] Thus we might have here a Near Eastern prototype of the 'civic identity' dimension associated with archaic and classical cities minting coinage of the man-faced bull.[211] The river deity has chosen the city, and the city lives in joy because of him, as the river brings fertility and health.

Ultimately, the most interesting aspect to Asallúhi is indeed the name itself. If the word underwent some sort of quasi-centumization, in which the *s* morphed into a *k*, one can very easily see that Akallúhi becomes the Greek Acheloios without much effort. Thus, in Asallúhi there appear to be mythological, etymological, and potential iconographic links to the later Greek (and Etruscan) cult of Acheloios. One issue prohibiting a more direct link is that man-faced bull iconography significantly predates the appearance of Asallúhi in the literary tradition. But this is easily reconcilable given the nature of Mesopotamian mythology, which, as many have attested, often does not fit into a strict ideological framework. Thus the iconography of the man-faced bull, which becomes very popular in the Ur III period, might have been adopted to represent Asallúhi, who emerges in the literature at the same time (it will last through the Neo-Assyrian period and is even recorded in Seleukid times).

Preliminary Conclusions: Near East

The Near East confronts observers with a significant problem yet at the same time points to a tentative resolution. On the one hand, there are many different creatures, all of which share an indisputable relation to the iconography and mythology of the Greek man-faced bull yet none of which can be demonstrated to have a direct connection. On the other hand, the very similarity

196 'Asallúhi' is the later term, employed first in the 18th century BC. See T. Oshima, *Babylonian Prayers to Marduk*, Orientalische Religionen in der Antike. Vol.7 (Tübingen :Mohr Siebeck, 2011), 191.

197 G. Whittaker, 'Milking the Udder of Heaven,' 130.

198 See **Fig. 11.**

199 G. Whittaker, 'Milking the Udder of Heaven,' 130.

200 G. Whittaker, 'Milking the Udder of Heaven,' 130, citing J. Black and A. Green, *Gods, Demons and Symbols of Ancient Mesopotamia,* 36.

201 M.J. Geller, *Forerunners to Udug-hul. Sumerian Exorcistic Incantations, Freiburger Altorientalische Studien,* 12 (Stuttgart,1985), 13.

202 G. Whittaker, 'Milking the Udder of Heaven,' 131.

203 G. Whittaker, 'Milking the Udder of Heaven,' 131, citing Å. W. Sjöberg and E. Bergmann, *The Collection of the Summerian Temple Hymns. Texts from Cuneiform Sources*, Vol. III (Lucust Valley, 1969), 80. In the Etruscan man-faced bull tradition the figure often has astral connotations, and the word Αυκηλως means 'overseer of sunrise.See below, pg. 94-5.

204 G. Whittaker, 'Milking the Udder of Heaven,' 127-137.

205 D. Charpin, *Le Clergé d'Ur au siècle d'Hammurapi* (Genève: Droz, 1986), 357-366, lines 20-20.

206 G. Whittaker, 'Milking the Udder of Heaven,' 131.

207 Pausanias, *Description of Greece,* 8.38.10, wherein ἄρχον is translated as 'prince.' (Pausanias, W.H.S. Jones and H.A. Ormerod, *Description of Greece* (Cambridge (MA): Harvard University Press, 1918)).

208 F.A.M. Wiggermann, *Mesopotamian Protective Spirits,* 66.

209 W. H. Hallo, 'More Incantations and Rituals from the Yale Babylonian Collection,' in *Mesopotamian Magic: Textual, Historical, and Interpretative Perspectives,* Volume 1, edited by I. T. Abusch and K. Van Der Toorn (Groningen: Styx, 1999), 295.

210 D.Charpin, *Le Clergé d'Ur au siècle d'Hammurapi,* lines 37-41.

211 Carina Weiss suggests a specific apotropaic dimension in this respect, wherein the man-faced bull, as a river god and when depicted on coinage, takes on the role of protecting the city (C. Weiss, *Griechische Flußgottheiten in vorhellenistischer Zeit* (Würzburg, 1984), 21-22).

of these different man-bull manifestations and their apparent sharing of common names[212] suggests an earlier mythological and iconographic prototype. Wiggermann argues that the Mesopotamian man-faced bull and bull-man share features 'that must go back to the time before they split into two separate figures,' which might be attested on the late Ubaid seals mentioned above. Thus, it seems as though man-faced bull iconography was adapted and slightly altered for different purposes in the Near East over a span of nearly three millennia: in some cases serving as an apotropaic deity guarding entranceways, protecting and purifying houses and their inhabitants; in another case representing one of the eleven creatures created by Tiamat; in another case representing deities with chthonic or fluvial connotations; and in another protecting a child in his journey to the afterlife.[213] All of these identities and their associated meanings, along with the accompanying mythological and iconographic underpinnings, might have been incorporated into a single figure, Asallúhi, whose name, mythology, and physical description strongly suggest he served as the central figure for the transference of the tradition into the Greek and Etruscan worlds.

Egypt

Not long after the appearance of man-faced bulls in the Near East we find a man-faced bull and some human-faced cows in Egypt, around the time of the Early First Dynasty, c. 3000 to 2600 BC.[214]

What looks to be an ithyphallic man-faced bull appears on a piece from Djer with full body shown standing right, head in profile.[215] The face looks human insofar as it matches that of the sarcophagus in the scene above. The man-faced bull stands on a raised platform (**Fig. 14**) supported by a man (standard bearer?), and is part of a much larger scene, apparently some sort of funeral procession, indicating a general liminal-chthonic association. Its position on a platform or as part of a standard may indicate an apotropaic facet as well. This is the only apparent man-faced bull the authors have found in Egyptian art before the spread of Greek culture in the area.

On the so-called Hathor bowl there is another figure that is either a man-faced bull or a human-faced female cow.[216] Other pieces also said to depict Hathor have a distinctly tauriform head, usually without a human face, and are often found in tombs, such as at Gerzeh.[217] The figure is usually surrounded by celestial iconography.[218] There are also Egyptian mirrors that feature the head of a horned, female-faced cow at the base, similar to later depictions of Acheloios on Etruscan mirrors.[219]

The human-faced female cow is often depicted in pairs,[220] such as on the Narmer Palette (**Fig. 15**), and has been identified as Hathor or possibly Bat. There are many symbolic functions shared among the Near Eastern man-faced bull tradition, the later western man-faced bull tradition, and the tradition surrounding Hathor: an apotropaic function[221] and associations with fertility;[222] similar complementary iconography including the sacred mound and celestial motifs;[223] chthonic connotations involving mediation between the living and the dead;[224] and other 'Dionysian' connotations, such as sexuality, fertility, music, dance, and alcohol.[225] Moreover, Hathor,

212 The bull-man and man-faced bull were both identified by the term GUD-ALIM (R.M. van Dijk, 'The Motif of the Bull,' 158). According to D.P. Hansen, in 'The Reclining Human-faced Bison Sculpture from Area SS,' 261, the man-faced bull is a visual image used to express the idea of Kusarikku. Many scholars use the term Kusarikku to describe both the Near Eastern bull-man and man-faced bull. In fact, J. Black and A. Green, 51, state, 'It is possible, but not certain, that the bull with human head was, like the bull-man, known in Akkadian as Kusarikku. The more usual identification with figures called by the Assyrians Aladlammu (or Lamassu or Sēdu) is also possible.'

213 Scholars have often observed that Mesopotamian ancient texts seem to show a lack of logic. According to Wiggermann, logical explanation was not commonly practiced in ancient Mesopotamia, and not accepted in the explanation of the facts of life and nature (F.A.M. Wiggermann, 'Mythological Foundations of Nature,' note 4). R.M. van Dijk, 'The Motif of the Bull,' 85, suggests that Mesopotamian mythological representations do not present ideologies which are mutually exclusive, rather variations of the same concept. At the same time there is not a single meaning behind the same scenes (ibid., 86).

214 R.M. van Dijk, 'The Motif of the Bull,' 189-191.

215 W. B. Emery and Z.Y. Saad, *The Tomb of Hemaka* (Cairo: Government Press, 1938), 35-39, fig. 8, Pl. 17A, 18A.

216 Fragment of the Hathor Bowl, from E.M. Burgess & A.J. Arkell, 'The Reconstruction of the Hathor Bowl,' in *The Journal of Egyptian Archaeology*, 44 (1958), Plate IX, fig.3; R.M. van Dijk, 'The Motif of the Bull,' 190, fig.11.

217 See e.g. the Gerzeh Palette, Cairo Mus. no. 34173, Gerzeh Tomb 59 (S.D. 47-77), Naqada IIc-d1. For general Hathor/Bat iconography, see S. Hendrick, 'Bovines in Egyptian Predynastic and Early Dynastic Iconography,' in *Droughts, Food and Culture: Ecological Change and Food Security in Africa's Later Prehistory*, edited by F. A. Hassan (New York: Kluwer Academic - Plenum Publishers, 2002), 310, Appendix H.

218 Ibid.

219 See, for example, Metropolitan Museum of Art, accession no. 26.8.97, from the New Kingdom Dynasty, 1479 to 1425 BC. Found in Thebes, from where, interestingly, the oracle at Dodona is said to have been kidnapped by Phoenicians. The oracle at Dodona instructed all patrons to make a sacrifice to Acheloios (this is discussed in the Greek chapter). Also, compare to the Etruscan mirrors featuring Acheloios, H.P. Isler, *Acheloos*, no.273-278.

220 Top of the Narmer Palette, Egyptian Museum, Cairo, CG 14716. For similar iconography see the ivory carving from the tomb of First Dynasty Pharaoh Anedjib at Abydos (R.M. van Dijk, 'The Motif of the Bull,' 190, fig.10).

221 R.M. van Dijk, 'The Motif of the Bull,' 98-9. See also D. Wengrow, 'Rethinking 'Cattle Cults' in Early Egypt: Towards a Prehistoric Perspective on the Narmer Palette,' in *Cambridge Archaeological Journal*, 11:1 (2001), 94.

222 R.M. van Dijk, 'The Motif of the Bull,' 185.

223 R.M. van Dijk, 'The Motif of the Bull,' 188, fig.8; ibid., 190, fig.11; ibid., 191, fig.12; ibid., 190, fig.11.; ibid., 191, fig.12. For the celestial/solar/astral meanings related to the iconography of the man-faced bull in the ancient world, see below pg. 51-2 and Fig. 54 and Fig. 59 (Etruria); pg. 70-1, Fig. 115-6 (Greek world). For the presence of astral/solar symbols on Greek bronze coinage see catalog entries for Agyrion, Panormos, Cales, Neapolis, etc.

224 Ibid.,193. 'Hathor acted as a mediator between the living and the dead, welcoming the dead to the afterlife. Because death was seen as a continuation of life in Egyptian thought, by helping the deceased reach the afterlife, Hathor can be said to be renewing life, and another aspect of her fertility is demonstrated' (Ibid., 193 & 187).

225 Ibid., 185, and reported bibliography. In the chapter on Greek man-faced bulls (Chpt. IV) we will discuss the similar meanings associated with the later western cult of the man-faced bull: rites of passage for

like the Near Eastern man-faced bull, has the important characteristic of absorbing other deities, like Smithis, who helped the deceased reach the afterlife; Mehurt, goddess of fertility who allegedly arose from the primeval waters; or Bat, the celestial deity associated with fertility.[226]

Ultimately, with the Egyptian man-faced bull and human-faced cows there is an undeniable iconographic relation to the Near Eastern tradition. Coupled with the remarkable similarities in the surrounding mythology of Hathor, it seems likely the Egyptian figures were influenced by earlier man-faced bull traditions, especially since Hathor is said to have very early origins associated with nature and fertility.[227] Thus, it seems likely that the Egyptian iconography and mythology stem from earlier Near Eastern practices, which when coupled with the local cattle cults already in place, provided a very rich mythology for later generations.

India

Although no true man-faced bulls from the Indus Valley exist, several examples of remarkably similar iconography prompt questions of inter-cultural influence. Among such examples are a man-faced Markhor Ram (**Fig. 16**),[228] which we originally thought was a man-faced bull,[229] and a Chimera[230] that is essentially a man-faced bull with the addition of a tiger's tail and an elephant's trunk (**Fig.17**).[231] There are also composite bull-man representations from the Indus Valley. A Harappan stamp-seal dated to the second half of the 3rd millennium, found at Mohenjo-Daro, depicts a standing bull-man,[232] and a human-headed horned creature is depicted in one very elaborate scene of worship on another seal from Mohenjo-Daro.[233] A. Parpola associated such scenes with rites of seasonal renewal, and water and vegetation are common motifs for the time period.[234]

In isolation one might consider such images 'common human responses to the natural environment.'[235] However, evidence exists of trade connections between Mesopotamia and the Indus Valley in the 3rd to 2nd millennium BC.[236] For example, a stone bowl dated 2600 to 2400 BC,[237] found at Khafajeh, which is located on a major ancient Mesopotamian trade route, depicts a figure kneeling on two hump-backed bulls, which are not native to Mesopotamia but instead to the Indus Valley. Other evidence comes from the abundance of Indian Ocean shells found in deposits in Mesopotamia.[238] Moreover, man-faced bulls carved from shells presumably imported from the Indus Valley exist, including a mother-of-pearl amulet appearing to depict a man-faced bull from a deposit dated to the 3rd millennium, found during excavations at Tell Brak.[239] According to Oates, other specimens of mother-of-pearl man-faced bulls are known elsewhere in the Khabur area, and a larger example, today stored at the Aleppo Museum, was found in a temple deposit at Qara Quzaq on the Euphrates.

While all of this makes for interesting reading, one must ask: What is the connection to the origin and development of the man-faced bull? One possible answer comes with an examination of Kamadhenu, a deity worshiped in Hinduism that is often portrayed as a winged cow with female head who brings fertility and prosperity (**Fig. 18**),[240] which appears to have been influenced by the Near Eastern tradition just as the Greek tradition would be. The myth of Kamadhenu describes how the goddess arose from the turbulent cosmic ocean, for instance.[241] This origination story is strikingly similar to the Near Eastern creation story of Kusarikku, who emerges from Tiamat. In both the Indus and Greek traditions, it must be pointed out that gender identity is not a clearly defined feature for such deities. As mentioned above, at least one statue of Acheloios in feminine dress exists.[242] Ultimately, both the Indians and the Greeks have human-headed bovine figures that are affiliated with water, fertility, and abundance. And thus it is reasonable to suggest that the early Near Eastern mythology of the man-faced bull, and elements of the iconography as well, made their way into India and are manifested in the art of the Indus Valley and the religious traditions that emerged much later. Unfortunately, this project cannot investigate Kamadhenu further, but instead examines the same phenomenon in the Greek world.

---

women as lustratio, connotations linked to fertility and sexuality, and the presence of Acheloios in Dionysian processions depicted on reliefs.

[226] Ibid.,188-9. A similar characteristic will be seen in India, with the female-faced cow goddess Kamadhenu, in whose belly are contained all other deities.

[227] D. Redford (ed.), *Oxford Guide to Egyptian Mythology* (Oxford: University Press, 2003), 157–161.

[228] Islamabad Museum, NMP 50.295; Mohenjo-Daro DK 6847.

[229] Dr. J. M. Kenoyer kindly provided the proper identification of this figure.

[230] See also D. Frenez and M. Vidale, 'Harappan Chimaeras as 'Symbolic Hypertexts'. Some Thoughts on Plato, Chimaera and the Indus Civilization,' in *South Asian Studies*, Vol. 28, No. 2 (September 2012), 107-130.

[231] Lahore Museum, L.P.-1727, published in J. Aruz and R. Wallenfels, *Art of the First Cities: the Third Millennium B.C. from the Mediterranean to the Indus*, 408, no. 300d.

[232] Karachi National Museum, NMP 50.214, in J. Aruz and R. Wallenfels, *Art of the First Cities,* 407, no. 300a.

[233] Ibid., 409, no. 294.

[234] A. Parpola, *New Correspondences between Harappan and Near Eastern Glyptic Art* (Cambridge: University Press, 1984), 184-5; J. Aruz and R. Wallenfels, *Art of the First Cities,* 409.

[235] J. M. Kenoyer, 'Master of Animals and Animal Masters in the Iconography of the Indus Tradition,' in *The Master of Animals in Old World Iconography*, edited by D. Counts and B. Arnold (Budapest, 2010), 39b.

[236] P.D. Curtin, *Cross-Cultural Trade in World History* (Cambridge: University Press, 1984) 66.

[237] British Museum ANE128887.

[238] J. Oates, 'The Evidence of the Sealings,' 296-7. J. Oates, 'Organic Material,' in *Excavations at Tell Brak*, Vol. 2, 295-9.

[239] Ibid., 296-7, fig.317.

[240] Depictions of the creature date from the 3rd century BC. However, the early myths about the creature are from Vedic times.

[241] V. Mani, *Puranic Encyclopaedia: A Comprehensive Dictionary With Special Reference to the Epic and Puranic Literature* (Delhi, 1975) 379.

[242] H.P. Isler, 'Acheloos,' in *LIMC*, no.77.

Chapter II: The Westward Migrations of Man-Faced Bull Iconography

Introduction

If anything could be more complex than tracing the origin and development of man-faced bull iconography from Neolithic times through the Near Eastern Dynastic periods, it is tracing the migration of the iconography westward. That there was an interplay between the Greek and Near Eastern worlds starting as early as the Iron Age has been well established.[1] Although some argue, mostly in the realm of historiography,[2] how exactly to conceptualize this phenomenon, the influence itself is clear enough and touches on nearly all aspects of civilized life. Religious iconography is no exception: 'The chimeras,' writes Burkert, 'can clearly be linked to Hittite representations, while Triton- a man with a fish's tail- seems to come straight from Mesopotamia.'[3] The man-faced bull should be added to this list, as it was in earlier publications, first by E. Curtius[4] and later, H.P. Isler.[5] Words, too, made the journey west. Burkert highlights a few: the Greek *harpe* and Aramaic *harba* (scimitar/sword); the Greek *skylon* and the Aramaic *sylan* (looted weapon/looting), among others.[6] From the 8th century on such influences become even clearer, when the ties between East and West begin to exhibit themselves in the literary and archaeological record much more regularly. There is no need to review all the evidence here. For the purpose of this project, only an examination of a few key elements of this East-West interplay is necessary: in particular, the focus on a specific location, Cyprus, followed by an examination of two essential archaic figures, seer-healers and mercenaries.

Cyprus

Man-faced bulls **(Fig. 20)** of a style unique to Cyprus appear as early as the Bronze Age. Throughout the centuries the man-faced bull and other bull men, including the bull centaur similar to some early depictions of Acheloios in the Greek cultural world, appear in ritual contexts associated with water, fertility, and death, just as they did in the Near East and just as they would in the Greek world. Ultimately, Cyprus plays both an active and passive role in the transference of the iconography: active via merchants and other itinerant craftsmen establishing contacts throughout the western Mediterranean; and passive, as a microcosmic reflection of a global, multi-generational and inter-cultural phenomenon, its own identity constantly evolving due to its location, much like the figure of the man-faced bull and its surrounding mythology and related iconography.

Located about 120 km west of the Levantine coast and 70 km south of the Anatolian coast, Cyprus occupies a spot between the eastern and western cultural worlds at a time of increased contact between the two. Its rich natural resources (most importantly copper, from which the island gets its name) facilitated trade contacts with many different locations throughout the Mediterranean.[7] Moreover, from very early on, waves of migrants arrived on its shores. According to Gjerstad's hypothesis, formulated on the basis of strong similarities between Cypriot pottery and contemporary Carian and north-Syrian pottery, there was a massive migration of Anatolian people to Cyprus in the mid 3rd millennium BC, who initiated a process of heterogenization of Cypriot culture that would characterize the subsequent centuries of the island.[8] Shortly thereafter, our first man-faced bulls appear.

Bronze and Iron Age Cult Activity and Related Art

One of the earliest pieces which might be a man-faced bull has been described as a 'fantastic' animal figure from Souskiou near Palaiapaphos, dated 2300 to 1900 BC **(Fig. 19)**.[9] It is unclear if the animal once

[1] For a general overview, see: W. Burkert, *The Orientalizing Revolution: Near Eastern Influence on Greek Culture in the Early Archaic Age,* translated by Margaret E. Pindar and Walter Burkert (Cambridge: Harvard UP, 1992). See also W. Burrkert, *Babylon, Memphis, Persepolis: Eastern Contexts of Greek Culture* (Cambridge: Harvard UP, 2004); M.L. West, *The East Face of Helicon: West Asiatic Elements in Greek Poetry and Myth* (Oxford: Clarendon Press, 1999).

[2] K. Momrak, 'Greeks and the East in the Iron Age: interpreting interaction in the Eastern Mediterranean,' Unpublished (pre-print) manuscript, accessed Fall 2014 via academia.edu.

[3] W. Burkert, *The Orientalizing Revolution*, 19.

[4] E. Curtius, *Gesammelte Abhandlungen*, 2 (1894), 77ff, 131.

[5] H.P. Isler, *Acheloos*, 92-108.

[6] W. Burkert, *The Orientalizing Revolution*, 39.

[7] For evidence of prehistoric contacts between Cyprus, the Anatolian area, and the Near East, see: G.E. Kenna, 'The seal use of Cyprus in the Bronze Age,' in *Bulletin de correspondance hellénique,* Volume 91, livraison 1 (1967), 255-268; C.J. Bergoffen, 'The Cypriote pottery from Alalakh: Chronological Considerations,' in *The Synchronization of Civilizations in the Eastern Mediterranean in the Second Millennium BC*, II (Wien, 2003), 395-410; K.O. Eriksson, 'Cypriote Proto White Slip and White Slip I: Chronological Beacons on Relations between Late Cypriote I Cyprus and Contemporary Societies of the Eastern Mediterranean,' in *The White Slip Ware of Late Bronze Age Cyprus*, edited by V. Karageorghis (Wien, 2001), 51-64; K.O. Eriksson, 'A Preliminary Synthesis of Recent Chronological Observations on the Relations Between Cyprus and Other Eastern Mediterranean Societies During the Late Middle Bronze - Late Bronze II Periods,' in *The Synchronization of Civilizations in the II Millennium BC*, 411-430; V. Karageorghis, *Cipro. Crocevia del Mediterraneo Orientale 1600 – 500 a.C.* (Milan: Electa, 2002); E. D. Oren, *The Hyksos: New Historical and Archaeological Perspectives. International Seminar on Cultural Interconnections in the Ancient Near East.* Museum Monographs No. 96 (Philadelphia: University of Pennsylvania, 1997).

[8] E. Gjerstad, *The Swedish Cyprus Expedition. Finds and results of the excavations in Cyprus 1927-1931*, Vols. I-III (Stockholm, 1934-37). For a revision of the old position of a major migration of Aegean people to Cyprus during the 12th to 11th centuries, which suggests an amalgamation of Cypriot, Aegean and Levantine trends, see I. Voskos and A. Bernard Knapp, 'Cyprus at the end of the Late Bronze Age: Crisis and Colonization or Continuity and Hybridization?,' in *American Journal of Archaeology*, 112 (2008), 659-84. For evidence of contact between Cyprus and the Western Mediterranean since the Bronze Age, see pg. 33, note 22.

[9] A.T. Reyes, 'The Iconography of Deities and Demons in Cyprus,' Electronic Pre-Publication (2007 Edition), Fig.10, http://www.religionswissenschaft.uzh.ch/idd/prepublication.php.

had horns, but it appears so. There is evidence from nearby Palaiapaphos dating to the 3rd millennium BC that indicates there were cultic activities including ritual bathing and oracular pronouncements related to the worship of natural fertility deities, performed during rites of passage, and it has been demonstrated that such cults were influenced by Near Eastern religions.[10]

The general association of bulls and water, and their use in cultic and funerary contexts, is widespread from a very early date. One particularly important example of this phenomenon is the use of little clay plaques representing models of sanctuaries, found in burials at Vounos and Kotchati,[11] which show bucrania mounted on walls above shrines. Karageorghis sees in the two models in question evidence of the existence of Cypriot chthonic cults associated with representations of the serpent and the bull, interpreting the latter also as the representation of a deity linked to fertility, worshiped in Cyprus since the Early Bronze Age.[12] The plaques are dated to the late 3rd millennium BC, and a similar artifact has been found at the Canaanite site of Megiddo in northern Israel.[13] It is worth noting that these plaques also show vessels used in ritual ablutions, and that such plaques were found in tombs.[14]

Numerous examples of basins for ablutions and cultic kernoi with bull shaped plastic decorations have been found within sacred areas both in the Near East and Cyprus.[15] The first examples of bull-shaped kernoi found in Cyprus come from tombs at Vounous, dated Early Cypriot I (2300 to 2075 BC), and examples with schematic representations of hybrid bull-men exist.[16] In fact, a late dated (Early Cypriot III to Middle Cypriot I) example of a red-polished ware jug in the form of an ithyphallic man-faced bull hybridization (**Fig. 22**) is a clear example that already in the Early Cypriot Bronze Age a funerary nexus existed with the symbolism of water closely associated with the man-faced bull.[17] The first known Cypriot kernos with a distinct man-faced bull protome is dated 1200 to 1050 BC, probably found in a grave at Akhera.[18] Ultimately, this overall employment of bull and man-faced bull shaped kernoi, when taking into account the symbolic value of the cultic kernos as a ceremonial vase, is strongly suggestive of water-related aspects of fertility, in both sacred and funerary contexts, in Late Bronze Age Cyprus through the Iron Age.[19] As with India, the abundance of evidence of close and consistent contact with neighbors sharing the same practices indicates that such activities were not simply common human responses, developed in isolation.

The most important manifestations of the use of man-faced bull iconography on Cyprus are askoi, occupying a significant place in ritual funerary art of the end of Middle Cypriot Period (1750 to 1600 BC) (**Fig. 20**).[20] According to Felice Lo Porto[21] the style of a nearly identical piece stored in Turin is reminiscent of the Chalcolithic Age, with Syro-Anatolian influences. Another example, also part of the Cesnola Collection and now in the Metropolitan Museum, is a piece dating to the same period which has remarkably similar features.[22] In total there are 17 man-faced bull pieces from Cyprus in the Cesnola Collection,

[10] P.H. Young, 'The Cypriot Aphrodite Cult: Paphos, Rantidi, and Saint Barnabas,' in *Journal of Near Eastern Studies*, Vol.64 (2005), 23-44. There is an abundance of archaeological evidence to demonstrate the influence of the Near East and Levantine coast on Cyprus, especially after the work of the Swedish Excavation Team led by E. Gjerstad. For further references on the matter, see: I. Voskos and A. B. Knapp, 'Cyprus at the end of the Late Bronze Age: Crisis and Colonization or Continuity and Hybridization?,' 659-84.

[11] V. Karageorghis, 'Two religious Documents of the Early Cypriote Bronze Age,' in *RDAC* (1970), 10ff.

[12] Ibid. For a summary of evidence of the worship of a bull-deity at Vounos, see G. Hill, *A History of Cyprus*, Vol.1 (Cambridge: University Press, 2010), 57ff.

[13] R.M. van Dijk, 'The Motif of the Bull,' 30-31.

[14] The form of such plaques, with a projection at the bottom, suggests they were used during rituals as a reservoir for libations (R.M. van Dijk, 'The Motif of the Bull,' 31).

[15] A. Bignasca, I kernoi circolari in Oriente e in Occidente: strumenti di culto e immagini cosmiche. (Freiburg, 2000), 107-109, and note 804. For an example of an Italic late archaic kernos with the protome of a man-faced bull, and other Italic kernoi influenced by Cypriot style, see below, pg. 42ff.

[16] J.M. Webb and D. Frankel, 'Social Strategies, Ritual and Cosmology in Early Bronze Age Cyprus: An Investigation of Burial Data from the North Coast,' in *Levant*, 42, 2 (2010), 200, fig.14.a.

[17] From Christie's Sale 2232, lot 80. The catalogue reports the following reference for a similar example: D. Morris, *The Art of Ancient Cyprus* (Oxford: Phaidon, 1985), Pl. 220. For a similar ithyphallic bull jug see Christie's 9296, lot 76, dated 1400 to 1200 BC. For a small clay statuette of a man-faced bull see also **Fig. 23** from Christie's 9296, part of lot 74, dated 1400 to 1200 BC.

[18] A. Bignasca, 'I kernoi circolari in Oriente e in Occidente: strumenti di culto e immagini cosmiche,' 109, note 828, no.C17.

[19] A crater found in 2013 at Hala Sultan Tekke, on the south-eastern coast of the island and dated to the 13th century BC shows a 'Horned God' with raised arms, serpent to right. On the right field of the painting a fish is depicted below the belly of a bull, suggesting the connection of the cult with a water element (See the online report of the 2013 campaign of the New Swedish Cyprus Expedition, http://www.fischerarchaeology.se/?page_id=1613).

[20] Cypriot White Painted Ware Askos, Bronze Age, Museo di Antichità, Turin, Italy (Cypriot Collection, donated by Cesnola, 1870), no. 4834. Published in F.G. Lo Porto, *La collezione Cipriota del Museo di Antichità di Torino* (Rome: Bretshneider 1986), no.43. Lo Porto dates the piece to 2200 to 1600 BC. He also reports similar pieces published by other scholars (E. Gjerstad, *Studies on Prehistoric Cyprus* (Uppsala, 1926), 176, no.2).

[21] F. G. Lo Porto, *La collezione Cipriota del Museo di Antichità di Torino*, no. 43; Museo di Antichità di Torino, Inv. no. 4834), described as White Painted Ware, zoomorphic askos, dated 2200 to 1600 BC; E. Gjerstad et al., 'The Middle Cypriot Bronze Age,' in *Swedish Cyprus Expedition*, Vol. IV, Part I-b, (Lund 1972), fig. XVII, I, reports that this type of askos is datable to the White Painted V Period: 1750 to 1600 BC. L. A. Campbell Gagné, 'Middle Cypriot White Painted Ware: A Study of Ceramic Production and Distribution in Middle Bronze Age Cyprus,' Unpublished Doctoral Thesis (University of Toronto, 2012), listed another specimen of this 'bovine askos' (no.303; 2B.125), and she reports that it was found in a tomb at Kazaphani (tomb 2B). The piece is listed as 2B.34 by Nicolaou, who dated the tomb to the end of the Middle Bronze Age or at the beginning of the Late Bronze Age, so there is accordance with the dating to the Swedish Expedition. This type of Cypriot askos must have been very widespread, insofar as dozens of specimens were found during archaeological excavations of burials. For an additional example, see: E. Gjerstad, *Studies on Prehistoric Cyprus*, 176, no.2.

[22] Accession no. 74.51.791

all of relatively similar style.[23] Gagné writes, 'It is possible that some of the attributes, namely the pouring-spout tail, three legs, and even choice of animal, were culturally determined, since Middle Cypriot animal askoi across the island seem to have these things in common.'[24] It is striking to note how similar features, like the pouring-spout tail, are found on Italic and Sardinian askoi dated from the 10th to 8th century BC,[25] but they are rarely attested in mainland Greece. Such pieces are clear evidence of the association of the man-faced bull with water and death (and in effect, rebirth) in Cyprus, representing a culminating midpoint for the man-faced bull tradition: the many threads of man-faced bull and bull man mythology and iconography in the Near East are becoming further intertwined on the relatively small island of Cyprus in the Late Bronze to Early Iron Age.

In terms of fertility, while the earliest examples of theriomorphic askoi used during rituals of fertility in Syria and Mesopotamia are from the Early Bronze Age,[26] winged man-headed bulls are used in this ritual context only at the end of the Bronze Age in Cyprus. Kourou identifies such figures as male 'bull-sphinxes,' specifically in reference to two winged man-headed bulls wearing a cap (or crown), depicted on a crater from a tomb excavated at Enkomi and dated 1250 to 1200 BC (**Fig. 25**).[27] The bovine hooves indicate these are stylized, winged man-headed bulls, often seen in pairs in the Near East. The author notes that 'In Cyprus oriental styles are more closely followed, while such close imitations of oriental originals are never attested in the art of the Aegean.'[28] A similar crowned and winged man-headed bull appears some five centuries later, on a painted jug, c. 8th to 7th centuries BC, today displayed at the Metropolitan Museum (**Fig. 26**).[29] In his recent essay, Sørensen discusses numerous other man-headed 'bull-sphinxes' and related bull men, drawing the conclusion that such creatures all represent different figures but at the same time are intimately related.[30]

Another important example of the influence of Mesopotamian culture on Cyprus is the early adoption of imagery from ancient cylinder seals, beginning in the 15th century BC.[31] A common element is a bull's head or bucrania, and bovine figures are also very common.[32] Just as in the Near East, some of them also show hybrid bull-man creatures.[33] A Cypriot seal dated c. 14th to 12th century BC, for instance, shows quadrupeds closely resembling recumbent bearded man-faced bulls (in fact, they might be stylized man-faced bulls).[34] According to Knapp,[35] much of the iconography used on Cypriot cylinder seals was foreign (Levantine, Near Eastern and Aegean) in derivation, but associated with local ideological constructs.[36] Many Cypriot bull-men are described on cylinder seals dated to the Late Bronze Age as well.[37]

Other, later examples for the cultic importance of the bull and man-faced bull in Cyprus exist. For instance, bucrania used as masks during religious ceremonies,

[23] The various catalogues consulted do not dwell on what the shape represents, they simply list it as 'zoomorphic askos' or 'bovine askos.' The specimen stored in Turin clearly shows human features of the face, in particular the eyes and the lower painting pattern that represents a beard. Moreover, the nose of all specimens is far too small to be a bovine snout.

[24] L.A.Campbell Gagné, 'Middle Cypriot White Painted Ware: A Study of Ceramic Production and Distribution in Middle Bronze Age Cyprus,' 134.

[25] There are many examples: For Sardinia, see Museo Archeologico di Nuoro Sala III, Vetrina 4 (M.A. Fadda, *Il Museo Archeologico Nazionale di Nuoro, Collana 'Sardegna Archeologica,' Serie Guide e Itinerari* (Carlo Delfino Editore, 2006), fig.54. For an additional Sardinian example, see: J. M. Eisenberg, 'The Art of the Italic Peoples. A Major Exhibition in Paris,' in *Minerva*, Vol.5, No.2 (London: Aurora, 1994), fig.16. A piece from Etruria was exhibited in 2013 at Vetulonia: S. Rafanelli, *Vetulonia, Pontecagnano e Capua. Vita parallele di tre città etrusche, Ara Edizioni* (2013). An additional example is in R. Cecchelin, *Guida Al Museo Nazionale Etrusco Di Tarquinia* (Edizioni Mediterranee, 1987), fig.9. There is an Etruscan piece at the Archaeological Museum of Bologna (no. 12791). The zoomorphic askoi were probably introduced into Italic culture by Cypro-Phoenician traders at the beginning of the Iron Age. For an example of a Cypriot zoomorphic askos with pouring-spout tail found in a grave in Cerveteri, see: V. Belleli, 'Caere e il Mondo Greco. Appunti di Archeologia e di Storia,' in *Incidenza dell'Antico*, 10 (2012), 139, fig.2.

[26] For examples from Tell Brak and Tell al-Rimah, see: C. Postgate, D. Oates and J. Oates, *The Excavations at Tell al-Rimah: The Pottery*. Iraq Archaeological Reports, Vol. 4, BSAI (London 1997), Pl. 99, no. 1189-1190. For a different example of a Cypriot bull-shaped askos showing anthropomorphic features of the face, see British Museum no. 1982,0726.26, from the Cesnola Collection.

[27] N. Kourou, 'Aegean Orientalizing versus Oriental Art: the Evidence of the Monsters,' in *The Civilizations of the Aegean and Their Diffusion in Cyprus and in the Eastern Mediterranean, 2000-600 BC. Proceedings of the International Symposium at Larnaka, 18-24 September 1989* (Pierides Foundation, 1989), PL.XXVIII:1; British Museum no. 1897,0401.1260 (**Fig. 24**). Kourou argues for a proto-orientalizing wave in Cyprus and the Aegean as early as 1300 to 1200 BC (N. Kourou, 'Aegean Orientalizing versus Oriental Art,' 112-4; V. Karagheorgis and J. Des Gagniers, *La céramique chypriote de style figuré, Âge du Fer (1050-500 Av. J. C.)* (Roma: Edizioni dell'Ateneo, 1974), 39-41).

[28] N.Kourou, 'Aegean Orientalizing,' 112.

[29] From the Cesnola Collection, BM no. 74.51.512. The piece shows distinct Near Eastern iconographical influences.

[30] L.W. Sørensen, 'Here There be Monsters: Hybrids Painted on Cypriot Iron Age Pottery,' in *Tradition: Transmission of Culture in the Ancient World* (Copenhagen: Museum Tusculanum Press, 2015), 427-450.

[31] E. Porada, 'The Cylinder Seals of the Late Cypriote Bronze Age,' in *American Journal of Archaeology*, Vol. 52, No. 1 (1948), 178-198.

[32] Examples stored at the British Museum: no. 1897,0401.743, no.1900,0615.53, no.1966,1103.2; Metropolitan Museum no.74.51.4323, no.74.51.4322, and Johns Hopkins Archaeological Museum seals A.1011, A.1015, 1271.

[33] Spurlock Museum, no. 1900.53.0056A; British Museum no.1900,0615.53, no.1898,1201.198, no.1962,1212.1; Metropolitan Museum no.1999.325.206.

[34] Metropolitan Museum no.74.51.4318.

[35] A.B. Knapp, *The Archaeology of Cyprus: From Earliest Prehistory Through the Bronze Age* (Cambridge: University Press, 2013) 460.

[36] For a hypothesis concerning the 'revival' use of Early Dynastic Mesopotamian motifs by Phoenician engravers of the first half of 1st millennium BC, see W.A. Ward, 'A Sumerian Motif on a Phoenician Seal,' in *Archéologie au Levant. Recueil à la mémoire de R. Saidah* (Lyon, 1982), 221-224.

[37] V.G.E. Kenna, 'The seal use of Cyprus in the Bronze Age,' in *Bulletin de correspondance hellénique*, Volume 91, livraison 2 (1967) 552-577; J.M. Webb, *Ritual Architecture, Iconography and Practice in the Late Cypriot Bronze Age*. Studies in Mediterranean Archaeology, Vol. 75 (Lund, 1999), 270-1.

found in a sanctuary area at Kition within the structure of a building dated to the 12th century BC.[38] Additional examples of the worship of a horned deity in which bucrania were used as masks comes from the sites of Enkomi and Ayia Irini.[39] Karageorghis[40] identified a bull-god cult at the Ashlar Building sanctuary, also known as 'Sanctuary of the Horned God,' where fifteen bucrania used as ritual masks were found. Most importantly, also at Enkomi,[41] from the Ingot-god sanctuary, and dated to the 12th century BC, are terracotta fragments of two double-headed androcephalic quadrupeds (**Fig. 27**),[42] identified as centaurs[43] or sphinxes[44] by some authors, but later as man-headed bulls incorporating both masculine and feminine elements.[45] According to Nikolaou, they were found against the northern wall of the court, among twenty-six bucrania placed antithetically in pairs.[46]

The central role of Cypriot and Cypro-Phoenician traders acting as intermediaries between the eastern and western Mediterranean has been suggested by many scholars recently.[47] In the 9th century BC Phoenicians occupied a portion of the island, and later traveled west along the North African coast, arriving intermittently along the coastal areas of the Tyrrhenian Sea and even further, in Spain.[48] In this regard it is interesting to mention the discovery of some examples of Phoenician faience amulets shaped as heads of man-faced bulls (also referred to as 'masks'), found in graves at the southern Cypriot site of Amathus, among other Phoenician artifacts (**Fig. 32**).[49] The single broken horn indicates this is probably a very early depiction of Acheloios as a man-faced bull. The earliest examples of such amulets are dated to the mid 8th century BC, while the later examples are dated to the latter half of the 6th century BC.[50] These pendants were mostly made of faience, but there is also a silver pendant dated to the 6th century BC, found at Marion.[51] Such amulets served as apotropaic devices.[52] According to Clerc, earlier examples of faience 'horned mask' pendants have been found in archaeological excavations at Phoenician sites of the Levantine Mediterranean coasts, like Tell Keisan, or Byblos (first half of the 1st millennium BC), and Tell Fara (from a tomb dated 1070 to 945 BC).[53] The same type of man-faced bull mask amulets are found in many western Mediterranean sites occupied by Phoenicians. An example was found in a tomb dated to the end of the 7th to early 6th century BC, from the Dermech Necropolis at Carthage.[54] An additional four examples from the same necropolis were found in a tomb dated to the 6th century BC.[55] Similar mask-amulets have also been found at the Phoenician site of Tharros in Sardinia, and at Ibiza in Spain.[56] As pointed out by Knapp, several faience objects found on Cyprus form part of an 'interregional artistic koiné' that is 'by [its] nature hybridized.'[57]

---

[38] R.M. van Dijk, 'The Motif of the Bull,' 28-33. For statuettes of 'priests wearing bull mask' from Amathus in Cyprus, see ibid., 28, fig.20.

[39] A. Hermary, 'Statuette d'un 'pretre' masqué,' in *BCH*, 103 (1979), 734ff, fig.6-11; V. Karageorghis, 'Notes on Some Cypriote Priests Wearing Bull-Masks,' in *The Harvard Theological Review* 64 (1971), 261-270, fig. 2-9.

[40] Ibid., 263.

[41] The site is named after a famous bronze statuette of a horned deity standing on an ingot-shaped pedestal. C.F.A. Schaeffer, *Alasia I* (Paris: Klincksieck, 1971), Pl. III.

[42] Ibid., 293, fig. 123.

[43] Ibid., 293-99, fig. 123-127 (about 1100 BC); V. Karageorghis, 'Notes on some Centaurs from Cyprus,' in *Χαριστήριον είς Α. Κ. Όρλάνδον*, Vol.II (Athens, 1964), Pl.XXI:a.

[44] J.M. Webb, 'Ritual Architecture, Iconography and Practice in the late Cypriot Bronze Age,' 218.

[45] S. Sophocleus, 'L'Aphrodite en tant qu'androgyne,' in *Archaeologia Cypria*, I (1985), 86; S. Sophocleus, *Atlas des représentations chypro-archaïques des divinités, Studies in Mediterranean Archaeology* (Göteborg, 1985), 20-23. For the statuette of an androgynous bull-man as a centaur found at Ayia Irini, see: ibid., 96, Pl.XVI, fig.10.

[46] K. Nikolaou, 'Archaeology in Cyprus, 1961-1966,' in *Archaeological Reports*, No. 12 (The Society for the Promotion of Hellenic Studies, 1965 – 1966), 30.

[47] G. Graziadio, 'Le presenze cipriote in Italia nel quadro del commercio mediterraneo dei secoli XIV e XIII a.C.,' in *Studi Classici e Orientali*, XLVI (1997), 681-719; V. Karageorghis, 'Aspects of Trade Between Cyprus and the West During the 14th- 13th Centuries BC,' in *The Point Iria Wreck: Interconnections in the Mediterranean ca. 1200 BC: Proceedings of the International Conference, Island of Spetses, 19 September 1998*, edited by W. Phelps, Y. Lolos and Y. Vichos (Athens, 1999), 121-30; A. Kanta 'The Aegean World Between the East and the West. Aspects of Common Cultural Elements, 16th - 6th c. BC,' in Πλοες. Sea routes. Interconnections in the Mediterranean, *16th-6th c. BC: Proceedings of the international symposium held at Rethymnon, Crete, September 29th-October 2nd 2002*, edited by N.C. Stampolidis and V. Karageorghis (Athens, 2003), 27-40; G. Graziadio and R. Guglielmino, 'The Aegean and Cypriot Imports to Italy as Evidence for Direct and Indirect Trade in the 14th and 13th Centuries BC,' in *Intercultural Contacts In The Ancient Mediterranean. Proceedings Of The International Conference At the Netherlands-Flemish Institute in Cairo, 25th to 29th October 2008* (2011), 309-326.

[48] For the interplay with Etruscan culture specifically, see R. D'Oriano and A. Sanciu, 'Phoenician and Punic Sardinia and the Etruscans,' in *The Etruscan World*, edited by Jean M. Turfa (London: Routledge, 2013), 231-243. For Phoenician influence throughout the Mediterranean, see M. Yon, *Studia Phoenicia*, Vol.V (1987), 369; M. Guidetti, *Storia del Mediterraneo nell'antichità: 9.-1. secolo a.C.* (Editoriale Jaca Book, 2004); V. Karageorghis, S. Hadjisavvas, and F.G. Maier, 'L'archeologia del Vicino Oriente antico. Cipro,' in *Il mondo dell'archeologia, Istituto dell'Enciclopedia Italiana Treccani* (Rome, 2005).

[49] **Fig. 32** was found at Amathus, site E, Tomb 88, today stored at the British Museum (no. 1894,1101.271). For two further examples, one of which is bearded, see G. Clerc, 'Démons Cornus' in *La Necropole d'Amathonte. Tombes 110-385. Études chypriotes*, Vol. XIII (Nicosia, 1991), 100-102, No. T.242/20.2 and 242/21.1.

[50] Ibid., 101.

[51] E. Gjerstad, *Swedish Cyprus Expedition*, Vol IV, 2 (1948), 158, fig.31.

[52] G. Clerc, 'Démons Cornus,' 100. The horned and bearded figures shown on the Phoenician pendants were clearly inspired by apotropaic deities employed in Mesopotamia and Assyria, and they likely even had a later influence on the Greek representations of Gorgons, Satyrs and Selinus (ibid.).

[53] G. Clerc, 'Démons Cornus,' 101, and notes 64-6.

[54] Z. Cherif, 'Le pectoral à Carthage à l'époque punique: origine et diffusion,' in *L'Africa Romana*, Vol.III (2006), 1494.

[55] Ibid., 1495. For other examples from Carthage dated to the 7th century BC, see: G. Clerc, 'Démons Cornus,' 102, note 67; P. Cintas, *Amulettes puniques* (1946), 56-60; A.L. Delattre, 'Notes sur la nécropole punique voisine du Serapeum, à Carthage, communiquées par M. Héron de Villefosse,' in *Comptes rendus des séances de l'Académie des Inscriptions et Belles-Lettres*, 38e année, No. 6 (1894), 440.

[56] G. Clerc, 'Démons Cornus,' 102, and notes 68 and 69 for additional references.

[57] A.B. Knapp, *The Archaeology of Cyprus*, 461.

Another example of Cyprus' involvement in the transference of man-faced bull and bull-man iconography is an askos from the Cesnola Collection (**Fig. 21**),[58] dated Middle Cypriot (1900 to 1600 BC), which depicts a man-faced bull that is somewhat centaur-like, with arms protruding from the top of the shoulder areas and an unidentified structure emerging from the head, right between the bull horns. On a schematic level this piece is similar to the later Bronze of Nule, in Sardinia, where Cypriot traders are known to have traveled extensively (**Fig. 44**).[59] No other man-faced bulls or man-bull hybrids share these basic characteristics. Another example: the earliest man-faced bull of the Greek cultural world, from Ionia, has distinct Cypriot influences (**Fig. 67**). Notice, in particular, the facial features in comparison to the (nearly contemporaneous) bull-masked priest of **Fig. 34**, and the black lines on the torso, reminiscent of the (albeit much earlier) askoi (**Fig. 20**).

Archaic Cult Activity and Related Art

Evidence exists of the image of the man-faced bull on plastic pottery found in Cypriot graves during the archaic period. Although at this point the man-faced bull had breached the shores of Western Civilization, cross-cultural influences were surely instrumental in its further development. These pieces are aryballoi (or balsamarii) in the shape of the man-faced bull's head (e.g., **Fig. 60**).[60] For an example found at Melousha during excavations at the archaic sanctuary area, see Karageorghis.[61] Interestingly, he attributed the piece to a middle 6th century Rhodian workshop,[62] and he notes that identical aryballoi are found in Italy.[63]

A Cypriot terracotta statuette, recently displayed in Rome,[64] gives additional substance to the hypothesis concerning an ancient cult of the bull-man hybrid in Cyprus. The statuette (**Fig. 28**) is dated to about 750 to 600 BC.[65] It depicts a hybrid creature with the body of a bull, a human torso, and a bearded and horned head, with arms raised and outstretched in benediction.[66] It comes from excavations at the Ayia Irini sanctuary,[67] which was dedicated to a fertility god worshipped from 1200 to 500 BC, who was (naturally) very closely associated with the bull.[68] Other similar statuettes of centaur-bull creatures have been found at the same site,[69] some of them are horned, some have snakes encompassing them,[70] and some of them show androgynous features.[71] There is no agreement among scholars on the exact dating of these pieces, but the earliest examples were found at a level of the sanctuary containing pottery from the 10th and 9th centuries.[72] According to Hill,[73] horned centaurs were also found at other Cypriot sites, such as Amathus. Rice notes how the humanoid features of those pieces have common elements to bull-men from Near Eastern cultures: 'A beard but no moustache, like the earlier Mesopotamian examples from seals, long lappets of hair, prominent ears and rather bland, almost vacant facial expression.'[74] There is also a fragment of a Cypriot horned centaur dated to the first half of the 6th century BC (**Fig. 29**) which was found at the site of the Temple of Aphrodite in Naukratis,[75] in Egypt.[76] These centaur-bulls have strong similarities with key early depictions of Acheloios on Greek Black Painted Ware, where he is struggling with Herakles (**Fig. 30**). On such pieces, Acheloios is depicted as a horned, bearded centaur, often with similar posture, as he has one or both arms raised.[77] This particular depiction of Acheloios is later abandoned in favor of the man-faced bull.[78] Incidentally, Semerano argues that the Greek κενταυροι comes from the Semitic *ken-* (as well as, such as) and *tora* (bull),[79] but still connects the figure with water, as he had earlier, referring back to the use of the 'M' iconography on such

[58] J. Myres, *Handbook of the Cesnola Collection of Antiquities from Cyprus* (New York: 1914), no. 222. Museum no. 74.51.796

[59] See below, pg. 36ff.

[60] V. Karageorghis, 'Chronique des fouilles et découvertes archéologiques à Chypre en 1961' in *Bulletin de correspondance hellénique*, Volume 86, livraison 1 (1962), 327-414; see also Inv. no. 1961/VIII-II/3 in, K. Nikolaou, 'Archaeology in Cyprus,' 27-43.

[61] V. Karageorghis, 'Chronique des fouilles et découvertes archéologiques à Chypre en 1961,' 350, fig.30.

[62] For a discussion of the problems of dating these aryballoi, also known as balsamarii, see below, pg. 56ff.

[63] M. I. Maximova, *Les Vases Plastiques dans l'Antiquité*, Vol. II (Paris 1927), Pl. XVIII, no.73.

[64] 'Mostri. Creature fantastiche della paura e del mito,' Exhibition at Palazzo Massimo in Rome, from December 20th, 2013 to June 1st, 2014.

[65] E. Gjerstad, *Swedish Cyprus Expedition,* Vol II, 710F, Pl.228-5, no.1122.

[66] Again, the resemblance to the Sardinian bronze of Nule is striking.

[67] At the same site small clay figurines representing men wearing bull masks were found (V. Karageorghis, 'Notes on Some Cypriote Priests Wearing Bull-Masks,' 262).

[68] G. Bourogiannis, 'The Sanctuary of Ayia Irini: looking beyond the figurines,' in *Pasiphae,* Vol.VII (Fabrizio Serra Editore, 2013), 37. The worship of a bull-deity associated with snakes and a fertility cult is attested in Cyprus since the 3rd millennium BC (G. Hill, *A History of Cyprus,* 58).

[69] E. Gjerstad, *Swedish Cyprus Expedition,* Vol II, 753, Pl.2281.1, no.2101.

[70] G. Hill, *A History of Cyprus,* 61. From the same site come bull statuettes with snakes wrapped around their necks (ibid., 60). Interestingly, plastic oinochai of Cypro-Phoenician style found in Etruria, shaped like bull heads with anthropomorphic features, show the same detail of serpents around the neck. They are dated to the 7th century BC. For example, see F. Sciacca, *La tomba Calabresi e la tomba del tripode di Cerveteri* (Città del Vaticano, 2003), no.12.

[71] E. Gjerstad, *Swedish Cyprus Eexpedition,* Vol. II, 749, Pl.227.1, no.2031, no.2361; S. Sophocleus, 'L'Aphrodite en tant qu'androgyne,' 86; S. Sophocleus, *Atlas des représentations chypro-archaïques des divinités. Studies in Mediterranean Archaeology* (Göteborg, 1985), 96, Pl.XVI, fig.10.

[72] E. Gjerstad, *Swedish Cyprus Expedition,* Vol II, Pl.227, no.1 & 4.

[73] Ibid., 61.

[74] M. Rice, *The Power of the Bull,* 271.

[75] Naukratis was a place where intense cultural exchanges occurred between Phoenicians, Greeks and Egyptians.

[76] BM EA50125, reg. no. 1911,0710.100, published in A. Villing, M. Bergeron, G. Bourogiannis, and A. Johnston, *Naukratis: Greeks in Egypt* (New York, 2013), TF.029.

[77] For example, see H.P. Isler, *Acheloos,* no. 74-76 and no.85.

[78] Cf. H.P. Isler, 'Acheloos,' in *LIMC,* for a chronology.

[79] G. Semerano, *L'infinito,* 14.

figures in Bronze Age Old European cultures and other prehistoric evidence.[80]

Another interesting specimen from the Cesnola Collection is described by Myres[81] as a 'human-headed bull and lion' sculpture, probably the fragment of an arm to a throne. The piece is dated to the years of the Assyrian domination of Cyprus (c. 700 to 560 BC). The man-headed bull is described as winged, and wearing a pointed helmet, and Myres compares it with the Assyrian winged man-headed bulls, but mentions that the stylistic features of the piece are entirely Cypriote.[82]

There is also a fragment of a bronze candelabrum (**Fig 31**) dated to the 6th century BC, found at the site of ancient Marion in Cyprus.[83] Cypriot bronze candelabra were the first ever produced in the Mediterranean, during the 6th century BC, then exported to Italy,[84] where Etruscan craftsmen produced similar artifacts from the end of 6th century,[85] whose tall stalks stand on elegantly-made animal legs. The first Etruscan pieces of Cypriot influence were made in Vulci. They were used in graves to symbolically illuminate the tomb, believed to be the 'house of the dead.' [86] The most famous and beautiful Etruscan example of a lighting object found in a grave, depicting many man-faced bulls, is the 'Lampadario di Cortona' (**Fig. 43**).[87]

One final object representing the man-faced bull in Cyprus, dated to the 6th century BC,[88] is a fragment of a terracotta mask perforated for suspension (**Fig.33**). It was found in a tomb at Amathus, the same area from which we find the faience amulets shaped as man-faced bull masks, and the same location where figurines of 'priests wearing [man-faced] bull masks' were found (**Fig. 34**). In fact, there is one extant priest mask with large human-like eyes and a distinctly human nose.[89] According to Nys, the use of ritual masks in Cyprus since the Late Bronze Age is connected with indigenous rituals involving the transition from childhood to adulthood.[90] Together with the aryballos and the candelabrum mentioned in the previous paragraph, there is an interesting demonstration of the lifespan of the connection of the image of the man-faced bull with funerary practices and rites of passage in Cyprus.

Altogether, it appears that in Cyprus, Near Eastern man-faced bull iconography is continuously re-incorporated into the already established traditions of the Bronze Age involving purification, ritual ablutions, and divinatory practices, which made use of bucrania, bull-men, and even man-faced bulls likely imported from Anatolia in the mid 3rd millennium BC. For thousands of years these rituals and iconographies persevered, and on the first coinage of Cyprus, minted at Paphos, we find the man-faced bull paired with an astragalos, a knuckle bone used in oracular activity in ancient times, which is fitting indeed since what appears to be the first Cypriot man-faced bull, one that was also associated with oracular activity, emerged just down the road in Souskiou.[91] And most importantly, there is compelling evidence that Cypriot man-faced bulls and related iconography made their way west during the Orientalizing Period, indicated by the distinct iconographical devices and stylistic signatures employed by the former and reflected in the latter.[92]

Iron Age Seer-Healers

A more specific avenue of migration that must be followed is quite obvious: since the Near Eastern man-faced bull has many religious connotations and is deeply involved in ritual practices, the ancient men whose daily work was to engage in such practices is a good place to look for the source of the man-faced bull's migration.

As indicated in Homer, seers were the first social group to make the long journey from East to West, which was probably facilitated by their esoteric knowledge and special skill sets, no doubt sought after inter-culturally,

[80] Originally, Semerano argued the etymology of κενταυροι was based on Semitic words for family (*kintu*) and river (*harru*). Cf. G. Semerano, *Le Origini della Cultura Europea. Dizionari Etimologici*, Vol. II (Olschki: Firenze, 1994), 137.

[81] no. 1021

[82] Ibid., 148.

[83] V. Karageorghis, 'Chronique des fouilles et découvertes archéologiques à Chypre en 1961,' 345, fig.24.

[84] H. U . Cain, 'Candelabro,' in *Enciclopedia dell'Arte Antica Treccani*, Vol. II (1994), 304. Cain states that Cypriot candelabrums were also exported from Cyprus to Asia Minor, Palestine, Greece, and Spain, and influenced the production of similar objects not only in Etruria, but also in Ionia and mainland Greece, since the end of the 6th century BC

[85] E. Oriani, *I candelabri etruschi in bronzo*, Vol.II, 4 (1980), 19-22.

[86] Cf. L. Ambrosini, *Thymiateria etruschi in bronzo: di età tardo classica, alto e medio ellenistica. Studia Archeologica 113* (Rome: Bretschneider, 2002), 329. It is striking to note how the presence of lighting objects found in graves is attested for Etruria and the Levantine Area, especially in the areas of Phoenician influence (see M.P. Nilsson, 'Lampen und Kerzen im Kult der Antike,' in *Opuscula archeologica*, 6 (Lund, 1950), 104 ff)), but they are not found in any Greek burials, nor in mainland Greece or its colonies (see A. Testa, 'Considerazioni sull'uso del candelabro in Etruria nel V e IV sec., Mélanges de l'Ecole française de Rome,' in *Antiquité*, Vol.95-2 (Paris, 1983), 610).

[87] See below, pg. 51ff.

[88] BMC no.1894,1101.202 (V. Karageorghis, *The Coroplastic Art of Ancient Cyprus*, Vol. III (1991), 117, no.33, Pl.LXVIII:1).

[89] See A. Ciasca, 'Le Protomi e le Maschere,' in *I Fenici* (Milano: Bompiani, 1988), 356. The object is Phoenician and dated to the 6th century BC.

[90] K. Nys, 'The use of Masks in Cyprus during the Late Bronze Age,' in *Journal of Prehistoric Religion*, Vol.9 (1995), 19-34.

[91] Even in Roman times, Chariton of Aphrodisias reports that at the sanctuary of Aphrodite in Paphos rites of divination were performed by priests, 'who were also prophets.' (Ibid., 27). For evidence of the link between the man-faced bull and female goddesses related to fertility/chthonic sphere, see M. R. Ciuccarelli, 'Acheloo ctonio dalla Magna Grecia all'Etruria?,' in *Meditarranea* (Pisa- Roma: Fabrizio Serra, 2007), 121-140.

[92] The Bronze of Nule, in Sardinia, and its counterpart in the Cesnola Collection; the candelabra and similar Etruscan works; the various Cypro-Phoenician man-faced bull amulets and their Greek and Etruscan counterparts, and the Ionian Greek askos with Cypriot facial features and painting pattern.

as Burkert tells us.[93] In fact, he goes so far as to label such figures the 'intellectual elite' of the time period, and there may be some truth to that. Plato, for instance, who hated such figures, acknowledges that they were able to convince entire cities of the truth of their prophecies.[94] Evidence of the migrations of said seer-healers is commonplace.[95] Moreover, these individuals traveled freely,[96] with bonds to members of their 'family'- an apprentice is essentially adopted by a mentor, instead of a specific polis.[97]

Although no direct archaeological evidence of Near Eastern seer-healers operating in the West exists, there is an abundance of evidence that demonstrates their influence in later Greek and Etruscan culture, e.g. Mesopotamian clay liver models dating from as early as the 18th century BC, and their much later Etruscan counterparts of the 3rd century BC. Cults concerned with the healing powers of water were active in Etruria from at least 500 BC, and although evidence exists of similar practices in Bronze Age central Italy, the latter were certainly influenced during the Orientalizing Period.[98] The use of astragaloi in seer activity is also attested in eastern and western Mediterranean cultures, and the former probably influenced the latter.[99] The practice of sacrificing suckling piglets to atone for sins exists in both cultures as well, and the occurrence of substitute sacrifices in general, widespread in Mesopotamia, finds counterparts in the Greek tradition.[100] Finally, the family-orientation amongst healers and the secrecy of the techne described in the *Hippocratic Oath* finds its parallel in a much earlier source, the *Papyrus Ebers*.[101]

In terms of the actual craft, Iron Age seer-healers often operated as both seers and healers, as the line between the two, which would not even begin to be established until after Hippocrates, had not yet been conceived of.[102]Although some delineations in seer activity existed in the Near East in the Bronze Age, whereby specific seers had specific functions (e.g. purification), in the Iron Age and throughout the Archaic Age seer activity was much more generalized.[103] Furthermore, because demons that cause illness were a fundamental component to Mesopotamian healing magic,[104] there was always a specifically apotropaic dimension to healing which certainly carried over into the practices of Iron Age and Archaic seer-healers. Put simply, the spiritual repulsion of evil by a seer is tantamount to curing a person of disease. Thus, the man-faced bull, as an apotropaic deity with special cleansing properties, is particularly relevant to the seer-healer of the Iron Age and Orientalizing Period, when the transference of the iconography from East to West began to occur. In fact, as discussed in the examination of Cyprus, the use of apotropaic amulets of man-faced bull heads was relatively widespread throughout the Mediterranean during this time period, and it is reasonable to think that seer-healers were associated with their distribution. Finally, recall that the texts relating to Kusarikku, who is often depicted as a bull-man and a man-faced bull/bison, have the very phrase 'Be gone, Evil! Come in, Well Being!,'[105] which was likewise shared, at least in spirit, by the Greek world in apotropaic ritual practices.[106] Likewise, Asallúhi, probably depicted as a man-faced bull, was the supervisor of the priests of Apsu (the subterranean waters), adding another promising connection between seer-healers and the man-faced bull.

Additional evidence of their association with the man-faced bull comes in the form of an important intercultural form of cleansing a person's misdeeds which specifically involves purifying waters (which the Near Eastern Asallúhi and later Etruscan and Greek Acheloios definitely represent): a piglet would be slaughtered over the guilty person and then its blood washed away with fresh water.[107] The 'sin' itself is absorbed into the blood and the purifying waters remove it. The famous purification of Orestes is perhaps the most well known example in the Greek world. In the *Asakki marsuti*, nearly the same ritual is described by Anu to Marduk, in which he says, 'then cleanse that man with pure water from the Deep and wash him clean.'[108] Moreover, the earlier traditions of Kusarriku involve the very same practices.[109] This notion of cleansing waters persists beyond the story of Orestes and is in fact strengthened in the cult of Acheloios,[110] where the practice of ritual purification is well documented. In fact, presented in the later chapter on identity, there is evidence that the Semitic origin of the word Αχ–ελώϊος means 'a sacred water deity associated with ritual cleansing.' Finally, the very founding of Oiniadai, at the mouth of the Acheloios River, involves a story of prophecy and

[93] W. Burkert, *The Orientalizing Revolution*, 41.
[94] Ibid., citing Plato, *Laws*.
[95] Ibid., 42.
[96] Ibid.
[97] Ibid., 43-46. See also, M.A. Flower, *The Seer in Ancient Greece* (Oakland: University of California Press, 2008). 37.
[98] E. Macnamara, *Everyday Life of the Etruscans* (London: Batsford, 1973) 45.
[99] See below pg., 66ff.
[100] W. Burkert, *The Orientalizing Revolution*, 73.
[101] See M.J. Geller, 'West Meets East: Early Greek and Babylonian Diagnostics' in *Archiv für Orientforschung, Bd. 48/49* (2001/2002), 50-75.
[102] See also M.A. Flower, *The Seer in Ancient Greece*, 27-28.
[103] Ibid., 27.
[104] W. Burkert, *The Orientalizing Revolution*, 59.
[105] See above, pg. 14ff. Sometimes translated as 'go out death, enter life.'
[106] See e.g., Plut. *Q.Conv.*, 693 f. As cited in W. Burkert, *The Orientalizing Revolution*, 60.
[107] W. Burkert, *The Orientalizing Revolution*, 58-60.
[108] Ibid.
[109] F.A.M. Wiggermann, *Mesopotamian Protective Spirits*, 66: 'take the bucket, the hoisting device with the wooden bail, bring water from the mouth of the twin rivers, over that water cast your holy spell, purify it with your holy incantation, and sprinkle that water over the man, the son of his god.' This last line, 'the son of his god,' might refer to Asalúhi. See above, pg. 14ff.
[110] See below, pg. 62ff.

purification: Alkmaion, after murdering his mother, was instructed by the priestess of Delphi to seek out a new area to free himself from his sin. He did, and there married Acheloios' daughter, Kallirhoe, who gave birth to Akarnan, the namesake of the area.[111] Moreover, Oiniadai was probably the first mint in Greece proper to issue coinage of the man-faced bull.[112]

The prophetic knowledge acquired from grappling with 'Old Men of the Sea' might also have been influential in the mythos surrounding the early seer-healers in their relation to the man-faced bull. These watery figures, Proteus, Nereus, and Glaucus, were shape-shifters just like Acheloios.[113] Nereus is even depicted as a fish-tailed man grappling with Herakles.[114] Taylor suggests these figures might have been older than Acheloios,[115] but based on the evidence provided in earlier sections, it seems that, instead, the 'Old Men of the Sea' emerged around the same time, possibly evolving from the previously discussed fish-*apkallu*. These earlier prophetic figures, usually depicted as old men with fish-head headdresses and fish-like gowns, are known to have shared attributes with the winged man-headed bull, like the aforementioned Ashurnasirpal lamassu, which is adorned with the same fish-head headdress and has fish scales on his stomach. Whatever the exact evolution, the oracular nature of such figures combined with the fluvial dimension suggests some intermingling early on. Coupled with the iconographic similarities and the notion of seizing water to produce benefit, and the relation is rather obvious.

Ultimately, clear similarities exist in the practices of the ancient seer-healers in the Near Eastern, Greek, and Etruscan traditions, the first no doubt migrating far beyond their own borders, as Homer and others have described, and influencing the other two. It makes sense that elements of their iconography traveled with them, examples of which we find in the practice of hepatoscopy and its use of liver models, and also in the use of bucrania, bull-men, and probably even the man-faced bulls appearing in foundation deposits and graves,[116] and used as wearable apotropaic devices. Moreover, in Cyprus, which played an important role during this period of transmission, 'priests' often wore bucrania and man-faced bull masks, and there are even statuettes of such activity (**Fig. 34**). These Cypriot priests were probably tantamount to Iron Age seer-healers. They were certainly involved in divinatory practices through Roman times.[117] So the idea that the iconography of the man-faced bull traveled with seer-healers is quite likely, as the apotropaic image and its association with ritual purification with fresh water were essential to their daily operations.

Empedocles

Perhaps the best indication of Near Eastern and Cypriot seer-healer practices and their association with man-faced bull iconography transferring West is exhibited through a discussion of Empedocles, the seer-healer and philosopher of Sicily, active in the 5th century BC. Empedocles of Akragas appears to be the only ancient Greek writer to mention the man-faced bull in descriptive terms, juxtaposing 'man-faced ox-progeny' and 'ox-headed offspring of man' (βουγενῆ ἀνδρόπρῳρα/ ἀνδροφυῆ βούκρανα).[118] He does so in the context of his zoogony, whereby at Stage 2,[119] through the special provenance of Love, we begin to see the unification of things (albeit mixed-up in certain cases). Even though he uses the iconography to illustrate his theory on the emergence and evolution of living things, other aspects of his life indicate an affiliation with the man-faced bull and its surrounding mythos as an ancient river god: He lived not far north of Gela, which steadily employed the iconography on its coinage throughout Empedocles' life.[120] He was known as a spiritual healer[121] whose approaches to medicine were criticized by the authors of the Hippocratic treatise,[122] much like the aforementioned traveling seer-healers. His second work, of which only a small fraction remains, was entitled *Purifications*, and therein he speaks about sin and redemption.[123] He considered the sacrifice of animals, specifically bulls, as tantamount to murder, and eating their flesh tantamount to cannibalism.[124] Moreover, he describes the words he speaks as flowing like a 'stream.'[125] Although many ancient authors use such descriptive terminology, an Attic Red-Figure Vase found at Akragas and dating to middle of the 5th century BC (coinciding exactly with Empedocles' life) depicts Herakles and Acheloios,[126]

[111] B. Powell, 'Oeniadae: I. History and Topography,' in *AJA*, Vol. 8, No. 2 (1904), 137-139.
[112] See below, pg. 71.
[113] R. Taylor, 'River Raptures,' 30.
[114] M. Pipili, 'Nereus,' in *LIMC*, Vol.6 (Zürich, 1992), 826-27 and 835.
[115] R. Taylor, 'River Raptures,' 30.
[116] W. Burkert, *The Orientalizing Revolution*, 46-53.
[117] H.P. Young, 'The Cypriot Aphrodite Cult,' 27.

[118] Fr. 61, Aelian, *Nat. anim.*, XVI, 29.
[119] See Fr. 59, from Simplicius, *de caelo*, 587, 20.
[120] Diogenes Laertius VIII, 51.
[121] Fr. 111, Diogenes Laertius VIII, 59; Fr. 112, Diogenes Laertius VIII, 62 (lines 1-10) and Clement, *Strom.* VI, 30 (lines 9-11).
[122] Hippocrates, *On Ancient Medicine*, Part 20.
[123] Empedocles, and M.R. Wright, *Empedocles: The Extant Fragments* (Indianapolis: Hackett, 1995), Fr.122 (136) & 124 (137).
[124] Empedocles, Fr.118 (128).
[125] Empedocles, *On Nature*, 2 (3); see also *Purifications*, 103 (114).
[126] In the *Derveni Papyrus* (c. 350 BC, discussed below, pg. 61.), which some argue was written by a seer (*mantis*), Acheloios is referred to as the god of all water, while Okeanus is equated with air and Zeus (K. Tsantsanoglou, 'The First Columns of the Derveni Papyrus and their Religious Significance,' in *Studies on the Derveni Papyrus*, edited by A. Laks and G. Most (Oxford, University Press, 1997), 93-128, especially 98-9). Empedocles was certainly aware of the tradition mentioned in the *Derveni Papyrus*, since he imitated a line from the same Orphic theogony presumably influencing this later text (K. Tsantsanoglou, 'The First Columns of the Derveni Papyrus and their Religious Significance,' 125) and therefore surely knew that Acheloios, like Asallúhi, was equated with all water.

with water streaming from the latter's mouth.[127] This iconographic motif is also seen on the coinage of Alontion, Mylai, and possibly Neapolis. [128]

Additional evidence that Empedocles carried on traditions from Cyprus and the aforementioned bull-men cults: In fragment 118(128), he praises the worship of queen Kypris, specifically mentions the painted animal figurines affiliated with her, and discusses how her followers did not drench their altars with the slaughter of bulls, which he claims is the greatest defilement among men- 'to bereave of life and eat noble limbs.'[129]

Empedocles is also said to have purified the river closest to Selinous by diverting, at his own expense, two nearby rivers.[130] Shortly after this event, Diogenes informs us,[131] the people of Selinous were having a festival on the banks of the river and Empedocles appeared, was worshipped as a god, and then jumped into the fire to confirm his god-like status. Commentators have remarked how the word used for 'appearance' in the text is one usually reserved for a god, namely, ἐπιφανῆναι.[132] However, what has not been mentioned is that, in the passive voice, as it is used here by Diogenes, the word takes the literal meaning of 'to appear upon the surface.'[133] Even if this literal interpretation goes too far, we must recall Taylor's observation of the pattern of figures dying in or beside a river and being reborn as river gods.[134] Thus, when Empedocles describes himself using terms that are reminiscent of man-faced bull iconography and mythology, it might be more than a mere coincidence: 'I go about honored by all...crowned with ribbons and fresh garlands[135]... [men and women] follow me in their thousands, asking wherein lies the road to profit,[136] some desiring prophecies;[137] while others ask to hear the word of healing[138] of every kind of illness.'[139] Individually, any of these indicators might seem like an exaggeration, but taken together Empedocles appears to be closely associated with the man-faced bull and the religious beliefs and ritual practices associated with it, and thus provides us with a convenient example that seer-healers were indeed instrumental in the transference of the man-faced bull.[140]

Mercenaries

A final, closely related avenue for explaining how and why the man-faced bull, specifically, made this journey west comes in the social phenomenon that was active around the entire Mediterranean throughout the Iron Age and during the period of the Peloponnesian War and beyond: the emergence of mercenaries from the western Mediterranean, including Greece, western Asia Minor, and most significantly Sardinia, Sicily, and the Italian Peninsula.[141] In this section the migrations of man-faced bull iconography are followed through an analysis of the employment of western mercenaries in the eastern Mediterranean during the Iron Age and the importance of man-faced bull mythology to the mercenary soldier.

Western Mercenaries in the East

Western mercenaries have a long history in the East, starting in at least the 7th century BC, although itinerant warriors may have been exploring those regions as much as 500 years earlier. Over the centuries they seem to have made a living serving various empires.[142] There is evidence of their use in Assyria, Babylonia, Egypt, Judah,[143] and Tyre,[144] and it has been suggested that the Greek mercenary tradition evolved out of Ionian trader-

[127] On display at Musée du Louvre, Department of Greek, Etruscan and Roman Antiquities, Sully, first floor, room 39, case 4.

[128] Cf. MSP I, 22-3 and 46 (this abbreviation is for Molinari Sisci Potamikon Vol. 1). The Neapolis coin is illustrated in Garrucci, but we have yet to confirm I ts existence (**Fig. 163**).

[129] Ibid., 118(128).

[130] Diogenes Laertius, and R.D. Hicks, *Lives of Eminent Philosophers* (Cambridge: Harvard University Press, 1972), 70.

[131] Ibid.

[132] Empedocles, and B. Inwood, *The Poem of Empedocles* (Toronto: University Press, 2001), 159, note 9.

[133] H. Liddell and R. Scott, *A Greek-English Lexicon* (Oxford: Clarendon Press, 1996), 669, under ἐπιφαίνω, 3rd meaning, wherein it cites Ti.Locr.101d.

[134] R. Taylor, 'River Raptures,' 21-23.

[135] The ribbons are seen on the iconography of man-faced bulls from Neapolis (e.g., Sambon 423) and Metropolis (Moustaka 138; Rogers 411; SNG München 119); The garland makes its appearance in Neapolis on silver and bronze issues that depict a winged nymph crowning the man-faced bull, but also in Gela (G.K. Jenkins, *The Coinage of Gela*, Group V, 371). See Empedocles, *Purifications*, 102 (112).

[136] The man-faced bull has always been a symbol of abundance, and as discussed in the section on mercenaries, likely connected with the pursuit of wealth and abundance.

[137] The man-faced bull is associated with divination, as indicated by his pairing with the astragaloi on the coinage of Cyprus (BMC Cyprus, 35, 1-3, Taf. 7., 1-3; 21, 1-3; Head 740; F. Imhoof-Blumer, 'Fluß- und Meergötter auf griechischen und römischen Münzen. (Personifikationen der Gewässer),' in *Schweizerische Numismatische Rundschau*, Band 23 (Bern, 1923), 228, 136, Taf. 4, 34), and astragaloi in tombs at Lokris, where the cult of the man-faced bull is well attested (discussed in Chapter 4).

[138] As demonstrated throughout Chapter 1, the man-faced bull is thoroughly intertwined with the practices of ritual healing, from the earlier Near Eastern tradition into the Greek cultural world.

[139] Fr. 112, Diogenes Laertius VIII, 62 (lines 1-10) and Clement, *Strom.* VI, 30 (lines 9-11).

[140] See also pg. 87ff for a discussion of the apotheosis of Euthymos of Locri in relation to river gods and man-faced bull iconography.

[141] W. Burkert, *The Orientalizing Revolution,* 39: 'another area in which there were prolonged and close contact: the military sphere of mercenaries.' For specific examples from Sicily, Sardinia, and Italy, see below, pg. 41.

[142] W. Burkert, *The Orientalizing Revolution*, 25.

[143] W. D. Niemeier, 'Archaic Greeks in the Orient: Textual and Archaeological Evidence,' in *Bulletin of the American Schools of Oriental Research*, No. 322 (South Hadley, 2001), 11-18, who relates that an inscription mentioning KTYM (Kittim) indicates the use of Greek mercenaries. He cites W.F. Albright, 'Palestinian Inscriptions,' in *Ancient Near Eastern Texts Relating to the Old Testament*, edited by J.B. Pritchard (Princeton: UP, 1969), 320-22; Y. Aharoni, J. Naveh, and A. F. Rainey, *Arad inscriptions* (Jerusalem: Israel Exploration Society, 1981), 12-13. Greek presence in Judah and Tyre is not investigated in this essay.

[144] W.D. Niemeier, 'Archaic Greeks in the Orient: Textual and Archaeological Evidence,' 18, who cites Ezekiel 27. Scholars debate whether or not the names mentioned can be equated with mercenaries. See reported bibliography for details of debate.

pirates active in the Levant during the second half of the 8th century.[145] In fact, according to Herodotus, Pharaoh Psammetichus I (664 to 610 BC) employed mercenaries from Ionia and Caria, and such soldiers-for-hire began their careers raiding the Delta.[146] And it is in Miletos, an Ionian city, where the man-faced bull first appears on Greek coinage, in the first half of the 6th century BC.[147]

In the Near East, which is most important for the purposes of this project, from textual evidence we know of a group of 'Ionian' opponents to the Assyrian kings in the 8th and 7th centuries, who were later pressed into service under the king.[148] The term 'Ionian' is used synonymously for 'Greeks.'[149] Moreover, the Assyrian king at the time, Sennacherib, was the son of Sargon II, who constructed the colossal winged man-headed bull statues and had them at the entrance of his throne room.[150] Thus there were definitely Greek mercenaries serving under an Assyrian king at the time the motif was popular in Near Eastern art. Annus goes so far as to identify these winged man-headed bulls with Kusarriku, and suggests they represent the king's vanquished enemies now bound to service.[151] This sounds remarkably similar to the situation encountered with our earliest mercenaries. Moreover, the same Psammetichus I of Egypt who employed Greek mercenaries against his rivals in the area,[152] was originally an Assyrian vassal king.[153] Niemeier argues, convincingly, that Psammetichus I employed Carian mercenaries when in charge of the Assyrian army, basing his argument on an analysis of the reliability of Polyainos' *Strategica,*[154] in which it says Psammetichus I had a Carian advisor by the name of Pigres, and employed many Carian mercenaries.[155] In fact, the winged man-headed bull has a prominent place on later (5th century) Carian coinage.[156]

In terms of archaeological evidence, the earliest indication of Greeks fighting in the east comes from a sword of Naue II type of central Mediterranean origin found in Ugarit and dating to the 12th century BC, and some scholars have claimed this sword is evidence of Sardinian mercenaries fighting in Ugarit.[157] Moreover, evidence of Sicilians, Sardinians, and Thyrrenians captured in Egypt and allegedly forced into service exists from c. 1200 BC.[158] Later evidence, reported by Niemeier, is an archaic Greek bronze greave found at Carchemish, from c. 630 to 550 BC;[159] and an archaic Greek bronze shield, also found at Carchemish, and dating to the second half of the 7th century.[160] Another important item, a Cypro-Phoenician silver bowl,[161] indicates the Babylonians and Egyptians were both employing Greek mercenaries against each other.[162]

Ultimately, there is no doubt that the colossal winged man-headed bulls of the time period made an impact on western observers, and as demonstrated from the relief of Sargon II,[163] the figure was an important deity in military expeditions. Surely, then, beginning at least in the 7th century BC, and possibly a few hundred years earlier, western mercenaries were exposed to the iconography of the Near Eastern man-faced bull.

On the Man-Faced Bull as a Mercenary Deity

Although the fact that mercenaries acted as 'mediators in the continuing oriental influx' into Greece is obvious,[164]

[145] N. Luraghi, 'Traders, Pirates, Warriors: The Proto-History of Greek Mercenary Soldiers in the Eastern Mediterranean,' in *Phoenix*, Vol. 60, No. 1/2(2006), 35.

[146] Herodotus II, 152-54, and Diodorus I, 66.12-67.2.

[147] C. Seltmann, *Greek Coins* (London: Methuen, 1933) Pl.1, no.25.

[148] W.D. Niemeier, 'Archaic Greeks in the Orient: Textual and Archaeological Evidence,' 18. See also T.F.R.G. Braun, 'The Greeks in the Near East,' in *Cambridge Ancient History*, III (Cambridge: University Press, 1982), 14-21; R.A. Kearsley, 'Greeks overseas in the 8th century B.C.: Euboeans, Al Mina and Assyrian imperialism,' in *Ancient Greeks West and East*, edited by G.R. Tsetskhladze (Leiden: Brill, 1999), 119-22. In reference to the documents of Sargon II, see D.D. Luckenbill, *Ancient Records of Assyria and Babylonia. Vol 2: Historical Records of Assyria from Sargon to the End* (Chicago: UP, 1927), 30, 62-63, 79-80; A.L. Oppenheim, 'Babylonian and Assyrian Historical Texts,' in *Ancient Near Eastern Texts Relating to the Old Testament*, edited by J.B. Pritchard (Princeton: University Press, 1969), 285-86.

[149] Ibid., 16.

[150] 'King Sargon's son and successor Sennacherib defeated a Greek army in a land battle in Cilicia, probably in 696 B.C. Two years later Sennacherib is said to have repelled an Ionian fleet in an engagement off the Cilician coast. The royal annals of the year 694 B.C. record that Ionian seafarers had been captured by the king and subsequently pressed into service in the Assyrian army. These Greek warriors then continued their military careers under new management, far from home' (J.Hale, 'Not Patriots, Not Farmers, Not Amateurs: Greek Soldiers of Fortune and the Origin of Hoplite Warfare,' in *Men of Bronze: Hoplite Warfare in Ancient Greece*, edited by D. Kagan and G. F. Viggiano (Princeton, 2013) 181).

[151] A. Annus, *The God Ninurta: in the Mythology and Royal Ideology of Ancient Mesopotamia*, 117; R.M. van Dijk, 'The Motif of the Bull,' 254.

[152] Herodotus II.152-54 and Diodorus I.66.12-67.2.

[153] A. Spalinger, 'Psametichus, King of Egypt: I,' in *Journal of the American Research Center in Egypt*, 13 (Boston, 1976), 138.

[154] Polyainos' *Strategica*, VII.3; W.D. Niemeier, 'Archaic Greeks in the Orient: Textual and Archaeological Evidence,' 17.

[155] Ibid.

[156] SNG Copenhagen Supp. 4301; BMC Lycia 7; K. Konuk, 'Orou, dynaste de Carie,' in *Scripta Anatolica, Mélanges en l'honneur de Pierre Debord*, edited by P. Brun (Bordeaux, 2007), 2.2.

[157] R. Jung and M. Mehofer, 'A Sword of Naue II Type from Ugarit and the Historical Significance of Italian type Weaponry in the Eastern Mediterranean,' in *Aegean Archaeology*, 8 (2008), 111–136 (see in particular 111 (in which the authors argue it is not an example of the exchange of goods) and 134 (in which the authors argue it is evidence of Sardinian mercenaries employed by Mycenaeans). Museum Latakia, inv. no. M /231.

[158] See below, pg. 41.

[159] W.D. Niemeier, 'Archaic Greeks in the Orient: Textual and Archaeological Evidence,' 19.

[160] Ibid. See also E. Kunze, 'Schildbeschläge,' in *Bericht über die Ausgrabungen in Olympia* (Berlin: de Gruyter, 1956), 48-50; J. Boardman, *The Greeks Overseas: Their Early Colonies and Trade* (New York: Thames and Hudson, 1980), 51, fig. 20.

[161] R.D. Barnett, 'The Amathus Shield-Boss Rediscovered and the Amathus Bowl Reconsidered,' in *Report of the Department of Antiquities, Cyprus* (1977), fig. 3.

[162] W.D. Niemeier, 'Archaic Greeks in the Orient: Textual and Archaeological Evidence,' 21. See also J.L. Myres, 'The Amathus Bowl: A Long Lost Engraving,' in *Journal of Hellenic Studies* 53 (1933), 35-36.

[163] See above, pg. 12-3ff.

[164] W.D. Niemeier, 'Archaic Greeks in the Orient: Textual and

the rationale for their adoption of man-faced bull iconography needs explanation (here we focus primarily on Greek examples, but the same rationale applies to earlier Sardinian, Sikel, and Thyrrenian mercenaries also adventuring around the eastern Mediterranean). Given what was observed about the mythology surrounding man-faced bull iconography in the Near East and Cyprus, it should be no surprise that it was especially appealing to mercenaries. The man-faced bull touches on nearly every aspect of a mercenary's life, from his reasons for finding employment as a soldier of fortune, to his protection on the very battlefield that will earn him his day's wages.

As a symbol of abundance[165] the man-faced bull embodies a significant aspect of the rationale for taking up arms. In the earliest, Iron Age examples of mercenary use there is some debate about the reasons for seeking employment in such a dangerous occupation, with reasons ranging from local political disturbances[166] to thrill seeking.[167] However, Nino Luraghi convincingly argues against the prevailing opinion that mercenary employment was reserved for the aristocratic elite.[168] Luraghi claims that the literature is only reflecting a small aspect of the greater reality, because a single mercenary would not be very marketable, whereas the hoplite, whose tactics are group-based, made the Greek mercenary desirable to foreign powers.[169] In addition, Luraghi mentions post-Peloponnesian War mercenaries, the bulk of whom were certainly not from the aristocratic elite, and extends this fact to reflect on the likely background of pre-Peloponnesian War mercenaries. Finally, Lughari suggests that many of the Greek mercenaries likely came from rural areas, if again one takes into consideration the history of mercenaries from the Peloponnesian War to modern times.[170] Thus, it is very likely that the majority of mercenaries were not wealthy thrill seekers but relatively ordinary men seeking wealth through a very dangerous occupation. Ultimately, the notion that economic reasons, coupled of course with some sense of adventure, opportunity, and entrepreneurship, were the main impetus for the Greek individual to seek employment as a mercenary are convincing even for the Iron Age, and so the man-faced bull as a symbol of abundance would be particularly appealing to the Greek individual who was risking his life for daily work.[171]

As a mediating, chthonic deity,[172] the man-faced bull acts as a facilitator for a mercenary's journey into the afterlife, should he not fare well on the battlefield. Engaged in such dangerous activity on a daily basis, an individual would constantly be aware that each new day could be one's last. Under such extreme circumstances, paying homage to a liminal god is only natural, ensuring that his spirit would be looked after should he die. Moreover, we know from stories as early as Homer that the fate of one's soul is of the utmost importance to the warrior, whose fear of becoming a *menima* should not be understated.[173]

On a related note, as a general fluvial deity the man-faced bull represents the originating and final principles of life, particularly important to soldiers and also exhibited

Archaeological Evidence,' 11. See also J. Seibert, *Die politischen Flüchtlinge und Verbannten in der griechischen Geschichte: von d. Anfängen bis zur Unterwerfung durch d. Römer* (Darmstadt: Wissenschaftliche Buchgesellschaft, 1979), 7-26; E. Stein-Hölkeskamp, *Adelskultur und Polisgesellschaft: Studien zum griechischen Adel in archaischer und klassischer Zeit* (Stuttgart: Steiner, 1989), 24, and 81-84. The topic of accepting new gods was recently taken up by Robert Parker in *On Greek Religion*, where he outlines four major avenues for the incorporation of new gods into a region: an assembly agreeing to honor a god, likely 'in return for favors received;' the recommendation by an oracle; granting land to foreigners so they could build a temple and worship their own gods; and establishing private altars throughout cities (R. Parker, *On Greek Religion* (Ithaca: Cornell University Press, 2011) 273-274). All except the last of these factors probably comes into play with the man-faced bull. The figure was no doubt worshipped by mercenaries, for many reasons that will become immediately apparent, and therefore upon returning home or colonizing a new area he was honored 'for favors received.' The oracle at Dodona almost always issued the instruction to offer sacrifices to Acheloios, so an oracular dimension is probably also operative. Insofar as mercenaries were often engaged in assimilation with pre-existing municipalities, Parker's third point is also relevant. Finally, one must consider the rural nature of man-faced bull worship, in which case, as Parker recounts, 'Beyond this assembly-controlled central area there was a hinterland where private cults and gods, both Greek and foreign, came and went freely; some of them would eventually become sufficiently recognized to acquire public priesthood.' Thus the idea that mercenaries brought back with them cultural elements from a distant land and incorporated those foreign elements back home is quite intuitive.

165 See below, pg. 63ff.

166 W.D. Niemeier, 'Archaic Greeks in the Orient: Textual and Archaeological Evidence,' 24.

167 Ibid. See also M. Bettalli, *I mercenari nel mondo greco, Vol. 1: Dalle origine alla fine del V. secolo a.C., Studi e testi di storia antica*, 5 (Pisa: Edizioni ETS, 1995), 26, 108-109.

168 N. Luraghi, 'Traders, Pirates, Warriors: The Proto-History of Greek Mercenary Soldiers in the Eastern Mediterranean,' 21-47. The arguments for mercenary elites concerns the following: the ancient accounts of mercenaries in the East are of aristocratic elites(Alcaeus of Mytilene Fragment 133; Herodotus II.152-54; Diodoros I.66.12-67.2.); mercenary equipment is very expensive (P. Kaplan, 'The Social Status of the Mercenary in Archaic Greece,' in *Oiskistes: Studies in Constitutions, Colonies, and Military Power in the Ancient World. Offered in Honor of A.J. Graham*, edited by V. Gorman and E.W. Robinson (Leiden: Brill, 2002), 241. See also G. Viggiano and H.Van Wees, 'The Arms, Armor, and Iconography of Early Greek Hoplite Warfare,' in *Men of Bronze*, 57-73); mercenaries would need to undergo expensive tactical training to be effective (ibid.); and mercenaries would have to be educated enough to survive in a foreign land and market themselves to others (ibid).

169 N. Luraghi, 'Traders, Pirates, Warriors: The Proto-History of Greek Mercenary Soldiers in the Eastern Mediterranean,' 24.

170 Ibid., 23. There might also be here an indication as to why the man-faced bull becomes a predominantly rural god once fully incorporated into the Greek world.

171 In later times, particularly from the time of the Peloponnesian War onward, the reasons are almost entirely economic. See e.g., H.F. Miller, 'The Practical and Economic Background to the Greek Mercenary Explosion,' in *Greece & Rome, Second Series*, Vol. 31, No. 2 (Cambridge: University Press, 1984), 153-160.

172 Especially in the Etruscan world. See Chapter 4.

173 W. Burkert, *The Orientalizing Revolution*, 66.

in Homer,[174] in which the fallen heroes are returned to the river of their birth. Incidentally, John Hale argues, convincingly, that many of the early mercenaries were promising young Greeks who were led (trained and funded) by aristocratic elites.[175] As a river deity in the Greek world, the man-faced bull is associated with the upbringing of youths, ensuring their protection.[176] Thus, this particular dimension of the man-faced bull would be appealing to a young mercenary.[177] In fact, for boys, the koureion ritual of the Greek world specifically indicated becoming a warrior, and perhaps the entire custom springs from these early, youthful mercenaries.[178]

In a more spiritual sense, the fluvial connotations, like those related to ablutions, take on a meaning of cleansing the soul for past misdeeds. There is textual evidence (albeit later) that beyond exile some of those who became mercenaries had been 'wandering about for lack of even daily bread, and destroying those with whom they come in contact...they have become equal danger to barbarian and Greek'[179] and, 'each seeking to get himself some kind of competence to be rid of the prevailing penury'[180] Thus the notion of rebirth, implicit in a fluvial, chthonic deity, is especially important in the Greek world, when mercenaries were seeking, in at least some instances, a new life because of a life gone awry in their homeland.[181] Put simply, for many mercenaries, engaging in such activity operated as a cleansing of depravity and a rebirth into a life of honor,[182] and therefore the man-faced bull's fluvial connotations of cleansing are particularly fitting. Ultimately, it is through the man-faced bull that they are 'purified and reborn into a new identity,' a phenomenon Taylor has correctly recognized was pervasive in Greek culture.[183]

It is also important to note that mercenaries are themselves apotropaic, protecting the kings they serve, much like Annus' aforementioned winged man-headed bulls.[184] Thus the notion of acquiring a new identity and assimilating with the god himself, which is clearly reflected in the later practices of lustratio and stories of apotheosis in the Greek world,[185] respectively, is indicated here in the basic apotropaic function which mercenaries shared with their god. There may also be evidence of this 'assimilation' in the use of horned helmets among the Nuragic Sardinians, later adopted by Italic natives.[186] Iconographically, the apotropaic function exhibits its ties directly to mercenaries on ornamental Etruscan shields of the 6th century BC, when some Etruscans were heavily employed in mercenary service and aligned with Carthage.[187] Moreover, on coinage, Weiss suggests a specific apotropaic dimension when a city employs the iconography, wherein the man-faced bull, as a river god, takes on the role of protecting the city and its inhabitants.[188] This, too, no doubt stems from the earlier association of mercenaries with man-faced bulls.

Select Numismatic Evidence

Mercenary affinity for the man-faced bull becomes even more iconographically apparent in the later use of the image on coinage, particularly in Sicily. There one sees the man-faced bull very often appear on the coinage of a municipality established by retired mercenaries. One must ask: Whom better to put on a new city's coinage than the god who (in some cases) brought them out of poverty, protected them, and offered them a new life? Taylor suggests that such images might have been used by a culture 'that required an initial expiatory sacrifice to accompany the acquisition of new territory,' which makes perfect sense for a mercenary group who needed purification after a life of bloodshed.[189] We will see many examples of this phenomenon in the accompanying catalog, and in Agyrion in particular, mercenary graves have been found dating to the exact time period the man-faced bull appears on its coinage.[190]

Also in terms of numismatic evidence: Any man-faced bull enthusiast will undoubtedly notice that he is often paired with Apollo, particularly in Campania, a veritable breeding-ground of mercenaries in the ancient world at the end of the 5th century BC.[191] Apollo himself has very interesting ties to mercenaries, and some believe he was considered a 'protector of mercenaries.'[192] In his essay,

---

174 For a discussion of this, see L. Posteraro, 'Origine di Alife. Simbolismo delle sue tradizioni e della sua moneta,' 318.

175 J.R. Hale, 'Not Patriots, Not Farmers, Not Amateurs: Greek Soldiers of Fortune and the Origins of Hoplite Warfare,' 190.

176 See below, pg. 62ff.

177 J.R. Hale, 'Not Patriots, Not Farmers, Not Amateurs: Greek Soldiers of Fortune and the Origins of Hoplite Warfare,' 190.

178 E. J. Håland, 'Take, Skamandros, My Virginity,' in *The Nature and Function of Water, Baths, Bathing, and Hygiene from Antiquity through the Renaissance* (Leiden: Brill, 2009), 125.

179 Isocrates 5.121.

180 Demosthenes 14.31.

181 'They were members of the elite who had been driven out of their native country by war,[or] exile following staseis' (W.D. Niemeier, 'Archaic Greeks in the Orient: Textual and Archaeological Evidence,' 24).

182 H.F. Miller, 'The Practical and Economic Background to the Greek Mercenary Explosion,' 154.

183 R. Taylor, 'River Raptures,' 38.

184 In fact, the very first man-faced bulls of Sicily were issued by Gelon, who before becoming tyrant of Gela was employed as the body guard of Hippocrates, the previous tyrant.

185 This will be explored in depth in the Chapter 6, particularly when we examine Euthymos of Locri, pg.96.

186 See below, pg. 45ff.

187 Cf. M. Sannibale, 'Orientalizing Etruria,' in *The Etruscan World*, edited by Jean Turfa (Routledge, 2013), 99-133; R. D'Oriano and A. Sanciu, 'Phoenician and Punic Sardinia and the Etruscans,' in *The Etruscan World*, 231-243. According to Artistotle, the Etruscans and Carthaginians had a military alliance (Aristotle, *Politics*, 3.5.10-11).

188 C. Weiss, *Griechische Flussgottheiten in vorhellenistischer Zeit: Ikonographie und Bedeutung* (Würzburg: K. Triltsch, 1984), 21-22.

189 R. Taylor, 'River Raptures: Containment and Control of Water in Greek and Roman Constructions of Identity,' 36-37.

190 See catalog.

191 D. Castrizio, *La monetazione mercenariale in Sicilia*, 20.

192 See N. Fields, 'Apollo: God of War, Protector of Mercenaries,' in *Archaeology in the Peloponnese, New Excavations and Research*, edited by K. Sheedy (Oxford: Oxbow Books, 1994), 95-113.

Fields draws attention to miniature bronze votive objects with specific military themes that are found in shrines to Apollo, particularly at the site of Apollo Epikourios at Bassai.[193] A statue of Apollo in Metropolis dating to the 6th century BC actually shows him fully clad in hoplite armor,[194] and Metropolis pairs Apollo with the man-faced bull on a bronze issue of the 4th to 3rd century BC.[195] Incidentally, the common pairing with Apollo also adds another interesting component to the seer-healer-mercenary phenomenon, insofar as many epithets label Apollo as a god of prophecy and healing: Thearios, Proopsios, Kledones, Paian, and Oulios, for example.[196] Thus, it appears that Apollo's pairing with the man-faced bull on coinage finds compelling rationale when one reevaluates the iconography based on its appeal to mercenaries (and seer-healers). Now, it makes perfect sense why the two are so often paired together.

A fascinating countermark on a bronze coin of Antiochos II, Theos,[197] offers an excellent example of the phenomenon of man-faced bull migration as it continued in the Greek world, serving as a veritable reflection of the earlier patterns of migration (**Fig. 35**). Within the countermark we see an Indian humped man-faced bull, just like the type on a Seleukid issue from either Ai Khanoum or Bactra (294-281 BC),[198] only this one is standing, not charging or (more likely) kneeling in submission. The coin was found in Asia Minor and dates 20 to 50 years later than the Ai Khanoum/ Bactra humped man-faced bull coin, thus supporting the notion that a mercenary group, which had served in the Eastern Empire under an earlier Seleukid King (probably Seleukos I or Antiochos I, who jointly issued the aforementioned Ai Khanoum/Bactra coin), decided to pay homage to the Oxus river god upon returning home for favors received while abroad. Moreover, above the bull we see a meander symbol, indicating the group was probably allotted some land on the Meander River (probably somewhere in Ionia, near Magnesia) after service to the king.[199] They therefore reissued a coin of a later Seleukid king with the group's adopted countermark, thereby incorporating the foreign concept back home, and essentially merging the foreign river god with their own, just as their ancestors had done when the iconography originally migrated west.[200] This return home is reinforced by Bernard's observation: 'In the eyes of a Seleukid ruler the real grandeur was to extend his power over the old towns of Asia Minor and the islands, to beautify them through his generosity and receive honors from them. This was much more important to him than to reign in Bactra over all the colonies that the first two kings [Seleukos I and Antiochos I] ...had had the political instinct to make their eastern satrapies.'[201] It should therefore be no surprise that the later Seleukid kings transported mercenaries back to the area of Asia Minor.

Conclusion

Ultimately, it seems that, one particularly important agent in the man-faced bull's journey from East to West was the mercenary, who likely adopted the iconography because of its appealing connotations, and, if lucky enough to survive and return home, made special arrangement to incorporate the god into the local pantheon. Moreover, when Greek and other western mercenaries colonized various areas, they transferred 'the cult ideas of their home city to local springs or rivers,'[202] as indicated in the many later examples of the figure's use on mercenary coinage of the 5th to 3rd centuries BC. Thus, in the end, it should be no surprise that none other than mighty Ares comes to the aide of Acheloios during his fight with Herakles![203]

[193] Many miniature iron soldiers were also found at the site (A.M. Snodgrass, *Early Greek Armour and Weapons, from the End of the Bronze Age to 600 B.C.* (Edinburgh: University Press, 1964), 110), in addition to a significant amount of slag. Fields interprets the slag to signify small metal workshops near the site that produced such votive objects for mercenaries to offer to the gods, without having to sacrifice the arms and armor that would keep them employed and alive (N. Fields, 'Apollo: God of War, Protector of Mercenaries,' 104). Additional examples exist of small votive objects from various shrines to Apollo (Ibid., Delphi (108); Crete (105); Dreros (105)), which the author differentiates from the large, inscribed pieces most likely offered by ordinary citizens of a particular polis(Ibid., 100). See also, A.M. Snodgrass, *Early Greek Armour and Weapons, from the End of the Bronze Age to 600 B.C.*, 74.

[194] C. Morgan, *Early Greek States Beyond the Polis* (London: Routledge, 2003), 141-2.

[195] MSP I, 496-500.

[196] For an extensive list of Apollo's many epithets, see Aaron J. Atsma's 'Theoi Greek Mythology: Exploring Mythology in Classical Literature and Art,' available at www.theoi.com.

[197] Original coin minted 261 to 246 BC. A. Houghton, C. Lorber, and O. Hoover, *Seleucid Coins: a Comprehensive Catalogue* (New York: The American Numismatic Society, 2002), no. 537, uncertain mint, possibly Tralles.

[198] Ibid., no. 283A. For an attribution to Bactra, see O. Bopearachchi, 'The Seleukid Coins of Central Asia and the Bactra Mint,' reprinted from *Travaux de Numismatique Grecques Offerts à Georges Le Rider*, edited by M.Amandry and S. Hurter (London: Spink, 1999) 17-37; O. Bopearachchi, 'The Monetary Policy of Bactria under the Seleukids,' reprinted from *Topoi, Suppl.* 6 (2004), 43-60.

[199] See catalog below for a full attribution. The meander symbol on this countermark, with long, straight segments, is similar to coins issued earlier in Magnesia (**Fig.36**), which further assists in the attribution. Incidentally, a statue of Marysas, a god originating in the area of the Meander, was found in Ai Khanoum. Cf. O. Bopearachchi, 'The Monetary Policy of Bactria under the Seleukids,' reprinted from *Topoi, Suppl.* 6 (2004), 54.

[200] We will discuss how this man-faced bull is probably Acheloios Oxus Meander in Chapter 7, where we present our theory of locative epithets.

[201] P. Bernard, 'L'Asie Centrale et l'Empire séleucide,' in *Topoi*, 4/2 (1994), 507.

[202] R. Taylor, 'River Raptures,' 37.

[203] Pausanias, and Sir James George Frazer, *Descriptions of Greece*, Vol. I (Macmillan, 1898), 312. Incidentally, the Mamar of Sicily, whose name probably stems from a worship of Mars, were a group of Campanian mercenaries that employed man-faced bull iconography when they began to issue coinage in Sicily, after service to a Syracusan tyrant.

Conclusions

Altogether, it seems that seer-healers and mercenaries played a pivotal role as the leading exponents in the migration of man-faced bull iconography from East to West. However, as we have indicated, these two avenues are not isolated tracks. In fact, it is likely that both commonly interacted in their roles as mediators of the Oriental influx. Who would have more demand for a seer-healer than a mercenary? Flower goes so far as to say, 'The most important role for the seer in ancient Greek society was arguably on the field of battle,'[204] and argues that the seer was on a level close to that of the general. And as the piglet sacrifice indicated, blood for blood is required for atonement, and it is the seer-healer who performs this act with cleansing waters. Thus, if a mercenary sought redemption after a bloody day on the battlefield, he likely sought out a seer-healer for ritual purification. In fact, there are even amphorai from the late 6th century that depict seers engaged in hepatoscopy and interacting with hoplites **(Fig. 37)**.[205] Seer-healers probably also helped protect mercenaries from black magic,[206] and, insofar as they were concerned with actual natural medicine, probably accompanied mercenaries in order to help clean their wounds and fight off infection. Moreover, the seer-healer needed the mercenary for steady income and physical protection, and the two likely had somewhat of a symbiotic relationship. Finally, in terms of the protection of one's soul at the point of death, which is a common concern for warriors: Who else helps ensure the proper rituals are performed to offer such protection? Probably seer-healers. Ultimately, it is the interplay of seer-healers and mercenaries, acting as complementary agents when traveling about the Mediterranean during the Iron Age, that greatly facilitated the incorporation of the man-faced bull, a deity very closely associated with both occupations, into the western world.

[204] M. Flower, *The Seer in Ancient* Greece, 153. See also H. Popp, 'Die Einwirkung von Vorzeichen,' Unpublished Dissertation (Erlangen, 1957); R. Lonis, *Guerre et religion en Grèce à l'époque classique* (Paris, 1979); W.K. Pritchett, *The Greek State at War*, Vol. 3 (Berkeley, 1979); M.H. Jameson, 'Sacrifice before Battle,' in *Hoplites: The Classical Greek Battle Experience*, edited by V.D. Hanson (London, 1991), 197-228; R. Parker, 'Sacrifice and Battle,' in *War and Violence in Ancient Greece*; edited by Han van Wees (London, 2000), 299-314.

[205] See, e.g., F.T. Van Straten (ed.), *Hiera kala: Images of Animal Sacrifice in Archaic and Classical Greece* (Leiden, 1995), V 242, V 243, V 247, V262.

[206] For a discussion of black magic and its use during this time period, see W. Burkert, *The Orientalizing Revolution*, 68-69.

Chapter III: The Man-Faced Bull and Related Topics in Early Western Mediterranean Cultures

Introduction

The iconography of the man-faced bull in Italy and Sicily was not entirely transplanted from the East during the Orientalizing Period, and neither was the underlying mythology of Acheloios.[1] In fact, strong evidence exists to demonstrate that a first wave of diffusion from East to West occured during the Bronze Age and continued to have ramifications throughout the Iron Age, with Cypriot peoples traveling about the Mediteraenean and bringing with them elements of Near Eastern culture. Early itinerant warriors from Sardinia, Sicily, and Italy, much like Greek mercenaries, also played an important role in the subsequent waves of transmission. Thus, while there were two major waves of diffusion, in the Bronze Age and during the Orientalizing Period, various smaller ripples no doubt occured as the iconography and mythology developed and took on various forms, never quite fully articulated but still undeniably related to the later traditions of Acheloios and the man-faced bull. This early diffusion resulted in a prolonged interplay among various cultural groups, eventually leading to the Etruscan and Greek figures of Acheloios. It was therefore the original wave that essentially plowed the soil for the second major wave that would occur much later. For, as we will see, the very same cultural phenomena operative in the later Etruscan and Greek traditions, namely, the worship of a shape-shifting bull, bull-man, and even man-faced bull water deity in caves and water-related temples, who has special healing and psychopomp attributes, was first deeply embedded in earlier cultures in Italy and the surrounding area.

Overview of Early Western Cult Practices

The basic association between undercurrent water and chthonic cults practicing in caves is attested in Italy and Sicily as early as Paleolithic times, and in some cases these caves were also used for burials.[2] In Neolithic times, after the introduction of agriculture and cattle breeding, evidence reveals various forms of worship of sacred water in caves, distinctly linked to agricultural and chthonic cults.[3] Starting in the Early Bronze Age in Sicily, Sardinia, and the Italian Peninsula, these chthonic practices acquired a distinct healing dimension, demonstrated by numerous archaeological excavations.[4] The clearest manifestations are found in caves in which subterraenean water flowed, which represents an important link to the underworld. This has prompted many authors to assume a connection between water cults, fertility, and burial rituals, demonstrating the dual function of some caves that were used in both religious rituals and funerary rites.[5] Numerous studies have addressed the Italian context in particular, focusing on the subject of rituals or religious beliefs connected with the agrarian sphere (death-rebirth cycle) and the underworld, where the sacred value of water appears as a dynamic symbol of regeneration, fecundity, germination and, in some cases, sanition.[6] Often these archaeological contexts have returned vases with distinct ritual functions, in which they were placed under stalactites in order to collect dripping subterraenean water to which the Neolithic people attributed healing and rejuvenating properties.[7]

[1] There is no evidence that the early Greek cultic depictions of Acheloios, like those reported by Plato and Pausanias, are shaped as man-faced bulls. In fact, ancient authors never described the statues they mention. Moreover, it is worth noting that the oldest known cultic image of Acheloios discovered in mainland Greece was not shaped as a man-faced bull; it is the aforementioned bronze statuette showing Acheloios wearing women's clothing, holding a cornucopia (H.P. Isler, 'Acheloos,' in *LIMC*, no.77; M. M. Lee, 'Acheloos Peplophoros. A lost statuette of a River God in Feminine Dress,' in *Hesperia*, Vol.75 (2006), 317-325). The statuette is dated between 480 and 450 BC and was found together with an inscription naming the figure as 'Acheloios' (IG XII, 9, 135), made on a boundary marker from a local sanctuary of Acheloios and the nymphs. Another example of a votive relief from Athens, dated to the end of the 5th century BC, shows Acheloios depicted as a horned human, not a man-faced bull (H.P. Isler, 'Acheloos,' in *LIMC*, no. 210). For additional examples of Acheloios as a horned human on later Attic reliefs see H.P. Isler, 'Acheloos,' in *LIMC*, no. 211-212. The unique known example from Magna Graecia is the stater of Metapontion (S. Noe, *The Coinage of Metapontum*, no. 311).

[2] S. Bianco, 'Il culto delle acque nella preistoria,' in *Archeologia dell'acqua in Basilicata* (Potenza, 1999), 13-24.

[3] Ibid., 18ff.

[4] Cf. R.D.Whitehouse, *Underground Religion: Cult and Culture in Prehistoric Italy* (London, 1992), 132ff and 164ff, which discusses the importance of water as an element intimately related to cultural practice. For the cult of water in caves in Bronze Age southern Italy, see also U. Rellini, 'La Caverna di Latronico e il culto delle acque salutari nell'età del bronzo,' in *Monumenti Antichi pubblicati per cura della Reale Accademia dei Lincei*, Vol. XXV (Roma: 1918), 461ff.

[5] See, for example, M. G. Melis, 'Osservazioni sul ruolo dell'acqua nei rituali della Sardegna preistorica,' in *Rivista di Scienze Preistoriche*, LVIII (2008), 111–124.

[6] L. Pigorini, 'Uso delle acque salutari nell'età del Bronzo,' in *Bullettino di paletnologia italiana*, Anno XXIV, no.9-12 (Parma: Battei, 1908), 169-191; U. Rellini, 'La Caverna di Latronico e il culto delle acque salutari nell'età del bronzo,' 461-618; A. Guidi, 'Luoghi di culto dell'età del Bronzo finale e della Prima età del Ferro nel Lazio meridionale,' in *Archeologia Laziale*, Vol. 3 (Roma: CNR, 1980), 148-155; A. Guidi, 'Alcune ossevazioni sulla problematica delle offerte nella protostoria dell'Italia centrale,' in *Scienze dell'Antichità*, III-IV (1990), 403-414; R. Grifoni Cremonesi, 'Alcuni dati relativi a fenomeni funerari con implicazioni cultuali nella Preistoria e problemi di interpretazione,' in *Prospettive storico-antropologiche in archeologia preistorica*. Part 2, Vol. 4, No.2 (1986), 265-269; R. Grifoni Cremonesi, 'Témoignages de cultes dans le néolithique ancienne des Abruzzes,' in *Prémières communautés paysannes de la Méditerranée occidentale* (Paris, 1987), 413-418; R. Grifoni Cremonesi, 'Observations on the Problems Related to Certain Cult Phenomena during the Neolithic in the Italian Peninsula,' in *Journal of European Archaeology*, 2, 2 (1994), 179–197; T. Di Fraia and R. Grifoni Cremonesi (eds.), *La Grotta S. Angelo sulla Montagna dei Fiori e il problema delle frequentazioni cultuali in grotta* (Rome, 1996), 350ff.; S. Bianco, 'Il culto delle acque nella preistoria,' in *Archeologia dell'acqua in Basilicata* (Potenza, 1999), 13-24.

[7] Interestingly, Sicilian examples of this phenomenon are similar to practices attested in Çatal Hüyük, in Anatolia, as demonstrated by M. Bernabei and R. Grifoni Cremonesi, 'I culti delle acque nella Preistoria dell'Italia peninsulare,' in *Rivista di Scienze Preistoriche*, XLVII (Firenze, 1996), 331-366. See also, M. G. Melis, 'Osservazioni sul ruolo dell'acqua nei rituali della Sardegna preistorica,' in *Rivista di Scienze Preistoriche*, LVIII (2008), 115.

A key element in the divine status of bull iconography in relation to water is that the same water that emerges from the earth descends back into the ground, thus in contact with the world of the dead and the afterlife, to which chthonic deities also have access. This element should be considered the basis of the link between the worship of water and chthonic-funerary-divinatory dimensions in the ancient world, which are an essential component to man-faced bull mythology and related ritual practices in the Etruscan and Greek traditions. What this section shows, in part, is that the symbolic interplay between the worship of water, the imagery of the bull (and man-faced bull) and chthonic, healing, and fertility dimensions was already operative among the prehistoric natives in Italy, Sicily, and Sardinia, centuries before the arrival of Greek culture, indicating that the content of the mythology of Acheloios was not purely Greek, as Isler maintains.

Incidentally, in the Minoan and Mycenaean worlds, no traces exist of such distinct religious associations of water and bulls as the cornerstone or object of worship, and instead bulls usually appear as substitute sacrifices in part of a much larger scheme.[8] It is therefore no coincidence that the more western areas, namely, Italy and Sicily, where people of Cyprus traveled extensively, are those which steadily employed representations of Acheloios in numismatics, painting, sculpture, and architecture in historical times.[9] In fact, by our calculations, some 70% of Isler's *Acheloos* entries are from Italy, Sicily, and further west, as opposed to mainland and eastern Greece. It also appears from our study that this division closely parrallels the early influences of Cypriot and Mycenean travelers, respectively.

Sicilian Traditions in Relation to Water Cults and the Man-Faced Bull

Early Evidence

Prehistoric Sicilian water cults linked to chthonic and funerary rituals, often performed in caves, have a long and well documented history in Sicily, dating from at least the 4th millennium BC.[10] The religious symbolism of bull iconography used in cultic practices related to water is also well attested since the late Neolithic period, suggesting the relation of bulls and water was well established in these early cults. An early example of this phenomenon comes from the most appropriate of places, Gela, at the Chalcolithic Necropolis of Molino a Vento, where a great ritual bowl adorned with seven plastic pairs of bull horns was discovered.[11] In fact, Carmela Raccuia goes so far as to attribute a specific apotropaic function to the horns adorning the ritual bowl.[12]

Sicily also offers the earliest Western-Mediterranean example of a man-faced bull, dating c. 3300 to 2800 BC (**Fig 38**).[13] The specimen was found in the votive deposit of Tomb 17 at the Necropolis of Piano Vento[14] (Palma Montechiaro), indicating an early chthonic association. Vincenzo La Rosa observed that the horns of the man-faced bull are intentionally broken.[15] He analyzes the related symbological meanings of the artifact, stating the associated qualities of death and rebirth, cyclicality, and general effectiveness in the sphere of fecundity.[16] The geometric paintings on this man-faced bull strongly resemble earlier Cypriot pottery style. In fact, Castellana compares the man-faced bull of Piano Vento with a plastic zoomorphic vase from Souskiou, in Cyprus, dating to the first half of the 4th millenium BC,[17] and La Rosa

---

[8] For the use of bull iconography in Minoan civilization, specifically in its relation to water, see L. A. Houseman, 'Fluid Metaphors: Exploring the Management, Meaning and Perception of Fresh Water in Minoan Crete' (Doctoral Thesis, The University of Manchester, 2014). Although bull iconography appears in ritual contexts involving water in Minoan civilization, it does not play a central role as the subject of worship directly connected to water. For the Myeanaean world, see C. Gallou, 'The Cult of the Dead in Central Greece during the Mycenaean Period' (Doctoral Thesis, University of Nottingham, 2002). Gallou presents interesting evidence that links the use of bulls and bull iconography to death rituals usually in the form of substitute sacrifices (ibid., 294-314). Sometimes the bull symbol is associated with a solar motif in LM IIIB Period (ibid., 134-135), and various bovine figures form part of greater ritual settings in the LH IIIA Period (ibid., 153-154). However, like Minoan civilization, the bull iconography of the Mycenaeans is not a central feature of water temples or utilized in caves with specific healing properties, as it is further west, in particular in Sardinia and Sicily. Therefore, although the notion of expiatory sacrifice in its relation to the man-faced bull tradition was undoubtedly influenced by Minoan and Mycenaean civilizations, the primary influence is from further east.

[9] An interesting survey of the existing evidence with informative statistics is found in E. Mussini, 'La diffusione dell'iconografia di Acheloo in Magna Grecia e Sicilia. Tracce per l'individuazione di un culto,' in *Studi Etruschi*, 65-68 (2002), 95-8.

[10] For the use of Chalcolithic Sicilian caves containing natural water sources as the setting for funerary and cultic rituals involving communication with chthonic forces, see: M.Cultraro, 'The Grotta del Vecchiuzzo (Petralia Sottana, Palermo): a multi-purpose cave in a karst system,' in *From Cave to Dolmen. Ritual and symbolic aspects in the prehistory between Sciacca, Sicily and the central Mediterranean* (Oxford: Archaeopress, 2014), 137ff; A. Crispino and M. Cultraro, 'Exploring underground paths. Caves and human landscape in the Siracusa district during prehistory,' in *From Cave to Dolmen*, 179ff; D. Gulli, 'The meanings of caves in the prehistory and protohistory of the Agrigento territory,' in *From Cave to Dolmen*, 73ff; O. Adamo and D. Gulli, 'Cracks, crevices and caves in the Serraferlicchio hill,' in *From Cave to Dolmen*, 69ff.

[11] C. Raccuia, 'Presenze e contatti fra le genti nell'area di Gela nelle età preistorica e protostorica,' in *Origine e incontri di culture nell'antichità. Magna Grecia e Sicilia. Stato degli studi e prospettive di ricerca* (Messina: Di.Sc.A.M., 1999), 322.

[12] Ibid.

[13] V. La Rosa, 'Ultra Mortem: Nuove Testimonianze di Età Preistorica dalla Sicilia,' in *SICVLORVM GYMNASIVM: Studi in ricordo di Rosario Contarino* (Università di Catania, 1995), 202, fig. 1. We sincerely thank Prof. La Rosa for his help and attention during the writing of this book. See also, D. Cocchi Genick, 'Le evidenze di contrada Scintilia nell'ambito dei rituali funerari dell'eta' del rame,' in *Storie Sepolte. Riti, culti e vita quotidiana all'alba del IV millennio a.C. La necropoli dell'età del rame di contrada Scintilia di Favara*, edited by D. Gulli (Agrigento, 2014), 46, fig.1f.

[14] Ibid., 46.

[15] V. La Rosa, 'A proposito di una recente pubblicazione di preistoria siciliana,' in *Archivio Storico per la Sicilia Orientale*, XCIII (Catania, 1997), 289, f.I-III; V. La Rosa, 'Ultra Mortem: Nuove Testimonianze di Età Preistorica dalla Sicilia,' 194.

[16] V. La Rosa, 'Ultra Mortem: Nuove Testimonianze di Età Preistorica dalla Sicilia,' 195.

[17] G. Castellana, 'Le fosse votive della necropoli e credenze religiose,' in *La necropoli protoeneolitica di Piano Vento nel territorio di Palma di Montechiaro* (1995), 67-80.

recognizes the same interesting connections.[18] Even the type of rock-cut tombs found in the Necropolis of Piano Vento are linked to the Anatolian area.[19] Interestingly, a second fragment of plastic bull-shaped pottery found in the same tomb, also intentionally broken, demonstrates the funerary ritual use of water which, in this case, pours from the mouth of a bull.[20] Daniela Genick comments that at Piano Vento the performance of rituals is attested by the intentional breaking of pottery and precious items, including 'an original statuette with anthropo-theriomorphic features, probably with the intention to emphasize the close relationship with the deceased by symbolic ritual acts.'[21] Ultimately, the evidence from Piano Vento gives substance to the notion of an initial wave of diffusion of man-faced bull iconography and related cultic practices from the Levant to Sicily via Cyprus.[22]

The early worship of rivers also emerges in Sicily around the same time. In fact, the relationship between the image of the bull and watercourses is documented in many archaeological contexts. For example, a large bowl with a plastic handle shaped as a bull protome, found in the Late Bronze Age ritual deposit of the spring of St. Giovanni di Ferla in the area of Syracuse,[23] near the Anapos River,[24] lead Cultraro to argue for the existence of early Sicilian water and river bull-cults at Ferla. The same author, by morphological comparisons, highlighted similar evidence from contemporary contexts on the Italian Peninsula, all concerning the connection of the symbol of the bull with native beliefs implying cultic water practices and rites of lustratio.[25]

During the transition from the Bronze Age to the Iron Age, an important indication of the bull-water association in ritual practice are the so-called *scodella a grandi corna*, ceremonial dishes with plastic bull protomes.[26] The practices involving these dishes is common in Ausonio I culture, 14th to 13th century BC, in Lipara and Sicily,[27] and similar examples are known for the Late Bronze Age in Campania and Etruria.[28] Moreover, from this cultural

[18] V. La Rosa, 'A proposito di una recente pubblicazione di preistoria siciliana,' 283-289.

[19] S. Tiné, 'L'origine delle tombe a forno della Sicilia,' in *Kokalos*, 9 (1963), 73-92. The earliest examples of rock-cut tombs are also known in Chalcolithic Campania, Latium, and Tuscany (J. Robb, 'Burial and Human Body Representation in the Mediterranean Neolithic,' in *The Oxford Handbook of Neolithic Europe*, edited by C. Fowler, J. Harding, D. Hofmann (Oxford: University Press, 2015), 962), and among the oldest known examples are the Sardinian 'Domus de Janas,' discussed below.

[20] Ibid.

[21] D. Cocchi Genick, 'Le evidenze di contrada Scintilia nell'ambito dei rituali funerari dell'eta` del rame,' 46.

[22] Evidence of pottery classes from Western Sicily (the area between the Platani and Salso rivers) comparable to pottery of Palestine are dated to the late 4th millennium BC (A. Cazzella, M. Cultraro and G. Recchia, 'Relazioni tra l'Italia centro-meridionale, la Sicilia e l'area egeo-balcanica durante l'Eneolitico,' in *Atti della XLIII Riunione scientifica: l'età del rame in Italia : dedicata a Gianni Bailo Modesti: Bologna, 26-29 novembre 2008* (Firenze: Istituto italiano di preistoria e protostoria, 2011), 159). For the 3rd millenium BC, many elements of cultural affinity between Sicily, Malta Archipelago, North Africa and the Aegean-Anatolian area, lead scholars to shift focus on the route of transmission to North Africa, rather than on the Aegean-Balkan avenue, to explain these similarities (ibid., 160). For clear evidence of cultural contacts between Sicily and the Anatolian cultural environment between the 3rd and 2nd millennium BC, see L. Bernabò Brea, 'Eolie, Sicilia, e Malta nell'età del Bronzo,' in *Kokalos*, 22-23 (Rome, 1978), 52; L. Bernabò Brea and M. Cavalier, *Meligunìs-Lipára*, 4 (Palermo, 1980), 688. Recently, Gianmarco Alberti argued for a revision of some classes of pottery found in Middle Bronze Age tombs of south-eastern Sicily, previously attributed to Cypriot workshops, but probably local products made in Sicily by Cypriot potters. Alberti's work provides strong evidence of early direct cultural contacts between Cyprus and Sicily along North African/southern Mediterranean routes not involving the mediation of mainland Greece (G. Alberti, 'Brocche Base Ring II da contesti del Bronzo Medio in Sicilia: produzione levantina, cipriota, o locale? Alcune considerazioni,' (unpublished, forthcoming). We sincerely thank the author for providing us with a copy of the essay. For the south-Mediterranean route and evidence of proto-histroical cultural contacts concerning Cypriots in native centers of Sicily, see the excellent dissertation and related bibliography of M. Cultraro, 'Prima di Cartagine. Forme di contatto tra Sicilia, Nord Africa e Mediterraneo orientale nella Protostoria recente,' in *Traffici, commerci e vie di distribuzione nel Mediterraneo tra Protostoria e V secolo a.C. Atti del Convegno Internazionale Gela, maggio 2009* (Palermo, 2009), 55-66. On the same topic, see, L. Vagnetti, 'I bacili di Bronzo di Caldare sono Ciprioti?,' in *Studi Micenei ed Egeo-Anatolici*, Vol.7 (1968), 129-138. Also among the most relevant early evidence of the connection of the symbolic value of the bull in relation to chthonic water cults is the hoard at the spring of Ciavolaro di Ribera, in the area of Akragas (G.Castellana, *La stipe votiva del Ciavolaro nel quadro del Bronzo Antico siciliano* (Palermo, 1996)). The same symbolic interconnections are seen in the area of Katane during the Middle Bronze age (M. Cultraro, 'Catania Prima di Evarco. Per una carta archeologica delle evidenze preistoriche nell'area urbana,' in *Tradizione, Tecnologia e Territorio. Topografia Antica*, 3 (Rome: Bonanno, 2014), 69).

[23] The topic is exhaustively discussed in a work by A. Crispino and M. Cultraro, 'Il deposito votivo di Ferla (Sr) e il culto delle acque nella Sicilia protostorica,' in *Santuari indigeni di Sicilia e Magna Grecia. Modelli di organizzaione e regime delle offerte a confronto, Atti del convegno (aprile 2011)*, forthcoming. The topic is also mentioned in M. Cultraro, 'Quis Deus? Su alcune rappresentazioni di carattere cultuale nella Sicilia dell'età del ferro,' in *Antropologia e Archeologia a confronto: rappresentazioni e pratiche del sacro. Atti dell'incontro internazionale di studi Roma, Museo Nazionale Preistorico Etnografico 'Luigi Pigorini' 20-21 maggio 2011* (Rome, 2012), 389.

[24] The Anapos River was later worshipped as a deity in Greek Sicily (Ovid, *Metamorphoses*, 5. 417 ff).

[25] M. Cultraro, 'I Siculi all'ombra del vulcano,' in *Dal mito alla storia. La Sicilia nell'Archaiologhia di Tucidide. Atti del VIII Congresso di Studi* (Rome: Sciascia Editore, 2012), 198. For additional bibliographic resources concerning the iconography of the bull as it is used in vessels found in funerary contexts dating to the Middle and Late Bronze Age in southern Italy and Sicily, see: M. Cultraro, 'Catania Prima di Evarco. Per una carta archeologica delle evidenze preistoriche nell'area urbana,' 69 and specifically note 179.

[26] Examples are stored at the Museo Archeologico Regionale Eoliano, in Lipara.

[27] In Lipara, excavations at the later Ausonio II site of Castello have revealed a Nuragic Ship which is discussed in detail below (A. Depalmas, *Le navicelle di bronzo della Sardegna nuragica* (Cagliari: Gasperini, 2005), 227). For Lipara, Mussini also reports a discovery (albeit late) 'of exceptional interest,' dated to the 4th century BC: a funerary mask of Acheloios made locally, 'showing no formal affinities with the Greek coroplastic' (E. Mussini, 'La diffusione dell'iconografia di Acheloo in Magna Grecia e Sicilia. Tracce per l'individuazione di un culto,' 109).

[28] G. Poggesi, E. Bocci, L. Pagnini, and F. Lo Schiavo, 'Rapporti fra l'Etruria settentrionale interna e il territorio di Capua: i kyathoi con anse a corna tronche e cave,' in *Gli Etruschi e la Campania settentrionale: atti del XXVI Convegno di studi etruschi ed italici, Caserta, Santa Maria Capua Vetere, Capua, Teano, 11-15 novembre 2007. Istituto Nazionale di Studi Etruschi ed Italici, Atti di convegni, 26. Pisa*, edited by O. Paoletti and M. C. Bettini (Rome: Fabrizio Serra Editore, 2011), 167ff. It is plausible that Ausonio culture in Sicily had its origins in the arrival of people maintaining Italic culture at the end of the Bronze

climate emerges the later appearance of what appears to be the head of another Late Bronze Age man-faced bull[29] in western Sicily, this one from Ausonio II culture, dating from the 12th to 10th century BC **(Fig 39)**.[30] Another, slightly later example that is also likely a man-faced bull head is from the Iron Age native populations of Sicily. It is a fragment of vase found at Capodarso, described as 'stylistically influenced by Cypriot art' and 'shaped as a horned human protome,' by La Rosa.[31]

Later Evidence

In the 1st millennium BC, the cultural relation of bulls and water is still visible in the traditions of the Sikan native populations of Sicily, showing additional cultural influence from Cyprus but now also the Aegean. This connection is attested by amphorae with plastic bull protomes dated to the 9th century BC found near Mussomeli at the site of Polizzello, a place identified as 'a major cultic place for Sikan populations of the island since the Early Iron Age.'[32] The site is located almost exactly at the center of Sicily. Cultraro connects the symbol of the bull on the examples from Polizzello with native beliefs concerning concepts of abundance and fertility and a complex of cultural water-related practices and lustratio rites,[33] which began to take a distinct shape in the Bronze Age.[34] Most importantly, Dario Palermo, analyzing the known representations of bull protomes on pottery and bronze plaques found at Polizzello and other Sikan sites of the area,[35] realized that the bull protomes on the Sikan amphorae sometimes render the impression of a human face, arguing that 'these representations allude to a divine or semi-divine being, joining in himself human traits and animal features; and that the schematic face of such a hybrid being, placed on the belly of the vessel, had an apotropaic function.'[36] Palermo assumes that the Sikan bull-man deity 'was linked to the sacred context in which the vessel is found,'[37] which is a water-cultic context.[38] Palermo also recognizes that the representations of the hybrid bull-man deity on the bronze plaques indicate his worship among warriors, who when wearing the plaques on the chest or abdomen, intended to keep the vital parts of their body under the protection of the god.[39] Palermo suggests a foreign (presumably eastern) influence, questioning 'how this presumed creature with apotropaic functions would fit into the framework of the religious beliefs of the Sikan people?'[40]

In the second quarter of the 1st millennium BC we see from the same Sikan site a later oinochoe, dated to the 7th century BC, which depicts a bull-man (**Fig. 40**).[41] The piece was first published by Gabrici in 1925,[42] who incorrectly thought the horns were a hat. However, the figure is clearly a bull-man, indicated by the horns,[43] the human face in profile with pointed beard, the tail (or ithyphallic representation), and animalistic hind legs. What Gabrici interpreted as a shield might be a representation of the sun, plausible indeed if we consider the solar connotations of eastern man-faced bulls (and later western man-faced bulls) and the fact that there is

Age (V. La Rosa, 'Considerazioni sul problema siculo,' in *Sileno*, Vol.III (1977), 65-81. In terms of Ausonio II culture, scholars have recognized the presence of Nuragic and peninsular proto-Villanovan elements, in addition to those from the eastern Mediterranean (A. Zanini, 'Contributo alla rilettura della necropoli del Bronzo Finale di Milazzo – ME,' in *Dai Ciclopi agli Ecisti. Società e Territorio nella Sicilia Preistorica e Protostorica. Atti della XII Riunione Scientifica. San Cipirello (PA), 16-19 novembre 2006* (Firenze: 2012), 899-900).

[29] Usually if a bull-man is intended instead of a man-faced bull, there is a distinct human chin and neck. Thus, many of the antefixes from Etruria can be identified as man-faced bulls, because artists made specific alterations to signify if they intended something else. This phenomenon is seen throughout the Greek world and especially on coinage. See, for example, the coinage of Istros, MSP I, 491-4, where both bull bodies and human necks are attached to bearded and horned human heads on different dies. The same phenomenon is seen in Metapontion (S. Noe, *The Coinage of Metapontum*, no. 311), where the artist made a deliberate effort to depict the entire human body of Acheloios, since the head had bovine ears and horns, and if alone would have signified a man-faced bull, as depicted on other varieties from Metapontion (ibid., no. 347, etc.).

[30] F. Nicoletti, S.Tusa, 'L'età del Bronzo nella Sicilia occidentale,' in *Dai Ciclopi agli Ecisti. Società e Territorio nella Sicilia Preistorica e Protostorica. Atti della XII Riunione Scientifica. San Cipirello (PA), 16-19 novembre 2006* (Firenze: 2012), 105-30.

[31] V. La Rosa, 'Un frammento fittile da Capodarso e il problema delle sopravvivenze micenee in Sicilia,' in *Cronache di Archeologia e Storia dell'Arte*, Vol.8 (1969), 33-46.

[32] G. Falsone, 'Per salvare Entella,' in *Sicilia Archeologica*, Vol.43 (1980), 21-26; E. De Miro, 'Eredità Egeo-Micenee e alto arcaismo in Sicilia,' in *La transizione dal miceneo all'alto arcaismo. Atti convegno Roma 1988* (Rome, 1991), 593-617; M. Cultraro, 'Quis Deus?,' 389ff.

[33] M. Cultraro, 'Quis Deus?,' 394.

[34] Ibid.

[35] Following a previous study by R. Leighton, *Sicily Before History* (New York, 1999).

[36] D. Palermo, 'Doni votivi e aspetti del culto nel santuario indigeno della Montagna di Polizzello,' in *Doni agli dei. Il sistema dei doni votivi nei santuari* (Naus: 2008), 261.

[37] Ibid.

[38] M. Cultraro, 'Quis Deus?,' 394.

[39] D. Palermo, 'Il gesto e la maschera. Rappresentazioni umane dal centro indigeno della Montagna di Polizzello,' in *Annali della Facoltà di Scienze della Formazione. Università degli Studi di Catania* (C.U.E.C.M., 2003), 150. See the previous chapter for a discussion of the man-faced bull as a mercenary deity.

[40] D. Palermo, 'Doni votivi e aspetti del culto nel santuario indigeno della Montagna di Polizzello,' 262. The original assumptions by Palermo have been confirmed by subsequent discoveries of Levantine objects at the site of Polizzello, suggesting 'cultural exchanges between Sikans and Eastern populations, maybe Phoenicians, in a time pre-dating (earlier) the foundations of the first Greek colonies' (D. Palermo and D. Tanasi, 'Diodoro a Polizzello' in *Diodoro Siculo e la Sicilia indigena. Atti del convegno di studi*, edited by C. Miccichè, S. Modeo and L. Santagati (Palermo: 2006) 95, tab.2, fig.5-6). A further interesting element is seen at Polizzello. In the excavation reports by Palermo there is a clay pinax on which a horned door is depicted (ibid., 99, fig. 10), strikingly similar to the entrance doors of the Sardinian Domus de Janas discussed below, pg.36ff.

[41] D. Palermo, 'Polizzello,' in *Contributi alla conoscenza dell'età del Ferro in Sicilia. Monte Finocchito e Polizzello. Cronache di Archeologia*, Vol.XX (Catania, 1981), 136, fig.10. The Cypriot influence on the piece is clear. Dario Palermo observed that the use of decorations on the side of vessels, especially oinochoai, with similar large isolated motifs, is typical of Cyprus in the Geometric Period (ibid).

[42] E.Gabrici, 'Polizzello. Abitato preistorico presso Mussomeli,' in *Atti R. Accad. Sc. Lett. Arti*, Vol.XIV (1925), Pl.II.

[43] Massimo Cultraro argues that the figure could wear a cap with bull horns (M. Cultraro,'Quis Deus?,' 392).

no evidence of the use of shields among Sikan warriors. Another similar representation is seen in **Fig.41a**,[44] on a crater of indigenous fabric, once stored in a private collection in Sicily, and now lost. The surviving drawing shows a group of five horned figures (perhaps wearing horned caps), led by one figure distinguished by his beard and erect phallus.[45] Ultimately, the oinochoe from Polizzello and related evidence further indicate the Cypriot transference of ancient Near Eastern iconographies to the West.[46]

Altogether, the evidence from excavation reports and analyses of finds and contexts show that in Sicily, at Polizzello, an ithyphallic hybrid bull-man deity with solar connotations was probably worshipped. This unknown deity had apotropaic qualities, was popular among warriors, and his cult employed complex water-related rituals, all derived from native beliefs concerning concepts of abundance and fertility. The plastic figures and paintings in silhouette suggest a hybrid bull-man form for this god, but perhaps, like the later Acheloios or other shape-shifting water deities, this is just one of the forms by which this prehistoric Sicilian deity could manifest itself. In other cases, such as at Piano Vento, he might have been shaped like a man-faced bull, especially since both Piano Vento and Polizzello have Cypriot influences. Thus, this unknown deity discovered by archaeologists is an important Sicilian predecessor to the later Etruscan and Greek Acheloios.

There is later evidence that indicates the importance of these early Sicilian traditions in the formulation of the cult of Acheloios. From Akragas, about 70 km south of Polizzello, comes a non-Greek plastic jar, manufactured locally.[47] Isler described it as a seated figure with human face, showing monstrous features and horns, stating it 'must be identified as Acheloos.'[48] In his analysis he proposed comparisons with sitting ithyphallic silens seen on an Attic vase painting of the last quarter of the 6th century BC and on coins of Naxos dated to the first half of the 5th century BC. Isler maintained that there were no parallels for the piece, and proposed a dating to the first quarter of the 5th century BC. An example not mentioned by Isler, slightly different but clearly from the same pottery tradition, is preserved at the Museum of Fine Arts in Budapest.[49] This second piece shows the same hybrid ithyphallic creature rendered as a plastic vase.[50] Moreover, comparison to the aforementioned oinochoe reveal additional similarities- the figure is bearded, horned, and ithyphallic, which, if we follow Isler's methodology, 'must be identified as Acheloios.' Isler's comparison with the sileni of Naxos or the Attic vase painting is not far-fetched, but we saw the imagery of the horned, bearded, ithyphallic being already at Polizzello in the first quarter of the 1st millennium. Thus, instead of looking at those later examples as imitative of Greek models, as Isler did, they all probably derive from earlier models from Cyprus. In fact, the oldest known example of a clay seated ityphallic figurine was made at Souskiou in Cyprus, dated to the Chalcolithic period.[51] Moreover, from the same Cypriot site and dated to the same time period comes the earliest example of a Cypriot man-faced quadruped (**Fig.18**).[52] Thus the two Cypriot iconographies from Souskiou seem to be reflected in the later traditions demonstrated by the Sikan piece identified as Acheloios by Isler.

Interestingly, archaeologists have noted that the same places used by chthnoic bull-water cults in Bronze Age Sicily were used again in the Archaic period by native populations and for essentially the same purposes.[53] In fact, the use of man-faced bull iconography by Sicilian natives is demonstrated in historic times. An askos shaped as a man-faced bull at the Cleveland Museum and dated to 480 BC attests to this.[54] Moreover, a comparison with other native zoomorphic askoi of the same fabric found in tombs dated to c. 500 BC helps us to re-attribute the Cleveland Museum piece to a Sikan workshop in the area of Selinous.[55] Ultimately, the evidence of native Sikans

[44] Ibid., 399, fig.7-8.

[45] Ibid., 390. If Cultraro is correct about the figure wearing a horned cap, the comparison with contemporary bronze figurines from Sardinia and Cyprus is striking.

[46] On Cypriot-style pottery from the site, see the reconstruction proposed by Palermo, who describes the Geloan mediation for the eastern Mediterranean influence on native pottery of the inland site of Polizzello (D. Palermo, 'Polizzello,' 135, 139, and 144). There are some convincing examples for a substantial Cypriot presence at Gela around the years of the foundation of the polis, discussed below.

[47] H.P. Isler, *Acheloos*, 47-8, no.125.

[48] Ibid., 48.

[49] Said to be from Sicily but of unknown provenance, from the Szépművészeti Múzeum collection. Image available at : http://www.szepmuveszeti.hu/data/cikk/859/cikk_859/2009.57.A_01_k.jpg)

[50] The narrow spout on these two plastic vases indicates the vessels were used to slowly drip water during rituals, or even for feeding a child. The same function is exhibited later on Greek and Etruscan gutti with the image of Acheloios in relief, discussed below. If the child-feeding function for these native plastic vessels is accurate, it is further evidence that the aforementioned examples are not simply imitations of Greek motifs, but rather a sign of the effective rooting of the man-faced bull and related traditions in local culture, because such a specific use, reminiscent of the man-faced bull's quality as a protector of youth, suggests a deeper awareness of the tradition for natives.

[51] From A. T. Reyes, 'Iconography of Deities and Demons in Cyprus,' as part of *Iconography of Deities and Demons in the Ancient Near East: An Iconographic Dictionary with Special Emphasis on First-Millenium BCE Palestine/Israel* (Electronic Pre-publication. University of Zurich), fig.9, available at http://www.religionswissenschaft.uzh.ch/idd/prepublication.php

[52] Ibid., fig.10.

[53] M. Cultraro, 'I Siculi all'ombra del vulcano,' 181-203.

[54] Cleveland Museum of Art, item no. 2.2012

[55] There are two examples for comparison: the first from C. Trombi, 'Il materiale indigeno presente nelle colonie Greche di Sicilia La Sicilia occidentale. Parte I,' in *Quaderni di Archeologia dell'Università di Messina*, No. 3 (Soveria Mannelli: Rubbettino, 2003), Pl.XXI, no.92; V. Tusa, 'Le Necropoli di Selinunte,' in *Odeon e altri monumenti archeologici*, edited by V. Tusa (Palermo, 1971), Pl. XV.e.. Another example of the same style, said to be from Sicily but of unknown provenance, is stored at the Museum of Fine Arts at Budapest, see: M. Dági, 'A Sicilian askos. Highlighted Works of Art – Spring, 2013,' on the Museum of Fine Arts at Budapest webpage, available at http://www.szepmuveszeti.hu/classical_antiquities/highlighted-works-of-art-859.

using a man-faced bull askoi[56] should not be explained by simplistic schemes in which barbarian populations imitated more evolved ones,[57] but instead emerged via the dynamics of contacts of cultures probably starting before Greek transfusion of the iconography.[58]

Another example from non-Hellenic Sicily to help illustrate this phenomenon is a protome of the man-faced bull from Syracuse (**Fig. 41b**).[59] The piece was found under the area where later Syracusans built their Athenaion, within layers dating before the foundation of the Greek polis.[60] This suggests the existence of a pre-Greek tradition of the man-faced bull in the area, where the iconography was already known by natives before the arrival of the Greek settlers.

Numismatic evidence also prompts questions on the native traditions of the man-faced bull. The earliest (c. 460 BC) 'barbarian imitations' known for Sicily copy Geloan litrai depicting a man-faced bull obverse with a solar wheel on the reverse.[61] Christof Boehringer[62] proposed these coins originate from the territories ruled by the native leader Ducezio during the famous decade of wars between Greeks and Sikels, known as the Sikel Revolt, from 460 to 450 BC. It is obvious that Sikel barbarians were influenced by the Greek polis when they started to mint these imitations, but the question is: Why would they chose to imitate the types of Gela to represent the new revolutionary Sikel state on their coins? It is probably because the iconography and mythology of the man-faced bull is not exclusively Greek, as Isler maintained for Sicilian manifestations of Acheloios as a man-faced bull. Altogether, we can therefore propose that the widespread imagery of Acheloios, which will later flourish among Greeks, natives and mercenaries on the island, retains elements of the religious practices of indigenous prehistoric people who were exposed to man-faced bull iconography from Cyprus from a very early date, and incorporated it into their cultic practices.[63]

Traditions of Sardinia

Sardinia played an important role in the development and diffusion of man-faced bull-related iconography and mythology from East to West. In fact, in Sardinia there is evidence since the Bronze Age of the existence of a water cult employing the image of the bull as a deity of water. This is not a simple symbolic relation of water to bulls or the ritual use of water as attested in other European areas, but the worship of the bull as a chthonic-healing-funerary water deity. Throughout the centuries, various indications emerge to suggest a direct relation between the Etruscan, Sikan, and Greek Acheloios and the earlier Sardinian and Cypriot traditions. The *Bronzetto di Nule* is perhaps the most obvious link in the chain, but it was certainly not an isolated phenomenon. Analyzing the greater Sardinian context, it appears to have been in contact with Cyprus and the Near East from a very early date, and also Sicily and Etruria, acting as a mediator between these areas and thus providing a plausible framework for the hypothesis of a pre-Greek cult of proto-Acheloios in the West.[64]

Early Traditions

The use of the symbol of the bull in connection with the ritual use of water is attested in Sardinia since the 5th millennium BC.[65] Throughout the 4th millennium

[56] For the Greek world only two specimens of man-faced bull-shaped askoi are known, described as Ionian and dated to the 6th century BC, one of which comes from Emporion in Iberia (**Fig.67**, from H.P. Isler, *Acheloos*, no. 124), and the other a fragment from Massalia in France (H.P. Isler, Acheloos, no. 125). Isler recognizes that they are unique examples of Greek askoi shaped as Acheloios (H.P. Isler, *Acheloos*, no. 47). The only earlier use of man-faced bull-shaped askoi are Bronze Age examples from Cyprus, discussed above. Moreover, the geometric ornamental syntax of the painting on **Fig. 67** seems to follow the earlier Cypriot examples.

[57] No man-faced bull askoi are known for Magna Graecia and mainland Greece.

[58] The form of the askos was adopted by prehistoric natives of Sicily under the influence of Cypriots, the first vectors of this class of pottery to the West (D. Palermo, 'Askoi ornitomorfi della Sicilia indigena,' in *Cronache di Archeologia*, Vol.22 (1983), 93-97. In fact, during the second half of the 2nd millennium BC, man-faced bull shaped askoi were found in Cypriot tombs.

[59] P. Orsi, 'Gli scavi intorno a l'Athenaion di Siracusa,' in *Monumenti Antichi Linc*, XXV (1918), 517-8, fig. 108.

[60] L. Bernabò Brea, 'Leggenda e Archeologia nella protostoria siciliana,' in *Kokalos*, 10-11 (1965), 11; S. Lagona, 'Il tipo del toro androprosopo a Gela,' in *Cronache di archeologia e Storia dell'Arte*, Vol. 7 (Catania, 1968), 137-142.

[61] G.K. Jenkins, *The Coinage of Gela*, no. B21 - B29.

[62] C. Boehringer, 'Die Barbarisierten muenzen von Akragas, Gela, Leontinoi und Syrakus im 5. Jahrhundert v. Chr.,' in *Le emissioni dei centri Siculi fina all'epoca di Timoleonte e i loro rapporti con la monetazione delle colonie Greche di Sicilia Atti del IV Convegno del centro internazionale di studi numismatici - Napoli 9-14 Aprile 1973. Istituto Italiano di Numismatica - Supplemento al Volume 20 degli 'Annali'* (Rome, 1975), 157-190.

[63] T. Alfieri Tonini, 'Riflessi del sincretismo religioso della Sicilia orientale nelle testimonianze scritte,' in *Convivenze etniche, scontri e contatti di culture in Sicilia e Magna Grecia. Aristonothos. Scritti per il Mediterraneo antico*, Vol. 7 (Trento: Tangram, 2012), 201.

[64] There are no ancient text relating to early Sardinian, native Sicilian, or Italic cults. Thus, it is in the archaeological evidence that we must seek the roots of the prehistoric cult of a proto-Acheloios. The only sources we have for Sardinian traditions are Roman, and therefore much later. Nonetheless, some of them refer to proto-historical Sardinian traditions, reporting the particular virtues of Sardinian rivers and springs, believed to heal fractured bones (Prisciano, *Periegesis*, 466ff) or even 'infirmis medellam praebentes, furibus caecitatem', 'healing the sick, giving thieves blindness' (Isidore of Seville, *Isidori Hispalensis Episcopi Etymologiarum Sive Originum*. Liber XIV, Chapter Vi. De Insvlis, Line 40).

[65] See ceramic and stone vases from the sites of Puisteris-Mogoro, Ludosu-Riola, Bingia Eccia-Dolianova, and Grotta Rifugio-Oliena, reported in R.H. Tykot, 'Radiocarbon Dating and absolute Chronology in Sardinia and Corsica,' in *Radiocarbon Dating and Italian Prehistory. Accordia Specialist Studies on Italy*, 3, edited by R. Skeates and R. D. Whitehouse (London: British School at Rome- Accordia Research, 1994), 121-122. For pre-Nuragic populations (4th millennium BC) using the symbol of the bull protome on pottery with religious significance, see: G. Lilliu, *Arte e religione della Sardegna prenuragica. Idoletti, ceramiche, oggetti d'ornamento* (Delfino Editore, 1999), no.149-153. The author highlights the symbolic importance and the thaumaturgical value of the bull protomes represented on prehistoric Sardinian pottery and noticed that for ancient Sardinian populations the bull represents almost exclusively *the* sacred animal, often in connection with cults

we also have several examples of the use of the bull in funerary ritual practices, especially in its liminal dimension, as attested by the numerous entrance gates (**Fig.42**)[66] in hypogeous tombs, the so-called 'Domus de Janas,'[67] literally 'Houses of Fairies,' and from the bull-shaped clay containers and ornaments used in these houses during 'rituals of spiritual communication with the dead.'[68] The symbol of the bull protome in these cases is clearly linked to the passage from the world of living to the world of the dead.[69] Giuseppa Tanda emphasizes the symbolism of the doors, which are identified with the head of the bull deity itself. Consequently 'the introduction, through it, of the deceased, assumes a magic ritual value of purification.'[70] Looking at **Fig.42** it seems clear that the door represents the protome of the bull, so the bull-god's head or face is the door, the 'liminal' god, and here we find perhaps the most ancient known example for the cultic water-bull-funerary connection which will later become embodied in the cult of Acheloios, which in Etruria, expecially, will include chthonic, funerary, and liminal connotations.[71] In fact, many 'Houses of Fairies' have cupules carved in the floor at the entrance, in perfect correspondace to the liminal bull-deity's virtual head,[72] testifying to ritual libations of water for those who enter the tomb.[73] This ritual environment provides a strong indication of the symbolic significance of water as a link to the subterranean underworld.

The early cultic and ritual function of water at various 'Houses of Faries' is the basis for the later widespread cult of water, typical of Bronze Age Sardinia. In fact, there are clear archaeological attestations for water cults in Sardinia since the Middle Bronze Age, and during the Final Bronze Age the evidence of water-bull cults becomes abundant. Water cults are essentially pervasive in Nuragic Sardinia, and this lead some scholars to speculate about an island-wide religion expressed in water rites.[74] Maud Webster recently provided a comprehensive analysis for the archaeological evidence of Sardinian water temples.[75] Before him, G. Ugas identified a widespread Sardinian water-based cult,[76] categorizing two types of places in which rituals were performed: sacred springs and sacred wells.[77] The pre-Nuragic water-cult rituals performed at those sites is characterized by the frequent recurrence of the symbol of bull horns or protomes.[78] Moreover, the symbolic value of water in these prehistoric Sardinian cults is related to the fertility of the earth and its purifying and healing qualities. In fact, some miniature vases involved in the rituals were clearly used as aspergillum, leading Maria Melis to state that the 'use of water within tombs is part of funerary cults, which brings the concepts of death and rebirth, contained in agrarian rituals connected with the production cycles.'[79]

Later Traditions

At the dawn of the Iron Age the Sardinian framework is even clearer: water cult rituals are the main religious practices performed on the island, and the archaeological discoveries of water temples, sacred springs, and sacred wells number in the dozens. At Funtana 'e Deus there is a temple frequented since the Final Bronze Age which was still operative during the Early Iron Age, and has been interpreted by Webster as a water-temple[80] (specifically, he mentions a water basin under a tholos, a beehive-shaped tomb, and the remains of a floor canal), and in the ritual deposits there were several dozen bronze and lead statuettes of bulls[81] among large amounts of ritual pottery. Melis noted that the same types of Bronze Age ritual miniaturistic pottery used in water cults and ritual funerary practices in Sardinia (Monte D'Accodi), have been found in Campania (Taurasi) and Anatolia

of chthonic female deities, since the Neolithic period (G. Lilliu, *Arte e religione della Sardegna prenuragica. Idoletti, ceramiche, oggetti d'ornamento,* 83-87). Clay molded handles with the symbol of a bull head are documented in contemporary cultures of other areas of the western Mediterranean and typological similarities were found within contemporary Levantine productions (G. Lilliu, *La civiltà dei sardi dal Paleolitico all'età dei nuraghi* (Torino: Nuova E.R.I., 1988), 215ff).

[66] For example, see G. Tanda, 'L'Arte del Neolitico recente in Sardegna: origine, sviluppo ed esiti finali,' in *Preistoria Alpina*, 46, I (Trento, 2012), 133-152, fig.11-15.

[67] G. Tanda, 'L'Arte del Neolitico recente in Sardegna: origine, sviluppo ed esiti finali,' 148, reports 258 examples of horned doors from 93 Sardinian sites dated from the Neolithic Period to the Bronze Age.

[68] G. Tanda, 'Arte e religione in Sardegna. Rapporti fra i dati monumentali e gli elementi della cultura materiale (Nota preliminare),' in *Atti del Valcamonica Symposium 'International Symposium on the Intellectual Expressions of Preistoric Man: Art and Religion'. Valcamonica, 28 july-3 August 1979, Capo di Ponte* (Brescia, 1983), 261- 280; G. Tanda, 'L'ipogeismo in Sardegna: Arte, Simbologia, Religione,' in *Atti del Congresso internazionale L'ipogeismo nel Mediterraneo. Origini, sviluppo, quadri culturali* (Sassari, 2000), 423, fig. 12.

[69] G. Tanda, 'L'Arte del Neolitico recente in Sardegna: origine, sviluppo ed esiti finali,' 149.

[70] Ibid.

[71] M. R. Ciuccarelli, 'Acheloo ctonio dalla Magna Grecia all'Etruria?,' 121-140.

[72] A view from the tomb interior is provided in, E. Blake, 'The Material Expression of Cult, Ritual, and Feasting,' in *The Archaeology of Mediterranean Prehistory*, edited by E. Blake and A. B. Knapp (Blackwell: 2005), 112, fig.5.1.

[73] E.Blake, 'The Material Expression of Cult, Ritual, and Feasting,' 111.

[74] A. Moravetti, *Sardegna archeologica dal cielo. Dai circoli megalitici alle torri nuragiche* (Sassari, 2012), 47ff; M.A.Fadda, *Nel segno dell'acqua. Santuari e bronzi votivi della Sardegna nuragica* (Sassari, 2013).

[75] M. Webster, 'Water-temples of Sardinia: identification, inventory and interpretation' (Uppsala University. Deparment of Archaeology and Ancient History, Master's Degree Thesis, 2014).

[76] G. Ugas, *L'Alba dei Nuraghi* (Cagliari: Fabula, 2005), 84-5.

[77] In terms of sacred wells, a similar phenomenon is attested in Bronze Age central-south Italy (M. Minoja, 'Elementi rituali in pozzi per acqua nell'età del bronzo: il caso dell'abitato del C.I.R.A (Capua - Ce),' in *Preistoria e protostoria in Etruria. Paesaggi d'acque. Atti del quinto incontro di studi*, Vol. II (Milan, 2002), 465 ff.).

[78] M. G. Melis, 'Osservazioni sul ruolo dell'acqua nei rituali della Sardegna preistorica,' 112.

[79] Ibid., 115.

[80] M. Webster, 'Water-temples of Sardinia: identification, inventory and interpretation,' 63.

[81] M.A. Fadda, *Nel segno dell'acqua. Santuari e bronzi votivi della Sardegna nuragica* (Sassari, 2013), 145.

(Acemhöyük, in a child's grave).[82] This evidence strongly suggests very early direct cultural contacts related to water cults from the eastern Mediterranean to the Tyrrhenian area.[83]

At Camposanto-Olmedo a bronze statuette of a bull was found in a ritual deposit at a sacred well[84] dated to the Early Iron Age.[85] From the same sacred well came a discovery which leaves no doubt as to the existence of a Sardinian cult of a bull deity worshipped by a water cult: a bronze model of a taurine idol, clearly showing a cultic function because of its adjoining pedestal.[86] Interestingly, the central part of the protome seems to be missing, and perhaps it once had a human face, as seen on the processional standards discussed below.

At Santa Vittoria, the greatest known Nuragic sanctuary of Sardinia,[87] excavations revealed a water- temple dated to the Early Iron Age, and the stone bull heads carved in high relief on the facade blocks have been interpreted as cultic images for a bull-deity.[88] A similar function is plausible for the bronze statuettes of bulls found in a sacred well at the contemporary water-temple of Predio Canopoli, near the ancient Silanis River.[89] For both temples, scholars have argued for cultural contacts from the Levantine area.[90]

As noted by A. Antona, the location of many of these Sardinian water temples, placed near the coastline, indicate they were probably visible from boats even at a great distance. Antona suggests a direct relationship between the monuments and the transmarine traffic, which intensified at the end of the Bronze Age.[91] Sanna et al., on this basis, argue for possible analogies with

[82] M. G. Melis, 'Osservazioni sul ruolo dell'acqua nei rituali della Sardegna preistorica,' 111, 114, 124.

[83] At the sanctuary of Monte D'accodi, in addition to the water cult, metallurgy was practiced during the 2nd millennium, as attested by crucibles found within (M. G. Melis, 'Osservazioni sul ruolo dell'acqua nei rituali della Sardegna preistorica,' 115). There is also clear evidence for a transmission of metallurgic techniques directly from Cyprus to Sardinia and Etruria during the 2nd millenium BC, as demonstrated by the western discoveries of Cypriot copper ingots and smithing tools (F. Lo Schiavo, P. Falchi and M. Milletti, 'Sardegna ed Etruria tirrenica: identità in formazione. Ripostigli e scambi della fase di transizione fra la fine del Bronzo Finale e la prima età del Ferro,' in Δόσις δ'ολίγη τε φίλη τε, Studi per Antonella Romualdi (Firenze, 2013), 371-416). An eastern Semitic influence for the cult of water in Sardinia also resonates in the etymology of the names of the sites at which these cults are attested, for example the worship of water, related to a deity still unidentified by scholars, at the natural source of Mitza Salamu, where *mitza* is the Phoenician word for 'spring,' and *salamu* has its root in the semitic *sml* (healing). Thus, the toponym means 'spring of healing' (G. Garbati and C. Peri, 'Considerazioni sul 'culto delle acque' nella Sardegna punica e tardo-punica: l'esempio di Mitza Salamu (Dolianova -Ca),' in *Saturnia Tellus: definizioni dello spazio consacrato in ambiente etrusco, italico, fenicio-punico, iberico e celtico. Conference proceedings* (Roma, 2008), 389). On the significance of water in Phoenician sanctuaries, see: E. Groenewoud, 'Use of Water in Phoenician Sanctuaries,' in *ANES*, Vol. 38 (2001), 139-159.

[84] A.Taramelli, 'Tempietto protosardo nel Camposanto di Olmedo (Sassari),' in *Bullettino di Paletnologia Italiana*, Vol.53 (Roma: Museo Preistorico Etnografico, 1933),110–122.

[85] At the same site a bronze statuette was found that also suggests the Levantine derivation of the Nuragic traditions at those temples (M. Melis, 'Osservazioni sul ruolo dell'acqua nei rituali della Sardegna preistorica,' 365-7, no.175). Although locally made, it shows a scheme identical to early Egyptian statuettes, later adopted in Syria, Anatolia, and Cyprus. This evidence gives further substance to the theory of the Shardana identified as Sardinian warriors among the 'People of the Sea' attacking Egypt at the dawn of the Iron Age, discussed below. There was probably movement of people from the Levant into Sardiania during this time as well, demonstrated by Nuragic centers of local production manned by immigrant Levantine peoples, as recently stated by S. Masetti, after archaeological discoveries at Irgoli (S. Masetti 'Monumenti Nuragici di Culto sulle montagne di Irgoli,' in *Archeologia Viva*, XXXIII, n.165 (Firenze: Giunti, 2014), 68). Even more striking are the discoveries at the Nuragic water temple of Nurdole, where dozens of bronze statuettes of bulls and Nuragic ships with bull protomes, donated by pilgrims since 1200 BC, have been found at the site of the sanctuary where a water deity was worshipped. The symbols carved in the block stones of the same temple lead G. Garbini to identify the presence of Philistine people at the site at the time the friezes were made, between the 10th and 9th century BC. After further recent discoveries of stone carvings in Philistine script at different inland sites of Sardinia, Garbini stated that the 'History of Sardinia will have to be re-written' (M. A. Fadda 'Il Sacro monte di Nurdole' in *Archeologia Viva*, XXXIII, n.167 (Firenze: Giunti, 2014), 32-35).

[86] M. Melis, 'Osservazioni sul ruolo dell'acqua nei rituali della Sardegna preistorica,' no.265.

[87] Cf R. Zucca, *Il santuario nuragico di S. Vittoria di Serri, Sardegna Archeologica*, Guide e Itinerari 7 (Sassari: Delfino, 1988).

[88] Cf. M.A. Fadda, *Nel segno dell'acqua. Santuari e bronzi votivi della Sardegna nuragica*; L. Usai, 'Il complesso cultuale di Santa Vittoria-Serri,' in *Simbolo di un simbolo: i modelli di nuraghe*, edited by F. Campus and V. Leonelli (Monteriggioni, 2012), 314–322.

[89] A. Taramelli, 'Perfugas. Tempietto a pozzo di carattere preromano scoperto nell'abitato,' in *Notizie degli Scavi di Antichità* (1924), 522–533; F. Campus and G. Pitzalis, 'Il complesso cultuale di Predio Canopoli,' in *Simbolo di un simbolo: i modelli di nuraghe,*edited by F. Campus & V. Leonelli (Monteriggioni, 2012), 157–160. The Silanis River has the same etymological root as the Sileraioi, as discussed in that section of the catalog.

[90] For Santa Vittoria, see: A. Taramelli, 'Il tempio nuragico ed i monumenti primitivi di S. Vittoria di Serri (Cagliari),' in *Monumenti Antichi della Reale Accademia dei Lincei*, 23 (1915), 346; A. Taramelli, 'Nuovi scavi nel santuario nuragico presso la chiesa di Santa Maria della Vittoria sull'altopiano della giara,' in *Notizie degli Scavi di Antichità* (1922), 330–332. For Predio Canopoli, see: G. Pitzalis, "Un athyrma dal pozzo sacro di Predio Canopoli-Perfugas,' in *Etruria e Sardegna centro-settentrionale tra l'età del bronzo finale e l'arcaismo. Atti del XXI Convegno di Studi Etruschi ed Italici. Sassari, Alghero, Oristano, Torralba, 13–17 ottobre 1998*, edited by O. Paoletti and L. Tamagno Perna (Rome, 2002), 563–568. The temple of Predio Canopoli shows the same isodomic flooring previously attested in Cyprus. Isodomic ashlar masonry is commonly considered a ritual correlate for pre- and proto-historic buildings in Sardinia, in particular for those in which water-cults were operative. This building technique was already established in Bronze Age Cyprus before it appeared in Sardinia, and its origins are Near Eastern (A. Foschi Nieddu, 'Il 'pozzo sacro' di Riu Salliu (Guasila-Cagliari). Osservazioni sull'opera isodoma negli edifici cultuali di età nuragica,' in *La Civiltà Nuragica. Nuove Acquisizioni, Atti del Convegno a Senorbì 2000*, II, edited by Soprintendenza per i Beni Archeologici di Cagliari (Dolianova, 2008), 379–390; G. Hult, *Bronze Age ashlar masonry in the eastern Mediterranean. Cyprus, Ugarit, and neighbouring regions* (Göteborg, 1983), 74ff, 109ff). For the crucial role of Cypriots in connecting Near Eastern cultures with the Tyrrhenian area during the Bronze Age, in particular for Sardinia, see: P. Bernardini, 'Considerazioni sui rapporti tra la Sardegna, Cipro e l'area egeo-orientale nell'età del Bronzo,' in *Quaderni della Soprintendenza Archeologica per le Province di Cagliari e Oristano*, 10 (1993), 29–67.

[91] A. Antona, 'Monumenti nuragici nel territorio di Olbia,' in *Omaggio a Doro Levi. Quaderni della Soprintendenza Archeologica di Sassari e Nuoro*, Vol. 19 (Ozieri, 1994), 34–35.

contemporary coastal sanctuaries in Cyprus which became significant places for cultural interactions.[92]

To get an even clearer idea of the Iron Age traditions in Sardinia one must consider the appearance of bronze processional standards featuring the head of a man-faced bull (**Fig.43**),[93] dated to the 8th century BC.[94] One was found in a votive hoard from a Nuragic sanctuary at St. Maria di Tergu.[95] Another is stored at the Museum of Cagliari.[96] These pieces provide evidence for a proto-cult of the man-faced bull in Iron Age Sardinia. The piece from Sassari was described by Lilliu as a 'bull protome, with an anthropomorphic head embossed on it, [the] symbol of a being embodying a dual nature, with both human and animalistic traits, [in] the same manner as the monster of Nule.'[97] These kinds of standards were used in Sardinia during processions in water cult practices, and a clay statuette was found at the site of a Nuragic sacred well, showing a man holding a standard of the same type.[98] An identical scene is also depicted on a Sardinian bronze statuette.[99] We can therefore propose the Nuragic people employed the iconography of the man-faced bull during their cultic practices, with the protome used at the head of the procession, as the figure who facilitates the liminal dimension of the ritual. The only other man-faced bull used as a processional standard is from Egypt, discussed above (**Fig. 14**). Interestingly, iconographic and epigraphic evidence suggests Nuragic warriors were captured in Egypt and possibly served under one of the pharoahs, much like the aforementioned mercenaries.[100]

To continue, Melis, in the course of the stylistical analysis of the standards,[101] mentions the similar 'pommel' horns seen on many examples of Sardinian statuettes depicting horned warrior deities and Nuragic ships found in water-cult and funerary contexts.[102] This interesting phenomenon of the placement of ships in graves and cultic sites demonstrates the value of the bull deity during funerary practices. The Nuragic ship is symbolic of the journey of the dead to the chthonic waters of the underworld, accompanied by the bull protome-shaped prow in many known Sardinian examples.[103] It is also plausible to associate these artifacts with the function of containing water libations offered to the dead. In any case, their use was certainly widespread in Iron Age Sardinia. In fact, in her recent study, Anna Depalmas listed 146 examples found in sacred wells, tombs, and votive deposits.[104]

The famous *Bronzetto di Nule* (**Fig. 44**),[105] from Sardinia, adds another dimension to the diffusion of man-faced bull-related iconography from East to West. It shows a man-headed bull wearing a strange cap,[106] with raised arms emerging from the shoulders of a bovine body. The Near Eastern influence on this piece is unquestionable. The piece is dated to the 8th century BC[107] and was made

92 B.Sanna, E. Usai and R. Zucca, 'Il Santuario costiero di Orri (Arborea),' in *Tharros Felix*, Vol.3 (2009), 238–239.

93 P. Melis, 'L'area nuragica di S. Maria di Tergu (Sassari),' in *Etruria e Sardegna centro-settentrionale tra l'Età del Bronzo finale e l'Arcaismo, Atti del XXI Convegno di Studi Etruschi e Italici, Sassari 13-17 ottobre 1998* (Rome: Istituti Editoriali e Poligrafici Internazionali, 2002), 454, fig. 1. **Fig.43** is from M. Pallottino, *La Sardegna Nuragica* (Nuoro: Ilisso Edizioni, 2000), 149, fig. 49.

94 G. Lilliu, *La civiltà nuragica* (Sassari: Carlo Delfino, 1982), 98.

95 A.Taramelli, 'Il tempio nuragico e i monumenti primitivi di S. Vittoria di Serri,' 96-104, fig.95. The author reports from the same site a stone bull head he interprets as a sign of the worship of a bull-deity at the Nuragic sanctuary.

96 P. Melis, 'L'area nuragica di S. Maria di Tergu (Sassari),'454.

97 G. Lilliu, *La civiltà nuragica* , 184.

98 G. Lilliu, 'Bronzi figurati esistenti nelle Collezioni pubbliche e private non insulari,' in *Studi Sardi,* Vol.VI (Sassari: 1945) 331, Pl.XV.

99 G. Lilliu, *Sculture della Sardegna Nuragica,* no.62. Lilliu argues also that his no.265 represents the same type of standard.

100 R. Drews, *The End of the Bronze Age: Changes in Warfare and the Catastrophe Ca. 1200 B.C.* (Princeton: University Press, 1995), 48-51.

101 P. Melis, 'L'area nuragica di S. Maria di Tergu (Sassari),' 455.

102 G. Lilliu, *Sculture della Sardegna Nuragica,* 271, no.104, is a horned warrior deity with four eyes and four arms. See ibid., 273, for comparisons with statuettes from Lusristan and Cyprus. See also ibid., 492, no.289, for a Nuragic ship.

103 The earliest instances of boat model deposits with the dead are attested in the mortuary traditions of Mesopotamia (in the predynastic Royal Cemetery of Ur two boats were found, one silver and one copper). More common, however, were boats made of argil or bitumen, such as those uncovered in Farah, Tello, Kish, Obeid, Ur, Eridu and Abu Hatab (J. Vanschoonwinkel, 'La barque dans le culte et la religion cretomyceniens,' in *Revue des archeologues et historiens d' art de Louvain*, No.15 (1982), 21-24). Similar practices are attested for Egypt (J.H. Taylor, *Death and the Afterlife in Ancient Egypt* (London: British Museum Press, 2001), 103-105). The tradition of the ship of the dead is also attested in prehistoric Europe, with examples in rock carvings from Italy and France (L. V. Grinsell, 'The Boat of the Dead in the Bronze Age,' in *Antiquity*, 15 (1941), 360-369. Grinsell argues a Near Eastern origin transmitted to Europe by Aegean vectors (ibid.). Models of ships in graves are also attested in Minoan and Mycenaean sites, but there is no agreement among scholars about their signtificance. For example, 'boats are appropriate gifts to the dead of a seafaring people and keen fishermen' (B.C. Dietrich, 'Death and Afterlife in Minoan Religion,' in *Kernos*, 10 (1997), 27). Other scholars have considered the interpretation of Minoan-Mycenaean funerary boats in eschatological terms as arbitrary and illegitimate and interpreted the offering as a reference to the deceased's past profession: I. Pini, *Beiträge zur minoischen Gräberkunde* (Wiesbaden: Steiner, 1968), 74; C. Sourvinou-Inwood, *'Reading' Greek Death to the End of the Classical Period* (Oxford: Clarendon, 1996), 45-48. Also, Sakellarakis rejected the idea that all Minoan-Mycenaean funerary model boats functioned as a means of transportation to the Underworld. However, there is no trace of bull protomes or horn symbology on the boats found in Minoan and Mycenaean graves (Y.A. Sakellarakis, 'Ἐλεφάντινον πλοίον εκ Μυκηνων,' in *Archaiologike Ephemeris* (Athens: Estia, 1971), 222).

104 A. Depalmas, *Le navicelle di bronzo della Sardegna nuragica* (Cagliari: Gasperini, 2005), 353-357. Examples from proto-historic Latium indicate the use of the symbol of the boat in chthonic cults of Levantine origin, found at proto-historic sanctuaries (M. Bettelli, "Divinità migranti'? Possibili influssi dal Mediterraneo orientale nell'iconografia dell'età del Bronzo italiana,' in *Miti simboli decorazioni. Ricerche e scavi, Atti del Secondo Incontro di Studi. Pitignano - Valentano, 13-15 settembre 2002*, edited by N. Negroni Catacchio (Milan, 2004), 247-260.

105 G.Lilliu, *Sculture della Sardegna Nuragica* (Nuoro: Ilisso, 2008), 467-472, no. 267.

106 The strange structure on the cap worn by the *Bronzetto di Nule* is similar to that of another Nuragic group showing two human figures, one of which is a warrior wearing a horned cap (Cf. G. Lilliu, *Sculture della Sardegna Nuragica*, 90).

107 G. Lilliu, *Sculture della Sardegna Nuragica*, 471; H.P.Isler, *Acheloos,*166, no.267. Surprisingly, Isler dated the piece to the 6th century BC, without any explanation for lowering the date. The dating of the Sardinian bronze statuettes, of which there are about

locally in Sardinia. It was found in 1937 at the site of Su Casteddu de Santu Lisèi,[108] in the area of Nule, near modern Sassari. The first reports indicate a burial area as the place of discovery,[109] probably from the votive deposit adjoining the tomb. Lilliu assumed the statuette was a cultic object representing a deity.[110] The author stylistically analyzed the piece, recognizing a mixture of influences, namely, Assyrian and northern Syrian[111] intermingled with Etruscan-Italic derivations.[112]

Another artifact published by Lilliu shows an interesting iconographical scheme.[113] The author states that the human figure shows 'the body confused with that of the bull, so as to give the impression, when viewed in profile, of a kind of centaur.'[114] The human figure is standing aside a bull, grasping its horn.[115] This iconography is similar to that seen on a Villanovian vase showing the earliest Italic man-faced bull, discussed below **(Fig. 45)**. Thus, in light of the Nuragic ships, we can infer that the image of the bull accompanies the soul of the deceased who clings to the horns on his journey toward death, understood here as an aquatic voyage, a concept reminiscent of the Mesopotamian cult of Apsu. Moreover, this psychopomp association, as a conveyor of souls, is related to later iconographic schemes of the man-faced bull otherwise difficult to explain, such as an Etruscan gem dated to the 5th century BC (**Fig.46**), and another Etruscan gem dated to the 4th century BC, described by Isler as the fight between Herakles and Acheloios (**Fig.47**).[116]

An even more striking comparison is revealed in the tetradrachms minted in Katane in the mid 5th century BC (**Fig. 48**), where the positioning of the man-faced bull's legs is exactly the same as on the aforementioned gems. Thus, the type from Katane has nothing to do with 'bull leaping' practices as commonly believed. It probably had a deeper symbological meaning related to the psychopomp dimension of the man-faced bull, as a liminal deity in his role as 'conductor,' driving souls to the afterlife. On these Katanian tetradrachms, the crown likely represents ciclicality and rebirth, and the winged female on the reverse of similar types is probably a chthonic nymph, rather than Nike, as commonly believed. Finally, there are small silver coins from Panormos/*Sys*, the Punic stronghold of Sicily, dated to the end of the 5th century, that show a figure riding utop a man-faced bull and grasping its horns.[117]

The Sardinian production of bronzetti and Nuragic ships probably started earlier than previosly believed. Depalmas identifies the derivation of Nuragic bronze art from Cypriot models of the 2nd millenium BC.[118] She provides many examples of Cypriot artifacts found in

500 specimens known, mainly depicting horned warriors and Nuragic ships with bull protomes, has been debated by scholars, and it has not been established with certainty until recent years. In the past they were commonly dated 9th to 7th century BC, but many academic studies suggested an earlier date for the beginning of production, to the last quarter of the 2nd millennium BC (F. Lo Schiavo, 'Bronzetti di età nuragica dalla Gallura,' in *Archeologia del territorio, territorio dell'Archeologia* (Sassari: Delfino, 1996), 65ff.; V. Santoni, *Il Nuraghe Su Nuraxi di Barumini*. Guide e studi, Vol.2 (Cagliari, 2001), 5ff; F. Campus, V., Leonelli, F. Lo Schiavo, 'La transizione culturale dall'età del bronzo all'età del ferro nella Sardegna nuragica in relazione con l'Italia tirrenica,' in *Meetings between cultures in the ancient Mediterranean*. Bollettino di Archeologia online, I (2010), 62-76). This has been confirmed by recent discoveries in controlled stratigraphy (M.R. Manunza, 'La stratigrafia del vano a di Funtana Coberta (Ballao - CA),' in *F.O.D.R* (2008), 120), the most recent one at Orroli, within a layer dated to the 13th century BC (Online report by the Italian Ministry of Cultural Heritage, http://www.archeossnu.beniculturali.it). For a comprehensive study of cultural contacts between Sardinians, Phoenicians and Cypriots based on Assyrian influences in Sardinian bronzes from the first quarter of the 1st millennium BC, in which the *Bronzetto di Nule* is also mentioned, see: P. Bernardini and M. Botto, 'I bronzi 'fenici' della Penisola Italiana e della Sardegna,' in *Rivista di Studi Fenici*, Vol. XXXVIII, 1 (Rome: Fabrizio Serra, 2011), 17-117. The beginning of production of *bronzetti* in Sardinia should be determined in connection with the contemporary participation of 'Shardana' in the incursions of the 'Peoples of the Sea' in the eastern Mediterranean. This would explain the strong Levantine influences on Nuragic Art. Beyond the *Bronzetto di Nule* is a fragment of a Nuragic bronze statuette from the Dessì collection, today displayed at the Archaeological Museum of Sassari (G. Lilliu, *Sculture della Sardegna Nuragica,* no.114), which shows an interesting similarity to Assyrian depictions, as the head is crowned with a horned tiara seen on winged man-headed bulls and other Near Eastern deities. For a dissertation on Neo-Assyrian influence on Iron Age Sardinian culture, see: M. Rendeli 'Monte 'e Prama: 4875 punti interrogativi,' in *Meetings between cultures in the Ancient Mediterranean. Conference Proceedings. 17th International Congress of Classical Archaeology Rome 2008* (Bollettino di Archeologia Online I, 2010), 58-72.

[108] D.Levi, 'Nule. Bronzi protosardi rinvenuti fortuitamente in località Santu Lisei presso Nule,' in *Notizie degli Scavi di Antichità* (1937), 83-90.

[109] P. Bernardini and M. Botto, 'I bronzi 'fenici' della Penisola Italiana e della Sardegna,' 60.

[110] G. Lilliu, *Sculture della Sardegna Nuragica,* 471

[111] Lilliu also mentions the Assyrian winged man-headed bull (Lamassu), and he ultimately connects some stylistical features of the Sardinian piece with Urartian artifacts (G. Lilliu, *Sculture della Sardegna Nuragica,* 468). For an excellent essay on the cultural interconnections between Sardinia, Etruria, and Urartu, see: M. Pallottino, 'Urartu, Greece and Etruria,' in *East and West*, Vol. 9, No. 1/2 (1958), 29-52.

[112] The piece was recently displayed in Rome ('Mostri. Creature fantastiche della paura e del mito,' December 17th 2013-June 1st, 2014) and it is worth noting the insightfulness of curators Rita Paris and Elisabetta Setari who compared the *Bronzetto di Nule* and the Cypriot bull-man centaur discussed above (**Fig.28**), placing them next to each other, clearly suggesting the connections recognized in this book. Levi, when making the discovery at Nule, suggested a Cypriot derivation of the type (D.Levi, 'Nule. Bronzi protosardi rinvenuti fortuitamente in località Santu Lisei presso Nule,' 84).

[113] G. Lilliu, *Sculture della Sardegna Nuragica*, 493, no. 289.

[114] Ibid.

[115] Comparison of this scheme with an Etruscan bronze applique dated to the 5th century BC (H.P. Isler, 'Acheloos,' in *LIMC*, no.238) and with a late Etruscan mirror dated c. 4th century BC (showing the fight of Herakles vs an uncommon young beardless Acheloios, labeled 'Achlae', from E. Gerhard, *Etruskische Spiegel*, Vol. IV. (Berlin: G. Reimer, 1867), 83, Pl. CCCXL), reveal that both use an iconographic scheme very similar to the one seen on the Sardinian ship, with the human figure standing sideways, grasping both horns of the bull.

[116] The style of the last gem suggests an earlier date, and the iconographic scheme is not convincing for the fight with Herakles as described by Isler. In fact, it is very similar with the other gem showing a female figure (**Fig. 46**).

[117] G.K.Jenkins, 'Coins of Punic Sicily,' in *SNR*, 50 (1971), Plate 24, no. 5 & 6. Jenkins describes the creature as a 'goat' (ibid., 74).

[118] A. Depalmas, *Le navicelle di bronzo della Sardegna nuragica*, 221-224, for discussion and bibliography.

Sardinia at that time, and also notes the strong Cypriot features of a Nuragic ship found at Vetulonia in Etruria.[119] She also states that the oldest ships produced in Sardinia show a close affinity with the motifs of Late Cypriot III art (1200 to 1050 BC). Finally, the most paradigmatic example of the network of cultural relations between Cyprus, Sardinia, and Etruria comes from the site of Sa Sedda 'e Sos Carros, where 10 Nuragic ships have been found, among other Cypriot bronze artifacts dated from the 12th to 11th century BC, and also Etruscan bronze artifacts dated to the 8th century BC.[120]

An appealing explanation for some of these early cultural interconnections are the Shardana, Shekelesh, and Teresh peoples named in Egyptian inscriptions among the 'People of the Sea,' fighting in the Levant around 1200 BC. The aforementioned ethnics are probably Sardinians, Sikels, and Tyrrhenians (respectively) used as mercenaries in the Levant at the dawn of the Iron Age.[121] The movements of these soldiers, mercenaries, and other people[122] was probably the basis for the spread of the proto-cult of the man-faced bull from the Levant and Cyprus to the West, especially when we consider the rationale provided for the early itinerant mercenary tradition above. Recall, also, the bronze plaques at Polizzello in Sicily, used to protect the abdomen of warriors. Thus, if we consider the widespread evidence of the particular warlike connotation in Sardinian traditions, as indicated by dozens of discoveries in water-cultic contexts of Nuragic horned gods like those seen in Cyprus, it seems reasonable to infer a sort of Cypro-Sikel-Nuragic-Italic cultural *koine*,[123] emerging from direct connections between the islands, sharing the use of bull-horned deities with similar qualities and iconographies, sometimes hybridizating man and bull features. This parallel non-Greek *koine*, when encountering the Greek tradition, ultimately produces the tradition of Acheloios as man-faced bull in the Archaic and Classical worlds.

[119] Ibid., 225. The Nuragic ship was discovered in Tomb 74 of Montevetrano, dated to the 8th century BC, among other artifacts from Sardinia and the Eastern Mediterranean. Pellegrino and Rafanelli pointed out that in the tombs of Vetulonia there is a strong presence of metal artifacts coming from Syria that influenced local production, citing in particular the feminine figures representing Ishtar, as seen in Vetulonian tombs on gold artifacts, and the bronze fittings for cauldrons shaped in form of sirens (C. T. Pellegrino and S. Rafanelli 'Vetulonia, Pontecagnano, Capua. Vite parallele di tre città Etrusche,' in *Archeologia Viva*, XXXII, n.162 (Firenze: Giunti, 2013), 37-38).

[120] Ibid., 223-224. Sardinian traditions also had an influence on Italic peninsular populations, as attested by the discoveries of Nuragic *bronzetti* in Italy (G. Bartoloni, 'Bronzetti nuragici importati nell'Italia peninsulare,' in *Dal Bronzo al Ferro. Il II millennio a.C. nella Toscana centro-occidentale, Catalogo della mostra*, edited by A. Zanini (Pisa, 1997), 27-31). For other reports of Nuragic ships found in Etruria and south Italy, see: A. Depalmas, *Le navicelle di bronzo della Sardegna nuragica*, 224. The report of Sardinian bronze artifacts in Campania is also interesting, among which was found a bronze ring with a bull protome (A. Depalmas, *Le navicelle di bronzo della Sardegna nuragica*, 229). For Etruria, examples of Nuragic *bronzetti* are known from discoveries in cultic contexts at Vetulonia, Gravisca, Tarquinia, and Vulci (G. Lilliu, *Arte e religione della Sardegna prenuragica. Idoletti, ceramiche, oggetti d'ornamento*, 21-22). The most famous Italian discovery is probably the Nuragic ship adorned with bulls from Capo Colonna near Croton (ibid., 23), at the site of a temple in which a later antefix of a man-faced bull head was discovered (E. Mussini, 'La diffusione dell'iconografia di Acheloo in Magna Grecia e Sicilia. Tracce per l'individuazione di un culto,' 100, Pl.XVIII.a). An iconographic symbol very similar to that of Nuragic ships, in which the journey of the deceased is centered upon a boat with bull protome at the top, is seen on a beautiful Etruscan fibula found in a royal tomb at Pizzoli (Aq), dated to the 8th century BC, now displayed at the Museum of Vetulonia (M.C. De Angelis 'Circoli di Pietre. Gli Etruschi e l'ideologia della Casta,' in *Archeologia Viva*, XXXIV, n.169 (Firenze: Giunti, 2015), 26).

[121] R. Drews, *The End of the Bronze Age: Changes in Warfare and the Catastrophe Ca. 1200 B.C.*, 48-51. A relief from Medinet Habu shows some of the 'People of the Sea' captured by the Pharaoh, labeled with their respective ethnics on the original relief (**Fig.48b**, from: M. Cultraro, 'Ex Parte Orientis: i Teresh e la questione dell'origine anatolica degli Etruschi,' in *Le origini degli Etruschi. Storia, archeologia, antropologia,* edited by Vincenzo Bellelli (Rome: Bretschneider, 2012), 111, fig.5). The comparison between the depiction of the Shardana on the relief and Nuragic bronzetti, who also wear horned helmets, indicates a likely connection. Recent discoveries at the site of Pyla-Kokkinokremos in Cyprus demonstrate that Sardinian and Sicilian people moved East in the 13th century BC. In fact, a great number of large storage vessels of the type known as 'Handmade Burnished Ware' dating back to the foundation of Pyla-Kokkinokremos have been discovered, and this pottery was originally produced in Sardinia, Sicily, and the Italian Peninsula. This suggests that a large group of people coming from the West settled in Cyprus around the 13th century BC, carrying with them their pottery traditions. According to Karageorghis and Karageorghis this evidence is connected with the contemporary Egyptian records concerning the People of the Sea (T. V. Karageorghis and J. Karageorghis 'Sull'isola di Afrodite. Cipro fra Oriente e Occidente,' in *Archeologia Viva,* XXXII, n.159 (Firenze: Giunti, 2013), 47). This gives even further substance to the crucial role of Cyprus in the early contacts between the Near East and Italy, suggesting the possibility of a Cypro-Sikel-Nuragic-Italic cultural *koine*.

[122] For Levantine artisans and metal-smiths traveling between Etruria, Sardinia and other areas of the western Mediterranean in the wake of Phoenician traders, see: M. Botto, 'Artigiani al seguito di mercanti: considerazioni su un aspetto del commercio fenicio nel Mediterraneo,' in *Archaeologica Pisana. Scritti per Orlanda Pancrazzi*, edited by S. Bruni, T. Caruso, and M. Massa (Pisa, 2004), 31-38. For Sardinia in particular, see: P. Bernardini and R. D'Oriano, *Argyròphleps nesos. L'isola dalle vene d'argento. Esploratori, mercanti e coloni in Sardegna tra il XIV e il VI sec. a.C.* (Fiorano Modenese, 2001). For Etruria, see: L. Drago Troccoli, 'Veio tra villanoviano e tardo arcaismo. Appunti sulla necropoli di Casale del Fosso,' in *Etruria e Italia preromana. Studi in onore di Giovannangelo Camporeale (Studia erudita, 4)*, edited by S. Bruni (Rome, 2009), 350; M. Pallottino, 'Urartu, Greece And Etruria,' in *East And West*, Vol. 9, No. 1/2 (March-June 1958), 49.

[123] The importance of Sardinia as a step along the Phoenician and Cypriot routes, and its ramifications in the West, has been clearly established by scholars (S. Celestino, N. Rafel, and X. L. Armada, (eds.), *Contacto cultural entre el Mediterraneo y el Atlantico (siglos XII-VIII ane: la precolonizacion a debate)* (Madrid, 2008)). For the importance of Sardinia as a center of cultural transmission to the Tyrrhenian coasts of Italy and Sicily, see: M. Milletti, 'Riflessioni sul tema dei contatti tra la Sardegna e l'Etruria tra bronzo finale e prima età del ferro,' in *Gli Etruschi e la Sardegna tra la fine dell'età del bronzo e gli inizi dell'età del ferro, Catalogo della mostra*, edited by F. Lo Schiavo, P. Falchi, and M. Milletti (Cagliari, 2008), 17-24; M. Botto, 'I rapporti fra la Sardegna e le coste medio-tirreniche della Penisola Italiana nella prima metà del I millennio a.C.,' in *Etruschi, Greci, Fenici e Cartaginesi nel Mediterraneo centrale. Atti del XIV Convegno Internazionale di Studi sulla Storia e l'Archeologia dell'Etruria* (Rome: Quasar, 2007), 75-136; O. Paoletti and L. Tamagno Perna, *Etruria e Sardegna centro-settentrionale tra l'età del Bronzo finale e l'Arcaismo, Atti del XXI Congresso di Studi Etruschi e Italici (Sassari-Alghero-Oristano-Torralba, 13-17 ottobre 1998), Istituto nazionale di studi etruschi ed italici, Istituti Editoriali e Poligrafici Internazionali* (Rome, 2002).

Early Italic Traditions

Introduction

The historical cult of the Etruscan man-faced bull has its early origins in prehistoric Levantine influences largely mediated by Cypriot and Sardinian vectors, before the arrival of Greek settlers in Southern Italy. Only later are the bull and bull-man water cults conflated with the Greek myth of Acheloios, and it is from the contact between Etruscan and Greek traditions that the imagery and mythology of Acheloios as a man-faced bull was finally formalized. Without this more local explanation, it is difficult to explain the later, almost obsessive popularity of the man-faced bull in Italy during the historical age. Jenkins seems to have noticed the same thing, but 'resisted the temptation' of attributing the popularity of the man-faced bull on the coins of Magna Graecia to Etruria, probably because of the pervasive hellenocentrism of the time.

Early Evidence

Since Palaeolothic times one finds traces of the veneration of water in caves in Peninsular Italy,[124] but it is during the Neolithic period that, initiated by agricultural practices, water becomes widely worshipped for its vivifying and healing properties.[125] Cultish forms for the Neolithic period are known mainly from labyrinthine caves, with deposits of vessels near small lakes or subterranean springs, often placed under the sources of dripping water. Within these caves various wall paintings and artifacts, mainly engraved fragments of bones, often depict serpentine motifs or representations of bulls related to the presence of running water, fertility and the vitality of nature.[126] In fact, the bone fragments were probably used in divination and oracular rites, along with carved shoulder blades and astragaloi sometimes found in the same contexts. Especially in central-south Italy, the many votive offerings in water-cultic contexts are related to agrarian rituals and funerary practices associated with birth, life, and death in a dimension of ciclicality.[127]

During the Copper Age the known evidence of water cults exhibits a connection to springs, river sources, and waterfalls, and in this context the exploitation of therapeutic waters emerges, with the first Italic evidence of man-made sacred wells in which ritual vessels appear, interpreted as offerings to the sacred medicinal source.[128]

Starting in the Bronze Age, water cults are even more common in Peninsular Italy, both in caves and now even in surface-water contexts by rivers and lakes.[129] For the Tyrrhenian peninsular area evidence exists for cults of therapeutic waters operating since the early Bronze Age, in Latium.[130] During the Late Bronze Age in the same area the ritual of cremation appears, a practice which is accompanied, in ceramics, with the symbolism of bull protomes and horns[131] in relation to water-cults as in contemporary Sicily.[132]

Torelli, in his studies on archaic Rome, detected the presence of two religious conceptions about sacred water. The first was based on chthonic-netherworld dimensions, connected to underground water and internal sources. The other was based on chthonic-solar beliefs linked to 'living' waters, i.e. rivers and watercourses.[133] The roots of these religious conceptions are in Bronze Age central Italy, where the places of worship are mainly caves with natural springs.[134] In these contexts there are numerous reports of swords, helmets, and valuable objects deposited in rivers and springs, testifying to the existence of widespread rituals which, according to Nuccia Catacchio et al., were performed to honor and appease the potentially terrible ire of the river-deity.[135] This practice is still popular in historical times, with the phenomenon of offering coins, often depicting

[124] Cf. R. Whitehouse, *Underground Religion. Cult and cultures in Prehistoric Italy.*

[125] R. Grifoni Cremonesi, 'Notes on some cultic aspects of Italian Prehistory,' in *Documenta Praehistorica*, Vol. XXXIV (2007), 223. Some examples worthy of mention are: Lattaia (Tuscany), Buca del Rospo (Tuscany), Grotta dell'Orso (Tuscany), Pozzi della Piana (Umbria), Grotta dei Meri (Latium), and Grotta Scaloria (Apulia). At Pozzi della Piana the ritual vessels were placed upside-down within the crevices of the rock near a large pool of water, which is probably the first known Italic trace for a symbolic value of communication with the chthonic underworld attributed to water (S. Bianco, 'Il culto delle acque nella preistoria,' in *Archeologia dell'acqua in Basilicata* (Potenza, 1999), 19.

[126] Ibid., 16. For southern Italy, the author mentions the following sites: Grotta di Papasidero, Grotta Romanelli presso Castro Marina, Grotta Paglicci o di Levanzo nelle isole Egadi, Grotta dell' Addaura presso Palermo, Grotta Polesini preso Tivoli, Grotta Paglicci, Grotte Romanelli, and Cavallo nel Salento.

[127] R. Grifoni Cremonesi, 'Notes on some cultic aspects of Italian Prehistory,' 221-225.

[128] Ibid., 225ff.

[129] Ibid.

[130] Z.Mari and M. Sperandio, 'L'insediamento dell'età del bronzo presso il lago delle Colonnelle nella piana delle acque albule (Tivoli),' in *atti e Memorie soc. Tiburtina Storia ed Arte*, Vol. LXXIX (2006), 81-111. In the same area, between the Late Bronze Age and Middle Bronze Age, there is evidence for the worship of chthonic deities in natural caves and propitiatory practices for agricultural activities (A. Guidi, 'Recenti ritrovamenti in grotta nel Lazio: un riesame critico del problema dell'utilizzazione delle cavità naturali,' in *Rassegna di Archeologia*, Vol. 10 (1992), 427-437).

[131] A. Guidi, 'Aspetti della religione tra la fine dell'età del bronzo e la I età del ferro,' in *Il Lazio dai Colli Albani ai Monti Lepini tra preistoria ed età moderna* (Rome: Quasar, 2009), 143-151.

[132] For Late Bronze Age cults of chthonic water linked to the symbolism of the bull and the interrelationships between traditions in Sicily and the Italian peninsula, see: A. Crispino and M. Cultraro, 'Il deposito votivo di Ferla (Sr) e il culto delle acque nella Sicilia protostorica'.

[133] M Torelli, 'L'acqua degli Etruschi dalle forme ideologiche alle pratiche sociali,' in *Gli Etruschi maestri di idraulica*, edited by M. Bergamini (Perugia, 1991), 24.

[134] N. Negroni Catacchio, M. Cardosa, and M. R. Pitone, 'Dalla grotta naturale al tempio, tra natura e artificio: forma ed essenza del luogo sacro in Etruria durante l'età dei metalli,' in *Antropologia e Archeologia a confronto: rappresentazioni e pratiche del sacro. Atti dell'incontro internazionale di studi Roma, Museo Nazionale Preistorico Etnografico 'Luigi Pigorini' 20-21 maggio 2011* (Rome, 2012), 595 ff.

[135] Ibid.

man-faced bulls, to bodies of water.[136] Also in the area of Capua, where we will later find many traces for a cult of Acheloios, bowls with horned handles used in ceremonial contexts can be linked to similar examples from Late Bronze Age Campania, Etruria, and Terramare civilization.[137]

Later Evidence

Water cults in central Italy became very popular and widespread in the Iron Age.[138] The presence of the image of the bull is attested in locations in which pre-Roman cults concered with springs, therapeutic water and oracular practices operated during the Archaic and Classical Age.[139] Evidence of links between the image of the bull and the funerary ritual use and worship of water are exhibited through the many examples of late Villanovian kernoi shaped in the form of a bull.[140] During the 5th century BC, we see the image of the man-faced bull used by Italic populations of Lavinium on ritual plastic kernoi.[141] Noteworthy as a possible precursor of those kernoi is a discovery from early Iron Age Latium, found in a woman's grave[142] who has been identified as a priestess (Tomba I from Valvisciolo): a multi-pot vessel on which the plastic, rough representation of a horned figure showing hybrid human and animal features is visible.[143]

---

[136] Seneca (*Ep.* 4. 41, 3) reports that in Roman Italy the worship of rivers and natural springs was still practiced. This is confirmed by frequent archaeological attestations of offering of coins in rivers and natural water sources, clearly derived from the earlier offerings of precious metal objects in the Bronze Age (for a map of the distribution, see G. Facchinetti, 'L'offerta di monete nelle acque in Età Romana e Tardo-Antica: alcune riflessioni,' in *Acque per l'Utilitas, per la Salubritas, per l'Amoenitas* (Milan: Et, 2004), 49 and 276). The same author suggests that these coins represent 'a form of compensation to the gods for oracles received and for ritual connection with the underworld' (G. Facchinetti, 'Iactae stipes: l'offerta di monete nelle acque nella penisola italiana' in *R.I.N.*, 104 (2003), 36-37). In Etruscan locations where the phenomenon occurred, it is also interesting to note the frequent recurrence of coins depicting the man-faced bull minted in Campania (L. Ambrosini and L. Michetti, 'L'ultima frequentazione del santuario meridionale: Testimonianze dai contesti,' in *Riflessioni su Pyrgi. Scavi E Ricerche Nelle Aree Del Santuario* (Rome: Bretschneider, 2013), 126-33. The following list of references concerning discoveries of Campanian coinages depicting the man-faced bull in sacred waters indicates the depth of the phenomenon: D. Giorgetti, 'La Stipe Votiva del Titano,' in *Romanizzazione e Moneta. La testimonianza dei Rinvenimenti dall'Emilia Romagna*, edited by E. Ercolani Cocchi, A.L. Morelli, and D. Neri (Firenze, 2004), 43-45; A. Pautasso, 'Il deposito votivo presso la Porta nord a Vulci,' in *Corpus delle stipi votive in Italia*, 7, Regio VII, 3 (Rome, 1994), 91; S. Costantini and C. Angeletti, *Il deposito votivo del santuario campestre di Tessennano. Corpus delle stipi votive in Italia, 8, Regio VII, 4* (Rome: Bretschneider, 1995), 129; F. Catalli, 'Note sulla produzione e circolazione monetaria dell'Etruria meridionale in età romana,' in *Il Lazio nell'antichità romana* (Roma, 1982), 132; A.M. Comella, 'I materiali votivi di Falerii,' in *Corpus delle stipi votive in Italia*, 1, Regio VII, 1 (Roma, 1986), 148; G. Benedettini, F. Catalli, and M. A. de Lucia Broll, 'Rinvenimenti monetali nel territorio dell'antica Narce: il santuario suburbano in località Monte Li Santi-Le Rote,' in *Bollettino di Numismatica*, No. 32-33 (Roma, 1999), 57-58, no. 2-9 and 87, no.163, and also 90, no. 172; F. Di Gennaro and L. Ceccarelli, 'Fidene. Santuari urbani e del territorio,' in *Sacra Nominis Latini. I santuari del Lazio arcaico e repubblicano*, edited by E. Marroni (Napoli: Loffredo, 2012), 77; P. Romanelli, 'Tarquinia. – Scavi e ricerche nell'area della città,' in *NSc* (1948), 269; F. Catalli, *Le monete di Talamone (Orbetello, GR), 1801-1892. Collezioni numismatiche in Italia, Documentazione dei complessi* (Firenze: Soprintendenza per i Beni Archeologici della Toscana, 2010), 22, 28. All this evidence suggests offerings from Campanian worshippers travelling in Etruria, but it could also indicate the particular attention the Etruscans placed on the typology of man-faced bull coins for votive offerings in water cult sites.

[137] G. Poggesi, E. Bocci, L. Pagnini, and F. Lo Schiavo, 'Rapporti fra l'Etruria settentrionale interna e il territorio di Capua: i kyathoi con anse a corna tronche e cave,' 167ff.; M. Cattani, 'La Terramara di Rastellino,' in *Paesaggio ed economia nell'età del Bronzo. La pianura bolognese tra Samoggia e Panaro* (Bologna, 2010), 167, fig.7; M. Cattani, 'Una fornace per ceramica delle terramare,' in *Le terramare: la più antica civiltà padana* (Electa, 1997), 513, fig.288.

[138] For water cults in Italy during the Iron Age, see: D. Cocchi Genick, 'Dati relativi ai culti delle acque in età protostorica nell'Italia centrale tirrenica,' in *Preistoria e protostoria in Etruria. Paesaggi d'acque. Atti del quinto incontro di studi*, Vol. II (Milan, 2002), 405; A. Mastrocinque, 'Alcuni aspetti degli dei fluviali centro-italici,' in *Preistoria e protostoria in Etruria*, 417; A.Calderone (ed.), *Cultura e Religione delle Acque. Atti del convegno interdisciplinare Qui fresca l'acqua mormora... (S. Quasimodo, Sapph. fr. 2,5) Messina 29-30 marzo 2012* (Rome: Bretschneider, 2012); C. Giontella, *I luoghi dell'acqua 'divina'. Complessi santuariali e forme devozionali in Etruria e Umbria fra epoca arcaica ed età romana* (Rome, 2006); E. Arslan, 'Spiriti delle acque,' in *Anima dell'Acqua. Da Talete a Caravaggio da Segantini a Bill Viola, Catalogo della Mostra, Milano, Palazzo Reale*, edited by C.D. Fonseca and E. Fontanella (Rome: Bretschneider 2009), 100-106; G. Bailo Modesti, A. Frezza, A. Lupia, and M. Mancusi, 'Le acque intorno agli dei: rituali e offerte votive nel santuario settentrionale di Pontecagnano,' in *Offerte dal regno vegetale e dal regno animale nelle manifestazioni del sacro, Atti Incontro di Studio (Milano 2003), Tarchna*, Suppl. 1, edited by M. Bonghi Jovino and F. Chiesa (Rome, 2005), 37-64; M. Barra Bagnasco, 'Il culto delle acque in Magna Grecia dall'età arcaica alla romanizzazione. Documenti archeologici e fonti letterarie,' in *Archeologia dell'acqua in Basilicata, Soprintendenza Archeologica della Basilicata e Consiglio Regionale di Basilicat* (Lavello, 1999), 25-52; M. Barra Bagnasco, 'Il culto delle acque a Locri Epizefiri. Contesti e documenti,' in *Zona Archeologica: Festschrift für H.P. Isler zum 60. Geburtstag* (Bonn, 2001), 27-40; S. Collin Bouffier, 'Il culto delle acque nella Sicilia greca: mito o realtà?,' in *Storia dell'acqua. Mondi materiali e universi simbolici*, edited by V. Teti (Rome, 2003), 43-66; P.G. Guzzo, 'Fonti divine. Miti dell'acqua in Magna Grecia,' in *Storia dell'acqua. Mondi materiali e universi simbolici*, edited by V. Teti (Rome, 2003), 35-42; G. De Sensi Sestito, *Tra l'Amato e il Savuto. Tomo I. Terina e il Lametino nel contesto dell'Italia antica* (Soveria Mannelli: Rubbettino, 1999), 121-148; P. Poccetti, 'Culti delle acque e stadi della vita muliebre: dottrine misteriche e fondo religioso italico nella Tavola osca di Agnone,' in *La Tavola di Agnone nel contesto italico. Convegno di Studio, Agnone,13-15 aprile 1994* (Firenze, 1996), 219-241; E. Herring, 'Using your Religion. Native Ritual and Belief in Southern Italy in the 5th and 4th Centuries BC,' in *Approaches to the Study of Ritual (Italy and the Ancient Mediterranean)*, II, edited by J. B. Wilkins (London, 1996), 144-178.

[139] M.Rizzello, *I santuari della Media Valle del Liri, IV-II sec. a.C.* (Sora, 1980), 93-126; G.R. Bellini, 'Il santuario di Casale Pescarolo in Valle di Comino,' in *Religio: santuari ed ex voto nel Lazio meridionale* (Terracina, 2004), 95-107; N. Cassieri, 'Il deposito votivo di Tratturo Caniò a Sezze,' in *Religio. Santuari ed ex voto nel Lazio meridionale*, 163-181; L. Gatti Lo Guzzo, *Il deposito votivo dall'Esquilino detto di Minerva Medica* Firenze: Sansoni, 1978), 140-142.

[140] A.Bignasca, 'I kernoi circolari in Oriente e in Occidente: strumenti di culto e immagini cosmiche,' 109, no. W56, W60 and W61. For the same phenomenon in Iron Age Cyprus, see above, pg. 18ff.

[141] Getty Image 122322305.

[142] For water cults as a hypostasis of the divine specifically in relation to female rites of passage in the Italic communities of central and southern Italy, see: P. Poccetti, 'Culti delle acque e stadi della vita muliebre: dottrine misteriche e fondo religioso italico nella Tavola osca di Agnone,' 232-234.

[143] A. Guidi, 'Aspetti della religione tra la fine dell'età del bronzo e la I età del ferro,' 148, fig.6.

The worship of a water-bull hybrid deity linked to funerary rituals is already attested in Villanovan cemeteries before the flourishing of Etruscan civilization.[144] Iaia observed that in the Villanovian necropolis of Tarquinia 'the alternance of zoomorphic and anthropomorphic handles that is found in multiple vessels of this necropolis would suggest the worship of a deity having different forms - sometimes human sometimes animal.'[145] It is worth mentioning that from later orientalizing Tarquinia comes the unique known example of a man-faced bull depicted on a fresco, from the famous Tomb of the Bull, discussed below.[146] Another interesting case comes from the Villanovan tombs of Veii (where later the cult of the man-faced bull will appear at the Etruscan temple of Portonaccio), where the presence of bovine representations on plastic vessels used for water rituals is exibited in the graves of children and youths.[147]

It should therefore be no surprise that a direct predecessor of the Etruscan man-faced bull's cult appears in Villanovian culture, almost a century earlier than in mainland Greece.[148] Evidence consists of a brown impasto offering bowl, dated to the 8th century BC, featuring the head of a bearded man-faced bull and upon him, a figure grasps his horns (**Fig.45**).[149] This is the earliest known narrative scene in art from the proto-Etruscan world, probably made in a workshop in the area of Falerii.[150] One possible way to read the iconographical scheme is in connection to the psychopomp quality of the man-faced bull, as we proposed for the Nuragic ship and related comparisons discussed above. Another, more traditional interpretation of this piece is in connection with the myth of Herakles and Acheloios, although the first depictions of that myth are seen significantly later (early 6th century BC) in Ionian glyptics and on Greek pottery.[151] If the reading of the scene as Herakles and Acheloios is correct, its relation to the later Etruscan cultural world is clear: it is well known, for instance, that the Etruscans accomplished some remarkable architectural feats in terms of the collection and regulation of water,[152] which the Herakles-Acheloios

[144] C. Iaia, 'Gli oggetti di uso cerimoniale,' in *Tarquinia Etrusca. Una nuova storia.Catalogo della Mostra*, edited by A.M. Moretti Sgubini (Rome, 2001), 92-93; F. Trucco, D. De Angelis, and C. Iaia, 'Villa Bruschi Falgari: il sepolcreto villanoviano,' in *Tarquinia Etrusca*, 81-93.

[145] Ibid.

[146] The ancient chthonic-water association of the bull also emerges from sulphurous waters which still flow from the hot springs of the ancient site of Aquae Tauri, south of Tarquinia. In fact, it was said that these waters were born from the earth where it was pierced by a bull's horns, as reported by ancient sources (Rutilio Namaziano, *De reditu suo*, lines 237ff).

[147] L. Drago Troccoli, 'Ricerche sul tema del bestiario fantastico di età orientalizzante. I precedenti della prima età del Ferro: continuità o discontinuità?,' in *Il bestiario fantastico di età orientalizzante nella penisola italiana. Aristonothos. Scritti per il Mediterraneo antico Quaderni*, 1 (Trento: Tangram, 2012), 17.

[148] Indeed, man-faced bulls depicted on early 6th century Corinthian and Attic pottery cannot be considered a sign of cults in mainland Greece, as those pieces were made for western customers influencing the Greek potters' choice of the subjects depicted. Thus, the early depictions of the myth of Herakles and Acheloios on Attic and Corinthian pottery have commercial underpinnings, rather than cultic. For the Corinthian pottery, the attribution to Corinthian or western workshops is still controversial, and the existence of a class of 'Etrusco-Corinthian' pottery raises more questions. We will provide an alternative interpretation below, reattributing various early vases depicting the man-faced bull, e.g. the Pontic Vases, or other controversial attributions like the case of the pervasive balsamarii.

[149] J. M. Eisenberg, 'The Art of the Italic Peoples. A Major Exhibition in Paris,' in *Minerva*, Vol.5, No.2 (London: Aurora, 1994), 4, fig.3. The piece is also published in M. De Juliis (ed.), *I fondamenti dell'arte italica* (Bari: Laterza, 2000), fig.45.

[150] J. M. Eisenberg, 'The Art of the Italic Peoples. A Major Exhibition in Paris,'4.

[151] For archaeological evidence relating to the cult of the Italic Hercle in the Etruscan tradition, see: G.Colonna, *Bronzi votivi umbro-sabellici a figura umana, I, Periodo 'arcaico'* (Firenze: Sansoni, 1970); S. J. Schwarz, *The iconography of the Archaic Etruscan Herakles: a study of three adventures: Nessos, Pholos and Acheloos* (University of Maryland, 1974); A. Stibbe Twist, 'Herakles in Etrurien,' in *Thiasos. Sieben archäologische Arbeiten*, edited by T. Lorenz (Amsterdam: J.E. Zeylmans van Emmichoven, 1978), 80-107; E.Richardson, *Etruscan votive Bronzes. Geometric, Orientalizing, Archaic* (1983), 340-5; O. De Cazanove, 'Plastique votive et imagerie Dionysiaque: à propos de deux ex-voto de Vulci,' in *MEFRA*, 98 (1986), 7-36; G. Colonna, 'Note preliminari sui culti del santuario di Portonaccio a Veio,' in *Scienze dell'Antichità. Storia Archeologia Antropologia*, I (1987), 419-46. As noted by Schwarz, the Etruscan Hercle, despite the derivation of his name from the Greek world, does not match the Greek-Herakles seen in literary sources or figurative art of Hellenic manufacture. Instead, he is a conflation of the Greek mythological character with local Italic deities (S. J. Schwarz, 'Herakles/Hercle,' in *LIMC*, Vol.5, Part 1 (Zürich, 1990), 196-253 and specifically 197). The most interesting aspect of Schwarz's study, to the aims of our work, concerns the significance the cult had on the Italian peninsula, where evidence suggests the figure was linked to health sanctuaries since the Archaic Age. Especially in northern Etruria, sanctuaries exibit evidence of water cult votives coupled with Herakles votives. Even more interesting is the connection with water, typical of Etruscan and Italic traditions, which appears in many iconographic contexts near amphorae, fountains, and springs (Ibid.,197). Livy (*Ab Urbe Condita Libri*, 22.1.10) reports springs near Caere called *'fons Herculis.'* Water-healing cults of Etruscan and Campanian worshippers of Hercle are attested in Etruria (J. R. Jannot, *Religion in Ancient Etruria* (Wisconsin: University Press, 2005), 87). Herakles also had a chthonic connotation among the Italic populations (Cf. J. Bayet, 'Hercule funéraire,' in *MEFRA*, 40 (1923), 19-102). Some scholars proposed a Phoenician origin for the archaic cult of Hercle in central Italy (D. Van Berchem, 'Sanctuaires d'Hercule Melqart. Contribution à l'étude de l'expansion phénicienne en Méditerranée,' in *Syria* 44 (1967), 74-109, 307-38; R. Rebuffat, 'Les Phéniciens à Rome,' in *MEFRA*, 78 (1966), 7-48). It is plausible that the representation of the fight of Herakles and Acheloios has its origins in the circular feedback between Italic and Greek traditions during the early Archaic Age. In fact, the aforementioned evidence suggests a conflation of the Greek hero with a local Italic deity, which merged in Archaic times. Even the iconography suggests this: from the 5th century one of the most common attributes of the hero in Greek art is the club, but in Homer and Hesiod Herakles was always described as a bowman, and the first images in which he holds the club are dated to the 6th century BC, from Nola in Campania (J. Boardman, 'Herakles,' in *LIMC*, IV, 734, no.17) and Vulci in Etruria (Ibid., 735, no.40), and on contemporary Phoenician gems (Ibid., 734, no.19ff).

[152] In terms of Etruscan water works, it is worth mentioning the famous cuniculi, man-made underground tunnels for water drainage and irrigation, widespread in central Italy, particularly on the Tyrrhenian coastline north and south of Rome. The earlier dating proposed by scholars for their construction is around 800 BC (F. Ravelli and P. Howard, 'I cunicoli etrusco-latini: tunnel per la captazione di acqua pura,' in *Irrigazione e drenaggio* (Bologna: Edagricole, 1988) 57-70, while others proposed a later date, around 500 BC (G. Casoria, 'La flora e le risorse agricole,' in *Etruria meridionale: conoscenza, conservazione, fruizione* (Rome, 1988), 43-50). Some scholars noticed strong similarities between the Etruscan 'cuniculi' and the Near Eastern 'qanat,' broadly spread within the Persian Empire since the 7th century BC (P.L. Viollet, *Water Engineering in Ancient Civilizations:*

pairing often symbolizes[153] (Incidentally, there were also many Etruscan water cults concerned specifically with the healing properties of water,[154] and such cults were deeply influenced during the early Iron Age and later Orientalizing Revolution,[155] as there was extensive contact between the populations of Tyrrhenian Italy and the Near East and Cyprus[156]). Perhaps both explanations are correct. In fact, in the section on Greek man-faced bulls, we will see examples of Herakles wrestling Acheloios on the walls of underground tombs, indicating the liminal function of the figures.[157]

Another artifact interesting to the aims of our work is an acroterium[158] depicting an unknown deity, discovered by F. Di Mario. It comes from Ardea in Latium,[159] a coastal area facing the Tyrrhenian coast of Sardinia. The acroterium was part of the architectural terracotta devices of a coastal temple dated to the last quarter of the 6th century BC. It shows a bearded man wearing a helmet with bull horns and bovine ears.[160] Di Mario suggested the piece might be the unique known depiction of the local god Inuo,[161] and he places it in relation to similar representations of a female deity from a sanctuary at Satricum identified as Juno Sospita.[162] However, looking at the iconographical scheme of the sanctuary of Satricum it clearly suggests a Near Eastern influence on these local Italic religious traditions, also confirmed by the discovery of Levantine bronze statuettes at the site.[163] The strong warlike connotation of the deity from Ardea is reminiscent of the earlier Nuragic bronzetti from Sardinia discussed above. In the Italic world, similar iconography emerges in the later representation of a

---

5,000 Years of History (CRC Press, 2007), 129). If the dating of Etruscan cuniculi proposed by Ravelli and Howard is correct, the technology was likely invented in Etruria, and later transferred to the East via cultural contacts. In any event, the matter is still controversal and needs further analyses, as recent studies proposed for the earliest examples of qanat known in Iran date contemporaneously with Etruscan cuniculi, around 800 BC (P. Magee, 'The chronology and environmental background of Iron Age settlement in southeastern Iran and the question of the origin of the qanat irrigation system,' in *Iranica Antiqua*, Vol.XL (2015), 217-231). According to Goblot, despite the similarities, the Etruscan cuniculi and Near Eastern qanat are both original inventions, independent of each other (H. Goblot, *Les Qanat. Une technique d'acquisition de l'eau* (Paris: Mouton, 1979).

153 E. Macnamara, *Everyday Life of the Etruscans* (London: Batsford, 1973), 45.

154 Ibid., 45.

155 Cf. M. Sannibale, 'Orientalizing Etruria,' in *The Etruscan World*, 99-133; R. D'Oriano and A. Sanciu, 'Phoenician and Punic Sardinia and the Etruscans,' in *The Etruscan World*, 231-243. According to Artistotle, the Etruscans and Carthaginians had a military alliance (Aristotle, *Politics*, 3.5.10-11).

156 G. Camporeale, 'Artigiani e mercanti stranieri in Etruria ed Etruschi fuori d'Etruria,' in *Mobilità geografica e mercenariato nell'Italia Preromana* (Rome: Quasar, 2013), 24. The author provides a reconstruction of the cultural contacts between the Levant and Villanovian Etruria during the 9th to 8th century BC, assuming the presence of eastern Mediterranean craftsmen in Italy since that time period. At the end of his dissertation, he inferred the following conclusions: Etruria was already open to foreign individuals or groups since the Villanovian age, consisting of foreigners from countries ranging from the western Mediterranean to the Levant. Those groups mainly operated in the fields of arts and crafts, working in local workshops while introducing advanced ideas, and acquiring a local education. They were easily integrated into the social fabric of Villanovan Etruria and participated in the organization of the the urban ideology that marks the passage from Villanovian culture to Etruscan civilization, contributing concretely to the formation of a distinct Etruscan world, which was at its core multicultural since its earliest manifestations. These recent analyses suggest one 'reconsider the phenomenon of 'orientalizing' in Etruria, not as a mere imitation of motifs seen on imported objects, but as an artistic and cultural phenomenon to which Etruria gave an active contribution as a result of its multi-cultural basis' (our translation of G. Camporeale, 'Artigiani e mercanti stranieri in Etruria ed Etruschi fuori d'Etruria,' 39). For a comprehensive bibliography and many examples of evidence concerning a direct cultural influence on Etruria since the 8th century BC, from Cyprus and the Levant, see: A. Naso, 'Gli influssi del Vicino Oriente sull'Etruria nell'VIII-VII sec. a.C.: un bilancio,' in *Origine degli Etruschi. Storia archeologia antropologia*, edited by V. Bellelli (Rome, 2012), 433-453. For the presence of Cypro-Phoenician people in Tyrrhenian Italy since the early Iron Age and their influence on local traditions, see: M. Botto, 'Le più antiche presenze fenicie nell'Italia meridionale,' in *Fenici e Italici, Cartagine e la Magna Grecia. Popoli a contatto, culture a confronto. Atti del Convegno Internazionale, Rivista di Studi Fenici, (Cosenza, 27-28 maggio 2008)*, Vol. 36, edited by M. Intrieri and S. Ribichini (Rome, 2011), 157-179; M. Botto, 'I bronzi di produzione orientale del tumulo F di Satricum,' in *Annali di Archeologia e Storia Antica* (Napoli: Istituto Universitario Orientale, 1993), 9-22; M. Martelli, 'Bronzi ciprioti dall'Etruria,' in *Studi in memoria di Lucia Guerrini*, edited by M.G. Picozzi and F. Carinci (Rome, 1996), 47-60; H. Mattha, 'Studies on the Interrelations of Cyprus and Italy During the 11th to 9th Centuries BC: A Pan-Mediterranean Perspective,' in *Italy and Cyprus in Antiquity: 1500 - 450 BC*, edited by L. Bonfante and V. Karageorghis (Nicosia, 2001), 153-214. Indeed, one might expect such foreign presence in central Italy, being on the same route discussed in the previous paragraph for the Cypriot influences on Nuragic traditions. Recent publications have shown convincing evidence for a movement of Cypriot and Levantine craftsmen between Sardinia and Etruria since the Early Iron Age, before Greek colonization of Magna Graecia (L. Drago Troccoli, 'Rapporti tra Sardegna e Italia medio-tirrenica nell'età del Ferro: aspetti inediti del ruolo e delle interrelazioni tra aristocrazie, mercanti e artigiani,' in *La preistoria e la protostoria della Sardegna. Atti della XLIV riunione scientifica. Cagliari, Barumini, Sassari 23-28 novembre 2009* (Firenze: I.I.P.P., 2012), 1087-1093). Colonna, on the basis of recent evidence from Etruria, has suggested a direct contribution by the Phoenicians on the Etruscan alphabet, meaning an introduction of writing in Italy before the Euboean presence in Campania (G. Colonna, 'Discussione e interventi,' in *Oriente e Occidente: metodi e discipline a confronto. Riflessioni sulla cronologia dell'età del ferro italiana, Atti dell'Incontro di Studi, Mediterranea*, I (Rome, 2005), 478-483; L. Drago Troccoli, 'Rapporti tra Sardegna e Italia medio-tirrenica nell'età del Ferro: aspetti inediti del ruolo e delle interrelazioni tra aristocrazie, mercanti e artigiani,' 1091). All this evidence, in addition to the comparisons discussed in our study, suggest that some elements of man-faced bull and related iconography and mythology came to the West through these Cypro-Phoenician carriers, along the same routes on which traders, artisans, and especially seer-healers and mercenaries moved since the end of the Bronze Age.

157 See below, pg. 66ff.

158 Excavation report by the Italian Ministry of Cultural Heritage: F. Di Mario, 'Sito archeologico del Fosso dell'Incastro 'Castrum Inui',' Excavation Report (Rome: Direzione Generale Archeologia, 2011).

159 Ardea is located in the same area from which comes the kernos mentioned above (**Fig.49**).

160 F. Di Mario, 'Sito archeologico del Fosso dell'Incastro 'Castrum Inui',' fig. 5.

161 The identification of Inuo is based on the hypothesis that the place of discovery corresponds to the ancient site of Castrum Inui mentioned by ancient sources. Scholars know very little about this Italic deity, mentioned by Macrobius (Macr., *Sat.* 22.2-7). He was a god embodying the representation of the sun in his chthonic winter phase (L. Ceccarelli and E. Marroni, *Repertorio dei Santuari del Lazio* (Rome: Bretschneider, 2011), 52). Scholars have recognized traces of his cult in the coastal area of Latium between Ardea and Satricum.

162 G. Bellucci and S.Cristofoli, 'Satricum,' on the website *Studi e ricerche di Giocando ancora nel Tempo* (Rome, 2011), fig. 6.

163 Ibid., fig.2.

Samnite warrior wearing a horned helmet, from a fresco in a tomb at Nola in Campania, dated to the 4th century BC.[164] Thus, perhaps the figure is not Inuo, but another bull-man related to the Near Eastern tradition. Moreover, it is worth noting that the Iberian site of Arse-Saguntum, where we will later find numismatic representations of man-faced bulls, was founded by Ardeans.[165]

The most striking comparison for the acroterium from Ardea is an earlier piece showing an ityphallic warrior wearing a similar helm with horns and bovine ears, found in Picenum and today exhibited at Pesaro, Museo Oliveriano.[166] It is a bronze applique for a hydria, a large jar used to store water, dated to the first half of the 6th century BC. The iconographic scheme of this applique indicates an influence from Mesopotamian glyptics, in which the 'Master of Animals' is often represented in association with bull-men and man-faced bulls.[167] In fact, Picenum is a very interesting area for the earlier diffusion of man-faced bull iconography in archaic Italy. In that area evidence was found demonstrating the existence of an archaic local tradition of the man-faced bull: it is a bronze artifact, probably a mobile terminal vase handle, dated to Piceno III Period, 7th century BC (**Fig. 50**),[168] which shows a man-faced bull protome with stylistic features of local manufacture but also influences from oriental types. The attribution to a local workshop is confirmed by the stylistical appearence of the piece, characterized by the tendency to synthesize the human and animal figures until they become almost abstract, typical of the art of Piceno III Period. The function of the piece is probably ritual, as a reusable attachment for ceremonial vessels.

Incidentally, since the Bronze Age, caves, lakes, and water sources in the area of Piceno were places in which collective worship rituals were performed by local communities, which later merged with forms of heroic and celebratory cults.[169] According to K. Kilian, the first religious expressions established for the natives of Piceno consisted of figurines of bulls discovered in Ancona, dated to the Late Bronze Age.[170] The known evidence indicates fresh water as the object of these early cults.[171] We find traces of these water cults in the Iron Age, as demonstrated by archaeological findings. For instance, in many places votive deposits were discovered[172] away from the villages and usually located on the banks of rivers and streams (Isola di Fano e Castelbellino), or near natural water springs (Coltone di Cagli e Montefortino).[173]

Particularly interesting is the site of Cupramarittima Piceno, where evidence lead archaeologists to state that in this area from the 8th to 6th century BC rituals of purification and healing were performed using water, and such activity was linked to beliefs concerning the transition between the world of the living and the dead.[174] Moreover, at the aforementioned sites of Montefortino and Cupramarittima, and also inland at the site of Cupramontana, materials were discovered documenting the existence of a sacred place in which water-healing practices were performed in relation to the cult of a

[164] F. Weege, *Oskische Grabmalerei* (1909), no.30, today stored at the Museo Archeologico Nazionale di Napoli (inv. no. 9363). See also a Samnite warrior from Nola, on a fresco from Tomba di Via del Crocifisso (A. Chierici, 'Armati e tombe con armi nella società dell'Etruria padana: analisi di alcuni documenti,' in *Annali della Fondazione per il Museo Claudio Faina*, Vol.XV (Quasar, 2008), 243, fig.56).

[165] L. Ceccarelli et al., *Repertorio dei Santuari del Lazio*, 52.

[166] A. Naso, *Piceni. Storia e archeologia delle Marche in epoca preromana* (Milano: Longanesi, 2000), 197, Pl.54.

[167] For a comprehensive essay on the iconography of the 'Master of Animals' in Akkadian glyptics, see: N. Manassero, 'Il Signore degli animali nella glittica di età accadica. Indagine iconografica ed analisi delle fonti,' in *Mesopotamia. Rivista di Archeologia, Epigrafia e Storia orientale antica*, Vol. XXXIX (Firenze, 2004), 71-92.

[168] Displayed at the Museo Archeologico Nazionale delle Marche, Palazzo Ferretti, Ancona (AN), inv. 7059 (1961).

[169] G. Colonna and L. Franchi dell'Orto 'Le forme della devozione,' in *Eroi e Regine. Piceni. Popolo d'Europa* (Rome: De Luca, 2001), 89-92. The first epigraphic evidence for Picenum reveals an unknown language not of the Italic Umbrian-Sabellic derivation used later by the Piceni, beginning in the 6th century BC. There are four inscriptions on the stele found in the Necropolis of Novillara, written in this strange language, known as 'language of Novillara,' from the place of discovery (A. Naso, *Piceni. Storia e archeologia delle Marche in epoca preromana,* 233). K. Beinhauer dated the oldest of the four inscriptions (*PID* 344, Pl. 70) from 690 to 630 BC on the basis of the chronological study of the necropolis in which they were found (K.W. Beinhauer, *Untersuchungen zu den eisenzeitlichen Bestattungsplätzen von Novilara. (Provinz Pesaro und Urbino, Italien). Archäologie, Anthropologie, Demographie. Methoden und Modelle.* Band 1 (Frankfurt am Main, 1985). According to Villar, the 'language of Novillara' is not of Indo-European origins, but also, given the paucity of evidence, possibly not even used by the people of the area, and instead demonstrates the presence of foreign travelers. In this case the oldest inscription might be a funeral stele made by a group of foreigners in honor of a comrade who died during the trip (F.Villar, *Gli indoeuropei e le origini dell'Europa: lingua e storia* (Bologna: Il Mulino, 2008), 492.

[170] Cited in A. Naso, *Piceni. Storia e archeologia delle Marche in epoca preromana,* 235.

[171] Ibid.

[172] Representations of horns are among the recognizable symbols in the decorations of the objects found in the votive deposits near springs and in the Necropolis of Picenum. These are interpreted as religious and apotropaic symbols connected to the chthonic and aquatic dimension of performative rituals in the places in question. Other recurring symbols are always associated with fertility and female fecundity (G. Colonna and L. Franchi dell'Orto 'Le forme della devozione,' 91; C. Chiaramonte Treré, 'Symboli nella necropoli orientalizzante ed arcaica di Campovalano. Ornamenti rituali e propiziatori nei corredi femminili,' in *I Piceni e l'Italia medioadriatica, Atti del XXII Convegno di Studi Etruschi ed Italici. Ascoli Piceno · Teramo · Ancona, 9-13 aprile 2000* (Rome: Istituti Editoriali e Poligrafici Internazionali 2003), 473). These water cults are found in Picenum even in Roman times. The continuity and overlap in the oldest local cults is well established for some of the excavated sites, e.g. the votive hoards of Montefortino d'Arcevia and Isola di Fano, and the thermal shrines of Cupramarittima and San Vittore di Cingoli (G. Baldelli, 'I luoghi di culto,' in *Eroi e Regine. Piceni. Popolo d'Europa* (Rome: De Luca, 2001), 87; M. Landolfi and G. Baldelli, 'San Vittore di Cingoli,' in *Acque, grotte e dei, 3000 anni di culti preromani in Romagna, Marche e Abruzzo*, edited by M. Pacciarelli (Imola: Musei Civici, 1997), 180-183).

[173] G.Baldelli, 'I luoghi di culto,' 86-87. The author states that the name of the deity worshipped at those water sites is still unknown.

[174] G. Baldelli, 'Deposito votivo da Cupra Marittima, località Sant'Andrea,' in *Acque, grotte e Dei. 3000 anni di culti preromani in Romagna, Marche e Abruzzo*, 161-171.

local goddess of fertility.[175] This evidence from Picenum is consistent with the observations by Ciuccarelli and Mussini about a strong chthonic dimension of Etruscan-Italic Acheloios, often related to the cult of female goddesses of the same dimension.

Ultimately, we can suggest that the extreme popularity of the man-faced bull type on the later coinage of Campanian and Oscan mints, while undoubtedly influenced by Greek culture, also has roots in the earlier traditions of central-south Italy,[176] insofar as the Oscans had the same cultural roots as the Etruscans and Picenii, and the Greek poleis of Campania likewise had significant cultural interrelations with the Etruscans. Thus, while we cannot say there was a definitive cult of Acheloios in this area (or Sicily or Sardinia), a proto-Acheloios figure stemming from very early Near Eastern influences was present, providing the fertile soil necessary for the true cult of Acheloios to emerge and flourish.

[175] A. Naso, *Piceni. Storia e archeologia delle Marche in epoca preromana*, 239. Scholars attribute this activity to the worship of the goddess Cupra of the Umbrian-Picenum pantheon. Interestingly, the name of the goddess refers to the island of Cyprus, which resonates in the names of the sites mentioned above: Cupramarittima and Cupramontana. In fact, ancient sources mention the existence of a sanctuary dedicated to the mother goddess Cupra 'founded by Tyrrhenians who gave Hera the name of Cupra' (Strabo, *Geographica*, 5.4.2). See also: M. Landolfi, 'Montefortino di Arcevia,' in *Acque, grotte e Dei. 3000 anni di culti preromani in Romagna, Marche e Abruzzo*, 172-179. Two epigraphs testify to the worship of the goddess by the Picenii (found at the sites of Colfiorito and Fossato di Vico), which were affixed to bronze plates originally applied to containers of water and on a sacred wellhead, documenting the close ties of the cult of the goddess with water and fecundity (A. Naso, *Piceni. Storia e archeologia delle Marche in epoca preromana,* 244). An interesting aspect to the inscription of Colfiorito is the epithet '*plestinas*,' attributed to Cupra, probably due to the ethnic of a local tribe (ibid., 244), indicating a distorted form of 'Palestine,' suggestive of Levantine influences on religious culture and the art of the Piceno, presumably already noticed by ancient authors (Antonio Brandimarte and Giovanni Battista Cipriani, *Plinio seniore illustrato nella descrizione del Piceno* (Roma, 1815), 93). In 1980 M. Verzàr wrote an extensive essay on the cult of a Levantine goddess identified as Cupra at Pyrgi in Etruria, on the basis of Cypriot cultural elements in the architectural style of the sanctuary (M. Verzár, 'Pyrgi e l'Afrodite di Cipro considerazioni sul programma decorativo del tempio B.,' in *Mélanges de l'Ecole française de Rome. Antiquité*, T. 92, No.1 (1980), 35-86.). See below for the cult of Acheloios at Pyrgi. Even more interesting are the links with Sicily, in particular from Syracuse and Morgantina, where Kupara is likely the Sikel name used for female deities later assimilated with Greek water nymphs (C. M. Antonaccio, 'Kupara, a Sikel Nymph?,' in *Zeitschrift fur Papyrologie und Epigraphik*, Vol.126 (Bonn, 1999),177–185). In fact, Kupara was the Sikel name of the spring later named Arethousa by the Greeks, which, according to Agostiniani, was derived from the Italic theonym *Kupra* (L. Agostiniani, 'Epigrafia e linguistica anelleniche in Sicilia: bilancio di un quadriennio,' in *Kokalos* 30-31, Tomo I, (Roma: Bretschneider, 1987), 193-222). Antonaccio also mentions ancient literary sources recording Kupara as the local name for Arethousa, and hence a divinity in Sicily. The common ancestral origins of Italic populations and Sikels from central Italy could lend further support to this hypothesis. Many historians of religion have made the assumption that indigenous cults of natural forces, like springs, rivers, or agricultural fertility, were celebrated in pre-Greek Sicily and Magna Graecia. The arrival of the Greeks brought congruent cults of Demeter, Persephone, the Nymphs, and other figures to which native cults were easily assimilated (C. M. Antonaccio, 'Kupara, a Sikel Nymph?,' 183 with references). This suggests a local proto-cult of the nymphs in Sicily before Greek colonization. The origin of the theonym Kupara-Cupra, interestingly, is not Indo-European. On this topic, see: M. Mertens-Horn, 'Una nuova antefissa a testa femminile da Akrai ed alcune considerazioni sulle Ninfe di Sicilia,' in *Bollettino d'Arte del Ministero della Pubblica Istruzione*, Vol.76 (Milano, 1991), 9-28; E. Epifanio Vanni, 'Terravecchia di Cuti. Campagne di scavo 1984, 1986, 1987,' in *Kokalos*, 34-35 (Rome: 1993), 669-678. See the introduction to the chapter on the coinage of Sicily for documentation of Gelon of Gela, the first to employ man-faced bulls in Sicily, as a priest of the chthonic godesses, likely including Kupara.

[176] For southern Italy, further traces of the existence of an Italic bull-deity of springs and rivers is found in the area of Greek Poseidonia. According to Astone, the Sybaritic settlers would have dedicated the city to the Greek god, influenced by previous Etruscan cults existing in the area which were related to 'a god of fresh waters, springs and rivers, characterized by bull attributes' (F. Astone, 'Poseidon e Poseidonia: le acque, il paesaggio, gli insediamenti, il culto, il nome della città,' in *Annali Storici di Principato Citra XI,* 1 (2013), 34-61). Still in Lucania, an amber pendant (BM no.1856,1226.1442) from Armento, attributed by Isler to an unidentified artisan in Magna Graecia, and dated by him to 500 BC, demonstrates the presence of man-faced bull imagery among the Italic peoples of Armento, more isolated inland, halfway between Campania and Bruttium, where Greek cults are known to have merged with local cults at the end of the 4th century BC (A. Russo Tagliente, 'Il santuario Lucano di Armento-Serra Lustrante,' in *I Greci in Occidente. Greci Enotri e Lucani nella Basilicata meridionale* (Napoli, 1996), 190-93). Thus, we propose, on the basis of stylistic comparisons with other examples of amber pendants, to attribute the pendant to an Etruscan artisan rather than a Greek one, and to an earlier date. For comparisons in style see the Etruscan lion-shaped amber pendant found in a tomb dated to the 6th century BC, recently featured in an exhibition (M.L. Nava and A. Salerno (eds.), *Ambre.Trasparenze dall'antico. Catalogo della mostra, Napoli, Museo Archeologico Nazionale* (Milano: Mondadori-Electa: 2007), 43). From Garaguso in Lucania, there is evidence of a pre-Greek cult of water, with water works inside a place of worship in which bull skulls were found, likely traces of cultic rites of reparation (C. Masseria, 'Garaguso. Santuari e culti di un centro Enotrio,' in *Il mondo Enotrio tra VI e V sec. a.C.*, Quaderni di Ostraka I, 1, edited by M. Bugno and C. Masseria (Napoli, 2001), 83-107). We also know that Acheloios had a cult near Metapontion and games were held in his honor, and moreover the evidence suggests water works began in the area when it was minted (discussed below). In many other centers in Magna Graecia and Sicily, and also in Republican Rome, evidence indicates the image of the man-faced bull was linked to water works in the area. Thus, the evidence from Garaguso is a good example of a cultic fertile ground in which the Greek myth of Acheloios is rooted.

Chapter IV: The Etruscan and Greek Worlds

Etruscan Man-Faced Bulls

Introduction

Finally, we have reached more familiar soil. Starting in the 6th century BC the image of the man-faced bull becomes very popular in peninsular Italy, particularly in Etruria. The use of the iconography in the Etruscan world is diverse, and the figure is exhibited on many works of art: armor fittings,[1] votive 'shields',[2] engraved gems,[3] mirrors,[4] bronze statuettes,[5] situla fittings,[6] ornamental stamnos handles,[7] skyphoi,[8] painted pottery,[9] plastic vases,[10] a tomb fresco,[11] incense holders,[12] sarcophagi,[13] cinerary urns,[14] memorial stones,[15] antefixes,[16] gold charms[17] and other jewelry,[18] and even a chandelier.[19] Despite the near complete absence of Etruscan literature to guide the investigator,[20] some familiar themes are immediately apparent, like water, death, rebirth, fertility, and the repulsion of evil. There are very clear Near Eastern influences as well, indicating that both the form and elements of the content are foreign in derivation and only further articulated in the Etruscan and Greek worlds.[21] Moreover, Etruscan man-faced bulls are not mere 'degraded forms'[22] copying Greek models, but have distinct associations that the Greek tradition later merged with, each contributing their own traditions that formed the later tradition of the man-faced bull in Classical times. Thus, as we will demonstrate, the iconography of the man-faced bull and mythology of Acheloios initially arrived in the Etruscan world without a Greek filter.

As we saw in the previous section with the Villanovian bowl from Falerii,[23] the Italic evidence of man-faced bull iconography is earlier than in Greece proper,[24] especially in plastic arts. In fact, the earliest example of a plastic representation of the man-faced bull found in Attica is not even Greek, but Etruscan: a bronze fitting found during excavations at the Akropolis in Athens, from a tripod showing Hercle (Herakles), Menerva (Athena), Turms (Hermes) and a female figure playing the aulos (Uni or Kupra?) at the head of the procession, the whole group standing on a pedestal adorned with heads of man-faced bulls at the corners.[25] The piece is dated 500 to 490 BC. It is likely that Attic artists, who at the end of the 5th century[26] started creating votive reliefs with

1 H.P. Isler, *Acheloos*, no. 205-228.

2 Ibid., no. 183-197.

3 Ibid., no. 293-294, no. 301-305.

4 Ibid., no. 273-278.

5 Ibid., no. 198-204.

6 Ibid., no. 205-228.

7 Ibid., no. 248-263.

8 H.P. Isler, 'Acheloos,' in *LIMC*, no. 116.

9 H.P. Isler, *Acheloos*, no. 59, no. 64-66, no. 92.

10 Ibid., no. 93-95, no. 116, no. 121-122.

11 Ibid., no. 311.

12 Ibid., no. 233.

13 Ibid., no. 45-48. L. A. Constans, 'Récentes découvertes archéologiques en Italie. Deuxième et dernier article,' in *Journal des savants*, 19e année (1921), 215.

14 H.P. Isler, *Acheloos*, no. 40-44.

15 J.R. Jannot, *Les reliefs archaïques de Chiusi* (Rome: École Française de Rome, 1984), fig.598, no. H.II.1 and fig.219, no. C.I.40.

16 H.P. Isler, *Acheloos*, no.150-157.

17 H.P. Isler, 'Acheloos,' in *LIMC*, no. 136.

18 Ibid., no. 160; H.P. Isler, *Acheloos*, no. 283-290.

19 H.P. Isler, *Acheloos*, no. 239; A. De Ridder, *Catalogue des bronzes trouvés sur l'Acropole d'Athènes* (Cambridge: Harvard University, 1896), No.760, Pl.V, fig.269.

20 There are some epigraphic sources dealt with in the chapter on the identity of the man-faced bull.

21 Isler (*Acheloos*, 92) and Jenkins (*The Coinage of Gela*, 165, note 3), while recognizing the undeniable derivation of the representation of Acheloios from Mesopotamian glyptic models, have both stressed the difficulty in establishing precise similarities between the Greek and Near Eastern figures, stating that the Mesopotamian versions are not involved in the worship of water. In fact, Isler states that the form and content of the Greek myth of Acheloios have completely separate origins, the first coming from the Near East, the latter being purely Greek (H.P. Isler, *Acheloos*, 92). However, the evidence given in this book demonstrates that some part of the content definitely arrived in the West embedded in the form and other related traditions of bull and bull-man water cults.

22 J. R. Jannot 'Achéloos, le taureau androcéphale et les masques cornus dans l'Etrurie archaique' in *Latomus* 33, 4 (Bruxelles: 1974), 117-8.

23 Also from Falerii comes a famous archaic gem (Fig.51) attributed to an Ionian workshop, dated to the early 6th century BC (H.P. Isler, *Acheloos*, no.291), which is the first known representation of the fight of Herakles and Acheloios in the entire Greek world. A later interesting example of an offering bowl from Etruscan Falerii (H.P. Isler, *Acheloos*, no.93), testifies to the permanence of the imagery of the man-faced bull in the cultic plastic pottery of the area. The piece is made locally, and described by Isler as 'Three connected vessels on a single foot. On supporting handles three Acheloios protomes between rams' heads. Between the vessels are seated figures' (H.P. Isler, *Acheloos*, 140).

24 The earliest Attic example of a man-faced bull is seen on Black Figure Pottery dated to the mid 6th century BC, which depicts Acheloios as a man-faced bull in his struggle with Herakles for the hand of Deianeira (cf. H.P. Isler, *Acheloos*, no.68, dated 560 to 550 BC), just as it continued to be exclusively represented in the Attic vase paintings of the 5th and 4th centuries (H.P. Isler, *Acheloos* , no. 69-89). In the Tyrrhenian area, the man-faced bull is much less often characterized by this mythological episode, albeit sometimes represented together with Hercle in Etruscan art. The Etruscan man-faced bull, instead, is more often represented as an isolated subject. According to many authors (Jannot first, and later Mussini and Ciuccarelli), the man-faced bull in Etruria mainly embodied the apotropaic, chthonic-funerary, and fertility associations when represented as an isolated protome or mask. However, Jannot is incorrect in his understanding that the Etruscan man-faced bull is a 'degraded form' of representation derived from the Greek tradition, the contents of which were misunderstood by Etruscan artists (J. R. Jannot 'Achéloos, le taureau androcéphale et les masques cornus dans l'Etrurie archaique,' 117-8). Oleson, alternatively, supported a much less Hellenocentric point of view when discussing the Tomb of the Bulls at Tarquinia: 'It is, however, now clear that the iconography of the tomb's frescoes is not the result of promiscuous, unintelligent copying of Greek vase-painting' (J.P. Oleson, 'Greek Myth and Etruscan Imagery in the Tomb of the Bulls at Tarquinia,' in *American Journal of Archaeology*, Vol. 79, No. 3 (1975), 200). Tom Rasmussen adds similar observations: 'Etruscan religion is not Greek religion or Roman religion in modified form, and can and should be explained on its own terms and without all the Greek and Roman terminology that is often used. Moreover, although the Etruscans were very interested in Greek mythology, there does exist a real Etruscan mythology which can, but only with much patient observation, be extricated from it. Future progress is also very likely to be moulded by new discoveries' (T. Rasmussen, 'Etruscan ritual and religion,' in *The Oxford Handbook of the Archaeology of Ritual and Religion*, edited by T. Insoll (Oxford: University Press, 2011), 718).

25 A. D. Ridder, *Catalogue des bronzes trouvés sur l'Acropole d'Athènes*, No.760, Pl.V, fig.269.

26 In Greek sculpture the man-faced bull appears isolated only later, with the Attic reliefs listed by H.P. Isler, *Acheloos*, no. 1-39.

processions of gods and Acheloios' head at the borders, were influenced by this Etruscan piece, supposedly displayed somewhere in the Akropolis at least 60 years before the Greek renditions begin to appear. Moreover, from existing archaeological evidence it appears that during the 6th and 5th centuries the man-faced bull had been mostly depicted in multiples (on single pieces) in Etruria, while in Greece proper he is represented almost exclusively as a singular figure on didactic vase paintings of the myth of his battle with Herakles. The Greeks would not adopt a more multifaceted and complex function related to chthonic cults and rites of passage until the end of the 5th century, indicating a further merging of the Etruscan tradition with that of the Greeks.

Evidence from Pyrgi

The man-faced bulls of Pyrgi are ideal for summarizing the key components of the overall Etruscan conceptual scheme. Giovanni Colonna[27] wrote about four acroteria shaped as rampant man-faced bulls (**Fig.52**)[28] from the shrine of Beta at Pyrgi, which is the oldest component of the sanctuary, dating back to the third quarter of the 6th century BC. The acroteria were placed at the four corners of the roof of the sanctuary, in prominent positions and indicating an apotropaic function, which is the predominant dimension of man-faced bull iconography in the Etruscan world. The temple of Pyrgi also had several antefixes shaped as man-faced bull heads,[29] alternating with other antefixes shaped as nymph heads and allegedly signifying the securing of the plain against the danger of flooding, obtained with the construction of a channel near the sanctuary. Such figures also celebrated the benefits of fresh water, gushing from a copious nearby spring that is still active today.[30] Colonna suggests that the precise meaning of the use of 'Acheloios' iconography is to indicate oracular activities at the site, in association with the possible location of the oracle of Tethis.[31] This understanding is founded upon the direct association with the nearby nymphs.[32]

As demonstrated by the many votive inscriptions found at the site, the sanctuary of Pyrgi was consecrated to two major Italic deities, Śuri and Cavatha.[33] Śuri was usually assimilated by the Greeks with Hades, but in this setting, probably Apollo, while Cavatha was assimilated with Persephone.[34] Archaeological evidence from Pyrgi testifies to the use of astragaloi in divinatory practices as a highly distinctive form of worship officiated at the sanctuary.[35] This oracular dimension was probably the reason why the Greeks visiting the Etruscan sanctuary interpreted it as a shrine to Apollo, and perhaps the Greek assimilation was based on the similarity of the name Śuri with 'Sourios,' the epithet of Apollo worshipped at the oriental Greek temple at Sura in Lycia.[36] In addition, there are various solar connotations of the Etruscan god that suggest a likely Greek assimilation with Apollo.[37] This assimilation is highly significant in terms of the interplay of cultural contacts between the Etruscan and Greek worlds, even more so when we consider the very frequent association of Apollo and the man-faced bull on later Campanian coinage.

Also at Pyrgi, there are many references to the journey of water as an allusion to the eschatological beliefs of the chthonic cults of the sanctuary, demonstrated by Claudia Antonetti et al. during their studies of the sacred

[27] G. Colonna, 'Il pantheon degli Etruschi 'i più religiosi degli uomini' alla luce delle scoperte di Pyrgi,' in *Mem. Acc. Linc.*, IX, XXIX, 3 (2012), 557-595. For the identification of the Etruscan man-faced bull as a river deity, based on the the location of a sanctuarial waterway near the iconography, see: G. Colonna,'Note preliminari sui culti del santuario di Portonaccio a Veio,' in *Scienze dell'Antichità. Storia Archeologia Antropologia*, 1 (1987), 437-441; Giuseppe Sassatelli, 'Spina nelle immagini etrusche: Eracle, Dedalo e il problema dell'acqua,' in *Spina. Storia di una Città tra Greci ed Etruschi* (Ferrara, 1993), 127.

[28] B. Belelli Marchesini, 'Le linee di sviluppo topografico del Santuario Meridionale,' in *Riflessioni su Pyrgi. Scavi E Ricerche Nelle Aree Del Santuario* (Rome: Bretschneider, 2013), 17, fig.2.

[29] G. Colonna, 'Note preliminari sui culti del santuario del Portonaccio a Veio,' 437-441.

[30] G. Colonna, 'Il santuario di Pyrgi dalle origini mitistoriche agli altorilievi frontonali dei Sette e di Leucotea,' in *Scienze dell'Antichità*, Vol.10 (2002), 251-336. For the sacred spring see ibid., 260.

[31] Ibid., 266-275. The argument for an oracular dimension of the sanctuary in relation to the man-faced bull acroteria is also mentioned in B. Belelli Marchesini, 'Le linee di sviluppo topografico del Santuario Meridionale,' 16-17.

[32] Ibid. A cult of Kupra has also been proposed by scholars for the area of the sanctuary of Pyrgi (M. Verzár, 'Pyrgi e l'Afrodite di Cipro considerazioni sul programma decorativo del tempio B,' 35-86).

[33] G. Colonna, 'Il pantheon degli Etruschi 'i più religiosi degli uomini' alla luce delle scoperte di Pyrgi,' 12.

[34] Ibid., 13. On the connection of the Etruscan man-faced bulls with cults of a female chthonic goddess in Etruria and Magna Graecia, see M. R. Ciuccarelli, 'Acheloo ctonio dalla Magna Grecia all'Etruria?,' 121-40.

[35] G. Colonna, 'Altari e sacelli. L'area sud di Pyrgi dopo otto anni di ricerche,' in *Rend. Pont. Acc.*, Vol.LXIV (Rome, 1994), 101, fig.41. For the use of astragaloi in connection with the man-faced bull traditions at Lokris in Magna Graecia, see below, pg. 66ff.

[36] G. Colonna, 'Il pantheon degli Etruschi 'i più religiosi degli uomini' alla luce delle scoperte di Pyrgi,' 12.

[37] The association of solar and chthonic qualities in the same deity is not uncommon in Etruscan religion, as seen above in the description of Inuo (allegedly depicted at Satricum). For an Italo-Corinthian plastic vase from Satricum, see H.P. Isler, *Acheloos*, no.122, dated 560 to 540 BC. For an additional specimen from Veii, found at the sanctuary of Portonaccio, see: G. Colonna, in *Archeologia Classica* vol.13 (1961) 25, cited in H.P. Isler, *Acheloos*, 144. For the solar and chthonic dimensions of the cult of Suri in central Italy, see: E. Marroni, 'Considerazioni sul santuario di Circei,' in *Sacra Nominis Latini. I santuari del Lazio arcaico e repubblicano* (Naples: Loffredo, 2012), 623; D. Maras, 'Suri il nero signore degli inferi,' in *Archeo* (2010), 108-115, no. 305; S. Fortunelli, *Gravisca. Scavi nel santuario greco* (Bari, 2007), 324-334. For the associations between chthonic and solar connotations of Etruscan deities it is worthwhile to cite Oleson: 'The connection of the setting sun with human death is a natural one, but in the context of the Etruscan religion, with its large component of celestial interpretation and its emphasis on the underworld, the image must have had extraordinary power. [...] As the sun sets, a man dies: this is the principle of universal cosmic sympathy on which the Etruscan science of hepatoscopy was founded' (J.P. Oleson 'Greek Myth and Etruscan Imagery in the Tomb of the Bulls at Tarquinia,' 196-7).

places of Etruria.[38] Ultimately, for the Etruscans, death is a journey into the afterlife waters, as seen in Sardinia and still further back in the Mesopotamian cult of Apsu. It is thus probably not a coincidence that the same eschatological symbolism is exhibited in the earliest known example of a depiction of sacred waters on an Etruscan tomb painting, which also includes an eastern-style man-faced bull, on the tympanum of the entrance door of the Tomb of the Bulls at Tarquinia. Here we see a representation of the journey of the soul into water, which is depicted as a pale blue veil in the bottom half of the fresco.[39] The existence of bothroi made to contain liquid offerings for the chthonic deities worshipped at the sanctuary[40] is also reminescent of the cupules seen in the prehistoric Sardinian Domus de Janas, discussed above. There is also probably a cultural link between the sacred wells of Sardinia and the sacred wells in Etruscan sites where the later cult of the man-faced bull is attested. For instance, at the sacred wells of the sanctuaries of Pyrgi[41] and Cerveteri,[42] where connections to prehistoric water cults have been suggested,[43] dozens of representations of Etruscan man-faced bulls have been found.

Other Important Evidence

Additional funerary associations of the man-faced bull are indicated in the Tomb of the Bulls at Tarquinia,[44] usually dated c. 540 BC (**Fig. 53**).[45] Here the man-faced bull appears as part of a larger fresco incorporating scenes from the Eastern Greek tradition,[46] likely by mediation of Cyprus.[47] The use of the iconography

[38] C. Antonetti, S. De Vido, and L.D. Troccoli, 'Lithoi, Semata, Anathemata. Connotare lo lpazio Sacro: contesti esemplari tra Grecia ed Etruria,' in *Epigrammata 2. Definire, descrivere, proteggere lo spazio sacro. Atti convegno Roma Ottobre 2012* (Rome, 2013), 29.

[39] C. Pizzirani, 'Il mare nell'immaginario funebre degli Etruschi,' in *Il viaggio oltre la vita. Gli etruschi e l'aldilà tra capolavori e realtà virtuale*, edited by G. Sassatelli and A. Russo Tagliente (Bologna:Bononia University Press, 2014), 76, fig.70.

[40] L. Ambrosini and L. Michetti, 'L'ultima frequentazione del santuario meridionale: Testimonianze dai contesti,' in *Riflessioni su Pyrgi. Scavi E Ricerche Nelle Aree Del Santuario* (Rome: Bretschneider, 2013),133. Of great interest is the comparison made by scholars for a particular ritual involving the burial of vases placed upside down. We already mentioned above other western contexts with identical practices at two cultic sites of Campania (Pontecagnano and St. Nicholas of Albanella), and two in Sicily (at Licata and Gela). In particular, the authors state that at Gela 'the phenomenon takes on striking proportions' (ibid., and note 147 for bibliography). These connections are also interesting if we consider that Gelas was the first Sicilian mint to issue coins with the iconography of the man-faced bull. For water-cults at Pontecagnano, see: G. Bailo Modesti, A. Frezza, A. Lupia, and M. Mancusi, 'Le acque intorno agli dei: rituali e offerte votive nel santuario settentrionale di Pontecagnano,' in *Offerte dal regno vegetale e dal regno animale nelle manifestazioni del sacro, Atti Incontro di Studio, Tarchna*, Suppl. 1, edited by M. Bonghi Jovino and F. Chiesa (Rome, 2005), 37-64.

[41] G. Colonna, 'I due pozzi antistanti il tempio A; La struttura e i dati stratigrafici,' in *Notizie degli Scavi di antichità*, Serie 8, Vol. XLII-XLIII, Suppl. II (Roma: Accademia Nazionale dei Lincei,1992) 11-20. For Neolithic ritual practices see G. Colonna, 'Il giacimento preistorico della zona del Templio A,' in *Notizie Scavi*, XXIV, Supplemento II (Rome, 1970), 267-274.

[42] A. Maggiani, 'Culti delle acque e culti in grotta in Etruria,' in *Ocnus*, 7 (1999), 188, 188.

[43] M. A. Fugazzola Delfino, 'Le acque interne: appunti di archeologia preistorica,' in *Etruria Meridionale. Conoscenza, conservazione, fruizione. Atti del Convegno Viterbo* (Rome: Quasar, 1988), 19.

[44] For the worship of a deity having different forms, sometimes human, sometimes animal,in Villanovian Tarquinia, see: C. Iaia, 'Gli oggetti di uso cerimoniale,' in *Tarquinia Etrusca. Una nuova storia. Catalogo della Mostra*, edited by A.M. Moretti Sgubini (Rome, 2001), 92-93; F. Trucco, D. De Angelis, and C. Iaia, 'Villa Bruschi Falgari: il sepolcreto villanoviano,' in *Tarquinia Etrusca*, 81-93.

[45] S. Rafanelli, 'Miti e divinita` del mare, creature simbolo e fantastiche del mare,' in *Il mare degli Etruschi*, Atti del Convegno, Piombino – Orbetello, 18-20 Settembre 2009 (Firenze: 2010), 43.

[46] The lower part of the fresco allegedly depicts Achilles and Troilus. As observed by Oleson, the depiction of the scene includes not only Greek traditions but also local religious beliefs. In fact, it is clear that the representation of the incident in the fresco closely corresponds to its treatment in the *Kypria*, and it is suggested that the artist received his inspiration directly from the literary sources rather than from imported Greek vase-paintings (J. P. Oleson, 'Greek Myth and Etruscan Imagery in the Tomb of the Bulls at Tarquinia,' in *AJA*, Vol. 79, No. 3 (1975), 191-194). As Oleson puts it: 'The motif of the setting sun in the Tomb of the Bulls can thus be interpreted as the literal reproduction of the context of the story in the *Kypria*. Since this detail cannot be found in any of the numerous surviving representations of the death of Troilos in earlier, contemporary, or subsequent Greek or Etruscan vase-painting or bronze relief work, there is no reason to infer that the tomb fresco is part of the visual rather than the literary tradition surrounding the incident' (ibid., 194). The title of the poem, *Kypria*, clearly indicates an origin in Cypriot culture. Moreover, Burkert noted that the *Kypria* has clear correspondences with Mesopotamian culture, and he concludes that the influences 'must then refer to the time when Cyprus, although rich and powerful, was still formally submitted to Assyrian domination' (W. Burkert, *The Orientalizing Revolution*, 103). For many examples of depictions on Etruscan pottery demonstrating a local elaboration of foreign visual themes directly inspired by the text of *Kypria*, rather than a mere imitative iconographic derivation from Greek vase paintings, see the bibliography in J.P. Oleson, 'Greek Myth and Etruscan Imagery in the Tomb of the Bulls at Tarquinia,' 199, especially note 84.

[47] For the connections between the funerary architecture of Tarquinia and Levantine examples, see A. Zifferero, 'Forme di possesso della terra e tumuli orientalizzanti nell'Italia centrale tirrenica,' in *The Archaeology of Power, Papers of the Fourth Conference of Italian Archaeology. London, January 1990*, Vol. 1, 1 (London, 1991), 107-134. Already in Villanovian times, at the coastal area between Civitavecchia and Tarquinia, there were six settlements, demonstrating a capillary control of the coast that certainly could not have been unaffected by early Mediterranean trade routes and related influences (L.G. Perego, *Il territorio tarquiniese. Ricerche di topografia storica* (Milan, 2005), 209-210). In fact, the presence of archaeological evidence of Near Eastern artifacts in Tarquinia indicates it was one of the main ports of trade on the Levantine and Phoenician traders' routes throughout the Orientalizing Period (L.G.Perego, 'Rileggendo vecchi dati. Spunti sull'Orientalizzante Tarquiniese,' in *Aristonothos*, 3 (2008), 186). Moreover, a clear Cypriot derivation for the archaic tombs of Tarquinia has been suggested by archaeologists in a preliminary report of the discovery of the Tomb of the Queen, the most ancient Etruscan painted tomb discovered in Italy (R. Masci, 'Tarquinia, scoperta la più antica tomba dipinta dagli etruschi,' in *La Stampa. Arte* (August, 2010). For discussion and extensive bibliography concerning the Cypriot influences on the tombs of Tarquinia, see: A. Mandolesi and D. De Angelis, 'Il Tumulo della Regina di Tarquinia fra tradizioni levantine e innovazioni etrusche,' in *Archeologia Classica*, Vol. LXII, 1 (Rome: Bretschneider, 2011), 7-39; D. Cianfaloni, 'Nota sulle tipologie architettoniche e murarie tarquiniesi. Ulteriori corrispondenze con il Vicino Oriente antico,' in *Tarquinia e le civiltà del Mediterraneo*, Vol.77, edited by M. Bonghi Jovino (Milan, 2006), 145-161; M. Bonghi Jovino and G. Bagnasco, *Tarquinia. Testimonianze archeologiche e ricostruzione storica. Scavi sistematici nell'abitato. Campagne 1982-1988* (Rome: Bretschneider, 2001), 346. For the funerary traditions of Tarquinia, which since the Archaic Age merged with architectural categories and votive practices from the Near East, particularly from Syria and Palestine, which in turn were influenced by earlier Mesopotamian examples, see: M. Bonghi Jovino, 'Tantum ratio sacrorum gerebatur. l'edificio beta di Tarquinia in epoca orientalizzante e alto arcaica. Ancora in merito alle tecniche

in a subterranean tomb indicates he was a god closely affiliated with death,[48] symbolic of rebirth or chthonic transformation. The central scene of the fresco, depicting Achilles ambushing Troilus, suggests a military role of the deceased.[49] In the iconographic scheme of the tomb we also see both solar[50] and water symbols.[51]

The presence of erotic scenes on the same level as the man-faced bull is difficult to interpret,[52] beyond the traditional generic reference to the sphere of human fecundity.[53] However, analyzing the fresco we can see that both scenes are placed above the two doors, probably to emphasize their liminal significance. To left we see the heterosexual and homosexual 'normal' habits of Etruscan people, accompanied by a regular, calm bull.[54] To the right, it is probably not a mere homosexual act, especially since homosexuality is already present in the left scene. On the contrary, we likely see the subversion of the reality of the living which is based on binary logic, such as male/female. Instead, we see the liminal ithyphallic man-faced bull, a hybrid creature, accompanied by the passive figure in the same scene who is also a hybrid, liminal creature, half-male and half-female. This hybrid nature is indicated in the pink color of the skin, which suggests a combination of the male (brown) and female (white) skin colors of the other characters of the fresco. Thus, the figure probably represents the 'third sex' that ancients believed existed in a divine dimension,[55] with Silen-like features of the head. Ultimately, the fresco appears to exhibit a structural dualism between the earthly left and the otherworldly right, paired with a regular quiet reclining bull and an aggressive ithyphallic man-faced bull, respectively. This 'third sex' interpretation is an appealing choice to be paired with what is presumably Acheloios as a man-faced bull, who is depicted in woman's clothing in the statue from Greece. Thus, the man-faced bull also appears to be a liminal figure in relation to the sexes, which is further confirmed in the Greek rites of passage for boys and girls discussed below.

The *Lampadario di Cortona* (**Fig. 54**)[56] is perhaps the greatest indication of an important liminal association with the man-faced bull in the Etruscan world. The massive bronze artifact was found at Fratta, near Cortona, in 1840. It was probably originally made for a funerary setting in the Late Archaic Era.[57] There are multiple man-faced bulls depicted on the lamp,[58] which is of the finest style. As mentioned in the section on Cyprus, such a device was used to literally and symbolically illuminate the tomb, believed to be the house of the dead. Thus the man-faced bull plays a liminal role (mediating between light and dark and life and death) in this subterranean realm of the Etruscan world. The notion of illumination also sheds light on the issue of identity, as Aukhlwς is believed to mean 'overseer of sunrise' in the Etruscan tradition, discussed in the chapter on identity.

The *Lampadario di Cortona* also has cosmic and oracular associations. In fact, the quantity of man-faced bulls and sirens depicted, each numbering sixteen, is the same number by which Etruscan seers divided the sky for their oracular practices.[59] In fact, we see the same division on the famous Etruscan bronze liver found at Piacenza, used as a divinatory device, where on the edge sixteen parts

edilizie, agli aspetti architettonici, sacri e culturali con comparanda mediterranei,' in *Koina. Miscellanea di studi archeologici in onore di Piero Orlandini*, edited by M. Castoldi (Milan: E.T., 1999), 87-103). For similar examples from Cyprus and Sardinia, see ibid., 95. For funerary and temple architecture at Tarquinia where altar-canalizations are reminiscent of previous examples from Bronze Age Sardinia and the Italian Peninsula, see: ibid., 99.

48 For the symbology of the fresco depicted in the tomb in connection with protection against the Evil Eye and the voyage of the dead to the Underworld, see: R. Ross Holloway, 'The Bulls in the 'Tomb of the Bulls' at Tarquinia,' in *AJA*, Vol. 90, No. 4 (1986), 447-452.

49 An even stronger warlike connotation of the man-faced bull for Etruria is exhibited in the so-called 'Tomb of the Warrior,' a rich grave found at the Osteria Necropolis of Vulci, dated to the last quarter of 6th century BC. The tomb takes its name because of the bronze panoply of the dead commander buried in it. Two man-faced bull protomes mark the center, front, and back of the commander's helm. Interestingly, in the same tomb a bronze plaque describes the same scene seen in Tarquinia with Achilles and Troilus at the fountain (S. Haynes, *Etruscan Civilization: A Cultural History* (Los Angeles: Getty Publications, 2000), 162).

50 J.P. Oleson, 'Greek Myth and Etruscan Imagery in the Tomb of the Bulls at Tarquinia,' 189.

51 C. Pizzirani, 'Il mare nell'immaginario funebre degli Etruschi,' 76, fig.70.

52 R. Ross Holloway, 'The Bulls in the 'Tomb of the Bulls' at Tarquinia,' 447; J.P. Oleson, 'Greek Myth and Etruscan Imagery in the Tomb of the Bulls at Tarquinia,' 197; A. Giuliano, 'Osservazioni sulle pitture della 'Tomba dei tori' a Tarquinia,' in *Studi Etruschi*, Vol.37 (Roma: Olschki, 1969), 11. Giuliano also noted that the erotic groups were derived from similar depictions on Pontic vases locally made in Etruria (ibid., 22).

53 For an example of a sexual scene related to fertility and celestial motifs, see the Cypriot cylinder seal dated to the Late Cypriot IIC Period, displayed at the British Museum (item no. 1899, 1229.39). Erotic scenes similar to those exhibited in the Tomb of the Bulls are also depicted on the enigmatic stele discussed above from Novillara in Picenum.

54 'The heterosexual label for the group on the left, however, may not be completely correct, because the artist's preliminary sketch strongly suggests that he intended the male supporting the woman to be engaged in fellatio with another male reclining on the ground in front of him' (A. Giuliano, 'Osservazioni sulle pitture della 'Tomba dei tori' a Tarquinia,' 11). However, Giuliano denies that the bulls are somehow connected with the erotic groups, assuming instead that all are unconnected parts of a purely decorative ornament (ibid).

55 Plato, *Symposium*, 189c-193e.

56 Displayed at the Museo dell'Accademia Etrusca in Cortona.

57 The piece was later re-used, as attested by an inscribed bronze plaque with a votive inscription (Etruscan: *(t)inscvil* = Belonging to Tinia, or more generically 'sacred, divine'), added in the Hellenistic era (S. Haynes, *Etruscan Civilization: A Cultural History*, 303).

58 The man-faced bull heads alternate with winged female creatures, possibly sirens, figures closely associated with the chthonic dimension of the man-faced bull. Moreover, the evidence of the use of multiple representations in Etruria confirms the prevailing apotropaic value of the man-faced bull, as seen in Near Eastern examples.

59 Cicero, *De Divinatione*, 2.42.

of the oracular sky[60] are engraved.[61] This all indicates the apparently ambivalent nature of the Etruscan man-faced bull, which encompasses both chthonic-subterranean and solar-celestial dimensions, here combined in one artifact.

Etruscan round 'shields,'[62] some examples being upwards of 70 cm in diameter, further emphasize the aforementioned connection to the underworld. They are found in graves[63] and feature the head of the man-faced bull at the center (**Fig. 55**).[64] According to Jannot, they were used as apotropaic devices hanging from the walls of tombs.[65] Jannot suggests they should be named '*disques*,' and not 'shields,' as they had no military use.[66] Some scholars even described these objects as 'basins,'[67] suggesting a ritual use in funerary rites involving water. However, the association with the military realm cannot be entirely ignored, especially in light of the role of mercenaries in the transference of the iconography.

Frequent multiple representations on antefixes, necklaces, and the aforementioned chandelier, all indicate the predominant apotropaic value of the man-faced bull. In fact, the vast majority of known representations for Acheloios represent him simply as a mask or isolated head, fitting indeed since Pausanias reports that chthonic deities were often represented with masks.[68] Mussini[69] calculated that for all the known images of Acheloios, 41.84% were masks or heads, 23.85% depict the fight with Herakles, 19.5% are reliefs with nymphs or other deities, 13.39% show him alone, either protome or full body, and only 1.67% show a bull-headed man. This data is striking when we consider only the Etruscan area, where 52.44% are masks,[70] or Magna Graecia, where 58.7% are masks,[71] compared with mainland Greece, where only 13.3% are masks. This evidence supports the predominant chthonic and apotropaic connotation of man-faced bull iconography in the areas west of Greece proper, indicating direct contact with the East for the Etruscans in their early, predominately independent adoption of man-faced bull iconography. The 'guardian of the gate' function demonstrated in these pieces is strongly reminiscent of the representations of man-faced bulls and winged human-headed bulls from the ancient Near East. In fact, the presence of the man-faced bull on many examples of cinerary urns and sarcophagi in Etruria[72] indicates both an apotropaic dimension, as guardian of the tomb or ashes, and a psychopomp function, as carrier of the soul to the afterlife, likely adopted from the Sardinian tradition.[73]

Further evidence confirming these associations are memorial stone reliefs found in Chiusi, dated to the mid 6th century BC (**Fig. 56 & Fig. 57**).[74] The stone in

[60] In a Late Babylonian text from Uruk, reported by Koch Westenholz, a section of the liver is associated with Shamash, the sun god, the month Ayaru (April-May) and the constellation Taurus (U. K. Westenholz, *Babylonian Liver Omens, the Chapters Manzāzu, Padānu and Pān tākalti of the Babylonian Extispicy Series Mainly from Aššurbanipal's Library*, C.N.I. Publications No. 25 (Copenhagen: University Press, 2000), 24).The tutelary deity of oracular disciplines for the Near East is often identified as Tarhu, while other regions use Taru, Tarhui, Tarhun or Tarhunt, and he was often depicted as a bull. In Anatolia this deity was also responsible for fertility, oaths, the conclusion of treaties, and compliance with the law. It is likely that the Etruscan city Tarchuna (Tarquinia) derives its name from this god. Likewise, its eponymous founder Tarchun, in the Etruscan legend reported by Roman texts, emigrated from Anatolia to Central Italy. His name is linked to Tarchies (*Tagete*), the divine child that emerged from the soil of Tarquinia and dictated the precepts of haruspicy at Tarchun (A. Palmucci, *Aruspicina Etrusca ed Orientale a confronto. Tarquinia e i libri Tagetici, con traduzione dei frammenti greci e latini, Collana di Etruscologia*, Vol.1 (Rome, 2010), 14-15 and bibliography). Finally, in terms of the Etruscan oracular practice based on thunder and lightning (brontoscopy): a late Roman source, Giovanni Lido, in *Traduzione letterale del Trattato di Broncoscopia del romano Fonteio*, reported texts clearly showing connections between the oracular dimension, celestial representations of the bull, rivers, fecundity, prosperity, and fertility, as stated in Etruscan divinatory texts: 'With the Moon in Taurus, thunders at day announces heavy rains, hail and diversion of rivers. [...] If thunders at night, women will abort children, and fresh water will be missing. Also serious upheavals of armies will occurr, and an unhappy tyrant will molest the East without obtaining his intentions'... 'With the Sun in Taurus. If it happens that there is an earthquake in Asia, both the Ethiopians and those at the shores of Asia Minor, and at the Cyclades islands and in Cyprus will occur ruin due to infection. So especially the cattle of these regions will die; There will be heavy heat and pestilences, huge floods of rivers, and absence of river waters in summer' (A. Palmucci, *Aruspicina Etrusca ed Orientale a confronto. Tarquinia e i libri Tagetici, con traduzione dei frammenti greci e latini, Collana di Etruscologia*, 174-177). Altogether, this provides additional indications of the role of seer-healers in the transmission of man-faced bull iconography, insofar as the same elements listed here are associated with the man-faced bull in later times.

[61] A. Palmucci, *Aruspicina Etrusca ed Orientale a confronto. Tarquinia e i libri Tagetici, con traduzione dei frammenti greci e latini, Collana di Etruscologia*, 101, fig.28. For the Mesopotamian origins of the divinatory practices and influences on the Etruscan tradition, see: ibid., 15-39. For Near Eastern models of livers compared with the Etruscan example, see: ibid., 22, fig.4 (Babylonian); ibid., 30-31, fig.6, British Museum, item no. 50494 (Babylonian); ibid., 35, fig.8, Berlin Museum v.a.t. 8320 (Hittite); ibid., 48, fig.9 (Hittite); ibid., 53, fig.11 (Syrian).

[62] Such pieces date from the 6th century BC, and might be related to Etruscan mercenaries and their incorporation of the image based on the previously provided rationale.

[63] Jannot listed fifteen specimens, mainly from Tarquinia (J.R. Jannot, 'Acheloos, le taureau androcéphale et les masques cornus dans l'Etrurie archaique,' 780-782).

[64] Dallas Museum of Art, Object No. 135.2012.5-6.

[65] J.R. Jannot, 'Acheloos, le taureau androcéphale et les masques cornus dans l'Etrurie archaique,' 780-782; O. Brendel, *Etruscan Art* (New Haven: Yale University Press, 1995), 214.

[66] J.R. Jannot, 'Acheloos, le taureau androcéphale et les masques cornus dans l'Etrurie archaique,' 780.

[67] A. Della Seta, *Italia Antica* (Bergamo, 1922), 232, fig.259.

[68] Pausanias, *Descriptions of Greece*, 1.2.4 /2.1.3 /8.15.3.

[69] E. Mussini, 'La diffusione dell'iconografia di Acheloo in Magna Grecia e Sicilia. Tracce per l'individuazione di un culto,' in *Studi Etruschi*, 65-68 (2002), 95-6.

[70] Ibid., 97.

[71] Ibid., 98.

[72] H.P. Isler, *Acheloos*, no.41-48; J.R. Jannot, *Les reliefs archaïques de Chiusi* (Rome: École Française de Rome, 1984), 135, no. C.40, and ibid., 180, no. H.II.1, H.II.2, H.III.2-H.III.14.

[73] J.R. Jannot, *Les reliefs archaïques de Chiusi*, 313.

[74] Fig.56. J. Jannot, *Les reliefs archaïques de Chiusi*, fig.598, and no. H.II.I; ibid., fig.219, no. C.I.40. Isler dated the first reliefs from Chiusi to the first quarter of the 5th century BC (H.P. Isler, *Acheloos*, no.40ff.), but today there is agreement among scholars for an earlier date, starting in the first quarter of the 6th century BC (cf. A. Minetti, *L'orientalizzante a Chiusi e nel suo territorio* (Rome: Bretschneider, 2004), 457; E. Pezzini, 'La scultura funeraria,' in *Gli Etruschi a Palermo. Museo Casuccini, Palermo, 17 ottobre 2012-6 gennaio*

Fig.56 helps further remove the illusion that Etruscan man-faced bulls were imitations of Greek traditions, because the full recumbent posture of the man-faced bull is never attested in the Greek world, but very often in the Near East.[75] In terms of the western Mediteranean, the Etruscan use of the recumbent scheme[76] is comparable to the famous Iberian *Bicha de Balazote*, from Spain.[77] Moreover, **Fig.57** provides strong evidence for a definitive cult of the man-faced bull in the area. It is not a cinerarium urn, as described by Isler,[78] insofar as it is not a hollow object and the roof is attached to the body of the structure, so could not possibly function as an urn. Jannot was not sure about the real function of the object, defining it as 'an enigmatic monument,' and argues it is the representation of a temple, probably a naiskos.[79] Thus, what we have here is the head of a man-faced bull operating as the centerpiece for a miniature Etruscan temple.

A large number of man-faced bull-shaped antefixes come from various cultic sites in Campania and Etruria,[80] suggesting widespread cult activity since the Late Archaic Age. The Etruscan site of Capua, for example, has a temple dated to the last quarter of 6th century BC equipped with man-faced bull acroteria and antefixes.[81] The pieces appear to have spread from Capua throughout the surrounding area, with examples at Minturne, Teanum, Cales, Suessula, and Fratte.[82] All of these places are non-Greek native centers of Campania,[83] some of which will later use the man-faced bull on their coinage. Colonna also mentions man-faced bull heads from Capua decorating wooden coffins and klinai displayed during funerals.[84] The author also mentions the discovery of a clay 'chest' consisting of three female busts linked shoulder-to-shoulder, found in the layers chronologically preceding the construction of the sanctuary,[85] testifying to an archaic cult of the nymphs in the area.[86] All this suggests that the southern Etruscan center of Capua had a predominant role in the transmission of the iconography of the man-faced bull to the Greek and Italic cultures of the area, where the man-faced bull flourishes on coinage.

Ciuccarelli, mostly following the old Hellenocentric hypothesis of transmission of the iconography from the Greek world to Etruria,[87] still leaves some room for the hypothesis of an Etruscan contribution to the matter. In fact, she mentions Veio[88]

2013, Exposition (Milan: Silvana, 2012), 9). The archaic style of the man-faced bull depicted on the specimens shown in **Fig.56** and **Fig.57** suggests they are among the earliest examples.

75 J. Aruz and R. Wallenfels, *Art of the First Cities: The Third Millenium B.C. from the Mediterranean to the Indus* (New York: The Metropolitan Museum of Art, 2003), 440, no. 313.

76 For two additional examples, see J.R. Jannot, 'Acheloos, le taureau androcéphale et les masques cornus dans l'Etrurie archaique,' Pl.II, fig.6-7. Ostrowski already noticed that the earlier non-Mesopotamian example the of reclining man-faced bull is the archaic statue from Balazote (H.P. Isler, *Acheloos*, no.50), appearing also in 5th century Etruscan urn reliefs (H.P. Isler, 'Acheloos,' in *LIMC*, no.61-63) and small bronzes (H.P. Isler, 'Acheloos,' in *LIMC*, no.65-67). The unique example of a reclining man-faced bull from the Greek world was found in Taras (H.P. Isler, *Acheloos*, no.173), on a terracotta applique dated end of the 5th century BC (J.A. Ostrowski, *Personifications of rivers in Greek and roman art*. Studia ad Archaeologiam Mediterraneam Pertinentia, Vol. XII (Warszawa-Krakòw: Sumptibus Universitatis Iagellonicae, 1991),18).

77 T. Chapa Brunet, 'El Toro Androcefalo de Balazote: Nueva Puesta a Punto de su Problematica,' in *Revista de Estudios Albacetenses*, No.10 (1981), 145-158, fig. P. The Bicha de Balazote is likely another example of a western man-faced bull influenced by Levantine contacts, showing essentially no influence from Greek archaic sculpture. In fact, William N. Bates noted that the piece 'clearly shows Chaldaean influence' (W. N. Bates, 'Archaeological Discussions,' in *AJA*, Vol. 15, No. 4 (1911), 563). The Chaldeans were a Semitic people, living in the southern part of Mesopotamia, whose existence is attested in Assyrian texts of the 9th century BC. The Iberian piece is dated to the mid 6th century BC. When discussing a possible model of diffusion for the scheme of the reclining man-faced bull, Ostrowski states: 'Most probably the development of suchlike images was influenced by Oriental currents penetrating Etruria and from there radiating to the regions of southern Italy, Sicily and even Spain' (J.A. Ostrowski, *Personifications of rivers in Greek and roman art*, 18).

78 H.P. Isler, *Acheloos*, no.40.

79 J.R. Jannot, *Les reliefs archaïques de Chiusi*, 214-215.

80 H.P. Isler, *Acheloos*, no. 144-165

81 G. Colonna, 'Le civiltà anelleniche,' in *Storia e Civiltà della Campania. L'evo Antico*, edited by G. Pugliese Carratelli (Naples: Electa, 1991), 57. It appears there was a direct influence from Asia Minor on the archaic antefixes of Capua and southern Etruscan centers, manifested in the architectural production by means of Velia (B. D'Agostino, 'Il mondo periferico della Magna Grecia,' in *Popoli e Civiltà dell'Italia Antica*, Vol. II (Rome, 1974), 179-215).

82 Fratte, in particular, is an interesting place in which different cultures intermingled, as citizens used both the Etruscan and Greek alphabets. For the iconography of the man-faced bull at Fratte, see: C. Pellegrino, 'La Campania degli Etruschi,' in *Vetulonia, Pontecagnano e Capua. Vite parallele di tre città Etrusche*, edited by S.Rafanelli (Monteriggioni: ARA Edizioni, 2013), 38; H.P. Isler, *Acheloos*, no. 149.

83 G. Colonna, 'Le civiltà anelleniche,' 60.

84 Ibid. Johannowsky states that the Capuan terracotta attachments for funerary coffins probably had the same arrangement as clay decorations on Etruscan sacred buildings, on the basis of the disposition of those attachments found in Tomb 201 at Capua (W. Johannowsky, *Capua antica*, (Napoli, 1989), 50.

85 Ibid., 59

86 This evidence suggests that the worship of the nymphs in Campania had early origins, rooted locally in the area before Greek colonization. For an interesting comparison of the archaic evidence from Capua with later triple herms from Grotta Caruso at Lokris, see below, pg. 64, note 239.

87 Ciuccarelli argues for a strong funerary dimension for the man-faced bull in Etruria arriving west by the import of Ionian balsamarii during the first half of 6th BC, which were 'reworked in the Etruscan culture,' as demonstrated in the examples from Pyrgy or Veii during the second half of the 6th century 'in the great southern Etruscan sanctuaries, where its further processing found fertile ground thanks to a similar religious milieu' (M.R. Ciuccarelli, 'Acheloo ctonio dalla Magna Grecia all'Etruria?,' 136). Ciuccarelli does not agree with Mussini's study, stating on more than one occasion that Mussini's dating is too late, both for the first examples of balsamarii (ibid., 126, no.5) and the diffusion of the cult of Acheloios in Etruria (ibid., 136, no.2).

88 The cult of the man-faced bull is attested at Veii by the architectural terracotta devices of the great temple at Portonaccio (H.P. Isler, *Acheloos*, no.152-154; see also no. 141), votive statuettes, and one oscillum (M.R. Ciuccarelli, 'Acheloo ctonio dalla Magna Grecia all'Etruria?,' 133). As in Pyrgi, a solar-chthonic-oracular cult was also operative at the sanctuary of Portonaccio at Veii, in relation to a deity named Rath, assimilated with the Greek Apollo (ibid.) At the same sanctuary the worship of a female goddess named Turan is attested, assimilated with the Greek Aphrodite (ibid., 135, no.5). Already very early with Villanovian bull-shaped askoi there is an emphasis for a strong symbolic allusion to the sphere of regenerative capacity and

and Pyrgi[89] as important places for 'the process of elaboration of the mythical figure of Acheloos,'[90] pointing out that there are clear traces of oracular practices performed for the solar-chthonic gods worshipped at the sanctuaries.[91] Similar cultic associations are attested by discoveries of representations of man-faced bulls at sites with oracular-chthonic religious dimensions like Caere,[92] Populonia, and Cerveteri.[93]

The Near Eastern connection with these cultic dimensions is even clearer if we analyze the appearance of some pieces made by Etruscan bronze workers. In fact, a clear Urartian influence can be seen on a pair of situla fittings depicting the head of the man-faced bull with wings on each side (**Fig. 59a and 59b**).[94] Situlas are often found in graves in which water or other liquid offerings were required. Thus, these pieces offer a glimpse of the Etruscan man-faced bull phenomenon in its entirety: the wings indicate both a solar and apotropaic aspect derived from Near Eastern prototypes,[95] the fact they were likely found in a tomb indicates a subterranean aspect, the attachment to a situla indicates a fluvial aspect, and insofar as they were involved in a ritual funerary practice, they indicate the man-faced bull is a liminal figure. Many extant stamnoi handles are also adorned with images of the man-faced bull.[96] Since these figures appear in pairs on containers used to hold liquids, and were likely used in graves, the same characteristics for the situla fittings are applicable. In fact, the stamnoi are visually reminiscent of urns, and were occasionally used as such,[97] making the perfect vessel for one's ashes.

Another interesting piece is an Etruscan handle in bronze in the shape of a 'despotes theron' mastering two man-faced bulls and a siren, found together with a Punic ivory plaque in a deposit at Malaga in Spain. Both votive offerings are attributable to a sanctuary erected on the summit of the citadel and date to the 6th century BC.[98] The piece is a clear sign for the direct Near Eastern influence on the Etruscan tradition of the man-faced bull, in this case likely mediated by Phoenicians, as such schemes

---

the deities presiding over it (L. Drago Troccoli 'Ricerche sul tema del bestiario fantastico di età orientalizzante. I precedenti della prima età del Ferro: continuità o discontinuità?,' in *Il bestiario fantastico di età orientalizzante nella penisola italiana. Aristonothos. Scritti per il Mediterraneo antico Quaderni*, 1 (Trento: Tangram, 2012), 16. See the section on early Italic traditions for the frequent recurrence of bull-askoi in children's graves at Veii. The presence of clear signs of Levantine funerary culture at the Necropolis of Veii led some scholars to assume the existence of an enclave of Asian artists, architects and sculptors, active since the early 7th century BC, 'as a prerequisite for the production of certain filigree decoration and granulation on jewelry of local form' (G. Bartoloni, 'Le città etrusche e gli altri: l'esempio di Veio,' in *Meetings between cultures in the ancient Mediterranean, 17th International Congres of Classical Archaeology (Rome, 2008).* Bollettino di Archeologia online, I (2010), 4). According to Bartoloni, the incredible flowering of Etruscan jewelery indicates a diaspora of artisans from northeastern Syria after the Assyrian conquest of the 8th century BC (ibid.). Etruscan jewelry depicting the man-faced bull is widespread. Amulets were worn about the neck and functioned as apotropaic devices. The most famous example is a stunning piece in the Louvre (**Fig.58**), dating to the 5th century BC. The material (gold) and level of artistry indicate this piece was made by an expert craftsman for an important individual, which in turn indicates the man-faced bull, here identified as Acheloios from the single broken horn, was an important part of Etruscan culture (M. Cristofani and M. Martelli, *L'Oro degli Etruschi* (Novara: Istituto geografico de Agostini, 1983), 295-296, no. 163)

89 For the cult of the man-faced bull at the sanctuary of Pyrgi, see above. For the oracular dimension of the cults at the sanctuary, see G. Colonna, 'L'Apollo di Pyrgi, Sur/Suri (il 'nero') e l'Apollo Sourios,' in *Studi Etruschi*, Vol.LXXIII (2009),101-134.

90 M.R. Ciuccarelli, 'Acheloo ctonio dalla Magna Grecia all'Etruria?,' 133. She also mentions the two sanctuaries with man-faced bull iconography used in relation to flowing waters and water works attested near the sites.

91 Ibid. The comparison of the iconographic scheme of the temples of solar deities at Pyrgi and Veio Portonaccio (with alternating man-faced bull heads and female figures) to the Near Eastern examples is striking, 'Shilhak-Inshushinak, king of Elam during the second half of the twelfth century, built the temple in Susa dedicated to Inshushinak, the city's patron deity. The facade of this temple was made of moulded bricks and depicted bull-men and intercession goddesses called lamas. In Mesopotamia bull-men were associated with the Sun God Shamash. Inshushinak is often invoked with the Elamite Sun God in legal documents from Susa. This suggests a similar association between Inshushinak and bull-men to that between Shamash and the bullmen, and their appearance on the facade of his temple wall is therefore fitting. That the bull-men served a beneficent and protective function is made clear by their accompaniment by the lamas' (R.M.van Dijk, 'The Motif of the Bull,' 249). Even more striking is the similar scheme of man-faced bulls alternating with winged female figures, as seen in the *Lampadario di Cortona*, with the image of the man-faced bull used in Mesopotamia for cultic and funerary lamps, as found at the Royal Cemetery of Ur, mentioned above.

92 G. Colonna, 'Divinazione e culto di Rath/Apollo a Caere (a proposito del santuario in località S. Antonio),' in *Archeologia Classica*, Vol.LII (2001), 151-173.

93 M.R.Ciuccarelli, 'Acheloo ctonio dalla Magna Grecia all'Etruria?,' 134-5.

94 Private Collection. For another winged example, see H.P. Isler, *Acheloos*, no.244.

95 For the solar connotation of ancient Mesopotamian and Syrian bull-men, see: R.M.van Dijk, 'The Motif of the Bull,' 69 and 249. For the merging of those aspects with the representation lahmu, a spirit of the rivers who mastered wild animals, especially in Anatolia, see ibid., 70. For the lamassu, the apotropaic protective figures which were originally associated with the Sun God Shamash, see ibid., 243. There are also Urartian Cauldron Handles shaped as winged bull heads (ibid., fig.23). Examples come from sites including southern Turkey, northern Syria and Etruria.

96 H.P. Isler, 'Acheloos,' in *LIMC*, no. 126-135.

97 J. Frel, 'Preface,' in *Stamnoi: An Exhibition at the J. Paul Getty Museum*, edited by C. Isler-Kerényi and J. Frel (Malibu: The J. Paul Getty Museum, 1980).

98 Surprisingly Isler proposed, although doubtfully, to attribute the piece as Tarentine (H.P. Isler, *Acheloos, 154, no.178*) despite the fact that the style is in no way consistent with the bronze productions of the Greek polis. A correct attribution to Etruscan fabric was proposed by J. Gran-Aymerich, 'Etruria Marittima: Massalia and Gaul, Carthage and Iberia,' in *The Etruscan World,* edited by Jean MacIntosh Turfa. (London: Routledge: 2013), 334-335. Gran-Aymerich finds close parallels with an artifact found in Carthage, and another from Schwartzenbach in the Celtic hinterland (ibid.) The diffusion of man-faced bull iconography into Celtic culture can be attributed to Etruscan influences, as demonstrated by the recent discovery of a large feasting cauldron adorned with a man-faced bull, unearthed in northern France, from the tomb of a Celtic ruler in Lavau (N. Bianca Fàbry and D.Vitali, 'Il Principe Celtico di Lavau. Dentro lo scavo,' in *Archeologia Viva*, No.171 (Firenze: Giunti, 2015), 58ff. This piece incorporates the symbolism of abundance and, insofar as it is a burial item, a chthonic association as well. Another Etruscan bronze situla fitting depicting the head of Acheloios was found in France, at Lezoux, in 1988 (A. H. de Villefosse, 'Une tête de bronze récemment découverte à Lezoux (Puy-de-Dôme) par M. le Dr Plicque,' in *Comptes rendus des séances de l'Académie des Inscriptions et Belles Lettres*, 32e année, No. 4 (1888), 308).

are never seen on Greek artifacts depicting Acheloios.[99] In fact, the same scheme appears on a decorated tube from Luristan, dated from the 10th to mid 6th century BC, which shows a female figure with man-faced bull heads emerging from her shoulders as she grasps the beards of the bulls.[100]

A further important indication of the Etruscan man-faced bull's eastern origin is exhibited on a bronze helmet fitting in which two figures with clubs attack the man-faced bull.[101] Clearly, it is not the usual Herakles-Acheloios battle, but instead reminiscent of the Gilgamesh-Enkidu-Gugalanna battle, sometimes represent on cylinder seals **(Fig. 13).** The fact that the man-faced bull has wings, just like the aforementioned situla fittings, reinforces this point. Some scholars suggest Herakles and Uni are represented by the two human figures.[102] This identification is certainly plausible if we consider that at the aforementioned sanctuary of Pyrgi, archaeologists discovered three inscribed gold plates with bilingual inscriptions in Etruscan and Phoenician, with a dedication to a goddess named Uni in the Etruscan text, and Astarte[103] in the Phoenician.[104]

Ultimately, cultic imagery of the man-faced bull was very widespread in Etruria and actually earlier than the archaeological findings reveal for the Greek mainland, where the diffusion of the specific cult of Acheloios is not attested in art before the Classical Age. This indicates, at the very least, that the iconography arrived in Italy from the Levantine world without a Greek filter (although the same phenomenon was also occurring in the Greek world with other itinerant mercenaries and seer-healers). The routes followed by these initial carriers to Etruria were quite possibly North African. In fact, the later numismatic evidence seems to confirm this model of diffusion, since the first coins with man-faced bull type are minted in similar order: Asia Minor, Cyprus, Kyrene, Rhegion, and Gelas, and only later Akarnania. Although cultic practices involving the man-faced bull were articulated in several different, though intermingled, ways, archaeological data proves that in Etruria and South Italy he was revered especially as a chthonic deity in relation to beliefs about the afterlife, and that the image had a strong apotropaic meaning, just like the Near Eastern winged man-headed bulls.

Despite the widespread use of man-faced bull iconography in the Etruscan world, it is interesting to note that he appears nowhere in the corpus of Etruscan numismatics.[105] It might be because Etruscan coinage is not often tied to religious iconography and more closely related to the heraldic symbols of the aristocratic families who started issuing silver coins.[106]

The Greek Man-Faced Bull

Introduction

After about 4,400 years and apparently having traveled several thousand miles through various cultures, the man-faced bull finally arrives in the Greek world in the first half of the 6th century BC.[107] In Magna Graecia and the western Greek world the iconography of the man-faced bull becomes extremely popular, as indicated in the spread of balsamarii starting in the early 6th century, and the slightly later flourishing of coins featuring the man-faced bull type. In contemporary mainland Greece, for the earliest examples, the man-faced bull is predominantely represented as a supporting actor in the myth of Herakles in painted pottery and glyptic art.[108] In fact, only in the early to mid 5th century do we see

[99] Interestingly, the earliest iconography of the 'Master of Animals' comes from Mesopotamia: he was a protective and beneficent deity, was a spirit of the rivers, and took care of domesticated herds with water. He was originally associated with Enki or his Akkadian counterpart Ea, and later with Marduk (R.M.van Dijk, 'The Motif of the Bull,' 68 and bibliography).

[100] From the Los Angeles County Museum of Art, Item no. M.76.97.73.

[101] H.P. Isler, 'Acheloos,' in *LIMC,* no. 142.

[102] Unfortunately, we were unable to relocate the specific reference that made this attribution by the time of publication.

[103] The Phoenician Astarte shared with Hathor the epithet *Baalat-Gebal,* the 'Lady of Byblos.' Astarte borrowed some of the attributes of Hathor, including the headdress of the sun-disc between a pair of cow's horns. A relief of Nectanebo II depicts Astarte as a female riding a bull (R.M.van Dijk, 'The Motif of the Bull,' 194).

[104] G.Colonna, 'Il santuario di Pyrgi dalle origini mitistoriche agli altorilievi frontonali dei Sette e di Leucotea,' in *Scienze dell'Antichità,* Vol.10 (2002), 294-298 and 336). The presence of Levantine craftsmen in Etruria since the early Archaic period has been repeatedly proposed by archaeologists, based on the striking similarities of local artistic products, whose fine workmanship does not allow classification as mere imitations of Levantine objects. Already Colonna and von Hase spoke explicitly of both sedentary and itinerant craftsmen, in particular sculptors from Syria, in Etruscan cities (G.Colonna and F.W. Von Hase, 'Alle origini della statuaria etrusca: la tomba delle statue presso Ceri,' in *Studi Etruschi,* Vol.LII (1984), 52-53). Prayon has suggested a similar phenomenon to explain the architectural evidence (F. Prayon, 'L'architettura funeraria Etrusca. La situazione attuale delle ricerche e problemi aperti,' in *Atti del II Congresso Internazionale Etrusco* (Rome, 1989), 441-9). The same dynamics for potters is apparent since the 8th century BC, suggested in M. Bonghi Jovino et al., *Tarquinia. Testimonianze archeologiche e ricostruzione storica. Scavi sistematici nell'abitato. Campagne 1982-1988* (Rome: Bretschneider, 2001), 346). Some scholars suggest a revision of the date for the beginning of the Orientalizing Period in Etruria to an earlier time on the basis of existing evidence (R. Peroni, *Introduzione alla protostoria italiana* (Bari, 1994), 212-216; A.M. Bietti Sestieri, I. Damiani, J. De Grossi Mazzorin, A. De Santis, G. Recchia, and E. Remotti, 'Un edificio della I età del Ferro nell'abitato di Fidene (Roma): posizione stratigrafica, caratteristiche strutturali, materiali,' in *Proceedings of the XIII International Congress of Prehistoric and Protohistoric Sciences* (Forlì, 1996), 595-604; A.J. Nijboer, J. Van Der Plicht, A.M. Bietti Sestieri, and A. De Santis, 'A high chronology for the early Iron Age in central Italy,' in *Palaeohistoria,* Vol.41-42 (2000), 163-176.

[105] Cf. I. Vecchi, *Etruscan Coinage,* Part I (Milan, 2012).Unless we consider the Etruscan contribution to the coinage of Irnthi, on which the legend has mixed Greek-Oscan-Etruscan letters. These coins were probably issued in a cultic context for the needs of the sanctuary of Punta Campanella, a meeting place for cultural and economic exchanges and the recruitment of mercenaries (see catalog entry for discussion).

[106] F. Catalli, *Monete Etrusche* (Rome: Istituto Poligrafico e Zecca dello Stato, 1998).

[107] For a general discussion of the notion of cultural continuity in its relation to the man-faced bull, see pg. 97ff.

[108] H.P. Isler, 'Acheloos,' in *LIMC,* no.213-228, and no.246-259.

the first traces for a cult of the man-faced bull in Greece proper.[109] Shortly after this adoption of the iconography around the second half of the 5th century BC, it appears to have become the standard cultic image for Acheloios throughout the entire Greek world.

Despite the incredibly long journey the iconography appears to have traveled, the man-faced bull maintains his associations with water, fertility, death, rebirth, and liminal-related qualities involved in rites of passage, all of which seem to have been with him, in one way or another, since his emergence in prehistory. The known evidence for the Greek world indicates less of a focus on the man-faced bull's chthonic qualities (especially in Greece proper), unlike what we saw in Etruria. This absence is filled with an important layer previously unseen elsewhere, in which he becomes intimately related both to civic identity and to the identity of the individual. This is particularly fitting, for it is in the Greek world, as discussed in the next Chapter, that the identity of the man-faced bull becomes clear.[110]

H.P. Isler's *Acheloos*[111] and subsequent *LIMC*[112] entry offer a comprehensive overview of the distribution of man-faced bull iconography in the Greek world from its inception to decline. He has appeared either alone, with Herakles, with Nike (or more likely a winged nymph) crowning him, or within a larger group of deities as seen on Attic marble reliefs, in which case often just his forepart is shown. There are examples of the man-faced bull on both functional and decorative items: gems,[113] painted pottery,[114] plastic pottery (kernoi,[115] askoi,[116] and balsamarii[117]), marble votive reliefs,[118] bronze statuettes,[119] masks,[120] terracotta appliqués,[121] antefixes,[122] jewelry,[123]and, of course, coins.[124] In fact, as a clear indication of the general pervasiveness of the image in Greek culture, it is worthwhile to list the mints issuing man-faced bull coinage: Abakainon, Aesernia, Ai Khanoum (issued under the Seleukid Empire), Agyrion, Alaisa Archonidea (?), Alaisa Katane, Allifae, Alontion, Ambrakia, Anaktorion, Arse, Assorus (depicting two man-faced bulls), Brettii, Cales, the Campani, Compulteria, Cumae, Emporion, Entella, Hodoi Gela, Halykiai, Herbessos, Hyria, Iaitas, Ionia (two uncertain mints), Irnthi, Istros, Katane, the Kersini, Koronta, Kyrene, Kyzikos, Laos, Larinum, Leukas, Lycia (uncertain mint), Macedon (Amphipolis?), Malies, Mallos, the Mamar, Megara Hyblaia, Metapontion, Methylion, Metropolis (Thessaly), Motya, Mylai, Neapolis, Nola, Oiniadai, Panormos, Paphos, Phaselis, Phistelia, Phokaia, Rhegion, Rome (probably minted at Neapolis), Selinunte, the Sergetaians, Sichas (?), the Sileraians, Stiela, Stratos, Suessa Aurunca, Syracuse, Tauromenion, Teanum Sidicinum, Tiati Apulorum, Thyrreion, Torybeion, and one uncertain Sicilian mint. The winged man-faced bull also appears in some areas, mostly in Asia Minor, such as Miletos and Lycia.[125] The earliest example emerges in the mid 6th century BC in Ionia, followed closely by issues from Cyprus, Kyrene, Rhegion, Gelas and Laos. By the mid 5th century the iconography is remarkably widespread throughout the Greek world, particularly in Campania, Sicily, and Akarnania, and examples can still be found in Roman times. There are even examples of man-faced bulls on Roman oil lamps and bronze appliqués, when the iconography had largely gone out of fashion.[126]

Early Representations on Pottery: Origins, Diffusion, and Commissioning

Plastic Pottery

Ionian balsamarii (**Fig.60**)[127] featuring the head of the man-faced bull are found spread throughout the Greek colonies of the western Mediterranean and Etruria in significantly greater numbers than in eastern and mainland Greece. They were offered in sanctuaries and as part of the grave goods in burials.[128] Ciuccarelli argues

[109] According to Isler, the earliest archaeological evidence for a cult of Acheloios in mainland Greece is a marble mask dated to 470 BC (H.P. Isler, *Acheloos*, 36-7, no.51). We have no evidence that the mask is a depiction of Acheloios. Even Jenkins is dubitative when stating it 'may be' Acheloios (G.K. Jenkins, *The Coinage of Gela*, 166). In fact, all we have is a bearded face, no bovine ears and no horns, and the lead insertions on the right side of the forehead could have been used to support a wreath, which might indicate Dionysus.

[110] To overcome the obstacle of the ambiguity of identity in this chapter, Acheloios, unidentified man-faced bulls, and water/river god mythology are all examined together. This will all seem perfectly acceptable by the end of Chapter 7, when we present our theory of locative epithets ('Sinews of Acheloios') to explain the identity of the man-faced bull.

[111] H.P. Isler, *Acheloos: Eine Monographie* (Bern, 1970).

[112] H.P. Isler, 'Acheloos,' in *LIMC*, 12-36.

[113] H.P. Isler, *Acheloos*, no. 291-292, no. 296 (winged), no. 297-300.

[114] Ibid., no. 57-58, no. 60-63, no. 67-91.

[115] British Museum, Reg. Number 1849,1122.4.

[116] H.P. Isler, *Acheloos*, no. 123-124.

[117] Ibid., no.96-122.

[118] Ibid., no. 1-39.

[119] H.P. Isler, 'Acheloos,' in *LIMC*, no.56 and no. 113-114.

[120] H.P. Isler, *Acheloos*, no.51 (marble); H.P. Isler, 'Acheloos,' in *LIMC*, no.86-91 (terracotta).

[121] H.P. Isler, 'Acheloos,' in *LIMC*, no.13.

[122] Ibid., no. 84; **Fig. 61 and Fig. 62.**

[123] H.P. Isler, *Acheloos*, no.279.

[124] H.P. Isler, 'Acheloos,' in *LIMC*, no.14-50, no. 92-99.

[125] For an example of a winged man-faced bull depicted on an Ionian glyptic gem, see: H.P. Isler, *Acheloos*, no. 296.

[126] After being absorbed into the world of Republican Rome, the man-faced bull maintains similar fluvial connotations. There is an angular tile dated to the late 4th, early 3rd century BC, adorned with a man-faced bull head which was found in Rome during excavations for the new Auditorium. The find site has been identified as a temple of Anna Perenna and the Nymphs, and there is evidence of the deviation of the Tiber near the sanctuary, indicated in this piece by the broken horn (M. J. Strazzulla, 'La tegola con Acheloo,' in *Il Santuario della Musica e il Bosco Sacro di Anna Perenna* (Rome: Electa, 2002), 79-83. See also, H. Di Giuseppe, 'L'Acheloo e gli altri indicatori religiosi della villa,' in *La fattoria e la villa dell'Auditorium nel quartiere Flaminio di Roma* (Rome : Bretschneider, 2006), 465-470.The discussion of the man-faced bull on Rome's first coinage can be found in the accompanying catalog.

[127] From the Dallas Museum of Art, S. Kotz, *Dallas Museum of Art: A Guide to the Collection* (New Haven: Yale University Press, 2012), 137.

[128] M.R. Ciuccarelli, 'Due nuovi balsamari greco-orientali da

that the great interest in the figure among the western colonies likely had a significant impact on the shaping of Acheloios that 'influenced the character of the God in terms of cultic and ritual symbology.'[129] It was therefore probably the western colonies, not Greece proper, that played the greatest role in the association between the man-faced bull and Acheloios, which should be no surprise given that the bulk of our aforementioned mercenaries and seer-healers likely came from that area. Isler dated the earliest balsamarii found in Italy from 580 to 570 BC.[130] In *Acheloos*, he listed 21 specimens,[131] five of which are described as 'Samo-Milesian,'[132] nine as 'Rhodian?,'[133] four as 'provincial,'[134] two as 'uncertain,'[135] and one as an 'Italian imitation of Ionic types.'[136] The classifications provided by Isler indicate the difficulty of attribution to a clearly identified area of manufacture, a problem still debated among scholars. In fact, there were probably a few different production workshops.[137]

Merging data from the catalogues of Isler and Ciuccarelli of items with known provenance, we can see that nine specimens were found in Italy,[138] three in Sicily,[139] three in Rhodes,[140] two in North Africa,[141] one in Thera,[142] one in Athens,[143] and one in Cyprus.[144] There are now a total of seven with unknown provenance.[145] Altogether, they can be chronologically ordered into six groups. The earliest known examples, dating from 595 to 580 BC, were found in Etruria and Magna Graecia.[146] The examples from Rhodes, according to Ducat, cannot be dated before 550 to 540 BC, and Higgins went so far as to propose 520 BC.[147] Ciuccarelli noted that beyond the three examples from Rhodes, no trace of these balsamarii were found in the Greek colonies of Asia Minor.[148]

On the basis of all this data, one must reconsider the proposed area of production of the balsamarii, originally attributed by Ducat to Rhodian or Samo-Milesian workshops.[149] First and foremost, not a single example has ever been found in Samos or Miletos, or any other Greek site in Ionia outside the area of Rhodes. Secondly, the overwhelming presence of these artifacts in Italy, combined with the evidence that the earliest examples are found there, suggests that the specimens described by Isler as 'Italian imitations of Ionic type' and 'provincial' might have been produced in the areas west of Anatolia and Greece proper, probably in some Etruscan workshop.[150] This proposed re-attribution should not be overly controversial. In fact, another interesting example for re-attribution concerns the man-faced bull plastic vases identified as Italo-Corinthian,[151] previously attributed to Corinth by H. Payne in his 1931 essay.[152] In 1963, Jean Ducat, based on his analysis of previous studies by Higgins, correctly re-attributed the 'proto-Corinthian' man-faced bull plastic vases to Etruscan workshops.[153]

However, Strabo does inform us that the people of Gela and Neapolis, both of whom employed man-faced bull

Cerveteri,' in *Agoge. Atti della Scuola di specializzazione in archeologia*, Vol. IV-V (Pisa: University Press, 2010), 163.

[129] M.R. Ciuccarelli, 'Acheloo ctonio dalla Magna Grecia all'Etruria?,'126.

[130] H.P. Isler, 'Acheloos,' in *LIMC*, no.101. Indeed, the dates here are earlier than stated by Isler in *Acheloos*. Today, the earliest man-faced bull balsamarii are dated to 595 BC, on the basis of rigorous cross analysis of the contexts of discovery (M.R. Ciuccarelli, 'Due nuovi balsamari greco-orientali da Cerveteri,' 177-180).

[131] H.P. Isler, *Acheloos*, no.96-116. Accounting for new discoveries, there are now 26 known specimens, all listed in: M.R. Ciuccarelli, 'Due nuovi balsamari greco-orientali da Cerveteri,' 169ff.

[132] H.P. Isler, *Acheloos*, no. 96-100.

[133] Ibid., no. 101-109.

[134] Ibid., no. 110-113. It is not entirely clear what Isler means by 'provincial,' since in the Archaic Greek world a central power, as in Roman times, never existed. By provincial he might mean 'made locally,' and in this regard it is interesting to note that the three specimens with known provenance match the North African route of distribution that mirrors the spread of the man-faced bull on coinage: Tocra in North Africa (dated 570 to 560 BC, ibid., no.110), Capua in Etruria (dated 560 to 550 BC, ibid., no.111), Lokris in Magna Graecia (dated 560 to 550 BC, ibid., no.112), and Rhodes in Asia Minor (dated 550 BC, ibid., no.113).

[135] Ibid., no. 114-115.

[136] Ibid., no. 116.

[137] M.R. Ciuccarelli, 'Due nuovi balsamari greco-orientali da Cerveteri,' 174, no.51.

[138] Etruria: ibid., no. 7, no. 9-10, no. 24-26; Magna Graecia: ibid., no. 21-23.

[139] Ibid., no. 18-20.

[140] Ibid., no. 14-16.

[141] Ibid., no. 12; H.P. Isler, *Acheloos*, no.110.

[142] M.R. Ciuccarelli, 'Due nuovi balsamari greco-orientali da Cerveteri,' no. 17.

[143] Ibid., no. 11. The author 'doubtfully included the specimen in the catalog,' as it was impossible to find, and thus it is equally impossible to assign it to any of the six chronological classes she identified. The piece is also listed by Isler with the specification 'no available photos' (H.P. Isler, *Acheloos*, no. 115).

[144] M.R. Ciuccarelli, 'Due nuovi balsamari greco-orientali da Cerveteri,' no. 13.

[145] Ibid., no. 1-6, no. 8.

[146] Ibid., 177-180.

[147] For a bibliography, see ibid., 179, footnotes 84 and 85. Ciuccarelli does not agree with the later dating of the pieces.

[148] Ibid., 181.

[149] J. Ducat, *Les vases plastiques rhodiens archaiques en terre cuite* (Paris, 1966), 58.

[150] Another recent example of reattribution from Greece to Etruria, although not concerning the man-faced bull, comes from fragments of pottery found at Katane and Gela, previously identified as Ionian or eastern-Aegean imports, reattributed in 2009 to local workshops on the basis of scientific archaeometric analyses (M. Kerschner and H. Mommsen, 'Imports of East Greek pottery to Sicily and Sicilian production of East Greek type. Archaeometrical analyses of finds from the votive deposit in Katane,' in *Stipe votiva del santuario di Demetra a Catania. La ceramica Greco-Orientale*, edited by Antonella Pautasso (Catania: IBAM, 2009), 125-154.

[151] H.P. Isler, *Acheloos*, no.121-122. Even for the four 'Corinthian' examples listed by Isler (*Acheloos*, no.117-120) there are no certified provenances from the area of Corinth: we only know the provenance of no.120, from Magna Graecia. Two of those with unknown provenance, no.117-118, are stored in Rome, which indicates they might have been found in Italy.

[152] H. Payne, *Necrocotinthia* (1931).

[153] J. Ducat, 'Les vases plastiques corinthiens,' in *Bulletin de correspondance hellénique*, Vol. 87, Livraison 2 (1963), 435. For an example of such a vase from the 6th century, now identified as Etruscan, see British Museum No. 1836,0224.367. For a similar vase which should be reattributed to an Etruscan worshop, see *Corpus Vasorum Antiquorum. Oxford, Ashmolean Museum* 2, 73, PL.(390) 7.5-6.

iconography obsessively, have Rhodian origins.[154] Thus, we should not adopt an Italocentric point of view to combat the earlier Hellencocentric point of view. Instead, both the Etruscans and Rhodians probably made these artifacts. Thus, it is important to recognize that when the man-faced bull arrived with the Rhodians, it found a culture that had already been exposed to its mythology and iconography, and this commonality contributed to the assimilation of these different groups and the great popularity of the man-faced bull thereafter.

Painted Pottery: Man-Faced Bull Alone

According to Isler, the earliest known depiction of Acheloios alone on Greek Black Figure Pottery was found in Sicily, on a proto-Corinthian style jug, dated to the second quarter of the 7th century BC.[155] The piece was discovered by Paolo Orsi during excavations at Syracuse and attributed to the Tolouse Group.[156] Despite the fact that Isler included this piece in his study of Acheloios, the image is not described as a man-faced bull: the legs are actually feline and above the forehead are two 'pedicles,' not horns.[157] Isler himself was not entirely convinced of the identification, claiming it 'could have been Acheloos, the Minotaur, or some other mythological character.'[158] Thus, the earliest Greek example presented by Isler as Acheloios is not a man-faced bull, adding further significance to the Etruscan man-faced bull tradition and its impact on that of the Greeks.

The case is similar for the two Ionian Black Figure vases found in south Russia (*Acheloos*, no. 61-62), where Isler identified Acheloios among the creatures depicted in the decorative patterns showing animal friezes derived from Mesopotamian glyptics of processions of animals. In this case, too, there is no clear evidence of man-faced bulls, as no.61 is described as a bull showing some details resembling human feaures (like a beard, and possibly lips and a nose, **Fig.63**), and no.62 can not in any way be confused with a man-faced bull, as it is clearly a man-faced ibex, attested in other animal friezes from the Greek Orientalizing Period dated to the early 6th century BC.[159] Ultimately, despite Isler's evidence of early Greek representations of Acheloios as a man-faced bull, which would support his theory that Etruscan man-faced bulls copy those of the Greeks, the evidence falls short. Indeed, Isler himself admits that the images depicted on Corinthian and Ionian animal friezes cannot indicate a cult or the representation of religious deities or mythological traditions, which clearly emerge in the Classical Greek marble reliefs, and should be understood instead as decorative elements of uncertain meaning, inspired by Near Eastern glyptic art.[160]

The most convincing early man-faced bull listed by Isler for the Greek world is dated to the second quarter of 6th century BC (**Fig.64**).[161] It is a fragment showing a human forehead with bovine ears and horns. The provenance of the piece is unknown. Unfortunately, due to the fragmentary state, it is unclear whether the figure had a bovine or human body, though the top of the head seems like it would continue onto a bull's body. It is described as 'Ionian,' but there is nothing of similar style in Ionian pottery from the Archaic Period. Moreover, as acknowledged by Isler, it resembles Etruscan representations of man-faced bulls seen on Caeretan hydriai.[162]

---

[154] Strabo, *Geographica*, 6.1.14. For the theory that the Rhodians were responsible for the diffusion of the iconography, see E. Gabrici, *Problemi di Numismatica Greca* (Napoli, 1959), 85-88.

[155] H.P. Isler, *Acheloos*, no. 60.

[156] Ibid. The Tolouse Painter lived in the first half of the 7th century BC, and was among the first potters to use the proto-Corinthian Black Figure technique. His workshop is called the Tolouse Group, in connection with the Cumae Group, which probably represents the earliest works of the painter (L. Banti, 'Tolosa, Pittore di,' in *Enciclopedia dell'Arte antica classica e orientale*, Vol. VII (Rome, 1966). J.L. Benson, a major 20th century scholar of proto-Corinthian pottery, wrote: 'The torsional and curvilinear plant ornament of the Cumae and Toulouse Groups constitutes more than a particular theme (thought it is one): it was a fundamental deeply felt experience through which Corinthian artists liberated themselves from Geometric habitude. By this I mean the change from a mentality engrossed in rectilinear abstract ornaments to the same mentality caught up in substantive curvilinear ornamentation. I see the first stirrings of this already in the running spiral of the Thapsos Class vases, and then in its implementation in Egyptian-derived plant and animal forms leading directly to the Cumae-Toulouse aesthetic in question' (J. L. Benson, *Earlier Corinthian Workshops. A Study of Corinthian Geometric and Protocorinthian Stylistic Groups* (Amsterdam, 1989) as cited in M. Shanks, *The Classical Archaeology of Greece: Experiences of the Discipline* (Routledge, 2003), 26). Thus, Benson suggests a rather sudden change of the style of the Corinthian potters in the years in which they were frequenting Sicily and the Tyrrhenian area, correlating with influences from the East. The so-called Thapsos Class proto-Corinthian pottery are named from the Sicilian location of some major discoveries of objects with this style, whose ultimate origin is still debated. In fact, evidence emerged for the manufacture of this class of pottery in Etruria and Campania already at the earliest stages of production. Thus, the identification of Corinth as the unique center of production and transmission for the Thapsos Class is uncertain, even moreso when one considers the great presence of finds in Italy and Sicily in relation to the less frequent appearances in the Corinthian area (For a bibliography on the topic, see: M.S. Vullo, 'Produzioni specializzate di età arcaica a Policoro,' in *Amphi Sirios Roas: Nuove ricerche su Eraclea e la Siritide* (Venosa: Osanna, 2013), 69-87; M. Cuozzo, B. d'Agostino and L. Del Verme, *Cuma. Le fortificazioni 2. I materiali dai terrapieni arcaici* (Naples: 2006); C. Zaccagnino, 'La ceramica di periodo orientalzzante,' in *Science and Technology for Cultural Heritage*, 12 (Rome, 2004), 47-63; M. Cuozzo, 'Pontecagnano e i centri greci della Campania: osservazioni sulle produzioni ceramiche di età orientalizzante,' in *Meetings between Cultures in the Ancient Mediterranean, 17th International Congress of Classical Archaeology, Rome, 2008, Bollettino di Archeologia Online*, Vol. I (2010), 59-65; E. Mangani and O. Paoletti, *Corpus Vasorum Antiquorum: Italia. Grosseto-Museo archeologico e d'arte della Maremma*, Part 1 (Rome: Bretschneider, 1986), 36.

[157] H.P. Isler, *Acheloos*, 48.

[158] Ibid., 49. The identification of the depiction as a man-faced bull has already been judged as 'disputable' by J. A. Ostrowski, *Personifications of rivers in Greek and roman art*, 16.

[159] Ibid., 134. From the Staatliche Antikensammlungen Munich, dated 580 BC.

[160] Ibid., 50-51.

[161] Ibid., no. 63.

[162] Ibid., 51, for the Caeretan hydria see: ibid., no.58.

Ultimately, on the basis of the three earliest artifacts presented by Isler, it is impossible to state that the Etruscan man-faced bull is a derivation from Greek figurative art. Indeed, the earliest known examples of the man-faced bull (alone) on painted pottery are entirely Etruscan.[163] This particular class is categorized as Pontic Vases, incorrectly attributed by older scholars to Ionian workshops. Today, it is widely accepted that such vases have an Italic origin, and were made at Cerveteri and Vulci in Etruria, starting in the late second quarter of the 6th century BC.[164]

Painted Pottery: Fight with Herakles

The earliest example of a Black Figure Vase depicting the fight of Acheloios and Herakles[165] was found in Sicily, not Greece, on a Black Figure Attic amphora attributed to the Ptoon Painter, and dated 570 to 560 BC.[166] Another early example is dated to the mid 6th century BC,[167] this one attributed to the Boston Painter.[168] On the Ptoon piece the hero fights without weapons, as seen in later depictions from Lokris and Etruria.[169] On the Boston piece, Herakles holds a sword, which is an uncommon attribute, more often associated with Theseus. Isler noted that the earliest model for the iconography of the battle was derived from gems of the first quarter of the 6th century BC,[170] of which we know only two examples. The only one with a known provenance was found in Etruria.[171]

Production and Commissioning

From the analysis of the pieces with known provenance from Isler's catalog entries, it appears that, apart from a 'lost piece,' which is impossible to date,[172] no man-faced bulls have been found in mainland Greece dating to the 6th century BC.[173] In terms of the 5th century BC, excluding the marble mask dated to 470 BC (**Fig. 62**, whose identification as a man-faced bull is uncertain), the earliest evidence definitely found in Greece is a Red Figure Vase dated to 450 BC (no.90).[174] All other known representations from mainland Greece are dated from 425 BC on (no. 2-6, no. 9-13, no. 15-17, no. 19-25, no. 30-31, and no. 33-36). On the other hand, there are man-faced bull depictions from the 6th century BC that were made in mainland and eastern Greece but were found in Sicily (no.67), Magna Graecia (no.120) and Etruria (no.69-70, no.72-74, no.82, no.84, no.87, no.117-118). Finally, as mentioned above, approximately 70% of the entries in Isler's catalog are related to Italy and Sicily, either as local products or by direct provenance.

In the face of all this, one must ask: Why are all the oldest examples of the man-faced bull on plastic and painted pottery found in Italy and Sicily?[175] Even if some of them were manufactured in mainland or eastern Greece, they were clearly made for customers from further west,[176] who made specific requests relating to the

---

163 Ibid., no. 64 and no.65, stored at Rome and Orvieto.

164 For notes on the debate and related bibliography, see: D. Williams, 'The beginnings of the so-called 'Pontic' Group and other Italian black-figure fabrics,' in *Aeimnestos: miscellanea di studi per Mauro Cristofani*, edited by B. Adembri (Florence, 2005), 352-360.

165 The earliest depictions of the fight of the 'hero' with the man-faced bull come from Mesopotamian and later Assyrian glyptic traditions, as mentioned above. Incidentally, the earliest western depiction of the 'hero' vs. man-faced bull was an Ionian gem from the Archaic Age, but found at Falerii, in Etruria (H.P. Isler, *Acheloos*, no. 291, dated to the first quarter of the 6th century BC). It was discovered in a grave near Perugia (D. Cardella, *Lotta di Ercole con Acheloo incisa sopra uno scarabeo arcaico* (Orvieto: Marsili, 1894), 1). The earliest Italic man-faced bull is also from Falerii, and it shows a similar scheme (discussed above). Another early example is seen on an Attic Black Figure amphora found in Sicily, also of Ionian style and from the Ptoon Painter (H.P. Isler, *Acheloos*, no. 67, dated 570 to 560 BC).

166 Ibid., no. 67.

167 Ibid., no. 68. Although Isler seemed sure of a Theban provenance, there are no archeological records. The MFA Boston acquired it from a private collection, and accordingly wrote 'said to be from Thebes' (Museum of Fine Arts, Boston, item no. 99.519). See M. M. Lee, 'Acheloos Peplophoros. A lost statuette of a River God in Feminine Dress,' 319.

168 It is widely accepted that the Boston Painter and the Ptoon Painter were active in Attica, but they were also the protagonists of the great change in Attic vase painting which occurred around the mid 6th century BC, characterized by the switch from Corinthian style to Ionian style. Thus, these pieces are likely the first attempts of painters of Ionian culture to adapt the image of the man-faced bull to the myth of Herakles and Acheloios, using predominately eastern imagery. The other side of the Boston piece is also significant in this sense, as the artist is employing eastern hybrid figure iconography commonly seen on Levantine glyptics to depict the Greek narrative of the metamorphosis of Ulysses' friends. In fact, both the Ptoon and Boston painters might have been Ionian immigrants working in Attica.

169 See below, pg. 66ff, for Lokrian evidence from the Contrada Lucifero Necropolis and Etruscan comparisons.

170 H.P. Isler, *Acheloos*,15.

171 The specimen stored at Berlin is the aforementioned gem found in a tomb at Falerii (H.P. Isler, *Acheloos*, no.291). The other one, stored at the British Museum (ibid., no. 292) is of unknown provenance. The gems are identified as 'Ionian' by Isler based on style, but there is no real evidence that gems depicting the man-faced bull were ever produced in Ionia. In fact, we know of a total of 5 gems depicting the battle, one 'Ionian' found in Etruria (ibid., no. 291), one 'Ionian' of unknown provenance (ibid., no. 292), and three Etruscan (ibid., no. 293-295). For gems depicting the man-faced bull alone we have no known provenances, attributed by Isler as follows: one Ionian (ibid., no. 296), four Magna Graecian (ibid., no. 297-300), and six Etruscan (ibid., no. 301-305).

172 Ibid., no. 115.

173 According to Isler, the unique known example would be the Boston piece.

174 The other Red Figure vases of known provenance are two specimens found in Etruria (Cerveteri, dated 510 BC, H.P. Isler, *Acheloos*, no.84; and Vulci, dated 470 BC, ibid., no.87).

175 Emma Aston recognized the same interesting phenomenon: 'In terms of location and distribution of worship, Acheloos presents us with an interesting dichotomy. On the one hand, as a deity he seems unusually localised: he is the god of the river Acheloos wich runs between Akarnania and Aitolia in northern Greece. At the same time, some of the earliest representations of Acheloos on his own come from outside 'Greece proper' and far away from Akarnania: from Asia Minor and the western Greek world, south Italy and Sicily. Only rather later do we find widespread worship in Greece… How the two processes really relate is extremely uncertain' (E. Aston, *Mixanthropoi. Animal-human hybrid deities in Greek religion.* Kernos Supplement 23 (Liège, 2011), 79).

176 This general topic of Archaic Etruria in its relation to Greek pottery has already been discussed in: V. Belleli, 'Ceramiche e bronzi laconici nel Mediterraneo arcaico: osservazioni su un libro recente da una prospettiva occidentale,' in *Archeologia Classica*, Vol. LXII (Rome: Bretschneider, 2011), 362. M. De Cesare's thoughts on the matter of

specific traditions of local cults and beliefs concerning the afterlife, many of which are discussed above. Therefore, the man-faced bulls of the Etruscan world were certainly not mere copies of Greek man-faced bulls, and one could argue that the Etruscan adoption of man-faced bull iconography to represent Acheloios preceeded that of the Greeks, and played an important role in the Classical Greek development.[177]

Water Deity

In terms of the Greek man-faced bull, as Acheloios, he is first and foremost a water deity- the deity of all fresh water, in fact. The origins of this notion stem from Homer,[178] but it is also demonstrated insofar as the poets operative during the time man-faced bull iconography flourished in Greek culture all refer to fresh water as Ἀχελώϊος: Sophocles (c. 497 to 405 BC),[179] Euripides (c. 480 to 406 BC),[180] Aristophones (c. 446 to 386 BC),[181] Achaeus (born c. 484 BC),[182] and Ephorius (c. 400 to 330 BC),[183] who claims the tradition stems from Dodonean rituals.[184] Even later authors, such as Virgil,[185] continue to describe fresh water this way. Hesiod,[186] on the contrary, simply says Acheloios is the son of Okeanos[187] and is the eldest and greatest of all 3000 river gods, but not necessarily their source. However, the manuscripts

Attic pottery found outside of Greece are also relevant: 'Indeed the context of production can not always give definite answers about the ideological intent behind the choices of themes, while sometimes more explicit data are provided by the contexts of use and fruition, which can in some cases even help to understand the motivations causing the spread of a particular subject and a particular figurative variant in the Attic artisanship' (M. De Cesare, 'Pittura vascolare e politica ad Atene e in Occidente: vecchie teorie e nuove riflessioni,' in *Arte-Potere. Forme artistiche, istituzioni, paradigmi interpretativi*, edited by M. Castiglione and A. Poggio (Milan: LED, 2012), 106). For Etruscan and Magna Graecian clients influencing Attic productions, not only for aesthetic reasons, but specifically in relation to the portrayed myths and symbolic interpretations underlying them, see: E. Mussini, 'La diffusione dell'iconografia di Acheloo in Magna Grecia e Sicilia. Tracce per l'individuazione di un culto,' 98-99, note 20.

177 On the problem of iconographic influences between mainland Greece and Italy and on the subject of the Etruscan, Italic and Sicilian clients influencing the iconographic choices of Attic and Ionian potters, see: E. Mugione, 'Problemi di trasmissioni iconografiche,' in *Miti della ceramica Attica in Occidente. Problemi di trasmissioni iconografiche nelle produzioni Italiote* (Taranto: Scorpione, 2000), 123-152; D. Paleothodoros, 'Commercial Networks in the Mediterranean and the Diffusion of Early Attic Red-figure Pottery (525-490 BCE),' in *Mediterranean Historical Review*, 22.2 (2007), 165-182; A. Rathje, 'Murlo, Images and Archaeology,' in *Etruscan Studies*, Vol. 10 (2007), 175-184; L. Cerchiai, 'Euphronios, Kleophrades, Brygos: circolazione e committenza della ceramica attica a figure rosse in Occidente,' in *Workshop di archeologia classica. Paesaggi, costruzioni, reperti* (Rome: Serra, 2008), 9-28; M.R. Ciuccarelli, 'Due nuovi balsamari greco-orientali da Cerveteri,' 181; G.M. Della Fina, *Artisti, committenti e fruitori in etruria tra VIII e V secolo a.C., Atti del XXI Convegno Internazionale di Studi sulla Storia e l'Archeologia dell'Etruria* (Rome: Quasar 2014); J. Boardman, 'Copies of Pottery: by and for Whom?,' in *Greek identity in the Western Mediterranean. Papers in honour of Brian Shefton*, Suppl. 'Mnemosyne,' edited by C. Lomas (2004), 149-162. Some direct citations are worthwhile: 'there were direct links between Attic potters and particular overseas markets for Greek wine pottery which influenced Attic potters or painters to produce material in particular styles for particular consumers' (D. Robinson and A. Wilson, 'Introduction: Maritime archaeology and the ancient economy,' in *Maritime Archaeology and Ancient Trade in the Mediterranean*, Vol. 6 (Oxford: Oxford Centre for Maritime Archaeology, 2011), 3); 'We must also recognise a conceptual issue, i.e. the attempts of the artists to visualise in a different way the eschatological hope of the customers' (M. Harari, 'The Imagery of the Etrusco-Faliscan Pantheon Between Architectural Sculpture and Vase-painting,' in *Material Aspects of Etruscan Religion: Proceedings of the International Colloquium, Leiden, May 29 and 30, 2008*, Suppl. 16, edited by L.B. van der Meer (Leuven, 2010), 90). The thoughts reflected in the aforementioned quotes are likely true for the Etruscan commision of work from Attic painters depicting the iconography of the man-faced bull.

178 Homer, *Iliad*, 21.194-197.

179 Sophocles, *Fragmenta*, 5.

180 Euripides, *Bacchae*, 625.

181 Aristophones, *Fragmenta*, 351.

182 Achaeus, *Athens*, 4.9.

183 Ephorius, *FGrH* 70, F 20.

184 G.B. D'Alessio, 'Textual Fluctuations,' 20.

185 Virgil, *Georgics*, 1.9.

186 Hesiod, *Theogony*, 367.

187 J. Rudhardt discussed the important role that water deities played in all the major Greek cosmogonies since the Archaic period (J.Rudhardt, *Le thème de l'eau primordiale dans la mythologie grecque* (Bern, 1971)). The divine nature of waterways is already apparent in the passage of Hesiod, who warns the reader never to cross a river without first saying a prayer to the flowing waters, and he even warns that 'Gods hate those who cross a river with their hands still stained with evil' (Hesiod, *Works and Days*, 737 ff). As described by Homer and Hesiod, as well as in other later sources, the primordial water is first and foremost a passage, a symbol of transition from one place to another (M.A. Beaulieu, 'The Sea as a Two-Way Passage between Life and Death in Greek Mythology,' Doctoral Dissertation, The University of Texas (Austin, 2008), 11.) In fact, early Greek cosmogonic myths represent Pontus as a navigable path marking the boundary between distant countries (Ibid). Okeanos, on the other hand, is described as a great fresh-water stream encircling the earth (Aeschylus, *Prometheus*, 139ff), thus marking the boundary between the world of the living and that of the dead (M.A. Beaulieu, 'The Sea as a Two-Way Passage,' 11). In this pre-Olympian conception, Okeanos is the gateway to a region of plenty in which the gods reside, and where humans spend the afterlife. Therefore he represents the boundary between life and death and between men and gods (Ibid.). Okeanos' liminal chthonic quality is also seen in his origins, as he is described by Hesiod as the son of Gaia and Uranus (Hesiod, *Theogony*, 133). Beaulieu pointed out that in Greek literature, sailing beyond Okeanus is equivalent to descending into Hades, essentially dying. Some examples: Odysseus had to cross Okeanos to reach Hades. The dead suitors follow Hermes above the water of Okeanos. Herakles does the same to reach the Island of the Hesperides. Those voyages bring the heroes to the land of the dead and back, symbolizing their victory over mortality (M.A. Beaulieu, 'The Sea as a Two-Way Passage,' 14-15 and bibliography). This suggests that the Archaic Greek Okeanos embodied elements of the chthonic-funerary dimension seen in the archaic man-faced bull tradition, at least as it appeared in the Etruscan world. This dimension is present in the early Greek Acheloios, too, but is less distinct, as he is more clearly associated with other liminal qualities related to the civic identity of living people. Ultimately, it seems clear that in the archaic Greek traditions a conflation between the representations of Okeanos and Acheloios occurred, as seen in Euripides, who mentions 'Okeanus taurokranos' (Euripedes, *Orestes*, 1377), or in the iconographical overlapping of common features as bearded, horned heads, and serpent-fish appearance (Cf. Attic Black Figure Dinos, dated to the first quarter of 6th century BC, British Museum no.1971.11-1.1). For the iconography of Okeanus, see also: J.Rudhardt, *Le thème de l'eau primordiale dans la mythologie grecque*, 77ff. The horns of Okeanos are sometimes represented as crab-claws, especially in later Roman art. Although geographically distant, the iconography of Okeanos is similar to that seen on a tattoo showing the forepart of a bearded long-haired man-faced hoofed creature with claw-like horns, discovered on a well-preserved body from a burial at Altai in Siberia, dated from the 5th to 4th century BC, and attributed to a chieftan of Pazyryk, a culture who had strong ties with Scythian groups located further west (N. Ranieri, *Archeologia della Morte* (Rome: Carocci, 2011), 42-43, fig. 2). Despite these similarities, in the *Derveni Papyrus*, as discussed on the following page, Okeanus is equated with air and Zeus.

recording Hesiod are late, with the earliest being c. 1st century AD.[188]

Part of the reason for following the (presumably) earliest Homeric tradition is the idea that Acheloios might be the origin of all water, as some recent publications indicate. Fowler,[189] following D'Alessio's original argument,[190] states that Akousilaos (6th century BC) knew of a text lacking Homer *Il.*.21.195, an omission which places emphasis on Acheloios as the original source and god of all water, not Okeanos, as Hesiod believed. In fact, 'the scholia on these lines (5.165-70 Erbse) reveal that Zenodotos (280 BC) athetized l. 195, and that the pre-Alexandrian critic Megakleides (c. 350 BC) did not have it in his text.'[191] In addition, Seleukos (*P.Oxy*, 0221, IX, 8-11) equates Acheloios and Okeanos, and Wilamowitz, attributing the lines to Panyassis (*fr.*, 13), suggests Acheloios was the original god.[192] Moreover, in the *Derveni Papyrus* (xxiii), the oldest surviving Greek manuscript (c. 350 BC), Zeus creates Acheloios independently of Okeanos, also contrary to the tradition of Hesiod.[193] In fact, Okeanus is equated with air and Zeus in that document.[194]

Additionally, we must consider the Orphic ἱερὸς λόγος (also exhibited in xxiii of the *Derveni*)[195] in which we see the expression ἶνας...Ἀχελωίου, probably later abbreviated as ἶς Ἀχελωίου,[196] which West,[197] Laks and Most,[198] and most recently Janko[199] and D'Alessio,[200] take to mean 'the sinews...of Acheloios,' in reference to the world's waterways.[201] As D'Alessio states, 'Both for the Greek poet of this age and for his public, the words ἶνας...Ἀχελωίου would unavoidably evoke the meaning 'the sinews of Acheloios'.[202] Herein there might also be an explanation of the pervasive use of IΣ as a control mark placed beneath or behind the man-faced bull on Campanian coinage (**Fig. 65**). In fact, IΣ is only present with the man-faced bull, never appearing on the obverse or on any other types of Campanian coinage. It is also important to note that Hesiod is said to have despised mercenaries,[203] so perhaps lowering the status of a god they found particularly important was deliberate on his part. Thus, not only was Acheloios the source of all fresh water in the early Homeric tradition, but very likely the original god of all water.

Further evidence to this effect is provided by ancient sources, in which the name Acheloios was not strictly and exclusively related to the Akarnanian River (modern Aspropotamos), but at least six different rivers.[204] There appears to be only one other river that still carries the original name Acheloios, located in modern Bulgaria.[205] Even Homer recorded the location of the Acheloios River as being in Lydia, saying it was near mount Sipylos.[206] This geographic data supports the hypothesis that originally Acheloios is described as the primal source of fresh-water, and was only afterwards applied to the Akarnanian river by Greek mythographical traditions.

Outside of the general water association, further iconographic and geographical evidence of fluvial connotations is abundant: for instance, the appearance of the man-faced bull on the Launderer's Relief (launderers were men and women who worked near or in the river);[207] the votive relief from Eleusis is pierced in the center for use as a water spout;[208] Caruso Cave at *Lokroi Epizephyroi* was originally a water source for the locals, and has many herms featuring man-faced bulls (**Fig. 66**);[209] and the Xenokrateia relief depicting the man-faced bull

188 Hesiod, F. Solmsen, R. Merkelbach, and M. L. West, *Hesiodi Theogonia; Opera et dies; Scvtvm* (Oxonii: Clarendon, 1990), ix-xxiii.
189 R.L. Fowler, *Early Greek Mythography*, 2 (Oxford: UP, 2013).
190 G.B. D'Alessio, 'Textual Fluctuations,' 20.
191 R.L. Fowler, *Early Greek Mythography*, 12.
192 Ibid. B. P. Grenfell and A. S. Hunt, *P.Oxy.II 0221. Scholia on Iliad XXI* (London, 1899).
193 Ibid.
194 It is worthwhile to quote Column XXIII: 'This verse has been made misleading and it is unclear to many, but to those who understand correctly it is quite clear that Ocean is the air and the air is Zeus. It is not the case that one Zeus contrived another Zeus but the same one (contrived) for himself great strength. But those who do not understand think that Ocean is a river because he added 'broadly flowing'. But he indicates his intention in current and customary expressions. For they say that the very powerful among men 'flowed great'. And the next verse, '...the sinews of silver-eddying Achelous.' to the water... the name Achelous...and the sinews...is the...each...' (A. Laks and G. Most, 'A Translation of the Derveni Papyrus,' in *Studies on the Derveni Papyrus*, 20).
195 This phrase is nearly identical to the *London Papyrus*. See G.B. D'Alessio, 'Textual Fluctuations,' 20-1 for discussion.
196 G.B. D'Alessio, 'Textual Fluctuations,' 23-4.
197 M.L. West, *The Orphic Poems* (Oxford: Clarendon Press, 1983).
198 A. Laks, and G.W. Most, 'A Translation of the Derveni Papyrus,' in *Studies on the Derveni Papyrus*; edited by A. Laks and G.W. Most (Oxford: Clarendon Press, 1997).
199 R. Janko, 'The Derveni Papyrus: an interim text,' *ZPE*, 141 (2002), 47. Janko changed his opinion, originally arguing for 'strength' rather than 'sinew'.
200 G.B. D'Alessio, 'Textual Fluctuations,' 24.
201 Ibid., 23-24.

202 Ibid., 24. D'Alessio indicates there was probably a semantic overlap in which 'strength of Acheloios' is also meant.
203 J.R. Hale, 'Not Patriots, Not Farmers, Not Amateurs: Greek Soldiers of Fortune and the Origins of Hoplite Warfare,' 189.
204 E. Mussini, 'La diffusione dell'iconografia di Acheloo in Magna Grecia e Sicilia. Tracce per l'individuazione di un culto,' 92 and bibliography.
205 E.Golovinski, 'Ахелой,' in Българска енциклопедия А-Я, БАН (Труд, Сирма, 2002), 917.
206 Homer, *Iliad*, 24.616
207 J. Larson, *Greek Nymphs: Myth, Cult, Lore*, 128-129, fig. 4.1.
208 Ibid., 249, fig. 5.12. National Archaeological Museum, Athens.
209 Ibid. 251-255, fig. 5.15. Museo di Reggio Calabria. For discussion see also E. Mussini, 'La diffusione dell'iconografia di Acheloo in Magna Grecia e Sicilia. Tracce per l'individuazione di un culto,' 103-104. She indicates that the sanctuary was active since the 6th century BC. For the most recent dating of the triple herms, see: G. Genovese, *I santuari rurali della Calabria Greca* (Rome: Bretschneider: 1999).The earliest triple herms with man-faced bulls found at the cave are dated to the 5th century BC, not the 4th, as previously believed (ibid., 105). The cults in the cave are attested since the early 6th century BC, indicated by the discovery of statuettes of reclining females which are also attested in Sicily (Gela, Akragas and Morgantina), Magna Graecia (Rhegion, Taras), Etruria (Capua), Cirenaica, and Asia Minor, but no comparisons are reported for mainland Greece (ibid., 106).The cult of the man-faced bull exhibited on triple herms was also attested by subsequent excavations in other sites of the area of Lokris. In fact, herms with nymphs and bearded man-faced bulls have been discovered in a cave

from New Phaleron occupied a spot adjacent to a river.[210] Moreover, on certain Greek coinage of Italy, Sicily and Asia Minor the man-faced bull is depicted above water or with water flowing from his mouth.[211] Kernoi, askoi, and situla fittings found in western sites are other strong indications of water-funerary associations.[212] Altogether, the various items and locations of shrines indicate the use of man-faced bull iconography is intimately related to ritual practices involving water in the Greek world, starting in the late 5th century BC.

Secondary Qualities

There are some secondary qualities stemming from the primary water-deity dimesion of the man-faced bull. As we already pointed out, some of these are more clearly seen in the western areas, especially the apotropaic and funerary dimensions, while other dimensions are shared by both Etruscan and Greek cultures, like the oracular quality and the liminal qualities related to water cults. Other qualities, like the identity dimension, seem more strictly linked to the Greek traditions. It is likely that these different 'nuances' of the man-faced bull mythos result from territorial specificities linked to pre-existing local traditions.

Oracular Dimension

One very interesting secondary quality is the man-faced bull's association with oracular activity. The most important indication of the Greek oracular dimension comes from Ephorus. He claims that Acheloios is worshipped as the god of all water precisely because the oracle of Dodona instructs patrons to offer sacrifices to him, in almost all cases.[213] This is confirmed by a scholiast on Homer *Il.* 24.616.[214] What is more, Herodotus informs us that the oracle at Dodona has its origins in the eastern Mediterranean, and much like man-faced bull iconography, was transferred west by Phoenicians who kidnapped the oracle from Thebes.[215] This eastern influence on the oracular dimension of Acheloios is also attested in Etruria, as seen above. Further indications of the man-faced bull's oracular involvement are the Greek coins from Cyprus that pair the man-faced bull with an astragalos,[216] and there are even examples of astragaloi found in caves of the nymphs in which the cult of Acheloios is also attested (the case of Lokris in particular is discussed at the end of this chapter).[217]

Individual and Civic Identity

The most important secondary quality that stems from the primary identification as the god of fresh water, and one that takes precedence in Greek culture in particular, has to do with individual and civic identity. In Greek culture it is rivers, not towns or cities, that are associated with the birthplace of a man, and often heroes are born beside rivers, which is an important aspect of their loyalty and identity.[218] As Evy Håland explains, 'just as initiation is about the allocation of civic identity and the perpetuation of the community, rivers and springs frequently figure in the rites and mythology that mark rites of passage.'[219] In fact, in the koureion ritual youths dedicated a lock of hair to the river upon reaching maturity.[220] This was seen as a way of paying homage to the river god for ensuring their proper growth and development.[221] For boys, it meant initiation as citizens and warriors; for girls, it meant fertility in married life.[222] An archaeological remnant of such practices in relation to the man-faced bull is the aforementioned Xenokrateia relief, which contains a specific dedication to the gods (including the man-faced bull) for the sake of her son Xeniades' education. Ritual baths were also performed for purifying purposes[223] before the consummation of marriage and the birth of a child.[224]

at Contrada Imperatore at Portiglia and in a cave at the site of Galatro (ibid., 108).

210 J. Larson, *Greek Nymphs: Myth, Cult, Lore*, 131.

211 Neapolis (Fig. 163); Alontion (MSP I, 21-3); Mylai (MSP I, 46).

212 Askoi from Spain (**Fig. 67**, of Ionian manufacture) and France dated to the mid 6th century BC (H.P. Isler, *Acheloos*, no.123-124); a kernos from an Italic workshop of Lavinium, dated to the 5th century BC; a kernos from Tarentum, dated to the 2nd century BC, BM item n.1849,1122.4.

213 Ephorus, *FgrH* 70, F20; Macrobius, *Saturnalia*, v.18. 6 *sqq*.

214 Pausanias, 'Commentary on book 1: Attica. Appendix: The pre-Persian temple on the Acropolis,' in *Description of Greece*, translated by Sir James George Frazer (MacMillan, 1898), 527.

215 Herodotus, *Histories*, 2.54-57.

216 H.P. Isler, *Acheloos*, no.319. Astragaloi were used in divinatory rites and as fortune-telling objects during rituals of passage performed by the youth in caves. Since the Archaic Period nymphs were believed to have the power to inspire oracular powers in people seized by them, the so-called *nympholepts* (J. Larson, *Ancient Greek Cults: A Guide* (London: Routledge, 2007), 154).

217 P. Amandry, 'Astragalo,' in *Enciclopedia dell'Arte Antica, Secondo Supplemento, 1971-1994* (Rome, 1994), 492-494.

218 J. Larson, *Greek Nymphs*, 98. See also E.J. Håland, 'Take, Skamandros, My Virginity,' 109-148; K. Dowden, *Death and the Maiden: Girls' Initiation Rites in Greek Mythology* (London, 1989), 123; F.T. van Straten, 'Gifts for the Gods,' in *Faith, Hope and Worship: Aspects of Religious Mentality in the Ancient World*, edited by Hendrik S. Versnel (Leiden, 1981), 90-91; Louis Gernet, *The Anthropology of Ancient Greece*, trans. Johan Hamilton and Blaise Nagy (Baltimore, 1981), 22-23, 29, 31, 154.

219 E.J. Håland, 'Take, Skamandros, My Virginity,' 125.

220 There is even a marble relief depicting such hair offerings, see E.J. Håland, 'Take, Skamandros, My Virginity,' 126, Fig. 6, British Museum, no. 798.

221 J. Larson, *Greek Nymphs: Myth, Cult, Lore*, 98.

222 E.J. Håland, 'Take, Skamandros, My Virginity,' 125.

223 For the purifying quality of Acheloios it is worth mentioning the Greek myth in which he purified Alcmaeon (Pausanias, *Hellados Periegesis*, 8.24.9). Another trace of the purifying qualities of Acheloios, in relation to sexual vigor and animal wildness, is pointed out in Werner's analysis of Plato's *Phaedrus* (D.S. Werner, *Myth and Philosophy in Plato's Phaedrus* (Cambridge: University Press, 2012), 22).

224 J. Larson, *Greek Nymphs*, 100. There are gutti with relief depictions of man-faced bull heads dated to the 4th centuy BC, listed in: Fernando Gilotta, *Gutti e Askoi a rilievo Italioti ed Etruschi* (Rome: Bretschneider, 1985), fig.1 (Campani); fig.93 (Northen Apulia); fig.94 (Etruscan). Gutti were a particular class of pottery, made to slowly drip liquid during rituals, and even in everyday life to feed infants. They are also often found in childrens' graves (V. Bologa, 'Gutti (biberoane) romane din sticlă,' in *Omagiu lui Constantin Daicoviciu cu prilejul împlinirii a 60 de ani* (Bucharest, 1960), 55-61).

Further evidence of rites of pre-nuptial lustratio involving water are demonstrated in the painted ware from Nola and the Caruso Cave at Lokris.[225] Ultimately, these pre-nuptial rites of lustratio are a paradigmatic example of the dimension of 'passage' attributed to water. By those rites, women performed the symbolic, one-way transformation from *parthenos* to *gynê,* separating them forever from their families, and undergoing a symbolic death that allowed them, by entering in contact with the divine, to change their social status as they were now ready for marriage. The same is true for young males, during those rites they died as children and were reborn as men, ready to take weapons and defend their polis. Thus, as a result of this symbolic death and subsequent return to life, youths underwent their transition to adulthood and returned to their communities as proper citizens.[226]

The man-faced bull on many coins of Magna Graecia and Sicily served as a symbol of civic identity since the late 6th century BC. It symbolized not only the strength and power of rulers, but also that of the poleis.[227] Akarnania, however, is perhaps the best indication of the use of the iconography as a symbol of civic identity. The obvious reason for this is that the Acheloios River flows through the area, seperating it from the Aetolians to the east (who never employed the iconography). But more importantly, using a symbol associated with individual identity as the civic emblem, represents the binding of an individual to the community. This is what Håland referred to in the above quote: the rites of passage associated with an individual are precisely those that incorporate the individual into the community. The Akarnanian Federation, in which multiple cities were alligned under a single force, serves as a macrocosm for this phenomenon: just as the individual is to the city, so the city is to the Federation.

Rebirth

The man-faced bull on Greek coinage also serves as a symbol of rebirth, which is implicit with any chthonic, liminal deity. In fact, often times the man-faced bull appears on the coinage of areas in which mercenaries either took over a town or established a new town: the Kersini, the Sileraians, and Halykiai, among others.[228] In these cases the mercenaries are finding rebirth after a life on the battle field, and paying homage to the man-faced bull for protecting them on said battle fields. There are also examples of man-faced bull countermarks from Gela, and others on the coinage of Segesta (but applied at Iaitos), probably connected to the rebirth of the two cities (for Gela, after its destruction by Carthage in the last decade of 5th century BC, for instance). Moreover, in Tauromenion, which was a colony established after the destruction of Naxos, the man-faced bull appears on its coinage. Naturally, this characteristic of rebirth is certainly intertwined with the aforementioned associations of birth and death rituals, but it is also an important indication of the man-faced bull's association with civic identity. Megara Hyblaia should also be added to the list, because they produced only one coin type[229] and did so just after the refoundation of the city as part of the policies of Timoleon, the Corinthian general.[230]

Rural God

In terms of distributive demographics, aside from his appearance on the coinage of some major cities, the Greek man-faced bull appears to be a figure predominantly worshipped in the countryside, and not within the walls of cities as part of the official pantheon. Isler mentions the importance of water for rural people, not simply as a natural element, but for its vital necessity in a farmer's life. Thus, Acheloios was revered as the god who gives the people water and with it, life.[231] The places in which the Greek cult is attested fall into the broad category of 'suburban' sanctuaries, which operate as borders, essentially meeting places between Greeks and natives especially in western colonial areas. Scholarly debate has often addressed the meaning and origin of such categories of sanctuaries,[232] linked both to the polis which the territory belonged, and to factors extraneous

---

[225] A good synthesis of this liminal quality of the man-faced bull is seen on the famous amphora from Nola (H.P. Isler, *Acheloos*, no.5) showing Eros crowning a young female riding a man-faced bull who walks towards a loutherion, the symbol of lustratio. The Nolan piece is of great importance, as the iconographical scheme has no comparisons in Greek art. The association of the man-faced bull with the loutherion is also visible on the triple herms from Caruso Cave at Lokris (H.P. Isler, *Acheloos*, no. 206)

[226] M. Beaulieu 'The Sea as a Two-Way Passage between Life and Death in Greek Mythology,' 55.

[227] The notion of identity for Greek communities is probably also related to the common etymological bases of Acheloios and Achaeans, discussed in Chapter 7 of this book. Interestingly, even in the Persian world there are traces of similar etymological associations, as *achl-achal* is the Tajik word for 'people' (A. E. Santangelo, *Radici Scite degli Etruschi* (Sabaini: Milano, 2002), 18). Following Santangelo's etymological study it is likely that Persians were named *Achaemenids* based on this same root. Thus, the same Tajik derivation is seen in the Etruscan word *acale-thur,* meaning 'born, son,' given by Santangelo among other etymological evidence concerning the Near Eastern origins of Etruscans (ibid.). This civic-identity connotation is somewhat reminiscent of earlier Mesopotamian traditions, in which some cities were compared to bulls. As reported by R.M. van Dijk, the Mesopotamian text *Enmerkar and the Lord of Aratta* describes the city of Uruk as a 'majestic bull bearing vigour and great awesome splendour' (R.M. Van Dijk, 'The Motif of the Bull,' 108).

[228] The iconography also symbolizes renewal and rebirth at a number of other mints: Abakainon, Alontion, Katane, etc.

[229] Silver litra with Demeter/man-faced bull, minted 339/8 to 330 BC (SNG ANS (4) no. 287).

[230] See below, pg. 123, for discussion of the *symmachia* of Timoleon.

[231] H.P. Isler, *Acheloos*, 112. Another argument Isler mentions for identifying Acheloios as a rural deity is the Dionysian connotations of his cult (H.P. Isler, *Acheloos*, 113ff).

[232] For an extensive bibliography, see: F. Veronese, *Lo spazio e la dimensione del sacro. Santuari e territorio nella Sicilia arcaica* (Padova, 2006), 29-34.

to it, such as the pre-existing indigenous cults,[233] or cults imported by pre-colonial visitors.[234]

An important characteristic for almost all contexts examined for both Magna Graecia and mainland Greece are the environmental features such as water and caves.[235] It is also likely that the rural nature of man-faced bull worship stems in part from the early incorporation of the iconography by mercenaries, many of whom likely resided in such areas, as already demonstrated. Moreover, the basic agricultural connotations of man-faced bull iconography find a natural fit in agrarian, rural areas of the Greek cultural world. This rural setting is well illustrated in Plato's *Phaedrus*, for example, in which Socrates and his interlocutor find the shrine of Acheloios outside the city walls on the bank of a river.[236] The earliest known Greek marble reliefs on which the forepart of a man-faced bull appears are almost contemporary to Plato's work, from the rural sanctuary of the river god Kephisos, in New Phaleron.[237] As Larson recounts, 'Kallirhoë and the shrine of the nymphs and Achelous on the Ilissos are part of a group of shrines and cults that could be said to exist on the margin of the old city, in a quasi-rural setting where one would expect to find nymphs.'[238]

There are additional examples of sites that also support this notion. The Launderer's Relief depicts the man-faced bull[239] and comes from an area known as the Agrai (the fields).[240] There is also a relief from Parsos above the entry to a rural quarry, where the mask of the man-faced bull occupies a central position surrounded by other gods.[241] Another relief, from a cave near Eleusis, prominently depicts the head of the man-faced bull.[242] For south Italy the most relevant examples are from Caruso Cave at *Locri Epifiziri*, where many man-faced bulls are found, and where the cult operating at the cave was 'initially of a rural, agrarian character.'[243] Lokris also offers various connections between the man-faced bull and Kybele, indicative of eastern influence.[244]

Nymph Pairing

The Greek man-faced bull's apotropaic nature is also apparent in the many depictions of a winged, female figure crowning or accompanying him. As briefly mentioned in the Near East section, Christian European cherubs have been linked to early Near Eastern traditions of winged figures, including the man-faced bull, as a protector against evil: 'The 'cherubim' who 'stood on the right side of the house when the man went in' and by the throne of God in Ezekiel 10:14 are known in Akkadian as *kurību*, a generic term meaning 'blessed' which refers to the winged, guardian spirits of the kinds that stood to left and right of monumental entrances at Assyrian courts.'[245] The Greek man-faced bull, appearing between the winged man-faced bulls

[233] The problem was already discussed by Ciaceri in 1927 (E. Ciaceri, *Storia della Magna Grecia, Vol. II. La grande civiltà del Mezzogiorno d'Italia* (Rome, 1927), 20-23). Some examples from Magna Graecia are discussed in: M. Barbanera, 'Altre presenze. Stranieri nei luoghi di culto in Magna Grecia,' in *Stranieri e non cittadini nei santuari greci. Atti del Convegno Internazionale*, edited by A. Naso (Firenze: Le Monnier, 2006), 364-375. For Sicily: A. Brelich, 'La religione greca in Sicilia,' in *Kokalos*, 10-11 (1964-1965), 35-62. The evidence already discussed confirms that Archaic cultural traditions of natives of Sicily and Italy played an important role in the later encoding of the cult and myth of the Greek Acheloios.

[234] G. Pugliese Carratelli, 'I santuari extramurani,' in *Magna Grecia, III. Vita religiosa e cultura letteraria, filosofica e scientifica*, edited by G.P. Carratelli (Milan, 1988), 149-158.

[235] One must also consider that water and caves carry significant chthonic connotations, and the various caves in which the man-faced bull was worshipped along with nymphs are another indication of his importance as a chthonic deity: Caruso Cave, the Parian quarry, and the cave at Eleusis, for example (J. Larson, *Greek Nymphs*, 179-180, 251-257, 248-249). This translates well into the funerary ritual functions of the man-faced bull, who was deeply embedded in such rituals throughout the ancient Mediterranean, expecially west of Greece proper.

[236] Plato, *Phaedrus*, 230.

[237] Xenokrateia relief, dated around the mid 5th century BC (H.P. Isler, 'Acheloos,' in *LIMC*, 197; J. Larson, *Greek Nymphs*, 131). Other known Greek reliefs are dated from 410 BC on (H.P. Isler, 'Acheloos,' in *LIMC*, 166-196).

[238] J. Larson, *Greek Nymphs*, 128. Caruso Cave is also outside the city (ibid., 251).

[239] Some authors have recently questioned the importance of Acheloios in the Attic cultic practices, on the basis of the iconographic analysis of the schemes depicted on marble reliefs, pointing out that 'a differentiation is to be made between minor and mainly decorative figures such as the Satyrs, Silenos, Acheloos, and the Kouretes, and the main addressees of worship in these caves, mainly the Nymphs and to a lesser degree Pan. The marginal depiction on the votive reliefs, the lesser number of their representations among the clay votive offerings, and mainly their rare mentions in the written dedications, can be taken as signs of a less common worship' (K. Sporn, 'Mapping Greek Sacred Caves: Sources, Features, Cults' in *Stable Places and Changing Perceptions: Cave Archaeology in Greece*, edited by F. Mavridis and J. Tae Jensen (Oxford: Archaeopress, 2013), 203). Following Sporn's line of thought we should suppose that the cult of the man-faced bull was much stronger in Magna Graecia, as he occupies a prominent role in the representations discovered at Caruso Cave, represented in full-body at the center of the field, and even on pedestals. In terms of Sicily, the cult of the man-faced bull is clearly attested in several examples: From the sanctuary of Demeter at Katane we know of a hand-modeled plastic terracotta mask of the man-faced bull (E. Mussini, 'La diffusione dell'iconografia di Acheloo in Magna Grecia e Sicilia. Tracce per l'individuazione di un culto,' 108, no.47). At Akragas, a matrix for a mask of the man-faced bull was found at excavations of the workshop of an artisan, placed close to the perimeter walls of the sanctuary of the chthonic deities and indicating local production for the worship of the man-faced bull (E. Mussini, 'La diffusione dell'iconografia di Acheloo in Magna Grecia e Sicilia. Tracce per l'individuazione di un culto,' 108, no.48). For other traces of the cult in Sicily, see H.P. Isler, 'Acheloos,' in *LIMC*, no. 12 and no. 220, and also H.P. Isler, *Acheloos*, no. 179. Pre-Greek evidence published by Colonna and mentioned by Lagona are discussed above. Evidence for a cult of the man-faced bull are attested even on the small island of Lipara (E. Mussini, 'La diffusione dell'iconografia di Acheloo in Magna Grecia e Sicilia. Tracce per l'individuazione di un culto,' 109 and bibliography in note 51).

[240] J. Larson, *Greek Nymphs*, 128.

[241] Ibid., 179-180, fig. 4.11.

[242] Ibid., 248-249, fig. 5.12.

[243] Ibid., 251.

[244] For a votive dedication to Kybele from Contrada Centocamere at Lokris, see G. Genovese, *I santuari rurali Calabria Greca*, Pl. 85, fig. 2. For statuettes of Kybele discovered at Caruso Cave, see ibid., 107.

[245] S. Dalley, 'The Influence of Mesopotamia upon Israel and the Bible,' in *The Legacy of Mesopotamia*, edited by S. Dalley (Oxford: Oxford University Press, 1998), 57-83.

and much later cherubs, seems a reasonable link in this chain insofar as both elements, the winged 'angel' and the man-faced bull, appear together. In fact, Grazia Salamone argues that many winged female figures appearing in Sicily and Magna Graecia are nymphs and not Nike,[246] just as Gabrici had previously argued.[247] Much like the origin and development of man-faced bull iconography, Salmone traces the origins of such winged nymphs, usually carrying wreaths, to Cypriot and Near Eastern prototypes **(Fig. 68)**. Following her rationale, which is very convincing, on Neapolitan coinage it is not Nike crowning the man-faced bull but a winged nymph, perhaps Parthenope herself. This alternative is very appealing, as the rationale for including Nike has always been troublesome (as Taylor asks, why have 'Victory' crowining the loser of an epic fight?).[248]

The same identification would apply to other areas beyond Campania pairing a winged female figure with the man-faced bull, like the mysterious Mamar of Sicily.[249] On a Campanian amphora from Nola the man-faced bull appears to be surrounded by nymphs, one of them winged and holding a crown.[250] If indeed the winged figure crowning the man-faced bull is a nymph, this also further reinforces the healing properties of water and its association with Acheloios and the nymphs. There are also wing-shaped ears depicted on Acheloios on some coins of Akarnania **(Fig. 69)**. These wings are clearly similar to those seen on the winged figure crowning the man-faced bull on Campanian coinage, and likely stem from the early winged man-faced bulls instrumental in the transference of the iconography from East to West, as seen in the aforementioned Etruscan situla and helmet fittings. Thus, the wings on the figures who crown or accompany the man-faced bull need not necessarily indicate Nike, particularly because his natural pairing, especially in Etruria, Magna Graecia, and Sicily, is with nymphs.

Herakles and the Man-Faced Bull

Another important aspect of the Greek man-faced bull is his association with Herakles, with whom he is often depicted,[251] and the accompanying notion of fertility and abundance. In fact, apart from the Attic votive reliefs and on coinage, the fight with Herakles is how the man-faced bull is most frequently represented in the Greek world. To recap, in the Greek myth Herakles is described as having torn Acheloios' horn from his head, and in order to get the horn back, Acheloios must give Herakles the horn of Amalthea.[252] Thus is born the tradition of the cornucopia, a nearly universal symbol of plenty that survives up to the present day.[253] In other traditions it is Acheloios' own horn that becomes the cornucopia.[254]

[246] Cf. G. Salamone, *'Una' e 'molteplice'. La ninfa eponima di città, Iconografie monetali e semantica* (Reggio Calabria: Falzea 2013).

[247] E. Gabrici, *Problemi di Numismatica Greca*, 111-120. See the catalog section for Neapolis for further discussion.

[248] R. Taylor, 'The Early Coinage of Neapolis,' 3.

[249] See catalog entry for the Mamar. See also a coin from Gela (G.K. Jenkins, *The Coinage of Gela*, Group V, no. 371) in which a nymph labeled ΣΟΣΙΓΟΛΙΣ crowns the man-faced bull with a wreath, demonstrating that Nike does not hold exclusive rights to the practice. Isler, on the other hand, argued the inscription means ‹savior of the city,› claiming the type was issued after the city was resqued from serious danger, perhaps an epidemic (H.P. Isler, *Acheloos*, 85).

[250] H.P. Isler, 'Acheloos,' in *LIMC*, no. 5.

[251] H.P. Isler, 'Acheloos,' in *LIMC*, no. 214-263.

[252] Anakreon, *PMG*, 361, Phokylides, *Fragmenta*, 7; Archilocus, *Fragmenta*, 287; Pindar, *Fragmenta*, 249a; Sophocles, *Trachiniae*, 9-26.

[253] Some comedians also mention the horn: Kratinus, *Fragmenta*, 261; Aristophones, *Fragmenta*, 707; Philemon, *Fragmenta*, 68; Antiphanes, *Fragmenta*, 108; Menander, *Fragmenta*, 838.6.

[254] Diodorus Siculus, *The Library of History*, 4.35.3-4; Strabo, *Geographica*, 10.2.19; Ovid, *Metamorphosis*, 9.1-88; Hyginus, *Fabulae*, 31.7. An interesting aspect of the liminal qualities of Acheloios is seen in the iconography of a bronze statuette representing Acheloios as a 'peplophoros,' holding a cornucopia and wearing women's clothing (H.P. Isler, 'Acheloos,' in *LIMC*, no.77). The piece, dated to the second quarter of the 5th century BC, was discovered in 1909 at Oichalia in Euboia. The god's ambivalent, liminal nature is emphasized through cross-dressing. Mireille Lee argues that cross-dressing can be interpreted 'as emphasizing the benevolent side of his character, which is also suggested by the cornucopia, a symbol of fertility. In this way, the destructive capacities of the river are counterbalanced by its life-giving aspects' (M. Lee, 'Acheloos Peplophoros,' 323). Taylor's interpretation is also appealing, 'I see it in starker terms, as an adjunct to his emasculation in the loss to Herakles. The cornucopia, a material reminder of his personal injury commuted to an abundant sacrifice, is equally suggestive' (R. Taylor, 'River Raptures,' 36). Indeed, from a psychoanalytic point of view, the horn that is broken off by Herakles and magically filled with fruit and flowers is a representation of castration, understood in its symbolic quality of limit (one that brings abundance). The wild component of existence is thus limited by the culture of people, a limit that civilization imposes on primal instincts, emerging also in the rationalistic explanation given by ancient authors: the myth of Acheloios as a celebration of the regimentation of the water, the 'limit' of the banks against flooding. Even from an etymological point of view this 'limit' appears to be present in the name of the deity himself, discussed below (See pg. 92ff). Lee also speculates that the cross-dressed Acheloios embodies 'multiple categories of crisis: animal/human; destructive/ beneficient; virile/feminine.' Finally, it should be stressed that the existence of cross dressing is well documented in literature, in particular for the worshippers of Cybele (J.B. Rutter, 'The Three Phases of the Taurobolium,' in *Phoenix*, Vol.22, No.3 (Toronto, 1968), 226-249). The priests of the cult (named Gallus), inspired by Attis, castrated themselves and dressed as women in honor of the goddess. The self-castration occurred on altars adorned with bull protomes called *Taurobolium*. Cybele is a Near Eastern chthonic goddess linked to fertility, whose cult is still preserved today in Campania, where it remains stratified in the Marian cult of the Madonna Schiavona of Montevergine, worshipped by Italian transgender people (N. Sisci, 'La Candelora a Montevergine, Nuove tradizioni e antichi diritti,' Videodocumentario Prodotto da Univerisità degli Studi di Napoli Federico II, in collaborazione con Sof-Tel. (Naples, 2008); P. Valerio, N. Sisci, and S. Ferrara, 'The Myth of Cibele and Attis: New Theoretical Hypothesis about Transsexualism,' in *Childhood-Adulthood, Culture and Brain. The World Professional Association for Transgender Health, WPATH XXI Biennial Symposium* (Oslo, 2009), 82; P. Valerio, N. Sisci, S. Ferrara, and A. Cuomo, 'A Particular Expression of Gender Identity in Italian Southern Culture: The Neapolitan Femminielli,' in *Childhood-Adulthood, Culture and Brain. The World Professional Association for Transgender Health, WPATH 2009 XXI Biennial Symposium* (Oslo, 2009), 79). Interestingly, there is even a link between Cybele and the man-faced bull, as Acheloios is often represented together with the goddess on votive reliefs dedicated to her (H.P. Isler, *Acheloos*, no.32-34; H.P. Isler, 'Acheloos,' in *LIMC*, no. 199-201). We also have an ancient literary source giving additional substance to the association of Acheloios and Cybele/Attis, specifically in the chthonic dimension of the cult of the nymphs: 'But when he [Attis, Gallus] passed beyond this limit and came even to the lowest region, the myth said that he had descended

Either way, Strabo offers a reasonable explanation, by connecting the struggle of Herakles and Acheloios with the taming of rivers: the meanders of rivers are referred to as 'horns' in ancient Greek, and by eliminating these meanders, which often flood, one tames the river.[255] Therefore, the story of Herakles conquering Acheloios is essentially an allegory about mankind conquering rivers, and the results are success in agricultural endeavors.[256] Surprisingly, on only two coin types do Herakles and Acheloios (as a man-faced bull) appear together in the same scene: an early stater from Pharselis[257] and a bronze issue from an unknown location, found in and probably attributable to Thessaly, originally identified as depicting Thessalos grappling with a man-faced bull, but clearly the club/bow pairing on the obverse links the reverse figure to Herakles.[258] On some coins Herakles and the man-faced bull are paired on obverse and reverse, such as at Agyrion.[259]

Lokris

The iconography of Herakles and Acheloios also had a symbolic meaning linked to funerary ritual practices and afterlife beliefs, at least in the archaic western Greek world. This is indicated at the Necropolis of Contrada Lucifero at Lokris, in Bruttium, where there is also closely related evidence concerning the apotropaic-funerary use of astragaloi. Marcella Bagna Bagnasco and her team have discovered a strong presence of the man-faced bull in the traditions of the polis, much earlier than the aforementioned rites of passage for living citizens seen in the same area at Caruso Cave. In fact, at the sites of Contrada Centocamere and Contrada Lucifero, sixteen arulas[260] of terracotta[261] depicting the fight of Herakles and Acheloios have been found in graves and votive deposits.[262] Origlia identified two types chronologically differentiated: Group B Type I,[263] dated to the last quarter of the 6th century BC (**Fig. 70**), and Group B Type II,[264] dated to the second quarter of the 5th century BC.[265] There are no other examples of arulas depicting Herakles and Acheloios in the entire Greek world, so this appears to be a peculiar Lokrian tradition.[266]

The overwhelming presence of arulas in the necropolis surely carries a symbolic meaning, linked to the chthonic, psychopomp and apotropaic dimensions of the man-faced bull. This is mostly derived from the Etruscan and Tyrrhenian traditions discussed above, especially considering that the representations of man-faced bulls in tombs from mainland Greece are rare in the archaeological records. Moreover, interesting evidence suggesting the role of Acheloios as a protector of children, in relation to a cultic and funerary dimension, has also been discovered at the site: a Type I arula was found used as the 'wall' of the small tomb of a child.[267] In Tomb 11 at the same necropolis another child grave had three Type II arulas, also used as 'walls'.[268]

---

into the cave, and had wedded the nymph. And the nymph is to be interpreted as the dampness of matter. [...] Indeed Heraclitus also says: 'It is death to souls to become wet' (Julian the Emperor, 'Hymn to the Mother of the Gods,' 5.15.D, from Wilmer Wright, *The Works of the Emperor Julian,* I (London: Heinemann, 1913), 462-3). Attis is also often paired with water symbols (cf. SNG France 291) and bulls (cf. SNG von Aulock 7336–7) on the coinage of Asia Minor.

255 Strabo, *Geographica,*10-458.

256 There are even rituals associated with the completion of water control projects that involve Acheloios, as reported by Pausanias for the tyrant Theagenes, who built an altar to Acheloios after diverting a river to Megara (Pausanias, *Descriptions of* Greece, 1.41.2, however, Pausanias does not describe the altar as adorned by man-faced bull statues, and we cannot know the shape by which Acheloios was depicted on the monument mentioned). There is also archaeological evidence documenting such activity: the nomos from Metapontion (H.P. Isler 'Acheloos,' in *LIMC*, 23, fig. 75). Here Acheloios is depicted with the body and face of a man, and bovine horns and ears), and a piece found at Villa dell'Auditorium at Rome, dating to Roman Republican times (H. Di Giuseppe, 'Acheloo e le acque deviate,' 79-86.)

257 BMC Lycia 79, no. 2.

258 Bronze coin attributed to Methylion, CNG eAuction 251, lot 18.

259 See catalog entry.

260 The arulas from Lokris are a clear sign of worship, as the cultic and ritual function of the arulas in the ancient world is widely accepted by scholars.

261 Evidence shows that contemporaneously in the Etruscan world man-faced bull iconography was repeated in multiple series on clay objects. The phenomenon is also attested at Akragas in Sicily, where a matrix was found at the site of a workshop annex for the sanctuary of the chthonic deities (these items were discussed above).

262 V. Origlia, 'Le arule a Locri Epifiziri,' in *Locri Epifiziri III. Cultura materiale e vita quotidiana*, edited by M. Barra Bagnasco (Firenze: Le Lettere, 1989), 135-144, no.168-183, Pl.XXVIII-XXIX.

263 Ibid., 135.

264 Ibid., 140. Here Herakles is depicted strangling the man-faced bull with both arms, not grasping his horn.

265 As noted by Origlia, the closest comparison for the scheme of the earlier examples (Type I) is with a contemporary Etruscan bronze piece from Vulci (J.R. Jannot, 'Acheloos, le taureau androcéphale et les masques cornus dans l'Etrurie archaique,' fig.1). A possible model for similar schemes showing Herakles fighting without weapons is on an Etruscan Black Figured amphora dated to the second half of the 6th century BC, found at Saturnia (T. Dohrn, *Die schwarzfigurigen etruskischen vasen aus der 2. Halfte des 6. Jh.* (1937), no. 284). An earlier example with a similar scheme is depicted on the aforementioned Attic Black Figure amphora dated 570 to 560 BC, found in western Sicily (H.P. Isler, *Acheloos*, no.67). For the style of rendering of Acheloios' head on the Lokrian arulas, we can make comparisons with the contemporary antefix from Lokris (H.P. Isler, *Acheloos*, no.140, dated 525 BC), and even with the incuse man-faced bull type issued in Rhegion (C.M. Kraay, *Archaic and Classical Greek Coins* (Berkeley: University of California Press), no. 779).

266 V. Origlia, 'Le arule a Locri Epifiziri,' 137. Another example of Lokrian fabric was discovered in Kroton (H.P. Isler, *Acheloos*, no.142). The numerous finds at Lokris are from contexts dating across a time span of about 70 years, and Origlia highlights the exceptional nature of the case, the unique example attested in Italy in which an artisans' production remains popular for so long (V. Origlia, 'Le arule a Locri Epifiziri,' 141). This unique phenomenon confirms the importance of the man-faced bull in the Lokrian religious framework. Other evidence for the cult at Lokris was one of the aforementioned balsamarii defined by Isler as 'provincial,' dated 560 to 550 BC (H.P. Isler, *Acheloos*, no.112). This 'provincial' specimen was probably made in Lokris. There is also the discovery of an Archaic antefix of local manufacture (H.P. Isler, *Acheloos*, no.140), which demonstrates the existence of a cult likely operating at a lost sanctuary. For the area of Bruttium we also have an example of an antefix from Croton (H.P. Isler, *Acheloos*, no.142). A later example of an antefix is the aforementioned specimen from Taras, while we have no evidence for antefixes from mainland Greece. There are also coins of the man-faced bull minted in Bruttium (see catalog entry for 'Brettii').

267 Tomb 1347, in: V. Origlia, 'Le arule a Locri Epifiziri,' 135, note 24, and no.169.

268 Tomb 11, in: V. Origlia, 'Le arule a Locri Epifiziri,' 140, note 43,

This evidence is even more striking if we consider the use of astragaloi at the Necropolis of Lucifero. The attempt to find a clear correlation between the man-faced bull and oracular or funerary use of astragaloi[269] is complex, in part due to the lack of attention normally reserved by archaeological reports for these kinds of discoveries.[270] Fortunately, the evidence from Contrada Lucifero demonstrates the widespread use of the iconography of the man-faced bull and the typically Lokrian phenomenon which archaeologists defined as 'astragalomania'.[271] In fact, if we look at excavation reports by Caré,[272] most of the tombs had astragaloi numbering between a dozen and four hundred specimens,[273] and in some graves the number of astragaloi was between 500 and 1000 specimens.[274]The most striking discovery was a child's grave filled with 1,002 astragaloi.[275]

The Lokrian funerary habit mainly consisted in placing the astragaloi around the head and body of the deceased, forming an apotropaic protective barrier. In some cases hundreds of astragaloi are placed outside the grave, over clay tile casings to improve the protective power.[276] The particular arrangement around the bodies of the deceased lead Paolo Orsi to assume a psychopompic function of such practices.[277] Put simply, astragaloi were liminal symbols insofar as they were linked to prophecies, oracles, and funerary practices.[278] For the Greek use as instruments of divination, the most famous evidence comes from Delphi, and Pausanias even reports the practice of astragalomancy in a sanctuary dedicated to Herakles.[279] Moreover, the association between representations of bulls, the ritual use of water, and astragaloi is exhibited in the plastic kernos discovered at the heraion of Samos, where the astragalos is visible under the plastic bull's head.[280]

Ultimately, in the case of Lokris, the use of astragaloi reveals a funerary, apotropaic, and psychopompic

and no. 179.

[269] Traces for a connection between the man-faced bull, oracular practices, and astragaloi come from the Etruscan sanctuaries discussed above. For the finds of astragaloi at the sanctuaries of Pyrgi and Veii, see: M.P. Baglione, 'Considerazioni sui santuari di Pyrgi e di Veio-Portonaccio,' in *Anathema* (1989-90), 651-667. In terms of the Greek world the associations appear on the silver and bronze coinage of Neapolis in Campania, where the astragalus often appear among the secondary symbols in obverse field (Cf. A. Sambon, *Les monnaies antiques de l'Italie*, no. 463, no.464, no.469, and no.478). The connection is also suggested by the earliest coinage of Cyprus. For the link between oracular and funerary meanings of the astragaloi in Cyprus, M. Cultraro has proposed that the discoveries in children's graves indicate cleromancy practiced by young practitioners of the sacred shrines (M. Cultraro, 'Giovani operatori del sacro: infanzia e divinazione a Cipro nella tarda età del Bronzo,' paper presented during the conference: Gli operatori cultuali. Secondo Incontro di studio del Gruppo di Contatto CNR per lo studio delle religioni mediterranee, Rome, 2005, forthcoming).

[270] B. Caré, 'L'astragalo nel sepolcro 'μειρακίων τε και παρθένων παίγνιον'? riflessioni per la rilettura di un costume funerario: i casi di Locri e Caulonia,' in *Caulonia tra Crotone e Locri. Tomo 2. Atti del Convegno Internazionale, Firenze, 30 maggio – 1 giugno 2007* (Firenze: University Press, 2010), 459-467, in particular 463ff and bibliography, in which the author recalls that sometimes the discoveries of astragaloi are totally unrecorded, or often archaeologists merely record the presence in generic terms, omitting exact indications regarding the quantities of finds and their distribution, a habit resulting in the loss of fundamental elements of evaluation for properly understanding and interpretating the phenomenon.

[271] Roland Hampe defined the funeral habit of Lokrians at the Necropolis of Lucifero as 'astragalomania' (D. Elia and B. Caré, 'Ancora sull''astragalomania' a Locri Epizefiri. La documentazione dalla necropoli in contrada Lucifero,' in *Orizzonti* Vol.V (Pisa: 2004) 77-90.

[272] Paolo Orsi, during excavations at the Necropolis of Lucifero, wrote, 'it is worth noting that no other necropolis ever gave us so many astragaloi as found here at Lucifero' (P. Orsi, 'Rapporto preliminare sulla quinta campagna di scavi nelle Calabrie durante l'anno 1910. Locri Epizephyrii,' in *Notizie Scavi Suppl.* (1911), 25, and the year after he commented on 'the singular predilection that the Locrians felt for this symbolic object' (P. Orsi, 'Scavi di Calabria nel 1911 (relazione provvisoria),' in *Notizie Scavi Suppl.* (1912), 17.

[273] B. Caré, 'L'astragalo nel sepolcro 'μειρακίων τε και παρθένων παίγνιον'? riflessioni per la rilettura di un costume funerario: i casi di Locri e Caulonia,' fig.31.3.

[274] B. Caré, 'L'astragalo nel sepolcro 'μειρακίων τε και παρθένων παίγνιον'? riflessioni per la rilettura di un costume funerario: i casi di Locri e Caulonia,' fig.31.2.

[275] Also mentioned in P. Amandry, 'Astragalo,' in *Enciclopedia dell'Arte Antica, Secondo Supplemento, 1971-1994* (Rome, 1994), 492-494. For discoveries of astragaloi in children and youth burials from other sites in Magna Graecia, see: B. Caré, 'Alcune osservazioni sulle sepolture di defunti in età pre-adulta nelle necropoli greche d'Occidente: la diffusione dell'astragalo,' in *Orizzonti* Vol.7 (Pisa: 2006), 143-151.

[276] B. Caré, 'L'astragalo nel sepolcro 'μειρακίων τε και παρθένων παίγνιον'? riflessioni per la rilettura di un costume funerario: i casi di Locri e Caulonia,' 31.3.

[277] P. Orsi, 'Scavi di Calabria nel 1911 (relazione provvisoria),' 17. A similar phenomenon, although of less impressive proportions, has been observed at the Necropolis of Caulonia, a few miles south of Lokris (B. Caré 'L'astragalo nel sepolcro 'μειρακίων τε και παρθένων παίγνιον'? riflessioni per la rilettura di un costume funerario: i casi di Locri e Caulonia,' 461).

[278] The phenomenon has its origins in the Near East and spread throughout Anatolia and Cyprus during the Bronze Age. For the early use of astragaloi in cultic, funerary, and oracular practices in the Near East and Levant, see: G.H. Gilmour, 'The nature and function of astragalus bones from archaeological contexts in the Levant and Eastern Mediterranean,' in *Oxford Journal of Archaeology*, 16, 2 (Blackwell: Oxford, 1997), 167-175. For interesting evidence from Ebla dated 2000 to 1600 BC, where 150 astragaloi were discovered in a child's grave, see: C. Minniti and L. Peyronel, 'L'uso degli astragali a Tell Mardikh-Ebla (Siria): oggetti simbolici o funzionali?,' in *Uomini, piante e animali nella dimensione del sacro* (Lecce-Bari: Edipuglia, 2008), 171-192. For the 'astragalomanteia,' the ancient use of astragaloi for divination to obtain prophetic messages and to consult and interpret the opinion of the gods, see: B. Caré, 'Knucklebones from the Greek Necropolis of Locri Epifiziri, Southern Italy (VI-III century BC). Typological and Functional Analysis,' in *The Sound of Bones. Proceedings of the 8th Meeting of the ICAZ Worked Bone Research Group* (Salzburg: Felix Lang, 2013), 93 and bibliography. The use of astragaloi in adult tombs has also been interpreted as a sign that the deceased had been previously initiated into mystery cults (L. Tondo, 'Riflessi numismatici della vittoria di Dionysos,' in *Dionysos. Mito e mistero, Atti del convegno internazionale, Comacchio 3-5 novembre 1989*, edited by F. Berti (Ferrara, 1991), 209-215; H. Hoffmann, *Sotades. Symbols of Immortality on Greek vases* (Oxford: University Press, 1997), 112; B. Caré, 'L'astragalo in tomba nel mondo greco: un indicatore infantile? Vecchi problemi e nuove osservazioni a proposito di un aspetto del costume funerario' in *L'Enfant et la Mort dans l'Antiquité. III. Le matériel associé aux tombes d'enfants. Actes de la table ronde internationale* (Aix-en-Provence, 2012), 410, note 35. For astragaloi on ancient coins, see: B. Tahberer, 'Astragaloi on Ancient Coins: Game Pieces or Agents of Prophecy?,' in *The Celator*, Vol.26, No.4 (2012), 6ff.

[279] Pausanias, *Descriptions of Greece*, 7. 35.10.

[280] J. De Grossi Mazzorin and C. Minniti, 'L'uso degli astragali nell'antichita' tra ludo e divinazione,' in *Atti del VI Convegno Nazionale di Archeozoologia. Orecchiella, 2009* (Pisa, 2012), 219, fig.8.

dimension associated with the religious dimensions related to the cult of the man-faced bull in the West, in all likelyhood originating from Cypriot and Nuragic traditions. Thus at Lucifero, astragaloi are 'characterized by a plurality of values, designating them more properly as 'polysemic' indicators of a ritual complexity that the case of Locri points out to be extremely strong.'[281] The case of Lokris is even more interesting if we consider the pairing of the man-faced bull with the astragalos seen on early types of archaic Cypriot coinage,[282] indicating a clear connection between the two areas and their religious traditions.

Conclusions

It is difficult to formulate concluding thoughts concerning a multifaceted figure like the man-faced bull. On the one hand, the figure is very simple in that he represents water. On the other hand, and resulting from this primary identification, he is a god involved with all sorts of things: the underworld, social transitions, guiding the soul, wealth and abundance, protection from evil and physical harm, oracular knowledge, healing, and rebirth- essentially, life, death, and nearly everything in between. And it is this special combination of attributes that makes the man-faced bull primarily an auxiliary god, and differentiates him from other deities. The Greek man-faced bull, more so than any other god, was distinctly linked to the theme of the uncanny border, operative at critical margins, and tied to transitional phases of biological, social, and metaphysical status. As such, the iconography and underlying mythos were easily spread from one culture to the next, and the figure becomes extremely popular among itinerant mercenaries, seer-healers, and rural people in general. This popularity is especially evident in his appearance on coinage, an overview of which we are now ready to present.

[281] B. Caré, 'L'astragalo nel sepolcro 'μειρακίων τε και παρθένων παίγνιον'? riflessioni per la rilettura di un costume funerario: i casi di Locri e Caulonia,' 463

[282] H.P. Isler, *Acheloos*, no. 319. The earliest evidence for an oracular use of astragaloi in Cyprus comes from the late 2nd millennium BC at Kition, found together with liver models (D.S. Reese, 'Shells, Ostrich Eggshells and Other Exotic Faunal Remains from Kition,' in *Excavation at Kition V. The pre-Phoenician levels*, Part II, edited by V. Karageorghis, and M. Demas (Nicosia, 1985), 388ff). For elements of Levantine culture in Lokrian traditions, with particular emphasis on Cypriot influence and the worship of the goddess Cupra, see: G. Capriotti Vitozzi, 'Elementi di tradizione egizia nella documentazione di Locri,' in *Rivista di Studi Fenici*, Vol.XXXVI (Rome: Serra, 2011), 124). For evidence of contact between Cyprus and Bruttium (the author mentions them in relation to the winged nymph Terina as derived from the Cypro-Phoenician Ishtar), with bibliography for discoveries of Cypriot pottery among other Levantine artifacts in Bruttium, between the 10th and 8th century BC, see: M. Caccamo Caltabiano, 'La moneta dei Bretii e l'identità di Nika' in *Enotri e Brettii in Magna Grecia. Modi e forme di interazione culturale*, edited by G. De Sensi Sestito and S. Mancuso (Soveria Mannelli: Rubbettino, 2011), 465). Caltabiano attributed this evidence to the geographical position of Bruttium, along the 'metal routes' between the Levant and Etruria. In particular, she mentions Tropea as 'a site of landing and exchange for Cypriot and Phoenician traders who, once they arrived in the Tyrrhenian Sea, continued along the route to Campania, Etruria, Sardinia and Spain.'

Chapter V: The Man-Faced Bull on Greek Coins

Eastern Mediterranean Man-Faced Bull Types

It should be no surprise that the man-faced bull appears on coinage in Ionia before anywhere else, for it was in Ionia that Thales, not long before, identified water as the governing origin of nature, and many of the mercenaries responsible for the transmission of the iconography came from that very area. The first man-faced bull coin is an electrum stater featuring a winged, kneeling man-faced bull,[1] probably minted around the mid 6th century BC (**Fig. 98**).[2] In the same area of Ionia just a few decades later an unidentified mint issued a silver coin of uncertain denomination, featuring a winged protome of the man-faced bull, dated 530 to 510 BC,[3] of which the unique known specimen comes from the Demanhur hoard in Egypt.[4]

Paphos in Cyprus issued the next type around 520 BC, and this one in several denominations.[5] It shows an obverse depicting a man-faced bull with kneeling forelegs and head turned back,[6] supposedly labeled with the Cypriot inscription '*BO-KA-RO-SE*.'[7] The reverse type features an astragalos (**Fig.101**).[8] On some varieties an ankh is engraved as a secondary symbol in the obverse field (**Fig.102**),[9] probably indicative of the life-renewing associations of the man-faced bull. At the same time or slightly later the man-faced bull appears on the silver coinage of Kyrene (**Fig.103**),[10] on drachms issued in the late 6th century.[11]

A coin minted at Phaselis on the southern coast of Asia Minor (**Fig. 104**),[12] shows a rare numismatic representation of the fight of Herakles and Acheloios, dated to the early 5th century BC.[13] Meanwhile, Phokaia issued electrum coins with the protome of the man-faced bull: the earliest types (**Fig.105**)[14] are dated 500 to 480 BC,[15] and the later types (**Fig.106**)[16] date after 480 BC.[17] Phokaia also appears to have issued a small silver fractional (.14g) featuring the head of the man-faced bull, but the attribution is still uncertain.[18]

At Kyzikos in Mysia, the man-faced bull is popular on electrum coin types. In fact, by examining the staters issued by the Greek mint we witness an interesting phenomenon: the earliest types are very similar to the types minted contemporaneously at Phokaia during the first half of the 5th century, but around the mid 5th century and later, the types seem to be inspired by the mints of Sicily and Magna Graecia, as Isler noted in his dissertation.[19] The earliest types show the head of the man-faced bull left (**Fig. 107**),[20] dated 500 to 460 BC,

[1] Jenkins did not consider the Ionian types with winged man-faced bulls relavent to the discussion of 'River God' iconography (G.K. Jenkins, *The Coinage of Gela*, 166). However, he must have been unaware that Acheloios was sometimes represented as a winged man-faced bull even in later depictions dated to the first half of the 5th century BC (Cf. H.P. Isler, 'Acheloos,' in *LIMC*, no. 142).

[2] C. Seltmann, *Greek Coins*, Pl.1, no.25, dated this coin to the first half of the 6th century BC. This early date was followed by Isler (H.P. Isler, 'Acheloos,' in *LIMC*, no.14). The dating might be lowered to the second half of the 6th century BC, especially if we compare the iconographic scheme with an Ionian gem dated to around 500 BC (**Fig.99**, from H.P. Isler, 'Acheloos,' in *LIMC*, no.6). Although on the very earliest types from Asia Minor the man-faced bull is winged, two electrum coins appeared on the market with regular man-faced bulls (M&M Basel, 1986/Busso Peus 372/500; Pecunem 9/192). They have been dated by dealers to 'Circa 6th century BC' (**Fig. 100**).

[3] H.P. Isler, 'Acheloos,' in *LIMC*, no.15.

[4] H. Dressel and K. Regling, 'Zwei ägyptische Funde altgriechischer Silbermünzen,' in *Zeitschrift für Numismatik der Numismatischen Gesellschaft Berlin* (Berlin, 1927), 72.

[5] BMC Cyprus, Pl. VII, no.1-3. Isler dated the type to the second quarter of the 5th century BC without providing any rationale for such a late date (H.P. Isler, *Acheloos*, no. 319). The evidence for our earlier date is the discovery of such coins in the Apadana hoard from Persepolis (*IGCH* 1789), which allows us to date the first man-faced bull emissions of Paphos sometime before 510 BC (M. Caccamo Caltabiano, *La monetazione di Messana. Antike Münzen und Geschnittene Steine*, Bd.13 (Berlin, 1993), 14, no.17).

[6] This particular orientation of the head is also shown on the silver coins minted at Laos in south Italy, in the early 5th century.

[7] Scholars have demonstrated that 'BO-KA-RO-SE' is a misreading of the legend. Cf. H. A. Troxell and W. F. Spengler, 'A hoard of early Greek coins from Afghanistan,' in *ANS Museum Notes*, No.15 (New York, 1969), 6, no.18; M. J. Price, 'Greek coin hoards in the British Museum,' in *Numismatic Chronicle* (London, 1969), 1; O. Masson, *Les inscriptions chypriotes syllabiques* (E. de Boccard, 1983), 116-117.

[8] ANS 1951.143.3.

[9] O. Masson, *Notes de Numismatique Chypriote. Opuscola Atheniensa*, Vol. VIII (Lund, 1968), 115, f.1.

[10] CNG, eAuction 292, lot 219.

[11] BMC Cyrenaica, Pl. IV, no.9-10. The south Mediterranean route is now clearly defined, as immediately after Cyprus and contemporary with Kyrene we see the type appearing on the coinage of Rhegion in south Italy, dated 510 BC.

[12] F. Imhoof-Blumer, 'Fluß- und Meergötter auf griechischen und römischen Münzen. (Personifikationen der Gewässer),' 226-227, no.133, Pl.IV, no.31.

[13] Isler dated the type to the second quarter of the 6th century BC (H.P. Isler, *Acheloos*, no. 315). Some years later in *LIMC* (no. 227), he revised the date following Jenkins (*The Coinage of Gela*, 169), to the early 5th century BC. Jenkins mentions that the Lycian town of Phaselis was related to Sicily, having been founded by the brother of Antiphemos, the founder of Gela (ibid.).

[14] Numismatik Lanz München, Auction 154, lot 175.

[15] S. Mani Hurter and H.J. Liewald, 'Neue münztypen der Kyzikener Elektronprägung,' in *Schweizerische numismatische Rundschau*, Band 81 (Bern, 2002), 25; F. Bodenstedt, *Die Elektronmünzen von Phokaia und Mytilene* (Tübingen, 1981), no.16.

[16] Roma Numismatics Limited, Auction 3, lot 208.

[17] S. Mani Hurter and H.J. Liewald, 'Neue münztypen der Kyzikener Elektronprägung,' Pl.4, E. Isler (*Acheloos*, no. 317) dated the oldest dies to the last quarter of the 6th century BC. Later, in *LIMC* (no.93), he lowered the dates for both types to 500 BC.

[18] Potamikon Collection, 6mm, .14g, unique. Head of man-faced bull to right/ bird(?) in incuse punch mark.

[19] H.P. Isler, *Acheloos*, no. 322. In the case of Kyzikus, Greenwell identified the man-faced bull minted on electrum coinage with the river Aesepos, flowing in the area of the ancient polis (W. Greenwell, 'The electrum coinage of Cyzicus,' in *Numismatic Chronicle*, VII (London, 1887), 73).

[20] Numismatik Lanz München, Auction 155, lot 264. The coin is not listed in Isler's works, as it was still unknown to scholars at that time. In fact, the existence of the type was disclosed only in 1989, with the publishing of the specimen in: G. K. Jenkins and M. de Castro Hipólito, *A Catalogue of the Calouste Gulbenkian Collection of Greek Coins: Greece to East*, Part 2 (Lisbon: Fundação Calouste Gulbenkian, 1989), no. 606. In the following years other specimens have appeared on the market, probably coming from illegal excavations in Turkey. However, the authenticity of the type is confirmed by subsequent studies (S. Mani Hurter and H.J. Liewald, 'Neue münztypen der Kyzikener

just like the contemporary issues of Phokaia (**Fig. 105-6**). The later type, featuring a protome of the man-faced bull kneeling right (**Fig.108**),[21] dated 460 to 400 BC,[22] show an iconographic scheme that appears to copy the contemporary silver coinage of Gela.[23] Moreover, on another electrum stater from Kyzikos (**Fig.109**),[24] dated to the first half of the 4th century BC, the inspiration comes from Neapolis in Campania,[25] as indicated by the full-body man-faced bull walking left with head facing. Finally for Kyzikos there is a unique specimen which recently appeared on the market (**Fig. 110**).[26] According to Hurter and Liewald, this 'baroque' protome can be dated 380 to 360 BC, and it 'can be compared to the Sicilian bronzes of Herbessus,'[27] which are slightly later (339 to 335 BC).

The image of the man-faced bull in Asia Minor was not only adopted by Greek cities, but also the dynasties of Lycia, who started issuing protomes of man-faced bulls (with or without wings) during the first quarter of the 5th century BC. Isler attributed the types with non-winged protomes paired with boar heads at first to Samnos, dating them to the third quarter of the 6th century BC,[28] based on some stylistical affinities with the coinage of that mint.[29] Some years later he revised the first attribution,[30] reassigning the coin type to an 'unknown mint,' but maintaining the early date. These fractionals, of which there are several variants with different orientations of obverse and reverse types, were later attributed by Mørkholm and Neumann to an uncertain dynast of Lycia but dated 480 to 450 BC (**Fig. 111**).[31]

Many other types, issued in various denominations by several dynasts and associated mints over the course of the 5th century BC, show winged full figures of the man-faced bull (**Fig.112**)[32] or winged protomes of the man-faced bull paired with triskeles,[33] female heads (Caria, **Fig.113**),[34] and, at the end of the century, helmeted heads of Athena (**Fig. 114**).[35] These Lycian types are strongly reminescent of gate-guardian winged man-headed bulls from Assyrian palaces.

Finally, for the dynasties of Asia Minor we have the interesting case of Mallos, where on types minted in the early 5th century BC,[36] the man-faced bull is associated with solar symbology (**Fig.115 and 116**),[37] discussed above in relation to the archaic Etruscan traditions. The style of the man-faced bull protome is clearly derived from the types minted in Gela, as noted by Isler.[38] This is suggestive of the direct contacts between the Levant and Italy explored in the previous sections of this book, even moreso if we consider that on the coinage of Mallos one often finds symbols of the ankh[39] and astragalos.[40] The man-faced bull will continue to appear on the coinage of Mallos during the second half of the 5th century, paired with a swan, the head of Janus, or a female head.[41]

The man-faced bull reappears on bronze coins from the Eastern Greek world issued during the 3rd century BC: an interesting type showing a butting humped man-

Elektronprägung,' 25, no.11) and even by recent documented official archaeological discoveries in hoards, from which we can surely date the type to after 500 BC (Cf. M.G. Abramzon and N.A. Frolova, 'Le trésor de Myrmekion de statères cyzicènes,' in *Revue Numismatique*, 6e série – Tome 163 (2007), 15-44. See especially no.49, inv. no. KP-155500.

21 BnF E 3628.

22 Three specimens of this type have been found in the same hoard mentioned above (Cf. M.G. Abramzon and N.A. Frolova, 'Le trésor de Myrmekion de statères cyzicènes,' no. 92-94).

23 Ibid., 20. This phenomenon is a good example of mutual influence between eastern and western Mediterranean peoples, which contributed to enriching the representations of the man-faced bull and the symbolic meanings associated with it, especially during the Late Archaic Period and Proto-Classical Age. The phenomenon of the western influence on eastern coinage has also been noted and discussed by M. Caccamo Caltabiano. She mentions in particular the defeat of Athens by Syracuse as the historical fact which determined, at the end of the 5th century BC, the great influence of Sicilian coinage on some mints of Asia Minor, in particular Kyzikus. The scholar even mentions Thucydides' report of the final stages of the Peloponnesian War, when Siceliot ships took part in the decisive naval battles fought in the sea off the port of Kyzikus (M. Caccamo Caltabiano, 'Tipi monetali siracusani in Asia Minore,' in *Sicilia e Anatolia dalla preistoria all'età ellenistica*, (Palermo, 1996), 103-114; M. Caccamo Caltabiano, 'Il Pansicilianesimo e l'annuncio di un'era nuova. Su alcuni tipi monetali di Siracusa ed Erice dell'epoca dei maestri firmanti,' in *Quarte Giornate Internazionali Di Studi Sull'area Elima, Erice 1-4 dicembre 2000*, Atti Vol.I, (Pisa, 2003) 108-9 and bibliography. The hypothesis concerning the influence of Sicilian types on the mint of Kyzikus was first proposed by A. Holm, *Storia della Sicilia nell'antichità*, Vol. 3.2, edited by G. Kirner (Torino, 1906), 59. Three years later O. Waser proposed Sicilian influences for the man-faced bull types of Kyzikus and Mallos (O. Waser 'Flussgotter,' in *Real-Encyclopadie der classischen Altertumswissenschaft*, Vol. 6 (Stuttgart,1909), 2781. For the the most recent, comprehensive and detailed essay concerning the western influence on eastern issues, in partucular on the coinage of Ionia, Caria, Lycia, Cilicia and Cyprus, including evidence from archaic hoards, see: M. Caccamo Caltabiano, 'Monetazione e circolazione monetaria,' in *Magna Grecia e Oriente Mediterraneo prima dell'età Ellenistica. Atti del trentanovesimo convegno di studi sulla Magna Grecia*, (Taranto, 2000) 291-328.

24 CNG, 75, lot 339. F. Imhoof-Blumer, 'Fluß- und Meergötter auf griechischen und römischen Münzen. (Personifikationen der Gewässer),' 224, no.128, Pl.IV, no.26.

25 H.P. Isler, *Acheloos*, 81.

26 Bank Leu 91, 2004, lot 152.

27 S. Mani Hurter, H.J. Liewald, 'Neue Nominale in der Elektronprägung von Kyzikos,' in *Schweizerische numismatische Rundschau*, Band 83 (Bern, 2004), 35.

28 H.P. Isler, *Acheloos*, 316.

29 Ibid., 80.

30 H.P. Isler, 'Acheloos,' in *LIMC*, no. 92.

31 O. Mørkholm and G. Neumann, *Die lykischen Munzlegenden* (Gottingen, 1978), 5 f. CNG, eAuction 235, lot 215.

32 Kuprilli, Dynast, c. 480 to 440 BC. Silver Stater. Winged man-headed bull walking to right / Lycian letters 'KO-P-R,' triskeles within dotted incuse square. Hess-Leu, Auction 316, lot 480.

33 E. Babelon, *Traité des monnaies grecques et romaines*, Pl.XCVII, 1.

34 Ibid.; Gorny & Mosch 122, 2003, lot 1459; K. Konuk, 'Orou, dynaste de Carie,' in *Scripta Anatolica, Mélanges en l'honneur de Pierre Debord*, edited by P. Brun (Bordeaux, 2007), 2.2.

35 Kherei, Dynast, c. 425 to 400 BC. Silver stater, uncertain mint, SNG Cop. (Suppl.), 453.

36 G.K. Jenkins, *The Coinage of Gela*, 169.

37 The type shows a janiform bearded figure holding a solar disk with both hands, below is the protome of a man-faced bull. CNG eAuction 299, lot 192.

38 H.P. Isler, *Acheloos*, 82.

39 Paired with the man-faced bull on SNG Levante (1), 139.

40 SNG Levante (1), 165.

41 SNG Levante (1), 137-143.

faced bull was struck c. 285 to 281 BC under Seleukos I and Antiochos I, probably at Ai Khanoum.[42] Another interesting issue is the aforementioned humped man-faced bull countermark with an apparent meander symbol above, minted in an uncertain location in Ionia on the Meander River (likely Magnesia). The countermark was most likely issued by retired mercenaries who served under Seleukos I and Antiochos I, and were allotted some land in Ionia upon retirement. Finally for Asia Minor we have a bronze type from Tarsos in Cilicia,[43] issued after 164 BC, where the winged(?) man-faced bull is represented as a secondary symbol beneath Sandan and forming part of a celebratory pyre, embodying the promise of rebirth.

Mainland Greece[44] Man-Faced Bull Types

In his monograph on Acheloios Isler accurately stated that in mainland Greece it is rare to find early images of the man-faced bull, with archaic examples being non-existent.[45] The observation is still valid, despite the attempt made by Robinson to attribute an archaic type showing a man-faced bull head to a mint in mainland Greece.[46] The coin, stored in the Ashmolean Museum at Oxford, is part of a hoard said to have been discovered in the neighbourhood of Adana, in Cilicia (**Fig. 117**).[47] It weights 10.2g (Babylonian standard). Despite the provenance and weight, which indicates an attribution to some mint of Asia Minor, Robinson attributed the coin to the mint of Ennea Hodoi, a small polis located in the Thraco-Macedonian area, from which no ancient coinage is known and for which we have no evidence of the existence of an ancient mint.[48] The coin should instead be described as originating in Asia Minor from an unknown mint, dating to the first half of the 5th century BC, given the similarity to the aforementioned electrum issues from Phokaia.

The earliest coinage of the man-faced bull in mainland Greece therefore appears no earlier than 430 BC. Isler attributed the first coins to Oiniadai on which the head of the man-faced bull appears in profile (**Fig. 118**).[49] Although the debate over who issued the earliest silver fractionals featuring the head of the man-faced bull is still ongoing, recent evidence suggests Oiniadai minted the silver coins with digamma F,[50] whereas the coins featuring T came from various mints (Stratos, Koronta, etc.). Whether or not Oiniadai preceeded Stratos, from 430 BC on silver fractionals showing the head of Acheloios seen in profile appear,[51] and these types appear to derive from an earlier type from Metapontion (**Fig. 119**).[52] Silver fractionals with the same scheme were subsequently minted in the Akarnanian mints of Torybeion (425 to 400 BC),[53] Koronta (423 to 400 BC),[54] and Anaktorion (425 to 400 BC). Oiniadai or Stratos also minted other fractionals with the man-faced bull head seen three-quarters facing.[55] On bronze coinage of Stratos the man-faced bull head (in profile) appears around the mid 4th century BC.[56]

On the coinage of the Akarnanian Confederacy minted in Leukas, starting in the first half of the 3rd century BC and continuing until the fall of the league in 168 BC, two different man-faced bull types are issued: bearded (**Fig. 120**) and later beardless (**Fig. 121**) heads seen in profile. Leukas issued bronze coins with the head of the man-faced bull starting in the late 4th century (civic issues) ,[57] but also probably issued Federal types throughout the 3rd century. Later, the mint issued gold[58] and silver staters and drachms,[59] operating as the chief city of the Akarnanian Confederacy from 280 until 232 BC (though Akarnania was divided in the mid 3rd century).[60]

Following Leukas, the beardless type is seen on silver staters minted in Thyrreion (**Fig. 122**).[61] According to Jenkins, Thyrreion continued to issue man-faced bull types even after the fall of the league.[62] According to Isler, the choice of the beardless man-faced bull demonstrates that, in the Hellenistic age, Acheloios was identified more often as a local river god, with his image now resembling those of horned, beardless human river gods seen in the earliest coinage of Sicily.[63] However,

[42] O. Hoover *HGC* 9, 89.
[43] SNG Levante (1), 947.
[44] And adjacent areas.
[45] H.P. Isler, *Acheloos*, 80.
[46] E.S.G.Robinson, 'A hoard of Greek coins from Southern Anatolia ?,' in *Revue numismatique*, 6e serie, Tome 15 (1973), 229-237, Pl.XXV, 1.
[47] Ibid., 229.
[48] It is worth citing Robinson to have an idea of his rationale: 'If the being represented is a river-god, as indeed it must be, an obvious choice is Strymon, son of Okeanos and Tethys, whom Aeschylos more than once described as 'Hagnos', 'the Hallowed', so must have been struck at some place on or near'(Ibid., 230). Robinson then concludes: 'Of the three possible candidates close enough to the Strymon to claim the creation of the river-god himself, Eion, Myrkinos, Ennea Hodoi; Eion, by the mouth, would be the obvious choice, except that it had already a coinage of its own, consisting of small change with quite different but appropriate types, representing the wild geese of the marshes. Myrkinos was apparently suspended indefinitely. This leaves Ennea Hodoi as the most likely choice for this unique and hitherto unknown coin, which shows perhaps the earliest representation of a river-god on any coin' (Ibid., 233).
[49] H.P. Isler, *Acheloos*, 89, see also no. 363a.
[50] The argument is based on orthography, in which the F is interchangeable with W, used in the archaic 'Wakarnania,' and so, presumably, 'Woniadai,'. Support of this theory is a coin from the BnF collection featuring this inscription (**Fig. 118**). See S. Psôma, 'Le monnayage fédéral acarnanien de l'époque classique,' in *KLIO*, 89 (2007), 7-23.
[51] BCD Akarnania 1-6, 10-12, 357.
[52] S.Noe, *The Coinage of Metapontum*, no.347-9.
[53] O. Hoover, *HGC* 4, 932.
[54] O. Hoover, *HGC* 4, 809.
[55] BCD Acarnania 7-9, 355-6, 358-360.
[56] BCD Acarnania 362.
[57] B. Head, *Historia Nummorum* (1911), 330.
[58] BCD Akarnania 14.
[59] BCD Akarnania 16-21.
[60] B. Head, *Historia Nummorum*, 330.
[61] BCD Akarnania 387-401.
[62] G.K. Jenkins, *The Coinage of Gela*, 170.
[63] H.P. Isler, *Acheloos*, 90.

there are some images of Acheloios as a beardless man-faced bull in Italy outside of numismatics.[64]

Further north, the Corinthian colony of Ambrakia in Epirus, starting in 360 BC,[65] minted silver staters featuring Pegasus/Athena, with the head of a man-faced bull (facing or in profile) used as a secondary symbol on the reverse (**Fig. 123**).[66] Probably following a previous identification by Oberhummer,[67] Jenkins identified this man-faced bull as the Arachthos River.[68] On the other hand, Ravel stated that this man-faced bull is indeed Acheloios, interpreting the secondary symbol, like other symbols seen on the coins of the polis, as closely related to the temple of Dodona and the oracular practices involving Acheloios.[69]

Stratos imitated this Corinthian type from Ambrakia, with the secondary symbol of the man-faced bull's head in profile, around 350 to 345 BC (**Fig. 124**).[70] It seems that Stratos and Ambrakia influenced one another, as the latter originally copied the scheme from Stratos, and subsequentely Stratos adopted the Corinthian types with the same use of the secondary symbol of Ambrakia.

Finally for Ambrakia we have bronze coins issued after 220 BC,[71] featuring the head of the man-faced bull in profile. Interestingly, the reverse featuring a crab[72] or a butting bull show influences from earlier Sicilian types of Akragas and Syracuse.

The head of the man-faced bull also appeared as a secondary symbol on the coinage of the Kings of Macedon around the mid 4th century BC (**Fig. 125**). There are two such coins, both 1/5th tetrachdrachms from an uncertain mint, but probably Amphipolis, dating c. 315 to 275 BC.[73]

Finally, two Thessalian mints also employed man-faced bull iconography on their coinage. A bronze coin, known from only three specimens,[74] probably minted at Methylion in Thessaly in the early 4th century BC, which shows the man-faced bull and Herakles in a scheme similar to the one featured on the Etruscan bronze piece discussed in the section on the psychopomp dimension of Sardinian traditions.[75]

In the early 3rd century BC, Metropolis, in south-western Thessaly, issued coins featuring the protome of the man-faced bull on bronze coins.[76] The scheme seen on this type is unique in the Greek world, seemingly merging together various features from different mints.[77] For example, as in Stiela, the apparent leash around the neck of this man-faced bull could be interpreted as a symbol of a tamed river in the area.[78]

Western Mediterranean Man-Faced Bull Types

Early Italian Types

Isler acknowledged that the majority of man-faced bull coinage comes from the western Mediterranean.[79] The oldest of these are the drachms[80] of Rhegion, which appear no later than 510 BC (**Fig. 126**).[81] The posture of the man-faced bull's body on these coins is just like that on the Lokrian Type I arulas from the Necropolis of Lucifero discussed above: the positioning of the legs, the meandering of the tail, the muscles of the body, and even the small detail of three ribs protruding from the chest (**Fig. 127**). The resemblance is so striking that one must infer a connection between the Lokrian workshop producing these arulas and the engraver who made the die for the mint of Rhegion.[82]

---

64 See the section on Etruscan man-faced bulls for examples of a beardless Acheloios on mirrors, gutti, and triple herms.

65 O. Ravel, 'The 'Colts' of Ambracia,' in *NNM*, 37 (1928), no. 137-138, no. 142-143 (two reverse dies known: P88 and P89, dated by Ravel to Period V, i.e. 360 to 338 BC).

66 Isler suggests Ambrakia imitated the Oiniadai in depicting the head of the man-faced bull in profile. However, he claims this occurred in last third of the 5th century BC, whereas Ravel (ibid.) established that the first man-faced bull type from Ambrakia is dated to 360 BC (H.P. Isler, *Acheloos*, 89ff).

67 E. Oberhummer, *Akarnanien, Ambrakia, Amphilochien, Leukas im Altertum* (München, 1887), 231.

68 G.K. Jenkins, *The Coinage of Gela*, 170.

69 O. Ravel, 'The 'Colts' of Ambracia,' 135.

70 345 BC according to C. M. Kraay, *Archaic and Classical Greek Coins* (New York: H.N. Abrams, 1976), 361, no.437. 350 BC according to BCD Akarnania 356.

71 See catalogue entries below.

72 The crab is also seen under the exergue line of the reverse type dated 241 BC from Alontion in Sicily, minted just 3 years before, and also featuring a man-faced bull (SNG Cop. (4), 144).

73 G. Le Rider, *Le monnayage d'argent et d'or de Philippe II frappé en Macédoine de 359 à 294* (Paris: Bourgey, 1977), Pl.48, n.8-9.

74 Triton XV, lots 469-470; CNG e-auction 251, lot 18.

75 See above, pg. 44.

76 See catalog entries below.

77 See catalog description.

78 There is also a bronze kollybos featuring a man-faced bull from either Athens or Asia Minor, now stored in the British Museum (BMC 1920,0805.421. Two curators confirmed that the kollybos did indeed feature a man-faced bull. Since it is not an actual coin, it is not included in the catalog.

79 H.P. Isler, *Acheloos*, 80.

80 A specimen is stored in the Cabinet des Medailles in Paris. It is the only known example for which we have a clear image. A second fragmentary specimen was published in an auction catalogue in 1997 (Italo Vecchi, Auction 5, lot 81). The specimen published by Larizza (P. Larizza, *Rhegium Calcidense* (Rome: 1905), 99) has been condemned as a modern forgery (B. Carroccio, 'Il toro androprosopo, la cicala e l'incuso reggino,' in *Numismatica e Antichità classiche. Quaderni ticinesi*, Vol.XXIX (Lugano: 2000), 48).

81 We follow Rutter and Gorini in adopting the date of 510 BC, which they proposed on the basis of stylistical analysis (N.K. Rutter, *HN: Italy*, 187, no.2468; G. Gorini, *La monetazione incusa della Magna Grecia* (1975), 33, 222, no. 1). Earlier dates have been proposed by other scholars, also on the basis of stylistical comparisons: 530 BC (G.E. Rizzo, *Saggi Preliminari sull'arte della moneta nella Sicilia greca* (Rome, 1938), 53ff.); 520 BC (A. Cutroni Tusa, 'Sopravvivenza di un motivo miceneo su monete siceliote,' in *Atti e Memorie del I congresso internazionale di Micenologia* (Rome: 1968), 268).

82 The arulas have been dated by Origlia on the basis of accurate analysis of the layers of discovery, while for the drachm of Rhegion we have no archaeological data. It is possible that the date of issue could be slightly earlier, as the Lokrian arulas of Type I were first made in 525 BC (V. Origlia, 'Le arule a Locri Epifiziri,' 135). Isler stated the

In terms of style, there is also a strong resemblance to the aforementioned man-faced bull coins from Paphos,[83] in particular the rendering of the head (**Fig. 128**). Here, too, the posture of the kneeling forelegs is similar, and the only difference is in the orientation of the head which at Rhegion is straightforward, while on the staters of Paphos it is turned back.[84] The turned head is similar to the slightly later coinage of Laos,[85] for which the comparison is obvious (**Fig. 129**).[86]

The Laos coins appear about ten years after the man-faced bulls of Rhegion. Laos was a native Italic center located on the Tyrrhenian side of southern Italy, included in the political sphere of archaic Sybaris.[87] Interestingly, the earliest types from Laos, the staters and drachms, show the man-faced bull wearing a helmet (**Fig. 130**).[88] Later examples, issued in various denominations from 480 to 460 BC,[89] show the iconography of the man-faced bull without a helmet,[90] perhaps indicating the influence of Cyprus. Gorini pointed out that the decorative patterns exhibited on the dotted borders of incuse coinage of Magna Graecia are clearly derived from Levantine toreutics, in particular Rhodian, Samian, Milesian, and Cypriot fabrications.[91]

The hypothesis concerning the crucial role of Cyprus for a possible model of diffusion of coin standards to the West was proposed by Caccamo-Caltabiano in her 1993 essay, when she discussed the issue of the early weight standards used in Magna Graecia and Sicily.[92] Caltabiano noted that the weight of the man-faced bull types of Paphos were consistent with the Persian weight standard, and so were the earliest man-faced bull types of Rhegion (two incuse drachms of Rhegion corresponding to one stater of Paphos).[93] Previously, Laura Breglia,[94] and later Nicola Parise,[95] recognized that at the basis of the weight system used in the western Chalcidian colonies[96] was a direct influence of the Persian weight system of Mesopotamian origin. The authors both stressed the contacts of cultures along maritime routes that, from the Semitic world, directly reached the western Mediterranean area. In particular, Breglia proposed 'Tyrrhenian' and Cypro-Phoenician vectors who in the second half of the 2nd millenium BC came to Italy from the Levant,[97] here 'Tyrrhenian' referring to the migrants from Lydia who led to the formation of Etruscan civilization. Nicola Parise proposed Cyprus as a center

coin was issued at the beginning of the 5th century BC, without giving any rationale for the later date (H.P. Isler, *Acheloos*, no.325).

[83] According to Jenkins the issue from Rhegion is 'probably the oldest occurrence of the river-god type on any Greek coins' (G.K. Jenkins, *The Coinage of Gela*, 168), but he was certainly excluding the winged examples from Asia Minor, which he considered irrelevant to the discussion of river god iconography (ibid.,166). Jenkins (presumably) also does not take into account the coinage of Paphos, because he either believes that on those Cypriot types the man-faced bull does not represent a river god, or because he believes that the Cypriot types were minted later than those of Rhegion. An echoe of eastern cultural influences on the traditions of the man-faced bull of Rhegion also comes from the name of the represented deity: Acheloios Apsias (discussed also at the end of Chapter 7). We learn of the name of the local river of Rhegion from Diodorus Siculus, who referred to the Apsias as 'the holiest among rivers' (Diodorus Siculus, *The Library of History*, 8.23.2), pointing out that this river was characterized by an extraordinary sacredness over all other rivers. This lead Semerano (G. Semerano, *Le Origini della Cultura Europea*, I.1, XL) to propose for the etymology of Apsias the Akkadian base *apsu*, meaning 'deep water,' which is also the name of the Mesopotamian deity representing the underground primeval source of all sweetwater. For a discussion on the cult of Apsu in ancient Mesopotamia see above, pg.8, note 101. According to the scholar even the name of the city itself, Rhegion, comes from Akkadian *rehu*, meaning 'to flow, to pour,' which is also the etymological base for the Latin verb *rigo*, from which comes the modern verb 'to irrigate' (G. Semerano, *Le Origini della Cultura Europea*, I.1, XL).

[84] There is a fractional coin showing a protome with head straight (**Fig. 131**), from O. Masson, *Notes de Numismatique Chypriote. Opuscola Atheniensa*, Vol VIII (Lund: 1968), 115, f.3.8.

[85] The scheme of the head turned back has a strict comparison to the regular bulls minted at Sybaris starting in 550 BC, and is reflected in the later coinage of Laos starting in 500 BC, the native center where the surviving Sybarites sought refuge after the destruction of their polis by Kroton around 510 BC.

[86] Isler also noted the comparison with the coins of Cyprus when dealing with the coinage of Laos, questioning if there could have been 'a direct dependence from the eastern images?,' and aknowledging that 'an iconographic relation is likely' (H.P. Isler, *Acheloos*, 81 and 83). The representation of the bull embodying a symbolic value of fecundity and vitality, even in connection with celestial and astral dimensions, is already attested in a paleolithic cave-sanctuary at the Grotta del Romito at Papasidero, near Consentia (B. Carroccio, 'Il toro androprosopo, la cicala e l'incuso reggino,' 54).

[87] N.K. Rutter, *HN: Italy*, 177, no.2270-2.

[88] Silver drachm, from Artemide Aste, XXXIX, lot 51. The meaning of the helm on the coinage of Laos certainly emphasizes a military connotation that is natural considering the man-faced bull's mercenary affiliation.

[89] N.K. Rutter, *HN: Italy*, 177, no.2275-82.

[90] Laos is a rare case of a mint issuing images of the man-faced bull on both sides of the coin: N.K. Rutter, *HN: Italy*, 177 no.2275 (stater) and no.2276 (triobol). The same phenomenon appears on the later coinage of Agyrion around the mid 4th century BC (A. Campana, 'Agyrion,' in *Panorama Numismatico* (1993), no.8). A final note on Laos concerns the reuse of an old die for a triobol (N.K. Rutter, *HN: Italy*, 177, no.2278), altered to read VM by Sybarites re-founding their polis around 453 BC (ibid., 177, no.2282), who probably brought the die with them from Laos to immediately begin the coinage of their new city, here using the image of the man-faced bull as a symbol of rebirth and vitality.

[91] G. Gorini, *La monetazione incusa della Magna Grecia* (Bellinzona, 1975), 79.

[92] M. Caccamo Caltabiano, *La monetazione di Messana*, Antike Münzen und Geschnittene Steine, Bd.13 (Berlin: 1993), 12ff. The importance of Cyprus in the spread of iconographic schemes from the Levant to Magna Graecia was recognized early by Thomas Dunbabin (T.J. Dunbabin, *The Western Greeks: the History of Sicily and South Italy from the Foundation of the Greek Colonies to 480 B.C.* (Oxford, 1948), 4-5 and 21-23), also mentioned by Caltabiano when she discussed the origins of the dolphin iconography on the first coinage of Zankle (M. Caccamo Caltabiano, *La monetazione di Messana*, 12).

[93] M. Caccamo Caltabiano, *La monetazione di Messana*, 14.

[94] L. Breglia, *Le antiche rotte del mediterraneo documentate da monete e pesi. Studia Archaeologica. Vol. 8* (Roma: Bretschneider, 1966), 25-8.

[95] N. Parise, 'Unità ponderali orientali in Occidente. Osservazioni e postille intorno alle 'antiche rotte del Mediterraneo',' in *Il Commercio greco nel Tirreno in età arcaica: atti del seminario in memoria di Mario Napoli, Salerno 1977. Università degli studi, Facoltà di lettere e filosofia, Istituto di storia antica e archeologia* (Salerno, 1981), 97-110.

[96] For a convincing discussion of the Cypriot connection in the matter of the early coinage of the Tyrrhenian area of Italy, see: M. Caccamo Caltabiano, *La monetazione di Messana*, 13-15.

[97] L. Breglia, *Le antiche rotte del mediterraneo documentate da monete e pesi*, 97-100.

for the spread of the Persian weight system to the West,[98] which through Cypro-Phoenician vectors reached Sicily[99] and Etruria. These same vectors also transmitted typical Levantine cultural elements.[100] On this topic Caltabiano gives us very insightful observations: 'We cannot consider as just a casualty the evidence that in all the Mediterranean area, and in close chronological times, only the Chalcidian poleis of Sicily and Italy, and at the other side first Croesus, and later Persians, issued coins using the same weight standard.'[101] Caltabiano even states that, since the coinage of Croesus is chronologically precedent to the first coinage of Himera, and taking into account the relationships between the western Chalcidian colonies and Asia Minor, 'it is very likely that the experience of coinage by the Chalcidian colonies arose by direct influence of the Near Eastern poleis.'[102] Finally, archaeological discoveries of stone weights in Sardinia, of which we know at least three specimes dated from the 11th to 7th century BC,[103] provide further evidence for an early direct transmission of the Persian weight standard from the Levant to the Tyrrhenian area by Cypro-Phoenician vectors. Thus, upon this background it is easy to understand our proposed model of diffusion of the iconography of the regular man-faced bull in numismatics, since the first examples are seen in Cyprus and Rhegion, the latter being a Chalcidian colony minting the incuse drachm on the same weight system.

Sicilian Types

Gela

In Sicily, the man-faced bull appeared on coinage about 20 years after the first examples of peninsular Italy. In 490 BC the man-faced bull appears on the coinage of Gela (**Fig. 132**). The dating of these first emissions, mainly didrachms, was established by Jenkins in his famous work on the coinage of the mint.[104] The main iconographic scheme for Geloan man-faced bulls is the protome with bull kneeling in submission, which once again demonstrates a Cypriot connection since the same posture of the front legs is seen on their earlier coinage, too (**Fig. 131**).[105] Oddly, there has been no mention of the comparison between the Geloan and the Cypriot types in any numismatic publications. Perhaps this is due to the great distance between the two mints.[106] But how else does one interpret this striking evidence if not attributing it to direct connections?[107]

The earliest types minted in Gela were not strictly depictions of a protome. There is a scarce type issued at the earliest stage of the Geloan mint exhibiting the entire body of the man-faced bull (**Fig. 133**).[108] Although this scheme is also similar to the coins from Paphos, it closely resembles a Near Eastern cylinder seal from the Schoyen Collection mentioned above in the section on the Near East. On this seal both the posture of the legs and the very specific detail of long hair on the man-faced bull points to a direct Near Eastern influence (**Fig. 134**).[109]

---

98 N. Parise, 'Unità ponderali orientali in Occidente. Osservazioni e postille intorno alle 'antiche rotte del Mediterraneo',' 97-110.

99 The first Sicilian polis to issue coinage on that weight standard was Himera, around 550 BC (P.R. Franke and M. Hirmer, *Die griechische Münze* (München, 1964), no.62.

100 A later reflection of these early connections can been observed in the appliqué of an Etruscan bronze helmet dated to about 475 BC, found at Himera. Some authors have stressed the importance of this piece to establish the existence of cultural and commercial exchanges between the area of Himera and the Etruscan and Campanian cultural environment (E. Mussini, 'La diffusione dell'iconografia di Acheloo in Magna Grecia e Sicilia. Tracce per l'individuazione di un culto,' 102, note 29).

101 M. Caccamo Caltabiano, *La monetazione di Messana*, 15. The first silver coinage of Croesus was issued on a weight standard of 5.50 to 5.60g, and the same standard was later used by Persians until Darius began to issue the sigloi featuring the archer king.

102 Ibid.

103 C. Zaccagnini, 'Nuragic Sardinia: metrological notes,' in *Atti del secondo Congresso Internazionale di Studi Fenici e Punici* (Rome, 1991), 344. For the role of Cypriot sailors in the spread of Near Eastern weight standards from the Levant to the Tyrrhenian sea starting in the late Bronze Age, the very same weight values that will be used in the later coinage of Etruria, Cumae, Rhegion, and Chalcidian colonies of Sicily, see: N. Parise, 'Unità ponderali orientali in Occidente. Osservazioni e postille intorno alle 'antiche rotte del Mediterraneo',' 97-110.

104 G.K. Jenkins, *The Coinage of Gela*, 167. In detail: Group I (no.1-103) is dated 490/485 to 480/475 BC (Ibid., 177ff., Pl.1-6).

105 O. Masson, 'Notes de Numismatique Chypriote. Opuscola Atheniensa,' 115, f.3.8.

106 Another interesting case is Emporion, who in 480 BC issued silver coins with the same scheme (J.A. Chevillon and P.P. Ripollès Alegre, 'The Greek Far West: An Exceptional Adaptation of a Design from Asia Minor with Bull and Lion Foreparts,' in *Journal of the Numismatic Association of Australia*, Vol.25 (2014), 44, fig.12; M. Campo, 'Las emisiones de Emporion y su difusión en el entorno ibérico,' in *La monetazione dei Focei in Occidente : atti dell' XI convegno del Centro Internazionale di Studi Numismatici, Napoli 25-27 ottobre 1996* (Rome, 2002), Pl. XVI, no.3; L.Villaronga, 'La Troballa de l'Empordà,' in *Acta Numismatica*, 33, 7-13).

107 The first fifty years of life at the colony of Gela are unclear, since only small portions of the earliest layers of the colony have been excavated (C. Ingoglia, 'La più antica ceramica in Wild Goat Style da Gela,' in *Sicilia Antiqua. An International Journal of Archaeology*, Vol. III (Rome: Serra Editore, 2007), 22). The evidence does not confirm the tradition reported by ancient sources regarding a strong Cretan presence in the early stages of the development of the polis. In fact, more abundant are the archaeological attestations of pottery from Ionia and Cyprus in the decades immediately following the founding of the city. There is a strong presence of Cypriot pottery in the Akropolis of Gela, for instance, in sacred wells within the layers of the foundation of the Athenaion and more generally in layers dated to the 7th century BC. Massimo Cultraro further confirmed our hypothesis of a strong Cypriot influence on the archaic culture of Gela, informing us of recent archaeological discoveries not yet published, related to the presence of numerous fragments of Cypriot pottery from archaic layers dated in the years around the foundation. Other evidence reported by Ingoglia are suggestive of a Cypro-Phoenician presence in the years around the foundation of Gela, especially a vase found in the sanctuary of Bitalemi, offered by a patron from the earliest stages of existence of the sanctuary. The piece clearly indicates a connection with Tyre and is dated to the 8th century BC (P. M. Bikai, *The Pottery of Tyre* (Warminster: Aris and Phillips, 1978), Pl.5, no.19-23) and originated in contemporary Cyprus (Tomb 113-367 at the Necropolis of Amathus, cited Caterina Ingoglia, 'La più antica ceramica in Wild Goat Style da Gela,' 24). On the same topic, see: P. Astrom, 'Cocci ciprioti provenienti da Gela,' in *Kokalos*, 14-15 (1968-69), 332 ff, Pl. XLIX.

108 G.K. Jenkins, *The Coinage of Gela*, no.101-103, dated c.480 BC.

109 For cultural contacts between the area where the colony of Gela will later be established and the Mediterranean coasts of Anatolia since the beginning of the 3rd millennium BC, see: A. Cazzella, M.

The man-faced bull remains the main type employed by the mint of Gela until 405 BC.[110] An interesting piece recently published by Santelli and Campana[111] shows a countermark with the typical Geloan protome struck on a bronze unit of Akragas. The piece is probably dated to 397 BC. Finally, at Gelas, there were gold coins with the man-faced bull issued at the end of the 5th century BC.[112]

Katane

Starting in 464 BC[113] Katane issued beautiful tetradrachms depicting the kneeling man-faced bull, likely inspired by the earlier Geloan types. The historical context of the polis just before the beginning of coinage in silver, as well as the first coinage in bronze, suggests the strong symbolic value of the man-faced bull, related to rebirth and life-renewing dimensions embodied in the iconography. Some of the most artistic dies made by Katanian engravers[114] show a swimming man-faced bull who appears to tow a satyr that clutches the horn above him (**Fig. 48a**)[115] In some rare specimens the same interplay is exhibited with a winged figure in place of the satyr.[116] As mentioned above, this scene probably refers to the psychopomp quality of the man-faced bull. Because Katane was originally a native Sikan city, colonized by Greek settlers arriving from Naxos around 729 BC,[117] we can propose that the symbolic dimensions seen on the early coinage could be related to the native component of the Sikan/Sikel-Italic root of the city's culture.

Later Man-Faced Bulls

Around the mid 5th century BC, coinciding with the general spread of the use of coinage, we witness a veritable explosion in popularity of the man-faced bull. After Rhegion, Laos, Gela, and Katane, the man-faced bull appears further north on the coinage of Neapolis, where we first see him depicted as a protome only, clearly influenced by the types of Gela (**Fig. 135**). The dating for this first Neapolitan type is not easy. Rutter, in 1979, proposed circa 450 BC[118] based on stylistical comparisons: for the female head on obverse he compares it with Syracusan reverse types belonging to Boehringer's Series XIV, dated by Boheringer to 474 BC, but lowered by Rutter 'by at least a decade';[119] and for the man-faced bull protome he compares it with the reverse types of Geloan tetradrachms belonging to Jenkins group III, dated 465 to 450 BC.

Eleven years later Renata Cantilena, on the basis of crossed comparison between obverse and reverse dies from Syracuse, Velia, Cumae, and Gela, re-dated the first Neapolitan issue to around 470 BC.[120] Cantilena mentioned that the Neapolitan coin should be considered an 'act of deliberate polical claiming by the new born city.'[121] Founded around 475 BC, this would make terrific sense. However, twelve years later Giancarlo Alteri re-dated the coin to around 460 BC.[122] In *Historia Nummorum: Italy*, Rutter confirms 450 BC as the date for the first Neapolitan issue.[123]

Metapontion is the only known case in numismatics in which we see a depiction of Acheloios as a bearded man with bull horns and bovine ears.[124] The mint also issued silver diobols but with a man-faced bull head in profile (**Fig. 119**),[125] which is the first western evidence for the scheme, likely derived from the electrum types of Asia Minor by means of Kyrene in North Africa. The type later spread from Italy to Mainland Greece during the second half of the 5th century BC, as the coinage of Akarnania is probably 10 to 20 years later than the coins from Metapontion. Isler dates these diobols of Metapontion to the second half of the 4th century BC.[126] However, his dates are probably incorrect: the style of the head is clearly proto-classical, and the two anulets in the field of the die are clearly a stylistic continuation, or likely an indication of value, typical of the archaic coinage of the Metapontion mint, as they also occur on the types featuring the barley corn design.[127] Moreover, Noe stated that the dating of these diobols, 'is reasonable to place at

Cultraro and G. Recchia, 'Relazioni tra l'Italia centro-meridionale, la Sicilia e l'area egeo-balcanica durante l'Eneolitico,' in *Atti della XLIII Riunione scientifica : l'età del rame in Italia : dedicata a Gianni Bailo Modesti : Bologna, 26-29 novembre 2008* (Firenze, 2011), 159). Gela, according to ancient sources, was founded in the early 7th century BC by settlers coming from Rhodes and Crete (Herodotus, *Histories*, VII.153; Thucidides, *The Peloponnesian War*, VI.4.3). It is interesting that both Gela and Neapolis, who shared an obsessive fascination with man-faced bull iconography, both are reported to have been founded by Rhodians (Strabo, VI.1.14).

[110] G.K. Jenkins, *The Coinage of Gela*, 167.

[111] G. Santelli and A. Campana, 'Le prime contromarche siciliane su bronzo,' in *Monete Antiche*, Anno VII, No.38 (Cassino: Diana, 2008), 11-15. See catalog entry below for a discussion.

[112] G.K. Jenkins, *The Coinage of Gela*, no. 490-493.

[113] Isler dated the first types of Katane to 480 BC (H.P. Isler, *Acheloos*, no. 345), but later Arnold-Biucchi gave conclusive accounts to date the first emissions to 464 BC (C. Arnold-Biucchi, *The Randazzo Hoard 1980 and Sicilian Chronology in the Early Fifth Century B.C.*, 22-24).

[114] Ibid., no. 60-68.

[115] Ibid., no.62; CNG, Triton VIII, lot 62.

[116] C. Arnold-Biucchi, *The Randazzo Hoard 1980 and Sicilian Chronology in the Early Fifth Century B.C.*, no. 69.

[117] F. Giudice, E. Procelli, R. M. Albanese, and M. Frasca, 'Catania. Scavo all'interno del muro di cinta del Monastero dei Benedettini,' in *Cronache di Archeologia*, Vol. XVIII (Catania, 1984), 129-141.

[118] N.K. Rutter, *Campanian Coinages*, 475 to 380 B.C. (Edinburgh, 1979), 46.

[119] Ibid.

[120] R. Cantilena, *Monete della Campania antica* (Naples, 1988), 46-49.

[121] Ibid., 49.

[122] G. Alteri, *Le antiche monete di Neapolis* (Naples, 2000), 65.

[123] N.K. Rutter, *HN: Italy*, no.545.

[124] S. Noe, *The Coinage of Metapontum*, no. 311.

[125] Ibid., no. 247-350; SNG ANS (3), 290.

[126] H.P. Isler, *Acheloos*, 87. He states that the type is derived from Akarnanian types (ibid., no. 326), which he dates to 340 BC. In the same year Jenkins offered a more plausible dating to 450 BC (G.K. Jenkins, *The Coinage of Gela*, 168).

[127] See S. Noe, *The Coinage of Metapontum*, no. 297-309 for comparison.

the same time as the [aforementioned] stater (no.311),'[128] and therefore circa 460 BC. Rutter, however, dates both types c. 440 to 430 BC. We believe a date of c. 450 is most plausible. A similar type with the head in profile appears in bronze in South Italy much later, probably issued in Bruttium or Metapontion for the Brettians.[129]

During the 5th century BC the man-faced bull appears on the coinage of Emporion in Iberia.[130] This type, dated 480 BC,[131] was influenced by Gela, according to Chevillon et al. (**Fig.136**).[132] However, the rough incuse reverse suggests more direct influences from Levantine mints, and the scheme of the protome was used in Cyprus before Gela, as noted above. The same mint later issued silver obols.

The mint of Stiela in Sicily issued silver litrai with kneeling protomes starting in 440 BC, clearly influenced in style by Gela.[133] We know two types of man-faced bull coins minted in Stiela. The earliest are silver litrai dated 440 to 430 BC, showing the protome of the man-faced bull in Geloan style, with the addition of a new detail: a leash.[134] A second type of protome, this time walking, not kneeling, was issued by the mint around 413 to 408 BC, on silver drachms (**Fig. 137**).[135]

The indigenous town of Entella, located in the hinterland of Selinous, issued silver litrai with a standing man-faced bull starting in 440 BC (**Fig. 138**).[136] The Sikel Agyrion also issued various bronze denominations with the protome and full-body man-faced bull starting in the mid 4th century.[137]

The Siculo-Punic cities of Motya[138] and Panormos[139] issued silver and bronze fractionals featuring the man-faced bull starting at the end of the 5th century, using Punic inscriptions until the end of the 4th century. A particular type from *Zyz*-Panormos, a silver litra dated after 400 BC,[140] shows a boy riding a man-faced bull and signifying the psychopomp dimension discussed above (**Fig. 139**). During the 4th century BC Panormos issued bronze types strongly resembling Campanian coinage of the man-faced bull, depicting him as a protome, very similar to the Neapolitan examples.[141] On other coins appears the full body of the man-faced bull with facing head,[142] these types also featuring the head of Helios as a secondary symbol above, strongly reminiscent of the typical connotations of the Etrusco-Italic traditions. Panormos was also one of the two Sicilian mints, together with Gela, to issue gold coins with the type of the man-faced bull.[143]

Around the end of 5th century we see the man-faced bull appearing on the coinage of mercenaries fighting in Sicily. The mercenary group called the Mamar likely had Campanian origins and issued bronze types with the scheme of the kneeling protome, dated 409 to 403 BC.[144] It is probably not a mere coincidence that the origin of man-faced bull mercenary issues in Sicily coincides with Campanian mercenaries fighting in the area, since we also see the flourishing of the type in Campania. In fact, the walking man-faced bull type with head in profile, appearing first in the late 5th century BC in Neapolis (**Fig. 140**), spreads from there to many cities in Campania: Phistelia[145] (silver, c. 405 to 400 BC); Hyria[146] (silver, c. 405 to 385 BC); Allifae[147] (silver, c. 400 to 395 BC); and Nola (silver, c. 400 to 385 BC;[148] bronze, c. 300 to 250 BC).[149] The walking man-faced bull appears also on the coinage of the Kampanos, dating 415 to 400 BC.[150] As pointed out by Rutter, obverse dies were shared by different Campanian mints issuing silver coinage of the man-faced bull: Cumae, Kampanos, Neapolis, Nola,

[128] Ibid., 58.
[129] See catalog entry.
[130] J.A. Chevillon et al., 'The Greek Far West: an exceptional adaptation of a design from Asia Minor with bull and lion foreparts,' 44, fig.12; M. Campo 'Las emisiones de Emporion y su difusión en el entorno ibérico,' Pl. XVI, 3; L. Villaronga, 'La Troballa de l'Empordà,' no. 7-13.
[131] J.A. Chevillon et al., 'The Greek Far West: an exceptional adaptation of a design from Asia Minor with bull and lion foreparts,' 45.
[132] Ibid.
[133] As observed by Campana, there is a distinct similarity between the first types of Stiela and the reverse dies of Gela, listed by Jenkins in Group V, dated 440 to 430 BC (A. Campana, 'Sicilia: Stiela (440/430 e 413/405 a.C.),' in *Monete Antiche*, no. 57 (2011), 7).
[134] A. Campana, 'Sicilia: Stiela,' 8, no.1. Campana noted that the detail, previously believed to be a horizontal die break, does not show the progressive enlargement that should evolve from a real die break, despite the progressive wear of the die. Thus, it would seem instead to be a leash attached to a collar, perhaps symbolizing the regimentation of the usually unpredictable flow of water of the Akesines river (ibid., 8).
[135] Ibid., 11, no.3. A gold coin of the same type recently appeared on the market (CNG, Triton VI, lot 104), but has been condemned by Campana as a modern forgery (A. Campana, 'Sicilia: Stiela,' 10).
[136] Ibid., 180-1, no.1-2.
[137] Ibid.,173-178, no.3-8.
[138] A. Campana, 'Motya,' in *Panorama Numismatico* (2000), 377, no.12, dated 410 BC.
[139] G.K. Jenkins, 'The Coins of Punic Sicily,' 74-5.
[140] F. Imhoof-Blumer, 'Fluß- und Meergötter auf griechischen und römischen Münzen. (Personifikationen der Gewässer),' Pl.II, no.12a.
[141] R. Calciati, *Corpus Nummorum Siculorum* I, 274, no.10.
[142] Ibid., 270, no.5.
[143] A rare litra published in: L. Gandolfo, 'Note su due monete inedite del Museo Archeologico Regionale 'Antonino Salinas',' in *Atti del V Congresso Internazionale Di Studi Fenici e Punici, Marsala-Palermo, October 8th-9th, 2000,* Volume 2 (Palermo, 2005).
[144] SNG Cop. (1), 1072; A. Campana, 'MAMAR,' in *Panorama Numismatico* (2003), 158-9, no.1-2.
[145] N.K. Rutter, *HN: Italy*, no. 611.
[146] Ibid., no. 539-542.
[147] Ibid., no. 459.
[148] Ibid., no. 603-5.
[149] Ibid., no.607.
[150] A. Campana, 'Campania: Kampanos,' in *Kampanos* (Cassino: Editrice Diana, 2010), 33-55; N.K. Rutter, *HN: Italy*, no.476-8.

and Hyria.[151] The matter was also recently discussed by Alberto Campana.[152]

In the meantime, mercenaries in Sicily continued to issue man-faced bull coins. In fact, a new mercenary mint issuing such coins in bronze has been identified by Buceti: Alaisa Katane, dating to the late 4th, early 3rd century BC.[153] Another hitherto unpublished variant comes from a private collection, presented in the catalog.

The Sicilian polis of Selinous also issued silver litrai featuring a walking man-faced bull which date to c. 400 BC (**Fig. 152**),[154] similar in style and scheme to the earlier tetradrachms from Katane. Another peculiar type was issued around 400 BC and shows a running man-faced bull with head facing,[155] a scheme which seems to merge Sicilian and Campanian types into a new singular iconography.

Bronze fractionals with the type of a standing man-faced bull, previously attributed to Himera by Calciati,[156] have been recently re-attributed by Lazzarini[157] and Buceti[158] to a mercenary mint identified as Halykiai, minted c. 390 to 370 BC. Tauromenion also issued bronze coins featuring a walking man-faced bull, dated c. 357 to 345 BC.[159] In the same years the mercenary group called the Kersini[160] issued bronze tetrai. The mercenary group called the Sileraians issued bronze litrai and tetrai dated 357 to 339 BC.[161] There is another large bronze denomination, found at the same site of the main discoveries of Sileraian coins, of uncertain attribution.[162] Another mercenary group, the Sergetaians, in the mid 4th century BC, minted heavy bronze denominations featuring the head of the man-faced bull in profile.[163]

In 483 BC Megara Hyblaea was destroyed by Gelon.[164] The site remained uninhabited for more than a century, until, in the years of Timoleon, around 344 BC, the old site was re-populated[165] and the inhabitants issued silver litrai with the protome of the man-faced bull, of which a unique specimen is known, dated 344 to 339 BC.[166] The scheme mimics the types of Neapolis with a facing head.

Alaisa Archonidea (not Alaisa Katane) in Sicily also probably issued a type with the image of the man-faced bull, as Carmen Arnold-Biucchi reports a man-faced bull on a bronze coin with Greek inscription ALAISAS ARX, dated 344 to 317 BC and stored in the Museo Mandralisca at Cefalù.[167] Unfortunately, despite our repeated requests to the museum over the past two years, it was not possible to obtain a photographic reproduction of the apparently unique coin.

The Sikel city Abakainon started minting silver litrai with the protome of the man-faced bull in 339 BC.[168] They also contemporaneously issued bronze hemilitrai with the same scheme,[169] connected with the symmachia of Timoleon. The same mint later issued a heavy bronze of uncertain denomination with the type of a full body man-faced bull,[170] probably from the mid 2nd century BC. Near Abakainon another Sikel city, Alontion, started to mint bronze litrai in 339 BC,[171] whose types are clearly related to the contemporary types of Abakainon. Almost a century later an interesting image of a man-faced bull with water flowing from his mouth appears on a bronze series, probably issued during Roman times, c. 241 to 210 BC.[172]

After Alontion, there appears a contemporaneous coin in rough style which Imhoof-Blumer assigned to the city of Mylai.[173] The type shows a protome of a standing man-faced bull, who also has water flowing from his mouth. Sikel Herbessos also minted bronze litrai with protomes of beautiful style around 338 BC.[174] Another Sikel center, Iaitas, around 330 BC, issued man-faced[175] and man-headed[176] bulls of rough style.

The uncertain mint of Irnthi in Campania also minted bronze man-faced bull types.[177] The inscription on the coinage of Irnthi, discussed in the catalog, shows a

[151] See N.K. Rutter, *Campanian Coinages, 475–380 B.C.*, Pl.33-34 and key for die-transferences.

[152] A. Campana, 'Campania: Kampanos,' 33-55.

[153] E. Buceti, *Monete, storia e topografia della Sicilia greca* (Messina, 2010), no.1.

[154] SNG Cop. (5), 602; SNG ANS (4), 711.

[155] D. Bérend, 'Réflexions sur les fractions du monnayage grècques,' in *Studies in honor of Leo Mildenberg* (Wetteren, 1984), Pl. II, 27.

[156] R. Calciati, *Corpus Nummorum Siculorum* I, 46, no.44-45.

[157] L. Lazzarini, 'La monetazione e il sito Di Halykiai (Alicie),' in *Schweizerische numismatische Rundschau* 84 (Bern: 2005), 15-24.

[158] G. Buceti, *Alcune monete di bronzo inedite della Sicilia Greca*, 22-3.

[159] SNG Cop. (5), 916.

[160] A. Campana, 'Aggiornamento al Corpus Nummorum Antiquae Italiae. Sicilia: Kersini,' in *Monete Antiche* 36 (2007), 5.

[161] A. Campana, 'Sileraioi,' in *Panorama Numismatico* (2002), 88, no.1-2.

[162] R. Calciati, *Corpus Nummorum Siculorum* III, 321, no. 1

[163] A. Campana, 'Sergetai,' in *Panorama Numismatico* (2001), no.1.

[164] Herodotus, *Histories*, VI.156.

[165] A. Campana, 'Megara Hyblaea' in *Panorama Numismatico* n.135 (1999), 353.

[166] SNG ANS (4), 287.

[167] C. Arnold-Biucchi, 'Alaisos,' in *LIMC*, 479, no.1.

[168] A. Campana, 'Abakainon,' in *Panorama Numismatico* (1996), 19-20, no.26-27.

[169] A. Campana, 'Abakainon,' 20, no.28.

[170] R. Calciati, *Corpus Nummorum Siculorum* I, 74, no.6.

[171] A. Campana, 'Alontion,' in *Panorama Numismatico* (1996), 68, no.4.

[172] Ibid., 74, no.14.

[173] F. Imhoof-Blumer, 'Fluß- und Meergötter auf griechischen und römischen Münzen. (Personifikationen der Gewässer),' 192, no.48, Pl. II, n. 11.

[174] A. Campana, 'Erbessos,' in *Panorama Numismatico* (1998), 208, no.5.

[175] The authenticity of these types is uncertain, cf. S. Frey-Kupper, 'Ein 'neuer' Acheloos der Iaitiner. Ein Beitrag zur Erforschung der frühen Münzprägung von Iaitas,' in *Zona Archeologica: Festschrift für Hans Peter Isler zum 60. Geburtstag* (Bonn: Dr. Rudolf Habelt GMBH, 2001), 159-173.

[176] R. Calciati, *Corpus Nummorum Siculorum* I, 383, no.1.

[177] SNG France (6, Part 1), 631-4 (dated to the late 4th, early 3rd century BC); SNG Cop. (1), 596-8 (dated 300 to 250 BC); N.K. Rutter, *HN: Italy*, no.543 (dated 250 to 225 BC).

composit of Etruscan, Greek, and Oscan cultures, and the most likely location of the mint proposed by scholars is at a sanctuary at Punta Campanella in Campania, a place in which different cultures met, and also where mercenary recruitment occurred.[178]

As a result of mercenary activity, it is probably no coincidence that another wave of diffusion of man-faced bull iconography occurs among Italic mints of Peninsular Italy at the end of the 4th to the mid 3rd century BC: Cumae, no longer a Greek city after the occupation by the Kampanos (silver, 325 to 300 BC);[179] Teate in Apulia (bronze, 325 to 275 BC);[180] Larinum (bronze, 275 to 250 BC);[181] Teanum Sidicinum (bronze, 317 to 240 BC);[182] Suessa Aurunca (bronze, 265 to 240 BC);[183] Compulteria (bronze, 265 to 240 BC);[184] Cales (bronze, 317 to 240 BC);[185] Aesernia (bronze, 263 to 240 BC).[186] Beginning in the 3rd century BC the Italic Malies also issues a peculiar type (bronze, 300 to 275 BC)[187] which features a man-faced bull walking with facing head, and above him appears a mask or helmet.

During the last quarter of the 4th century BC the man-faced bull makes his first appearance on Roman coinage: first on the famous Neapolitan types with Apollo/protome of the man-faced bull, likely minted at Neapolis (bronze, c. 320/319 BC);[188] and some years later on a bronze coin showing on the reverse a standing man-faced bull with star above and Latin ROMANO in exergue (bronze, c. 297 BC).[189]

Some Sicilian mints of native Sikel origin continued to issue man-faced bull types under Roman rule. Sikel Assoros, for example, minted a bronze tetras on which two man-faced bulls appear together.[190] Also, Elymian Segesta features man-faced bulls on numerous countermarks dating to the 1st century BC, but these were probably applied at Iaitas.[191] In Iberia, we find the type on silver coins minted at Arse-Saguntum sometime in the 2nd century BC (**Fig.141**), which according to Jenkins may derive from Italian prototypes.[192]

Ultimately, surveying the chronological distribution of man-faced bull coinage reveals similar patterns to those we have already discussed in this book. The figure migrated west from Asia Minor and Cyprus into Magna Graecia, and eventually arrived on coinage in Greece proper in the late 5th century. Mercenaries found the iconography especially appealing and account for its spread and popularity throughout the ages, and many of the themes we are now familiar with- taming the river, psychopompic functions, rebirth, etc., are as apparent in numismatics as they are in other forms of ancient art featuring the man-faced bull. Now, having grasped the origin and development of man-faced bull iconography up to and including its appearance in numismatics, we can address the question of the identity of the man-faced bull on Greek coinage.

---

[178] A. Stazio, 'Monete a leggenda Irnthi,' in *Scritti di Numismatica* (Foggia: Claudio Grenzi Editore, 2011) 394-401.

[179] N.K. Rutter, *HN: Italy*, no.536-7.

[180] Ibid., no.698. According to Rutter it could belong to Teanum Sidicinum in Campania (Ibid., 81).

[181] Ibid., no. 622.

[182] Ibid., no. 454-6.

[183] Ibid., no. 450.

[184] Ibid., no. 437.

[185] Ibid., no. 436.

[186] Ibid., no. 431.

[187] Ibid., no. 438-9.

[188] Ibid., no. 251.

[189] Ibid., no. 252 .The man-faced bull will even appear on a Roman coin almost three centuries later, on a denarius dated 19/18 BC (RIC I, 319; RSC 432).

[190] BMC Sicily, 31, no.2.

[191] R. Calciati, *Corpus Nummorum Siculorum* I, 304, no. 54-55, struck on the undertype, SNG München (5) 872. G. Santelli, 'Monete d'epoca tardo repubblicana della zecca di Segesta: le contromarche ed il motivo dell'aquila,' in *Annotazioni Numismatiche Suppl.*, XV, Anno 10, Serie III (Milan: 2000), 4, f.2-3..

[192] G.K. Jenkins, *The Coinage of Gela*, 169.

Section Two

On the Identity of the Man-Faced Bull

Chapter VI: Past Arguments for the Identity of the Man-Faced Bull

The question of the identity of the man-faced bull on Greek coinage has been of interest to scholars for hundreds of years. As a result, he has been identified in numerous ways: the Minotaur, an agricultural allegory, Neptune, Jupiter, Dionysos Hebon, the harmony between Ceres and Dionysos, Dionysos Zagreus, a combination of Dionysos and Acheloios, a representation of individual local river gods, Euthymos of Locri, and, of course, Acheloios. While some arguments, such as those for the Minotaur, are almost certainly not correct, others are quite persuasive. Before we venture our own theory, however, we must first outline all the previous arguments that have been put forth for identifying the man-faced bull.

The Minotaur

Although the very first scholar to identify the man-faced bull as a Minotaur was Parisio,[1] we do not find any rationale until Agostini, who published a year later, in 1592.[2] Discussing the issue of Campanian coinage, he argued that each time an athlete of the polis won a competition at the Olympic Games, or whenever one of those cities won a battle, to celebrate the event they minted coins on which Nike crowns the man-faced bull, symbolizing 'victory over the Minotaur,' as if the entire population, after the victory, is identified with the hero Theseus.[3] In his essay on the subject, Eckhel[4] recounts how this tradition continued with such scholars as Gori,[5] Spanheim,[6] and Beger,[7] and Eckhel summarizes their views as an error of not recognizing the difference 'between a man-headed bull and a man with the head of a bull,'[8] or, in the case of Spanheim and Beger, choosing not to go against tradition, despite the contrary evidence.[9] Gori's argument is also founded upon a gem depicting a 'man-faced bull' within a labyrinth, but Eckhel,[10] and more recently Kern,[11] recognize the piece to be a forgery of the 16th century (**Fig. 142**, which actually depicts a centaur within a labyrinth). It is tempting to think that the man-faced bull is an artistic variation of the general Minotaur as man-bull theme, which is probably the assumption of most early commentators, even though the two are clearly opposites. Ovid's line in the *Ars Amatoria*[12] is unclear, describing the Minotaur as *semibovemque virum semivirumque bovem*, or 'half-bull man, half-man bull.'[13] Most other early literary sources consistently describe the Minotaur as a bull-headed man, as he is almost always depicted when fighting Theseus (**Fig. 143**).[14] The roles of the Minotaur and man-faced bull in Greek mythology are also very different, and in some cases opposites, much like their features. The Minotaur is a feared creature to whom the Athenian youths are sacrificed; whereas, if indeed the man-faced bull is a river god (surely, for Akarnania), he was responsible for the protection of youths,[15] who would offer locks of hair to the river in recognition of this role.

There are, however, two troublesome pithoi from the first quarter of the 7th century BC that allegedly depict the Minotaur as a man-faced bull, published most recently by Eva Sēmantōnē-Bournia.[16] However,

---

1 P. Parisio, *Rariora Magnae Graeciae Nomismata* (Roma, 1591).

2 A. Augustinus, *Discorsi del S. Don Antonio Agostini sopra le medaglie et altre anticaglie, divisi in XI dialoghi. tradotti dalla lingua Spagnuola nell'Italiana, con l'aggiunta di molti ritratti di belle, e rare medaglie* (Presso Ascanio, et Girolamo Donangeli, 1592).

3 Ibid., 95.

4 J. Eckhel, and C. Clay, 'Concerning the Man-Faced Bull,' in Appendix 1 of this publication, 292-3. Originally: J. Eckhel, 'De tauro cum facie humana' in *Doctrina Numorum Veterum*, Vol. 1 (Wien: Ignatius Alberti, 1792), 129-140.

5 A.F. Gori, *Gemmae antiquae ex thesauro mediceo et privatorum dactyliothecis Florentiae* (Florentiae, 1731).

6 E. Spanheim, *Dissertatio de praestantia et usu numismatum antiquorum* (Romae: Apud Blasium Deuersin, 1664).

7 L. Beger, *Thesaurus Brandenburgicus Selectus : sive gemmarum, et numismatum Græcorum, in cimeliarchio electorali Brandenburgico, elegantiorum series, commentario illustratæ* (Coloniae Marchicae, 1696).

8 J. Eckhel, 'Concerning the Man-Faced Bull,' 293.

9 The apparent confusion might stem from ancient times. A. Alföldi suggests the Roman Legionary Standard described by Pliny (*Naturalis Historia,* 10.16) as displaying a Minotaur is linked to the man-faced bull, but does not equate the two. See A. Alföldi, 'Zu den römischen Reiterscheiben,' in *Germania*, 30 (1952), 188, no. 1; as cited in S.B. Downey, *Architectural Terracottas from the Regia* (University of Michigan Press, 1995), 29.

10 J. Eckhel, 'Concerning the Man-Faced Bull,' 293.

11 H. Kern, *Through the Labyrinth: Designs and Meanings over 5,000 Years* (New York: Prestel, 2000), 202, item no.371.

12 Ovid, *Ars Amatoria,* 2.24. In his essay, J.S. Rusten suggests Ovid was combining the lines from Empedocles (Fr. 61, Aelian, *De Natura Animalium,* 16.29): 'man-faced bulls' and 'bull-headed men' (βουενῆ ἀνδόπῳρα / ἀνδρόφυῆ βούκρανα) (J.S. Rusten, 'Ovid, Empedocles and the Minotaur,' in *The American Journal of Philology*, Vol. 103, No. 3. (Baltimore, 1982), 332-333).

13 This ambiguity might have led to the tradition in Dante commentary in which commentators argue Dante conceived of the Minotaur as a man-faced bull. See R. Hollander's translation and commentary in R. Hollander and J. Hollander, *Dante, the Inferno* (New York: Random House, 2000), 228. In some cases, such as a wood carving by Pietro da Figino, Venice, 1520, Dante's Minotaur is depicted with a bull's body with the torso and head of a man, much like Gori's gem. William Blake's (1826) illustration shows the same type of Minotaur, but his has distinct bull horns. See also, R. Beal, 'Minotaur,' in *The Dante Encyclopedia*, edited by R. Lansing (2000), 615-616.

14 Attic Black Figure Amphora, c. 550 BC, High Archaic, The J. Paul Getty Museum, Malibu, California, USA, Malibu 85.AE.376.

15 J. Larson, *Greek Nymphs,* 100.

16 E. Simantoni Bournia, *La céramique grecque à reliefs. Ateliers insulaires du VIII au VI siècle avant J.C.* (Genève: Droz, 2004), 85-6,

the identification as a man-faced bull relies on the appearance of eastern-style hair and a horn; the face itself is completely missing.[17] Isler,[18] who believes the figures did have human faces, suggests these pieces are a good indication that at the beginning of the 7th century BC, when the imagery of Near Eastern human-bovine hybrids was transferring west, the same man-faced bull shape could have been used to represent either Acheloios or the Minotaur. Isler acknowledges that such evidence demonstrates that the form and content of the Greek myth of Acheloios have separate origins, the first coming from Near Eastern influences, the latter being purely Greek. Thus, these pithoi could be a sign that, at an earlier stage in the codification of Greek myth, some of the iconographies and surrounding myths were intermingled. We know, for example, that many of the myths of Theseus mirror those of Herakles,[19] and also that Acheloios, at least at Metapontion, was depicted as a bearded man with bovine ears and horns.[20]

The Agricultural Allegory

The notion of the man-faced bull as an agricultural allegory is straightforward: the bull in ancient times was often a symbol for agricultural production and so naturally the man-faced bull represents this. Eckhel cites Carrera,[21] Pighius,[22] Hardouin,[23] Wachter,[24] and la Chau and le Blond[25] as holding this view (**Fig. 144 & 145**). La Chau and Le Blond make some persuasive arguments against the identification of Campanian man-faced bulls as Acheloios. They claim that the iconography of Acheloios as a man-faced bull is only seen in Akarnania, where the god is depicted with one horn in accordance with the mythical narrative. In contrast, the man-faced bull is shown with two horns in Campania, and thus cannot represent Acheloios because he lost a horn in the battle with Herakles. This interpretation is confirmed by the Victory crowning the man-faced bull, which does not make sense for Acheloios, the loser of the battle.[26] Ultimately, the view that the man-faced bull is an agricultural allegory is somewhat unsatisfying, because an agricultural connotation is common for most of the other identities of the man-faced bull, with the exception of perhaps the Minotaur. As an example, Ignarra's argument that the man-faced bull is Acheloios begins with a preliminary argument that it is an agricultural allegory.[27] Moreover, Eckhel's argument that the man-faced bull is Dionysos Hebon is, according to him, perfectly consistent with the agricultural allegory.

Neptune[28]

The theory that the man-faced bull is in fact a depiction of Neptune is interesting. Eckhel cites only Mazochius[29] as espousing this view and claims that no other scholars were convinced of it. Mazochius' argument, however, is more concerned with demonstrating that the man-faced bull is not the Minotaur. He argues that if the man-faced bull's origins were in fact in Crete, then we would see the iconography there. He also insists that there is no legitimate rationale for the man-faced bull to be identified as the Minotaur. Aside from the ambiguity of Ovid's description, mentioned above, the Minotaur is a foul creature that has no business on Italian coinage. Instead, he suggests Neptune, arguing that most man-faced bull issues come from coastal areas and that the man-faced bull is often depicted with symbols associated with Neptune. Mazochius also speculates about the Italian peninsula appearing as a bull's head, in which Calabria and Bruttium are the horns. This theory was originally put forth by Pomponius Mela, who wrote during the 1st century AD.[30] Mazochius seems to recognize the limitations of his theory, however, and acknowledges that the case would be stronger if the coins of Poseidonia, on which he sees Neptune depicted

101-4, Pl. 42, fig.103, Pl. 58, fig.143.

[17] Ibid., fig. 143. Fig. 103 is entirely unclear.

[18] H.P.Isler, *Acheloos*, 94-95. He mentions also that the man-faced bull on a Proto-Corinthian vase could be either Acheloios or the Minotaur. See Ibid., no. 60.

[19] Certain aspects of the myth of Theseus were clearly modeled on the more prominent hero Herakles during the early 6th century BC (A. Greene, 'Theseus, Hero of Athens,' in *Heilbrunn Timeline of Art History* (New York: The Metropolitan Museum of Art, online publication, 2000)). Plutarch himself, in his work on the life of Theseus, stressed many times the similarities between some labors of Herakles and the deeds of Theseus 'in imitation of Herakles' (Plutarch, *Theseus*, 6, 8, 11, 25, 29). On the conflation/contamination of the two myths, see: J. Boardman, 'Herakles, Theseus and Amazons,' in *The Eye of Greece. Studies in the Art of Athens* (Cambridge: University Press, 1982), 1-28; F. Brommer, *Theseus. Die Taten des griechischen Helden in der antiken Kunst und Literatur* (Darmstadt: Wissenschaftliche Buchgesellschaft, 1982), 30; J. Neils, *The Youthful Deeds of Theseus* (Rome: Bretschnider, 1987), 144 ff. On the iconographic conflations of Herakles and Theseus, see: R.D. Von Dippe, *The Origin and Development of Continuous Narrative in Roman Art, 300 B.C. - A.D. 200* (University of Southern California: UMI Microfilm 3291874, Doctoral Dissertation, 2008), 53-6.

[20] S. Noe, *The Coinage of Metapontum*, no. 311.

[21] D. Petri Carreraæ, and Diodorus Siculus, *Monumentorum historicorum urbis Catanaœ libri quatuor. Adjunguntur Epistolaœ Diodori cum annotationibus ejusdem Petri Carraraœ. Ex Ital. Lat. vertit, recens. & illustr*; edited by Abrahamus Preigerus (Oxford: University Press, 1723).

[22] S. Vinandus Pighius, S. Pardo, and A. Schottus, *Annales Magistratvvm Et Provinciar..* (Antverpiae: Officina Plantiniana, 1615), T. I., 423.

[23] Pliny, and J. Hardouin, *Historiae naturalis* (Biponti: Ex typographia Societatis, 1783), T.I., 162.

[24] J.G. Wachter, *Archaeologia nummaria, continens praecognita nobilissimae artis, quae nummos antiquos interpretatur* (Lipsiae: Ex Officine Breitkopfiana, 1740), 95.

[25] G.de La Chau, and F.T.M. de Baculard d' Arnaud Le Blond, *Description des principales pierres gravées du cabinet de S.A.S. Monseigneur le duc d'Orleans,* (Paris: Pissot, 1780), T.I., 123.

[26] Ibid., 123-126. A special thanks to Bruno Lambert for his helpful translation of the original French document.

[27] N. Ignarra, *De palaestra Neapolitana* (Naples: Donati Campi, 1770), 232.

[28] This summary is based on the author's own rough translation of some particularly difficult Latin text.

[29] Alexius Symmachus Mazochius, *Commentariorum in Regii Herculanensis Musei aeneas tabulas Heracleenses: Pars I-II* (Neapoli: Ex Officina Benedicti Gessari, 1754), 512-13.

[30] P. Mela, *De Chorographia. Libri tres*, edited by P. Parroni (Roma: Ed. di Storia e Letteratura, 1984), 145, line 67.

as a regular bull with the label ΠΟΣΙΔΟΝ above, had human faces (**Fig. 146**).[31] Interestingly, a quarter-century later, in 1770, Nicola Ignarra published a work dedicated to Mazochius, in which he included a line drawing of just such a coin, the actual existence of which is unlikely (**Fig 147**).[32]

Jupiter

Two gems, one in the Florence cabinet[33] and the other published by Lévesque de Gravelle,[34] and both reproduced on plates included in Eckhel's *Doctrina,*[35] appear to show Jupiter in the guise of a man-faced bull as he carries off Europa (**Fig.148**). If the gems do in fact represent Jupiter, and the maritime themes along with the javelin, which was a gift from Jupiter to Europa, suggest they do, then such evidence supports the notion that the man-faced bull might have represented different things to different people depending on the context.[36] In one case it is Jupiter, in another case Neptune, and in another case Acheloios, etc. [37] However, the authenticity of these gems is highly uncertain, and they are most likely creations of the 1600 to 1700s.[38]

Dionysos

Dionysos Hebon

Giacomo Martorelli,[39] writing under the name of his friend D.M.V. Macciucca because his earlier antiquarian work had come under severe criticism, was the first to argue that the man-faced bull is Dionysos Hebon, who he claims came to Campania from Phoenicia.[40] His argument is based on philological evidence of a Levantine origin, and, to illustrate his position, he provides a line drawing of a non-existent statue of the man-faced bull as it is unloaded from a Phoenician ship onto the shores of Campania (**Fig. 149**).[41] Although the work is based on interesting etymological insights concerning Campanian toponyms, the book generally lacks any legitimate scientific underpinnings and is largely speculation on the part of the author. For instance, on one plate, we see what appears to be a man-faced bull with an inscription related to Dionysos. However, the text indicates the real statue has no head, and Martorelli simply assumed its head had a man's face (**Fig. 150**).[42]

Slightly later Eckhel, following Matthaeus Aegyptius,[43] also argues that the man-faced bull of Italy and Sicily is probably Dionysos Hebon, although the primary purpose of his argument, he informs us, is to demonstrate that it is definitely not a river god, Acheloios or the local variety. His argument in favor of it being Dionysos Hebon is based on the following: (1) Dionysos Hebon was often depicted as a bull; (2) A coin of Gela[44] seems to portray Dionysos approaching a woman who offers him a wreath, just as Plutarch's account illustrated[45] (**Fig. 151**); (3) Jupiter is represented as a bull with a man's face on two gems (see citation above) so Dionysos could be displayed this way too, in order to distinguish him from a regular bull; (4) He interprets a coin of Selinous[46] in the following way: it shows on the obverse Proserpine, who was a daughter of Jupiter and he impregnated her in the form of a serpent, also shown on the obverse, and the reverse depicts their child, Dionysos, as the man-faced bull (**Fig. 152**); (5) Dionysos was highly honored in Campania because of the wine produced; (6) Dionysos invented the diadem, and that is why he is frequently seen in the guise of a man-faced bull with a Victory[47] crowning him with a diadem (**Fig. 153**);[48] and finally, (7) This theory is compatible with the 'agricultural allegory' identification because Dionysos was believed to be the first to submit bulls to the yoke, which is why he is depicted with horns. That is Eckhel's argument in a nutshell.

[31] For similar coinage, except with the inscription ΡΟΣΕΙDONI as opposed to ΡΟΣΕΙDON, see SNG ANS (2) 691; CNG 60, lot 82*. Some man-faced bull coins have been mistakenly attributed to Poseidonia. See F. Imhoof-Blumer, 'Fluß- und Meergötter auf griechischen und römischen Münzen. (Personifikationen der Gewässer),' 181, no. 21. A similar mistake was made by the Berlin Museum with a silver issue from Phistelia. See S.W. Grose, *Catalogue of the McClean Collection of Greek Coins* (Cambridge: University Press, 1923), 51, footnote 2.

[32] N. Ignarra, *De palaestra Neapolitana*, no. 13. Even though the man-faced bull on Greek coinage is not Poseidon, Aeschylus (*Seven against Thebes*, line 309) equated Poseidon and Okeanos, and the latter shares some iconographic features and qualities of Acheloios, which may have contributed to the confusion of some early commentators.

[33] Tom. I. tab. 57. no. 2, as cited in J. Eckhel, 'Concerning the Man-Faced Bull,' 296.

[34] L. de Gravelle, M. Philippe, and P.J. Mariette, *Recueil de pierres gravées antiques* (À Paris: De l'imprimerie de P.J. Mariette, ruë S. Jacques, aux Colonnes d'Hercule, 1732), T. II. no. 45.

[35] J. Eckhel, 'De Tauro Cum Facie Humana,' Tab. III. ad. Vol. I. 136, no. 2 & 3.

[36] G. Lippold also identifies the figure as Jupiter, but doubts the authenticity of the piece. See G. Lippold, *Gemmen und Kameen*, (1922) plate 143, 2. H.P. Isler also doubts the authenticity of both pieces, personal correspondence, March 2014.

[37] H.P. Isler believes that the 'javelin' mentioned above might actually be a thyrsos. See H.P. Isler, *Acheloos*, 173-174, no. 308.

[38] See below, pg. 90.

[39] P. Matarazzo, 'Martorelli, Giacomo,' in *Dizionario Biografico degli Italiani* - Volume 71 (Roma: Istituto dell'Enciclopedia Italiana, 2008). See also F. Strazzullo, 'Il carteggio Martorelli-Vargas Macciucca,' in *Settecento napoletano: documenti II* (Napoli: Liguori, 1984).

[40] M. Vargas Macciucca, *Dell'Antiche colonie venute in Napoli, ed i primi si furono i Fenici [ed i secondi furono gli Euboici], opera del duca Michele Vargas Macciucca* (Napoli: presso i fratelli Simoni, 1764).

[41] Ibid., 1.

[42] Ibid., 255.

[43] M. Aegyptius, *Senatusconsulti de Bacchanalibus; sive, aeneae vetustae tabulae Musei Caesarei Vindobonensis explicatio* (Neapoli: apud F. Muscam, 1729), 232.

[44] G.K. Jenkins, *The Coinage of Gela*, Group V, 371 (O74/R150); CNG 82, Lot 269*

[45] For an alternative interpretation of the meaning of the scene see H.P. Isler, *Acheloos,* 85.

[46] SNG ANS 711; CNG, Triton VII, 79*

[47] For a proposal of a different identity for the winged female figure see above, pg.64ff.

[48] SNG ANS 327. Numismatica Ars Classica NAC AG, Auction P, 1008*.

The debate between Dionysos and local river gods reached its peak in the early 19th century. The main advocate for Dionysos Hebon during that period was Avellino, who more or less maintained the arguments already published.[49] More recently, modern scholarship has shed some light on the cult of Dionysos Hebon, which was restricted to Campania and apparently emerged only in Roman Imperial times.[50] There has been some confusion as to whether he was depicted strictly as a youth (as ἥβων indicates) or also as a bearded old man, as the phrase from Macrobius,[51] *praeterea barbata specie, senili quoque,* seems to indicate.[52] In his essay, Bowersock argues *praeterea barbata* refers to the god as a young man, since beards and vitality are often associated with one another,[53] and this guise of Dionysos corresponds to summer (Macrobius indicates there were four guises of Dionysos corresponding to the four seasons).[54] Thus, argues Bowersock, *senili quoque* must refer to a different guise of Dionysos as an old man, corresponding to autumn (and therefore the bearded, youthful Dionysos might be depicted as a man-faced bull).[55] Ultimately, the very late emergence of the cult makes it difficult to associate it with man-faced bull iconography on Campanian coinage of the 5th to 3rd centuries BC. Moreover, the earliest Roman coins, which feature a man-faced bull (RRC 1/1), probably did not depict Dionysos Hebon either, both because of the date of issue (c. 326 BC) and as indicated by the circumstances surrounding the Senatorial Decree Concerning the Bacchanalia of 186 BC.[56] Here we witness the persecution of members of the cult of Dionysos, which was allegedly so severe that some members committed suicide rather than face the wrath of their persecutors.[57] The Roman Senate would probably not issue a decree that severely persecuted the ceremonies of a cult whose central iconography was used on Rome's very first coins, and one that is also very popular with mercenaries.[58] This might be reason enough to conclude that no Dionysian epithet is represented by these man-faced bulls, not just Hebon.[59] However, because the cult of Dionysos Hebon emerged under Augustus,[60] one could attempt to identify the man-faced bull on the denarius from 19 to 18 BC with him.[61] In this case, the Hellenization occurring under Augustus is manifested in the use of an old Greek iconography now repurposed for the area's new cult.[62]

Representation of Harmony between Ceres and Dionysos

Eckhel mentions the possibility of this 'harmony' only in passing, but explains as follows: Dionysos and Ceres are the two principle deities of agriculture, and the horned head might represent Dionysos while the bull represents Ceres, since the bull was her favorite animal.[63]

Dionysos Zagreus

It was Gardner[64] who argued that the man-faced bull of Neapolis is Dionysos Zagreus. Rutter quotes the appropriate lines, ' 'we have no sufficient proof that streams were objects of special worship in Campania,' and, second, '...we have...ample proof that the cultus of Dionysos, especially Dionysos Zagreus, was there quite at home, and that the god was frequently worshipped in the form of a horned youth or a human-headed bull.'[65] Gardner also mentions that the man-faced bull is often seen with Dionysian emblems, presumably referring to the bunch of grapes or lyre seen above the man-faced bull on Neapolitan coinage (**Fig. 154**).[66] Rutter, however, demonstrates that there is at least one example of a river being worshipped in Campania and placed on a coin (the Sebethos),[67] and that the monuments recording the worship of Dionysos Zagreus in Campania are too late, coming from Hellenistic and Roman times. As for the Dionysian emblems accompanying the man-faced bull, this is highly debatable, especially since Gardner does not specify to which emblems he refers. If the lyre, it might instead accompany Apollo, seen on the obverse of the Neopolitan bronzes presumably in question. Ultimately, there are many emblems above the man-faced bull on the bronze coinage of Neapolis and even the grape bunches do not necessarily indicate the accompanying man-faced bull is Dionysos. Finally, there appears to be absolutely

[49] M. F. Avellino, 'Osservazioni sul toro dal volto umano, tipo di talune medaglie della Italia e della Sicilia,' in *Opuscoli I* (Napoli, 1826), 81 ff. See also M. Nassa and V. Nassa, *Cubulteria. Ragguagli sulla moneta attribuitagli e sul controverso simbolo del toro androprosopo* (Roma, 2010). The authors thank him for having kindly provided us copies of his valuable work, which offers an excellent review of the contemporary literature.

[50] For an overview of the cult, see G.W. Bowersock, 'The Barbarism of the Greeks,' in *HSCPh*, Vol. 97(1995), 3-14. For the only two known inscriptions recording the cult of Hebon at Neapolis see: E. Miranda, *Iscrizioni greche d'Italia, Napoli vol 2* (Roma, 1995), 14-19, no. 3-4 = *IG* XIV no. 716-717.

[51] Macrobius, *Saturnalia,* 1.18.9.

[52] G.W. Bowersock, 'The Barbarism of the Greeks,' 11.

[53] See, e.g., Ovid, *Ars Amatoria,* 1.518: *sit come, sit trita barba resecta manu,* as cited by G.W. Bowersock, 'The Barbarism of the Greeks,' 12, note 35.

[54] Macrobius, *Saturnalia,* 1.18.9.

[55] G.W. Bowersock, 'The Barbarism of the Greeks,' 11-13.

[56] Deutsche Akademie der Wissenschaften zu Berlin, *Corpus Inscriptionum Latinarum* (Berolini: Apud G. Reimerum, 1862), i^2 2, 581.

[57] Livy, *Ab Urbe Condita Libri,* 39.8-39.18.

[58] See above, pg. 25ff.

[59] Michael H Crawford, *Roman Republican Coinage* (Cambridge: University Press, 1974), no. 1/1.

[60] R. Schlesier, *A Different God? Dionysos and Ancient Polytheism* (Berlin: De Gruyter, 2011), 6.

[61] RIC I 319; RSC 432.

[62] It is worth mentioning that the image of Acheloios was still very popular in sculpture during Roman times, until c. 2nd cent. AD. For example, see: H.P. Isler, *Acheloos,* no.174 and no. 268-72; H.P. Isler, 'Acheloos,' in *LIMC*, no. 68-74, and no. 161-65.

[63] J. Eckhel, 'Concerning the Man-Faced Bull,' 298.

[64] P. Gardner, *The Types of Greek Coins; An Archaeological Essay* (Cambridge: University Press, 1883), 183.

[65] Ibid., as cited in N.K. Rutter, *Campanian Coinages 475-380 BC* (Edinburgh: University Press, 1979), 43.

[66] A. Sambon, *Les monnaies antiques de l'Italie*, no. 634. BnF Specimen*.

[67] A. Sambon, *Les monnaies antiques de l'Italie,* no. 422.

no evidence for Gardner's claim that Dionysos Zagreus was worshipped in the form of a 'human-headed bull.'

Dionysos Tauromorphos

The confusion surrounding Acheloios and Dionysos on coin types occurred for Kyzikus just as it did for Campania (discussed below). It was Baker who stated that the man-faced bull depicted on the electrum staters of Kyzikus represented Dionysos, his identification referring to Athenaeus of Naucratis (2nd to 3rd century AD), who in his work, *The Deipnosophistae*, tells us that in Kyzikus there was a statue of Dionysos Tauromorphos.[68] However, Athenaeus was probably referring to a much later style of statue, popular in Roman Anatolia, which depicts not a man-faced bull, but instead a young beardless man crowned with grape clusters, with two little horns slightly protruding from his forehead.[69]

The Acheloios-Dionysos Dynamic

Whereas Franz Strebers[70] went so far as to equate Dionysos and Acheloios, Arthur Sambon was more in-line with the Italian school when he addressed the issue of the identity of the man-faced bull,[71] arguing for a syncretism between Dionysos and Acheloios.[72] Ultimately, his position is that Dionysos was the original identity which was slowly overtaken by Acheloios through the centuries.

Isler writes about the intimate relation of Dionysos and Acheloios but does not equate the two, as Strebers did.[73] He argues that only Acheloios is represented as a man-faced bull on Greek coinage,[74] despite the fact that Acheloios can be seen as part of the omnipresent Dionysian cosmos of living nature,[75] since water exists within nature. One example he uses to illustrate this close connection between the two is the mixing of wine and water, which was the customary way in which Greeks drank wine during symposia, according to Athenaeus of Naucratis.[76] Another important example is the use of masks in funerary rituals and rites of passage, which both deities have in common.[77] This common cultic feature probably generated confusion between Acheloios and Dionysos in early dissertations on the iconography of the man-faced bull, as the ritual use of masks indicates specific qualities that likely steered speculations on identity. Ultimately, the common use of masks is a real phenomenon, which might have its roots in a syncretism that occurred in ancient times. Thus, Sambon's hypothesis is plausible and worthy of further investigations, and it finds confirmation in Gimbutas' arguments on prehistoric man-faced bulls as the earliest representations of young Dionysos.[78] It is also worth mentioning Moretti's remarks regarding the relief from Sabouroff discussed in the introduction to this book (**Fig. 1**).[79] Moretti points out that the mask of Acheloios and its central position surrounded by a semicircle of deities refers to very primitive habits in ritual, which demonstrate a close analogy to the rituals of Dionysos practiced in open fields, 'so that in this analogy one can almost see the original identity of the two primitive genes.'[80] In fact, one of the gods appears to hold a cornucopia. Although it is tempting to identify that figure with Acheloios and the man-faced bull as Dionysos, it is probably Plouton or Agathos Daimon, as Cook suggested.[81] Finally, it is worth mentioning that even Carroccio sees similarities between river cults and the Dionysian sphere, indicated by the presence of related accessory symbols on coins in combination with river god representations.[82]

Local River Gods

The case for man-faced bulls as representations of local river gods is a strong one, first taken up by Petrus Burmannus[83] and advanced by the Prince of Torremuzza.[84] Later on, in the early 19th century, the debate about the man-faced bull's identity focused on Dionysos versus local river gods. Millingen was the main advocate for the hypothesis of river deities, suggesting that the representation of Acheloios as a man-faced bull had become 'a prototype of the symbolic forms attributed to

[68] Athenaeus, and C. Burton Gulick, *The Deipnosophists* (Cambridge: Harvard University Press, 1927), 11.51. For another mention of Dionysus Tauromorphos, see Plutarch, *De Iside*, 35.

[69] For another statue identified as Dionysus Tauromorphos, see: L. Summerer, 'Topographies of Worship in Northern Anatolia,' in *Space, Place and Identity in Northern Anatolia* (Stutgard, 2014), 192, fig.5.

[70] F. Streber 'Über den Stier mit dem Menschengesichte auf den Münzen von Unteritalien und Sicilien,' in *K. Akademie der wissenschaften, Munich. Philosophisch-philologische classe. Abhandlung* (München: Verlag der Akademie, 1838), 444-555.

[71] The Italian school followed Giulio Minervini ('Moneta inedita di Napoli, che risolve la questione del toro androprosopo,' in *Bullettino Archeologico Napoletano. Nuova Serie. Anno primo*, No. 8 (Napoli: Cataneo, 1852), 57-58), and the man-faced bull was identified as Acheloios in Garrucci's famous work, P. R. Garrucci, *Le monete dell'Italia antica. Parte seconda: monete coniate* (Roma: Salvincci, 1885).

[72] A. Sambon, *Les monnaies antiques de L'Italie*, 173 and 181.

[73] H.P. Isler, *Acheloos*, 113, note 451.

[74] Ibid., 113-114.

[75] Ibid., 114, specifically note 460.

[76] Ibid., 115, specifically note 470 & 471. Athenaeus, *The Deipnosophists*, 11.51.

[77] H.P. Isler, *Acheloos*, 115.

[78] M. Gimbutas, 'Il linguaggio della Dea,' 79.

[79] G.Moretti, 'Terrecotte inedite del Museo delle Terme,' in *Bollettino d'Arte, anno VII, fasc.4* (Roma: P.Calzone, 1913), Pl.XXVII.

[80] Ibid., 140.

[81] A.B. Cook, *Zeus: A Study in Ancient Religion, Vol. II, Zeus: God of the Dark Sky* (Cambridge: University Press, 1925), 1117, note 7.

[82] B. Carroccio, 'Il dio fluviale giovane,' 71.

[83] J.P. d' Orville, P. Burman, G. Tielenburg, and J.V. Le Clerc, *Jacobi Philippi d'Orville Sicula, quibus Siciliae veteris rudera, additis antiquitatum tabulis, illustrantur* (Amstelaedami: apud Gerardum Tielenburg, 1764), 390.

[84] G.L. Castello, principe di Torremuzza, *Siciliae et obiacentium insularum veterum inscriptionum nova collectio* (Panormi: Bentivenga, 1769). Originally, Castello believed the man-faced bull was the Minotaur, but changed his view after reading the work of Pieter Burman.

all rivers.'[85] The river deity theory was proposed again at the beginning of the 20th century by Posterano,[86] and recently has been suggested by G.K. Jenkins,[87] C. Weiss,[88] A. Campana,[89] R. Taylor,[90] and several others.

The Learned Prince of Torremuzza[91]

The Prince's argument as summarized by Eckhel is as follows: (1) The ancients accorded divine honors to rivers; (2) Ancient rivers were depicted as bulls; (3) Rivers were also depicted as a human face [and human body] with horns; and (4) The Akarnanians and Ambrakians used a man-headed bull to depict their rivers, so it follows that other cities depicted their river god this way too.

The Man-Faced Bull of Gela

The argument that the man-faced bull on the coinage of Gela is a representation of the river Gelas is held by many numismatists today. At the outset, it should be noted that there is literary evidence that the river god of the Geloans was named Gelas, as we learn from Timaios of Tauromenion,[92] when he discusses the Phalaris Bull in the first *Pythian Ode*. However, some, including Eckhel, have still doubted this connection. Carina Weiss[93] points out that the inscription ΓΕΛΑΣ serves to acknowledge precisely that it is a local god and not Acheloios, since the Geloan tetradrachms are the earliest coins to show the man-faced bull in the West.[94] But the most convincing argument might come from a chronological overview of the inscriptions, again provided by Weiss. As she explains, the legend ΓΕΛΑΣ must be linked to the man-faced bull, because the Jenkins Group VII tetradrachms, which show a youthful horned river god, do not have the inscription ΓΕΛΑΣ, but instead on the obverse ΓΕΛΩΙΩΝ (**Fig. 155**).[95] Yet in the same series, when the man-faced bull reappears on the reverse, the inscription ΓΕΛΑΣ also returns (**Fig. 156**).[96] Weiss also takes note of the fact that the man-faced bull reappeared when Gela re-founded itself after the Carthaginian invasion, c. 405 to 339 BC. As for the later bronze units, which do not depict a man-faced bull but instead have a horned human river god on the obverse and a regular bull on the reverse, Jenkins[97] explains that it might indicate the dual nature of the river god (**Fig. 157**).[98] Ultimately, Weiss believes the man-faced bull of Gelas borrowed its iconography from Acheloios, just as Millingen proposed.

The Man-Faced Bull of Agyrion

According to Weiss, the man-faced bull depicted on the bronze coins of Agyrion represents the local river god Palagkaios (**Fig. 158**).[99] It is worth noting, first, that Eckhel mentions in the *Doctrina*, 'If I ever see the man-headed bull type labeled not with these ambiguous names [i.e. Gelas]...but with a name such as Amenanos...I will become an immediate convert to the theory of the learned Prince.'[100] Palagkaios of Agyrion might be such a name. Weiss argues first that the nominative *Palagkaios* does not correspond to the later forms of Agyrion magistrate legends, but her evidence is from after 241 BC, when Sicily was a Roman province. Secondly, Weiss suggests that it is probably not an artist's signature, since such signatures are usually tiny abbreviations, not large banners directly over the illustration. She also questions why an artist would sign a substandard bronze die in such a way. Finally, she cites Agyrion coinage from the period 339 to 300 BC in which a male head in laurel wreath carries the inscription ΞΕΥΣ ΕΛΕΥΘΕΡΙΟΣ, a clear label of the illustration (**Fig. 159**).[101] She then concludes that ΠΑΛΑΓΚΑΙΟΣ must also refer to the illustration, and therefore name the man-faced bull.

The most significant problem in Weiss' theory is that the two main rivers near Agyrion, the modern Dittaino and Salso rivers, were not known as Palagkaios in ancient times according to the literary sources. Diodorus Siculus (active 60 to 30 BC), who was from Agyrion, never mentions that the archaic name of the local river was Palagkaios, and instead refers to it as Chrysas.[102] Polybius,[103] too, does not give the name Palagkaios for an Agyrian river but instead gives us the name Kyamosoros. However, both of these sources are late, and since Agyrion was one of the earliest areas inhabited by native Sikels, it might have been a pre-Greek name for either of the aforementioned rivers. In fact, where Weiss could find no etymological basis for the name in

85 J. Millingen, *Recueil de quelques médailles grecques inédites* (De Romanis, 1812), 8 ff.

86 L. Posteraro, 'Origine di Alife: simbolismo delle sue tradizioni e della sua moneta,' in *Rivista Italiana di Numismatica* (1916), 307ff.

87 G.K. Jenkins, *The Coinage of Gela*, 165-175.

88 C. Weiss, *Griechische Flußgottheiten in vorhellenistischer Zeit* (Würzburg, 1984).

89 A. Campana, 'Sicilia: Agyrion (440 – circa 150 a.C.),' in *Panorama Numismatico*, no. 67 (Serravalle: Nomisma 1993) 173.

90 R. Taylor, 'Chapter Three- The Early Coinage of Neapolis,' in *A Documentary History of Naples: Ancient Naples*, forthcoming (accessed September 13th, 2010).

91 G.L. Castello, *Siciliae et obiacentium insularum veterum inscriptionum nova collectio*, XXVI-XXVIII, note b.

92 Scholiast of Pindar, *Pythian Ode*, 1.185, as cited by R. Taylor, 'The Early Coinage of Neapolis.'

93 C. Weiss, *Griechische Flussgottheiten*, 53-55.

94 This is not correct, as Rhegion or even Laos are earlier.

95 G.K. Jenkins, *The Coinage of Gela*, no. 454-456.

96 Ibid., no. 459 (O86/R175); CNG 66, 103*.

97 G.K. Jenkins, *The Coinage of Gela*, 103.

98 Ibid., no. 505; R. Calciati, *CNS* III, 14; CNG, Coin Shop*

99 R. Calciati, *CNS* III, 122, 6/; CNG, Triton V, 117*.

100 J. Eckhel, 'Concerning the Man-Faced Bull,' 295.

101 R. Calciati, *CNS* III, 127-128, no. 11-11/14. CNG 67, Lot 207*. For a revised dating of this type to pre-Timoleontic years, cf. M. Bertelli and R. Calciati, 'Considerazioni sulla serie bronzea Zeus Eleuterio/ Flumine di Siracusa e della symachia,' in *Numismatica e Antichà Classiche*, Quaderni ticinesi, XL (Lugano: Arti Grafiche Gaggini-Bizzozero, 2011), 1-12.

102 Χρύσαν ποταμὸν, Diodorus Siculus, *The Library of History*, 14.95.2. Most likely the modern day Dittaino River.

103 Κυαμόσωρον ποταμὸν, Polybius, *Histories*, 1.9.4. Most likely the modern day Salso River.

Greek, there is compelling evidence, presented in the catalog portion of this publication, that the name has Semitic roots.[104]

Taylor's Theory on Neapolitan Man-Faced Bulls

Rabun Taylor provides an argument that the Neapolitan man-faced bull represents Sebethos, and as such, he argues that it is a symbol of synoecism, or the cohabitation of two or more different peoples in one geographic area, which in the case of Neapolis would be Neapolitans and Parthenopēans.[105] Taylor's argument rests on the fact that the Sebethos River was probably the river that divided ancient Neapolis from Parthenopē, and the man-faced bull is therefore the appropriate synoecistic image for depicting the river god.[106] In his words, 'The early coinage could be seen to represent an accord between the classes and their respective settlements- a pact that overcame the river dividing them, thereby signaling a rebirth of the colony's vitality.'[107]

His argument also refers to a coin minted c. 400 to 380 BC, on which a youthful horned river god is surrounded by the inscription *Sepeithos*, naming the horned man as the river god outright (**Fig. 160**).[108] He therein recognizes a phenomenon similar to Gela, claiming both cities employed the man-faced bull and youthful, horned male heads to represent their rivers. Taylor also cites an inscription from the island of Kōs that claims the Neapolitans 'were using as an emblem for their civic identity 'a figure of a male animal.''[109]

In terms of Parthenope, the Siren appearing on the obverse of many of the city's silver coins, Taylor suggests that one need not necessarily pair her with Acheloios, her father. Here he argues that the affiliation of Acheloios with the Sirens is fully developed only in Roman times, whereas his affiliation with Nymphs is Greek.[110] With this connection severed, Taylor argues that there is no justification for Acheloios to appear continuously on the city's coinage.[111]

Taylor also makes reference to the triple herms from Locri that depict a beardless man-faced bull and the inscription labeling him as Euthymos, another indication that man-faced bull iconography can be adapted for various deities (**Fig. 161**).[112]

Another argument from Taylor is that the cult of Herakles is well-attested in Campania, and it seems strange to him that the Campanians would put Herakles' rival on the area's coinage, and also have Victory crown him.[113]

Ultimately, like Weiss, Taylor believes the strict dichotomy advocated by Isler is unnecessary, and many river gods could be represented as a man-faced bull.

Di Giuseppe's Theory

Helga Di Giuseppe advances the theory that the man-faced bull is only used to represent deviated rivers. In her view, once a local river has been deviated it becomes like Acheloios with his broken horn, and therefore the community adopts the iconography of a man-faced bull on its coinage to represent its deviated river, as a form of compensation for the harmed deity. Thus the coin types are both a form of political propaganda and religious reparation of local communities towards the local regulated waters. This recompense could also take the form of celebrative games, as one sees in Metapontion, the building of altars, as in Teagene, or even the antefixes in Etruscan shrines and temples built near locations that underwent water works.[114] Ultimately, Di Giuseppe argues that the image of the man-faced bull does not simply represent the local river, as many scholars suggest, but instead 'deviated, regimented, regulated local water, thus represented in the form of Acheloos, tamed river *par excellence*.'[115]

Jannot's theory

Jean Jannot, who began his work before Isler without the motive of disproving him, nonetheless disagrees with him in terms of the identification of Etruscan man-faced bulls as the Greek river-deity Acheloios, because he finds no river deity connotation in Etruscan culture.[116] In Jannot's mind, the Italic populations relegated the man-faced bull to a subordinate role, a mere decorative motif, deprived of any divine quality. He states that in Etruria 'the Greek myth withered, and the Akarnanian monster dissolved into the Italic-Etruscan culture, to resurrect and develop into a hybrid creature who shares the same external features of Acheloios, but in reality is a very different being.'[117]

[104] See catalog section for Agyrion.
[105] R. Taylor, 'River Raptures: Containment and Control of Water in Greek and Roman Constructions of Identity,' 21-42.
[106] Ibid., 38-39. See also M. Napoli, *Napoli Greco-romana*, 2nd ed. (Naples, 1979), 130-134.
[107] Ibid., 38.
[108] Ibid., 26.
[109] R. Taylor, 'The Early Coinage of Neapolis,' 4, in which he cites for the inscription *SEG* 12.378.
[110] R. Taylor, 'River Raptures,' 26. For Roman sources identifying Acheloios as father of the Sirens, he cites: Ovid, *Metamorphoses*, 5.552-53, 14.87-88; Silius Italicus, 12.33-36; Lucian, *The Dance*, 50; Libanius, *Progymnasmata: Narrationes*, 31, *Libanii opera*, 8. For Acheloios as father of the nymphs, he cites: Plato, *Phaedrus*, 263d; Euripides, *Bacchae*, 519-20; Vergil, *Copa*, 15; Columella, 10.263.
[111] Ibid., 26.
[112] Ibid., 27-29.
[113] R. Taylor, 'The Early Coinage of Neapolis,' 3. La Chau and Le Blond (see above) made the same argument about the use of Victory over Acheloios (Cf. G. de La Chau, and F.T.M. de Baculard d' Arnaud Le Blond, *Description des principales pierres gravées du cabinet de S.A.S. Monseigneur le duc d'Orleans*, 123ff).
[114] H. Di Giuseppe, 'Acheloo e le acque deviate,' 79-86.
[115] Ibid., 86.
[116] J.R. Jannot, 'Achéloos, le taureau androcéphale et les masques cornus dans l'Etrurie archaique,' 765-789.
[117] Ibid., 765.

However, Jannot's solution to the identity of the man-faced bull has many problems. In the article, the author assumes that the Etruscans copied the image of the Greek Acheloios, which is an antiquated, Helleno-centric point of view. As a result of this initial mistake, he then relegates the Etruscan man-faced bull to a 'modest symbol of vitality,'[118] misunderstood by 'Etruscan artisans' ignorance'[119] as a result of the 'degradation of Greek myths and religious beliefs.'[120] However, the different connotations of the Etruscan man-faced bull, as this work demonstrates, are a sign of earlier direct contacts with Near Eastern traditions. Jannot seems to completely ignore the similar qualities of Near Eastern man-faced bulls which perfectly match the qualities he observed in the Etruscan man-faced bull tradition. In fact, summarizing Jannot's observation of the phenomenon, the man-faced bull of Etruria is a symbol of power and vitality, a protector, guardian, lucky charm, and promise of rebirth,[121] precisely as he was described in the Near East. Ultimately, like many others, Jannot fails to recognize the difference between the Akarnanian river deity named Acheloios and the earlier, 'one and manifold'[122] Acheloios as lord of primeval waters, not linked to any specific location.

Guzzo's Theory

Pietro Giovanni Guzzo agrees with the local river god hypothesis for Magna Graecia and Sicily, recognizing the divine essence of such figures and describing the rivers themselves as the houses in which river gods live. His major example is the deification and worship of Euthymos at Lokris.[123] Guzzo also argues that the image of Acheloios was a sort of divine archetype used to represent the overwhelming charge of a river's current, so the local rivers were therefore represented as man-faced bulls to indicate the rough, downstream portion of the river course. On the other hand, Guzzo proposes that the youthful river gods on Greek coinage represent the river in its initial course, a more suitable, quieter 'house' for the deity.[124] There appears to be no geographical evidence for this theory.[125]

Carroccio's Theory

Benedetto Carroccio believes that the man-faced bulls of Magna Graecia and Sicily never represent Acheloios, and instead advances the theory that man-faced bulls and horned youthful river gods are both depictions of local rivers, ultimately explaining the differences in iconography as references to different religious meanings.[126] For example, whereas a man-faced bull would represent the wild, impetuous local river deity as both destructive and life-giving, the youthful, horned river god alluded to the notion of rebirth or kourotropic associations.[127] Carroccio also exhibits the contemporaneous appearance of man-faced bulls and youthful river gods, arguing against those who suggest a diachronic development of the iconography from man-faced bull to youthful river god with horns, since the youthful river gods and man-faced bulls simultaneously represented rivers for centuries.[128] Ultimately, he argues that such iconographies stem from pre-historic ancestral beliefs concerning water: power, fertility, regeneration, chthonic associations, etc.[129] Moreover, he suggests, following previous speculations by Giannelli,[130] that the human features attached to the bull's body originally alluded to the 'mutability' of water as the local object of cult, which was only later associated with the Akarnanian Acheloios.[131]

Carroccio's specific argument against the identification of Sicilian and Magna Graecian man-faced bulls as Acheloios is as follows: (1) The cult of Acheloios was unknown in western colonies at the time such coinage was issued;[132] (2) There are images of man-faced bulls with inscriptions naming them as local river gods, e.g. the Brettian Traente, Sicilian Palagkaios and Gelas;[133] (3) For Neapolis, Sebethos is the only river god mentioned in legend, never Acheloios;[134] and, (4) The coin from

[118] Ibid., 788.
[119] Jannot states this while referring to the iconographic confusion in Etruria of bearded horned heads and Silenic heads.
[120] Ibid., 789.
[121] Ibid.
[122] Here we have adopted the terminology of Grazia Salamone because it captures the essence of the cultural enterprise of Acheloios. Cf. G. Salamone, *'Una' e 'molteplice'. La ninfa eponima di città, Iconografie monetali e semantica.*
[123] P.G. Guzzo, 'Fonti divine. Miti dell'acqua in Magna Grecia,' in *Storia dell'aqua. Mondi Materiali e Universi Simbolici* (Roma: Donzelli 2013), 40-1.
[124] Ibid, 39.
[125] See also Carroccio's critique: B. Carroccio, 'Il dio fluviale giovane in Magna Grecia e Sicilia,' in *Polis, urbs, civitas: moneta e identità. Atti del convegno di studio del Lexicon Iconographicum Numismaticae (Milano 25 ottobre 2012)* edited by L. Travaini and G. Arrigoni (Rome: Quasar, 2013), 67.
[126] B. Carroccio, 'Il dio fluviale giovane in Magna Grecia e Sicilia,' 65-75. Originally, Carroccio believed that either (1) youthful, horned river gods were simply man-faced bulls in juvenile form, representing the nascent river at its origin, when it is more subdued, or, (2) youthful, horned river gods represented tributaries of major rivers. See B. Carroccio, 'Il Toro androprosopo, la cicala e l'incuso reggino,' in *Numismatica e Antichità Classiche*, Vol. XXIX (Quaderni Ticinesi, 2000). He abandoned this geological approach when no supporting evidence could be found.
[127] Carroccio presents compelling evidence that ties the appearance of youthful, horned river gods with various 'renovations' promoted throughout Sicily by Hermokrates and Timoleon. See Ibid., 71-72.
[128] Ibid., 66.
[129] B. Carroccio, 'Il Toro androprosopo, la cicala e l'incuso reggino,' 54-55.
[130] G. Giannelli, 'La figura taurina sulle monete della Magna Graecia,' in *Rivista italiana di Numismatica*, Vol. XXXIII (Milano: Società Numismatica Italiana, 1920), 105-140.
[131] According to Carroccio, Isler's identification of any man-faced bull with Acheloios emerges from 'references to the late encodings of myth and decorative schemes, given by literary sources' (B. Carroccio, 'Il Toro androprosopo, la cicala e l'incuso reggino,' 52).
[132] Ibid., 53.
[133] Ibid., 56-7.
[134] B. Carroccio, 'Il dio fluviale giovane in Magna Grecia e Sicilia,' 67.

Metapontion that depicts Acheloios with a bull's head is evidence against Isler's theory of a codified image of Acheloios, and he points out the fact that Acheloios is depicted on this coin just as Sophocles described.[135]

While there are undoubtedly pre-Greek roots to the man-faced bull tradition,[136] and a strong case can be made for local river gods by examining the inscriptions on coins such as those of the Brettians, there are some significant shortcomings with Carroccio's standpoint. One issue is that there is distinct evidence for the cult of Acheloios in the west at an early date, for example, the aforementioned stater from Metapontion (which actually shows a bearded man with bovine ears and horns, unlike Sophocles' description).[137] There are also numerous examples of Attic Painted Pottery found in Sicily and dating back to the 6th century BC that distinctly show Acheloios as a man-faced bull fighting Herakles.[138] If the Sicilians were purchasing this pottery, they must have recognized the painted subjects and therefore were well aware of the image of Acheloios when they (later) began to issue coinage. Finally, Carroccio does not consider the link between Acheloios and Parthenope, mentioned above, worthy of interest.[139]

Bouffier's Theory

Sophie Bouffier argues that the man-faced bulls of Sicily and Magna Graecia are not Acheloios, claiming that an Akarnanian river god has no business on the coinage of the area.[140] Instead, she takes the position that man-faced bulls are symbols of local rivers representing economic prosperity, fertility, and geo-political power, but are not actual deities. Her ultimate position in this respect is that 'personification does not mean deification,' meaning that the representations of rivers in Sicily were stripped of any divine quality.[141] She supports this position by examining youthful, horned personifications of rivers which are depicted performing sacrifices on coins. For Bouffier, it would not make sense for a deity to sacrifice to himself, and instead the figures must be sacrificing to the true Hellenic deities of Olympus.[142] Her justification is further supported by the accompanying symbols of major deities on such coins, evidence that the personified river is sacrificing to them on behalf of the community.[143]

Carroccio was the first to criticize Bouffier's theory, arguing that it is too Helleno-centric and was not attentive to the specificities of local cults. An additional problem, addressed in detail below, is that Bouffier, like others, presupposes that Acheloios is first and foremost an Akarnanian god whose iconography and mythology spread from that region, not a deity of all fresh water. In addition, she does not deem important the evidence of water cults and worship of rivers in Magna Graecia and Sicily, some of which she even mentions in her work. Finally, she seems to ignore that rivers are mentioned in ancient Greek sources concerning divine lineages, so there is little reason to strip Sicilian rivers of any divine connotation.

Euthymos of Locri

Another possible identification for at least some man-faced bulls is Euthymos of Locri. Euthymos was an actual person living in Locri[144] in the 5th century who won three Olympic boxing titles.[145] He is purported to have accomplished some legendary feats, too, including his most famous accomplishment of defeating the Hero of Temesa, the restless, virgin-hungry spirit that was once a member of Odysseus' crew.[146] It is interesting for our purposes to note that Euthymos never died, but instead was absorbed into the Kaikinos River,[147] the river of his birth.[148] Some modern scholars argue that Euthymos thereby became a river god and was worshipped as such,[149] at times in the guise of a man-faced bull. In terms of iconographical evidence, on some triple herms found at *Locri Epizephyrii* (c. 4th century BC) there appears a beardless man-faced bull before an altar, with the inscription Εὐθύμου ἱερά, with minor variants (**Fig. 161**). Thus, argues Bruno Currie, the people of Locri worshipped Euthymos in the form of a man-faced bull.[150] Isler disagrees, arguing that the inscription is Εὔθυμ[ος] (*sc.* ἀνέθηκε) or Εὐθύμ[ou] (*sc.* ἀνάθημα), and is therefore a dedication to Acheloios from a person named Euthymos who lived during the 4th century BC.[151]

135 S. Noe, *The Coinage of Metapontum,* no. 311. See also B. Carroccio, 'Il Toro androprosopo, la cicala e l'incuso reggino,' 53.

136 See above, Chapter 3.

137 S. Noe, *The Coinage of Metapontum,* no. 311. See the accompanying catalog entry for Metapontion for an enlargement of the BnF specimen, exhibiting a distinct human face.

138 H.P.Isler, *Acheloos*, 60, 166.

139 The Siren appearing on silver issues from Neapolis has been identified as Parthenope, the original namesake of the city before it became Neapolis.

140 S. Collin Bouffier, 'Il culto delle acque nella Sicilia greca: mito o realta?,' in *Storia dell'acqua. Mondi materiali e universi simbolici*; edited by V. Teti (Rome: Donzelli, 2013), 52. Bouffier also disagrees with Isler re the inscriptions on the coinage of Gela.

141 Ibid., 55.

142 Ibid., 54.

143 Ibid., 51.

144 Pausanias, *Descriptions of Greece*, 6.6.4; *CEG*, 1.399.

145 Ibid., and also, *P.Oxy*, 222, col.i.12, 25.

146 Callimachus, *Fragmenta*, 98 Pf and *Diegesis*, 4.6-17; Strabo, *Geographica*, 6.1.5 255; Pausanias, *Descriptions of Greece*, 6.6.7-11; Aelian, *Various Histories*, 8.18; Suda, *s.v.* Εὔθυμος .

147 Aelian, *Various Histories*, 8.18. Cf. Pausanias, *Descriptions of Greece*, 6.6.10.

148 Pausanias, *Descriptions of Greece*, 6.6.4. The etymology of Euthymos and Kaikinos (Lat. Caecinus), as the Etruscan city of Caecina, suggest a water course quietly (greek *eu-* 'good' and *-thymos* 'soul') flowing in the valley (semitic *gaj-* 'valley'), born on mountains (*-kinnu* is Akkadian for 'mountain'). G. Semerano, *Le Origini della Cultura Europea* (1984), I.1, XXXIX.

149 See B. Currie, 'Euthymos of Locri: A Case Study in Heroization in the Classical Period,' in *JHS*, 122 (2002); F. Costabile et al., *I ninfei di Locri Epizefiri* (Catanzaro, 1991) 195-238.

150 B. Currie, 'Euthymos of Locri,' 29.

151 H.P. Isler, *Acheloos*, 34 and 195, no. 103, as cited by B. Currie,

However, recent studies allegedly demonstrate Isler's view is incorrect.[152]

Acheloios

N. Ignarra and Other Early Commentators:While it is not disputed that the man-faced bull of Akarnania is Acheloios, others have extended this theory to apply far beyond that region (**Fig. 162**).[153] Nicola Ignarra[154] was the first to do this in his work De Palaestra Neapolitana, or 'Concerning the Wrestling School at Neapolis.' According to the summary provided by Curtis Clay, 'The Buthysia at Puteoli was a festival at which bulls were slaughtered. Therefore some scholars had connected this festival with the man-headed bulls that frequently appear on Campanian coins. Ignarra wants to reject this explanation, so is drawn into the question of what those man-headed bulls on the coins actually represent,' devoting some 45 pages to the topic.[155]

As for his actual argument, Ignarra explains that all depictions of the man-faced bull are Acheloios, since Acheloios represents rivers and water in the general sense and we can, as Eckhel recounts, refer to them as 'Acheloici.'[156] Thus, for Ignarra, Acheloios is much more than an Akarnanian river god.[157] His argument is based mostly on iconography, and in particular the beard of the man-faced bull, which Sophocles mentions in his *Trachiniae*, line 13, 'with ox-like face: and from his beard's dark shadows.' In addition, Ignarra argues against the notion that man-faced bulls are exclusively river gods, the crux of his argument being that many man-faced bulls were minted in areas not close to rivers. In fact, he sees the figure more as a symbol of abundance than strictly a river god.[158] As for the origin of the iconography, Ignarra points to the Chalcidians, and claims the iconography was spread by colonization, most notably to Cumae.[159] Unfortunately, Eckhel does not give this theory the credit it deserves, and instead dismisses it as a problem of overextending an example of an iconography and applying it to all examples of an iconography.

Many other scholars have argued that the man-faced bull is a depiction of Acheloios. Guilio Minervini is the most notable proponent of the 19th century. Originally completely convinced that the man-faced bull on the coinage of Campania was Dionysos,[160] he changed his opinion after seeing a coin from Neapolis published by Riccio, on which the man-faced bull is depicted above water with an apparent stream springing from his mouth (**Fig. 163**).[161] After seeing the coin, he wrote another work in which he stated that the man-faced bull on the coinage of Campania was 'undoubtedly' Acheloios, and that there should 'no longer [be] any doubts for the future.'[162]

N.K Rutter's Position

In his work, N.K. Rutter[163] suggests that the man-faced bull of Neapolis is Acheloios, which is probably the most widely-held view by contemporary numismatists. It should be mentioned that Rutter agrees with most contemporary scholars that the man-faced bulls on south Italian and Sicilian coinage represent local river gods and not Acheloios.[164] However, in the case of Neapolis he questions whether we see Sebethos or Acheloios. His argument that it is probably Acheloios is as follows: (1) There are iconographic parallels that display a very similar iconography and are certainly Acheloios; (2) There is definitive proof of a cult of Acheloios that was established in south Italy by the time Neapolis was founded;[165] and, (3) The obverse most likely shows Parthenope, Acheloios' daughter, whose tomb is allegedly in Neapolis and who had games held in her honor; hence the reverse shows her father and, on most issues, Victory crowns him (**Fig. 164**).[166]

H.P. Isler's Position

Isler's view is that all man-faced bulls are Acheloios, except those on the aforementioned pithoi of the 7th century BC and on the coinage of Lycia (and possibly Istros). His argument is based primarily in the area of hermeneutics.[167] Essentially, he claims

'Euthymos of Locri,' 29, footnote 52.

[152] F. Costabile et al, *I ninfei di Locri Epizefiri*, 195-238; *SEG*, 42.906, as cited by B. Currie, 'Euthymos of Locri,' 29. The Lokrian herms with the inscription Euthymos always depict a beardless man-faced bull, so perhaps this feature was used to differentiate that specific mythological character. It is likely that the tradition of Lokris also spread some miles northwest to its colony Medma, as attested by the discovery of a fragmentary herm featuring a beardless young man with bovine ears and horns (S. Settis, *Archeologia in Calabria. Figure e temi* (Roma, 1987), 263).

[153] For examples of such coinage, see BMC Thessaly, pg. 168; CNG 67, lot 526*.

[154] N. Ignarra, *De palaestra Neapolitana*, 232.

[155] Personal correspondence with authors, Spring 2015.

[156] J. Eckhel, 'Concerning the Man-Faced Bull,' 293.

[157] N. Ignarra, *De palaestra Neapolitana*, 238.

[158] Ibid., 232-238.

[159] Ibid., 238-243.

[160] G. Minervini, 'Osservazioni sulle monete di Napoli colla protome del Sebeto,' in *Bullettino Archeologico Napoletano. Nuova Serie. Anno primo*, No. 6 (Napoli: Cataneo, 1852), 45-48.

[161] G. Riccio, *Repertorio, ossia descrizione e tassa delle monete di città antiche: compresse ne' poerimetri delle province componenti l'attuale regno delle Due Sicilie al di qua del Faro, con la enunciazione delle altre inedite o nuove, venute in luce dopo il decesso del cav. Carelli* (Napoli: Tramater, 1852), Pl. I, No. 9.

[162] G. Minervini, 'Moneta inedita di Napoli, che risolve la questione del toro androprosopo,' 57ff.

[163] N.K. Rutter, *Campanian Coinages*, 42-45.

[164] N.K. Rutter, *Greek Coinages of Southern Italy and Sicily* (London: Spink, 1997), 118, 137, etc.

[165] R.Taylor claims the idea that there was a living cult to Acheloios in Neapolis is an 'unproven proposition' (R. Taylor, 'The early coinage of Neapolis,' 4a).

[166] A. Sambon, *Les monnaies antiques de l'Italie,* no. 336. Numismatica Ars Classica NAC AG, Auction 46, Lot 149*.

[167] H.P. Isler, personal correspondence, January 2014. See also H.P. Isler, *Acheloos*, 80-91; H.P. Isler, 'Acheloos,' in *LIMC*, 35.

that one cannot assume the same iconographic type has different meanings, because the public would be unable to understand the image. He refers specifically to an 'encoding' that occurred in the 6th century BC, whereby artists were no longer free to deal with the issue at will, and were forced to respect the traditional forms which became patterns to carry a specific and recognizable meaning for the images.[168] Deviating from the code, he argues, would therefore make the image incomprehensible.[169] This holds true for all except Lycian mints and Istros. In terms of Lycia, it is not clear if the mint copied an eastern man-faced bull or intended to represent Acheloios, specifically (presumably, this does not break the code since Lycia is under the influence of the east, and not subject to the code; also, all Lycian issues showing the creature's full body depict it as a winged man-faced bull, like the Near Eastern lamassus).[170] His basic hermeneutical argument is in striking contrast to the argument Eckhel advances against Ignarra, namely, that just because the Akarnanians depicted Acheloios as a man-faced bull does not mean all man-faced bulls are Acheloios.[171]

In terms of Sicilian coinage of the man-faced bull, Isler's position is more concrete. For the coinage of Gela, Isler argues that the inscription ΓΕΛΑΣ must be understood as a Doric genitive singular name for the city.[172] He argues that ΓΕΛΟΙΩΝ (genitive plural) would not be used in the early 5th century because such terminology is too democratic for a city ruled by a tyrant. Later on, the inscription does become, for a short time, ΓΕΛΟΙΩΝ, taking on the new meaning, 'of the citizens of Gela,' instead of, 'of the city of Gelas,' and reflecting the political environment more suitably.[173] Isler also points out: If the man-faced bull is a local river god, should not Akragas, a sub-colony of Gela, have employed the iconography as well? Therefore, according to Isler, we cannot connect the man-faced bull with local river gods. Isler also points to the coinage of Panormos, on the obverse of which is depicted a youthful, horned river god and on the reverse, the man-faced bull. Here he sees a clear example of the local river depicted as a young, horned man and the god Acheloios depicted as a man-faced bull. He also argues that there are coins depicting man-faced bulls in Sicily for which there is no known corresponding river.[174]

In terms of the removal of the beard of the man-faced bull on the coinage of Akarnania, Isler explains this as the lowering of Acheloios' status from a god of all water to a local river god, which occurred during the Hellenistic period.[175] As we saw with **Fig. 120**, the Akarnanians depicted Acheloios without a beard just as often as with a beard (**Fig. 165**) on the city's coinage.[176] Extending this same principle to Istros, Isler argues that their coinage depicting bearded, horned men or masks of 'Acheloos' may be a local river god and not Acheloios.[177] Perhaps Isler was not aware of the varieties that clearly show the neck of a bull attached to the bearded horned heads, differentiated from those with a human neck.[178] Otherwise, the idea that Istros, during the 3rd and 2nd century BC, could employ the iconography of the man-faced bull for a local river, while others, such as Neapolis, Nola, Cales, Compulteria, Suessa Aurunca, Teanum Sidicinum, Aesernia, Malies, Larinum, Rome, Teate (Magna Graecia), or Alontion, Abakainon, Katane, Panormos, Segesta (Sicily), or even Arse (Hiberia), could not, is inconsistent, since all those mints issued man-faced bull coinage contemporaneously.

One other significant issue with Isler's position is that tyrants of 5th century Sicily are unlike the tyrants of later times, and we must disconnect certain connotations from the Platonic tradition that influence our understanding.[179] Tyrants were often supported by the people in 5th century Sicily, and so an inscription such as ΓΕΛΟΙΩΝ would certainly not be out of the question. In his essay, Donald Kagan reinforces this point: 'It [tyranny] often came in the form of a popular rebellion against a ruling dynasty or an aristocracy led by a heroic leader who had gained eminence as a soldier or, as in Cylon's case, as an athlete.'[180] Furthermore, the case of Gelon of Syracuse confirms this point: According to Diodorus Siculus, after defending the city from the Carthaginians, Gelon called an assembly of the Syracusan demos and offered to relinquish his role as defender of the city. But the demos themselves refused the offer, proclaiming him 'benefactor, savior, and king (basileus).'[181] Moreover, when Gelon was tyrant of Syracuse, the inscription ΣΥΡΑΚΟΣΩΝ continued to appear on the city's coinage.[182]

In terms of the coinage of Panormos, Isler's argument is at its strongest, although the theory advanced by Benedetto

[168] H.P. Isler, *Acheloos*, 95.
[169] Ibid.
[170] Ibid., 82, in reference to his catalog no. 296.
[171] J. Eckhel, 'Concerning the Man-Faced Bull,' 293.
[172] H.P. Isler, *Acheloos*, 84.
[173] Ibid., 85.
[174] Ibid., 84. We could not find one Sicilian mint issuing coinage of the man-faced bull that had no corresponding river.

[175] H.P. Isler, *Acheloos*, 90.
[176] See, for example, BCD Akarnania 53.2; CNG 79, 207*.
[177] Ibid., 90.
[178] See MSP I, 491-494; CNG, eAuction 288, lot 99.
[179] The Greek túrannoς means ‹an absolute ruler.› Liddell-Scott-Jones, *Greek-English Lexicon* (Oxford: UP, 1996), 1863. It is in the Latin that a distinctly negative connotation appears, namely, 'a cruel or severe ruler, a despot.' See 2nd meaning, Lewis-Short, *A Latin Dictionary* (Oxford: UP, 1969), 1922.
[180] D. Kagan, *Pericles of Athens and the Birth of Democracy* (New York: Simon & Schuster, 1991), 12.
[181] S.L. Budin, *The Ancient Greeks: An Introduction* (Oxford: UP, 2009), 192-193. However, it must be noted that Diodorus' account is formulated in Hellenistic terms (Cf. N.K. Rutter, 'The myth of the Damareteion,' in *Chiron* 22 (1993), 171-88, esp. 177-8).
[182] Cf. SNG ANS 17; SNG München 927.

Carroccio that such depictions represent different aspects of the same river is an intriguing alternative.[183]

Intermediary Conclusions

All that has been determined so far is that the identity of the man-faced bull on Greek coinage is far from well established. We can be fairly certain that it is not an artistic variation of the Minotaur, for the reasons outlined by Mazochius and later by Eckhel. It probably is an agricultural allegory, but as we stated before, that does not really help in determining the actual identity. As for Neptune, the argument is more of a suggestion and is not very convincing, especially since the coin later illustrated by Ignarra is likely a fantasy. The gems depicted in Eckhel's plates are most likely not authentic: Isler has his doubts and gem expert Hadrien Rambach believes they were probably engraved in the 1600 to 1700s.[184] Eckhel's argument for Dionysos Hebon is considered outdated, but his reasoning is quite sound. Still, it is unsatisfying when we consider the persuasive evidence for alternative identifications. Gardner's argument for Dionysos Zagreus seems plausible, but lacks sufficient proof. The case for local river gods is indeed an interesting one, which is why the theory has become so popular today amongst scholars. Likewise, the case for Euthymos of Locri is equally convincing. Finally, Acheloios is in many cases represented as a man-faced bull, but the question we have to address is: Are all man-faced bulls Acheloios? We now turn to that and other questions as we formulate and present our own interpretation of the identity of the man-faced bull.

[183] B. Carroccio, 'Il dio fluviale giovane in Magna Grecia e Sicilia,' 65-75.

[184] Personal correspondence, Fall 2014.

Chapter VII: The Identity of the Greek Man-Faced Bull

There are two essential topics we will cover in this section in order to properly formulate our theory on the identity of the man-faced bull: the widespread use of locative epithets in the Greek world during the time period in which the man-faced bull appeared on Greek coinage, and the etymology of the word Ἀχελώϊος. In the end, we hope to demonstrate that the man-faced bulls on the coinage of the Greek world are probably Acheloios with qualifying locative epithets,[1] essentially building upon the work of N. Ignarra and H.P. Isler, and incorporating the work of C. Weiss, N.K. Rutter, R. Taylor, and others.

On Greek Epithets

The use of epithets in the Greek world was as important as it was pervasive. As Simon Pulleyn sums up in his article on the subject, 'It has become a commonplace to say that, in classical Greek and Roman religion, to know the name of a god was to have power over him.'[2] Whether one agrees or disagrees, it would be nearly impossible to find a deity that did not have many different epithets, some being employed nearly universally whereas others only occasionally. In fact, a deity may have many different epithets within the same city.[3] There are also various kinds of epithets employed by the ancient Greeks, the most common referring to either a special characteristic or title (Zeus the King) or a location (Delphian Apollo).[4] It is the latter that will be of special interest to us, but first we must give an overview of the general importance of the epithet.

Epithets are generally seen as an essential element to Greek religion, if not the cornerstone.[5] P. Brulé argues that gods without epithets are mere 'artifacts of language.'[6] In other words, without the epithet we have only some abstract notion that has no real, meaningful significance for the religious observer. Fields offers further confirmation of the pervasive use: 'Greek gods... were linked to specific domains and functions in two ways: by their epithet and through the personified abstractions in their retinue.'[7] Thus the use of the epithet was an integral component in connecting with a deity and this much is well established. In fact, the importance of having the proper name of a god is well attested in the ancient sources.[8] There are very few epigraphic exceptions to this general rule.[9]

In terms of everyday religious observances, if, for example, a Milesian wanted to pray to Apollo, he would normally pray to Apollo Milesius. Sometimes such local cults became so popular that they would travel: the cult of Venus Erycina in Rome is attested on the coinage of C. Considius Nonianus,[10] but was originally a cult from Eryx, Sicily. More importantly, an individual would not normally pray to just 'Apollo'- it would be his local Apollo or another epithet of Apollo associated with a specific function, like Apollo the Healer. In each case the Greeks ought to know to which epithet to pray. In Xenophon,[11] for instance, we learn that he is having financial trouble because he is praying to Zeus Basileos and not Zeus Meilichios.[12] Thus, in Greek religion, if one sought a specific remedy to a problem one prayed to a specific epithet. Finally, it should be noted that the use of epithets, and in particular locative epithets, was not restricted to just major deities. Asclepius Kaousios, for instance, is associated with the town of Kaous in Arkadia.[13] There are many other examples of this phenomenon among lesser gods.[14]

---

[1] H.P. Isler is the only other author to mention something like an epithet with the figure of the man-faced bull, but he conceptualizes it in just one case and in a totally different sense: on the coinage of Paphos he understands the inscription BO-KA-RO-SE to mean 'horned bull,' and takes that as a reference to Acheloios, suggesting that the two words were essentially synonymous, '*anderer Name fur Acheloos.*' He very distinctly disagrees with BO-KA-RO-SE referring to a local river god, however, '*Doch ist es ebenso möglich, das sich auch die Münzen von Paphos auf einen kult des Acheloos-Bokaros* in *dieser Stadt beziehen, ohne auf einen lokalen Fluss anzuspielen*' and thus his theory is entirely different from the one we will present, which is a theory of locative epithets/local manifestations, incorporating both Acheloios and local river gods. See H.P. Isler, *Acheloos*, 81-82, in reference to BMC Cyprus, 35, 1-3, Taf. 7., 1-3; 21, 1-3; Head 740; F. Imhoof-Blumer, 'Fluß- und Meergötter auf griechischen und römischen Münzen. (Personifikationen der Gewässer),' 228, 136, Taf. 4, 34.

[2] S. Pulleyn, 'The Power of Names in Classical Greek Religion,' in *Classical Quarterly*, New Series, Vol. 44, No. 1 (1994), 17. Pulleyn ultimately argues that the significance of knowing a god's name in the Greek world has been exaggerated.

[3] R. Parker, *On Greek Religion* (Cornell: UP, 2011), 67.

[4] Ibid. 67-69.

[5] J. Wallensten summarizes the general consensus that 'the use of epithets is a vital component of Greek Polytheism.' See J. Wallensten, 'Personal protection and tailor-made deities: the use of individual epithets,' in *Kernos*, 21 (2008), 82. See also R. Parker, *On Greek Religion*, 67.

[6] 'A god without an epithet is but 'un artefact du lange',' P. Brulé, 'Le lange des épiclèses dans le polythéisme hellénique,' *Kernos*, 11 (1998), 18-19, as cited in J. Wallensten, 'Personal protection and tailor-made deities,' 82.

[7] N. Fields, 'Apollo: God of War, Protector of Mercenaries,' in *Archaeology in the Peloponnese: New Excavations and Research*, edited by Kenneth Sheedy (Oxford: Oxbow Books, 1994), 95-113.

[8] S. Pulleyn, 'The Power of Names in Classical Greek Religion,' 18. Pulleyn argues that, in contrast to the Judeo-Christian tradition of the secret name of YHWH, the Greeks tradition simply emphasized that one must know the name of a god if one were to pray to him, and that it did not posses some 'magical' power.

[9] For example see Homer, *Iliad*, 10.462. As cited in S. Pulleyn, 'The Power of Names in Classical Greek Religion,' 18, note 6. In the passage Odysseus refers to Athena as simply θεά.

[10] For the basic type, see RRC 424/1. For identification of the reverse temple as that of Rome and not Sicily, see M. Harlan, *Roman Republican Moneyers and Their Coins 63 BC-49 BC*, (London, 1995), 92-93.

[11] Xenophon, *Anabasis*, 7.8.1-6, as cited in S. Pulleyn, 'The Power of Names in Classical Greek Religion,' 18.

[12] The story is recounted in S. Pulleyn, 'The Power of Names in Classical Greek Religion,' 18. Incidentally, Cook claims there was an association between Zeus Meilichios and Acheloios at Athens (A.B. Cook, *Zeus: A Study in Ancient Religion*, Vol. II, 1117-1118).

[13] A. J. Atsma, 'Asclepius Cult,' *The Theoi Project*. www.theoi[dot]com.

[14] See ibid. for a very useful site on ancient religion.

Ultimately, an epithet can be seen as the essential element of Greek religion that serves as the auxiliary between the individual and the divine, bringing the latter from a position of transcendence to one of imminence. Its use was pervasive, and its importance in Greek religion should not be understated. More significantly for our purposes, the use of epithets must be considered in questions of identity.

The Greek Man-Faced Bulls, Epithets of Acheloios

If the use of epithets in the Greek world was pervasive, one must ask: Why would the man-faced bull be any different? In our view, and we see no reason to think otherwise, he would be subject to the same use of epithets as every other deity. Thus, a potential resolution to the problem of the identity of the man-faced bull in the Greek world, and one that incorporates the two main views held today, concerns the use of locative epithets. We know, for example, that Apollo had many epithets and most of these indicated specific cities, ethnic groups, or even geological features such as mountains, rivers, and plains: Abaeus, Basses, Cataonius, Delphicus, Eftrisios, Granius, Hyperboræus, Ismenius, Karneos, Leucadius, Maleates, Onceates, Pæonian, Salganeus, Tegyræus, and Zirinthios, among many others.[15] Although only two in the above list refer to rivers, Granius and Ismenius, it is clear that the location of specific temples or shrines was very often the source of a particular epithet in the Greek world. In fact, as Parker claims, 'no two Greek political communities worshipped exactly the same gods.'[16]

In terms of the iconography of Acheloios, we have the problem pointed out by Isler: How is the viewer supposed to know who the figure is if a variety of different deities are represented by the same iconography?[17] One could argue that in some cases the iconography is labeled as such: Palagkaios of Agyrion and Gelas of Gela, for instance. But perhaps, if we consider the widespread use of locative epithets in the ancient world, we can infer that these 'labels' are simply epithets, and not proof against Ignarra and Isler's position. So, for example, the inscription ΠΑΛΑΓΚΑΙΟΣ does not name an individual river god Palagkaios, but instead names the local representation of Acheloios, Acheloios Palagkaios (**Fig. 158**). The same would be true for other locations: Acheloios Amenanos (Katane), Acheloios Traies (Brettian), etc. We know also that dropping the 'Acheloios' from such an inscription is perfectly acceptable, as we see the epithet for Apollo, ΑΡΞΑΓΕΤΑΣ, used as the inscription on a contemporaneous bronze coin from Tauromenion (**Fig. 166**).[18] Therefore, Acheloios Palagkaios, Acheloios Gelas, Acheloios Sebethos, and so on and so forth, would be more appropriate ways of identifying the man-faced bulls on the coinage of the Greek world. For without an epithet Acheloios is relegated to a mere 'artifact of language,' and we know from Isler's great work that he was far more than that in ancient Greek religion. For Acheloios was the embodiment of a physical element and the source of all fresh water,[19] and the poets active during the time of the emergence and popularization of man-faced bull iconography on coinage refer to water as Ἀχελώϊος.[20] Thus he is literally inseparable from fresh water,[21] and as such, the only conceivable way that Greek man-faced bulls can have an individual identity during that time period, is via a locative epithet (a sinews of Acheloios).[22]

Aside from the numismatic inscriptions mentioned above, additional archaeological evidence of the syncretism of seemingly separate river deities exists in the 'Temple of the Oxus' and related 'Oxus Treasure' of 1877 from the area of Ai Khanoum, further reinforcing the case for locative epithets.[23] In fact, a sword hilt engraved with Herakles fighting Acheloios was found within the treasure, which allegedly came from the temple.[24] Thus, Litvinskii and Pichikian argue for either a syncretism among some gods (they include the river god Silenus-Marsyas,[25] depicted on a statue dedicated to the Oxus) or the incorporation of Greek river god iconography as a way of paying homage to the foreign Oxus at the temple.[26] In either case, it seems clear that Acheloios was still venerated amongst the Greek inhabitants of Ai Khanoum, and so the Indian humped man-faced bull appearing on a bronze issue is probably Acheloios Oxus.[27] This identification pays homage to the new river god but still honors the underlying god of all water, keeping with the Greek tradition. In fact, we know from Paul Bernard, excavator of Ai Khanoum, that the Greeks

15 Some 48 locative epithets for Apollo are listed in Anonymous, *A Classical Manual, Being a Mythological, Historical, and Geographical Commentary on Pope's Homer, and Dryden's Æneid of Virgil* (1833), 20-24.

16 R. Parker, *On Greek Religion*, 70.

17 Summary of personal correspondence with H.P.Isler.

18 See catalog entry MSP I, 56a-60.

19 Homer, *Iliad*, 21.194-195.

20 Sophocles, *Fragmenta*, 5; Euripides, *Bacchae*, 625; Aristophones, *Fragmenta*, 351 ; Achaeus, *Athens*, IV, 9; Ephorius, *FGrH* 70, F 20.

21 For an analysis of all rivers in the Greek world being called Acheloios, see F.L.W. Schwartz, *Der Ursprung der Mythologie, dargelegt an griechischer und deutscher sage* (Berlin: W. Hertz, 1860), 60-61 and, P. Decharme, *Mythologie de la Grèce antique* (Paris: Garnier Frères, 1886), 542.

22 In the course of this book it will also be clear that some of those locative epithets, like Palagkaios and Apsias (Rhegion), refer to toponyms and hydronyms of non-Greek origin, which convey an earlier Semitic cultural background.

23 Brian Kritt, *New Discoveries in Bactrian Numismatics* (Lancaster, PA: CNG, 2015), 104.

24 In this case depicted as a horned bearded man. Ibid., 106.

25 Incidentally, Marsyas originates from Meander. Thus, just as the Greeks (probably from the region of the Meander) incorporated Marsyas into new traditions in Ai Khanoum/Bactra, when they returned home they incorporated the Oxus back with the Meander.

26 B. A. Litvinskij and I. R. Pičikjan, 'River-Deities of Greece Salute the God of the River Oxus-Vakhsh: Achelous and the Hippocampess,' in *In The Land of the Gryphons: Papers on Central Asian Archaeology in Antiquity* (Firenze: Le Lettere 1995), 129.

27 Or possibly Acheloios Bactra, if we follow one of Bopearachchi's suggestions. Cf. O. Bopearachchi, 'The Monetary Policy of Bactria under the Seleukids,' 50-54.

made special arrangement to incorporate and preserve their Greek heritage in their new surroundings.[28] The fact that Acheloios appears here on a sword hilt also further reinforces the association of the iconography with mercenaries. In fact, the same group of mercenaries responsible for the deposit of this sword hilt, some 20+ years later, very likely applied the humped man-faced bull countermark (with meander symbol) to a coin of Antiochos II,[29] once retired and back on familiar territory in Asia Minor **(Fig. 35).** On that coin, Acheloios is indicated in the man's face attached to a bull, the hump indicates Oxus, and the meander symbol informs the viewer of the incorporation of their 'new' river, thus Acheloios Oxus Meander.

Notes on Ancestry and Etymology

Arguably the most interesting etymological, mythological, and iconographic relative to Acheloios is Asallúhi, the Near Eastern god of the 'river of ordeal' that emerges onto the earth in rivers and springs, and is known both as the 'princely bison' and 'light of the gods.'[30] The figure may very well have been depicted as a man-faced bull, especially since his father, Enki, ruler of Apsu (the subterranean waters) is depicted above two man-faced bulls on cylinder seals, where he collects water from streams emerging from their heads (**e.g., Fig. 11**). If we allow for a common *s-k* changeover,[31] Asallúhi morphs to Akalluhi, and one very easily arrives at Ἀχελώϊος. Moreover, the line reported by Wiggermann, in which purified water is referred to as 'the son of his god (Enki),' indicates that Asallúhi might also have been equated with water itself.[32] Thus the mythological tradition surrounding Asallúhi (river god, healer, mediating figure, 'princely' bison) combined with the probable evolution of the name, are a good indication of Acheloios' closest Near Eastern ancestor. In fact, the very first man-faced bull to appear on coinage in the West, Acheloios Apsias of Rhegion (**Fig.167**), bears a remarkable similarity in name to the Semitic Asallúhi Apsu.

Further evidence of the Near Eastern influence on the name Acheloios comes from an examination of the root Αχ and the word-bases which were operative in its formulation. Not surprisingly, the Greek root Αχ probably has a Semitic origin, not an Indo-European one.[33] Semerano was the first to establish a relation between the Semitic *aḫu* and the Greek Αχ. The Semitic root means 'bank

[28] P. Bernard, 'An Ancient Greek City in Central Asia,' in *Scientific American*, 246 (1982), 157.

[29] MSP I, 491. The probable find spot and elongated meander symbol indicate somewhere in the area of Magnesia, in Ionia. The undertype, SC 537, is of an uncertain mint, possibly Tralles, indicated by the awkward 'N' in the inscription.

[30] See above, pg. 14ff.

[31] It is possible that the Greeks adopted the Near-Easten word through early contacts, substituting the velar stop in the place of palatal sibilant. For the phenomenon of replacement sibilar-palatovelar from Akkadian to Greek, see Malati N. Shende, *The Language of the Harappans: From Akkadian to Sanskrit* (New Delhi: Abhinav Publications , 1997), 94.

[32] F.A.M. Wiggermann, *Mesopotamian Protective Spirits*, 66.

[33] Isler connects the etymology of Ἀχελώϊος and ἀχέρων, presupposing an αχερ-αχελ root, insofar as both have to do with water. He further connects the etymological basis of ἀχιλλεύς insofar as Achilles was the son of the sea goddess, Thetis. However, Isler argues that, since no reasonable Indo-European root can be found, the words must all have Mycenaean origin, citing Mycenaean tablets that show the name Achilles. The interesting part about Isler's view is that he acknowledges the iconography of the man-faced bull stems from the east, but does not look there for the origin of the name. (H.P. Isler, *Acheloos*, 113). Ἀχιλλεύς has the same base as the Akkadian *aklu*, 'overseer,' sharing the semantic cross-base *akel*, 'chieftain;' so the name Achilles, according to Semerano, also has Near Eastern origins (G. Semerano , *Le Origini della Cultura Europea. Vol. II. Dizionari etimologici. Basi semitiche delle lingue indeuropee. Tomo 1: Dizionario della lingua greca; Tomo 2: Dizionario della lingua latina e di voci moderne.* Biblioteca dell' Archivum Romanicum, Serie II, Vol.43 (Firenze: Leo S. Olschki, 1994), 45). As Isler noted for the etymological root, there is also a clear link between the mythical figures of Acheloios and Acheron: ἀχέρων, was first described by Homer as one of the Underworld rivers flowing in Hades (*Odyssey,* 10.513). In later Roman tradition he is identified as the main river of the Underworld (cf. Virgil, *Aeneid*, 6.297), but even later the name is used to designate the entire Underworld. (Virgil, *Aeneid*, 7.312; Cicero, *Senat.*, 10.c; Nepos, *Dion*, 10.) In archaic Latin he is called *Acheruns*, derived from earlier Etruscan Aχrun. (G. Pasquali, 'Acheruns, Acheruntis,' in *Studi etruschi*, Vol I (Firenze: Olschki, 1927), 291). The Greek ἀχέρων was used as a name for many rivers in Greece, for example the Thesprotia of Epirus, which, after a wild mountain course, goes underground and reappears on the surface not far away from the sea, forming the swamp Acherusiade. This swamp was a location for ancient oracles (G. Calogero, 'Acheronte,' entry in *Enciclopedia Italiana Treccani*, Vol.I, (Roma: 1929)). Other similar rivers or marshes had the same name in Triphylia (Strabo, *Geographica*, 8.344), in Bruttium at Pandosia (Strabo, *Geographica*, 6.256), and at Cuma, near the site of a famous oracle (G. Calogero, 'Acheronte'). In the characteristic depiction of the afterlife that Plato gives (*Phaedo*, 107a-115a), souls seeking purification have to wait on the bank of the swamp Acherusiade (G. Calogero, 'Acheronte'). In ancient sources Acheron is also described as the river that marks the entrance into the realm of the dead, the limit that the souls of the dead must cross. However, Semerano noted some specific differences between the Greek 'αχερων and the Etruscan aχrun (Latin *Acheruns*), suggesting they originally had different connotations in the Greek and Etruscan traditions, insofar as the conflation ἀχέρων -*Acheruns* began later, with Lucretius, during the 1st century BC. The Greek term refers more to the fluvial connotation, as it derives from Akkadian *aḫarātu*, 'the western bank' or 'the far bank of the river,' still somewhat connected with the underworld insofar the west was linked with the dark world of the dead for ancient Mesopotamian culture. The Italic aχrun/*Acheruns*, one the other hand, was more often used to describe the entire underworld, with less of an association with fluvial qualities. These observations match the etymological evidence and ancient texts: We know from ancient sources that the Etruscan *Sacra Acheruntia* were rites that had to do with fate, the afterlife, the founding of cities, and the delimitation of boundaries (N.T. de Grummond, 'Haruspicy and Augury: Sources and Procedures,' in *The Etruscan World*, 539-556). We know very little about those rites, except that they were described in the Etruscan texts called the 'Acheruntic Books,' which contained instructions for divination and prophesy (Arnobius, *Adversus Nationes*, 2.62). Ultimately, the main connotations of the word aχrun are related to divination, prophesy, and afterlife, and this is clear by the etymology of the world given by Semerano: Akkadian feminine *aḫrûtu*, 'which comes after, posterity;' Ugaritic *aḫr* and Hebraic *aḥar*, 'after;' Hebraic *aḥaron*, 'which comes after, western, lastly;' and Hebraic *aḥarīt*, 'future, end.' The chthonic connotation is shown by the homophonic Akkadian base *ḫarûm*, 'to dig, digging work.' Semerano states that different Semitic bases can prevail in western and central Mediterranean areas, and this is a case in which the bases related to the 'after' connotation prevailed in Etruria, and those related to the 'fluvial' connotation prevailed in Greece. Altogether, there are some features shared by Acheloios and Acheron: both are chthonic and liminal rivers, both have purifying properties, and both are connected to oracular practices. Therefore, Isler was correct in recognizing a common etymological root for Acheloios and Acheron, he just looked in the wrong place.

of the river'[34] and its closely related word, *aḫû*, means 'seashore.'[35] Semerano connected this with the Greek Αχαίϝο (Achaeans), as 'people from the seashore.'[36] The Semitic *aḫu* is itself related to other significant Semitic roots, namely, *agû*, which mainly means 'water,' and is also used for 'river,' or 'flowing from the river;'[37] and *īku*, which also means 'river, riverbank, or dike.'[38] It is important to note that in Semerano's method, which this work follows, the Semitic velar *h* is interchangeable with *k* when determining Akkadian etymologies for Greek words, which applies for Greek *K* as well as Ξ.[39] Thus, given probable vocalic mutations and the similarity in meanings, it seems plausible that the Greek root αχ has its origin in the Semitic *aḫu, aḫû, agû, īku,* and, of course, *asal* (possibly from from Akkadian *sarum*, 'rich,' *sarrum* (and Hebrew *sar*) 'prince, king,' and *saratu*, 'to shine.'[40]

Examining the later part of the Greek word, ἐλώϊος, the case becomes even more obvious. In Akkadian *illu* means 'watercourse,' or 'water of the river invading land.'[41] The closely related words *elu* and *ilu* mean 'deity.'[42] In addition, we have the equally significant word *ellu*, which means 'holy, sacred,' and, 'clean and shining.'[43]

Altogether it is likely that the Greek word Ἀχελώϊος , much like man-faced bull iconography, has its roots deeply embedded in the Semitic tradition,[44] in which all of these bases were influential throughout the generations and ultimately, for the Greeks, emerged in a word embodying all of the old Semitic meanings: a sacred water deity associated with ritual cleansing.[45] This is further reinforced by our discussion of mercenaries in Chapter 2. As John Hale points out in his essay on the origin of the hoplite tradition, 'Certainly it is a truth, universally acknowledged, that a landing on a beach held by enemy troops constitutes one of the most difficult of all military challenges.'[46] Thus, by paying homage to the god associated with that type of landscape, mercenaries no doubt hoped for success on that very shore. This last point is also appealing when considering the earlier discussion on the primacy of Acheloios versus Okeanus and the notion that Acheloios might have been the original god of all water.[47]

But there is another side to the coin: the enigmatic world of Etruscan epigraphy. In an Etruscan epigram allegedly written by a young man for his beloved, one sees the phrase *Axlei Truies (x) θesθufarce*,[48] translated as 'the journey of the sun brought us the spring.' Semerano proposed that the root of *axlei* (genitive form meaning 'of the sun') is the Akkadian *aklu* (from Summerian *akil*) meaning 'chieftain' or 'overseer.'[49] Another Etruscan fragment from Hesychius reads Αυκηλως εως υπο Τυρρηνων, translated by Mangini as 'for the Tyrrhenians, Αυκηλως means dawn.'[50] Semerano takes this further and suggests that Αυκηλως means ‹overseer of sunrise,'[51] which, for the purpose of this work, makes perfect sense: Recall that in the man-faced bull tradition of the Near East, the figure is very often seen as a liminal deity, mediating between life and death and even the transition from dark to light.[52] Likewise, in the Etruscan world, man-faced bulls operate more as chthonic, liminal deities than fluvial figures. Moreover, from very early on in our story the sun-water dynamic has been operative: It was revealed first in the Near East, where

---

[34] G. Semerano, *Le Origini della Cultura Europea. Vol. I*, I.2, 429; G. Semerano, *L'infinito*, 16 and 21 (for genitive *aḫi*); G. Semerano, *Il popolo che sconfisse la morte. Gli Etruschi e la loro lingua* (Milano: Mondadori, 2003), 77.

[35] G. Semerano, *L'infinito*, 26

[36] Ibid.

[37] From Sumerian *a-gi6-a*, 'water,' cf. G. Semerano, *Le Origini della Cultura Europea*, Vol. I, 2, 453; *agûm* is Akkadian for 'wave' understood as 'flood wave of the river,' *agaḫu* is Akkadian for 'water flooding,' cf. ibid., 427-9, 435; G. Semerano, *Le Origini della Cultura Europea. Vol. II.*, 343; G. Semerano, *L'infinito*, 15. Latin *acqua* probably shares the same Akkadian root.

[38] G. Semerano, *Il popolo che sconfisse la morte*,75.

[39] G. Semerano, *L'infinito*, 26, also observed that Assyrian words with the initial letter *k* later came out as *h* in derived Hittite words.

[40] G. Semerano, *Le Origini della Cultura Europea*, Vol. II, II.1, 151. The original name for *Asallúhi* was *Asarlúhi.*

[41] G.Semerano, *La favola dell'indoeuropeo* (Milano: Mondadori, 2005), 85.

[42] G. Semerano, *Il popolo che sconfisse la morte*, 41, 113.

[43] G.Semerano, *L'infinito*, 29.

[44] Semerano's own view of the etymology of Acheloios is *aḫu* (bank of the river) + *elû* (tall, high), wherein he sees a relation to the notion of water control projects associated with the struggle of Herakles and Acheloios (G. Semerano, *Le Origini della Cultura Europea. Vol. I*, I.2, 429). It is worth mentioning that the Sanskrit *achamanna* (āchamanam) is almost certainly related to the Akkadian and Greek words, as it means 'sipping water from the hand before religious ceremonies.' See V.S. Apte, *The Student's Sanskrit-English Dictionary* (Delhi: Motilal Banarsidass, 2000), 76.

[45] An additional etymological connection can be seen in the the pre-nuptial rites of passage of the cult of Acheloios. The same etymological base of Acheloios appears in the Akkadian verb *aḫāzu*, 'to marry,' from which, according to Semerano, is derived the Greek words for husband ἀκοίτης and wife ἄκοιτις. This is also relevant as an additional demonstration of the interchangeability of the Semitic *aḫ-ak* with the Greek αχ-ak. See G. Semerano, *Le Origini della Cultura Europea. Vol. II*, II.1.18.

[46] J. Hale, 'Not Patriots, Not Farmers, Not Amateurs,' 189.

[47] See above, pg. 60ff. In terms of Okeanos, there appears to be no link to earlier Semitic words, further supporting the primacy of Acheloios and relegating Okeanus as the strictly Hellenic god. Moreover, according to Semerano the Greek word ποτᾰμός derives from Sumerian *pa6*, 'channel,' and Akkadian *pātum*, 'channel,' 'river,' + Akkadian *ammu, amûm*, 'swamp' (G. Semerano, *Le Origini della Cultura Europea. Vol. II*, II.1, 238-9) whereas the rivers spreading unregimented produced extensive wetlands (G. Semerano, *Le Origini della Cultura Europea*, Vol. I, 1, XVI). Póntoς shares the same Semitic etymology of ποτᾰμός (G.Semerano, *Le Origini della Cultura Europea*, Vol. II, 1, 238) as the Mesopotamians basically ignored the existence of a separate 'sea' and did not have a specific term for it.

[48] M. Pallottino, *Testimonia Linguae Etruscae. Biblioteca di Studi Superiori*, Vol. XXIX (Firenze: La Nuova Italia Editrice, 1954), TLE 329.

[49] G. Semerano, *La favola dell' indoeuropeo*, 77.

[50] L. Magini, *L'etrusco, lingua dall'oriente indoeuropeo, Studia Philologica*, Vol.21 (Roma: L'Erma di Bretschneider, 2007), 36, frag. TLE 815.

[51] G. Semerano, *La favola del''indoeuropeo*, 77.

[52] See above, pg.10, and specifically the lullaby in which the bull-man is named in a song that discusses the transition from dark to light, sleep to wakefulness, etc. A liminal connotation is implicit in any chthonic deity.

Anzu, the lion-headed bird monster (representing the sun) was frequently depicted attacking the man-faced bull (representing water) from above. Numerous Near Eastern examples of the man-faced bull with celestial motifs were also presented. There is even a mace head depicting the man-faced bull from Ur III dedicated to the sun god, Utu.[53] Herakles, too, has many associations with the sun (and lions) and thus he too forms a natural pairing with the man-faced bull as Acheloios.

In the Greek world this phenomenon occurs on coinage: celestial symbols attached to the man-faced bull, and the pairing with either Herakles or Apollo (also a solar deity) on issues of man-faced bull coinage. In fact, many of the mints issuing man-faced bull coinage on territory formerly occupied by the Etruscans use such celestial motifs.[54] There is even a coin from Mallos (440 to 390 BC) that offers a glimpse of the situation: On it, a winged man holds a solar disc above a man-faced bull (**Fig. 115 & 116**). But most importantly, there is a likely Near Eastern predecessor, Asallúhi, that is mentioned in ritual texts as both a fluvial deity and the 'light of the gods,' and he is recorded as early as Ur III and as late as Seleukid times. Thus, the Etruscan inscriptions simply remind us of the interplay and co-mingling of these figures and the carrying on of a natural pairing that has existed for thousands of years, in language, mythology, and iconography. In strictly linguistic terms, there are semantic crossings which are homophonically based, wherein multiple bases could have been carried by a single word. Thus, by these homophonic bases, which can sometimes interfere with each other, different and even seemingly ambivalent meanings emerge.[55] In the late Semerano's own words: 'Words, like stars, continue to radiate light even when the bodies that produced them no longer exist.[56] The names of deities will lend through the ages to be heard with new inflections and nuances, which will give new creative reasons to those names, and from renewed words new myths will be born.'[57]

Ultimately, throughout the centuries when all of these iconographies, word-bases, and cultic practices were traveling west, there eventually emerged two intimately related qualifications of Acheloios, both of which were still bound by the Semitic soil from which they came, and both of which employed the iconography of the man-faced bull.

Conclusions

With this solution we alleviate Isler's primary concern and make room for individual local rivers to maintain the level of honor they enjoyed in the ancient world, as sinews of Acheloios.[58] Robertson's notion of glocalization reveals just how this is possible.[59] Originally conceptualized as an economic theory, scholars in the humanities, such as Robert Holton,[60] began to conceptualize broader historical phenomena in terms of glocalization, in which there is a universalization of the particular, and a particularization of the universal, precisely what we are getting at with this theory of local embodiments of Acheloios. Thus, we must keep in mind that the man-faced bull is not an individual with an absolute 'identity', but rather a symbol that may contain several meanings or qualities, recognized in varying degrees in different places at different times. R. Parker's *On Greek Religion* makes a similar observation that is at the heart of glocalization: 'this greater particularity [from epithets] does not in itself make the god of cult an intrinsically different being,' but at the same time, 'even if in one perspective Zeus Meilichios was simply one aspect of Zeus, in another he had to be treated as a different figure.'[61] Thus, in cases outside Akarnania, the man-faced bull is probably both Acheloios and the local river god. In the specific case of Agyrion, Acheloios Palagkaios is especially important to its inhabitants because it is in the presumed Palagkaios

[53] F.A.M. Wiggerman, *Mesopotamian Protective Spirits*, 176 note 10, wherein the man-faced bull is described as an emblem of Utu.

[54] For an overview, see M. Cuozzo, 'Etruscans in Campania,' in *The Etruscan World* (London: Routledge: 2013), 301-318. Cales is notorious for depicting 16-rayed stars (the sun?) above the man-faced bull, and Neapolis goes so far as to place stars on the man-faced bull's body.

[55] G. Semerano, *Le Origini della Cultura Europea*. Vol. I, 2, 435ff. We highlight a few additional terms that all relate to the same roots ακ and αχ, as they demonstrate the interchangeability of velars K (κ) and ḫ (χ), as seen in Semerano's method: ἀκτή, meaning 'coast,' 'bank,' and 'shore' which apparently stem from the Akkadian *aḫātu*, 'bank, shore,' derived from *aḫu* (G. Semerano, *Le Origini della Cultura Europea*, Vol. II, 1, 20); ἄκτιος, an epithet used for Pan at Sybaris, Theocritus 5.14, which R. Lucca identifies as 'Pan of the River Bank' (R. Lucca, 'Il culto di παν ακτιος a Sibari e Turi,' in *Hesperìa*, 5 (Rome: Bretschneider, 1995), 233-7); ἀκεστωρ, meaning 'physician,' or 'mender' (C. Schrevel and J. Richardson, *Schrevelius' lexicon, in Greek and English, for the use of colleges and schools: to which is added, a copious English and Greek lexicon* (London: R. Baldwin, 1853)); ἀκέομαι, meaning 'to recover' and ἄκος, meaning 'cure' or 'remedy,' all of which are used in literature in relation to the practices of healing by water in the sanctuaries of Aesculapius; ἀκαλός, -η -ον, used as an adjective for rivers by Hesiod (*Fragmenta*, 218) and Sappho (*suppl.*, 19), and as an epithet of Okeanos by Homer (*Iliad*, 7. 422; *Odyssey*, 19.434), which Semerano suggests means 'the one who is quietly flowing' (G. Semerano, *Le Origini della Cultura Europea*, Vol. II, 1, 17); ἀκίς, the name of a Greek river (C. Schrevel and J. Richardson, *Schrevelius' lexicon*; Strab., VIII, 347); ἄκμων, meaning 'meteorite stone;' ἀκτίς, used by Homer for 'rays of the sun.'

[56] G.Semerano, *Le Origini della Cultura Europea. Vol. I Rivelazioni della linguistica storica*, I.1, XXXIX.

[57] Ibid., I, 1, XXXVI.

[58] See page 61, in which in the Orphic ἱερὸς λόγος, we see the expression να...Ἀχελωίου, later abbreviated as ἴς Ἀχελωίου, which M.L. West, in *The Orphic Poems,* and later A. Laks and G.W. Most, in 'A Translation of the Derveni Papyrus,' take to mean 'the sinews... of Acheloios.' G.B. D'Alessio, 'Textual Fluctuations and Cosmic Streams,' 23-24.

[59] R. Robertson, 'Glocalization: Time-Space and Homogeneity-Heterogeneity' in *Global Modernities* ((London: Sage, 1995). 25-44.

[60] R. Holton, 'Some comments on Cosmopolitanism and Europe' in *European Cosmopolitanism in Question* (Macmillan, 2012), 35. For the phenomenon of glocalization observed in Orientalizing Tarquinia, see also: A. Babbi and U. Peltz, *La tomba del guerriero di Tarquinia, Das Kriegergrab von Tarquinia*, Römisch-Germanisches Zentralmuseum, Monographien Vol. 109 (Mainz: Schnell & Steiner, 2013).

[61] R. Parker, *On Greek Religion*, 67. Parker still maintains, ultimately, that 'As far as I can tell (with the exception of Aegina) the Pan-Hellenic figures prevail over the local' (R. Parker, *On Greek Religion*, 72).

River that a local embodiment of Acheloios as Acheloios Palagkaios is worshipped.[62]

This solution also alleviates the problem faced when explaining why a particular group, for example, the Ambrakians, would adopt the god (or iconography) of their enemy, the Akarnanians, on the city's coinage. In this case it is not simply Acheloios on the coinage of the Ambrakians, but Acheloios Arachthos.[63] Campanian mercenary groups active in Sicily are another good indication of this. We know, for example, that Campanian mercenaries fought for various, sometimes competing groups throughout Sicily.[64] Moreover, the notion of locative epithets helps us to understand how the iconography spread so easily: instead of a colonizing force imposing their religious beliefs onto the customs of native inhabitants, both the beliefs of the natives and the colonizers are incorporated into one new god.

The issue of Euthymos of Locri, the man-faced bull apparently identified on triple herms mostly from Caruso Cave, finds an appealing solution here as well. It is not Acheloios or Euthymos on the triple herms, but probably Acheloios Kaikinos Euthymos. This identification stays true to the inseparability of Acheloios from fresh water, recognizes the river from which Euthymos came and to which he returned, and incorporates the extant epigraphic evidence identifying the beardless man-faced bull on the triple herms as Euthymos.

In addition, the debate about the identity of the Campanian man-faced bull is alleviated, insofar as both major streams of thought are incorporated into one: Acheloios Sebethos validates Rutter's argument for Acheloios and incorporates the extant evidence for the identification as Sebethos, as summarized and strengthened most recently by Taylor. Ultimately, we simply add another layer to the synoecism advocated by Taylor. Our solution is also further reflected in the extensive use of ΙΣ[65] as a 'control mark' throughout Campania, which we take as clearly indicating that the man-faced bull on the city's coinage is a sinew of Acheloios (ἴς Ἀχελωίου), namely, Acheloios Sebethos (for Neapolis).

We can also draw some tentative conclusions in terms of the nearly contemporaneous appearance on coinage of young, beardless, horned river gods. The young river gods exist within the overall omnipresent field of Acheloios, as god of all fresh water (and possibly all water), but each takes on its own identity and is depicted on coinage (and occasionally labeled[66]) as such, when a municipality decides to pay the local river special honor, probably, as Carroccio suggested, in its kourotrophic dimension. But when the man-faced bull appears, it is a special recognition of Acheloios, always embodied in the local river and indicated in some cases by the appearance in the inscription of the locative epithet. Moreover, the notion proposed by Isler of the man-faced bull as the civic symbol (*Wappen*) adopted by a city is still a valid one;[67] he simply failed to recognize the encompassing nature of Greek religion in its relation to Acheloios and, like others, adopted a delineating approach to the question of identity. Thus the coinage of Panormos, which in some cases depicts a youthful horned river god on the obverse and the man-faced bull on the reverse, probably represent the local river and Acheloios as embodied in the local river, respectively (though the youthful river god might also be Eleutherios, a minor river in the area, distinct from the Orethos).

Finally, some might object that it does not make sense for the iconography from a river in central Greece to appear all over the Greek world, as Eckhel did in response to Ignarra's argument. But this is a misunderstanding of chronology surrounding the application of the name to the geological feature. As we demonstrated with the etymology of Ἀχελώϊος, the word probably has very early Semitic roots, and thus was applied to the river only after it was applied to the iconography of the man-faced bull. In fact, Strabo informs us that the Acheloios River of Akarnania was originally called Thoas![68] Therefore, Acheloios as a man-faced bull and god of water emerged before 'Acheloios' was applied to the central river of Greece, which as we noted was a name applied to many rivers in the ancient world, and in the Etruscan tradition had a different (though related) meaning altogether. Therefore, both the form and content of Acheloios have earlier, pre-Greek origins, and by examining such features as they emerged in the Greek and Etruscan worlds, it seems reasonable to identify the man-faced bulls on the coinage of the Greek world as Acheloios embodied in the local river.

[62] 'As scholars working on ancient religion have collectively pointed out, it would be *variety*, not *uniformity* that was the norm in the ancient Mediterranean world. I would argue that it is both' (A. Nagel, 'Searching for the Gods at Ancient Akarnania: New Evidence From a Ritual Deposit Near Stratos,' in *Anodos: Studies of the Ancient World, 6-7* (2007), 299).

[63] BMC Thessaly, 95, no.18.

[64] J. Champion, *The Tyrants of Syracuse. War in Ancient Sicily. Volume I: 480-367 BC* (England: Pen & Sword, 2010), commentary for plate 9.

[65] See above, pg. 61ff.

[66] See, e.g., SNG ANS 1272, where the river god is labeled as ΑΜΕΝΑΝΟΣ on a bronze coin of Katane from the late 5th century BC.

[67] H.P. Isler understands the appearance of young, beardless river gods as proof that all man-faced bulls are Acheloios (H.P. Isler, *Acheloos*, 81).

[68] Strabo, *Geographica*, 10.2. Pseudo-Plutarch (3rd century AD) says the original name was Thestius (*De Fluvii*, 22).

Concluding Reflections on the Man-Faced Bull

We have come a long way since this book began, spanning thousands of miles and tens of thousands of years. We have exhibited the murky origins of the iconography to the greatest extent we could, and even came to some reasonable conclusions about the figure's identity in the Greek world. Along the way we have hinted at the notion of a common origin, though we have tried to remain cautious in asserting its existence. But we are at a point now where we can freely reflect on the enterprise of the man-faced bull in its entirety, and the potential ramifications this enterprise has for an understanding of ourselves and of our own origin.

Beauty, it is said, begets replication, and the beauty of the man-faced bull is certainly no exception.[1] It first emerged under the most appropriate of circumstances: not long after the Black Sea finished its transition from a freshwater lake into the saltwater sea we are familiar with today.[2] It is believed that this transition prompted a shift of the inhabitants of the area, from migrant communities close to the shores deeper into Europe and probably elsewhere.[3] In fact, by 5000 BC various cultures are spread throughout Old Europe, and we begin to see the man-faced bull at this time, toward the end of the 6th, beginning of the 5th millennium, first in Vinča, then Valač, Gumelniţa, and Karanovo cultures. What a fascinating coincidence that not long after the Black Sea finished its metamorphosis, the man-faced bull emerges in prehistoric art. It is the perfect fit for our new communities, who presumably had to rely on agricultural production and the state of rivers more so than ever before.[4] One could even say the man-faced bull is an echo of this early interplay of people and rivers, constantly reminding us that when regulated or appeased, they provide safety and abundance.

It was upon this background that the man-faced bull eventually migrated south, presumably through Anatolia and into the general area of the Near East.[5] It is certainly plausible, indeed it is our belief, that Near Eastern man-faced bulls were influenced by the original man-faced bulls of Old Europe, since contacts between these cultures within the spatio-temporal bounds of the 'Ubaid' have been reasonably well attested.[6] In fact, the

[1] For an essay on Beauty in its relation to the notion of replication, see E. Scary, *On Beauty and Being Just* (Princeton: University Press, 2001). A simple examination of the obsessive minting of man-faced bull types at Neapolis or Gela attests to the truth of this.

[2] Whether or not a catastrophic flood occurred is highly controversial and beside the point, but for the debate, see W. B. Ryan and W.C. Pitman, *Noah's Flood*, (New York: Simon & Schuster, 1999). For an opposing view, see e.g., A. Aksu et al., 'Persistent Holocene Outflow from the Black Sea to the Eastern Mediterranean Contradicts Noah's Flood Hypothesis,' in *GSA Today*, 12, 5 (2002), 4–10. In relation to ancient flood accounts, see, P. Dimitrov and D. Dimitrov, *The Black Sea, the flood, and the ancient myths* (Varna: Slavena, 2004). For a date of reconnection between the Black Sea and the Sea of Marmara around 7400 BC, see L. Giosan, F. Filip and S. Constantinescu, 'Was the Black Sea catastrophically flooded in the early Holocene?,' in *Quaternary Science Reviews*, 26 (2009), 1–6. For a recent study against a catastrophic flood, see K.N. Mertens et al., 'Quantitative estimation of Holocene surface salinity variation in the Black Sea using dinoflagellate cyst process length,' in *Quaternary Science Reviews*, Vol 39 (2012), 45–59. What is important is that conclusive proof that the Black Sea was once a smaller, freshwater lake, has been well established. For example, varieties of now-extinct freshwater shells, such as *Dreissena rostiformis*, were found dating to c. 7,600 years ago (cf. W. B. Ryan and W.C. Pitman, *Noah's Flood*, 153ff).

[3] Ryan and Pitman attributed the spread of agriculture to the Black Sea Deluge, but the reality of the matter was probably a much slower transition. For a more scientific analysis of the changes to the human experience in the c. 1,500 period following the change, see D.W. Bailey, 'Holocene Changes in the Level of the Black Sea: Consequences at a Human Scale,' in *The Black Sea Flood Question: Changes in Coastline, Climate, and Human Settlement*, edited by V. Yanko-Hombach, A.S. Gilbert, N. Panin, and P.M. Dolukhanov (Springer, 2007), 515-36, especially 526-7. In any case, our early ancestors could never return to the presumably pleasant environment they experienced on the shores of the original Black Sea, as they had been permanently expelled.

[4] For the general layout of Vinča cultural sites in relation to waterways, see M. Maric, 'Encircled in Water: Modelling watercourses of the late Neolithic- early Copper Age Vinča culture sites in the Danube region (c. 5300-4500 BC),' in *Quaternary International* XXX (2014), 1-10.

[5] Our hypothetical sketch of the earliest diffusion of the iconography also finds support in recent DNA evidence, which suggests something significant occurred in the mid 3rd millennium BC in Old Europe that fundamentally changed (genetically and culturally) the entire population, precisely when the iconography of the man-faced bull begins to flourish in the Near East (cf. P. Brotherton et al., 'Neolithic mitochondrial haplogroup H genomes and the genetic origins of Europeans,' in *Nature Communications*, 4, Article 1764 (2013). We will resist the temptation to place too much emphasis on the genetic path that follows the same lines as the iconography. However, a tentative outline is useful for future study: Scientists studying the genetics of the modern inhabitants of Italy and Anatolia revealed a common ancestor among these groups that split in 5600 BC (S. Ghirotto et al., 'Origins and Evolution of the Etruscans' mtDNA,' in *PLoS ONE*, 8(2): e55519 (2013), 4). It should not be overly controversial to suggest the split occurred in Old Europe, and the sub-groups migrated away from the area, especially since the language employed by these people (Vinča script, for example) and essentially their entire culture very abruptly disappears from the historical record, which Gimbutas attributed to belligerent northern invaders (cf. M. Gimbutas, M. Robbins Dexter, and K. Jones-Bley (eds.), *The Kurgan culture and the Indo-Europeanization of Europe* (Washington, DC: Institute for the Study of Man, 1997), 309, for one example). In fact, the most recent archeological evidence suggests that Ubaid 'culture,' which characterizes the general Near East, including Syria and even parts of northern Anatolia, from the early 7th to mid 4th millennium BC, had contact with Old Europe, particularly through pastoral farmers- those same people that likely developed man-faced bull iconography in their early interplay with rivers and cattle. As R.A. Carter and G. Philip point out: 'The importance of migration in the spread of people with associated material culture and behavior has regained prominence in archaeological discourse, supported by some recent isotopic and genetic analyses. For example, there is now isotopic evidence to argue that the Bell Beaker horizon of the European Bronze Age was associated with a spread of immigrants, while the distribution of figurines and painted pottery in Neolithic southern Europe follows that of certain Near Eastern Y-chromosome lineages, testifying to the spread of agriculturalists from the latter region' (R.A. Carter and G. Philip, 'Deconstructing the Ubaid,' in *Beyond the Ubaid: Transformation and Integration in the Late Prehistoric Societies of the Middle East*, 7. See also, R. King and P.A. Underhill, 'Congruent Distribution of Neolithic Painted Pottery and Ceramic Figurines with Y-chromosome Lineages,' in *Antiquity* 76 (2002), 707-14). Ultimately, the genetic evidence might someday reveal more about the migratory patterns of ethnic groups that employed man-faced bull iconography, since the initial evidence appears to confirm the general layout we have proposed for the diffusion of the iconography on strictly intercultural terms.

[6] For an overview of Near Eastern (Ubaid) and southern European (Old European) influences in Anatolia throughout the Chalcolithic and

man-faced bull is the ideal candidate for intercultural continuity precisely because water is utterly boundless. The very principles that indicate the worship of water and its association with bulls are common human behaviors also allow for interesting models of diffusion, insofar as the underlying mythos is appealing to people regardless of culture and can therefore be incorporated into a new religious framework with ease.[7] With such a strikingly peculiar iconography, it makes it even more likely. For there are no man-faced bulls in ancient Chinese civilization or among the Mayans, and we find none among the Australian natives or in central or southern Africa. Instead, they are all confined to the Mediterranean and areas immediately surrounding.

In the Near East, the man-faced bull adopted a predominantly apotropaic dimension (Gateway Guardians), was related to healing practices and incantations (Kusarikku and Gud-alim), was mentioned in lullabies for children (also Kusarikku and Gud-alim), exhibited astral-chthonic-fertility dimensions (Bull of Heaven), but also maintained the fluvial nature (at Susa and in the figure Asallúhi) that forms the core of the man-faced bull mythos. Although many of these other associations were present in Old Europe, the iconography would remain in the Near East for some 3,000 years, so its use in religious practices undoubtedly underwent some variation as it was adapted to local cults, just as it would later.

The iconography of the man-faced bull also arrived in the west, but it first passed through Cyprus. In Cyprus, the water-funerary dimension was at the forefront of cultic practices since the early Bronze Age, and the area was heavily influenced by Anatolian migrants. Throughout the Iron Age it operated as a veritable nexus of exchange for various traveling sea folk, and later on, in the Archaic Age, we witness (on coinage) the notions of oracular knowledge and expiatory sacrifice, which become hallmarks of the man-faced bull further west. Ultimately, Cyprus was instrumental in continuously promoting the iconography in the western Mediterranean for hundreds of years.

In the Tyrrhenian area itself we see distinct influences from the eastern Mediterranean in the art, architecture, and religious practices of native Sicilian and Italian groups, who were no doubt influenced over the centuries by successive waves of small groups of mercenaries, seer-healers, merchants, potters, metal craftsmen, and other itinerant folk. And all of these groups, when carrying the iconography west, found a fertile cultural landscape in the prehistoric western Mediterranean worship of chthonic river bull deities, on which the tradition of the man-faced bull flourished, especially from the Iron Age forward.[8] Of course, various 'nuances' of the original Old European, Near Eastern, and Cypriot connotations emerge depending on the areas in which the iconography took root: In Sardinia the water and funerary dimension was of the utmost importance. In archaic Etruria, on the other hand, the man-faced bull was mainly apotropaic and chthonic, though still bound to its fluvial underpinnings, especially at archaic Pyrgi, Veii, and Cerveteri.

Although the archaeological evidence shows that mainland Greece, in particular Lefkandi in Euboea, was exposed very early on to Levantine imports,[9] the Near Eastern imagery of the man-faced bull took root better in the Tyrrhenian area, where we see not simply an iconographic copying, but an effective reworking of the significance associated with the iconography and an incorporation of the image into the local cults. This is probably thanks to the mixture of cultures in the area, in particular the presence and intensive exchange of artifacts and culture among the Etruscans, Phoenicians, and Greeks.[10]

Exactly when Acheloios emerges to become the god of water is uncertain, but the mythology probably formalized in the Iron Age with all these itinerant 'People of the Sea'. We cannot say when man-faced bull

Bronze Age, which is when the iconography would have transferred, see S.R. Steadman and G. McMahon, *The Oxford Handbook of Ancient Anatolia: (10,000-323 BCE)* (Oxford: University Press, 2011), 159-66.

[7] In fact, enough elements have emerged to define the man-faced bull as 'migrant deity,' a description coined by Bettelli to highlight the transfer of religious iconography from East to West, which at the end of the 2nd millennium BC appears in the Italian peninsula, the result of routes connecting the area with the eastern Mediterranean (M. Bettalli, 'Divinità migranti'? Possibili influssi dal Mediterraneo orientale nell'iconografia dell'età del Bronzo italiana,' in *Miti simboli decorazioni. Ricerche e scavi, Atti del Secondo Incontro di Studi (Pitignano - Valentano, 13-15 settembre 2002)*, edited by N. Negroni Catacchio (Milano, 2004), 247-260). On the same topic see F. Rossi, *La dea sconosciuta e la barca solare. Una placchetta votiva dal santuario protostorico di Breno in Valle Camonica* (Milano, 2005).

[8] The eastern figurative tradition played a significant part in the development of a great number of representations in western art, some of which, in the course of the so-called Orientalizing period, reached a defined shape that remained thereafter fixed during the following centuries (G. Rocco, 'Modelli orientali e rielaborazioni Greche: originali iconografie di creature fantastiche nell'Orientalizzante,' in *Varia Iconographica ab Oriente ad Occidentem*, Studia Punica 14, (Roma, 2006), 29-40). Beyond the influence of Near Eastern models depicted on imported manufactured goods through trade, Levantine immigrant workers in the West also played an important role, attested since the beginning of the 1st millennium BC (E. Lipinski, *Itineraria Phoenicia* (Leuven, 2004), 146-188). In this process of assimilation of iconographic models by western archaic cultures it is possible that, in addition to the acquisition of subjects actually 'copied' from eastern images, there was some experimentation by Etruscan artists, who added new meanings to the imported forms, and gave new shapes to the characters and episodes already existing in the western epic-mythological traditions (G. Rocco, 'Modelli orientali e rielaborazioni Greche: originali iconografie di creature fantastiche nell'Orientalizzante,' 29-44).

[9] M. Popham and E. Milburn, 'The Late Helladic IIIC pottery of Xeropolis, Lefkandi: a summary,' in *Annual of the British School at Athens* (Cambridge: University Press, 1971) 333-352.

[10] Such contacts of cultures promoted the development of narratives and related mythological characters having common traits and common religious connotations in different cultures (G. Rocco, 'Modelli orientali e rielaborazioni Greche: originali iconografie di creature fantastiche nell'Orientalizzante,' 29-44).

iconography was first applied to the god, but probably during the late Iron Age into the Archaic Period for Asia Minor, Cyprus, North Africa, Italy, and Sicily, and only later, in the late 5th century, in Greece proper.

Ultimately, as surprising as it sounds, it is not until the end of his journey that the man-faced bull arrives in the area of the Acheloios River,[11] some 5,000 years after his emergence, and having essentially circled the entire Mediterranean to come to rest at a river just south of his birthplace so many years ago.[12] And although it is bold to suggest a common origin that prompted all other man-faced bulls, it would be unfair not to suggest some form of intercultural continuity, especially in regard to a figure whose mythos is universally appealing, and in the later traditions, as we have clearly demonstrated in the Greek world, actually facilitated the assimilation of newcomers among natives. Thus, although there was no mysterious cult of the man-faced bull persevering for thousands of years, the iconography's beauty reflects the very essence of the human condition, and it was this beauty that prompted the series of interactions of all these people who form the individual links in the chain, a chain forged by the very relation of nature and man itself.

And so we end with mighty Acheloios of the Greek world, and the ultimate crystallization of the mythology of the man-faced bull, an amalgamation of all past meanings gloriously emerging as the god of all water, the god who cleanses the soul, the god who protects us from evil and watches over us, the god who, most importantly, redeems us. And such an intercultural phenomenon, thousands of years in the making and reflective of broad patters of human cultural growth and development, would plow the soil for yet another, strikingly similar figure. That is the story of the man-faced bull's origin, development, and identity. That is the story of us.

[11] Hesiod and Homer are good indicators of the existence of a mythological character named Acheloios personifying water or a river, but this is not evidence of a cult of a deity shaped as a man-faced bull in early Iron Age mainland Greece, for which there is no evidence. He could just have easily been depicted as a man with a fish's tail, or something similar.

[12] Measuring from the southern vicinity of Vinča culture (modern day southern Macedonia) to central Akarnania, about 300 km.

Plates for Part I

Fig. 1: Greek, c. 370 BC, Pergamon Museum, Berlin (Redrawn by Molinari)

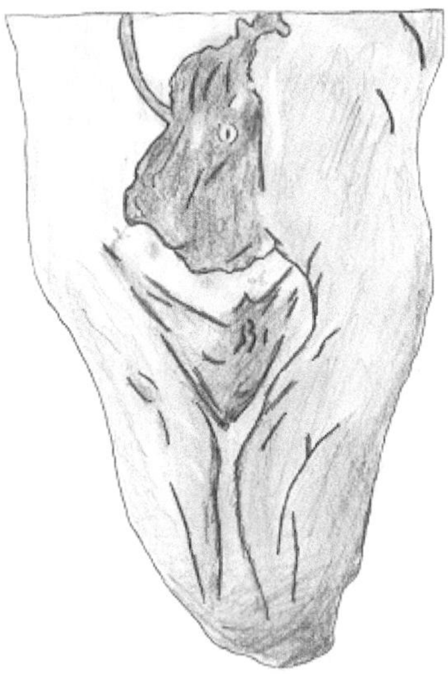

Fig. 2: Bison-man in Chauvet-Pont-d'Arc Cave of southern France, c. 30,000 BC (Redrawn by Molinari)

Fig. 3: Horned creature from la Pasiega, c. 16000 to 14000 BC, adaptation of José-Manuel Benito Álvarez's handmade sketch (Redrawn by Molinari)

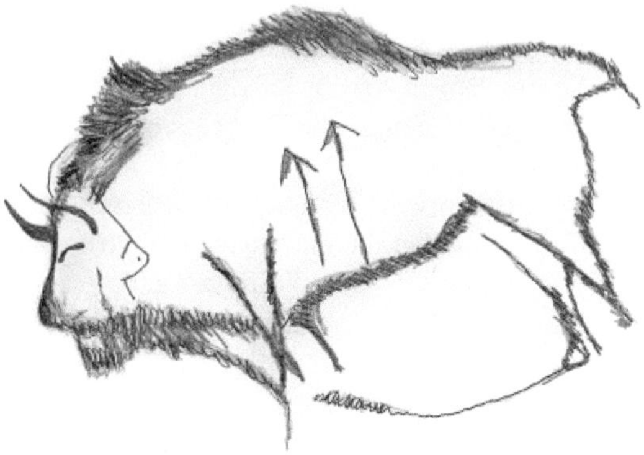

Fig. 4: Man-faced(?) bison from Niaux, Ariège, France, c. 17,000 to 12,000 BC (Redrawn by Molinari)

Fig. 5: Man-faced bull, Karanovo VI culture, second half of the 5th millennium BC (Redrawn by Molinari)

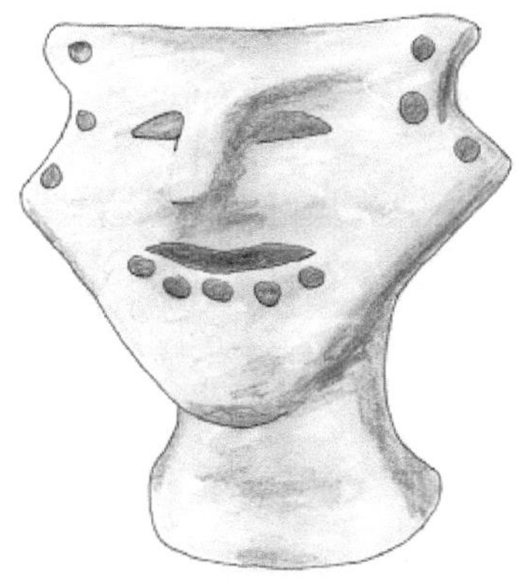

Fig. 6a: 'Female Death Goddess,' Karanovo Culture, 5th millennium BC (Redrawn by Molinari)

Fig. 6b: Late Ubaid seal featuring man-faced bulls, c. 3750 to 3500 BC (Courtesy of Frank Hole)

Fig. 6c: Late Ubaid seal featuring man-faced bulls, c. 3750 to 3500 BC (Courtesy of Frank Hole)

Fig. 7: Near-Eastern bull man, 2000 to 1600 BC (© Trustees of the British Museum)

Fig. 8: Segment of Cylinder seal, 2600 to 2400 BC (© Trustees of the British Museum).

Fig. 9: Great Lyre from Ur inlay, dated Early Dynastic Period II, c. 2650 BC (Redrawn by Molinari)

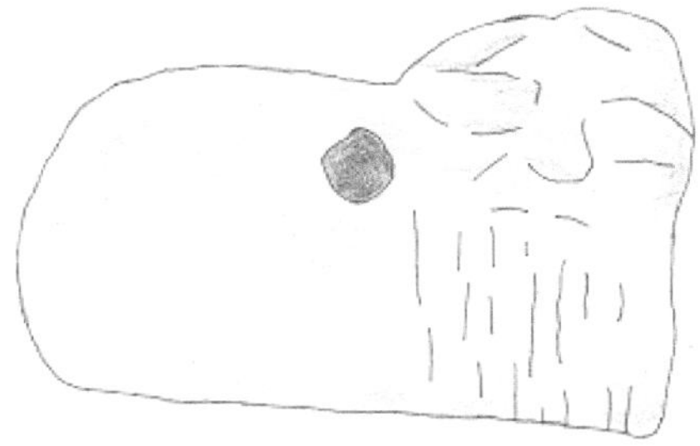

Fig. 10: Akkadian man-faced bull amulet, Tell Arbid, Sector S, Akkadian and Post-Akkadian Periods (Redrawn by Molinari)

Fig. 11: Early Syrian cylinder seal, c. 1800 to 1720 BC (Redrawn by Molinari)

Fig. 12: Colossal statue from the main entrance of the throne room of Ashurnasirpal II's Northwest Palace at Nimrud, early 9th century BC (Redrawn by Molinari)

Fig. 13: Assyrian cylinder seal, 7th century BC (Redrawn by Molinari)

FIG. 14: DJER 2, EARLY DYNASTIC, C. 3000 BC (IMAGE FROM JIMENEZ-SERRANO, REDRAWN BY MOLINARI)

FIG. 15: TOP OF THE NARMER PALETTE (REDRAWN BY MOLINARI)

FIG.16: RITUAL TABLET, C. 2000 BC (REDRAWN BY MOLINARI)

FIG. 17: INDUS VALLEY CHIMERA, 3RD TO 2ND MILLENNIUM BC (REDRAWN BY MOLINARI)

FIG. 18: MODERN ILLUSTRATION OF KAMADHENU (REDRAWN BY MOLINARI)

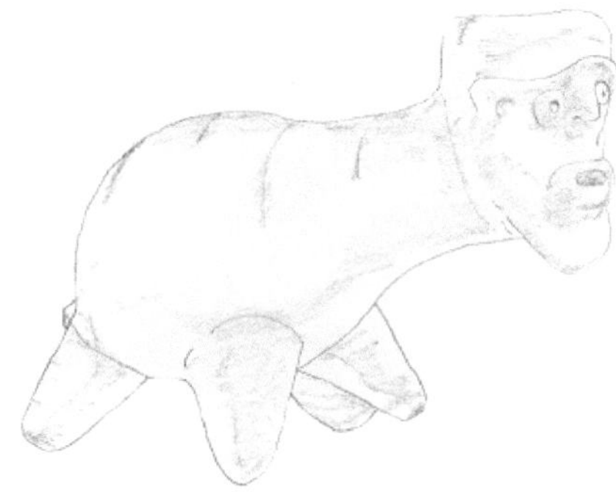

FIG. 19: 'FANTASTIC' ANDROCEPHALIC QUADRUPED, 2300 TO 1900 BC (REDRAWN BY MOLINARI)

FIG. 20: MAN-FACED BULL ASKOS, CYPRUS, 1750 TO 1600 BC (REDRAWN BY MOLINARI)

FIG. 21: MAN-FACED BULL CENTAUR, 1900 TO 1600 BC (REDRAWN BY MOLINARI)

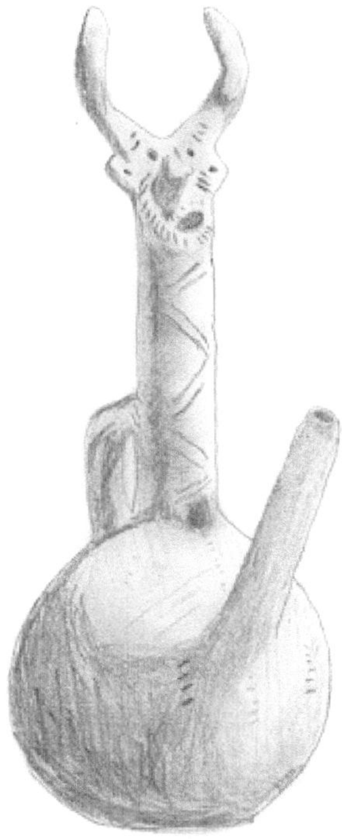

FIG. 22: MAN-FACED BULL VESSEL, CYPRUS, 2100 TO 1850 BC (REDRAWN BY N.MOLINARI)

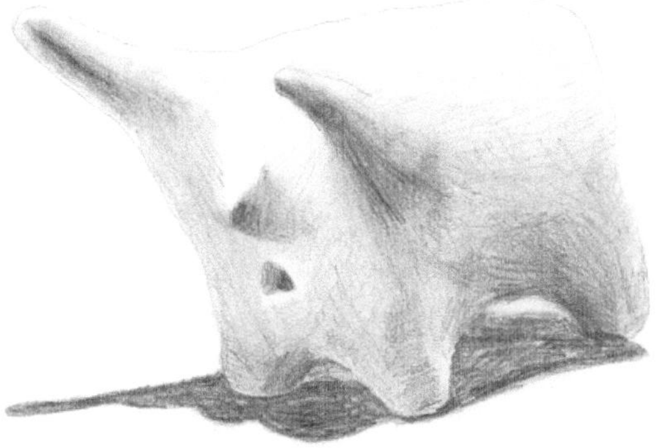

FIG. 23: MAN-FACED BULL FIGURINE, CYPRUS, 1400 TO 1200 BC (REDRAWN BY MOLINARI)

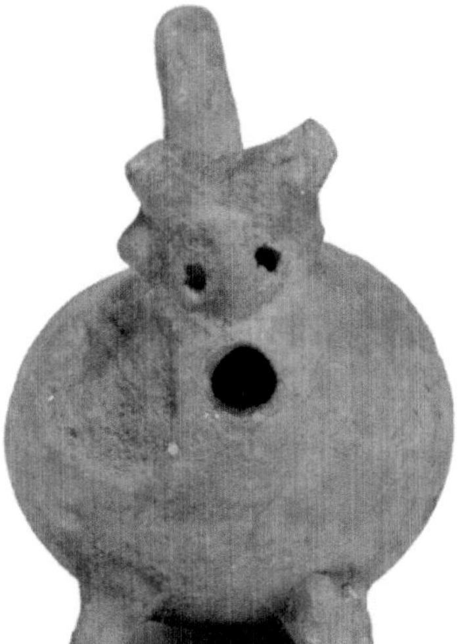

FIG. 24: CYPRIOT MAN-FACED BULL ASKOS, 1650 TO 1450 BC (© TRUSTEES OF THE BRITISH MUSEUM)

FIG. 25:, WINGED MAN-FACED BULL DECORATION, 1250 TO 1200 BC (REDRAWN BY MOLINARI)

FIG. 26: WINGED MAN-FACED BULL DECORATION, 7TH CENTURY BC (REDRAWN BY MOLINARI)

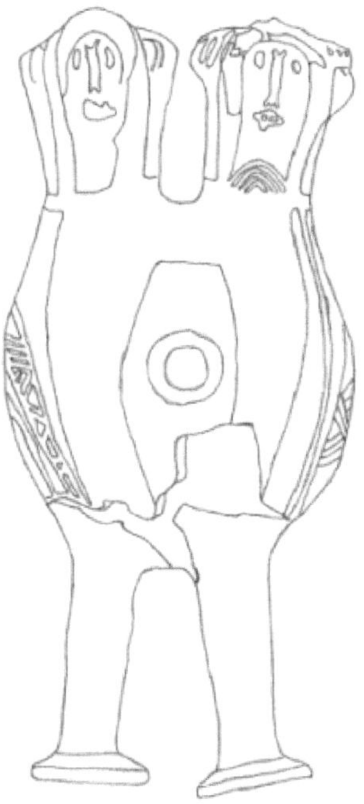

FIG. 27: DOUBLE-HEADED MAN-FACED BULL CREATURE, 12TH CENTURY BC (REDRAWN BY MOLINARI)

Fig. 28: Bull-man centaur, Cyprus, 750 to 600 BC (Redrawn by Molinari)

Fig. 29: Bull-man centaur(?), upper torso, first half of the 6th century BC (© Trustees of the British Museum)

Fig. 30: Herakles vs. Acheloios (as bull-centaur), 520 to 510 BC (Redrawn by Molinari)

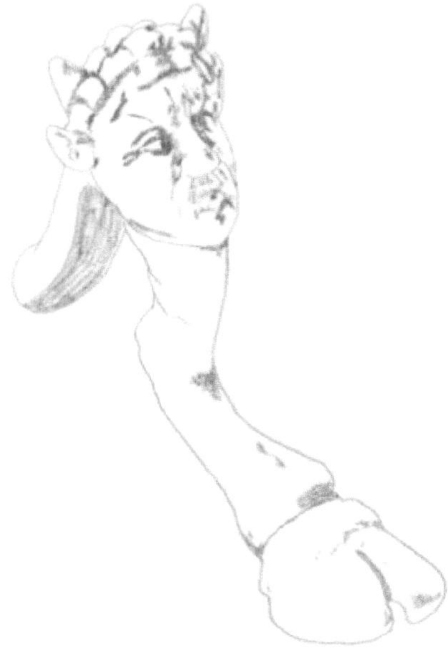

Fig. 31: Bronze candelabrum, Marion, Cyprus, 6th century BC (Redrawn by Molinari)

Fig. 32: Cypro-Phoenician faience amulet, 750 to 300 BC (Redrawn by Molinari)

Fig. 33: Cypriot clay sculpture of Acheloios, 6th century BC (Redrawn by Molinari)

Fig. 34: Cypriot priest idol wearing man-faced bull mask, 6th century BC (Redrawn by Molinari)

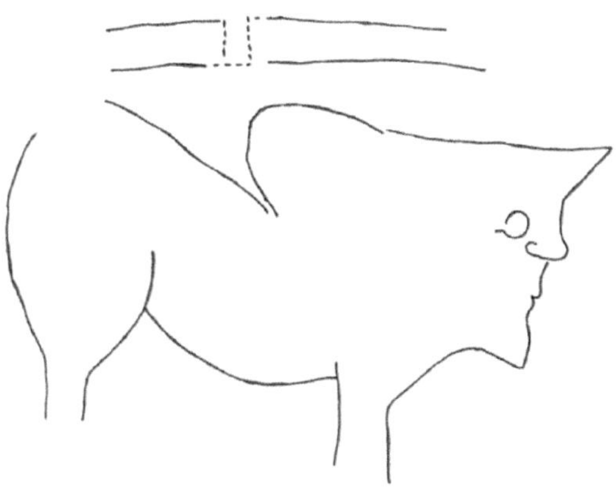

Fig. 35: Line-drawing of Humped Man-Faced Bull Countermark, late 3rd century BC (Redrawn by Molinari)

Fig.36: From Ionia, Magnesia on the Meander, c. 350 to 325 BC (CNG 96, lot 435)

Fig. 37: Amphora Depicting Seer Practicing Hepatoscopy with Hoplite (Redrawn by Molinari)

Fig.38: Sicilian Bronze Age Man-Faced Bull, 3300 to 2800 BC (Redrawn by Molinari)

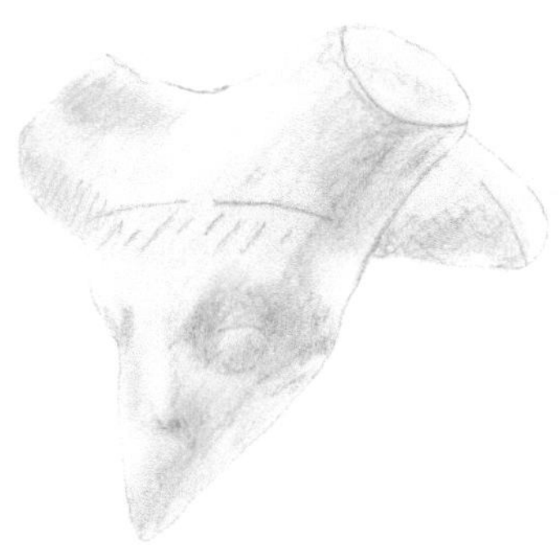

Fig. 39: Ausonio II man-faced bull handle, 12th to 10th century BC (Redrawn by Molinari)

Fig. 40: Sikan oinochoe decoration, 7th century BC (Redrawn by Molinari)

Fig. 41a: Sikan oinochoe decoration, 7th century BC? (Redrawn by Molinari)

Fig. 41b: Pre-Greek man-faced bull protome of Syracuse (from Paolo Orsi's 'Gli scavi intorno a l'Athenaion di Siracusa')

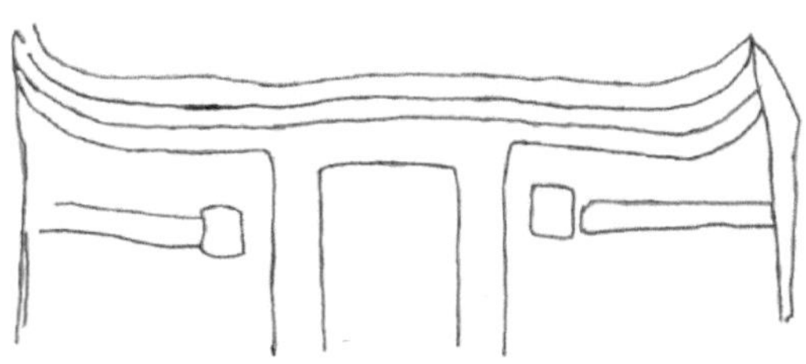

Fig. 42: Bull head entrance gate, Sardinia, 3400 to 2700 BC (Redrawn by Molinari)

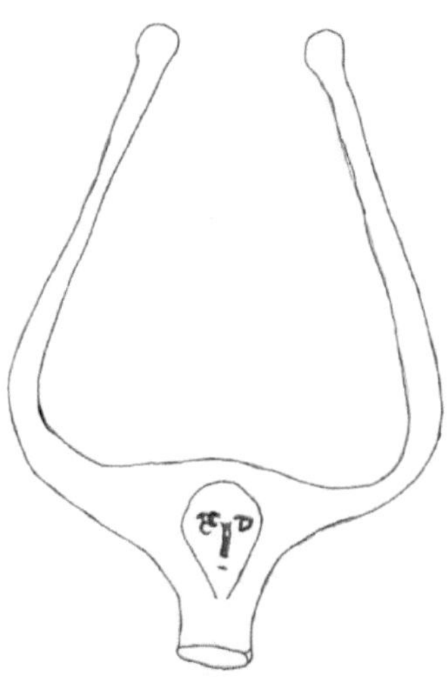

Fig. 43: Sardinian man-faced bull processional standard, 8th century BC (Redrawn by Molinari)

Fig. 44: Bronze man-faced bull-centaur from Nule, Sardinia, 8th century BC (Redrawn by Molinari)

Fig. 45: Etruscan bowl featuring the head of the man-faced bull and upon him, a Herakles-like figure, 8th century BC (Redrawn by Molinari)

Fig. 46: Etruscan gem, 5th century (Redrawn by Molinari)

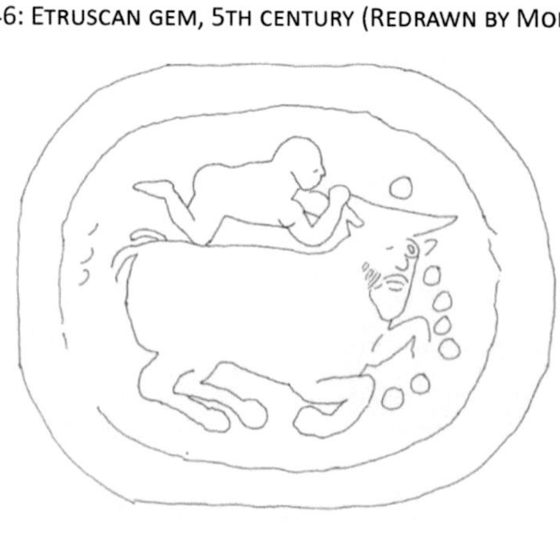

Fig. 47: Etruscan gem, 4th century (Redrawn by Molinari)

FIG. 48A: TETRADRACHM FROM KATANE, MID 5TH CENTURY BC (NOMOS AG, AUCTION 5, LOT 115)

FIG.48B: RELIEF FROM MEDINET HABU, 12TH CENTURY BC (REDRAWN BY MOLINARI)

FIG. 49: ETRUSCAN KERNOS (REDRAWN BY MOLINARI)

FIG. 50: PICENII TERMINAL VASE HANDLE, 7TH CENTURY BC (REDRAWN BY MOLINARI)

FIG. 51: ENGRAVED GEM FROM FALERII, EARLY 6TH CENTURY BC (REDRAWN BY MOLINARI)

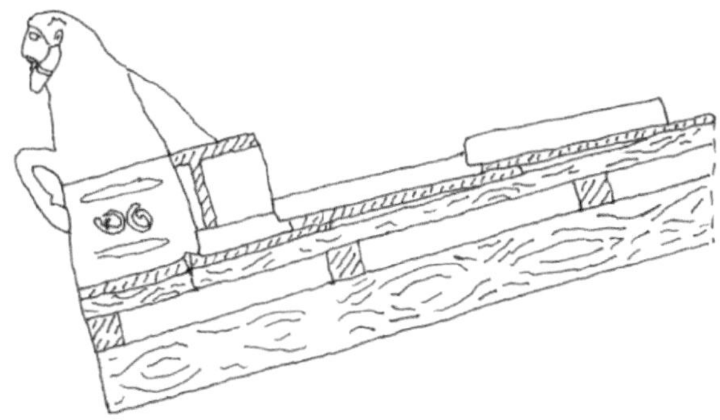

FIG. 52: ACROTERIA RECONSTRUCTION FROM B. MARCHESINI, 550 TO 525 BC (REDRAWN BY MOLINARI)

FIG.53: FRESCO PORTION FROM THE TOMB OF THE BULLS, 5TH CENTURY BC (REDRAWN BY MOLINARI)

FIG. 54: LAMPADARIO DI CORTONA, 5TH CENTURY BC (© MUSEO DELL'ACCADEMIA ETRUSCA E DELLA CITTÀ DI CORTONA)

Fig. 55: Etruscan shield, 6th century BC (© Dallas Museum of Art)

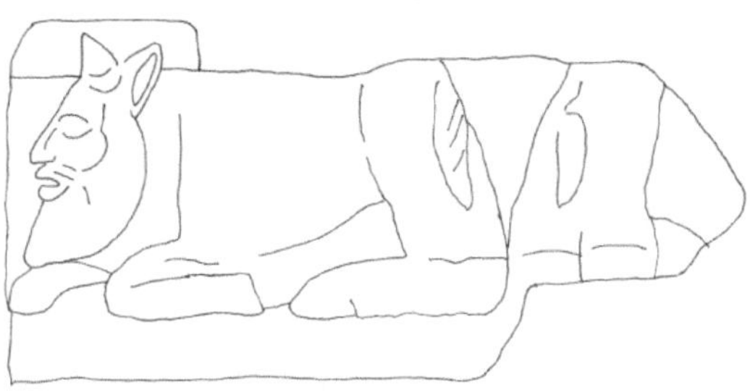

Fig. 56: Memorial relief from Chiusi, 6th century BC (Redrawn by Molinari)

Fig. 57: Man-faced bull 'temple' monument, 6th century BC (Redrawn by Molinari)

Fig. 58: Gold necklace, 5th century BC (Redrawn by Molinari)

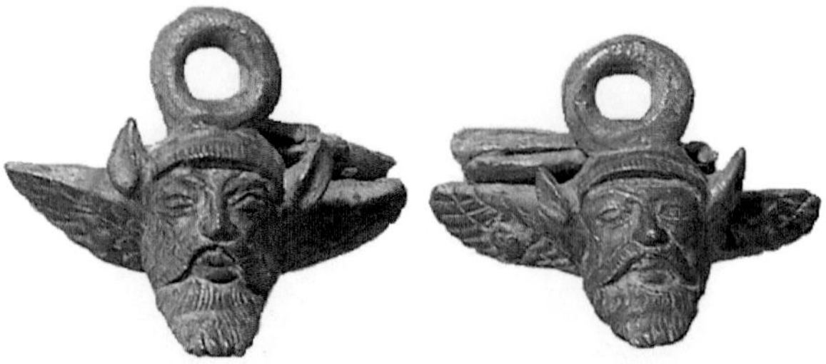

Fig. 59a & 59b: Etruscan situla fixtures, 5th century BC (Image courtesy of Mark Goodstein)

Fig. 60: Balsamarii, early 6th century BC (Redrawn by Molinari)

Fig.61: Greek Antefix, 420 to 400 BC (© Trustees of the British Museum).

Fig. 62: Mask of Acheloios?, 470 BC (Redrawn by Molinari)

Fig. 63: Black Figure Vase fragment, early 6th century BC (Redrawn by Molinari)

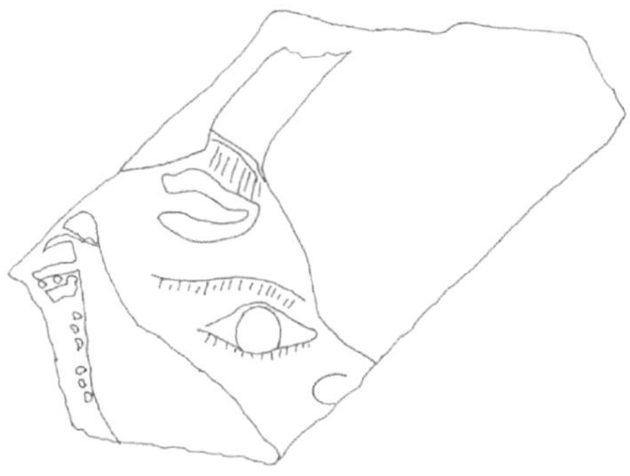

Fig. 64: Pottery fragment showing possible man-faced bull, 575 to 550 BC (Redrawn by Molinari)

Fig. 65: Neapolis, AE Obol, with IΣ control mark (CNG eAuction 288, lot. 32)

Fig. 66: Caruso Cave (Lokroi Epizephyroi), triple herm featuring man-faced bull, 4th century BC (Redrawn by Molinari)

Fig. 67: Ionian askos of Cypriot style, 6th century BC (Redrawn by Molinari)

Fig. 68: Cypriot 'Nymph,' 8th to 5th century BC (Redrawn by Molinari)

Fig. 69: Wing-like ear on man-faced bull from Leukas, late 3rd century (Potamikon Collection)

Fig. 70: Type I Arula, c. 525 BC (Redrawn by Molinari)[1]

[1] Nos. 71-97 not used

Fig. 98: Miletos, mid 6th century (C. Seltman,Greek Coins, Pl. 1, no. 25)

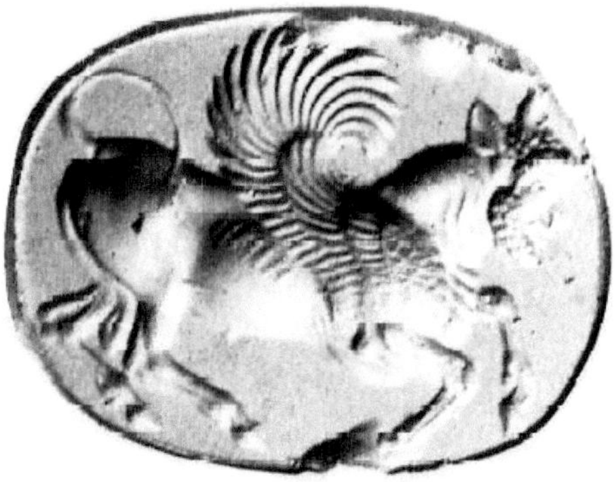

Fig. 99: Ionian gem, Late 6th to early 5th century (Image courtesy of H.P. Isler, from 'Acheloos,' in LIMC, no. 6)

Fig. 100: Uncertain Mint in Asia Minor, EL, mid 5th century(?) (Gitbud and Naumann, Pecunem 9, lot. 192)

Fig. 101: Cyprus, Paphos, late 6th century (BnF collection)

Fig.102: Cyprus, Paphos, c. 520 BC (BnF collection)

Fig. 103: Silver drachm, Kyrene, c. 510 BC (CNG eAuction 292, lot. 219)

Fig. 104: Phaselis, early 5th century (BnF Collection)

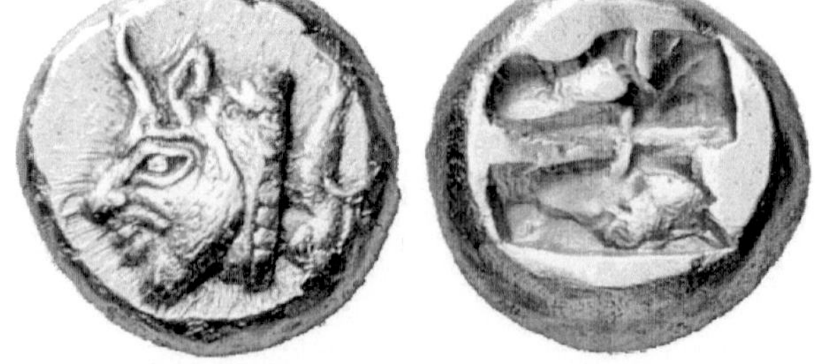

Fig. 105: Phokaia, 500 to 480 BC (Numismatik Lanz, Auction 154, lot 175)

Fig. 106: Phokaia, after 480 BC (Roma Numismatics, Auction 3, lot 208)

Fig. 107: Kyzikos, 500 to 460 BC (Numismatik Lanz, Auction 155, lot 264)

Fig. 108: Kyzikus, 460 to 400 BC (BnF Collection)

Fig. 109: Kyzikus, 400 to 350 BC (CNG Auction 75, lot 339)

Fig. 110: Kyzikus, 380 to 360 BC (Leu Numismatik AG, Auction 91, lot 152)

Fig. 111: Lycia, 480 to 450 BC (CNG eAuction 235, lot 215)

Fig. 112: Lycia, 480 to 440 BC (Hess-Leu Auction 316, lot 480)

Fig. 113: Caria, 5th century BC (Gorny & Mosch Auction 122, lot 1459)

Fig. 114: Lycia, 5th century BC (CNG, Triton VII, lot 284)

Fig. 115: Cilicia, Mallos, early 5th century (CNG eAuction 299, lot 122)

Fig. 116: Cilicia, Mallos, early 5th century BC

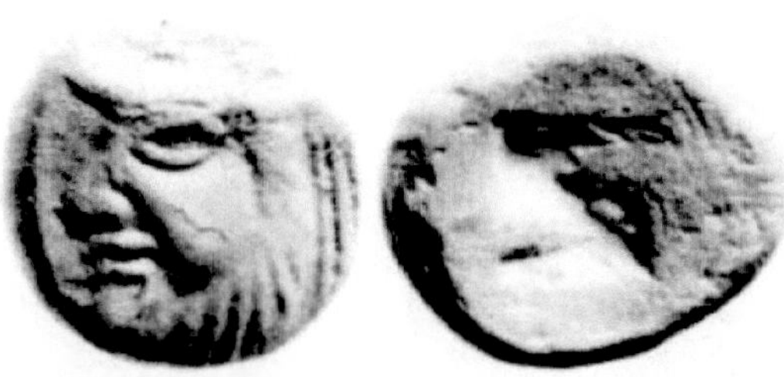

Fig. 117: Asia Minor, first half of the 5th century (E.S.G. Robinson, 'A hoard of Greek coins from Southern Anatolia?,' Pl. XXV, 1)

Fig. 118: Oiniadai, c. 430 BC (BnF Collection)

Fig. 119: Metapontion, c. 450 BC (H.D. Rauch GmbH, 87, 58)

Fig. 120: Akarnanian Confederacy (CNG Auction 67, lot 526)

Fig. 121: Akarnanian League (Roma Numismatics Limited 4, 1382)

FIG. 122: TETRADRACHM FROM THYRREION (DR. BUSSO PEUS NACHFOLGER, AUCTION 398, LOT 176)

FIG. 123: AMBRAKIA, C. 360 BC (NUMISMATIK LANZ, 117, 248)

FIG. 124: STRATOS, 350 TO 345 BC (GEMINI, AUCTION II, 101)

FIG. 125: AMPHIPOLIS (?), MID 4TH CENTURY (CNG COIN SHOP, 810271)

FIG. 126: RHEGION, 510 BC (BNF COLLECTION)

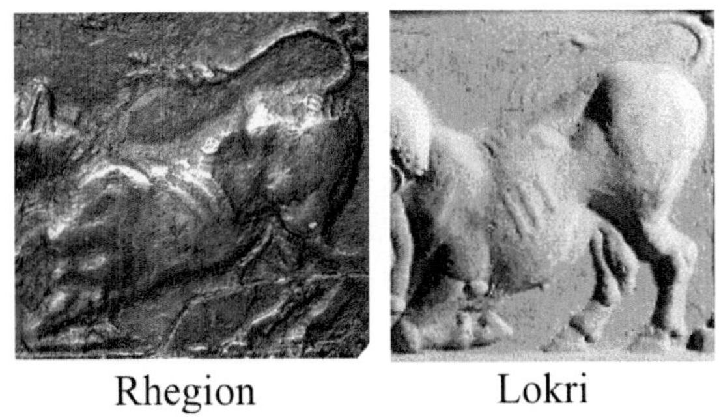

FIG. 127: RHEGION INCUSE-ARULA COMPARISON

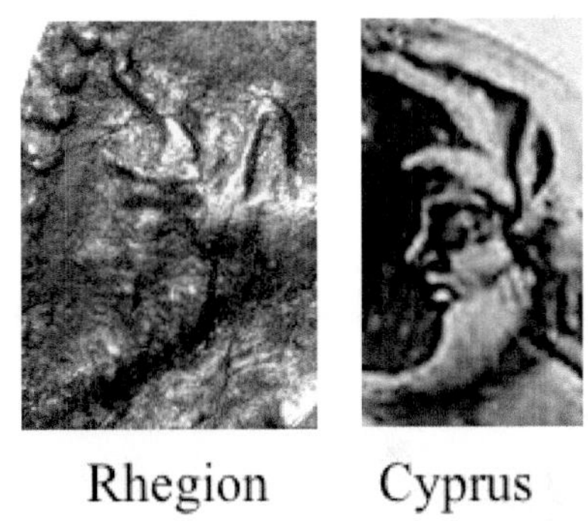

FIG. 128: RHEGION INCUSE-PAPHOS STATER COMPARISON

FIG. 129: PAPHOS-LAOS COMPARISON.

FIG. 130: LAOS, 500 BC (ARTEMIDE ASTE, XXXIX, LOT 51)

Fig. 131: Paphos, 500 BC (O. Mason, 'Notes de Numismatique Chypriot,' f.3.8)

Fig. 132: Didrachm from Gela, 490 BC (CNG, Triton XVI, 206)

Fig. 133: Gela, 480 BC (Leu Numismatik AG, Auction 81, lot 50)

Fig. 134: Tetradrachm-Schoyen Seal Comparison.

Fig. 135: Neapolis, c. 450 BC (BnF de Luynes Specimen)

Fig. 136: Emporion, 480 BC (CNG, Triton XVI, 168)

Fig. 137: Stiela, 413 to 408 BC (Numismatica Ars Classica NAC AG 64, 708)

Fig. 138: Entella, 440 BC (CNG, eAuction 238, 26)

Fig. 139: Panormos, after 400 BC (G.K. Jenkins, 'The Coins of Punic Sicily,' Pl. 24, no.6)

Fig. 140: Neapolis, late 5th century (Numismatica Ars Classica NAC AG, 27, 8)

FIG. 141: ARSE-SAGUNTO, 2ND CENTUY BC (IBERCOIN, AUCTION 22, LOT 3091)

FIG. 142: GORIUS' GEM WITH A CENTAUR, NOT A MAN-FACED BULL

FIG. 143: ATTIC BLACK FIGURE AMPHORA, C. 550 BC, THE J PAUL GETTY MUSEUM, 85.AE.376 (REDRAWN BY MOLINARI)

FIG. 144: LA CHAU AND LE BLOND ILLUSTRATION OF AGRICULTURAL ALLEGORY

FIG. 145: PIGIUS ILLUSTRATION OF AGRICULTURAL ALLEGORY

FIG. 146: COIN ALLEGEDLY LABELING A REGULAR BULL AS POSEIDON. (CNG 60, LOT 82)

FIG. 147: THE MAZOCHIUS-IGNARRA FANTASY COIN (LINE DRAWING FROM N. IGNARRA, PLATE 1, NO. 13)

FIG. 148: TAB. III. AD. VOL. I. PAG. 136, CITED IN ECKHEL AS PLATE III, 2-3 (REDRAWN BY MOLINARI)

Fig. 149: Vargas Ship Illustration

Fig. 150: Vargas 'Fantasy Head' illustration

Fig. 151: Tetradrachm of Gela (CNG 82, lot 269)

Fig. 152: Litra of Selinous (CNG, Triton VII, 79)

Fig. 153: Nomos of Neapolis (NAC, Auction P, lot 1008)

Fig. 154: Bronze Unit of Neapolis (BnF Collection)

Fig. 155: Tetradrachm of Gela (Numismatica Ars Classica NAC AG, 72, lot 310)

Fig. 156: Tetradrachm of Gela (CNG Auction 66, lot 103)

Fig. 157: Bronze Unit of Gela (CNG, Coin Shop)

Fig. 158: Bronze Unit of Agyrion (CNG, Triton V, lot 117)

Fig. 159: Bronze Unit Featuring Zeus Eleutherios (CNG Auction 67, lot 207)

Fig. 160: Silver Obol from Neapolis (Image courtesy of Rabun Taylor)

Fig. 161: Triple herm from Locri, 4th century BC (Redrawn by Molinari)

Fig. 162: Akarnanian Confederacy (CNG Auction 67, lot 526)

Fig. 163: Possible Bronze Unit of Neapolis (Riccio line drawing)

Fig. 164: Nomos of Neapolis. (NAC, Auction 46, lot 149)

Fig.165: AR Drachm from Leukas (CNG Auction 79, 207)

Fig. 166: AE Litra of Tauromenion, depicting Apollo Akragetas (NAC, Auction 64, lot 753)

Fig. 167: Incuse coin of Rhegion featuring Acheloios Apsias (BnF Collection)

Part II

Catalog of the Bronze Coinage of the Man-Faced Bull

Section Three

SICILY

As we saw in our brief essay on the coinage of the man-faced bull, the figure first appears in Sicily around 490 BC, on the didrachms of Gela. They were issued by the most appropriate of characters, Gelo, the bodyguard[1] of the tyrant Hippocrates who became a tyrant himself, ruling over much of southern Sicily, including Syracuse. Like the man-faced bull, Gelo is a binary character: a fierce general that decimated the Carthaginians at Himera, allegedly slaying some 150,000 men in the process,[2] he was also enormously popular amongst the people,[3] and Syracuse is said to have truly flourished under his leadership.[4] Indeed, Gelo offered to Sicily protection and abundance like no other, and so his choice of the man-faced bull to adorn the coinage of Gela is the perfect entrance for the iconography into the island's numismatic history. In fact, the abundance of mercenary soldiers that breached the shores of Sicily were no doubt paid in the coinage that honored their god,[5] and many of the later examples of man-faced bull coinage are issued by the mercenaries themselves, who incorporated the forepart depiction used first at Gela (who copied Cyprus). Altogether, for all metals, twenty-five mints issued some variety of man-faced bull coinage. These cities or issuing authorities are: Abakainon, Agyrion, Alaisa Archonidea, Alaisa Katane, Alontion, Assoros, Entella, Gela, Halykiai, Herbessos, Iaitas, Katane, the Kersini, the Mamar, Mylai, Megara Hyblaia, Motya, Panormos, Selinous, the Sergetaians, the Sileraians, Stiela, Syracuse, Tauromenion, and one unidentified group. In this catalogue we will list all known varieties of bronze coinage of the man-faced bull minted in Sicily.[6] The dates for bronze man-faced bull coinage in Sicily range from about 409 BC to roughly 150 BC. The earliest are those issued by a mercenary group named MAMAR while the latest are the latter issues of Alontion. A last sporadic appearance of the man-faced bull emerges at the end of the first century BC, but only as a countermark, which was probably applied at Iaitas on bronze coins of Segesta. As demonstrated in this catalog, the man-faced bull was very popular in Sicily, not only among Greek municipalities, but also among native towns and mercenary groups.

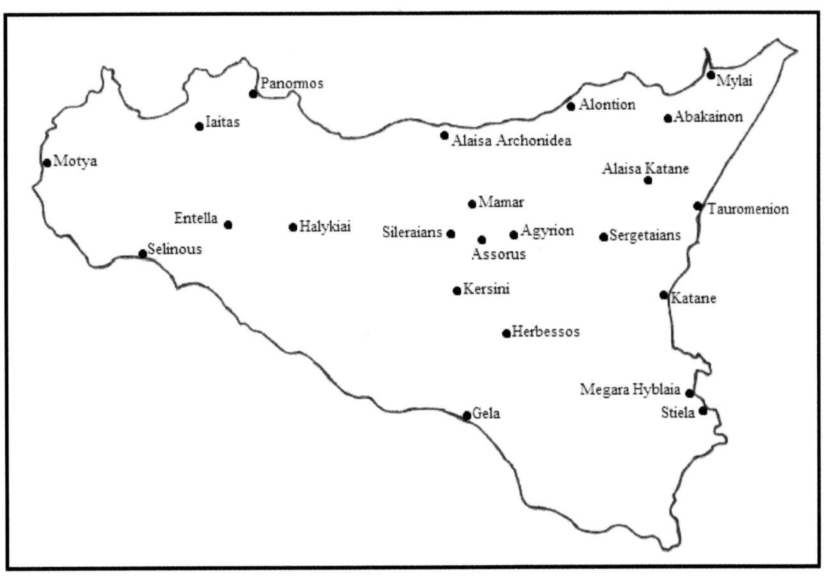

[1] Herodotus, *The Histories*, 7.154.

[2] Diodorus Siculus, *The Library of History*, 11.22.

[3] Ibid., 11.23.

[4] αἳ δὲ παραυτίκα ἀνά τ᾽ ἔδραμον καὶ ἔβλαστον (Herodotus, *The Histories*, 7.156). It is also interesting to note that Gelo descended from a line of priests of the female chthonic goddesses, often associated with man-faced bulls (e.g. Kypris), and probably occupied a position as priest himself (Herodotus, *The Histories*, 7.153-4).

[5] Gelo, for instance, is said to have marched with 50,000 men and 5,000 cavalry to Himera (Diodorus Siculus, *The Library of History*, 11.21).

[6] For the two main theses on the start date of bronze coinage in the Western Mediterranean, see: N.K. Rutter, 'South Italy and Messana,' in *Le origini della monetazione in bronzo in Sicilia e Magna Grecia, Atti VI Convegno del Centro Internazionale di Studi numismatici,* AIIN Vol. XXV, Suppl. 6 (Roma: Istituto Italiano di Numismatica), 194. Rutter proposes 425 to 420 BC. Maria Caccamo Caltabiano proposes 460 BC (M. Caccamo Caltabiano, 'Identità e peculiarità dell'esperienza monetale siciliana,' in *Magna Grecia e Sicilia Stato degli studi e prospettive di ricerca, Atti dell'Incontro di Studi Messina 2-4 dicembre 1996*, edited by M. Barra Bagnasco, E. De Miro, A. Pinzone (Messina, 1999), 299).

ABAKAINON

The Sikel Abakainon was located in north-east Sicily to the east of Alontion and just south of Tindaris. Archaeological discoveries at the site, situated on the top of a rocky hill[7] in the area of modern-day Tripi, attest to the very ancient origins of the town, with graves dating back to the Bronze Age and traces of human presence since Neolithic times.[8] In the historical period, Abakainon was a fairly significant independent Sikel center of northern Sicily, demonstrated in part by the abundant minting of silver coins since the mid 5th century BC.[9] Independence was taken from them in 396 BC,[10] when Dionysius I of Syracuse occupied the maritime area of Abakainon, and founded the colony of Tyndaris (all part of his overall plan against native Sikels).[11] As a result, in 393 BC Abakainon allied with Carthage against the tyrant, but succumbed the following year, in 392 BC. At that point, Abakainon stopped minting coins and remained politically and economically subservient to nearby Tyndaris (which was developing very quickly).

This situation lasted for decades until the arrival of Timoleon. He organized a *symmachia* against the Carthaginians, which resulted in a new found freedom for Abakainon. [12] In fact, in 343 BC Abakainon began to mint silver and bronze coins, and those featuring the man-faced bull appear shortly thereafter (no. 1-3). The use of man-faced bull iconography appropriately reflected the climate of rebirth linked to the aforementioned political events. After the years of Timoleon, Abakainon was able to maintain its autonomy and continued to mint bronze coins until 313 BC, when it fell back under the dominion of Syracuse at the hands of Agathocles.

The majority of coins from Abakainon do not show the man-faced bull, but he does appear on rare issues of the city's coinage. The known bronze varieties depict a classic forepart of the man-faced bull to right, paired with a female head on the obverse. Examples of coins copying Campana 36 have emerged recently and appear to show a man-faced bull, but are very likely forgeries (Campana 36 is a regular bull). The female is commonly believed to represent a nymph, probably a personification of Sikelia.[13]

The man-faced bull appearing on the coinage of Abakainon is probably a representation of Acheloios Helikon, the modern-day Mazzarrà.[14] These types share a stylistic similarity to an issue from nearby Alontion, and probably the common model for both coinages came from the earlier reverse type of Agyrion (which itself copies Gela).[15] Calciati incorrectly attributed another coin to Abakainon, with 'grotesque style'; however, an examination of the coin in the British Museum Collection (which Calciati uses in his catalog) reveals a T below the man-faced bull, indicating Alontion and not Abakainon.[16] Calciati doubtfully listed all these coins as '*Litrai*(?)'.[17] According to Campana, the correct denomination is hemilitron, as the average weight of 9.39g for the known specimens corresponds to the standard of the 18g litra adopted during Timoleon's restoration,[18] which took place after the battle of Krimissos.[19] Thus, the dating of the hemilitrai of Alontion with man-faced bull type must be lowered from the 343 to 336 BC range,[20] to the 339 to 317 BC range.

[7] The characteristics of the location resonate in the etymology of the city name, which is of non-Greek origin. Giovanni Massa, in 1709, proposed a Phoenician origin, noting the similarity with Carthaginian *abac*, meaning 'tall, steep' (G. Massa, *La Sicilia In Prospettiva Parte Seconda* (Palermo: Cichè, 1709), 1). We suggest Abakainon's roots are from the Akkadian *abnu* and *aban*, meaning 'stone, rock' (G. Semerano, *Le Origini della Cultura Europea. Vol. II*, 2, 331) and *kinnu*, meaning 'mount' (G. Semerano, *Le Origini della Cultura Europea. Vol. II*, 2, 332).

[8] A. Campana, 'Sicilia: Abakainon (460-27 a.C.),' in *Panorama Numismatico*, 95-96 (Serravalle: Nomisma, 1996), 1

[9] According to M. Caccamo Caltabiano, the emergence of coinage in the native cities of the island, including Abakainon, indicated a major awareness of a distinct political identity by non-Greek populations of Sicily, which should be considered in connection with the simultaneous political-military action of Ducetius (M. Caccamo Caltabiano,'Identità e peculiarità dell'esperienza monetale siciliana,' 301).

[10] Diodoros Siculus, *The Library of History*, 14.78.5-6.

[11] A. Campana, 'Sicilia: Abakainon,' 18.

[12] Ibid.

[13] The female head on the obverse has been identified by Campana as a personification of Sikelia, given the similarity with female heads on contemporary types from Alaisa Archonidea, which include the inscription 'Sikelia'. Moreover, the recurrence of the head of Sikelia on the obverse of many coins minted by different cities during the *symmachia* could be considered as a form of federal coinage (A. Campana, 'Sicilia: Abakainon,' 21)

[14] Ibid., 19.

[15] Ibid., 21.

[16] R. Calciati, *Corpus Nummorum Siculorum: La Monetazione di Bronzo*, Vol. I (Milano: Edizioni GM, 1983), 73, no. 1 mv 1 (abbreviated as 'CNS' in catalog entries)

[17] Ibid.

[18] A. Campana, 'Sicilia: Abakainon,' 21. Campana listed 15 specimens (ibid., 20).

[19] A. Campana 'Sicilia: Alaisa Archonidea,' in *Panorama Numismatico*, 102-103 (Serravalle: Nomisma, 1996), 90.

[20] R. Calciati, *Corpus Nummorum Siculorum I*, 73.

Coinage

1. AE Hemilitron, 13.59g, 23mm	c. 339 to 317 BC
	OBV: Head of Sikelia to right, hair in sphendone and wearing earrings. Dotted border. REV: Forepart of Acheloios Helikon as a man-faced bull to right, above, ABAK, in upper right field, (AI), in lower right field, N, and below, INΩN.[1] Dotted border. REF: Campana 28; CNS I, 73, 1/1; Castrizio I, 1; Moretti Collection=CNG 63, lot 67 *.

2. AE Hemilitron, unrecorded weight and size	c. 339 to 317 BC
	OBV: Head of Sikelia to right, hair in sphendone and wearing earrings. Dotted border. REV: Forepart of Acheloios Helikon as a man-faced bull to right, above, ABAK, to right, AIN, and below, INΩN. Dotted border. REF: Salinas Cat.32, Pl.II, no.1*.[2]

3. AE Hemilitron, unrecorded weight and size	c. 339 to 317 BC
	OBV: Head of Sikelia to right, hair in sphendone and wearing earrings. Dotted border. REV: Forepart of Acheloios Helikon as a man-faced bull to right, above, ABAKAI, to right, (N), and below, (INΩN). Dotted border. REF: Salinas Cat.33, Pl.II, no.2*.

21 The disposition of the legend on this specimen matches the description provided by F. Imhoof-Blumer, Fluss- *und Meergötter*,189

22 A. Salinas, Le monete delle an*tiche città di Sicilia descritte e illustrate* (Palermo, 1867).

AGYRION

Agyrion, like Abakainon, was a city originally composed of native Sikels that later came under the influence of Greek culture.[23] It was located in central-eastern Sicily, was relatively prosperous in ancient times, and the main road from central Sicily to Katane is said to have gone through it.[24] Its earliest origins are described by Diodorus, a native of Agyrion, who claims Herakles visited the city during his tenth labor and created a nearby lake, and is also credited with the foundation of Iolaos and Geryon, two precincts of the city.[25]

According to Campana, Agyrion was the first among Sikel cities to mint bronze coins.[26] Campana divided the coinage of the polis into five phases, stating that the earliest types with the man-faced bull featuring the inscription ΠΑΛΑΓΚΑΙΟΣ[27] were issued during Phase II (420 to 405 BC, no.6-12 and 14-16 below) and the later types during Phase III (357 to 344 BC, no. 4-5 and 13 below).[28] However, recent archaeological discoveries suggest that the dating of Campana's Phase II bronze coinage of the man-faced bull should be lowered to the same time frame as Phase III.[29]

The metrology of the coins of Agyrion has not been established with certainty. In this catalog we follow the denominations provided by Campana in his monograph, in which he theorizes a standard litra of 12g, similar to that in use at Himera and Piakos.[30]

According to La Delfa, during excavations at the acropolis, sealed strata were discovered in a portion of the ancient settlement located downstream from the acropolis, which allowed him to establish the absolute chronology of all coin series featuring the man-faced bull to between 355 and 344 BC, thanks to their presence with other coin series and pottery.

On the basis of La Delfa's work, it is also possible to argue the following relative chronology: In terms of the heavier denominations, litra no.4 predates no.5, which was already proposed by Campana, who noted the existence of a specimen of no.5 overstruck on the previously listed type.[31] The litrai of Agyrion are generally overstruck on Syracusan coinage, usually the Athena/dolphins and star type, minted between 357 and 344 BC.[32] During this time period, the practice of overstriking Syracusan coins is very common among native municipalities and mercenary mints.[33] The dating of no.4 is closer to the *terminus post quem* (355 BC), i.e. the collapse of the empire of Dionysius, while the dating of no.5 is closer to the *terminus ante quem* (344 BC), as demonstrated by an example overstruck on a coin of the Athena/star type, the latest issue of Syracuse, dated to 344 BC.

The smaller denominations (hemilitrai and tetrantes), unlike the litrai, were never overstruck, but instead minted on new blanks, and the materials used to manufacture these blanks were found during the aforementioned excavations.

The identity of the obverse portrait on these hemilitrai is unclear. Calciati described it as a young Herakles,[34] while Campana believes it is a depiction of one of the two local rivers,[35] the Chrysas or the Kyamosoros (we suggest Chrysas because it is smaller).[36] Calciati and Campana identified some dies exhibiting finer style (no.6-8, below), which feature a large, more stylized neck truncation, whereas the others have a rough style with a narrow neck truncation (no.9-12 below). According to La Delfa, the progressive degradation of style, and also the progressive weight reduction, helps us establish a relative chronology for these fractionals: no.6-8, because of the fine style, the articulate engraving of letters, and the heavier weights, are fractional issues of litra no.4, while no. 9-12 are probably fractional issues of litra no.5.

[23] G. Favaloro, 'Agyrium' (1922), 33f, accessed via Perseus Project, Tufts University.

[24] R. Stillwell et al, *The Princeton Encyclopedia of Classical Sites* (Princeton, N.J.: Princeton University Press, 1976). Accessed via Perseus Project, Tufts University.

[25] Diodorus Siculus, *The Library of History*, 4.24.80; 16.83.3.

[26] A. Campana, 'Sicilia: Agyrion (440 - circa 150 a.C.),' in *Panorama Numismatico*, 67-68 (Serravalle: Nomisma, 1993), 170.

[27] See above, Chapter 6 & 7 (on the identity of the man-faced bull), for a discussion of this issue.

[28] A. Campana, 'Sicilia: Agyrion,' 170. Campana was prudent, stating that the exact dating of Phase II coins has not been established with certainty (A. Campana, 'Sicilia: Agyrion,' 173). On the other hand, according to Calciati, all man-faced bull types of Agyrion were issued between 344 and 336 BC, during the years of Timoleon (R. Calciati, *Corpus Nummorum Siculorum III*, 120).

[29] We are grateful to Dr. Orazio La Delfa, who informed us about these recent discoveries which he presented in his unpublished degree thesis, entitled, 'Nuovi dati per lo studio della monetazione di Agyrion' (2010). Within the thesis La Delfa discusses the problem of the series' chronology in light of the three seasons of excavations directed by B. Basile at the acropolis of Agyrion, conducted by the Superintendence BB.CC.AA. of Enna and the regional Association Sicili Antica. The investigations have led to the identification of the actual mint operative in the 4th century BC, indicated by the discovery of artifacts related to bronze casting and the preparation of blanks.

[30] A. Campana, 'Sicilia: Agyrion,' 174.

[31] Ibid..

[32] A. Campana, 'Sicilia: Agyrion,' 174.

[33] During private correspondence with Dr. La Delfa an interesting element was revealed that serves as additional evidence for our theory concerning the spread of the iconography of the man-faced bull: The excavation campaign by Basile discovered tombs of mercenaries dating to the same time period the man-faced bull appears on the city's coinage.

[34] R. Calciati, *Corpus Nummorum Siculorum III*, 122.

[35] Campana recognizes the similarity of this type with the head of the river Amenanos represented on a bronze type from Katana, and also on the bronze types of Gela (A. Campana, 'Sicilia: Agyrion,' 174 and bibliography).

[36] F. Imhoof-Blumer, *Fluss und Meergötter*, 189.

The reverse type of no. 8-9 probably represents the link between the two series, as it shows the same orthogonal disposition of the legend on the reverse.

The tetrantes (no.14-16) and the unique known hexas (no.13) are probably linked to the earliest issues, and their relative chronology can also be gleaned from the progressive weight loss. On these types, the man-faced bull is paired with Herakles, no doubt as an acknowledgment of his role in the city's early history, and the natural pairing formed with Acheloios. On the unique example of the hexas the man-faced bull is paired with another man-faced bull,[37] a phenomenon seen earlier on the silver coinage of Laos,[38] and never again on any other man-faced bull coinage.

The man-faced bull depicted on the coinage of Agyrion probably represents the local manifestation of Acheloios, Acheloios Palagkaios.[39] According to Caltabiano, Palagkaios was probably the Sikel name for the larger of the two local rivers in the area, the Kyamosoros,[40] today named Salso Cimarosa (not to be confused with the modern-day Salso). We propose here a Semitic origin for the Sikel name, as *Palagkaios* primarily stems from the Akkadian *palag-āsû*, 'the gushing river.'[41] Akkadian *palag* is used for 'river' and 'stream;'[42] *palāsû* is Akkadian for 'erupting water, invading water.'[43] Even the name of Agyrion suggests a Semitic origin, as discussed in Chapter 2. To that discussion is added *agû* and *agâ-nari*, the Akkadian words describing the full wave of a river on the cusp of a flood.[44] Despite these ominous connotations, the binary aspect of water recognized by Taylor is still evident in the homophonic bases at the foundation of the word *Palagkaios*: Akkadian *palāsu* means 'protector (said of deities)' + *gā'u* 'people, nation,' indicating an apotropaic association with the river.[45]

[37] A. Campana, 'Sicilia: Agyrion,' no. 8 (Here listed as no. 13).

[38] See, e.g., SNG ANS 136 ; HN Italy 2277; Kraay & Hirmer 216.

[39] H.P. Isler identified the man-faced bull as Acheloios and not a local river (*Acheloos*, 84) resuming the old hypothesis of F. Imhoof-Blumer that Palagkaios was the name of a local magistrate (*Fluss und Meergötter*, 189). The opposing view, as outlined above, has been articulated most recently by C. Weiss (*Griechische Flussgottheiten in Vorhellenistischer Zeit*, 56-57).

[40] M. Caccamo Caltabiano, 'Palankaios' in *Lexicon Iconographicum Mythologiae Classicae, Vol. VII* (Zürich, 1994), 149-150. The author reads 'Palankaios' instead of 'Palagkaios'.

[41] G. Semerano, *Le Origini della Cultura Europea*, I.1, 183.

[42] G. Semerano, *Le Origini della Cultura Europea*, I.2, 435.

[43] Ibid.

[44] Ibid., 427-9. There are likely further crossings with homophonic bases that relate to the fertility of the fields, from Sumerian *agàr* and Akkadian *ugaru*, 'field, meadow,' which, according to Semerano, is the base of the Latin *ager* (G. Semerano, *Le Origini della Cultura Europea, II.2*, 336). Incidentally, the same base is probably connected to the original meaning of Akragas.

[45] Ibid., 435-49. The same etymology is probably shared with the Greek 'Palaimon,' the son/epithet of Herakles cited by ancient sources. In Attica, 'Palaimon' was a benevolent god of the Underworld depicted on reliefs and vase-paintings among other wealth-giving gods (R. Fowler, *Early Greek Mythography*, Volume II, 324, and bibliography). It is interesting that Fowler reports, on the same page but without further discussion, that 'the scholion quoting Pher. fr.76 suggests that the epithet could also derive from his wrestling match with Acheloos'. This enigmatic 'scholion' suggests some kind of unclear connection between Acheloios and the etymological base of Palagkaios, and ultimately reveals how much information concerning the ancient traditions of the man-faced bull is missing.

Coinage

4. AE Litra, 27.4g, 29mm	**355 to 344 BC**
	OBV: Head of young Herakles wearing Nemean Lion headdress to right, ΑΓΥΡΙΝΑ-ΙΟΝ before and behind. Linear border. REV: Forepart of Acheloios Palagkaios as a man-faced bull to right, ΠΑΛΑΓΚΑΙΟΣ above. Linear border. REF: CNS III, 121, 5/7 (this coin); Castrizio I, 1/2 (Castrizio lists six die varieties of this type); Campana 6; CNG 63, lot 69*.

5. AE Litra, 33.47g, 30mm	**355 to 344 BC**
	OBV: Head of young Herakles wearing Nemean Lion headdress to right, ΑΓΥΡΙΝΑΙΟΝ before. Linear border. REV: Acheloios Palagkaios as a man-faced bull to right, above, star with 8 rays, ΠΑΛΑΓΚΑΙΟΣ in exergue. Linear border. REF: CNS III, 120, 4 OS/1 (this coin); Castrizio II, 1/2 (Castrizio lists three die varieties of this type); Campana 7; CNG 63, Lot 68*.

6. AE Hemilitron, 5.33g, 20mm	**355 to 344 BC**
	OBV: Head of a young man (river god Chrysas?) to right, ΑΓΥΡΙΝΑΙΟΝ before. Linear border. REV: Forepart of Acheloios Palagkaios as a man-faced bull to right, ΠΑΛΑΓΚΑΙΟΣ (retrograde) above. REF: Pecunem 12, lot 22=Potamikon Collection*. *Previously unpublished variety. The rough flan design and retrograde legend indicate this might have been the first emission.*

7. AE Hemilitron, 6.84g, 19mm	**355 to 344 BC**
	OBV: Head of a young man (river god Chrysas?) to right, ΑΓΥΡΙΝΑΙΟ-Ν around, stylized neck. Linear border. REV: Forepart of Acheloios Palagkaios as a man-faced bull to right, ΠΑΛΑΓΚΑΙΟΣ above. Linear border. REF: CNS III, 122, 6/2 = Virzi 725 (this coin); Campana 3; CNG 63, lot 71*.

8. AE Hemilitron, 6.88g, 18mm	**355 to 344 BC**
	OBV: Head of a young man (river god Chrysas?) to right, ΑΓΥΡΙΝΑΙΟΝ before, stylized neck. Linear border. REV: Forepart of Acheloios Palagkaios as a man-faced bull to right, ΠΑΛ-ΑΓΚΑΙΟΣ behind and above. Linear border. REF: CNS III, 122, 6/1*.

9. AE Hemilitron, 6.12g, 18mm	**355 to 344 BC**
	OBV: Head of a young man (river god Chrysas?) to right, ΑΓΥΡΙΝΑΙΟΝ before. Linear border. REV: Forepart of Acheloios Palagkaios as a man-faced bull to right, ΠΑΛ-ΑΓΚΑΙΟΣ behind and above. Linear border. REF: CNS III, 123, 7/11; M&M GmbH, 21, Lot 54*.

10. AE Hemilitron, 4,73g, 20mm	**355 to 344 BC**
	OBV: Head of a young man (river god Chrysas?) to right, ΑΓΥΡΙΝΑΙΟΝ before. Linear border. REV: Forepart of Acheloios Palagkaios as a man-faced bull to right, ΠΑΛΑΓΚΑΙΟΣ above. Linear border. REF: CNS III, 124,7/7; Campana 3; M&M GmbH, 17, lot 150*.

11. AE Hemilitron, unrecorded weight and size — **355 to 344 BC**

OBV: Head of a young man (river god Chrysas?) to right, ΑΓΥΡΙΝΑΙΟ-Ν around. Linear border.
REV: Forepart of Acheloios Palagkaios as a man-faced bull to right, exergue line below, ΠΑΛΑΓΚΑΙΟΣ above.
REF: F. Imhoof-Blumer, Fluss und Meergötter, Pl.I, n.36*.

This image combines the reverse of the coin illustrated in Imhoof-Blumer with a hypothetical obverse (not depicted in Imhoof-Blumer) based on similar coins from the mint. The neck truncation style is uncertain, but probably crude rather than stylized, based on the reverse style man-faced bull. Apparently the reverse die for no. 10 was re-engraved to add the exergue line.

12. AE Hemilitron, 4.68g, 17mm — **355 to 344 BC**

OBV: Head of a young man (river god Chrysas?) to right, ΑΓΥΡΙΝΑΙΟΝ before. Linear border.
REV: Forepart of Acheloios Palagkaios as a man-faced bull to left, ΠΑΛΑΓΚΑΙΟΣ (retrograde) above. Linear border.
REF: CNS III, 124, 8; SNG Fitzwilliam 936; Campana 4; CNG, eAuction 199, lot 13*.

13. AE Hexas, 5.18g, 18mm — **355 to 344 BC**

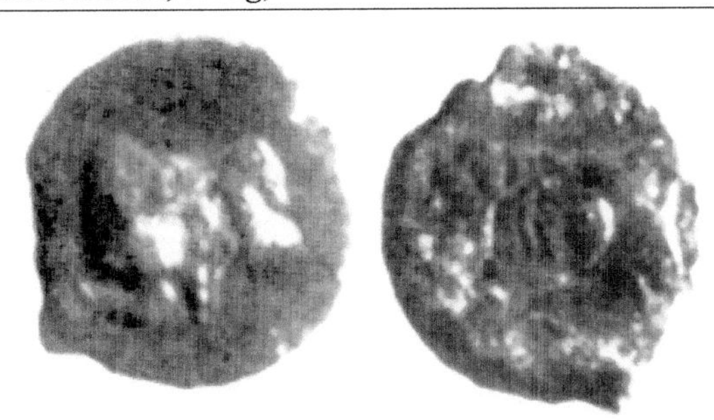

OBV: Forepart of Acheloios Chrysas(?) as a man-faced bull to right.
REV: Forepart of Acheloios Palagkaios as a man-faced bull to left, ΠΑΛΑΓΚΑΙΟΣ above.
REF: Campana 8*.

Unique

14. AE Tetras, 3.12g — **355 to 344 BC**

OBV: Head of Herakles wearing Nemean Lion headdress to left, ΑΓΥΡΙΝΑΙΟΝ before.
REV: Forepart of Acheloios Palagkaios as a man-faced bull to left, ΠΑΛΑΓΚΑΙΟΣ above. Dotted border.
REF: Campana 5A/a; CNS III, 125, 10/4; BnF 1991.45*.

15. AE Tetras, 3.53g, 14mm — **355 to 344 BC**

OBV: Head of Herakles wearing Nemean Lion headdress to left, ΑΓΥΡΙΝΑΙΟΝ and bow before.
REV: Forepart of Acheloios Palagkaios as a man-faced bull to left, ΠΑΛΑΓΚΑΙΟΣ above. Dotted (?) border.
REF: Campana 5 B/a; CNS III, 125, 9/1*.

16. AE Tetras, 2.88g, 14.5mm	**355 to 344 BC**
	OBV: Head of Herakles wearing Nemean Lion headdress to left, ΑΓΥΡΙΝΑΙΟΝ and bow before. REV: Forepart of Acheloios Palagkaios as a man-faced bull to left, ΠΑΛΑΓΚΑΙΟΣ above, olive sprig below. Dotted border. REF: Campana 5 B/b = CNG eAuction 365, lot 23*. *Unique*

ALAISA ARCHONIDEA (unconfirmed)

Alaisa Archonidea was founded on the banks of the river Alaisos (modern Tusa)[46] near the modern day town of Tusa,[47] which is in the area of Messina. The city was established in 403 BC by Archonides II,[48] tyrant of Herbita, the year after the peace treaty establishing the independence of Sikels was agreed to by Dionysius I and Carthage.[49]

Diodorus tells us that Alaisa Archonidea was founded on a hill lying eight stades from the sea by a mixed throng of refugees flowing into Herbita, many from the Greek and Sikel cities previously conquered by Dionysius. To this group were added destitute Herbitans and a large number of mercenaries.[50] Thus, Alaisa Arconidea was a polis with three major cultural contributors: the Greeks, Sikels, and (presumably Campanian) mercenaries.[51] In the 4th century BC it participated in the confederation of cities allied with Timoleon. Alaisa Archonidea remained famous in history, most notably as one of the first Sicilian cities to fall under Roman rule, with whom it voluntarily joined in 263 BC, the year in which the first Punic War began.[52]

According to Diodorus, the name 'Alaisa' was used for several places throughout Sicily,[53] likely to name those areas where Campanian mercenaries settled after services to the Sicilian tyrants of the 5th and 4th centuries BC. Campana, following a previous line of thought from Cavallaro, argued this could be explained through an examination of the etymology of the Greek αλαομαι: 'to be aimless, to be driven into exile.'[54]

[46] The ancient name of the river is mentioned in a famous inscription known as 'Tabula Alaesina' (cf. A.M. Prestianni Giallombardo, 'Per una edizione dei frammenti della Tabula Halaesina,' in *ASM*, XXVIII (1977), 209-212.

[47] A. Campana, 'Sicilia: Alaisa Archonidea (347 a.C. - 7 d.C.),' in *Panorama Numismatico*, n.102-103 (Serravalle: Nomisma, 1996), 81.

[48] Diodorus informs us that 'since there were other cities of Sicily with the same name, he called it Halaesa Archonidion after himself' (*The Library of History*, 14.16.2, C. H. Oldfather translation). The name of the city is also mentioned in the Tabula Alaesina (A.M. Prestianni Giallombardo, *Per una edizione dei frammenti della Tabula Halaesina*, 209-212).

[49] Diodorus Siculus, *The Library of History*, 13.111.3. According to another tradition Alaisa was founded by the Carthaginians when Himilcon concluded his peace with Dionysius (Diodorus Siculus, *The Library of History*, 14.16.4).

[50] Diodorus Siculus, *The Library of History* , 14.16.1-2.

[51] A. M. Prestianni Giallombardo, 'Ducezio, l'oracolo e la fondazione di Kala Akte,' in *Diodoro Siculo e la Sicilia indigena. Atti del convegno di studi, Caltanissetta 21-22 maggio 2005*, edited by C. Miccichè, S. Modeo, L. Santagati (Palermo, 2006), 145.

[52] A. Crisà, 'G. L. Castelli, principe di Torremuzza, numismatico ed antichista ad Halaesa Archonidea,' in *LANX* 2 (2009), 123.

[53] Diodorus Siculus, *The Library of History*, 14.16.2. Today we know the existence of at least two other 'Alaisa' cities issuing coins: Alaisa Etnea and Alaisa Katane (A. Campana, 'Sicilia: Alaisa Etnea (343-339 a.C.),' in *Panorama Numismatico*, n.105 (Serravalle: Nomisma, 1997), 113-115; G. Buceti, *Monete, storia e topografia della Sicilia greca* (Messina, 2010).

[54] A. Campana, 'Sicilia: Alaisa Archonidea,' 81 and bibliography.

It is not certain that Alaisa Archonidea ever minted man-faced bull types. The existence of an example is reported by Carmen Arnold-Biucchi,[55] following G. Tropea's 1901 description of a coin stored in the Mandralisca Museum at Cefalù.[56] Unfortunately, Tropea never published a picture of the coin he described, and despite repeated requests over the past two years, it was not possible to obtain an image of the specimen from the Mandralisca Museum or confirmation of its reverse type. However, we found a possible match listed by Campana.[57] On this coin the obverse type and reverse inscription are identical to Tropea's description. Moreover, rotating the reverse by 90 degrees counterclockwise the 'cuirass' looks like the protome of a man-faced bull to left. An examination of the (allegedly unique) coin in the British Museum reveals a cuirass, so Tropea's original identification may have been a misinterpretation of this reverse type.

In any event, the coin probably dates to the end of the 3rd century BC, and should be identified as an onkia.[58] Arnold-Biucchi dated the coin from 344 to 317 BC, but the legend definitely suggests a later start date, sometime after 339 BC, the year of the victory of Timoleon against Carthage at Krimissos. This is because the previous coins minted in Alaisa during the *symmachia* (344 to 339) always feature an ethnic in the genitive plural, Αλαισινον.[59]

If the existence of the type is ever confirmed, the man-faced bull on the reverse of this coin probably represents the local embodiment of Acheloios, namely, Acheloios Alaisos. Here the significance of man-faced bull iconography, similar to other mints, reflects the renaissance experienced in the polis during the years it was issued.

[55] C. Arnold-Biucchi, 'Alaisos,' in *LIMC, Vol. I*, 478-9.

[56] G. Tropea, 'Numismatica siceliota del Museo Mandralisca in Cefalù (Palermo), classificata e descritta,' in *Archivio Storico Messinese*, Vol. I, 3-4. (Messina: Tipografia d'Amico, 1901), 10, no.8.

[57] A. Campana, 'Sicilia: Alaisa Archonidea,' 102, no.29.

[58] Ibid.

[59] cf. A. Campana, 'Sicilia: Alaisa Archonidea,' no. 8-9

Coinage

17. AE Onkia?, unrecorded weight and size	**339-317 BC ?**
Image Not Available	OBV:Head of young Dionysos to left. Dotted border. REV: Forepart of Acheloios Alaisos as a man-faced bull to left, inscription ΑΛΑΙΣΑΣ ΑΡΧ. Dotted border. REF: Tropea 8; Arnold-Biucchi LIMC 1.

ALAISA KATANE

This Alaisa is the second known Alaisa to issue coinage of the man-faced bull, distinct from Alaisa Archonidea.

The dating of these coins to after 402 BC coincides with the relocation of Campanian mercenaries from Katane after the city was conquered and its inhabitants enslaved. The find spots of these coins on Mt. Aitna (modern Mt. Etna) indicate a new Alaisa in the same area as Alaisa Atnaia, named 'Alaisa Katane' by Buceti.[60] This one, however, is on the side of the volcano closest to Katane and supports the idea that its inhabitants were former mercenaries.[61] Buceti's rationale is that some of the mercenaries leaving Katane, instead of following the others to the northern location on Mt.Aitna, went to an area situated southeast of the mountain and established their own town, remaining close to Katane. Thus, this other town is an Alaisa born prior to Alaisa Aitnaia.[62]

Recently, Alberto Campana questioned the dating proposed by Buceti (personal correspondence), pointing out that the Kore/bull and dolphin are probably inspired by the types issued at Syracuse during the time of Agathocles, thereby proposing a lower date range to between the end of 4th and the early 3rd century BC. In this case, Buceti's narrative would need revision.

Four examples of no. 18 are known to exist, all in private collections but three significantly altered to appear in better grade for commercial purposes (or, perhaps, to avoid detection as forgeries). We publish here the unique untouched example. All four are of the same type and have on the obverse a nymph and on the reverse, a man-faced bull standing left, head in profile, with dolphin above. The coins carry the inscription ΑΛΑΙΣΑ on the obverse, but the most recent example to appear on the market had the inscription 'ΑΛΑΕΣΑ.'[63] This, however, was surely a misunderstanding on the part of the forger who manipulated the original coin's surfaces, as 'Alaesa' was the Roman spelling of the Greek 'Alaisa,' and the form 'Alaesa' appears on coinage inscriptions only during the time of Augustus.[64]

The man-faced bull on the reverse of these coins most likely represents the local embodiment of Acheloios, Acheloios Akis, after the river which flowed from Mt. Aitna into the Mediterranean. Alternatively, since the group stems from Katane, it might be Acheloios Amenanos Akis.

Coinage

18. AE Hemilitron(?), 4.88g, 16mm	**Late 4th to early 3rd century BC?**
	OBV: Head of nymph wearing necklace(?) to right, bee behind, ΑΛΑΙΣΑ before. REV: Acheloios Akis as a man-faced bull standing to left, head in profile, above, dolphin to right. Dotted border. REF: Buceti 1; Private collection* Image courtesy of Alberto Campana.

19. AE Hemilitron(?), 4.68g, 17.5mm	**Late 4th to early 3rd century BC?**
	OBV: Head of nymph to left. REV: Acheloios Akis as a man-faced bull standing to left, head in profile, above, dolphin to right. REF: Previously unpublished. Private collection* Image courtesy of Alberto Campana. *Unique*

[60] G. Buceti, *Monete, storia e topografia della Sicilia greca* (Messina, 2010).
[61] Ibid.
[62] Ibid.
[63] Fritz Rudolph Kunker 257, lot 8054.
[64] Cf. Phase V in A. Campana, 'Sicilia: Alaisa Archonidea (347 a.C. - 7 d.C.),' in *Panorama Numismatico*, n.102-103 (Serravalle: Nomisma, 1996), 104 ff.

ALONTION

The Sikel Alontion was located in north-east Sicily about 80km west of Abakainon, at the site of the modern day town of San Marco d'Alunzio.[65] The town has very early origins and archaeological finds indicate that it was frequented since the Bronze Age.[66] Ancient literary sources record that the legendary Patron Turio of Akarnania, after fighting in the Trojan War, followed Aeneas west and was persuaded by him to remain and settle in Sicily with his companions, thus founding the city.[67]

There are two types of man-faced bull coinage from Alontion, all bronze. The earliest example,[68] the hemilitron, was issued on the 18g litra standard, which was established during the monetary reform of Timoleon. It shows types similar to the aforementioned issue from Abakainon.[69] Alontion, along with other Sikel cities of northeastern Sicily, had lost the right to issue coinage after the peace between Dionysius and the Carthaginians and the division of the island in 392 BC.[70] Therefore, it makes perfect sense to use the man-faced bull, a symbol intimately related to the notion of rebirth, when the mint began to issue coins again during the time of Timoleon.

The second type, appearing over 100 years after the first, was struck under Roman rule, from 212 to 150 BC (Campana's dating). The dating is confirmed by the discovery of five specimens in a hoard[71] dating back to the end of the 3rd or early 2nd century BC.[72] The type shows on the obverse the mythical founder Patron Turio, whose Phrygian cap suggests an eastern connection, as the style was popular in the Levantine area. The coupling of Patron and the man-faced bull has a political intent, as the citizens of Alontion wanted to celebrate both their own city and Rome.[73] Moreover, the inclusion of the local hero demonstrates a common origin between the people of Alontion and the founding myth of Rome.[74] The man-faced bull is depicted with water flowing from his mouth on the later types, a phenomenon seen on only one other coin, an extremely rare bronze issue from nearby Mylai.[75] There is also a Red Vase Painting in the Louvre depicting the battle between Herakles and Acheloios, where the latter also has a stream of water flowing from his mouth, thus supporting the identification as Acheloios instead of a strictly local river god.[76] Incidentally, Milligen took the water feature to signify a local river god, and used this peculiar motif as support for his theory that many man-faced bulls are local river gods, in this case Chydas (the modern Rosmarino).[77] However, it is probably Acheloios Chydas (χύδας), for the reasons stated in Chpt. 7.

In fact, Chydas comes from the Greek χύδην, meaning 'words pouring from the mouth,'[78] and still today in modern Greek χύστε means 'pour out.' In addition, the ancient Greek χύδην refers specifically to water 'poured out, in floods,'[79] and thus the image of Acheloios Chydas with water flowing from his mouth is especially fitting. Incidentally, Alberto Campana suggested that the man-faced bull depicted on the types paired with Patron Turio could have been used to represent both Acheloios and the spring of a local river,[80] a forerunner to our own theory of locative epithets. His claim is that the man-faced bull represents Acheloios but the water signifies the head of the river Chydas, and therefore represents both.

The broad weight range (2.57g to 8.92g) makes any definite conclusion about the denomination of the second type difficult, but it is suggested by Campana that the issue might be a trias.[81]

65 A. Facella, 'San Marco d'Alunzio,' in *Bibliografia Topografica della Colonizzazione Greca in Italia e nelle Isole Tirreniche*, Vol.XVIII (Roma, 2010), 44-57.

66 For the discovery of prehistoric pottery and obsidian blades, see: F. Bianco, 'Il territorio di S. Agata Militello (ME) nell'antichità,' in *Archivio Storico Messinese*, Vol. XLIII (Messina: 1988), 167-8.

67 Dionysius of Halicarnassus, and E. Cary, *The Roman antiquities of Dionysius of Halicarnassus*, Vol. I (Harvard University Press: 1937), 1.51, 2.

68 The type is actually unique, despite the sporadic appearance on the market of specimens attributed to Alontion, which are actually more common coins of Abakainon with altered inscriptions.

69 Alberto Campana, on the basis of the typological and metrological affinities between the issues of the two Sikel cities, argued that among them there were close economic and commercial relations (A. Campana, 'Sicilia: Alontion (409 - ca. 150 a.C.),' in *Panorama Numismatico*, n.101 (Serravalle: Nomisma, 1996), 69).

70 A. Campana, 'Sicilia: Alontion,' 68.

71 *IGCH* 2246

72 E. Fabbricotti, 'Considerazioni su di un tesoretto di monete proveniente da S. Marco d'Alunzio,' in *Annali Istituto Italiano di Numismatica*, Vol. XV (1968), 83-90, no.2-6.

73 A. Crisà, 'Heroic Cults in Northern Sicily between Numismatics and Archaeology' in *Proceedings of the XIV International Numismatic Congress, Glasgow 2009*, edited by N. Holmes (Glasgow: International Numismatic Council, 2011), 116.

74 Ibid., 118.

75 See Mylai entry below. The existence of the coin from Neapolis illustrated by Riccio, featuring the same iconographic scheme of water flowing from the mouth of the man-faced bull, is uncertain (Fig. 163 of Part I).

76 Louvre Museum, found at Akragas, dated 450 BC, Museum Inventory no. G 365.

77 J. Millingen, 'On a Fictile Vase, Representing the Contest Between Hercules and the Achelous,' in *Transactions of the Royal Society of Literature of the United Kingdom*, Volume 2, Part 2 (London: Murray, 1834), 95-101.

78 E. M. Cope, *Commentary on the Rhetoric of Aristotle*, Vol.III (New York, 1970), 95.

79 Cf. 'χύδην› entry in ΛΟΓΕΙΟΝ, University of Chicago, Perseus Project at Chicago, available at http://logeion.uchicago.edu/.

80 A. Campana, 'Sicilia: Alontion,' 75.

81 Ibid., 74.

Coinage

20. AE Hemilitron, 7.5g, 21mm	**339 to 338 BC**
	OBV: Head of nymph to right. Dotted border. REV: Forepart of Acheloios Chydas as a man-faced bull to right, head in profile, above, ΑΛΟ, below, ИΤΙ, behind, ИΩИ. Dotted border. REF: CNS I, 68, 4; Campana CNAI, 69, 4; Private Collection*. *Unique*

21. AE Hemilitron, 8.1g, 20mm	**339 to 338 BC**
	OBV: Head of nymph to right. Dotted border. REV: Forepart of Acheloios Chydas as a man-faced bull to right, head in profile,uncertain inscription but with TI below forepart. Dotted border. REF: BM no. G.111*. *Incorrectly listed by Calciati under Abakainon (CNS I, 73, 1mv1)*

22. AE Trias?, 6.34g, 19mm	**212 to 150 BC**
	OBV: Head of Patron Turio wearing Phyrigian helmet to left. Dotted border. REV: ΑΛΟΝΤΙΝΩΝ to upper right, Acheloios Chydas as a man-faced bull standing to left on single line, water flowing from mouth, crab in exergue. Linear border. REF: CNS I, 67, 2 Rs1; Laffaille, 'Choix de Monnaies Grecques en Bronze,' 51 (this coin); Campana 14b; CNG, Triton V, lot 142*.

23. AE Trias?, 4.62g	**212 to 150 BC**
	OBV: Head of Patron Turio wearing Phyrigian helmet to left. Linear border. REV: ΑΛΟΝΤΙΝΩΝ to upper right, Acheloios Chydas as a man-faced bull standing to left on single line, water flowing from mouth. Linear border. REF: CNS I, 67, 2; Minì 3-4; Campana 14a; BMC 4 = BM no. TC, p60.1.Alu*.

ASSOROS

Assoros was an ancient Sikel city of central Sicily, just west of Agyrion. Little is known about its early history.[82] It began to issue coinage in the early 1st century BC and the inscriptions on this coinage, of which there are only two types, are in Latin, indicating significant Roman influence.[83]

Edgar L. Owen[84] was the first to question if the two bulls on the obverse of the bronze tetrantes of Assoros are in fact man-faced bulls, based on personal observation of a specimen in his inventory. In fact, all known examples display human-like features. For instance, all known specimens feature distinct human chins as opposed to bovine snouts, which is perhaps the most compelling evidence. Add to that the observation that both Virzi pieces feature distinct lines indicating human noses on the outermost figures.[85] Additionally, the example from the Continental Collection appears to show human-like eyes, particularly on the outermost figure.[86] On the example used here for the main catalog entry (from Owen's inventory) there are fairly distinct human eyes, noses, and chins, basically confirming the speculation that it is indeed two man-faced bulls depicted together in the same scene, a phenomenon seen nowhere else on Greek coinage.

Beyond the visual evidence, we know from Cicero[87] that the Chrysas river was particularly significant to the people of Assoros, and that there was a famous shrine to the river god outside the city walls. It seems that the Kyamosoros (modern day Salso Cimarosa) and the Chrysas (modern day Dittaino) are the most likely candidates for identification. Assoros was well protected on the plateau between these rivers,[88] thus the depiction of two river gods (as local embodiments of Acheloios) standing parallel just as the rivers ran is fitting indeed, and reminiscent of the much earlier Near Eastern practices of apotropaic winged man-headed bulls situated in pairs.[89]

The dating of the type is commonly placed in the late 1st century BC. However, this date is based on an old speculative hypothesis by Grant concerning a commemorative issue of the foundation of the Roman *municipium*.[90] The date was pushed back recently by Campana, who suggests c. 200 BC, arguing that Grant's speculations find no support in ancient sources.[91]

Coinage

24. AE Tetras?, (4.63-5.23g), 18mm	**c. 200 BC**
	OBV: Female head (nymph?) to right, wearing stephane, earrings and necklace, hair in knot behind. Dotted border. REV: Acheloios Kyamosoros and Acheloios Chrysas as man-faced bulls standing to right on single line, above, Latin ASSORV. REF: BMC Sicily, 31, 2; CNS III, 259, 3; Edgar L. Owen cat. No. 4968=Potamikon Collection*.

[82] The earliest source is Diodorus Siculus, reporting that Dionysius I of Syracuse struck a treaty with the Sikels of Assoros (*The Library of History*, 16.78.7), which occurred around 395 BC (A. Campana, 'Sicilia: Assoros (ca.200 a-C.),' in *Panorama Numismatico*, n.108. (Serravalle: Nomisma, 1997), 137).

[83] A. Burnett, M. Amandry, P. P. Ripollés Alegre, and Marguerite Spoerri Butcher, *Roman Provincial Coinage* (London: British Museum Press, 1998), no. 665 & 666.

[84] E. L. Owen, 'Ancient Greek Coins of Sicily, A-N,' no.4968 in his Online Catalog, available at www.edgarlowen.com.

[85] R. Calciati, *Corpus Nummorum Siculorum III*, 259, 3/2.

[86] CNG eAuction 327, lot. 370.

[87] Cicero, *Verr*. 4.44.

[88] R. Stillwell et al, 'Assorus,' in *The Princeton Encyclopedia of Classical Sites*.

[89] The practice of situating a village between rivers and its relation to apotropaic associations of man-faced bulls is first attested in Old Europe, as discussed in Chapter 1. The notion of two epithets appearing in the same scene is very early, first attested on the Syrian cylinder seal featuring two manifestations of Asallúhi (**Fig. 11**), who appears on the earth as rivers.

[90] M. Grant, *From imperium to auctoritas* (Cambridge: University press, 1969), 191.

[91] A. Campana, 'Sicilia: Assoros,' 138.

GELA

It is surprising that Gela issued no official bronze units depicting the man-faced bull, especially when the figure was featured so predominately on the city's silver coinage. Instead, bronze varieties show the head of a young, horned river god paired with a regular bull on the reverse.[92] Jenkins suggested this phenomenon related to the dual nature of the river god as part bull and part man. In his view, whereas on the silver it is depicted as one creature, on the bronze it appears as two.[93] There are, however, three known examples of the man-faced bull appearing as a large countermark of Geloan type.[94] These countermarks were struck on a bronze undertype from Akragas,[95] possibly from earlier dies that had been used for silver didrachms.[96]

It is difficult to understand the circumstances under which these coins emerged, which casts some doubt on their authenticity.

Santelli and Campana connect the countermarks with the invasion of Sicily by Carthage in 409 BC, arguing they were struck in Akragas to pay Geloan troops fighting in the army of the Greek alliance against Carthage. Moreover, they argue that it is very unlikely that an original Geloan didrachm die was re-used to countermark these bronze coins, pointing out that about 70 years had passed from the date of issue of the didrachms.[97] Instead, they suggest the countermark engraver copied the older silver coin types. Another possibility is that they were struck after the city was destroyed by the Cathaginians in 405 BC, under the leadership of Himilco.[98] In that case, these issues might have emerged c. 397 BC, when the surviving citizens of Gela joined Syracuse in a new war against Carthage,[99] reusing an old type as a symbol of rebirth.

Coinage

25. Didrachm Countermark, 19.03g	**Late 5th to Early 4th Century BC**
	OBV: Forepart of Acheloios Gelas as a man-faced bull to right, above beard, ΓΕ, between beard and front leg, Λ, and between front legs, A. REV: Blank. REF : G. Santelli and A. Campana, 'Le prime contromarche siciliane su bronzo,' in *Monete Antiche* anno VII, n.38 (March/April 2008), 37*. *Unconfirmed, uncertain authenticity. The countermarks measure about 17.5mm. All are overstruck on bronze hemilitrai of Akragras.*

Gela Didrachm Reverse:[100]

[92] See G.K. Jenkins, *The Coinage of Gela*, no. 499.

[93] Ibid., 103.

[94] G. Santelli and A. Campana, 'Le prime contromarche siciliane su bronzo,' in *Monete Antiche* 38 (2008), 11-15.

[95] R. Calciati, *Corpus Nummorum Siculorum I*, 174-176, no. 32-41.

[96] As pointed out by Santelli and Campana ('Le prime contromarche siciliane su bronzo,' 12, fig.6), there is a strong similarity between these countermarks and the reveres dies listed in G.K. Jenkins, *The Coinage of Gela*, group Ib, no. 7.

[97] G. Santelli and A. Campana, 'Le prime contromarche siciliane su bronzo,' 11-15.

[98] Diodorus Siculus, *The Library of History*, 13.111, 1-2.

[99] Ibid., 14.46-53.

[100] 100 G.K. Jenkins, *The Coinage of Gela*, group Ib, no. 7. Image Source: CNG, Triton XIV, 19.

HALYKIAI (ALICIE)

These interesting coins were attributed to Himera as late as Calciati,[101] but more recent scholarship places them in Halykiai, an Elymian town located at the top of Mount Polizzo near the modern-day village of Vita in western Sicily.[102] This new reattribution is based on coin finds in the area indicating an organized mint. The new location of the mint goes a step further than what Buceti proposed,[103] when he argued that the coins were not minted at Himera proper. Based on a coin with the inscription ΙΛΑ or ΑΛΙ (retrograde), Buceti hypothesized that the issue in question was minted by Campanian mercenaries on the site of the ruined Himera, which was given to them as a form of payment for services to Hannibal.[104] However, based on the research of Lazzarini, the inscription on the coin type, which is indeed ΑΛΙ, refers to Halykiai or Alicie,[105] the Elymian town mentioned by ancient sources.

The Elymians were a native population of western Sicily in close political and cultural relationships with Siculo-Punic peoples.[106] Diodorus informs us that during the military campaign of Dionysius I against the Carthaginians in 397/6 BC, the Halicyaeans refused to ally with the tyrant, instead sending ambassadors to the Carthaginian camp and concluding an alliance with Himilcon.[107]

According to Lazzarini, the tetrantes of Halykiai featuring the man-faced bull were issued from 390 to 370 BC,[108] in the years after Carthage rapidly retrieved the area of western Sicily, which brought freedom to the Elymian cities. Thus, once again the man-faced bull represents rebirth and renewal for a municipality.

There are at least four, but possibly six varieties of man-faced bull coinage issued at Halykiai. According to Lazzarini, all combine the obverse of a man-faced bull standing to left, head in profile, and three dots intermixed with the inscription ΑΛΙ (retrograde) above, with the reverse of a boar standing to left on single line, head in profile and leaf above.[109] Lazzarini argues the confusion about different varieties stems from poorly engraved dies or rough cleaning (or outright tooling), which explains the rare examples with clear letters.[110] Thus, in his view, many specimens appearing on the market seem to lack the inscription or the three dots, showing a blank field over the man-faced bull.[111] However, there are probably additional varieties of this type which we document below, which cannot be accounted for by Lazzarini's explanation (dot instead of leaf, etc.).

Another rare variety unlisted by Lazzarini shows the same types but oriented right.[112] The existence of a third type, featuring a dog standing to left on the reverse,[113] is still questionable. Another variety listed by Calciati[114] (for Himera) depicts a bull to right on the obverse and a man-faced bull to right on reverse, but is of a style unlike the others.

The man-faced bull on the coinage of Halykiai is likely a representation of the local embodiment of Acheloios, Acheloios Mazaro,[115] a river that originates on Mount Polizzo.

[101] R. Calciati, *Corpus Nummorum Siculorum I*, 46, no. 44-45. O. Hoover makes the same error in his handbook.
[102] L. Lazzarini, 'La monetazione e il sito di Halykiai (Alicie),' in *Schweizerische numismatische Rundschau* 84 (2005), 24.
[103] G. Buceti, *Alcune monete di bronzo inedite della Sicilia Greca* (Cassino, 2008), 22-3.
[104] Ibid.
[105] L. Lazzarini, 'La monetazione e il sito di Halykiai (Alicie),' 21
[106] For the eastern origins of the Elymians, see: V. Tusa, 'Il territorio degli Elimi. Stato attuale degli studi e delle ricerche,' in *Gli Elimi e l'area elima fino all'inizio della I guerra punica. Atti del Seminario di Studi* (Palermo, 1990), 9-15; M. Giuffrida, 'Rapporti tra l'area elima e il Mediterraneo orientale,' in *Gli Elimi e l'area elima fino all'inizio della I guerra punica. Atti del Seminario di Studi* (Palermo, 1990), 115-131; S. N. Consolo Langher, 'Erice e il koinon degli Elimi nella storia della Sicilia occidentale tra VI e IV sec. a. C.,' in *Atti delle Terze Giornate Internazionali di Studi sull'Area Elima, Gibellina-Erice-Contessa Entellina 1997* (Pisa, 2000), 287-310.
[107] Diodorus Siculus, *The Library of History*, 16.55.7.
[108] L. Lazzarini, 'La monetazione e il sito di Halykiai (Alicie),' 24.
[109] Ibid., Serie III.1
[110] Ibid., 23.
[111] Cf. Pecunem, Auction 14, lot 15; CNG eAuction 327, lot 420.
[112] R. Calciati, *Corpus Nummorum Siculorum III*, 412, no. 45/1.
[113] L. Lazzarini, 'La monetazione e il sito di Halykiai (Alicie),' Serie III.2.
[114] R. Calciati, *Corpus Nummorum Siculorum III*, 421, 44/1.
[115] E. Manni, *Geografia fisica e politica della Sicilia antica* (Roma, 1981), 115-116.

Coinage

26. AE Tetras, 3.52g, 15mm	**390 to 370 BC**
	OBV: Acheloios Mazaro as a man-faced bull standing to left on single line, head in profile, three dots above, inscription AΛI (retrograde). REV: Boar standing to left on single line, leaf above. REF: Lazzarini III.1; CNS I, 46, 44; Buceti 'inedited', p.23*. Image courtesy of Giuseppe Buceti.

27. AE Tetras, 4.40g, 19mm	**390 to 370 BC**
	OBV: Acheloios Mazaro as a man-faced bull standing to left on single line, head in profile, three dots above, inscription AΛI (retrograde). REV: Boar standing to left on single line, dot above. REF: CNG eAuction 327, lot 420*.

28. AE Tetras, 3.38g, 16mm	**390 to 370 BC**
	OBV: Acheloios Mazaro as a man-faced bull standing to left on single line, head in profile, nothing above. REV: Boar standing to left on single line, nothing above. REF: CNG eAuction 357, lot 55*. *Unconfirmed. It is possible this coin has some of the devices worn off, as Lazzarini proposed in his model, but it does not appear so.*

29. AE Tetras, 3.37g, 15mm	**390 to 370 BC**
	OBV: Acheloios Mazaro as a man-faced bull standing to right, head in profile. REV: Boar standing right on single line, (two?) dots above. REF: CNS III, 412, no. 45/1*.

30. AE Tetras, 4.62g, 17mm	**390 to 370 BC**
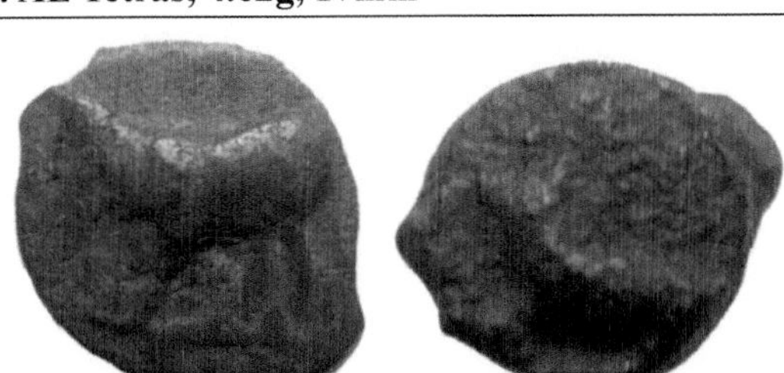	OBV: Acheloios Mazaro as a man-faced bull standing to left on single line, head in profile. REV: Dog(?) standing to left. REF: Lazzarini III, 2; D. Cavalli Collection*.

31. AE Tetras, 4.44g, 16mm	**390 to 370 BC**
	OBV: Acheloios Mazaro as a man-faced bull standing to right, head in profile. REV: Bull(man-faced?) moving right. REF: CNS III, 412, 44/1*.

HERBESSOS

Like many native Sikel populations, little is known about the Herbessenes, including their exact whereabouts. Current scholarship suggests the site of Montagna di Marzo,[116] in the general area of Gela. The site was apparently bordered by the modern Braemi River.

Herbessos issued five coin types, of which only one depicts the man-faced bull. From a metrological point of view there are two different issues of the same type, with obverse depicting a laureate female head to right, likely a representation of Sikelia, and the inscription ΕΡΒΕΣΣΙΝΩΝ. The reverse features the head and neck of a man-faced bull to right.[117] The two issues are differentiated by their weight, with the first being around 30g while the latter issue is about 18g. Campana lists these as two variations of the same denomination: the litra.[118] As is often the case, both issues are overstruck on earlier coins. The heavier litra was originally overstruck on two types: the coins of Syracuse of the Athena/star and dolphins type, [119] and the coins of the Tyrrhenoi, themselves overstruck on the same Syracusan types.[120] The reduced litra, on the other hand, was always overstruck on coins of Syracuse of the Zeus/horse and Archia/Pegasus type.[121]

Campana reconstructed an appealing historical framework for the two issues: the Tyrrhenoi, together with another group of mercenaries from Aitna, fought against Timoleon but were ultimately exterminated by the Corinthian ruler. Therefore, their coins became the spoils of war for the inhabitants of Herbessos, allies of Timoleon, and were overstruck just before the battle of Krimissos.[122] Soon after that episode came the official coinage reform of Timoleon, which provided a weight reduction of the bronze litra (from the previous standard of about 30g to the new standard of about 18g). Thus, the mint of Herbessos adopted the new standard for the litra and started to use coins weighing less as the undertype. In fact, the dies appear to show more wear on the later examples.

The man-faced bull depicted on Herbessene coinage is probably the local embodiment of Acheloios, Acheloios Herbessos. In fact, on an earlier litra from the same mint a bearded and horned man is named outright as ΕΡΒΗΣΣΟΣ, the ancient name of the modern-day Braemi.[123] A potential alternative identification is Acheloios Halykos. Diodorus, in his account of the First Punic War, mentions the river Halykos during the conquering of Herbessos by the Romans.[124] Halykos was another name for the southern portion of the Himera River, the modern day Salso, although ancient sources report a homonymy with the modern day Platani.[125]

[116] A. Campana, 'Sicilia: Erbessos (344-336 a.C.),' in *Panorama Numismatico,* 116 and 118 (Serravalle: Nomisma, 1998), 203. The hypothesis was first proposed by Cammarata, who in 1971 pointed out that at the site, among the coins discovered during the excavation, were three specimens of Herbessos, two of which feature the man-faced bull (E. Cammarata, 'L'importanza della numismatica per l'identificazione di Erbessos,' in *Bollettino nusmismatico,* VIII, No.2 (1971).

[117] Only one die is known for the obverse, and probably two dies for the reverse (E. Cammarata, 'L'importanza della numismatica per l'identificazione di Erbessos,' 208).

[118] A. Campana, 'Sicilia: Erbessos,' 208, no. 5a and 5b.

[119] R. Calciati, *Corpus Nummorum Siculorum II*, 111, 62, dated 395 BC.

[120] R. Calciati, *Corpus Nummorum Siculorum III,* 307, 1 (dated 357 to 336 BC); also overstruck on Syracusan Athena/star and dolphins (*Corpus Nummorum Siculorum II*, 111, no. 62).

[121] R. Calciati, *Corpus Nummorum Siculorum II*, 185, 80 (Zeus/horse); R. Calciati, *Corpus Nummorum Siculorum II*, 181,77 (Archia/pegasus) dated between 344 and 336 BC.

[122] A. Campana, 'Sicilia: Erbessos,' 208.

[123] Ibid., 205, no. 2.

[124] Diodorus Siculus, *The Library of History*, 23.9.5. This literary suggests Herbessos might have been located near the inland course of the southern Himera River, the Halykos (modern-day Salso), or along the Halykos River (modern-day Platani).

[125] The modern-day Salso River (Salso is Italian for 'salty') corresponds to the course of the ancient southern Himera River (not to be confused with the eponymous northern Himera, at whose mouth was located the Greek polis of Himera) defined as *Halykos potamos* by ancient sources. In fact, the etymology of Himera indicates the irregular taste of the river water, as the Semitic *hemar* means 'bitter', from the Akkadian *marru* 'bitter' (G. Semerano, *Le Origini della Cultura Europea*, Vol. II, Serie II, 189) closely related to the modern meaning of the Italian 'salso'. Thus, the adjective over time probably transitioned to a name, from *halykos* to Halykos, which is how it is mentioned by Diodorus. However, the debate is still open, because the name Halykos, based on the ancient sources, would also belong to the modern-day Platani River. For a discussion and exhaustive bibliography on the problem of homonyms between the two major Sicilian rivers, see: M.I. Gulletta, 'Kamisos/Lykos/Halykos. Da 'via del sale' a 'confine' tra le due eparchie (note di geografia storica nella Sicilia centro-occidentale),' in *Troianer sind wir gewesen - Migrationen in der antiken Welt, Geographica Historica*, Band 21, edited by E. Olshausen and H. Sonnabend (Stuttgart, 2006), 402-419. The Salso River had significant geographical and political importance in ancient Sicily, insofar as it cut through the central part of the island and therefore represented the natural border between Sikels and Sikans, the two major non-Greek populations of Sicily (M.I. Gulletta, 'Kamisos/Lykos/Halykos. Da 'via del sale' a 'confine' tra le due eparchie (note di geografia storica nella Sicilia centro-occidentale)' 408. The same river, in its early stages, flows through the site of Polizzello, an important site related to a proto-cult of the man-faced bull, as discussed in Chapter 3.

Coinage

32. AE Litra, 32,17g, 29mm	**338 BC**
	OBV: Head of Sikelia to right, wearing wreath of myrtle, ΕΡΒΕΣΣΙΝΩΝ before. Dotted border. REV: Head and neck of Acheoios Herbessos as a man-faced bull to right. Dotted border. REF: Campana 5a; Castrizio II, 1.1; CNS III, 252, 4; Moretti 297 (this coin); CNG 90, lot 346*. *Pre-Timoleontic Weight Standard*

33. AE Litra, 20.8g, 29mm	**338 to 336 BC**
	OBV: Head of Sikelia to right, wearing wreath of myrtle, ΕΡΒΕΣΣΙΝΩΝ before. Dotted border. REV: Head and neck of Acheoios Herbessos as a man-faced bull to right. Dotted border. REF: Campana 5b; Castrizio III, 1-2; CNS III, 253 5 OS/15 = CNG eAuction 327, lot 407=Potamikon Collection*. *Timoleontic Weight Standard*

IAITAS

Iaitas was a native town located on Mount Iato in north-western Sicily, between Panormos and Segesta, in the area of present day St. Giuseppe Iato and St. Cipirello.[126] It is positioned over the valley of the Iaitos River. The first archaeological traces date back to the 9th century BC, and attest to Elymian culture among the inhabitants.[127] According to Campana,[128] Iaitas prospered because of its exceptionally strategic position that dominated the main access roads of western Sicily. The Elymian city had contact with Greek culture since the Archaic Age,[129] and archaeological evidence has lead scholars to date the first contact with Selinous to the time period immediately after the founding of that Greek colony.[130] Selinous was destroyed in 409 BC and a new political and cultural reorganization occurred in the central-western region of the island, now ruled by the Carthaginians (especially after the treaty of 374 BC). This undoubtedly influenced the life and history of the settlements in the valley. In most cases, the major population centers experienced a new stage of economic and urban development, but the most significant examples are Iaitas and Entella, which began to truly thrive at the end of the 4th century BC.[131]

Upon this background, in 330 BC, Iaitas began to issue bronze coinage depicting the man-faced bull, presumably under the influence of the Carthaginians.[132] There are potentially three types of man-faced bull coinage from Iaitas. After these coins appear, which may have been minted as late as 260 BC, the mint apparently ceased operation for about 100 years.[133] On the onkia the man-faced bull is paired with a grain ear and barleycorn. The tetrantes, allegedly found on Mount Iato, pair the man-faced bull obverse with a lion to right on the reverse (this man-faced bull/lion pairing has been explored in other sections).[134] The man-faced bulls on the coinage of Iaitas probably represent Acheloios Iaitos.

It should be noted, however, that Suzanne Frey-Kupper[135] is very skeptical about the authenticity of the tetrantes coins and they will not be included in *Historia Nummorum Sicily and Adjacent Islands*.[136] Her rationale is as follows: (1) the surface of coins 23.1 and 23.3 seem to be heavily cleaned and possibly reworked; (2) the obverse dies of 23.2 and 23.3 are basically identical, but no inscription appears on 23.2, and the same problem applies to 23.1 and 23.3, where the body, double exergue line and right horn are identical, but the head of 23.1 is in profile, unlike 23.3, and, moreover, the reverse dies of all three appear to be identical, but 23.1 is missing the curved ground line beneath the lion. These features can only be explained by extensive re-engraving of the dies in antiquity, which she finds unlikely; (3) the double exergue line and the curved tail on the man-faced bull on coin 23.1 are stylistically incorrect; (4) during 42 years of extensive excavation at Iaitas not one of these types has been found, yet all other coin types from Iaitas have been revealed in the archaeological record.[137] She acknowledges, however, that the coins appear to be struck on genuine flans, and that the example from the Potamikon Collection has very convincing surfaces (See enlargement).[138]

In response to Frey-Kupper's compelling argument, we suggest: (1) evidence of harsh cleaning and reworking by a modern hand probably indicates a genuine coin has been manipulated; (2) many ancient dies were re-cut in antiquity; (3) the curved tail on 23.1 is stylistically strange but not enough to condemn the coin, especially since we see the same scheme at Abakainon, Panormos, and even Tarsos, and double exergue lines are extant; (4) there are numerous coins that are undoubtedly genuine but have not come from controlled archaeological digs.

There are also some countermarks from Iaitas that feature the man-faced bull. These were applied to undertypes from Segesta that date to the 1st century BC, although they were originally dated to the mid 3rd century BC or later by Calciati.[139] The depiction of Aeneas on the reverse stems from the founding story of Segesta, in which refugees from Troy along with the son of the local river, the Crimisus, were the first to occupy the city.[140] Thus, the Elymian Segestans and Romans found solidarity in common Trojan roots, symbolized by this reverse design.[141] Dating of the undertype to the 1st century BC is now broadly accepted.

---

126 A. Campana, 'Sicilia: Ietas (ca. 330 a.C.-20 d.C.),' in *Panorama Numismatico*, 126 (Serravalle: Nomisma, 1999), 273.

127 A. Campana, 'Sicilia: Ietas,' 273.

128 Ibid.

129 H. P. Isler, 'Monte Iato. Indigène et Grecs à l'époque archaïque,' in *Des Grecs en Sicile... Grecs et indigènes en Sicile occidentale d'après les fouilles archèologiques*, edited by F. Spatafora, S. Vassallo (Caltanissetta, 2006), 77-80.

130 F. Spatafora, 'Le Vie dell'acqua: città e villaggi nelle vallate fluviali della Sicilia centro-occidentale tra Età Arcaica ed Ellenismo,' in *Cultura e religione delle acque Atti del Convegno interdisciplinare, Qui fresca l'acqua mormora ... (S. Quasimodo, Sapph. fr. 2,5) Messina 29-30 marzo 2012*, edited by A. Calderone (Roma: Bretschneider, 2012), 304.

131 Ibid., 305.

132 In terms of metrology, the man-face bull/grain issue should be identified as a Siculo-Punic onkia (A. Campana, 'Sicilia: Ietas (ca. 330 a.C.-20 d.C.),' 274).

133 Ibid.

134 See index for page listings.

135 See S. Frey-Kupper, 'Ein 'neuer' Acheloos der Iaitiner : Ein Beitrag zur Erforschung der frühe Münzpraegung von Iaitas,' in *Zona Archeologica: Festschrift für Hans Peter Isler zum 60. Geburtstag* (Bonn: Dr. Rudolf Habelt GMBH, 2001), and also, S. Frey-Kupper, *Die antiken Fundmünzen vom Monte Iato 1971-1990. Ein Beitrag zur Geldgeschichte Westsizilien. Studia Ietina X* (Lausanne, 2013), 80-96 and 631-632, pl. 64 and pl. 65.

136 K. Rutter, J. Morcom, and S. Frey-Kupper, (eds.), *Historia Nummorum Sicily and Adjacent Islands* (Forthcoming, 2017).

137 S. Frey-Kupper, 'Ein 'neuer' Acheloos der Iaitiner,' 163-168.

138 Personal correspondence with author. See enlarged coin below, ex. ACR Auctions, Milan.

139 R. Calciati, *Corpus Nummorum Siculorum I*, 304, 54-55.

140 Virgil, *Aeneid*, 5.715-18, 746-58.

141 O. Hoover, *Handbook of Coins of Sicily*, 296.

The countermark itself is relatively abundant with about forty known examples. They are dated after Caesar's death, during the last years of the Republic, c. 27 BC. Interestingly, man-faced bull iconography appears nowhere else on the coinage of Segesta, so it seems strange that the Elymian city would employ the iconography, and also so late. This fact led Santelli to state that it is unlikely the countermarks were applied in Segesta, who highlighted Iaitas as the most probable candidate.[142] His rationale is that: (1) Iaitas already had a previous tradition of the man-faced bull on coin types; (2) the phenomenon of countermarks is present at Iaitas on contemporary issues from the same mint (i.e. countermarks applied at Iaitas on Segestan coins);[143] (3) the man-faced bull countermarks are always struck on the obverse side, demonstrating the intention to identify the countermark as a symbol of the new issuing authority, replacing the old issuing authority of the obverse undertype; (4) there are three different countermarks (dog, horse protome, and man-faced bull) all contemporaneously overstruck on the obverse side of the same Segestan undertypes, suggesting that there was a plurality of issuing authorities reusing these coins. Thus, the main hypothesis proposed by Santelli, which is very convincing, is that Iaitas and other neighboring issuing authorities (identified by the different countermarks) were originally administratively dependent on Segesta under Roman rule (Santelli speaks of 'joint municipality'), and that subsequently a division occurred in which each of these municipalities began to mark the available coins in circulation: Segesta employing the dog, Iaitas employing the man-faced bull, and a third mint, still unidentified, employing the horse protome.[144] The man-faced bulls on these countermarks are also probably Acheloios Iaitos.

Coinage

34. AE Onkia(?), 1.00g, 12mm	**330 to 260 BC**
	OBV: Acheloios Iaitos as a man-faced bull standing to right on single line, head in profile, IAITI above, NΩ before, N (retro) between legs. Linear border. REV: Grain ear with side-shoot to right. REFERENCES: CNS I, 383, 1; Minì 1; Pecunem 6, lot 115*.

35. AE Tetras (?), 5.24g	**330 to 260 BC**
	OBV: Acheloios Iaitos as a man-faced bull standing to right on double line, head in profile. Anepigraphic. REV: Lion to right. REF: Moretti Collection, Palermo, Museo Regionale, from Monte Iato, Inv. M 427 (1976); Frey-Kupper, Taf. 23, 1*. *Unconfirmed. This might be a tooled version of 36, in which the face was engraved in profile and the line beneath the lion was removed.*

36. AE Tetras (?), 4.91g	**330 to 260 BC**
	OBV: Acheloios Iaitos as a man-faced bull standing to right on double line, head facing, IAITIN-ΩN above and before. REV: Lion to right, single, curved line below. REF: Moretti Collection, Palermo, Museo Regionale, from Monte Iato, Inv. M 105 (1973); Frey-Kupper, Taf. 23, 3*.

142 G. Santelli, 'Monete d'epoca tardo-repubblicana della zecca siciliana di Segesta: le contromarche ed il motivo dell'aquila,' in *Annotazioni Numismatiche*, Suppl. XV, anno 10°, serie III (Milano, 2000), 3-24.

143 Ibid., 16-17.

144 Ibid., 20-22.

37. Countermark Type 1	**c.27 BC**
	OBV: Turreted and veiled bust of Segesta to right. Countermark: Acheloios Iaitos as a man-faced bull standing to right, head in profile. REV: Aeneas standing to right, holding sword and carrying his father, Anchises. REF: CNS I, 304, 55 CM; Santelli 2*. *Santelli reports 28 known specimens. Size of countermark: 7mm.*

38. Countermark Type 2	**c.27 BC**
	OBV: Turreted and veiled bust of Segesta to right. Countermark: Acheloios Iaitos as a man-faced bull standing to left, head in profile. REV: Aeneas standing right, holding sword and carrying his father, Anchises REF: CNS I, 304, 55 CM; Santelli 3*. *Santelli reports 11 known specimens. Size of countermark: 7mm.*

Enlargement of Countermark Type 1:

Enlargement of MSP I, 34b from the ΠΟΤΑΜΙΚΟΝ Collection (3.60g, 16mm):

KATANE

Katane was located on the eastern coast of Sicily, nearly equidistant between Syracuse to the south and Tauromenion to the north. Signs of life at the site appear in the late Chaclcolithic Period[145] and continue throughout the Bronze Age.[146] Archaeological evidence suggests that Katane was originally a native Sikan city[147] later occupied by Sikels,148 who were ultimately forced out by Chalkidian Greek settlers coming from Naxos149 around 729 BC.150

Katane has a rich numismatic history, reflecting the important part it played in the general narrative of Sicilian history. The very first coins of Katane were silver tetradrachms featuring the man-faced bull.[151] The series was struck after 466 BC, the year of the return of the Katanians from Leontini, where they had been relocated through force by the Syracusan tyrant, Hieron I,[152] in 476 BC.[153] Thus, the man-faced bull clearly operated as a symbol of rebirth for the Katanians in this early context.

After about half a century of independence Katane was sacked for a second time, in 403/402 BC, by Dionysius I of Syracuse. This time the inhabitants were sold as slaves and replaced by Campanian mercenaries.[154] About 60 years later a mercenary named Mamercos became tyrant of the city, but was defeated by Timoleon and apparently crucified in Syracuse in 338 BC.[155] It is probably just after this event that the man-faced bull appears on the bronze coinage of Katane, where again he symbolizes the renewal of the polis. Previous scholarship suggested either 405 to 402 BC,[156] or 344 to 336 BC.[157] However, a date of after 338 BC is the most likely, since we know that Timoleon reformed the monetary system after the battle of Krimissos.[158] Thus, it is for this reason that we can suggest that the bronze types of the man-faced bull were issued as a symbol of the rebirth of the city during the Timoleonic renaissance of Sicily. Ultimately, the Katanians issued two bronze types (both litrai) featuring the man-faced bull,[159] who is most likely a representation of the local embodiment of Acheloios, Acheloios Amenanos.[160]

[145] Late Chalcolithic pottery was found at Montevergine Hill, upon which the akropolis of the Greek city was built (S. Privitera, 'Lo sviluppo urbano di Catania dalla fondazione dell'apoikia alla fine del V secolo d.C,' in *Catania. L'identità urbana dall'antichità al settecento*, edited by L. Scalisi (Catania, 2009), 37.

[146] G. Rizza, 'Attività dell'Istituto di Archeologia dell'Università di Catania. Scavi e ricerche in Sicilia negli anni 1972-1975,' in *Kokalos*, 22-23 (Palermo, 1978), 644-645.

[147] R.M. Albanese Procelli, *Sicani, Siculi, Elimi: forme di identità, modi di contatto e processi di trasformazione,* (Milano: Longanesi 2003), 140.

[148] F. Giudice, E. Procelli, M. Frasca, R.M. Albanese, 'Catania. Scavo all'interno del muro di cinta del monastero dei Benedettini,' in *Cronache di Archeologia,* Vol.18 (1979), 131-135; E. Procelli, 'Appunti per una topografia di Catania pregreca,' in *Kokalos*, 38 (Roma, 1995), 69-78.

[149] Thucydides, *The Peloponesian War*, 6.3.3.

[150] A. Patané, 'Saggi di scavo all'interno del Castello Ursino di Catania,' in *Kokalos*, 39-40 (Roma, 1996), 901-907; L. Moscati Castelnuovo, 'Tucidide (VI 3, 3) e gli ecisti di Catane,' in *Hommages à Carl Deroux, III-Histoire et épigraphie, Droit*, edited by P. Defosse (Bruxelles, 2003), 321-327.

[151] C. Arnold-Biucchi, *The Randazzo Hoard and Sicilian Chronology in the Early Fifth Century BC* (New York: American Numismatic Society, 1990), 54-76.

[152] Diodorus Siculus, *The Library of History*, 11.49.1; 11.76.3.

[153] G. Manganaro, 'Per una storia della chora katanaia,' in *Catania Antica, Atti del Convegno della S.I.S.A.C. Catania 23-24 maggio 1992,* edited by B. Gentili (Pisa, 1996), 32-34. The tyrant Hieron I died at Katane in 466 BC (L. Braccesi and G. Millino, *La Sicilia greca* (Roma: Carocci, 2000), 229-230.

[154] G. Manganaro, 'Per una storia della chora katanaia,' 35-43. As elsewhere in Sicily, the new inhabitants eventually adopted a genuinely Greek lifestyle, transforming themselves from mercenaries to citizens (G. Tagliamonte, 'Rapporti tra società di immigrazione e mercenari italici nella Sicilia greca del IV secolo a.C.,' in *Confini e frontiera nella Grecia d'Occidente. Atti del trentasettesimo convegno di studi sulla Magna Grecia, Taranto 3-6 ottobre 1997* (Napoli: Arte Tipografica, 1999), 564).

[155] Plutarch, *Timoleon*, 34.4.

[156] R. Calciati, *Corpus Nummorum Siculorum III*, 91, 4. Calciati argued that the coins were struck by the Campanian mercenaries assigned to settle in Katane by Dionysius I.

[157] SNG Munchen 447; thus the German catalogers assumed that the coins were struck during the years of Timoleon

[158] M. Puglisi, 'Distribuzione e funzione della moneta bronzea in Sicilia dalla fine del V sec. a.C. all'età ellenistica,' in *XIII Congreso Internacional de Numismática, Madrid, 2003*, Vol. 1 (Madrid, 2005), 288.

[159] C. Boehringer, 'Die fruhen Bronzemunzen von Leontinoi und Katane,' in *Le origini della monetazione di bronzo in sicilia e Magna Grecia. Atti del VI Convegno del Centro Internazionale di Studi numismatici, Napoli 1977.* Suppl. Annali Istituto Numismatica Vol.25 (Roma, 1979), 145-179.

[160] The area with the richest votive deposits in Katane was at the mouth of the Amenanos River. The abundance and variety of the materials of the Archaic Age deposits, many of which were imported from the main centers of Greece, the Aegean, and Asia Minor, led scholars to compare the sanctuary of Katane with those distributed along the main commercial routes in Aegina, Cyrenaica, and Etruria (Cf. F. Giudice, 'Il ruolo di Catania nella rete dei traffici commerciali del Mediterraneo,' in *Catania Antica*, 97-148). The frequenting of the area by non-native Greeks may reflect its role as a 'gateway community' (Cf. R.M. Albanese Procelli, *Sicani, Siculi, Elimi: forme di identità, modi di contatto e processi di trasformazione* (Milano: Longanesi, 2003), 186; K. G. Hirth, 'Inter-regional trade and the formation of prehistoric gateway communities,' in *American Antiquity*, 43 (1978), 25-45).

Coinage

39. AE Litra, 13.03g, 24mm	**After 339 BC**
	OBV: Head of the nymph Katana wearing wreath of reeds to left, KATANA below neck, around, three dolphins. REV: Acheloios Amenanos as a man-faced bull standing to right on single line, head in profile. Dotted border. REF: Castrizio II, 1/1; CNS III, 94, 3/3 = NAC 64, Lot 680*.

40. AE Litra, 14.23g, 25mm	**After 339 BC**
	OBV: Head of the nymph Katana wearing wreath of reeds to left. Dotted border. REV: Acheloios Amenanos as a man-faced bull standing to left on single line, head in profile, KATANAIΩN in ex. REF: Hunterian Collection, Greek Coins, Volume I, Plate XII, 19; Castrizio I, 1; CNS III, 92, 2 A/5 = BM no. 1920,0305.1651*.

KERSINI

Originally identified as the Skeraioi,[161] the Kersini were probably a group of ancient mercenaries who were allotted land in central Sicily after service to Dionysius I of Syracuse.[162] No record of their name appears in the ancient texts, but it stems from the Greek word for peninsula, which lead Campana to suggest they might be Illyrian mercenaries from the more northern portion of that area, the ancient Cherso, today's Austria and Slovenia.[163]

There are two types issued by the Kersini, all found in the vicinity of Santa Caterina Villarmosa, at a site called Cozzo Scavo.[164] The tetras with man-faced bull reverse, with only six examples known, does not have a clear inscription. However, since the coins were found with another type of tetras, this one bearing the inscription ΚΕΡΣΙΝΩΝ, we can connect the two.[165]

The man-faced bull on the coinage of the Kersini is probably Acheloios as embodied in the local river of their new homeland. The nearest river to the site of Santa Caterina Villarmosa is the modern Salito, believed to be the initial trunk of the ancient Salso which was called Halykos in ancient times.[166] Thus, this man-faced bulls is Acheloios Halykos.

These coins all appear to be overstruck on tetrantes of Syracuse.[167] There are six known specimens, struck by a single reverse die and two obverse dies.[168] The denomination, according to Campana's metrological studies, corresponds to the tetras of the time of Dionysius I, before the reduced standard established by Timoleon.

Coinage

41. AE Tetras, 7.51g, 21mm	357 to 344 BC
	OBV: Bearded male head to right. Dotted border. REV: Forepart of Acheloios Halykos as a man-faced bull to right. Linear border. REF: CNS III, 322, 1; Campana 1; Cammarata 114; SNG München 14 (misattributed to Agyrion, appears to show an 'I' in inscription); CNG eAuction 327, lot 329 (misattributed to Agyrion)= Potamikon Collection*.

Enlarged Inscription:[169]

[161] A. Campana, 'Sicilia: Skeraioi,' in *Panorama Numismatico*, 176 (Serravalle: Nomisma, 2003), 153.

[162] A. Campana, 'Aggiornamento al Corpus Nummorum Antiquae Italiae. Sicilia: Kersini,' in *Monete Antiche*, 36 (Cassino: Diana, 2007), 5.

[163] Ibid., 6.

[164] R. Calciati, *Corpus Nummorum Siculorum III*, 322. Recently, S. Amata identified the mint of the Kersini at the site of Cozzo Scavo near S. Caterina Villarmosa (S. Amata, 'Cozzo Scavo. I rinvenimenti numismatici dalle campagne di scavo 1993-1996,' in *Kokalos*, Vol 43-44, Tomo II,1 (Roma, 2002), 41-54).

[165] A. Campana, 'Aggiornamento al Corpus Nummorum Antiquae Italiae. Sicilia: Kersini,' 7.

[166] M. I. Gulletta, 'Kamisos/Lykos/Halykos. Da 'via del sale' a 'confine' tra le due eparchie (note di geografia storica nella Sicilia centro-occidentale),' in *Troianer sind wir gewesen - Migrationen in der antiken Welt, Geographica Historica*, Band 21, edited by E. Olshausen and H. Sonnabend (Stuttgart, 2006), 413.

[167] R. Calciati, *Corpus Nummorum Siculorum II*, 86, 41.

[168] A. Campana, 'Aggiornamento al Corpus Nummorum Antiquae Italiae. Sicilia: Kersini,' 7.

[169] Ibid., 6. Image of obverse inscription on Campana Type 2, courtesy of Alberto Campana.

MAMAR

Two types of MAMAP coinage exist in two corresponding bronze denominations, the hemilitron and the tetras. All types show the forepart of a man-faced bull, which is a common feature for mercenary coinage of Sicily.[170] The MAMAP hemilitron was described for the first time by Imhoof-Blumer, who discovered a specimen in the Copenhagen Museum and an additional one in the British Museum.[171] The tetras, with two specimens known, was described for the first time by Gabrici, and subsequently published by Campana.[172]

The reverse type of the hemilitron recalls the series from Himera with Silenos riding a goat on the obverse and a winged 'Nike' to left on the reverse. The weight, however, is not consistent with the standard in use at Himera. MAMAP coins are slightly heavier, with a litra of about 16 to 18g, as opposed to the theoretical litra of 13g for Himera. Thus, the weight of MAMAP coinage is closer to the Siculo-Punic world rather than the Greek.[173]

No historical source cites a population or locality named Mamar. According Tagliamonte,[174] the linguistic root of MAMAP is not attributable to the Greek world, and instead is likely from the Osco-Italic world, probably referring to Mamars, the Oscan name for the god Mars. The same root is the basis for the names of the Marsi and the Mamertines,[175] both Italic peoples. Consequently, it is likely that the Mamar were a group of Italic mercenaries, presumably Campanians, devoted to the worship of Mars. This explanation is also appealing in light of the claim by Pausanias[176] that Ares came to the aid of Acheloios during his fight with Herakles, hence these worshippers of Mars feature the man-faced bull, a local embodiment of Acheloios, on their coinage.

It is possible that these MAMAP coins were minted by the same Campanian mercenaries cited by Diodorus Siculus.[177] He informs us that in 404 BC, Dionysius I of Syracuse, under siege by Rhegion and Messana, sought the help of some 1,200 Campanian mercenaries who had remained in Sicily as a garrison of a Punic fortress. Their intervention ultimately enabled the tyrant to end the siege. This hypothesis is supported by the existence of a specimen in a private collection, which was found in a hoard along with some hemilitrai of Himera and various ceramic fragments on a hill a few kilometers from Resuttano.[178] As reported by Campana, based on the archaeological dating of the pottery fragments and the Himera coin types, the MAMAP coinage was probably issued during the last decade of the 5th century BC and circulated in the area of Himera, which at that time was under the control of the Carthaginians. In fact, Resuttano is located on the road that leads from Himera to the inside of Sicily, and during the historical period related to the burial of the hoard, Resuttano was also in Carthaginian territory. Therefore, the most likely hypothesis concerning the MAMAP coinage is that they were struck for Campanian mercenaries formerly in the pay of the Carthaginians but later employed by Dionysius I, issued 409 to 403 BC.

The man-faced bull on the coinage of the Mamar is probably Acheloios as embodied in the southern Himera river, today named Salso, thus Acheloios Himera.

170 The following considerations follow the monograph of A. Campana (A. Campana, 'Sicilia: Mamar? (409/405-403 a-C.),' in *Panorama Numismatico* 176 (Serravalle: Nomisma, 2003), 156-160) and subsequent updates via personal correspondence, not yet formally published.

171 A. Campana, 'Sicilia: Mamar?,' 156-160.

172 Ibid.

173 Ibid.

174 G. Tagliamonte, *I figli di Marte. Mobilità, mercenari e mercenariato italici in Magna Grecia e Sicilia* (Roma, 1994), 137.

175 According to some scholars the MAMAP coins were issued by the Mamertines who settled in the area of Gelas (Cf. E. Galvagno, 'I Siculi: fine di un ethnos,' in *Diodoro Siculo e la Sicilia indigena. Atti del convegno di studi, Caltanissetta 21-22 maggio 2005*, edited by C. Miccichè, S. Modeo and L. Santagati (Palermo, 2006), 43, footnote 90).

176 Pausanias, and Sir J. G. Frazer, *Descriptions of Greece*, Vol. I (Macmillan, 1898), 312.

177 The presence of Campanian mercenaries in Sicily is attested as early as the end of the 5th century BC (see the bibliography in E. Galvagno, 'I Siculi: fine di un ethnos,' 41, note 61). Under Dionysius I and his son, their number grew larger until constituting a third of the army (Diodorus Siculus, *The Library of History*, 14.1.3; 58.2).

178 A. Campana, personal correspondence.

Coinage

42. AE Tetras, 5.47g, 15mm	**409 to 403 BC**
	OBV: Forepart of Acheloios Himera as a man-faced bull to left, MAMAP above. REV: Head of nymph to right, bandage in hair, three dots surrounding. REF: Campana 2*; Gorny and Mosch 237, Session I, lot 1133= Potamikon Collection*. *2 known specimens. Some areas on the top coin have been strengthened from cleaning, particularly the hair on the reverse.*

43. AE Hemilitron, 7.89g, 20mm	**409 to 403 BC**
	OBV: Forepart of Acheloios Himera as a man-faced bull to left, M-A-M-A-P surrounding, grain above (in-line with inscription). REV: Winged nymph holding bandage and flying to left, water spring(?) before, five dots surrounding. REF: SNG Cop 1072*. *2 known specimens.*

44. AE Hemilitron, 6.80g, 18mm	**409 to 403 BC**
	OBV: Forepart of Acheloios Himera as a man-faced bull to left, MA-M-A-P surrounding, grain just above back of bull's neck (not in-line with inscription). Dotted border. REV: Winged nymph holding bandage and flying to left, water spring(?) before, five dots surrounding, star to left. REF: Roma, e-Sale 4, lot 60*. *Questionable authenticity.*

45. AE Hemilitron, 6.76g, 22mm	**409 to 403 BC**
	OBV: Forepart of Acheloios Himera as a man-faced bull to left, MA-M-A-P surrounding, no grain ear. Dotted border. REV: Winged nymph holding bandage and flying to left, water spring(?) before, five dots surrounding. REF: F. Imhoof-Blumer, Monnaies Grecques (1883), 22, pl.B, no.7; BMC Sicily 240, no. 1; Campana 1 = Lanz (e-Bay item 230764837283)*. *This example is the coin found in Resuttano.* *6 known specimens.*

MYLAI (?)

Ancient Mylai lies beneath the site of the modern-day town of Milazzo, just south-west of Messana. A Bronze Age necropolis containing primarily Aegean and Levantine pottery dates the earliest inhabitants to the late 2nd millennium BC.[179] The graves within the necropolis also contained pottery from the Italian peninsula, but Mycenaean pottery was totally absent.[180] Interestingly, in this early multicultural climate, archaeologists also found traces of Ausonio II Culture,[181] with strong influences from Nuragic and peninsular proto-Villanovan civilizations dating to the 11th to 9th century BC.[182] This proto-Villanovan society of Milazzo never evolved into proper Villanovan culture,[183] but instead gave rise to the ethnos of Sikels. Mylai finally became a Greek town around 490 BC, when the Zankleans lost their city after a massive influx of Messenians, and decided to migrate to Mylai[184] and occupy the Sikel town.[185]

Only one unique bronze coin from Mylai depicting the man-faced bull exists, and the attribution is uncertain.[186] The man-faced bull iconography on this coin shows the forepart of the figure with a stream of water flowing from his mouth, just like the later issues from nearby Alontion.[187] Despite Manganaro's skepticism about the attribution to Mylai,[188] Imhoof-Blumer's attribution is adopted here. The coin probably dates to the first half of the 4th century BC, when ancient sources report that the people of Rhegion, in 394 BC, offered asylum to the inhabitants of Sicily that were active against Dionysius I, settling the surviving Naxians and Katanians at Mylai.[189] Thus the man-faced bull issued on this bronze coin symbolizes renewal and rebirth for the refugees coming to Mylai.

The man-faced bull is probably a representation of Acheloios as embodied in the local river, Mela, thus Acheloios Mela. In fact, the name of the city itself is linked to the river, coming from the Akkadian *mīlu*, meaning 'seasonal flooding of the river.'[190]

Coinage

46. AE, Unrecorded weight, 11mm	**4th century BC**
	OBV: YM over LA(?), Forepart of Acheloios Mela as a man-faced bull standing to right, water flowing from mouth. REV: Trident REF: F. Imhoof-Blumer, 'Fluss und Meergötter,' Pl. II, 11*.

[179] G. V. Gentili, 'Milazzo,' entry in *Enciclopedia dell' Arte Antica* (Treccani, 1963).
[180] Ibid.
[181] See Chapter 3 for a discussion of Ausonio Culture in relation to the man-faced bull.
[182] S. Levi, B. Prosdocimi, G. Tigano, A. Vanzetti, 'Il villaggio protostorico di Viale dei Cipressi e la facies Capo Graziano,' in *Mylai II*, edited by G. Tigano (Messina, 2009), 23-136; A. Zanini, 'Contributo alla rilettura della necropoli del Bronzo Finale di Milazzo – ME,' in *Dai Ciclopi agli Ecisti. Società e territorio nel la sicilia preistorica e protostorica. Atti della XLI riunione scientifica San Cipirello (PA), 16-19 novembre 2006* (Firenze, 2012), 899-900).
[183] N. Negroni Catacchio, 'l'alba dell'etruria nel territorio di Vulci dal bronzo medio alla prima età del ferro,' in *Quaderni di Acme*, 134 (Milano, 2012), 120.
[184] G. Manganaro, 'Dai mikrà kermata di argento al chalkokratos kassiteros in Sicilia nel V. sec. a.C,' in *Jahrbuch für Numismatik und Geldgeschichte. Herausgegeben von der Bayerischen Numismatischen Gesellschaft*, Band XXXIV (Munchen, 1984), 38.
[185] On the debate concerning Mylai as true Greek polis or mere stronghold, see: T. Heine Nielsen, 'Phourion. A note on the term in Classical Sources and in Diodorus Siculus,' in *Even More Studies in the Ancient Greek Polis*, Historia Einzel-schriften 162 (Stuttgart, 2002), 59-60.

[186] The unique known specimen is stored in Berlin. It was first published by Imhoof-Blumer, who attributed it to Mylai (F. Imhoof-Blumer, *Fluss und Meergötter*, 192, no.48, Pl. II, 11). According to Manganaro the attribution is dubious and he questions even its Sicilian origin (G. Manganaro, 'Metoikismos dei Danklaioi a Mylai,' in *Schweizerische numismatische Rundschau*, Band 80 (2001),18).
[187] MSP I, 21-3 .
[188] G. Manganaro, 'Metoikismos dei Danklaioi a Mylai,' 17.
[189] Diodorus Siculus, *The Library of History*, 14.87.1.
[190] G. Semerano, *Le Origini della Cultura Europea*, Vol. II, Serie II, 173. A semantic crossing on a homophonic base is also plausible in relation to the Akkadian *mil'u*, meaning 'fullness, abundance' (Ibid., 189). The same bases are probably operative in the formulation of Miletus in Ionia, Mylasa in Caria, and Mileto in the area of Rhegion.

PANORMOS

Panormos was originally a Phoenician colony known as *Sys*,[191] which probably means 'shining'.[192] It lies on the northern coast of Sicily in the area of Palermo. Panormos played a significant role in Sicilian history from the 5th to 1st centuries BC and its coinage is extensive. The man-faced bull appears on the city's coinage from the late 5th through the late 4th century BC on both silver and bronze issues.[193] Generally, but not always, they carry the Punic inscription *Sys*.

The use of man-faced bull iconography in Panormos is no doubt related to the enormous number of Italic and Libyan mercenaries employed by the Carthaginians, who used Panormos as a central hub for their operations.[194] Moreover, the iconography certainly found fertile soil in the earlier Cypro-Phoenician cultural traditions already in place, whose involvement in the transmission of man-faced bull iconography is discussed in Chapter 2.

The silver issues of Panormos often pair a young, beardless and horned male with the man-faced bull,[195] which led Isler to hypothesize that the man-faced bull is always Acheloios, since on these issues we see the local river god differentiated from Acheloios. However, the identity of the man-faced bull on the coinage of Panormos is probably Acheloios Orethos,[196] and the young, beardless and horned male Eleutherios, a minor river flowing in the area of Panormos.[197] On some silver issues the inscription šb'lsys appears under the man-faced bull and has been translated as 'Lord of *Sys*.'[198] However, recent scholarship indicates the appropriate translation is 'Of the Citizens of *Sys*,' where 'lord' should be taken to mean 'land owner'.[199]

The first bronze issue features on its reverse a man-faced bull standing to left, head facing, with head of Helios above and *Sys* below. Curiously, the style of this coin is much closer to Campanian nomoi of the same period, and does not resemble any contemporaneous Sicilian man-faced bull iconography. This is indeed fitting, since many of the mercenaries came from Italy, where this particular iconographic scheme was in use since the mid 5th century BC. The type was dated only generally by Calciati to the 'first half of the 4th century up to 260 BC'.[200] However, there is a specimen overstruck on a coin of Syracuse dated to 336 BC,[201] so the type must be dated contemporaneously to the other bronze man-faced bull issues from Panormos.

The other bronze man-faced bull issues are all onkiai of generally the same type, and are stylistically closer to Carthaginian issues of 370 to 340 BC (the 'free' horse iconography is nearly identical).[202] These small bronzes feature the forepart of the man-faced bull either left or right, paired with free horse. Occasionally, a grain ear appears in the field.

Finally, there is a type issued by an uncertain mint of Sicily, of which two specimens are known, both published by Buceti. The type shows a female head right on its obverse, and a man-faced bull walking right on the reverse. Buceti proposed to attribute the type to the mint of Panormos under roman rule.[203]

Ultimately, the coinage of Panormos featuring the man-faced bull represents the coinage of a Carthaginian stronghold (it was not captured until 276 BC, by Pyrrhus), and the iconography was probably employed for the sake of the aforementioned mercenary forces utilized by the Carthaginians throughout the 4th century.[204]

---

191 Despite the existence of silver litrai with double inscription *Sys*/Πανορμος, or *Sys*/Π (in which 'Sys' is the transliteration of [illegible]), not all scholars agree with the attribution to Panormos of the inscription *Sys* (for the coins, cf. G. Manganaro, 'Il paesaggio di Panormos riflesso nei dodici tipi delle serie frazionarie a legenda punica SYS, un nuovo kerma col polipo ed un triemiobolion a legenda SICHAS degli Ichaninoi,' in *Quarte Giornate Internazionali di Studi sull'Area Elima. Erice, 1-4 dicembre 2000*, Atti II (Pisa, 2003), 850-51, Pl.CXLI no.6, Pl.CXLIII no.6). Lo Cascio, for example, argued that *Sys* is the Punic equivalent for Sikelia, suggesting a political concept of *epikrateia*, and so the Sys coins could have been issued contemporaneously by different Punic mints of Sicily (E. Lo Cascio, 'La leggenda SYS delle monete siculo-puniche e il concetto politico di *epikrateia*,' in *La Parola del Passato. Rivista di Studi Antichi*, CLXI (Napoli, 1975), 156-161). For the alternative, more widely-held view, see G.K. Jenkins, 'Coins of Punic Sicily,' in *SNR* 50 (1971); G.K. Jenkins, 'Coins of Punic Sicily,' in *SNR* 57 (1978), 48-50.

192 G.K. Jenkins, 'Coins of Punic Sicily,' in *SNR* 50 (1971), 30. Alternative translations proposed by scholars are 'flower' (G. Manganaro, 'Il paesaggio di Panormos,' 850) and 'salty field' (G. Garbini, 'Sys 'campo salato' in ebraico,' in *Egitto e Vicino Oriente XIII* (Pisa, 1990), 139-141). Coacci Polselli proposed that *Sys* was not originally a Punic word, but derived from a native word with its meaning related to the local topography (G. Coacci Polselli, 'L'epigrafia punica in Sicilia,' in *Kokalos*, 26-27 (Roma, 1983), 476).

193 For the silver issues, see G.K. Jenkins, 'Coins of Punic Sicily,' in *SNR* 50 (1971), 30. For the bronze coins, see R. Calciati, *Corpus Nummorum Siculorum I*, 270-272. There is allegedly one electrum litra featuring a man-faced bull from Panormos, described in L. Gandolfo, 'Note sue due monete inedite del Museo Archaeologico Regionale 'Antonino Salinas',' in *Atti Del V Congresso Internazionale Di Studi Fenici e Punici, Marsala-Palermo, October 8th-9th, 2000*, Volume 2 (Palermo, 2005).

194 W. Fischer-Bossert, 'A Brief Numismatic History of Sicily,' in *Handbook of Coins of Sicily* (Lancaster, PA: Classical Numismatic Group, 2012), lvii.

195 Cf. SNG ANS 549.

196 The main hypothesis, formulated first by Imhoof-Blumer in 1915 ('Di alcune monete italiche e sicule,' in *Atti e Memorie dell'stituto Italiano di Numismatica,* Vol. 2 (Roma, 1915) 15), identifies the man-faced bull of Panormos as the local river Oreto, and the Oreto River is mentioned by Polybius (1.40. 4).

197 F. Spatafora, 'Indigeni, Punici e Greci sulla Montagnola di Marineo e nella valle dell'Eleuterio,' in *Atti delle Terze Giornate Internazionali di Studi sull'Area Elima, Gibellina - Erice - Contessa Entellina 1997* (Pisa, 2000), 895-918, 901, Pl.CLXVI.

198 O.Hoover, *Handbook of Coins of Sicily*, 273. For the translation 'Masters of the Mint,' see A.M. Honeyman, 'Varia Punica,' in *American Journal of Philology*, Vol.68 (1947), 81.

199 G. Manganaro, 'Il paesaggio di Panormos,' 847-860. See also L. I. Manfredi, 'Iconografia e leggenda. Il linguaggio monetale di Cartagine,' in *Mediterranea. Quaderni annuali dell'Istituto di Studi sul Mediterraneo antico. Vol VI* (Pisa: Fabrizio Serra, 2009), 203-218.

200 R. Calciati, *Corpus Nummorum Siculorum I*, 270.

201 L.Gandolfo, 'Monete,' in *Palermo Punica. Museo Archeologico Regionale Antonino Salinas* (Palermo: Sellerio, 1998), 349.

202 Cf. SNG Copenhagen 94-7.

203 G. Buceti, *Alcune monete di bronzo inedite della Sicilia Greca*, 44.

204 The iconography is also seen on a bronze weight from Panormos stored at the British Museum (Museum number: G1955,1105.2).

Coinage

47. AE Litra, 11.77g, 20mm	**336 to 330 BC**
	OBV: Head of Hera to left wearing single-pendant earring and stephane decorated with three fleur-de-lis. REV: Acheloios Orethos as a man-faced bull standing to left on double line, radiate head of Helios above, Punic 𐤑𐤉𐤑 in exergue. REF: Jenkins, 'Coins of Punic Sicily,' in SNR 50 (1971), pl. 24, 21, CNS I, 270, 5; CNG Triton V, lot 210*.

48. AE Onkia, c. 2.11g, 12mm	**336 to 330 BC**
 	OBV: Forepart of Acheloios Orethos as a man-faced bull to left, grain ear (?) above. REV: Free horse to right, line below, grain ear above. REF: Hoover HGC 2, 1062; Potamikon Collection*. *Unconfirmed. This is a troublesome coin type because the clearest example is also clearly tooled (bottom coin). David Sear remarked that the grain ear above the man-faced bull seemed original and not an invention of the tooler. The emergence of another specimen appears also to show a grain ear above (top coin). All examples might be forgeries(3 known).*

49. AE Onkia, 1.95g, 12mm	**336 to 330 BC**
	OBV: Forepart of Acheloios Orethos as a man-faced bull to left, Punic 𐤑𐤉𐤑 above. REV: Free horse to right, grain ear above. Linear border. REF: CNS I, 272, 11*.

50. AE Onkia, 1.67g, 13mm	**336 to 330 BC**
	OBV: Forepart of Acheloios Orethos as a man-faced bull to right, Punic 𐤑𐤉𐤑 above. REV: Free horse to right, grain ear above. Linear border. REF: CNS I, 272,10; SNG ANS 1362; CNG no. 724172*.

51. AE Onkia, 1.63g, 11mm	**336 to 330 BC**
	OBV: Free horse to right, line below, no grain ear. Dotted border. REV: Forepart of Acheloios Orethos as a man-faced bull to right, line below, nothing above. Linear border. REF: CNG eAuction 327, lot 516*. *CNG questions whether this piece is an imitation. An example from the same dies was listed by H. D. Rauch GmbH, Auction 86, lot 234, (1.32g).*

Uncertain: Panormos?

52. AE Unit, 0.88g, 10mm	**Roman Period?**
	OBV: Female head to right. REV: Acheloios Orethos as a man-faced bull to right. Irregular dotted border. REF: Buceti 'inedite', 44, Attribuzione incerta III*. *Unconfirmed.*

SERGETAIANS

The Sergetaians occupied a location on the right bank of the Chrysas river, at the site of Giardinella, near Agyrion and Menaion.[205] They were likely allotted land and issued coins shortly after serving Dionysius I, in the time of Timoleon, c. 357 to 340 BC.[206]

They issued one type of bronze coin, the litra.[207] These are overstruck on coins of Syracuse that date from 375 to 345 BC, the Athena/Dolphin type.[208] The pairing of Herakles and the man-faced bull suggests cultural and economic relations with nearby Agyrion, who employed the same iconographic pairing and also overstruck on the same undertypes.

Calciati suggests that the rarity of these coins results from some unknown event whereby the mint ceased operation permanently, basing his position on unstruck flans that were found in the area along with coins from other cities (bronzes of Kentoripai, Agyrion, and Entella).[209] Calciati observes some interesting aspects about these coins which differentiate them from other mercenary issues: the depiction of just the head of the man-faced bull, the dotted border on both sides of the coins, the dolphins before the head of the man-faced bull, and the large, neat inscription.[210]

The identity of the man-faced bull on the reverse of this coinage is likely Acheloios Chrysas.

Coinage

53. AE Litra, 32.54g, 25mm	**357 to 330 BC**
	OBV: ΣΕΡΓΕΤΑΙΩΝ, head of bearded Herakles to right. Dotted border. REV: ΣΕΡΓΕ-ΤΑΙΩΝ, above and behind head and neck of Acheloios Chrysas as a man-faced bull to left, before, two dolphins with crossed tails facing downward. Dotted border. REF: Campana 1; CNS III, 203, 1*.

Enlarged Line Drawing by Romolo Calciati:[211]

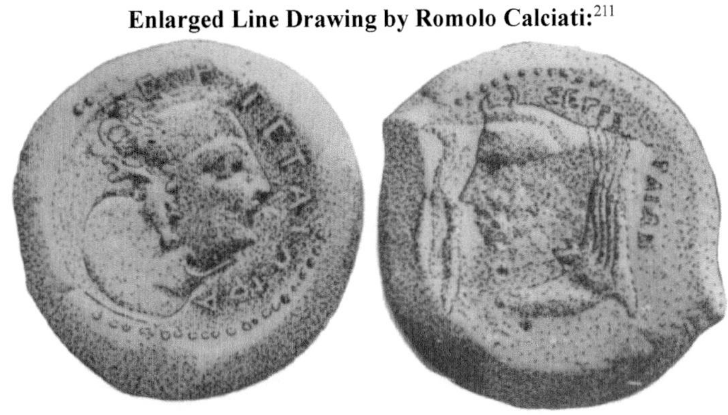

[205] R. Calciati, *Corpus Nummorum Siculorum III*, 201, who cites information about the city from the account of Cluverius (*Sicilia Antiqua* (Lugduni Patavorum, 1629), 337-339).

[206] A. Campana, 'Sicilia: Sergetai,' in *Panorama Numismatico*, 150 (Serravalle: Nomisma, 2001), 59-60.

[207] R. Calciati, *Corpus Nummorum Siculorum III*, 203.

[208] As pointed out and discussed by M. Caccamo Caltabiano, the evidence concerning mercenary coins always over-struck suggests that after the dissolution of the 'empire' of Dionysius I of Syracuse, these groups became autonomous and had many earlier coins available for reuse as flans for their own coins. The removal of Dionysius II from Sicily created a vacuum of power, from which sprang the various groups of mercenaries, not only the Sergetaians, but also: the Tyrrhenoi (CNS III, 307-310, 1-31); the Sileraians (MSP I, 52-4); the Kersini (MSP I, 39); and the Campanians at Tauromenion (CNS III, 327, 1-1/4). The area of this phenomenon appears to be limited to the north-eastern side of Sicily. Adjacent to this area is Kephaloidion, which was under Carthaginian domination. To the south these mercenary groups were bordered by the area of Akragas and the course of the southern Himera River (M. Caccamo Caltabiano, 'Identità e peculiarità dell'esperienza monetale siciliana,' in *Magna Grecia e Sicilia Stato degli studi e prospettive di ricerca, Atti dell'Incontro di Studi Messina 2-4 dicembre 1996*, edited by M. Barra Bagnasco, E. DeMiro, and A. Pinzone (Messina, 1999), 303.

[209] R. Calciati, *Corpus Nummorum Siculorum III*, 205. Perhaps the Sergetaians were defeated by Timoleon.

[210] Ibid.

[211] Ibid., 204. A special thanks to Alessandro Calciati for permission to use images from the magnificent work of his late father.

SILERAIANS

The Sileraians were a group of ancient mercenaries employed by one of the Sicilian tyrants of the 4th century BC, who were allotted some land or municipality after their service had ended. They began to issue coinage between the years 357 and 336 BC, and this coinage provides the only evidence we have of their existence.

Originally, the coinage of the Sileraians was cataloged as a variety from Himera by G. Lancillotto, based on a misreading of the inscription above the man-faced bull on the tetras.[212] Imhoof-Blumer corrected this original attribution and identified the group as the Sileraioi.[213] The interpretation that the Sileraians were named after the area of the Sila mountains in Bruttium is far from certain,[214] since the name *silerai* has its roots in Akkadian *sil'u*, 'the flowing water,'[215] and could therefore refer to any number of places in ancient Italy or Sicily that have flowing water.[216] More recent theories place the origin of the Sileraians on the border of Campania and Lucania, in this case deriving their name from the Silaros River (modern Sele).[217]

Recently, scholars have suggested that there was never an actual city of the Sileraians, but instead the group occupied a natural hilltop stronghold at a site now called Cozzo Mususino, which is located between modern-day Alimena and Resuttano.[218] This theory is supported by the amount of Sileraian coins found at that location, but it was probably more than a mere camp.[219]

Whatever their precise origins, eventually the group organized themselves enough to mint coinage,[220] as we see bronze coinage from Sicily with the inscription ΣΙΛΕΡΑΙΩΝ (it appears retrograde on all examples) on the obverse above the forepart of a man-faced bull. The reverse always depicts Leukapsis[221] with spear and the inscription ΣΙΛΑ, indicating again the group's probable relation to the Silaros River. The man-faced bull on the obverse is probably Acheloios Silaros Himera, recognizing the original god of water, the eponymous river of their homeland, and the southern Himera,[222] which is the river closest to Cozzo Mususino.

According to Castrizio, the entire series was struck with only two pairs of dies for the heavier denomination, and only one pair of dies for the lighter one.[223] However, Calciati lists a third type with no legend (no. 53),[224] but neither Castrizio nor Campana published it. Ultimately, based on our research, there is undoubtedly more than one obverse die for the smaller denomination and there appear to be at least three for the larger series. According to Campana's metrological studies the two denominations are Dionysian litrai and tetrantes.[225]

---

212 G.L. Castelli (Principe di Torremuzza), *Insularum veterum inscriptionum nova collectio prolegomenis, et notis illustrata*, (Palermo, 1769) Plate 4, no. 30.

213 F. Imhoof Blumer, *Monnaies Grecques* (Amsterdam, 1882), 28, 227. Also cited in A. Campana, 'Sicilia: Sileraioi (ca. 357-339 a.C.),' in *Panorama Numismatico* 159 (Serravalle: Nomisma, 2002), 87.

214 S. Garraffo, 'La monetazione dell'età dionigiana. Contromarche e riconiazioni,' in *La monetazione dell'età dionigiana. Atti dell'VIII Convegno del Centro Internazionale di Studi Numismatici Napoli 29 maggio – 1 giugno 1983* (Roma, 1993), 195; G. Manganaro, 'Intervento,' in *Kokalos*, Vol. 14-15 (1969),134. Tusa Cutroni proposed that the Sileraians were inhabitants of an unrecorded city named Silera (A. Tusa Cutroni, 'La riconiazione della litra siracusana nel IV a.C.,' in *Sicilia Archeologica* 4 (1968), 48). According to some theories the mint was located between Agrigento and Caltanissetta (E. Manni, 'Su alcune recenti proposte di identificazione di centri antichi della Sicilia,' in *L'Italie préromaine et la Rome républicaine. I. Mélanges offerts à Jacques Heurgon* (Roma: École Française de Rome, 1976), 605-617.

215 G. Semerano 'Il popolo che sconfisse la morte' (2003), 87. According to Semerano the Akkadian *sil'u-eni* means 'the springing of the watersource' (ibid., 80). According to Black et al., the Akkadian *silihtu* was the name of a canal at Nippur, and *silangitu* was the Akkadian name for a freshwater fish (see entries 'silihtu' and 'silangitu' in J. Black, A. George, and N. Postgate, *A Concise Dictionary of Akkadian* (Wiesbaden, 2000).

216 The original base *sil* is present in many places throughout the Mediterranean area and always indicates places with rich water sources, streams, and rivers (e.g. the Sele River in Campania; the Sile River in Venice; the Sila River in Romania, Sillara Lake in the Tuscan Appennines, the Sellena baths near Chianciano in Tuscany, and the Sila region of Bruttium, to name but a few). Among the earliest known examples of water cults in which the symbology of the bull was employed are those from the early Iron Age at Predio Canopoli in Sardinia, where the Silanis river flows (see above pg.38).

217 R. Calciati, *Corpus Nummorum Siculorum III*, 297; E.Pais, 'Le Colonie dei Sibariti alle foci del Silaro,' cited in: A. Campana, 'Sicilia: Sileraioi,' 87. See also R. Cantilena, 'Un gruzzolo di monete d'argento da Pontecagnano: l'offerta votiva di un mercenario?,' in *Incidenza dell'Antico*, Vol.6 (Napoli, 2008), 194; G. Tagliamonte, *I figli di Marte, mercenari e mercenariato italici in Magna Grecia e Sicilia* (Roma, 1994), 143.

218 E. Cammarta, *Da Dionisio a Timoleonte* (Modica, 1984), 118-119; A. Campana, 'Sicilia: Sileraioi,' 87.

219 These coins are said to be from the site of Cozzo Mususino. Castrizio and Puglisi assumed that there was a military camp upon the hill, essentially a place used by the troops of Dionysius I during his military campaigns against Carthage. This is based on the locations of hoards, in which the minting of such bronze coins during the time of Dioniysius I seems to follow the movements of his army, and the recipients of these coins were the mercenaries in the pay of the tyrant. This theory would essentially refute the hypothesis of autonomous communities of mercenaries settling around Sicily, and instead place the issues (Sileraians, Sergetaians, etc.) in relation to the activity of territorial control exercised by the tyrant (M. Puglisi, 'Distribuzione e funzione della moneta bronzea in Sicilia dalla fine del V sec. a.C. all'età ellenistica,' 285-294; D. Castrizio, 'Considerazioni sul pagamento del sîtos ai mercenari nella Sicilia tra Dionisio I e Timoleonte,' in *Polifemo. Rassegna bibliografica di storia delle religioni e storia antica*, Vol.XI (2011), 209-232). We do not agree with this position, because the ethnic appearing on the dies should be considered a sign of civic identity for an autonomous community.

220 These coins were always over-struck on other coins of the area, usually bronze litrai of Dionysius I, which also suggests that they were originally under his command, and that after the dissolution of the Dionysian empire these groups of mercenaries became autonomous and had great amounts of old coinage available for overstriking.

221 For the identification of Leukapsis, see R. Calciati, *Corpus Nummorum Siculorum III*, 303, where he compares the figure with a rare bronze from Syracuse (Museum of Fine Arts, Boston, A.B. Brett, no. 420).

222 A. Campana, 'Sicilia: Sileraioi,' 87.

223 D. Castrizio, *La monetazione mercenariale in Sicilia*, 109.

224 R. Calciati, *Corpus Nummorum Siculorum III*, 300, 1 lv 1.

225 A. Campana, 'Sicilia: Sileraioi,' 87-8. The metrological theories of Campana and Castrizio for the bronze coinage of Sicily are different. Castrizio suggested (while prudently asserting that it is just a hypothesis with no archaeological, numismatic, or literary evidence)

Coinage

54. AE Litra, 31.02g	**357 to 336 BC**
	OBV: Forepart of Acheloios Silaros Himera as a man-faced bull to left, ΣΙΛ behind, ΕΡΑΙΩΝ above, all retrograde. Linear border. REV: Naked Leukapsis wearing helmet and charging right with spear and shield, ΣΙΛΑ appearing retrograde from knee to shoulder. Linear border. REF: Campana 1; Calciati III, 297, 1; CNG Triton V, lot 224*.

55. AE Litra, 26.18g, 29mm	**357 to 336 BC**
	OBV: Forepart of Acheloios Silaros Himera as a man-faced bull to left. Anepigraphic. REV: Naked Leukapsis wearing helmet and charging to right with spear and shield. No legend. REF: CNS III, 300, 1 lv 1; Roma, E-Sale 10, lot 70*. *Unconfirmed.*

56. AE Tetras, 6.86g, 20mm	**357 to 336 BC**
	OBV: Forepart of Acheloios Silaros Himera as a man-faced bull to right, before, Σ, above, ΙΛΕΡΑΙΩ, behind, N, all retrograde. Linear border. REV: Naked Leukaspis wearing helmet and charging to right with spear and shield, ΣΙΛ-Α behind, from knee to shoulder. REF: Calciati III, 301, 2; Campana 2; Castrizio I, 2/1; Moretti 417; Lanz 153, Lot 0101= Potamikon Collection*. *Mechanically cleaned, some areas, especially the eye and parts of the beard, might have been slightly strengthened as a result.*

that the mercenary overstrikes on Dionysian litrai of c. 32g to 36 g were actually hemilitrai, implying a devaluation of them (D. Castrizio, *La monetazione mercenariale in Sicilia*, 44-46). Campana's theory is that the mercenary groups never changed the Dionysian denominations, and a metrological change occurred only after Timoleon's monetary reform. For these reasons Campana defined the heavier denomination issued by the Sileraians as the litra (hemilitron for Castrizio) and the lighter one as the tetras (hexas for Castrizio).

UNCERTAIN: SILERAIANS?

This coin, found in the vicinity of Sileraian coinage near Cozzo Mususino, is only tentatively attributed to the Sileraians, but might also have been issued by an unknown group of retired mercenaries.[226] Like other mercenary coinage, it was overstruck on a bronze litra of Dionysius I.

Calciati notes the pairing with female head on the obverse, unknown on mercenary issues but appearing at Herbessos, where the head of a man-faced bull is paired with the nymph Sikelia.[227]

Coinage

57. AE Litra, 33.33g, 29mm	**357-336 BC**
	OBV: Female head to right. Encircled. REV: Acheloios Silaros Himera(?) as a man-faced bull standing right, head in profile, uncertain symbol above. REF: CNS III, 321, 1 OS*

Enlargement of Line Drawing by Romolo Calciati:[228]

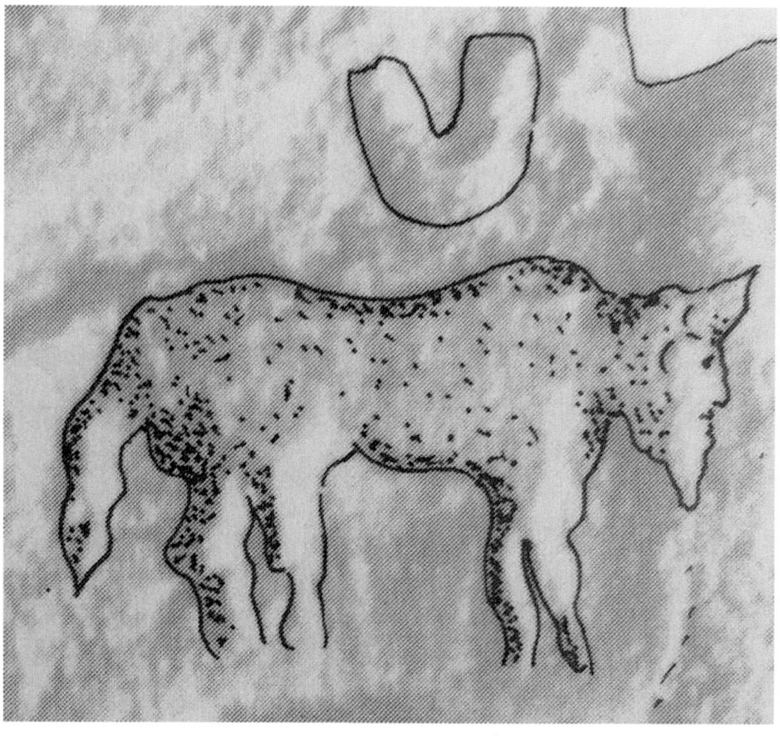

[226] R. Calciati, *Corpus Nummorum Siculorum III*, 321.

[227] Ibid.

[228] Ibid.

TAUROMENION

Tauromenion was originally a town of native Sikels established during the Late Bronze Age atop Mount Tauro,[229] which is located on the east coast of Sicily just north of the area of Naxos. The archaic Sikel town was conquered by Naxians[230] during the 7th century BC,[231] and remained occupied by the Greeks until the destruction of Naxos by Dionysius I in 403 BC.[232] In 396 BC the Carthaginian commander, Himilcon, desiring to create a center of resistance against Dionysius on the east coast of the island, forced the Sikels to resettle on Mount Tauro.[233] After a few years the stronghold was conquered by Syracuse, in 392 BC, and it became home to mercenaries employed by Dionysius I,[234] and later by the original Naxians themselves, who were led there in 358 BC by Andromachos.[235]

It was after this re-founding in 358 BC that the man-faced bull appears on the city's coinage,[236] dated between 357 and 315 BC,[237] and confirming earlier statements about the man-faced bull as a symbol of rebirth.

The coins come in two basic types, and pair an obverse featuring the head of Apollo Archagetas, labeled ΑΡΧΑΓΕΤΑΣ, with a reverse featuring the man-faced bull standing to left, head in profile, with the inscription ΤΑΥΡΟΜΕΝΙΤΑΝ. The use of Apollo's epithet 'Archagetes' is equally significant, insofar as he is affiliated with colonization. According to Campana, Apollo Archegetas served as protector of and guide for the Greek settlers, and later operated as protector of the city. [238] He was also previously worshipped in Naxos. Thus, the iconography forms the perfect pairing for the refugees from Naxos insofar as it symbolizes both rebirth and colonization. Moreover, the pairing also would be appealing to the Campanian mercenaries who remained at Tauromenion when the Naxians returned, for the reasons outlined in Chapter 2.

This series is particularly important because it shows only Apollo's epithet, not his name. In our view, the contemporaneous man-faced bull coins from Agyrion, which only feature ΠΑΛΑΓΚΑΙΟΣ, are also only showing a particular epithet, and indicate Acheloios Palagkaios just as on these coins ΑΡΧΑΓΕΤΑΣ indicates Apollo Archagetas.

The man-faced bull on the issues from Tauromenion probably represents the local embodiment of Acheloios, Acheloios Tauromenios.[239]

[229] In 1918 a Sikel necropolis dated to the 8th century BC was discovered at the site (M. I. Gulletta, 'Taormina,' in *Bibliografia Topografica della Colonizzazione Greca in Italia e nelle Isole Tirreniche*, Vol.XX (Pisa, 2011), 64).

[230] According to Diodorus Siculus, a Sikel settlement was located on top of Mount Tauro, which was later expelled by the Greeks of Naxos (Diodoros Siculus, *The Library of History*, 14.88.1).

[231] G.M. Bacci, 'Scavi e ricerche ad Avola, Grammichele, Portopalo, Taormina,' in *Kokalos*, 30-31 (Roma, 1987), 722-725.

[232] Diodoros Siculus, *The Library of History*, 14.88.1.

[233] Ibid., 14.59.1-2.

[234] According to the chronology of Diodorus, in 392 BC Dionysius I, after signing a peace agreement with Mago II, expelled the Sikels from the city, establishing at the site his mercenaries from Campania (Diodoros Siculus, *The Library of History*, 14.96.4).

[235] Diodoros Siculus, *The Library of History*, 14.96.4; 16.7.1. Information about Andromachos is unclear. The different interpretations identify him as: (1) a Zanclean from Ibla; (2) a mercenary of Dionysius I (possibly from Lucania, like the Sileraians); (3) a refugee from Naxos; or (4) a citizen of Syracuse (for a bibliography on this issue, see: E. Arena, 'La fondazione di Tauromenion fra i Dionisi ed Andromaco,' in *Sicilia Antiqua*, Vol.V (2008), 93-111; M. I. Gulletta, 'Taormina,' 42). We do know that Andromachos was the father of the historian Timaeus, and with his intervention Tauromenion developed rapidly, becoming very prosperous and famous all over the island (Diodoros Siculus, *The Library of History*, 16.7.1).

[236] Following Campana's metrological studies, the denomination should be the hemilitron, based on the Dionysian weight standard (A. Campana, 'Sicilia: Tauromenion (ca. 357-150 a.C.),' in *Panorama Numismatico*, 166-167 (Serravalle: Nomisma, 2002), 99).

[237] Consolo Langher's studies on the coinage of Tauromenion have established with great certainty the date ranges for the issues of Tauromenion (S.N. Consolo Langher, 'Numismatica tauromenitana (357-306),' in *Ricerche di numismatica* (Roma, 1967), 63-165; S.N. Consolo Langher, 'Tauromenio e le vicende siciliane tra Dionisio e Agatocle,' in *Archivio Storico Messinese,* Vol.XXXIII (Messina, 1983), 189-214; S.N. Consolo Langher, 'Andromaco e Tauromenio. Dalla indipendenza politica ed economica di età timoleontea alla sottomissione ad Agatocle,' in *Siracusa e la Sicilia greca tra età arcaica ed alto ellenismo* (Messina, 1996), 534-573.

[238] A. Campana, 'Sicilia: Tauromenion,' 99.

[239] According to Casagrandi-Orsini, in ancient times there was a local river named Tauromenios, mentioned by Vibus Sequestre (Vib. Seq., *geogr.*, 144, cited in: V. Casagrandi-Orsini, *Il fiume Taurominius in Vibo Sequestre* (Catania, 1898). The ancient river is also called Tauromenios in E. Manni, *Geografia fisica e politica della Sicilia antica* (Roma, 1981), 124.

Coinage

58. AE Hemilitron, 15.61g, 25mm	**357 to 345 BC**
	OBV: ΑΡΧΑΓΕΤΑΣ before laureate head of Apollo Archagetas to left, wearing laurel wreath with leaves in opposing pairs. Dotted border. REV: ΤΑΥΡΟΜ–ΕΝΙΤ–ΑΝ surrounding Acheloios Tauromenios as a man-faced bull to left on single line, head in profile. Dotted border. REF: Campana 1a; Castrizio III, 1a = CNS III, 209, 1/6 = Virzi 1990 = CNG E-auction 318, Lot: 40*.

59. AE Hemilitron, 15.26g	**357 to 345 BC**
	OBV: ΑΡΧΑΓΕΤΑΣ before laureate head of Apollo Archagetas to left, wearing laurel wreath with leaves in opposing pairs. Dotted border. REV: ΤΑΥΡΟΜ–ΕΝΙΤ–ΑΝ surrounding Acheloios Tauromenios as a man-faced bull to left on single line, head in profile. Dotted border. REF: CNS III, 209, 1/7; BM no. 1946,0101.1675*. *Same variety as last but finer style.*

60. AE Hemilitron, 16.34g, 25mm	**357 to 345 BC**
	OBV: ΑΡΧΑΓΕΤΑΣ before laureate head of Apollo Archagetas to left, wearing laurel wreath with leaves in opposing pairs. Dotted border. REV: ΤΑΥΡΟΜ–ΕΝΙ–ΤΑΝ surrounding Acheloios Tauromenios as a man-faced bull to left on single line, head in profile. Dotted border. REF: SNG Morcom 843; F. Imhoof-Blumer, 'Fluss und Meergötter,' Pl. II, n.18; CNS III, 209, 1/3*.

61. AE Hemilitron, 14.91g, 26mm	**357 to 345 BC**
	OBV: ΑΡΧΑΓΕΤΑΣ before laureate head of Apollo Archagetas to left, wearing laurel wreath with leaves in opposing pairs. Dotted border. REV: ΤΑΥΡΟΜΕΝ–ΙΤΑ–Ν surrounding Acheloios Tauromenios as a man-faced bull to left on single line, head in profile. Dotted border. REF:CNS III, 209, 1/4; M&M GmbH 17, lot 396*.

62. AE Hemilitron, 13.07g, 26mm	**357 to 345 BC**
	OBV: ΑΡΧΑΓΕΤΑΣ before laureate head of Apollo Archagetas to left, wearing laurel wreath with leaves in opposing pairs. Dotted border? REV: (ΤΑΥΡΟΜΕΝΙ) above, with -ΤΑΝ under exergue line, surrounding Acheloios Tauromenios as a man-faced bull to left on single line, head in profile. Dotted border. REF: Previously unpublished; NAC Q, lot 1276*.

63. AE Hemilitron, 16.81g, 25mm	**357 to 345 BC**
	OBV: ΑΡΧΑΓΕΤΑΣ before laureate head of Apollo Archagetas to left, wearing laurel wreath with leaves in opposing pairs. Dotted border. REV: ΤΑΥΡΟΜΕ–ΝΙΤΑΝ surrounding Acheloios Tauromenios as a man-faced bull to left on single line, head in profile, bunch of grapes in left field. Dotted border. REF: Castrizio III, 1b, 1; Campana 1b; CNS III, 211, 4 = CNG 97, lot 51=Potamikon Collection*.

Antiquarian Plate:[240]

[240] D. Petri Carreraæ, *Monumentorum historicorum urbis Catanaæ* (1723), misattributed no. 60 as a coin of Katane.

Section Four

ITALY

The very first coinage of the man-faced bull in Italy is an incuse silver drachm from Rhegion, minted c. 510 BC.[1] Laos quickly followed, c. 510 to 500 BC, issuing its own incuse coinage featuring a man-headed bull, iconographically distinct from the man-faced bull of Rhegion. The next man-faced bulls appear in Neapolis, c. 450 BC,[2] and Acheloios depicted as a bearded man with bovine ears and horns makes an appearance in Metapontion, c. 440 to 430 BC.[3]

Bronze coinage depicting the man-faced bull does not occur until c. 350 BC in Neapolis[4] and lasts until the last quarter of the 3rd century. One silver issue from Rome minted c. 19/18 BC depicts the man-faced bull. The map below features all mints issuing man-faced bull coinage in all metals.

One notable observation about man-faced bull coinage in the region is the steady employment of the control mark, ΙΣ. It was in use at Aesernia, Compulteria, Cales, Neapolis, Nola(?), and Suessa.

As discussed in the section on Greek man-faced bulls, this likely reflects the belief that rivers in the ancient world are sinews of Acheloios, a concept which has been advocated by a number of scholars recently. Again, the Orphic ἱερὸς λόγος contains the expression ἶνας...Αχελωίου, later abbreviated as ἴς Αχελωίου. Therefore, in the general area of Central Italy we see a quasi-confederation among cities employing the same iconographic devices, many clearly labeled with a device that would indicate they are all sinews of Acheloios, or smaller parts of a greater whole, much like the control marks of the Akarnanian confederacy.

It is very difficult, and sometimes impossible, to identify the names of the local rivers of Campania at the sites that issued man-faced bull coins. This is because the hydrographic layout of Campania, made up of many branches to form a complex network, has profoundly changed over time.[5]

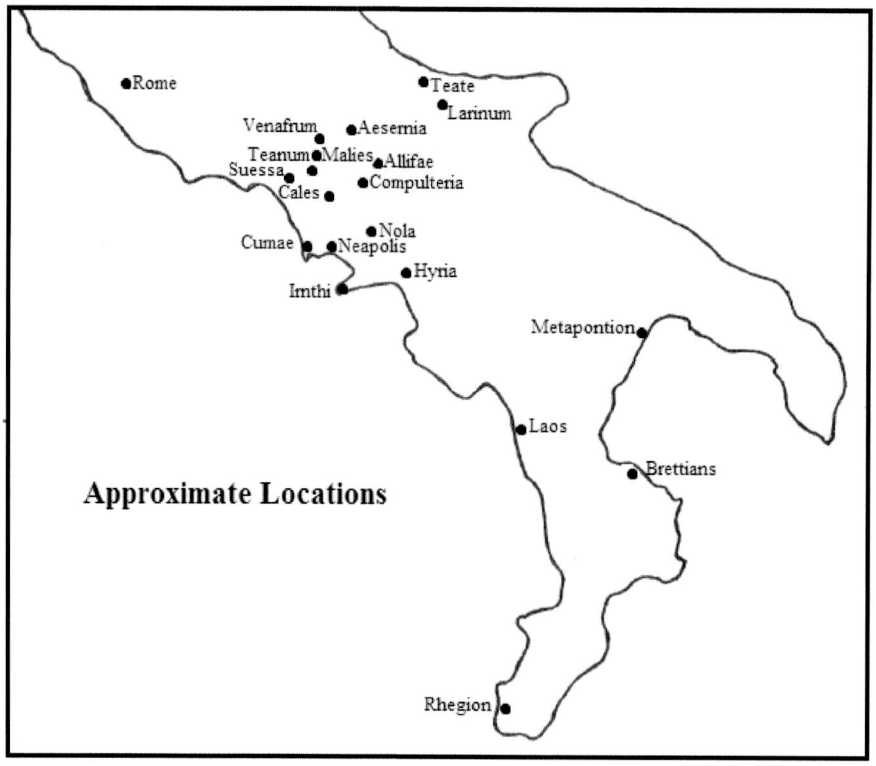

[1] N. K. Rutter, *Historia Numorum: Italy*, 187, no. 2468.

[2] Ibid., 68, no. 545-551.

[3] Ibid., 132, no. 1491.

[4] According to M. Taliercio Mensitieri, the first bronze series minted in Neapolis is dated shortly before the Roman issue featuring Apollo and the man-faced bull with legend ΡΩΜΑΙΩΝ, c. 326 BC (M. Taliercio Mensitieri, 'Il bronzo di Neapolis,' in *La monetazione di Neapolis nella Campania antica: atti del VII Convegno del Centro internazionale di studi numismatici, Napoli 20-24 aprile 1980*, edited by Attilio Stazio, Marina Taliercio Mensitieri, and Valeria Zagli (Napoli: Arte tipografica, 1987), 236-7).

[5] S. De Caro, *La terra nera degli antichi Campani* (Napoli, 2012), 1.

AESERNIA

Aesernia was located inland between the Carpino Valley and the Sordo Valley at the source of the Volturnus,[6] and traces of life at Aesernia extend back to Paleolithic times.[7] In historical times, the city was originally a Samnite center[8] until it was sacked by Rome in 295 BC.[9] Livy informs us the Samnites briefly pillaged the city[10] before it became an official Latin colony in 263 BC.[11] Allegedly, the city was a communication hub in the area.[12]

It was at the beginning of the First Punic War, in 263 BC, that Aesernia began to issue bronze coinage (Aesernia was loyal to Rome during the Punic Wars).[13] Some of the earliest bronze varieties from Aesernia depicting Vulcan/Jupiter (HN Italy 430) were overstruck at Neapolis with the Apollo/man-faced bull type (HN Italy 589).[14] This evidence lead Campana to argue that the first coinage minted in Aesernia was the Vulcan/Jupiter type, and only afterwards, during the First Punic War, Aesernia adopted the Apollo/man-faced bull type. His rationale is that the city had a need to fit into the economic sphere of Campania, and this need essentially sprang from the fact that Neapolis was supplying an enormous amount of coins in support of Roman troops, which penetrated the economies of the area.[15]

Rutter connects the mints of Aesernia, Compulteria, Suessa, Cales, Nola, and Neapolis by the use of the same types and even the same IΣ device appearing below the man-faced bull, a symbol which operates on practical and symbolic levels for the aforementioned reasons. He dates the Sinew (IΣ) coins of Neapolis to 275 to 255 BC. Recently Napoleone Stelluti published a comprehensive study on the coinage of Aesernia.[16]

The varieties below are listed with the assumption that the sequence must be identified on the basis of the marks below the man-faced bull. For this reason those without marks appear first (n.64-66), followed by those with the IΣ mark (n.67-70), which are linked to the previous and following series by the presence of the oval shield behind Apollo. Finally, those marked by letters below the man-faced bull are listed next (n.71-78). The later issues (n.73-78) move the ethnic to the obverse. There is a specimen in Paris (no. 64) which shows a round shield behind Apollo. Given the style and higher weight, we date this earlier than the oval shield varieties and identify it as Aesernia's first man-faced bull coin.

Because of its close proximity to the head of the Volturnus River,[17] the man-faced bull on the reverse of the city's coinage probably represents Acheloios Volturnus. The figure flying above the man-faced bull is more difficult to identify. On earlier issues from Neapolis it is probably a winged nymph (HN Italy 456, c. 420 BC), naturally associated with Acheloios and the notions of cyclicality (indicated in the laurel wreath) and rebirth. However, given the importance of these issues to soldiers and the series of wars in the area, it may be during this time (260 to 240 BC) that the iconography becomes associated with Nike.

---

[6] Livy, *Ab Urbe Condita Libri*, 10.31.2.

[7] M. Coltorti, M. Cremaschi, A. Guerreschi, B. Peretto, and C. Sala, 'L'accampamento preistorico di Isernia La Pineta,' in *Atti della XXIII Riunione Scientifica I.I.P.P. Firenze 7-9 Maggio 1980* (Firenze, 1982), 577-587; M. Cremaschi and C. Peretto, 'Les sols d'habitat du site paleolithique d'Isernia La Pineta (Molise, Italie centrale),' in *L'Anthropologie*, Vol.92 (Paris, 1988), 107-140.

[8] Strabo, *Geographica*, 5.3.10.

[9] G. Uggeri, 'Aesernia,' in *Brill's New Pauly*.

[10] Livy, *Ab Urbe Condita Libri*, 10.31.

[11] Livy, *Epit.*, 16.7; See A. La Regina, 'Contributo dell'Archaeologia alla Storia Sociale: I Territori Sabellici e Sannitici,' in Dialoghi di Archeologia, Vol. IV-V (Milano: Il Saggiatore, 1971), 443-59; A. Campana, 'Samnium: Aesernia (263-240 a.C.),' in *Panorama Numismatico*, 85 (Serravalle: Nomisma, 1995), 289.

[12] G.Uggeri, 'Aesernia,' in *Brill's New Pauly* (Brill Online, 2015).

[13] N.K. Rutter, *HN Italy*, 58.

[14] A.M. Burrnett and M.H. Crawford, 'Overstrikes at Neapolis and Coinage at Poseidonia-Paestum,' in *Studies in Greek Numismatics in memory of Martin Jessop Price*, edited by R. Ashton and S. Hurter (London: Spink, 1998), 55-6.

[15] A. Campana, 'Samnium: Aesernia,' 293.

[16] N.K. Rutter, *HN Italy*, 58, no. 431. However, we were unable to find a coin from Nola featuring the IΣ device. See also, N. Stelluti, *Monete della zecca di Aesernia, Venafrum, Bonavium, Aquilonia e Bellum Sociale* (Campobasso, 2015).

[17] Livy, *Ab Urbe Condita Libri*, 10.31.2.

Coinage

64. AE Unit, 8.49g, 19mm	**260 to 240 BC**
	OBV: Head of Apollo facing left, wearing laurel wreath with leaves in opposing pairs, round shield behind. Dotted border. REV: Acheloios Volturnus as a man-faced bull standing to right on single line, head facing, winged nymph above, (AI)SERNINO in exergue. REF: Stelluti 161; SNG France 276 = BnF 1966.453, n.FRBNF41843672*. *Unique*

65. AE Unit, 8.15g	**260 to 240 BC**
	OBV: Head of Apollo facing left, wearing laurel wreath with leaves in opposing pairs, oval shield behind. Dotted border. REV: Acheloios Volturnus as a man-faced bull standing to right on single line, head facing, winged nymph above, AIƧERNINO in exergue. REF: Santangelo 386-7; Sambon 178; Stelluti 151-2; BMC 7 = Campana 5/a*. *Unique*

66. AE Unit, 6.01g	**260 to 240 BC**
	OBV: Head of Apollo facing left, wearing laurel wreath with leaves in opposing pairs, oval shield behind. Dotted border. REV: Acheloios Volturnus as a man-faced bull standing to right on single line, head facing, winged nymph above, AISERNIO in exergue. REF: Sambon 179; Stelluti 161; KM Berlin 7; Campana 5/b*.

67. AE Unit, 6.60g	**260 to 240 BC**
	OBV: Head of Apollo facing left, wearing laurel wreath with leaves in opposing pairs, oval shield behind. Dotted border. REV: Acheloios Volturnus as a man-faced bull standing to right on single line, head facing, winged nymph above, IΣ below, AISERNINO in exergue. REF: Sambon 180; Campana 6/a; Stelluti 157; SNG France 279 = BnF Luynes 22*.

68. AE Unit, 5.82g	**260 to 240 BC**
	OBV: Head of Apollo facing left, wearing laurel wreath with leaves in opposing pairs, oval shield behind. Dotted border. REV: Acheloios Volturnus as a man-faced bull standing to right on single line, head facing, winged nymph above, IΣ below, ASERNINO in exergue. REF: Sambon 181; Campana 6/b; Stelluti 155; SNG Morcom 61; SNG France 281 = BnF Fonds general 79*.

69. AE Unit, 5.97g | **260 to 240 BC**

OBV: Head of Apollo facing left, wearing laurel wreath with leaves in opposing pairs, oval shield behind. Dotted border
REV: Acheloios Volturnus as a man-faced bull standing to right on single line, head facing, winged nymph above, IΣ below, ΛISERNINOM in exergue.
REF: Sambon 182; Santangelo 385; Fiorelli 637-8; Stelluti 144-6; Campana 6/c.

70. AE Unit | **260 to 240 BC**

OBV: Head of Apollo facing left, wearing laurel wreath with leaves in opposing pairs, lyre behind. Dotted border.
REV: Acheloios Volturnus as a man-faced bull standing to right on single line, head facing, winged nymph above, IΣ below, AISERNINO in exergue.
REF: Carelli Pl.LXI n.9*.
Unconfirmed, possibly a misreading of the shield or inscription by Carelli.

71. AE Unit, 7.19g | **260 to 240 BC**

OBV: Head of Apollo facing left, wearing laurel wreath with leaves in opposing pairs, oval shield behind. Dotted border.
REV: Acheloios Volturnus as a man-faced bull standing to right on single line, head facing, winged nymph above, A below, AISERNINO in exergue.
REF: Campana 7/a; Grose-McClean 152; SNG Cop. 262; NAC O, lot 1005*.

72. AE Unit, 6.41g | **260 to 240 BC**

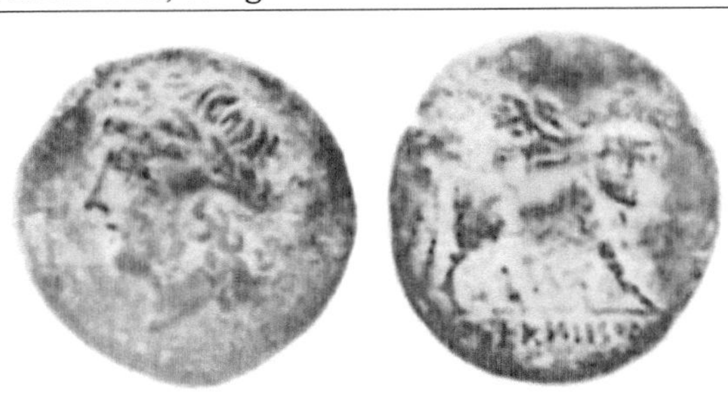

OBV: Head of Apollo facing left, wearing laurel wreath with leaves in opposing pairs, oval shield behind. Dotted border.
REV: Acheloios Volturnus as a man-faced bull standing to right on single line, head facing, winged nymph above, A below, AISERNINOM in exergue.
REF: Santangelo 385; Stelluti 150 and 153; SNG ANS 116 = Campana 7/b *.

73. AE Unit, 4.97g | **260 to 240 BC**

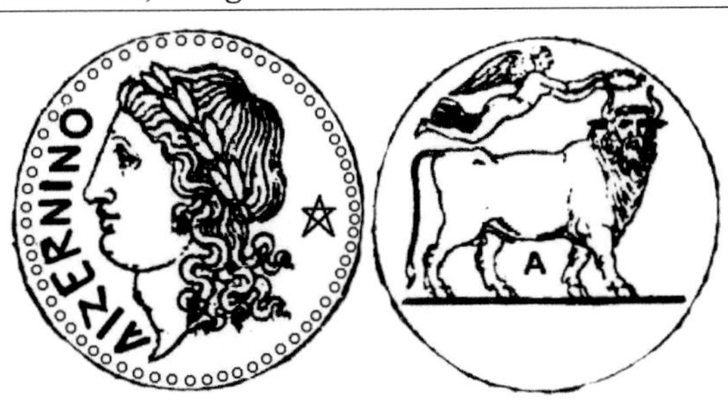

OBV: Head of Apollo facing left, wearing laurel wreath with leaves in opposing pairs, AIƧERNINO before, pentagram behind. Dotted border.
REV: Acheloios Volturnus as a man-faced bull standing to right on single line, head facing, winged nymph above, A below, no inscription in exergue.
REF: Stelluti 143; SNG Milano II, 1; Campana 8.
Unique

74. AE Unit, 6.68g	260 to 240 BC
	OBV: Head of Apollo facing left, wearing laurel wreath with leaves in opposing pairs, AISERNINO, retro N behind. Dotted border. REV: Acheloios Volturnus as a man-faced bull standing to right on single line, head facing, winged nymph above, N below, nothing in exergue. REF: Sambon 176var.; Fiorelli 639; Stelluti 147 and 156; Torino 597; Campana 11; SNG Cop 260; SNG France 274 = BnF Luynes 23*.

75. AE Unit, 6.42g, 19mm	260 to 240 BC
	OBV: Head of Apollo facing left, wearing laurel wreath with leaves in opposing pairs, AISERNINO, uncertain (N?) behind. Dotted border. REV: Acheloios Volturnus as a man-faced bull standing to right on single line, head facing, winged nymph above, N below, nothing in exergue. REF: Sambon 176var.; Stelluti 158 ; SNG France 275 = BNF Y 20243, Seymour de Ricci 1209*.

76. AE Unit, 6.30g	260 to 240 BC
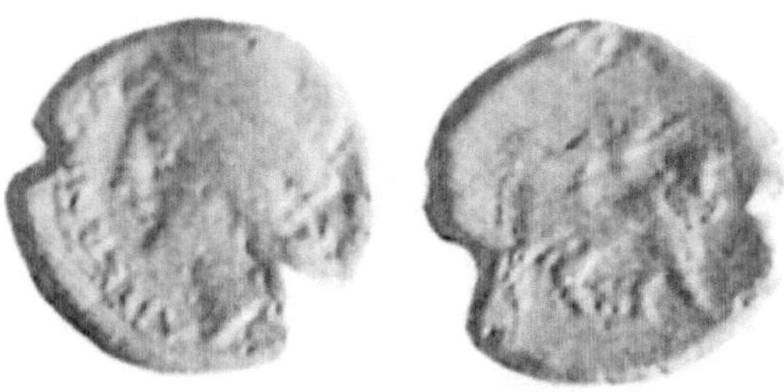	OBV: Head of Apollo facing left, wearing laurel wreath with leaves in opposing pairs, AI≲ERNINO before, pentagram behind. Dotted border. REV: Acheloios Volturnus as a man-faced bull standing to right on single line, head facing, winged nymph above, N below. Nothing in exergue. REF: Sambon 175; KM Berlin 4; SNG Cop 260 = Campana 9*.

77. AE Unit, 5.77-6.49g	260 to 240 BC
	OBV: Head of Apollo facing left, wearing laurel wreath with leaves in opposing pairs, AI≲ERNINO before, pentagram behind. Dotted border. REV: Acheloios Volturnus as a man-faced bull standing to right on single line, head facing, winged nymph above, T below, no inscription in exergue. REF: Sambon 177 var.; KM berlin 5; Campana 10; SNG München 118; Garrucci PL.XC, n.24(redrawn)*.

78. AE Unit, 6.46g	260 to 240 BC
	OBV: Head of Apollo facing left, wearing laurel wreath with leaves in opposing pairs, AISERNINO, N behind. Dotted border. REV: Acheloios Volturnus as a man-faced bull standing to right on single line, head facing, winged nymph above, T below, nothing in exergue. REF: Sambon 177; Fiorelli 640-1; Stelluti 138 and 148-9; Campana 12 = Sternberg 25, lot 13*.

THE BRETTII

Rare bronze coins featuring the head of the man-faced bull labeled as ΤΡΑΕΣ, and bearing the reverse inscription ΒΡΕΙΓ, were the subject of several studies in recent decades. Less than twenty specimens are known and according to Attianese, there are only two obverse dies and three reverse dies,[18] suggesting it was only issued for a short time. Most of these coins have been found on a hill at Cozzo Cerasello, located between Caloveto and Pietrapaola. This hill is on the southern shore of the Traeis River[19] (modern Trionto),[20] on the coastal area of modern Cosenza.[21]

The coins were originally dated to the late 4th century BC by Isler, who attributed them to Paestum, following Imhoof-Blumer.[22] Jenkins revealed his doubts about that attribution in the same year, not believing they were influenced by Campanian types, and lowering the tentative date to the 3rd century BC.[23] Taliano-Grasso later made a compelling argument based on an analysis of style, ancient literary sources and discoveries of specimens, ultimately proclaiming the coins were issued between 207 and 203 BC. He argued they might have been issued by a group of Metapontine citizens, relocated by Hannibal to the Traeis River in the area of his Brettian allies, after the conquest of Metapontion by the Romans in 207 BC.[24]

Carroccio, observing the features of the flans, re-dated these coins to the time of Pyrrhos,[25] arguing that the inscription ΒΡΕΙΓ would be an earlier version of ΒΡΕΤΤΙΩΝ, which is commonly seen on Brettian coinage.[26] Carroccio also suggests that the monogram ΣA on the reverse could be read as ΣΙΒΑ,[27] in support of the hypothesis that the mint was located at the site of the new 'Sybaris at Traente,' an area founded by Sybarite refugees,[28] and later conquered by Brettians in the 4th century BC. However, the same monogram was used by Taliano-Grasso for his assignment of dates, in which he compared them with a monogram appearing on other Brettian bronze types dated by Scheu to 211 to 203 BC.[29] Alternatively, Rutter suggests the coin was minted in Metapontion for the Brettians.[30] In fact, a similar type from Metapontion featuring the forepart of a man-faced bull and paired, like the ΤΡΑΕΣ coin, with a grain ear on reverse, appears in Garrucci's work, though its actual existence is still uncertain.[31] According to Paoletti, the denomination is probably a hemiobol.[32]

Although the meaning of K-A on the obverse is still uncertain, the inscription above the man-faced bull, ΤΡΑΕΣ, apparently names him outright. This has been used as evidence by proponents of the local river god theory, arguing that here we see the man-faced bull labeled as a local river god.[33] According to our theory, ΤΡΑΕΣ is a locative epithet, and so the man-faced bull is Acheloios as embodied in the local river, Acheloios Traeis, who probably symbolized rebirth for the Metapontine refugees living in Bruttium. The association of this coin with Metapontion is also appealing insofar as the cult of Acheloios is well attested there.[34]

---

18 P. Attianese, 'Una nuova zecca brettia?,' in *Panorama Numismatico*, 96 (Serravalle: Nomisma, 1996), 15.

19 The ancient river is referred to as Τράεντα by Diodorus Siculus (*The Library of History*, 12.22).

20 P. Attianese, 'Una nuova zecca brettia?,'14; A. Taliano-Grasso, 'Riflessioni sull'etnonimo dei Brettii,' in *Aitna. Quaderni di topografia antica*, Vol.3 (Messina, 1999), 184, note 6.

21 Corresponding to the ancient Consentia, the capital of the Brettian Federation.

22 H.P. Isler, *Acheloos*, no. 328.

23 G.K. Jenkins, *The Coinage of Gela*, 169.

24 For a discussion and references, see: A. Taliano-Grasso, 'La presenza brettia sul Traente attraverso nuovi documenti monetali,' in *I Brettii. Cultura, Lingua e Documentazione Storico-Archeologica* (Rubbettino, 1995), 203-204.

25 Therefore, about 50 years earlier than Taliano-Grasso's date. Morcom proposed 'early 300 BC' (J. Morcom, 'Some South Italian Questions,' 159-161).

26 The author argued that initially there must have been uncertainty among Brettian engravers on the transliteration of their original word into Greek letters, which according to Carroccio is derived from Oscan and defined by ancient sources as 'pitch dark' (B. Carroccio, 'A proposito di due nuove emissioni del koinon Brettio,' in *Panorama Numismatico*, 101 (Serravalle: Nomisma, 1996), 9). A totally different hypothesis is proposed by Taliano-Grasso, who offers a convincing argument that the Brettians derived from the earlier Oenotrians, a 'native' group of southern Italy for which scholars have proposed possible Anatolian origins. Ultimately, Βρειγ could be the original sound of the ethnic in the language of natives of Bruttium. The most interesting aspect of the matter is that Βρειγ is probably derived from 'Phrygian,' supporting the hypothesis of a Levantine origin of the Oenotrians (for a detailed discussion with bibliography and references to ancient sources, see: A. Taliano-Grasso, 'Riflessioni sull'etnonimo dei Brettii,' 181-183).

27 B. Carroccio 'A proposito di due nuove emissioni del koinon Brettio,' 8.

28 Diodorus Siculus, *The Library of History*, 12.22.

29 A. Taliano-Grasso, 'La presenza brettia,' 202 and footnote 19.

30 N.K. Rutter, *HN Italy*, 199, no. 2678. See also J. Morcom, 'Some South Italian Questions,' 159-61.

31 Cf. MSP I, 188.

32 M. Paoletti, 'Sibari sul Traente,' in *BTCGI* Vol.XVIII (Pisa, 2010), 788.

33 P. Attianese, 'Una nuova zecca Brettia?' 11-15; B. Carroccio, 'A proposito di due nuove emissioni del koinon Brettio,' 8-9.

34 L. Lacroix, *Monnaies et colonization dans l'occident grec* (Brussels, 1965), 82-3.

Coinage

79. AE Hemiobol, 3.78g	**Late 3th Century BC**
	OBV: Head and neck of Acheloios Traeis as a man-faced bull to right, above, ΤΡΑΕΣ, Κ-Α flanking. REV: Grain ear with leaf to right, above leaf, dolphin, below leaf, monogram, ΒΡΕΙΓ in left field. REF: HN Italy 2678; Taliano-Grasso (1995), 1-5; NAC 8, lot 450*.

CALES

Cales was originally a city of native Ausones,[35] located in the area of modern-day Calvi Risorta, near the Savo River (modern Savone). Archaeological discoveries of archaic pottery of eastern Mediterranean style exist, but were produced in local workshops. This pottery was inspired by Thapsos style, and also pottery from Asia Minor and Ionia, though it is not entirely clear if it was made by native or immigrant potters. The pottery is found along the course of the Savone River, which flows between Cales and Teanum Sidicinum. Between the 8th and 6th centuries BC, the river played an instrumental role in the spread of imported material from the coast of the Tyrrhenian Sea inland, indicated by the archeological finds of imported eastern and Etruscan materials found at the sites of Teanum Sidicinum and Cales.[36] On the basis of this evidence the etymological basis for Cales might be Akkadian *kallû-nāri*, 'the river courier'.[37]

The ancient city was situated at a central position for communication between the inland valleys of southern Latium, the Samnite territories, and the Campanian plains,[38] and probably for this reason it attracted the attention of Rome in the second half of the 4th century BC. In fact, the city's position as an independent center ended in 335 BC, when Rome defeated the combined armies of the Ausones and Sidicini. Cales was plundered at this time, and a Roman military garrison was imposed on the city. In the following year (334 BC) 2500 Roman citizens were settled there.[39]

It was after the re-foundation as a Roman colony that the man-faced bull appeared on many varieties of bronze coinage, always paired with Apollo. A recent extensive study on the coinage of Cales does not exist, and the main reference is still Sambon.[40]

All the man-faced bull varieties of Cales (all bronze) are lumped together and dated in accordance with later issues of Neapolis by Crawford and Rutter.[41] However, the style of both obverse and reverse on the star and lyre varieties are markedly superior to the later examples with winged nymph, which, coupled with the use of the same devices at Neapolis during Taliercio's Phase II, suggests a date range in line with those Neapolitan coins: 317/310 to 270 BC.[42] Thus, herein is proposed an earlier date for the beginning of the bronze coinage, from 317 to 272 BC (our Phase I).[43]

In the following catalog there are three chronological phases, the first and the third divided into two groups. The groups are identified on the basis of the main symbol above the man-faced bull, and the individual coins are listed according to the alphabetical order of the letters appearing on the reverse.

Phase I dates between 317 and 280 BC. For this phase the group with star above the man-faced bull is dated earlier than the group featuring a lyre above. Without this ordering, it is difficult to explain why the series with Apollo right/lyre (Phase II) exhibits an abrupt reduction of weight and size, which is attributable to the economic needs of the Pyrrhic war.[44] After the victory over Pyrrhus and the final conquer of Taras in 272 BC, which gave Rome and its allies significant financial resources, the weight was increased again for Phase III.

---

[35] Livy, *Ab Urbe Condita Libri*, 8.16. Ausones was the name used by ancient Greeks to indicate the pre-Roman native Italic people of the area. The Ausones themselves claimed to be descendants from a hybrid deity named Mares, later assimilated to centaurs by Latin authors (Aelianus, *Varia Historia*, 9.16). We know very little about the original Ausonian myth of the hybrid Mares, only that he lived for 123 years and that he died and was reborn three times. For the name Mares there is a probable etymology stemming from the Akkadian *mar'u*, meaning 'descendant'. Another possible semantic crossing is the Sumerian *amaru*, 'devastating flood' (G. Semerano, *Le Origini della Cultura Europea. Vol. II*, 468). Mares was strictly connected to the Ausonian nymph Marica, to which the Ausones built sanctuaries on the banks of rivers. Interestingly, the river sanctuaries of the Ausones were not only places of worship in which rites of passage are attested, but also meeting places for the various Ausonian tribes, where public collective functions were hosted (L. Cerchiai, *Gli antichi popoli della Campania, Archeologia e storia* (Roma: 2010), 86). Clearly, the Ausones produced a fertile cultural landscape in which the later tradition of Acheloios at Cales and Teanum was rooted, which was also influenced by the Etruscan culture of Capua and Pontecagnano.

[36] F. Sirano, 'Identità culturali nella Campania settentrionale: un aggiornamento,' in *Dalle sorgenti alla foce Il bacino del Liri-Garigliano nell'antichità: culture, contatti, scambi. Atti del convegno, Frosinone-Formia 10-12 novembre 2005*, edited by C. Corsi and E. Polito (Roma: Quasar, 2008), 47; F. Chiesa, *Aspetti dell'Orientalizzante recente in Campania. La tomba 1 di Cales*, Quaderni di ACME No.19 (Milano: Cisalpino, 1993), 63 and 112. For a study indicating that such discoveries testify not simply to a movement of materials between Etruria and the area of the Ausones, but indeed a 'common cultural imprint,' see: C. Passaro and G. Ciaccia, 'Cales: la necropoli dall'Orientalizzante recente all'eta` ellenistica,' in *Studi sull'Italia dei Sanniti* (Milano: 2000), 20-25.

[37] J. Black, A. George, and N. Postgate, 'kallû' in *A Concise Dictionary of Akkadian* (Wiesbaden: 2000), 142.

[38] S. Pantuliano, 'La monetazione della colonia latina di Cales,' in *XIII Congreso Internacional de Numismática. Madrid, 2003* (Madrid: 2005), 357.

[39] Livy, *Ab Urbe Condita Libri*, 8.16.

[40] A. Sambon, *Les monnaies antiques de l'Italie*, 354 ff.

[41] M. Crawford, *Coinage and Money under the Roman Republic: Italy and the Mediterranean Economy* (Berkeley: University of California Press, 1985), 47ff.; K. Rutter, *Historia Nummorum Italy*, 59. The two scholars dated all the coinage of Cales between 265 and 240 BC, in relation to the First Punic War.

[42] M. Taliercio Mensitieri, 'Il bronzo di Neapolis,' 227-238.

[43] Already in 1988 Renata Cantilena proposed an earlier date for the bronze coinage of Cales, based on the similarities of the devices with the coinage of Neapolis (R. Cantilena, *Monete della Campania antica* (Napoli: 1988), 157), which we try to further substantiate here.

[44] According to Cantilena, beginning with the war against Pyrrhus, the cities allied with Rome had to provide troops and to support them at their own expense, as reported by Polybius (R. Cantilena, 'Le prime monete di Roma e le colonie latine,' in *La collezione numismatica. Per una storia monetaria del Mezzogiorno* (Napoli: Electa, 2001), 47).

Phase I, Group Ia (star above) has 16 varieties (n. 80-95),[45] slightly more than the 14 listed by Sambon (Sambon 954-967). The varieties are marked first by letters ranging from A to Π. After these issues appears the presence of a star with 8 rays below the man-faced bull. The earliest varieties marked by letters probably reached Ω, but no specimens after P are known. Most of the varieties marked on the reverse by letters show a star of eight rays behind Apollo.

The next issue (n.91) shows a star with 8 rays on both obverse and reverse, which probably links the series with letters and the later ones (n.92-99) where a star of 8 rays appears in place of letters on the reverse. On the obverse the star disappears (n.88) and is replaced by various symbols (n. 93-95). Some of the series listed by Sambon are excluded, since they are probably non-existent types: the variant with star with eight rays above (Sambon 966) is certainly inaccurate: Sambon gives two references: Glasgow 20 (here referenced as Hunterian)[46] and Berlin 43 (here referenced as KM Berlin).[47] The reality of the matter is that their attribution was based on a misreading of Macdonald's listing by Sambon, where a normal specimen with 16 rays above and 8 rays below is listed as 'MacDonald 20'.[48] Moreover, the KM Berlin 43 description states that the coin is '*gänzlich oxydirt*' (completely oxidized), pointing out that the devices are poorly preserved.[49] The same goes for Sambon 954 (no symbol behind / 16 rays above, no symbol below). Sambon was surely confused, as he listed this variant also as Berlin 43, the coin already identified by him as having '8 rays above.'

Phase I, Group Ib (Apollo left/Lyre), is organized into 56 varieties (n.96-151), significantly more than the 33 recorded by Sambon (Sambon 921-953). The series is identified by a star with 8 rays below the man-faced bull (n.96-99), which places them in continuity with the previous series of Group Ia. These are followed by varieties with no letter (n.100-104), which themselves are followed by those featuring letters A through Ω (n.105-147).50 The final series is marked by the sign IS (n.148-151).51

Phase II (Apollo right/Lyre) dates from 280 to 272 BC, and this phase has no subdivisions based on types. There are eight varieties (n.152-159), six more than Sambon (919-920). This group shows types struck with dies of smaller size on three different sized flans: the first two issues (152-3) were on large heavy flans of the previous phase. The third issue (154) was struck on a heavy flan of very poor manufacture, indicating an issue struck in haste, probably due to the state of military emergency in connection with the Pyrrhic war. The remaining issues of this group (no. 155-159) exhibit both reduced size and weight of the flans, and also are of poor quality manufacture.

Thus, Phases I and II chronologically correspond to Taliercio Neapolis Phase II. In fact, the style and devices go well together. Moreover, the IS mark appears on Taliercio IIb and IIC, and this is congruent with the chronology established for the issues of Cales with lyre and IS, which comprise the later issues of our Phase I.

Phase III dates between 272 and 250 BC, from the victory of Rome over Pyrrhus to the years of the First Punic War. This phase is divided into two groups. Group IIIa (Apollo left/ no symbol) is known from a single specimen weighting 5.92g, with the letter A below the man-faced bull (n.160 = Sambon 968). Group IIIb features Apollo/man-faced bull crowned by a winged nymph. This type, typical of the Neapolitan bronzes of Phase IIIa (dated by Taliercio between 270 and 250 BC),[52] is very common in Campania and Samnium, as it appears on the bronze coinage of Neapolis, Nola, Suessa, Teanum, Compulteria, Aesernia, Larinum and even Venafrum.[53] For Cales we identified eight varieties (n.160-168), three more than Sambon (969-973). This group has two additional varieties (n.169-170), whose attribution to the mint of Cales is uncertain. No. 159 is the most common issue from Cales, and the large number of extant specimens indicates its connection with the military efforts of the first Punic war.[54]

[45] We include in this group the variants featuring a star of six rays above the man-faced bull (n. 78 and 79), as the star on obverse and the letter on reverse is consistent with the proposed chronological progression of the series.

[46] G. MacDonald, *Catalogue of Greek coins in the Hunterian Collection, University of Glasgow*, Vol.I (Glasgow: 1899).

[47] H. Dressel, *Konigliche Museen zu Berlin. Beschreibung der Antiken Munzen. Dritter Band*, Abtheilung 1 (Berlin: 1894).

[48] G. MacDonald, *Catalogue of Greek coins in the Hunterian Collection, University of Glasgow*, 28, no.20.

[49] H. Dressel, *Konigliche Museen zu Berlin. Beschreibung der Antiken Munzen*, 81, no.43.

[50] The symbols behind Apollo are variable, but in some cases the recurrence of the same symbol on specimens marked by different letters in the alphabetical progression confirms the chronological succession of the series identified in this cataog, cf. no.105-106 (kantharos) from B to Γ; no. 111-112 (cock) from Γ to Δ; no. 118-119 (serpent) and no. 117-120 (helmet) from Z to E; no. 129-130 (star) from K to Λ; 131-132 (delta) from Λ to M; and no. 142-143 (fly) from X to Ω.

[51] The sign IΣ appears on the bronze coinage of the man-faced bull minted at several Campanian cities: Neapolis, Suessa, Cales, Aesernia, Compulteria and Venafrum. This evidence lead Rutter to recognize 'a close co-operation in minting, possibly using a centralized system,' and probably issued by the same mint (Neapolis?) (Rutter *Historia Numorum Italy*, 58, where the scholar mentions Nola among the cities issuing IΣ coinage, but there appear to be no such issues from Nola, even in Rutter's work). The IΣ inscription is not consistent with the theory of contemporary issues by the same centralized issuing authority. In fact, it appears on types covering a very large span of time: the earliest being Taliercio Phase IIa (MSP I, 269), the latter from Aesernia (MSP I, n. 64-66b). The meaning of IΣ, always appearing below the man-faced bull, and never on the obverse behind Apollo nor on any other type of Campanian coinage, should not be considered as part of the normal chronological series of a mint but instead is related to the notion that the rivers of the ancient world are sinews of Acheloios, as discussed above and below.

[52] M. Taliercio Mensitieri, 'Il bronzo di Neapolis,' 238-245.

[53] See related entries for each mint in this catalog.

[54] We traced the following specimens in published collections: Fiorelli 827-33; Santangelo 682-3; KM Berlin 49-52; Hunterian 15; Grose-McClean 186-7; SNG Cop 321; SNG Munchen 153; SNG ANS 184-7; SNG UK VII 41; SNG France 470-3; SNG Sweden II 72; SNG

The man-faced bull depicted on the coinage of Cales is probably a representation of Acheloios Savo. The identification of this man-faced bull with the Savo River was first proposed in 1920 by Borrelli.[55] Moreover, the Savo River is mentioned by ancient sources,[56] and it was probably sacred to the natives of the area between Cales and Teanum Sidicinum. In fact, archaeological evidence records ancient temples built along the course of the river dating as early as the Archaic Age.[57]

The name Savo probably has a Semitic derivation related to the verb 'to drink,' as proposed in 1820 by Mattia Zona.[58] There are other possible etymological bases, namely, the Akkadian word *sahu*, 'basin for drinking',[59] and *saqu*, the Akkadian word used for both 'to give to drink' and 'to irrigate fields'.[60] A semantic crossing with the Akkadian base *sebu* and *sabu,* meaning 'to be satisfied with drink and food', 'long life' and 'plenty',[61] is probably shared with the nearby Sebethos River of Neapolis.

Coinage

PHASE I: c. 317 to 280 BC

GROUP IA (APOLLO LEFT/STAR)

80. AE Unit, 7.74g, 21mm	**317 to 280 BC**
	OBV: Head of Apollo facing left, wearing laurel wreath with leaves in opposing pairs, star with 8 rays behind, (CALENO) before. Dotted border. REV: Acheloios Savo as man-faced bull standing right on single line, head facing, star with 16 rays above, A below, CALENO in ex. Dotted border. REF: Sambon 957; Santangelo 691-2; KM Berlin 44; Artemide 29E, lot 3*.

81. AE Unit, 7.34g, 20mm	**317 to 280 BC**
	OBV: Head of Apollo facing left, wearing laurel wreath with leaves in opposing pairs, CALENO before, star with 8 rays behind. Dotted border. REV: Acheloios Savo as man-faced bull standing right on single line, head facing, star with 16 rays above, Γ below, CALENO in ex. Dotted border. REF: Sambon 958; Santangelo 693; Brunetti V, 2010, lot 24*.

82. AE Unit, 6.42g, 20mm	**317 to 280 BC**
	OBV: Head of Apollo left, wearing laurel wreath with leaves in opposing pairs, star with eight rays behind, CALENO before. Double dotted border. REV: Acheloios Savo as man-faced bull standing right on single line, head facing, star with 6 rays above, below, CALENO in ex. Dotted border. REF: Sambon 967; BMC 24; SNG Gale 36; Pozzi 155; SNG Morcom 80; SNG France 467 = BnF Fonds Général 188*.

Budapest 368; SNG Milano 11; Pozzi 157; Lindgren 182; British Museum n.1926,0204.58.

[55] N. Borrelli, 'La moneta dell'antica Cales' in *Bollettino del Circolo Numismatico Napoletano* (Napoli, 1920), 1-8.

[56] Statius, *Silvae*, 4.3.66.

[57] P.F. Talamo, *L'area aurunca nel quadro dell'Italia centromeridionale. Testimonianze archeologiche di eta` arcaica*, BAR, International Series, 384 (Oxford, 1987), 167-170.

[58] M. Zona, *Calvi antica e moderna o sia memorie istoriche dell'antichissima città di Calvi* (Napoli, 1820), 178-9.

[59] J. Black, A. George, and N. Postgate, *A Concise Dictionary of Akkadian*, 347.

[60] Ibid., 359.

[61] Ibid., 365.

83. AE Unit, 7.15g | **317 to 280 BC**

OBV: Head of Apollo facing left, wearing laurel wreath with leaves in opposing pairs, olive sprig (?) behind, CALENO before. Dotted border.
REV: Acheloios Savo as man-faced bull standing right on single line, head facing, star with 6 rays above, Γ below, CALENO in ex. Dotted border.
REF: SNG Lewis 64 = Graziano 47*.
Unique? The olive sprig might be a star that was not properly struck.

84. AE Unit, 7.01g | **317 to 280 BC**

OBV: Head of Apollo facing left, wearing laurel wreath with leaves in opposing pairs, CALENO before, star with 8 rays behind. Dotted border.
REV: Acheloios Savo as man-faced bull standing right on single line, head facing, star with 16 rays above, Δ below, CALENO in ex. Dotted border.
REF: Sambon 959; Hunterian 18; Elsen 93, lot. 37*.

85. AE Unit, 4.60g | **317 to 280 BC**

OBV: Head of Apollo facing left, wearing laurel wreath with leaves in opposing pairs, no inscription, star with 8 rays behind. Dotted border.
REV: Acheloios Savo as man-faced bull standing right on single line, head facing, star with 16 rays above, Δ below, CALENO in ex. Dotted border.
REF: Graziano 63*.

86. AE 6.88g, 21mm | **317 to 280 BC**

OBV: Head of Apollo facing left, wearing laurel wreath with leaves in opposing pairs, CALENO before, star with 8 rays behind. Dotted border.
REV: Acheloios Savo as man-faced bull standing right on single line, head facing, star with 16 rays above, K below, CALENO in ex. Dotted border.
REF: Sambon 961; SNG Sweden II, 75; SNG Cop. 310; Artemide 24.2 E, lot 1008*.

87. AE Unit, unrecorded weight | **317 to 280 BC**

OBV: Head of Apollo facing left, wearing laurel wreath with leaves in opposing pairs, CALENO before, no symbol behind. Dotted border.
REV: Acheloios Savo as man-faced bull standing right on single line, head facing, star with 16 rays above, Λ below, CALENO in ex.
REF: Sambon 962 = Carelli LXVIII.30*.
Unconfirmed. Sambon cites Carelli but incorrectly lists the variety with 'Star behind'.

88. AE Unit, 6.40g, 20mm | **317 to 280 BC**

OBV: Head of Apollo facing left, wearing laurel wreath with leaves in opposing pairs, CALENO before, (star with 8 rays?) behind. Dotted border.
REV: Acheloios Savo as man-faced bull standing right on single line, head facing, star with 16 rays above, N below, CALENO in ex.
REF: Sambon 963; KM Berlin 45; SNG Cop. 308; Private Collection*.

Sambon described the star behind Apollo, but KM Berlin and SNG Cop. do not.

89. AE Unit, 7.13g, 20mm | **317 to 280 BC**

OBV: Head of Apollo facing left, wearing laurel wreath with leaves in opposing pairs, CALENO before, star with 8 rays behind. Dotted border.
REV: Acheloios Savo as man-faced bull standing right on single line, head facing, star with 16 rays above, O below, CALENO in ex. Dotted border.
REF: Sambon 960 (Θ), 964 (O); Hunterian 19 (O); KM Berlin 46 (O); Santangelo 694 (O); SNG Cop.309 (Θ); SNG ANS 183 (O); ACR 5, Lot 10*.

The omicron is often incorrectly described as Θ

90. AE Unit, 7-09g | **317 to 280 BC**

OBV: Head of Apollo facing left, wearing laurel wreath with leaves in opposing pairs, CALENO before, star behind. Dotted border.
REV: Acheloios Savo as man-faced bull standing right on single line, head facing, star with 16 rays above, Π below, CALENO in ex. Dotted border.
REF: Sambon 965; KM Berlin 47-48; Santangelo 695; SNG Evelpidis 40; Munzen Ritter, VCoins SKU: 66023*.

91. AE Unit, 6.62g | **317 to 280 BC**

OBV: Head of Apollo facing left, wearing laurel wreath with leaves in opposing pairs, star with 8 rays behind, (CALENO) before. Dotted border.
REV: Acheloios Savo as man-faced bull standing right on single line, head facing, star with 16 rays above, star with 8 rays below, CALENO in ex. Dotted border.
REF: Fiorelli 817 (incorrectly described as 'sword behind'); BnF 1966.453*.

92. AE Unit, 5.79g, 19mm | **317 to 280 BC**

OBV: Head of Apollo facing left, wearing laurel wreath with leaves in opposing pairs, no symbol behind, (CALENO) before. Dotted border.
REV: Acheloios Savo as man-faced bull standing right on single line, head facing, star with 16 rays above, star with 8 rays below, CALENO in ex. Dotted border.
REF: Hunterian 20; SNG France 466 = BnF Fonds Général 186*.

93. AE Unit, 7.48g, 20mm	**317 to 280**
	OBV: Head of Apollo facing left, wearing laurel wreath with leaves in opposing pairs, club behind, CALENO before. Dotted border. REV: Acheloios Savo as man-faced bull standing right on single line, head facing, star with 16 rays above, star with 8 rays below, CALENO in ex. Dotted border. REF: Sambon 955; Alteri 150; SNG Morcom 81 = BM no. 2013,4030.12*.

94. AE Unit, unrecorded weight	**317 to 280**
	OBV: Head of Apollo facing left, wearing laurel wreath with leaves in opposing pairs, sword (?) behind, CALENO before. Dotted border. REV: Acheloios Savo as man-faced bull standing right on single line, head facing, star with 16 rays above, star with 8 rays below, CALENO in ex. Dotted border. REF: Sambon 956; Santangelo 696-7. *Unconfirmed, may be the same type as no. 90. Sambon cited Fiorelli 817, which itself was probably incorrectly described, as the coin in question seems to show a star with 8 rays behind Apollo, thus our variant no. 87.*

95. AE Unit, 7.59g	**317 to 280 BC**
	OBV: Head of Apollo facing left, wearing laurel wreath with leaves in opposing pairs, thyrsus behind, (CALENO?) before. Dotted border. REV: Acheloios Savo as man-faced bull standing right on single line, head facing, star with 16 rays above, star with 8 rays below, CALENO in ex. Dotted border. REF: SNG Morcom 82 = Graziano 53*.

Group Ib (Apollo left/Lyre)

96. AE Unit, 6.71g	**317 to 280 BC**
	OBV: Head of Apollo facing left, wearing laurel wreath with leaves in opposing pairs, lightning bolt behind, CALENO before. Dotted border. REV: Acheloios Savo as man-faced bull standing right on single line, head facing, lyre above, star with 8 rays below, CALENO in ex. Linear border. REF: Sambon 923; Fiorelli 815; Hunterian 14; Pozzi 156; SNG ANS 176; CNG 60, lot 29*.

97. AE Unit, 6.58g	**317 to 280 BC**
	OBV: Head of Apollo facing left, wearing laurel wreath with leaves in opposing pairs, winged nymph behind, CALENO before. Dotted border. REV: Acheloios Savo as man-faced bull standing right on single line, head facing, lyre above, star with 8 rays below, CALENO in ex. Linear border. REF: Sambon 924; SNG Cop 311; SNG Firenze 180; NAC 64, Lot 613*.

98. AE Unit, 7.48g	**317 to 280 BC**
	OBV: Head of Apollo facing left, wearing laurel wreath with leaves in opposing pairs, dolphin behind oriented downward, CALENO before. Dotted border. REV: Acheloios Savo as man-faced bull standing right on single line, head facing, lyre above, star with 8 rays below, CALENO in ex. Linear border. REF: BMC 21; SNG Firenze 180; SNG Ashmolean IA 44 = Graziano 76*.

99. AE Unit, 6.37g, 20mm	**317 to 280 BC**
	OBV: Head of Apollo facing left, wearing laurel wreath with leaves in opposing pairs, CALENO before, uncertain symbol [aphlaston?] behind. Dotted border. REV: Acheloios Savo as man-faced bull standing right on single line, head facing, lyre above, star with 8 rays below, (CALENO in ex.?). Linear border. REF: InAsta 36, lot 40*.

100. AE Unit, 6.40g, 21 mm	**317 to 280 BC**
	OBV: Head of Apollo facing left, wearing laurel wreath with leaves in opposing pairs, CALENO before, nothing behind. Dotted border. REV: Acheloios Savo as man-faced bull standing right on single line, head facing, lyre above, nothing below, CALENO in ex. Linear border. REF: CNG, eAuction 199, 3*.

101. AE Unit, 6.09g, 20 mm	**317 to 280 BC**
	OBV: Head of Apollo facing left, wearing laurel wreath with leaves in opposing pairs, laurel branch behind, CALENO before. Dotted border. REV: Acheloios Savo as man-faced bull standing right on single line, head facing, lyre above, nothing below (erased letter?), CALENO in ex. Linear border. REF: CNG, eAuction 201, 1*. *Unconfirmed variant, may be an obscured Θ below the man-faced bull.*

102. AE Unit, 6.18g, 21 mm	**317 to 280 BC**
	OBV: Head of Apollo facing left, wearing laurel wreath with leaves in opposing pairs, spearhead behind, CALENO before. Dotted border. REV: Acheloios Savo as man-faced bull standing right on single line, head facing, lyre above, nothing below, CALENO in ex. Linear border. REF: Sambon 922; Hunterian 13; KM Berlin 31; SNG ANS 175; CNG eAuction 199, 2*.

103. AE Unit, 6.67g	**317 to 280 BC**
	OBV: Head of Apollo facing left, wearing laurel wreath with leaves in opposing pairs, thyrsus behind, CALENO before. Dotted border. REV: Acheloios Savo as man-faced bull standing right on single line, head facing, lyre above, nothing below, CALENO in ex. Linear border. REF: KM Berlin 40; Graziano 96*.

104. AE Unit, 6.44g	**317 to 280 BC**
	OBV: Head of Apollo facing left, wearing laurel wreath with leaves in opposing pairs, club behind. Dotted border. REV: Acheloios Savo as man-faced bull standing right on single line, head facing, lyre above, nothing below, CALENO in ex. Linear (?) border. REF: Sambon 921; Fiorelli 816; Hunterian 12; Carelli LXVIII.24*.

105. AE Unit	**317 to 280 BC**
	OBV: Head of Apollo facing left, wearing laurel wreath with leaves in opposing pairs, nothing behind, CALENO before. Dotted border. REV: Acheloios Savo as man-faced bull standing right on single line, head facing, lyre above, A below, CALENO in ex. Linear (?) border. REF: Sambon 925. *Unique?*

106. AE Unit, 7.01g, 20mm	**317 to 280 BC**
	OBV: Head of Apollo facing left, wearing laurel wreath with leaves in opposing pairs, nothing behind, CALENO before. Dotted border. REV: Acheloios Savo as man-faced bull standing right on single line, head facing, lyre above, B below, CALENO in ex. Linear border. REF: SNG France 450 = BnF N3638; Potamikon Collection*.

107. AE Unit, 7.46g, 21mm	**317 to 270 BC**
	OBV: Head of Apollo facing left, wearing laurel wreath with leaves in opposing pairs, grain ear behind, CALENO before. Dotted border. REV: Acheloios Savo as man-faced bull standing right on single line, head facing, lyre above, B below, CALENO in ex. Linear border. REF: Sambon 926; Santangelo 688-9; KM Berlin 32; BMC 17; Torino 620; SNG Morcom 79; SNG Cop 316; SNG Firenze 175; SNG France 449; Artemide 21E, 18*.

108. AE Unit, 6.88g	**317 to 280 BC**
	OBV: Head of Apollo facing left, wearing laurel wreath with leaves in opposing pairs, pentagram behind, CALENO before. Dotted border. REV: Acheloios Savo as man-faced bull standing right on single line, head facing, lyre above, B below, CALENO in ex. Linear border. REF: Grose-McClean 185, Pl.10, n.7 *.

109. AE Unit, 6.36g	**317 to 270 BC**
	OBV: Head of Apollo facing left, wearing laurel wreath with leaves in opposing pairs, kantharos behind, CALENO before. Dotted border. REV: Acheloios Savo as man-faced bull standing right on single line, head facing, lyre above, B below, (CALENO?) in ex. Linear border. REF: SNG Ashmolean IA 40 = Graziano 102*. *Letter described as 'B' in SNG Ashmolean as 'E' in Graziano.*

110. AE Unit, 6.71g	**317 to 280 BC**
	OBV: Head of Apollo facing left, wearing laurel wreath with leaves in opposing pairs, kantharos behind, CALENO before. Dotted border. REV: Acheloios Savo as man-faced bull standing right on single line, head facing, lyre above, Γ below, CALENO in ex. Dotted border. REF: Sambon 928; HM Frankfurt 32; SNG Ashmolean IA 40; Lafaille 8; CNG, eAuction 305, lot 7*.

111. AE Unit, 7.71g	**317 to 280 BC**
	OBV: Head of Apollo facing left, wearing laurel wreath with leaves in opposing pairs, lightning bolt behind, CALENO before. Dotted border. REV: Acheloios Savo as man-faced bull standing right on single line, head facing, lyre above, Γ below. Dotted border. REF: SNG Ashmolean IA 41; Katane 8, lot100*.

112. AE Unit, 6.96g, 21mm	**317 to 280 BC**
	OBV: Head of Apollo facing left, wearing laurel wreath with leaves in opposing pairs, Phrygian helmet behind, CALENO before. Dotted border. REV: Acheloios Savo as man-faced bull standing right on single line, head facing, lyre above, Γ below. Dotted border. REF: Sambon 927; HM Frankfurt 31; Lindgren 181; SNG France 451; SNG Cop 315; CNG 79, 8*.

113. AE Unit, 6.80g	**317 to 280 BC**
	OBV: Head of Apollo facing left, wearing laurel wreath with leaves in opposing pairs, pentagram behind, CALENO before. Dotted border. REV: Acheloios Savo as man-faced bull standing right on single line, head facing, lyre above, Γ below. REF: British Museum n.EH,p59.6.Cal; SNG Ashmolean IA 42; SNG Ashmolean I 3*.

114. AE Unit, 7.44g	**317 to 280 BC**
	OBV: Apollo facing left, wearing laurel wreath with leaves in opposing pairs, CALENO before, serpent behind. Dotted border. REV: Acheloios Savo as man-faced bull standing right on single line, head facing, lyre above, Γ or Π below. REF: Sambon 944; KM Berlin 42, Pl.II n.32 *.

115. AE Unit, 8.19g, 20mm	**317 to 280 BC**
	OBV: Head of Apollo facing left, wearing laurel wreath with leaves in opposing pairs, CALENO before, cock behind. Dotted border. REV: Acheloios Savo as man-faced bull standing right on single line, head facing, lyre above, Γ below. Dotted border. REF: Sambon 945; BMC 14; SNG Cop 320; Hunterian 7-8; CNG, eAuction 305, lot. 8*.

116. AE Unit, 7.33g	**317 to 280 BC**
	OBV: Head of Apollo facing left, wearing laurel wreath with leaves in opposing pairs, CALENO before, cock behind. Dotted border. REV: Acheloios Savo as man-faced bull standing right on single line, head three-quarters facing, lyre above, Δ below. Dotted border. REF: Sambon 946; Grose-McClean 183, Pl.10, n.6; Monetiere Archeologico Firenze, inv. n. 83147; NAC auction P, lot 1002 = CNG #750588*.

117. AE Unit, 6.80g	**317 to 280 BC**
	OBV: Head of Apollo facing left, wearing laurel wreath with leaves in opposing pairs, bunch of grapes behind, CALENO before. Dotted border. REV: Acheloios Savo as man-faced bull standing right on single line, head facing, lyre above, Δ below, CALENO in ex. REF: Sambon 930; Fiorelli 818; SNG France 448; SNG München 149 = Graziano 91*.

118. AE Unit, 6.41g	**317 to 280 BC**
	OBV: Head of Apollo facing left, wearing laurel wreath with leaves in opposing pairs, sword oriented downwards behind, CALENO before. Dotted border. REV: Acheloios Savo as man-faced bull standing right on single line, head facing, lyre above, Δ below, CALENO in ex. REF: Sambon 929; Hunterian 11; Carelli LXVIII.25*.

119. AE Unit, 7.96g, 23mm	**317 to 280 BC**
	OBV: Head of Apollo facing left, wearing laurel wreath with leaves in opposing pairs, CALENO before, wing-shaped aphlaston behind. Dotted border. REV: Acheloios Savo as man-faced bull standing right on single line, head facing, lyre above, E below. Dotted border. REF: Sambon 947; Hunterian 9; SNG ANS 180; SNG Ashmolean I 1 10; Monetiere Archeologico Firenze, inv. n. 83148; NAC 33, lot 7*.

120. AE Unit, 7.25g	**317 to 280 BC**
	OBV: Head of Apollo facing left, wearing laurel wreath with leaves in opposing pairs, kantharos behind, CALENO before. Dotted border. REV: Acheloios Savo as man-faced bull standing right on single line, head facing, lyre above, E below. CALENO in ex. Dotted border (?). REF: Sambon 931; KM Berlin 34.

121. AE Unit, 6.92g, 21mm	**317 to 280 BC**
	OBV: Head of Apollo facing left, wearing laurel wreath with leaves in opposing pairs, Phrygian helmet behind, CALENO before. Dotted border. REV: Acheloios Savo as man-faced bull standing right on single line, head facing, lyre above, Z below. Dotted border. REF: Sambon 948; BMC 15; Grose-McClean 184; Hunterian 10; CNG, eAuction 305, 9*. *Sambon 934 has the ethnic under exergue line, citing BCM 15. However, that variety does not exist, cf. British Museum number RPK,p302B.2.Cal, which has no ethnic on the reverse.*

122. AE Unit, 7.01g	**317 to 280 BC**
	OBV: Head of Apollo facing left, wearing laurel wreath with leaves in opposing pairs, serpent behind, CALENO before. Dotted border. REV: Acheloios Savo as man-faced bull standing right on single line, head facing, lyre above, Z below. Dotted border. REF: Sambon 933; SNG France 453; SNG Morcom 78; CNG Triton V, lot 20*. *The letter below the man-faced bull is Z, not I. In fact, the Greek Iota was rendered as a single vertical line.*

123. AE Unit, 7.05g, 20mm	**317 to 280 BC**
	OBV: Head of Apollo facing left, wearing laurel wreath with leaves in opposing pairs, serpent behind, CALENO before. Dotted border. REV: Acheloios Savo as man-faced bull standing right on single line, head facing, lyre above, H below. Dotted border. REF: SNG München 147; SNG Cop.314; CNG, eAuction 129, lot 2*.

124. AE Unit, 7.64g, 22mm	**317 to 280 BC**
	OBV: Head of Apollo facing left, wearing laurel wreath with leaves in opposing pairs, CALENO before, Phrygian helmet behind. Dotted border. REV: Acheloios Savo as man-faced bull standing right on single line, head facing, lyre above, H below, nothing in ex. Dotted border. REF: SNG Firenze 179; Artemide 23E, lot 15*.

125. AE Unit, 5.98g	**317 to 280 BC**
	OBV: Head of Apollo facing left, wearing laurel wreath with leaves in opposing pairs, dolphin behind oriented downward, CALENO before. REV: Acheloios Savo as man-faced bull standing right on single line, head facing, lyre above, H below. Dotted border. REF: SNG Firenze 179 = Graziano 119*.

126. AE Unit, 6.11g, 19mm	**317 to 280 BC**
	OBV: Head of Apollo facing left, wearing laurel wreath with leaves in opposing pairs, unclear symbol behind, CALENO before. Dotted border. REV: Acheloios Savo as man-faced bull standing right on single line, head facing, lyre above, H below. Dotted border. REF: Sambon 932; SNG Evelpidis 39; SNG France 452 = BnF N 3639*.

127. AE Unit, 6.62g, 20mm	**317 to 280 BC**
	OBV: Head of Apollo facing left, wearing laurel wreath with leaves in opposing pairs, laurel branch behind, CALENO before. Dotted border. REV: Acheloios Savo as man-faced bull standing right on single line, head facing, lyre above, Θ below, CALENO in ex. Linear border. REF: Sambon 937; SNG France 457; SNG Gale 35; Basel 32; ACR 9 lot 6*.

128. AE Unit	**317 to 280 BC**
	OBV: Head of Apollo facing left, wearing laurel wreath with leaves in opposing pairs, kantharos behind, CALENO before. Dotted border. REV: Acheloios Savo as man-faced bull standing right on single line, head facing, lyre above, I below, CALENO in ex. Dotted border (?). REF: Sambon 936; Fiorelli 821.

129. AE Unit	**317 to 280 BC**
	OBV: Head of Apollo facing left, wearing laurel wreath with leaves in opposing pairs, amphora behind, CALENO before. Dotted border. REV: Acheloios Savo as man-faced bull standing right on single line, head facing, lyre above, I below, CALENO in ex. Dotted border (?). REF: Sambon 935; Fiorelli 820.

130. AE Unit	**317 to 280 BC**
	OBV: Head of Apollo facing left, wearing laurel wreath with leaves in opposing pairs, uncertain symbol (torch or sword?) behind, (CALENO?) before REV: Acheloios Savo as man-faced bull standing right on single line, head facing, lyre above, I below, CALENO in ex. Linear border. REF: Graziano 93* (described as sword).

131. AE Unit, 6.61g,	**317 to 280 BC**
	OBV: Head of Apollo facing left, wearing laurel wreath with leaves in opposing pairs, uncertain symbol (described as either sword or club, but probably a sword) behind, CALENO before. Dotted border. REV: Acheloios Savo as man-faced bull standing right on single line, head facing, lyre above, K below, CALENO in ex. Linear border. REF: HM Frankfurt 33 (club); SNG Ashmolean I 4 (sword); SNG München 150 (sword); Graziano 99 (caduceus); SNG France 456 (sword) = BnF Armand Valton 8*.

132. AE Unit, 7.06g	**317 to 280 BC**
	OBV: Head of Apollo facing left, wearing laurel wreath with leaves in opposing pairs, spearhead behind, CALENO before. Dotted border. REV: Acheloios Savo as man-faced bull standing right on single line, head facing, lyre above, K below, CALENO in ex. Linear border. REF: CNG, eAuction 130, lot 15*.

133. AE Unit, 6.27g, 21mm — **317 to 280 BC**

OBV: Head of Apollo facing left, wearing laurel wreath with leaves in opposing pairs, star with 8 rays behind, CALENO before. Dotted border.
REV: Acheloios Savo as man-faced bull standing right on single line, head facing, [lyre?] above, K below, CALENO in ex. Linear border.
REF: LAC Auction 8, lot 4*.
On this specimen the lyre above is not visible. If not a lyre, this could be the second known specimen without a main symbol on reverse, the other being no.156.

134. AE Unit, 6.17g — **317 to 280 BC**

OBV: Head of Apollo facing left, wearing laurel wreath with leaves in opposing pairs, star with 8 rays behind, CALENO before. Dotted border.
REV: Acheloios Savo as man-faced bull standing right on single line, head facing, lyre above, Λ below, CALENO in ex. Linear border.
REF: SNG München 151; BnF AA.GR.18271*.

135. AE Unit, 6.76g — **317 to 280 BC**

OBV: Head of Apollo facing left, wearing laurel wreath with leaves in opposing pairs, Δ behind. Dotted border.
REV: Acheloios Savo as man-faced bull standing right on single line, head facing, lyre above, Λ below, CALENO in ex. Linear border.
REF: Sambon 938; Naster-Hirsch 47; Mionnet I p.112, n.115; SNG Evelpidis 41; SNG France 458 = BnF Fonds Général 180*.

136. AE Unit, 6.35g — **317 to 280 BC**

OBV: Head of Apollo facing left, wearing laurel wreath with leaves in opposing pairs, Δ behind, CALENO before. Dotted border.
REV: Acheloios Savo as man-faced bull standing right on single line, head facing, lyre above, M below, CALENO in ex. Linear border.
REF: Sambon 939; KM Berlin 35; Fiorelli 822-3; Santangelo 690; SNG ANS 178; SNG Budapest 371; Gorbea Madrid 20; SNG France 459 = BnF Fonds Général 181*.

137. AE Unit, 6.68g — **317 to 280 BC**

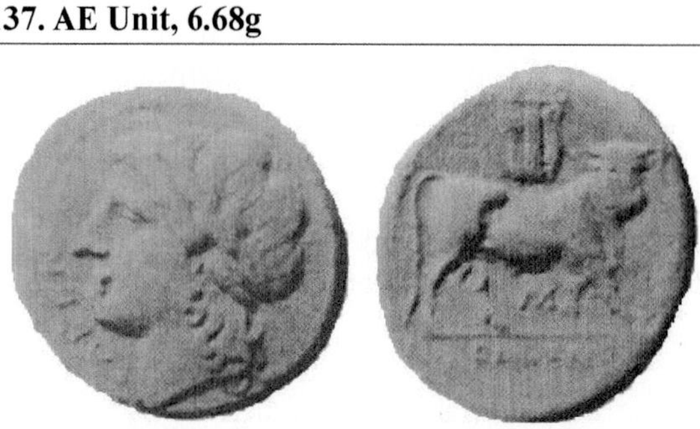

OBV: Head of Apollo facing left, wearing laurel wreath with leaves in opposing pairs, no symbol behind, CALENO before. Dotted border.
REV: Acheloios Savo as man-faced bull standing right on single line, head facing, lyre above, M below, CALENO in ex. Linear border.
REF: KM Berlin 36; SNG Lloyd 54*.

138. AE Unit, 6.07g — **317 to 280 BC**

OBV: Head of Apollo facing left, wearing laurel wreath with leaves in opposing pairs, uncertain symbol behind, CALENO before.
REV: Acheloios Savo as man-faced bull standing right on single line, head facing, lyre above, Π below, CALENO in ex.
REF: Sambon 940; SNG ANS 179 (described as 'bird? behind') = SNG France 460-1 (described as 'Δ behind'), 460 = BnF Fonds Général 182*.

The known specimens for this variety are all too worn to conclusively determine the symbol behind Apollo.

139. AE Unit — **317 to 280 BC**

OBV: Head of Apollo facing left, wearing laurel wreath with leaves in opposing pairs, helmet behind, CALENO before. Dotted border.
REV: Acheloios Savo as man-faced bull standing right on single line, head facing, lyre above, T below, CALENO in ex. Linear (?) border.
REF: Sambon 941 = Carelli, LXVII, 18*.

Unconfirmed

140. AE Unit — **317 to 280 BC**

OBV: Head of Apollo facing left, wearing laurel wreath with leaves in opposing pairs, triskeles behind, CALENO before. Dotted border.
REV: Acheloios Savo as man-faced bull standing right on single line, head facing, lyre above, Y below, CALENO in ex. Linear border (?).
REF: Sambon 942 = Carelli, LXVII, 21*.

Unconfirmed

141. AE Unit, 6.98g — **317 to 280 BC**

OBV: Head of Apollo facing left, wearing laurel wreath with leaves in opposing pairs, cornucopia behind, CALENO before. Dotted border (?).
REV: Acheloios Savo as man-faced bull standing right on single line, head facing, lyre above, Y below, CALENO in ex. Dotted border (?).
REF: Sambon 943; Fiorelli 824.

142. AE Unit, 6.23g, 21.9mm — **317 to 280 BC**

OBV: Head of Apollo facing left, wearing laurel wreath with leaves in opposing pairs, CALENO before, (eagle?) behind. Dotted border.
REV: Acheloios Savo as man-faced bull standing right on single line, head facing, lyre above, Y below, CALENO in ex.
REF: Forvm Ancient Coins Item n.GI18200*

Another specimen in SNG Milano P.II, n.19 shows an unclear symbol behind Apollo's head, which N. Vismara described as an eagle.

143. AE Unit, 20mm	**317 to 280 BC**
	OBV: Head of Apollo facing right, wearing laurel wreath with leaves in opposing pairs, A rotated 45 degrees counterclockwise behind. Dotted border. REV: Acheloios Savo as man-faced bull standing right on single line, head facing, lyre above, Φ below, CALENO in ex. REF: Private collection*. *SNG Cop 312 (not illustrated) lists a variant with* Φ below *and no further description for the obverse. For a similar orientation of the obverse A see Phase IIIb, no. 165.*

144. AE Unit, 6.51g	**317 to 280 BC**
	OBV: Head of Apollo facing left, wearing laurel wreath with leaves in opposing pairs, CALENO before, star with 8 rays behind. Dotted border. REV: Acheloios Savo as man-faced bull standing right on single line, head facing, lyre above, X below, CALENO in ex. Linear border. REF: SNG Morcom 77 = BM no. 2013,4030.10*.

145. AE Unit, 6.51g, 18mm	**317 to 280 BC**
	OBV: Head of Apollo facing left, wearing laurel wreath with leaves in opposing pairs, CALENO before, (M?) behind. Dotted border. REV: Acheloios Savo as man-faced bull standing right on single line, head facing, lyre above, X below, CALENO in ex. Linear border. REF: SNG Cop.317; SNG France 455 = BnF N3641*.

146. AE Unit, 5.71g, 22mm	**317 to 280 BC**
	OBV: Head of Apollo facing left, wearing laurel wreath with leaves in opposing pairs, fly behind, CALENO before. Dotted border. REV: Acheloios Savo as man-faced bull standing right on single line, head facing, lyre above, X below, CALENO in ex. Linear border. REF: SNG Budapest 384 (incorrectly attributed to Compulteria); Artemide XXXVI, lot 19*.

147. AE Unit, 6.81g, 22mm	**317 to 280 BC**
	OBV: Head of Apollo facing left, wearing laurel wreath with leaves in opposing pairs, fly behind, CALENO before. Dotted border. REV: Acheloios Savo as man-faced bull standing right on single line, head facing, lyre above, Ω below, CALENO in ex. Linear border. REF: SNG Cop 313; NAC P, lot 1002*. *This is probably the coin described by Sambon 949 and BMC 20 (uncertain symbol behind Apollo).*

148. AE Unit	**317 to 280 BC**
 	OBV: Head of Apollo facing left, wearing laurel wreath with leaves in opposing pairs, club behind. Dotted border (?). REV: Acheloios Savo as man-faced bull standing right on single line, head facing, lyre above, IΣ below, CALENO in ex. Linear border (?). REF: Sambon 950; Santangelo 685.

149. AE Unit, 7.62g	**317 to 280 BC**
	OBV: Head of Apollo facing left, wearing laurel wreath with leaves in opposing pairs, club behind, CALENO before. Dotted border. REV: Acheloios Savo as man-faced bull standing right on single line, head facing, lyre above, nothing below, IΣ in ex. Linear border. REF: Sambon 953 = Santangelo 686*.

150. AE Unit, 6.95g	**317 to 280 BC**
	OBV: Head of Apollo facing left, wearing laurel wreath with leaves in opposing pairs, Phrygian helmet behind, CALENO before. Dotted border. REV: Acheloios Savo as man-faced bull standing right on single line, head facing, lyre above, nothing below, IΣ in ex. Linear border. REF: Sambon 951; KM Berlin 41; Santangelo 687 SNG ANS 181 = Graziano 122*. *Sambon 951 incorrectly states 'IΣ below' as opposed to 'in ex.'*

151. AE Unit, 7.03g	**317 to 280 BC**
	OBV: Head of Apollo facing left, wearing laurel wreath with leaves in opposing pairs, dolphin behind oriented downward, CALENO before. Dotted border. REV: Acheloios Savo as man-faced bull standing right on single line, head facing, lyre above, nothing below, IΣ in ex. Linear border. REF: Sambon 952; BMC 16 (BM n.1851,0503.28); SNG France 462; Monetiere Archeol. Firenze, inv. n. 83146; Gorny & Mosch 147, lot 1074*.

PHASE II: (Apollo right/Lyre) c.280 to 272 BC

152. AE Unit, 6.09g, 20mm	**280 to 272 BC**
	OBV: Head of Apollo facing right, wearing laurel wreath with leaves in opposing pairs, grain ear behind, remnants of uncertain symbol (bird's head and neck?) before, no inscription. Dotted border. REV: Acheloios Savo as man-faced bull standing right on single line, head facing, lyre above, nothing below, CALENO in ex. Double linear border. REF: Artemide 21E, lot 19*.

153. AE Unit, 7.31g	**280 to 272 BC**
	OBV: Head of Apollo facing right, wearing laurel wreath with leaves in opposing pairs, no inscription before, grain ear behind. REV: Acheloios Savo as man-faced bull standing left, head facing, lyre above, cornucopia below, A in ex. REF: SNG Tubingen 336*.

154. AE Unit, 7.75g-8.81g	**280 to 272 BC**
	OBV: Head of Apollo facing right, wearing laurel wreath with leaves in opposing pairs, nothing behind, CALENO before (from top to bottom and in rough style). Dotted border. REV: Acheloios Savo as man-faced bull standing left, head facing, lyre above, cornucopia below, nothing in ex. REF: Sambon 920; Fiorelli 834; Moretti 46 = Graziano 132; Potamikon Collection (Photo by London Ancient Coins, Ltd.)*. *Sambon listed the variant as Fiorelli 834, and mentions a grain ear behind Apollo, but in Fiorelli's catalog there is no mention of that symbol. Moretti 46 shows the same rough features of CALENO.*

155. AE Unit, 5.62g	**280 to 272 BC**
	OBV: Head of Apollo facing right, wearing laurel wreath with leaves in opposing pairs, uncertain symbol behind (thyrsus or corn-ear?), CALENO before. REV: Acheloios Savo as man-faced bull standing right on single line, head facing, lyre above, nothing below, CALENO in ex. REF: BM no.1938, 1007.218.

156. AE Unit, 4.23g, 16mm	**280 to 272 BC**
	OBV: Head of Apollo facing right, wearing laurel wreath with leaves in opposing pairs, CALENO before, nothing behind. Dotted border surrounded by linear border. REV: Acheloios Savo as man-faced bull standing to right on single line, head facing, lyre above, CALENO in ex., uncertain symbol (A?) below. Dotted border. REF: Sambon 919; Fiorelli 835; SNG Cop. 319 (not illustrated); KM Berlin 30; SNG France 447 = BnF 1966.453; Potamikon Collection*.

157. AE Unit, 3.52g, 15mm	**280 to 272 BC**
	OBV: Head of Apollo facing right, wearing laurel wreath with leaves in opposing pairs, CALENO (written from top to bottom) before, uncertain symbol behind, if any. Dotted border. REV: Acheloios Savo as man-faced bull standing to right on single line, head facing, lyre above, exergue off flan. Dotted border. REF: SNG ANS 182. *If a star behind (area is off-flan on the known specimens) then this would be the same as the next coin.*

158. AE Unit	**280 to 272 BC**
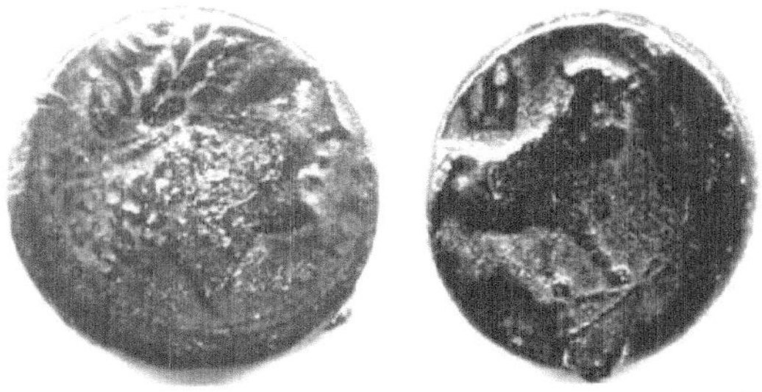	OBV: Head of Apollo facing right, wearing laurel wreath with leaves in opposing pairs, star with 8 rays behind, CALENO before (written from top to bottom). Double dotted border. REV: Acheloios Savo as man-faced bull standing to right on single line, head facing, lyre above, uncertain symbol below, if any, CALENO in ex. Dotted border. REF: SNG Firenze 181; Graziano 129*.

159. AE Unit, 5.22g	**280 to 272 BC**
	OBV: Head of Apollo facing right, wearing laurel wreath with leaves in opposing pairs, CALENO before. Dotted border. REV: Acheloios Savo as man-faced bull standing right on single line, head facing, lyre above, uncertain letter (Σ?) below, CALENO in ex. Dotted border. REF: Graziano 131*.

PHASE III: c.272 to 250 BC

GROUP IIIA

160. AE Unit, 5.90g	**c.272 to 250 BC**
	OBV: Head of Apollo facing left, wearing laurel wreath with leaves in opposing pairs, CALENO before. REV: Acheloios Savo as man-faced bull standing right on single line, head facing, A below. Dotted border. REF: Sambon 968; SNG France 469 = BnF Fonds Général 189*. *Apparently Unique*

GROUP IIIB

161. AE Unit, 6.14g, 20mm	**272 to 250 BC**
	OBV: Head of Apollo facing left, wearing laurel wreath with leaves in opposing pairs. Dotted border. REV: Acheloios Savo as a man-faced bull standing to right on single line, head facing, winged nymph above, CALENO in ex. REF: Sambon 969; Fiorelli 825-6; Hunterian 16-7; BMC 13; SNG Morcom 83; SNG München 152; CNG 60, lot 30*. *Torino 623 lists the head of Apollo to right, probably in error.*

162. AE Unit, 6.85g	**272 to 250 BC**
	OBV: Head of Apollo facing left, wearing laurel wreath with leaves in opposing pairs, club behind, CALENO before. Dotted border. REV: Acheloios Savo as a man-faced bull standing to right on single line, head facing, winged nymph above, CALENO in ex. Linear border. REF: SNG Budapest 367 = Graziano 142*. *Incorrectly described with 'shield behind'.*

163. AE Unit, 6.34g	**272 to 250 BC**
	OBV: Head of Apollo facing left, wearing laurel wreath with leaves in opposing pairs, shield behind. Dotted border. REV: Acheloios Savo as a man-faced bull standing to right on single line, head facing, winged nymph above, CALENO in ex. REF: Sambon 970; Fiorelli 827-33; Santangelo 682-3; KM Berlin 49-52; H.D. Rauch GmbH 85, lot 53*. *This is the most common issue from Cales. The large number of extant specimens indicates it is linked to military efforts during the first Punic War. See narrative above for references to additional specimens.*

164. AE Unit, 5.69g, 20mm	**272 to 250 BC**
	OBV: Head of Apollo facing left, wearing laurel wreath with leaves in opposing pairs, shield behind . Dotted border. REV: Acheloios Savo as a man-faced bull standing to right on single line, head facing, winged nymph above, A below, CALENO in ex. REF: Sambon 971; Santangelo 684; KM Berlin 53; Walter Holt's Old Money, Vcoins SKU 490359*.

165. AE Unit	**272 to 250 BC**
	OBV: Head of Apollo facing left, wearing laurel wreath with leaves in opposing pairs, shield behind. Dotted border. REV: Acheloios Savo as a man-faced bull standing to right on single line, head facing, winged nymph above, Z below, CALENO in ex. REF: Sambon 972; Carelli, LXVIII, 35*.

166. AE Unit 6.70g, 17mm	**272 to 250 BC**
	OBV: Head of Apollo facing left, wearing laurel wreath with leaves in opposing pairs, shield behind. Dotted border. REV: Acheloios Savo as a man-faced bull standing to right on single line, head facing, winged nymph above, uncertain letter (retrograde N?) below, CALENO in ex. Linear border. REF: Babelon-De Luynes 69 = SNG France 474 = BnF Luynes 69*.

167. AE Unit	**272 to 250 BC**
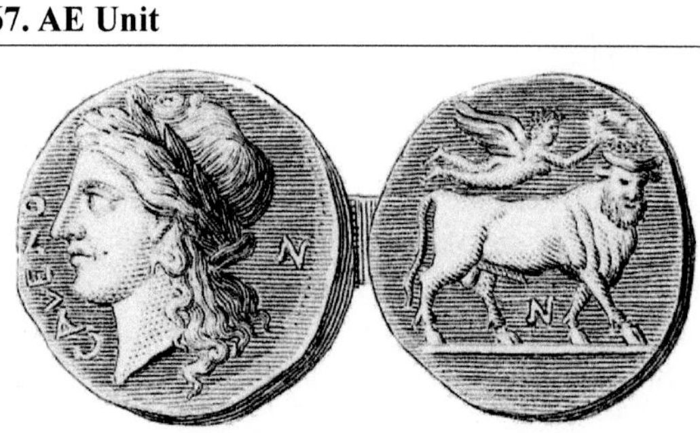	OBV: Head of Apollo facing left, wearing laurel wreath with leaves in opposing pairs, CALENO before, N behind. Dotted border. REV: Acheloios Savo as a man-faced bull standing to right on single line, head facing, winged nymph above, N below, CALENO in ex. REF: Sambon 973; Carelli, LXVII, 36*.

168. AE Unit, unrecorded weight	272 to 250 BC
	OBV: Head of Apollo facing left, wearing laurel wreath with leaves in opposing pairs, CALENO before, N behind. Dotted border. REV: Acheloios Savo as a man-faced bull standing to right on single line, head facing, winged nymph above, Π below. REF: HM Frankfurt 39; Graziano 147*.

UNCERTAIN: CALES?

169. AE Unit, 20mm	272 to 250 BC
	OBV: Head of Apollo facing left, wearing laurel wreath with leaves in opposing pairs, A rotated 45 degrees counterclockwise behind. Dotted border. REV: Acheloios Savo as a man-faced bull standing right on single line, head facing, winged nymph above, nothing below. REF: BM no. EH,p59.12.Cal = BMC 25*. *Despite the BMC attribution to Cales, it is ultimately uncertain as there is no ethnic and could be from another Samnite or Campanian mint. However, the existence of a similar obverse type with ethnic (no. 139) makes the attribution to Cales probable.*

170. AE Unit, 22mm	272 to 250 BC
	OBV: Head of Apollo facing left, wearing laurel wreath with leaves in opposing pairs, (CALENO?) before, uncertain symbol (A?) behind. Dotted border. REV: Acheloios Savo as a man-faced bull standing right on single line, head facing, winged nymph above, M below. REF: Heritage Auctions, 2004 June HWCA, part of lot 12427*.

COMPULTERIA

Compulteria, or Cubulteria,[62] was a Samnite city whose exact location has not yet been established. The most likely hypothesis is that it was located at Località San Ferdinando in the area of modern-day Alvignano, where today there is a medieval church whose original name was Santa Maria de Cubultere. Also in this location archaeologists found traces of Latin inscriptions, further indicating it is the ancient Compulteria.[63]

The only coinage issued by Compulteria features a man-faced bull and is dated after the end of the Pyrrhic War,[64] when the Samnite center came under the control of Rome and became a *civitas foederata.*[65]

Coinage

The coins show a retrograde inscription in Oscan letters: ꟽVИKƎT√ƎΠV⋊, transliterated as KUPELTERNUM. According to Mommsen, this is the genitive plural: 'of the citizens of Compulteria'.[66]

Because the town was situated on the upper Volturnus, the man-faced bull can be identified as Acheloios Volturnus. Like other mints in the area, the IΣ control mark indicates the man-faced bull is a sinew of Acheloios.[67]

171. AE Unit, 4.47g	**272 to 250 BC**
	OBV: Head of Apollo facing left, wearing laurel wreath with leaves in opposing pairs, oval shield behind, ꟽVИ⊲ƎT√ƎΠV⋊ before. Dotted border. REV: Acheloios Volturnus as a man-faced bull standing to right on single line, head facing, winged nymph above, nothing below. REF: Sambon 1069; BMC 3; Graziano 2*.

172. AE Unit	**272 to 250 BC**
	OBV: Head of Apollo facing left, wearing laurel wreath with leaves in opposing pairs, uncertain symbol (O or shield?) behind, ꟽVИ ⊲ƎT√ƎΠV⋊ before. Dotted border. REV: Acheloios Volturnus as a man-faced bull standing to right on single line, head facing, winged nymph above, ⋊ below. REF: Graziano 7*.

173. AE Unit, 5.10g, 18mm	**272 to 250 BC**
	OBV: Head of Apollo facing left, wearing laurel wreath with leaves in opposing pairs, uncertain symbol behind (if any), ꟽVИ⊲ƎT√ƎΠV⋊ before. Dotted border. REV: Acheloios Volturnus as a man-faced bull standing to right on single line, head facing, winged nymph above, M below. REF: SNG France 542 = BnF Fonds général 214*.

[62] The city is named 'Compulteria' by Livy (*Ab Urbe Condita Libri*, 24.20.4), but the inhabitants are named 'Cubulterini' by Pliny the Elder (*Naturalis Historia*, 3.63).
[63] G. Cera , 'Il territorio di Cubulteria,' in *Carta archeologica e ricerche in Campania*, Parte 1 (Roma: 2004), 204 ff.
[64] Ibid., 203.
[65] Ibid., 195.
[66] T. Mommsen, 'Sulle desinenze delle epigrafi nelle monete osche,' in *Annali di Numismatica*,Vol.I (Roma: 1846), 38. See also M. Nassa and V. Nassa, *Cubulteria. Ragguagli sulla moneta attribuitagli e sul controverso simbolo del toro andropros opo*, 225 (Cubulteria). We kindly thank Mario Nassa for providing us a copy of the manuscript.
[67] Discussed in Chpt. 4 and 7, but see index listings for 'Sinews' and 'IΣ' for particular pages.

174. AE Unit, 4.8g, 19mm | **272 to 250 BC**

OBV: Head of Apollo facing left, wearing laurel wreath with leaves in opposing pairs, nothing behind, (ᛘVИ⊲ƎT⊳Ǝ)ΠVꓘ before. Dotted border (?).
REV: Acheloios Volturnus as a man-faced bull standing to right on single line, head facing, winged nymph above, N below.
REF: Forum ancient coins item n.GB39084* (incorrectly attributed to Nola).

175. AE Unit, 5.31g, 20mm | **272 to 250 BC**

OBV: Head of Apollo facing left, wearing laurel wreath with leaves in opposing pairs, nothing behind, ᛘVИ⊲ƎT⊳ƎΠVꓘ before.
REV: Acheloios Volturnus as a man-faced bull standing to right on single line, head facing, winged nymph above, IΣ below.
REF: Auctiones GmbH, eAuction 17, lot 3*.

176. AE Unit, 3.99g, 20mm | **272 to 250 BC**

OBV: Head of Apollo facing left, wearing laurel wreath with leaves in opposing pairs, I behind, ᛘVИ⊲ƎT⊳ƎΠVꓘ before. Dotted border.
REV: Acheloios Volturnus as a man-faced bull standing to right on single line, head facing, winged nymph above, IΣ below.
REF: Sambon 1070; Santangelo 785; KM Berlin 8-9; SNG Gale 42-3; SNG Milano 57; M&M GmbH 13, lot 23*.

177. AE Unit, 5.99g | **272 to 250 BC**

OBV: Head of Apollo facing left, wearing laurel wreath with leaves in opposing pairs, O behind, ᛘVИ⊲ƎT⊳ƎΠVꓘ before. Dotted border.
REV: Acheloios Volturnus as a man-faced bull standing to right on single line, head facing, winged nymph above, IΣ below.
REF: Sambon 1071; Fiorelli 907-9; KM Berlin 8-9; Lindgren 192; SNG Evelpidis 50; SNG Cop.356; SNG Milano 52; SNG France 542-6; NAC 59, lot 1531*.

178. AE Unit, 4.96g | **272 to 250 BC**

OBV: Head of Apollo facing left, wearing laurel wreath with leaves in opposing pairs, O behind, ᛘVИ⊲ƎT⊳ƎΠVꓘ before. Dotted border.
REV: Acheloios Volturnus as a man-faced bull standing to right on single line, head facing, winged nymph above, nothing below.
REF: Sambon 1066; Santangelo 781-2; SNG Budapest 383; SNG Milano 53; NAC 72, lot 818*.

179. AE Unit, 7.41g, 18mm	**268 to 240 BC**
	OBV: Head of Apollo facing left, wearing laurel wreath with leaves in opposing pairs, O behind, nothing before. Dotted border. REV: Acheloios Volturnus as a man-faced bull standing to right on single line, head facing, winged nymph above, ꟽVИꓷƎTꓶƎПVꓘ in ex. REF: Sambon 1072; Santangelo 790; SNG Morcom 96; SNG France 547; LAC 23, lot 7*.

180. AE Unit	**268 to 240 BC**
	OBV: Head of Apollo facing left, wearing laurel wreath with leaves in opposing pairs, O behind, nothing before. Dotted border. REV: Acheloios Volturnus as a man-faced bull standing to right on single line, head facing, winged nymph above, IΣ below, ꟽVИꓷƎTꓶƎПVꓘ in ex. REF: Sambon 1073 = J. Friedlaender, *Die osckischen münzen*, Pl. I, n2.

181. AE Unit, 6.32g	**268 to 240 BC**
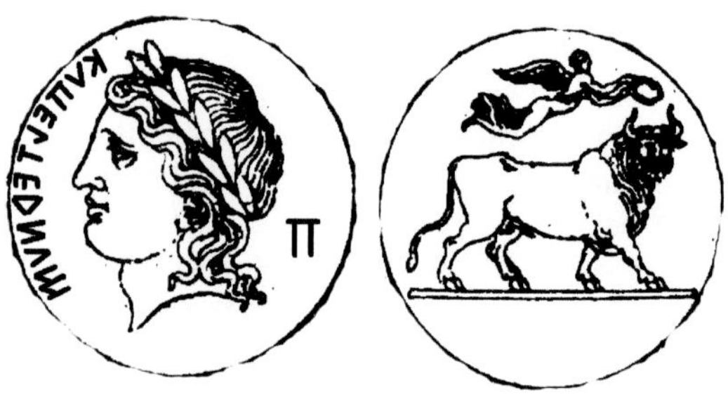	OBV: Head of Apollo facing left, wearing laurel wreath with leaves in opposing pairs, ꟽVИꓷƎTꓶƎПVꓘ before, Π or M behind. Dotted border. REV: Acheloios Volturnus as a man-faced bull standing to right on single line, head facing, winged nymph above. REF: Sambon 1067; Fiorelli 910-13; KM Berlin 11; SNG ANS 229.

182. AE Unit, 5.20-5.50g	**268 to 240 BC**
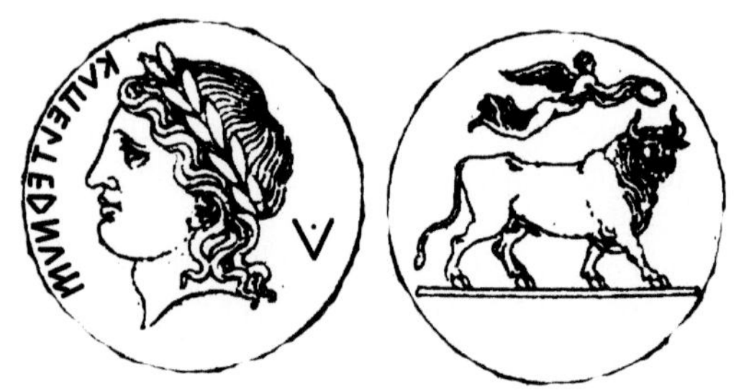	OBV: Head of Apollo facing left, wearing laurel wreath with leaves in opposing pairs, ꟽVИꓷƎTꓶƎПVꓘ before, V̇ behind. Dotted border. REV: Acheloios Volturnus as a man-faced bull standing to right on single line, head facing, winged nymph above. REF: Sambon 1068; Santangelo 783; KM Berlin 1-2.

IRNTHI

The man-faced bull issues from Irnthi are among the most enigmatic of the Campanian area, both for the uncertain location of the mint, and for the problems posed by the inscription: IÐN⊗H (or variant). It is certainly not Greek. It is generally believed to be Oscan by numismatists and collectors,[68] though the sign ⊗ (crossed Theta) does not appear on any known Oscan epigraph,[69] while it is present in the archaic Greek and Etruscan alphabets.[70] The sign Ð, likewise Oscan, is the Etruscan for 'Rho,' too. However, the problem with labeling the inscription as Etruscan is that in Etruscan epigraphy the sign ⊗ was no longer in use after the 6th century BC,[71] while the bronze coins in question cannot have been issued before the second half of the 4th century. In fact, the archaeological finds in graves are all datable to the 4th and 3rd centuries.[72] Ultimately, when we look at the coinage of Irnthi we have a coin from the late 4th century BC that employs an Etruscan alphabet out of use since the 6th century BC. Moreover, it was probably minted in a location that was under Etruscan influence in previous centuries but at the time of issue was probably under Samnite influence,[73] assuming that the place in question was the Sorrento peninsula (as we propose below).

In terms of earlier scholarship, it was G. Fiorelli[74] who argues the inscription and its variants belong to the ancient city of Irnum (modern-day Fratte, near Salerno), on the banks of the Irnum River. However, as reported by Attilio Stazio,[75] the connection of the mint to Irnum is not based on any archaeological evidence, but only on the existence of a river named Irno, which at the time of Fiorelli (1854) ran just south of Salerno. This prompted the antiquarian to postulate the existence of an eponymous town along the river. Fiorelli's thesis was accepted without reserve and resumed by almost all scholars that followed: R. Garrucci,[76] B. V. Head,[77] A. Sambon,[78] etc.

On the other hand, K. J. Beloch[79] located the city in Picenum, suggesting the name of Arinthe or Arnthe, as mentioned by Hecataeus. However, Hecataeus, whose fragments come to us from Stephanus Byzantius, wrote of Arinthe as an Oenotrian city in inland south Italy,[80] thus making Beloch's hypothesis very unlikely.

Later, V. Panebianco,[81] based on the thesis of Fiorelli, went so far as to derive the name of Salerno from 'Salum Irni' (the port of Irnum). However, P. Zancani Montuoro[82] proved beyond any doubt that the name of the Irno River is medieval, derived from the corruption of the ancient name of the Leirionos/Lirinus River, becoming, in Italian, 'L'Irno' ('the Irno'). Thus, the main argument in favor of the supposed existence of a city named Irnum has no consistent basis.

As a possible alternative to Irnum, in 1836 Avellino formulated a new hypothesis, ignored by his contemporaries and many later scholars, such as Sambon. In short, Avellino proposed to interpret 'IRNTHI' as corresponding to 'sIReNTHI', modern-day Sorrento.[83] Even if Avellino's etymological hypothesis is not

[68] The sign Ð is the Oscan for 'Rho'.

[69] G. Colonna, 'Nuovi dati epigrafici sulla protostoria della Campania,' in *Atti della XVII riunione scientifica Dell'Istituto Itaiano di preistoria e protostoria* (Firenze: 1975), 151ff; A. Morandi, *Epigrafia Italica. Guida alle scritture e alle lingue dell'Italia antica preromana* (Roma: 1982); R. Antonini, 'Materiali per un'indagine preliminare sull'alfabeto osco. Documenti, problemi, prospettive concernenti la riforma,' in *Quaderni dell'Istituto di Linguistica dell'Università di Urbino,* Vol.6 (Urbino: 1989), 33-91; M.H. Crawford, et al., *Imagines Italicae: a corpus of Italic inscriptions* (London: 2011). The only non-Etruscan Italic alphabet in which the crossed theta is attested on inscriptions dated from the 6th to 5th century BC is Messapian, cf. C. De Simone, 'Per una cronologia delle iscrizioni messapiche,' in *Studi Salentini*, Vol.23 (Lecce: 1966), 325.

[70] ⊗ was originally the sign for the Phoenician letter *Teth*, first appearing on Semitic texts dating to the early 1st millennium BC (O. Goldwasser, and J. Naveh, 'The origin of the Tet-Symbol,' in *Israel Exploration Journal*, 26 (Jerusalem: 1976), 16). During the 7th century BC the sign was adopted for the letter *theta* in southern Aegean islands and Etruria (for Greece, see: R.D. Woodard, 'Phoinikeia grammata: an alphabet for the Greek language,' in *A companion to the ancient Greek language*, edited by E.J. Bakker (Oxford: 2010), 26ff. For Etruria, see: D.F. Maras, 'Le iscrizioni,' in *Il museo delle Antichità Etrusche e Italiche*, Vol.II, edited by G.M. Benedettini (Roma: 2007), 555, no.28 and no.105). The sign was probably not adopted into the Oscan alphabet, itself derived from Etruscan and Greek influences, as the Oscan language lacks the corresponding aspirate sound (A. Ventriglia, 'L'Osco: un esempio perfetto di integrazione etnica e culturale,' in *Seminario Scuola Normale Superiore di Pisa, 22 giugno 2010*, Congress Presentation).

[71] It was used especially in southern Etruria and Etruscan Campania, where, except for the case of Irnthi, it was abandoned during the 6th century BC and replaced by the dotted *theta* (C. Pellegrino, 'Pontecagnano: la scrittura e l'onomastica in una comunità etrusca di frontiera,' in *La colonizzazione etrusca in Italia. Atti del XV Convegno Internazionale di Studi sulla Storia e l'Archeologia dell'Etruria*, edited by G. Della Fina (Roma: 2008), 427).

[72] A. Stazio, 'Monete a leggenda Irnthi,' in *Scritti di Numismatica* (Taranto-Foggia: 2011), 394ff; R. Cantilena, 'Presenza e funzioni della moneta nelle Chorai delle colonie greche della Campania,' in *Presenza e funzioni della moneta nelle chorai delle colonie greche dall'Iberia al Mar Nero*, Atti del XII Convegno organizzato dall'Università 'Federico II' e dal Centro Internazionale di Studi Numismatici (Roma: 2004), 171-193.

[73] A. Stazio, 'Monete a leggenda Irnthi,' 397.

[74] G. Fiorelli, *Monete Inedite dell'Italia Antica* (Napoli: 1845), 4.

[75] A. Stazio, 'Monete a leggenda Irnthi,' 394ff.

[76] R. Garrucci, *Le monete della Italia Antica, raccolta generale del P. Raffaele Garrucci. Parte seconda: monete coniate*, (Roma: 1885).

[77] B.V. Head, *Historia Numorum: A Manual of Greek Numismatics* (Oxford: 1887), 43.

[78] A. Sambon, 'Les monnaies antiques de l'Italie,' 337.

[79] K.J. Beloch, 'Sulla confederazione nocerina,' in *Archivio storico per le province napoletane* (Napoli: 1877), 285-298.

[80] Stephanus Byzantius, *Fragmenta*, 64.

[81] V. Panebianco, *La colonia Romana di Salernum* (Salerno: 1945), 14ff.

[82] P. Zancani Montuoro, 'Il fiume Lirino,' in *La Parola del Passato*, Vol.IV (Napoli: 1949), 61-68.

[83] F.M. Avellino, 'Secondo saggio di osservazioni numismatiche, Hyrium,' in *Opuscoli diversi. Tomo III* (Napoli: 1836), 109-114.

perfectly accurate (the ancient name was Syrrentón),[84] the documented findings seem to support his intuition. In fact, the map featured after the catalog of coins from Irnthi shows find spots and includes the number of specimens found at each location. The map is built with information from A. Sambon, A. Stazio, M. Russo, R. Cantilena, and P. Zancani Montuoro,[85] plus unpublished discussions with A. Campana and G. Benevento. Most of the finds are actually located on the Sorrento Peninsula or close by, which supports Avellino's original hypothesis, which was later resumed by Zancani Montuoro in 1949.[86]

The most likely location for the mint itself is the site of Punta Campanella, where according to ancient sources there once stood a sanctuary dedicated to Athena. In this case the issue in question might have been motivated by the needs of the sanctuary itself.[87] This sanctuary enjoyed its own autonomy[88] and was a multiethnic and multilingual site,[89] essentially a center for gatherings of people belonging to different cultures.[90] Interestingly, the coin finds in the area, which include coins from Panormos and other Punic mints,[91] suggest that the site was a place of passage and likely facilitated the recruitment of Campanian mercenaries by Sicilian and Punic rulers.

In terms of the actual coins, there are two main types featuring the man-faced bull standing either right or left, with several variants known for the inscription. Altogether, there are about 100 extant specimens. They must have been struck shortly after the mid 4th century BC, because Libero Mangieri records that some specimens were discovered in burials dated to 340 BC.[92] The mint probably ceased issuing these coins after the Romans conquered the Sorrento peninsula between 309 and 307 BC.[93] The denomination is best described as a half-unit in comparison to other Campanian mints issuing bronze coinage of the man-faced bull.

The identity of the man-faced bull featured on this coinage is difficult to state with certainty, since there are no reports of the names of the waterways running through the area (whose hydrography also changed significantly over the centuries due to the geographic features of the territory). In this catalog, we will call him Acheloios Syrrentón, assuming the town borrowed its name from the local water source.

[84] The ancient name of modern day Sorrento was not Sirenthi, but Syrrentón, coming from the Greek verb *syrréo*, 'to flow', in reference to the waters flowing down from the nearby narrow valleys (P. Zancani Montuoro, 'Συρρεντόν Surrentum-Sorrento,' in *Annali dell'Università degli Studi di Napoli 'L'Orientale'*, Rivista del Dipartimento del mondo classico. Sezione Linguistica, n.6 (Napoli,1985), 313ff.

[85] A. Sambon, 'Les monnaies antiques de l'Italie,' 337; A. Stazio, 'Monete a leggenda Irnthi,' 394ff; P. Zancani Montuoro, 'Riepilogo sui rinvenimenti e sul culto del santuario,' in *Punta della Campanella. Epigrafe rupestre osca e reperti vari dell'Athenaion* (Roma: Accademia Nazionale dei Lincei., 1990) 257-259.; R. Cantilena, 'Presenza e funzioni della moneta,' 171-193; R. Cantilena, 'La moneta in Penisola sorrentina tra IV e III sec. a.C.: dati acquisiti e problemi aperti,' in Sorrento e la Penisola Sorrentina tra Italici, etruschi e Greci nel contesto della Campania antica, edited by F. Senatore and M. Russo (Roma: 2010), 201-222.

[86] P. Zancani Montuoro, 'Il fiume Lirino,' 61-68. The hypothesis was also resumed by R. Cantilena, 'La moneta in Penisola sorrentina,' 201-222. Cantilena also advanced the idea that the mint of Irnthi was the same mint that, earlier, issued silver coinage of the man-faced bull with legends Hyrietes and Yrina, commonly attributed to the unknown mint of Hyria (ibid., 202ff.).

[87] A. Stazio, 'Monete a leggenda Irnthi,' 397.

[88] Ibid.

[89] R. Cantilena, 'La moneta in Penisola sorrentina,' 207.

[90] An appealing explanation for this numismatic and epigraphic rebus is that the coinage of Irnthi is evidence of the historical-geographical phenomenon defined by Pellegrino as 'Samnite Tyrrhenia,' documented by the persistence of Etruscan epigraphic traditions in a territory occupied by the Samnites, characterized by the so-called 'modified Etruscan alphabet of the Sorrento Peninsula,' the use of which lasts from the beginning of the 5th to at least the end of the 4th century BC (C. Pellegrino, 'Pontecagnano: l'uso della scrittura tra Etruschi, Greci e Italici,' in *Meetings between cultures in the ancient Mediterranean, 17th International Congress of Classical Archaeology*, Bollettino di Archeologia Online I, Volume speciale F/F3/2 (Roma, 2010)). It is likely that the site of Punta Campanella, an important seaport and home to one of the most important temples of the Tyrrhenian Sea, could have maintained a certain political and cultural autonomy, perhaps because of the sacredness attributed to the site and despite the succession of rulers (Etruscans, Greeks, Oscans), thereby preserving characteristics of the archaic Etruscan use of the alphabet, and at the same time absorbing the different cultural influences of the people who later became involved in the region.

[91] Cf. R. Cantilena, 'La moneta in Penisola sorrentina,' 216, in particular footnotes 50 and 51.

[92] G. Libero Mangieri, 'Problemi di circolazione monetaria a Nuceria Alfaterna dall'età classica a quella imperiale,' in *Nuceria Alfaterna e il suo territorio. Dalla fondazione ai Longobardi*. Vol.II, edited by A. Pecoraro (Salerno: 1994), 22.

[93] R. Cantilena, 'La moneta in Penisola sorrentina,' 215.

Coinage

183. AE half unit 3.15g, 15mm	340 to 309 BC
	OBV: Head of Apollo facing right, wearing laurel wreath with leaves in triple clusters. REV: Acheloios Syrrentón as a man-faced bull standing to left on single line, head forward and in profile, IDN⊗H above REF: Fiorelli 962; BMC 1-2; Stazio 1-2; SNG Morcom 97; SNG München 200-202; Sambon 848 and 849b; SNG Cop 596-7; SNG Milano 83-4; Weber 417-9; KM Berlin 1-6; SNG Dreer 102; SNG ANS 274-275; SNG France 632 = BnF Fonds général 250*. *Sambon 848 (IDN⊗H) and 849b (IDN⊗ ⊢) are the same variety. Examination of the cited specimens reveals that the H appears in various states of preservation, which Sambon took to be different letters entirely.*

184. AE half unit, 3.32g	340 to 309 BC
	OBV: Head of Apollo facing right, wearing laurel wreath with leaves in triple clusters. REV: Acheloios Syrrentón as a man-faced bull standing to left on single line, head forward and in profile, IDN⊗I⊣ above. REF: Sambon 849a, BnF Fonds général 251*.

185. AE half unit 2.98g, 16mm	340 to 309 BC
	OBV: Head of Apollo facing right, wearing laurel wreath with leaves in triple clusters. REV: Acheloios Syrrentón as a man-faced bull standing to left on single line, head down and in profile, I ᗡ⊗ИH above. REF: CNG eAuction 130, lot 24*.

186. AE half unit	340 to 309 BC
	OBV: Head of Apollo facing right, wearing laurel wreath with leaves in triple clusters. REV: Acheloios Syrrentón as a man-faced bull standing to left on single line, head down and in profile, IDN⊗NI? above. REF: Sambon 849d. Digitally reconfigured line drawing adapted from Sambon*. *Unconfirmed. This might be the same variety as the last coin but Sambon did not record the N as retrograde (a detail he missed with the next coin) and the final H is obscured.*

187. AE half unit 3.16g, 14mm	**340 to 309 BC**
	OBV: Head of Apollo facing right, wearing laurel wreath with leaves in triple clusters. REV: Acheloios Syrrentón as a man-faced bull standing to left on single line, head down and in profile, ΙD⊗ИΗ above. REF: Sambon 849c, SNG France 634 = BnF Fonds général 249*. *Sambon does not record that the N is retrograde.*

188. AE half unit, 3.85g	**340 to 309 BC**
	OBV: Head of Apollo facing right, wearing laurel wreath with leaves in triple clusters. REV: Acheloios Syrrentón as a man-faced bull standing to left on single line, head forward and in profile, Ͱ⊗ИDΙ above. REF: BMC 5 (BM n. 1867,0101.98); Sambon 850 = KM Berlin 3, pl.VII, 104. Digitally reconfigured line drawing adapted from Sambon*.

189. AE 15mm, 3.0g	**340 to 309 BC**
	OBV: Head of Apollo facing right, wearing laurel wreath with leaves in triple clusters. REV: Acheloios Syrrentón as a man-faced bull standing to left on single line, head forward and in profile, Ι ⊗ Ν ⊗ (?) above. REF: Unique, discovered in May of 2013 at Fractanova in Campania.

190. AE 16mm, 3.52-4.0g	**340 to 309 BC**
	OBV: Head of Apollo facing right, wearing laurel wreath with leaves in triple clusters. REV: Acheloios Syrrentón as a man-faced bull standing to right on single line, head forward and in profile, ΙͰΝ⊗DΙ above. REF: Garrucci pl.XC, 7; Stazio 12; HD Rauch GmbH 92, lot 1024*.

Map of find spots

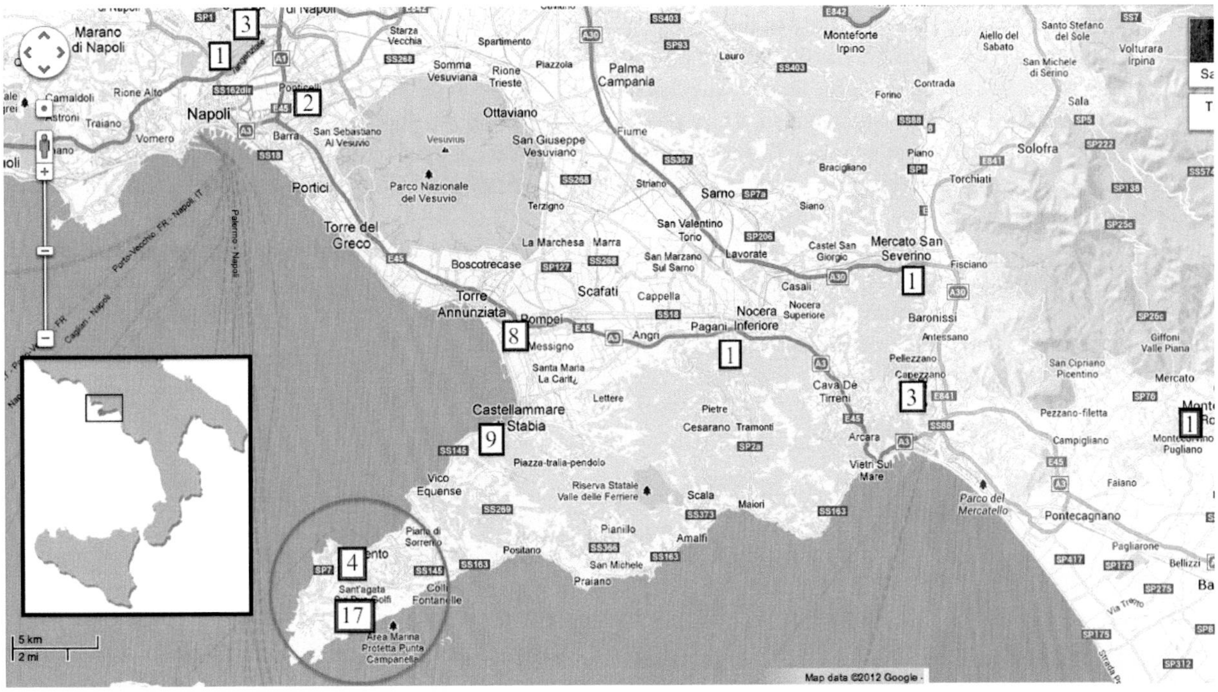

LARINUM

Larinum, the modern-day Larino, was a city of the Frentani[94] located in central eastern Italy in the valley of the Tifernum River[95] (modern Biferno). Archaeological excavations record that the earliest layers date back to the Archaic Age, but the city reached its peak of development during the 4th century BC. This was a time when the city had cultural exchanges with neighboring Daunia and Etruscan Campania.[96] Although they were defeated by Rome in 319 BC,[97] the Frentani later allied with the Romans in 304 BC, becoming *socii*. However, for unknown reasons Larinum was excluded from the treaty and remained an independent center, while retaining its ethnic identity linked to the Frentani.[98]

Larinum issued a significant amount of bronze coinage,[99] but only one issue copying Neapolitan types and depicting the man-faced bull. This was issued during the First Punic War.[100] This coin type is also the unique issue of Larinum bearing an inscription in Greek, all the other known types for the mint feature Oscan inscriptions. In total, only four specimens are known.[101]

As with other ancient cities featuring man-faced bulls on their coins, this one can be identified as the local manifestation of Acheloios: Acheloios Tifernum.

Coinage

191. AE Unit, 5.30g, 19mm	**272 to 250 BC**
	OBV: Head of Apollo facing left, wearing laurel wreath with leaves in opposing pairs, ΛΑΡΙΝΩΝ before. Dotted border. REV: Acheloios Tifernum as a man-faced bull standing to right on single line, head facing, winged nymph above. REF: Sambon 198; Fiorelli 748; Weber 244; BMC 1; HN Italy 622; Campana 1; Stelluti 86-89; CNG 61, Lot 5*.

Drawing from Sambon 198

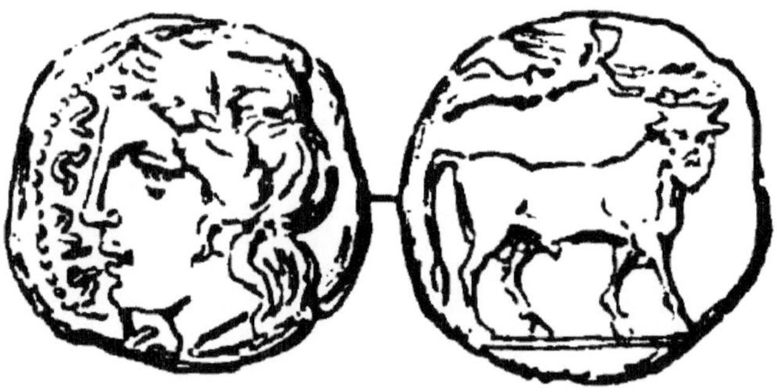

[94] Pliny, *Naturalis Historia*, 3.105. The Frentani were a population of Samnite ancestry (N. Stelluti, 'Monete della zecca di Frentrum, Larinum e Pallanum,' in *Proceedings of the 14th International Numismatic Congress, Glasgow 2009*, Vol.I, edited by N. Holmes (London: Spink, 2011), 1057).

[95] A Campana, 'Frentania: Larinum (268-208 a.C.),' in *Panorama Numismatico*, 79 (Serravalle: Nomisma, 1994), 257.

[96] Ibid.

[97] Livy, *Ab Urbe Condita Libri*, 9.16.1.

[98] A Campana, 'Frentania: Larinum (268-208 a.C.),' 257; A. Campana, 'Frentania: I Frentani (260-250 a.C.),' in *Panorama Numismatico*, 79 (Serravalle: Nomisma, 1994), 269.

[99] The main studies on the coinage of Larinum are those by Cantilena, Campana and Stelluti: R. Cantilena, 'Le emissioni monetali di Larino e dei Frentani,' in *Samnium, Archeologia del Molise* (Roma, 1991), 141-8; A Campana, 'Frentania: Larinum (268-208 a.C.),' 257-68; N. Stelluti, 'Monete della zecca di Frentrum, Larinum e Pallanum,' 1056-64.

[100] Rutter's *HN Italy* incorrectly states that the type from Larinum is 'paralleled at Neapolis in the issues before the introduction of the large symbols on the reverse (573)' (N.K. Rutter, *Historia Nummorum Italy*, 74, no.622). However, those types from Neapolis are dated c. 320 to 300 BC. What this should say is that this coin from Larinum coincides with the 'Nike' issues from Neapolis which, like the Larinum coins, were minted c. 272 to 250 BC.

[101] Weber 244; Fiorelli 748; British Museum n. 1840,1226.2; CNG Auction 61, Lot 5.

MALIES

The location of the ancient city issuing bronze coinage of the man-faced bull with the legend MALIEΣ is uncertain and still debated by scholars.[102] The coins are commonly attributed to the Samnite city of Maleventum before it became a Roman colony and changed its name to Beneventum.[103] However, this attribution is just an assumption by early antiquarians with no actual evidence to support it, since there is no surviving information from textual sources and the find spots are unknown for the few extant specimens.[104]

As a result, not all scholars agree the coinage of MALIEΣ is from Maleventum.[105] According to Campana, the most current belief is that Malies was a Samnite center totally distinct from Maleventum,[106] located on the hilly area of Montauro, on the right bank of the Volturno River, not far from Teanum Sidicinum and Cales.[107] In fact, Caiazza's description of the site where Malies was probably located suggests a possible etymological base in the Akkadian *melu* (hebraic *ma'ale*), meaning 'height, altitude'.[108]

It is interesting to note the presence of both Latin (L) and Greek (Σ) letters in the inscription, which indicates the different cultural influences operative in the formation and establishment of the city.

Two different man-faced bull types are known from Malies. The first coin below, no.192, is known from a single specimen published by Garrucci, once part of the Minervini collection and now lost. It depicts the head of Apollo right on obverse and a man-faced bull on the reverse, with a Phrygian helmet above and the inscription MAᛚIEΣ under the exergue line. There is a clear resemblance with a type from Neapolis dating between 310 and 270 BC, with an identical helmet (Taliercio, IIa, n.26/ MSP I, 253).

On the contemporaneous issue (no. 193) the inscription moves to the obverse. It depicts a female head right, perhaps the personification of the city.[109] On the reverse we again see a man-faced bull to right, head facing, with a bearded head above, commonly identified as the head of Silenos. However, a similar type from Phaselis features the head of Herakles during his struggle with Acheloios, so perhaps this head, too, represents Herakles.

The man-faced bull on the coinage of Malies is probably Acheloios Volturnus.

Coinage

192. AE Unit	**310 to 270 BC**
	OBV: Head of Apollo to right. Dotted border. REV: Acheloios Volturnus as a man-faced bull standing to right on single line, head facing, Phrygian helmet above, MAᛚIEΣ in ex. Dotted border. REF: Sambon 190 = Campana 1 = Garrucci Pl.XC, n.13* (redrawn).

[102] A valuable update of the related literature has been recently published by Alberto Campana (A. Campana, 'Aggiornamento al Corpus Nummorum Antiquae Italiae. Samnium: Malies (300-275 a.C.),' in *Popoli dell'Italia antica. Gentes Fortissimae Italiae. Samnium, Latium et Campania. Le antiche città scomparse.* Atti del II Convegno San Vittore del Lazio, 28 ottobre, 2007. Quaderni di Studi II dell'Associazione Culturale Italia Numismatica (Cassino: 2007), 267-271.

[103] This hypothesis, albeit tentative, was proposed by A. Sambon and B.V. Head, and later resumed by many scholars, such as K. Rutter (*HN Italy*, 59).

[104] Basing the attribution purely on a toponomastic point of view, the legend could indeed refer to several centers in the area between Campania and Samnium, like modern-day Malegno, Pietra Melara, Melito di Napoli, Melito Irpino, Melizzano, etc.

[105] N. Borrelli, 'Le monete di Malies,' in *Numismatica e Scienze affini* (Roma: Santamaria, 1935), 5-7; E.T. Salmon, *Il Sannio e i Sanniti* (Torino: 1985), 82; A. Campana, 'Samnium: Malies (300-275 a.C.),' 267.

[106] A. Campana, 'Samnium: Malies (300-275 a.C.),' 267.

[107] For an extensive dissertation, see: D. Caiazza, 'Contributo per l'identificazione dei siti di Phistelia e Malies,' in *Popoli dell'Italia antica. Gentes Fortissimae Italiae. Samnium, Latium et Campania. Le antiche città scomparse.* Atti del II Convegno San Vittore del Lazio, 28 ottobre, 2007. Quaderni di Studi II dell'Associazione Culturale Italia Numismatica (Cassino: 2007), 185-231.

[108] G. Semerano, *Le Origini della Cultura Europea. Vol. II*, 465.

[109] A. Campana, 'Aggiornamento al Corpus Nummorum Antiquae Italiae,' 269.

193. AE Unit, 4.07g	310-270 BC
	OBV: Female head to right, hair in sakkos, MALIEΣ before. Dotted border. REV: Acheoios Volturnus as a man-faced bull standing to right on single line, head facing, mask of Silenos or Herakles above. Linear border. REF: Sambon 191; KM Berlin 1; SNG Cop 265; BnF Fonds général 92; BMC p.127 n.6; Santangelo 417-8, 417 = Campana 2*.

BnF Fonds général 266, Silver Stater from Phaselis

METAPONTION

This coin was not included in Noe's *The Coinage of Metapontum* or even *HN Italy*, though Rutter says the omission was for no specific reason.[110] It is included in the main catalog here because the illustration appears to copy a real coin with clear inscription. Moreover, the only other man-faced bull coinage from Metapontion, a silver diobol from c. 440 to 430 BC, also pairs the figure with a grain ear.[111]

Interestingly, the single man-faced bull issue of the Brettii might have been minted by Metapontion refugees in Bruttium (or at Metapontion for the Brettii), and on that issue we also see the man-faced bull paired with grain ear and leaf.[112]

Acheloios appears in 'human form but with a bull's head' on a rare issue from Metapontion, with the inscription AXELOIO AEΘLON, and somewhat matching the description from Sophocles.[113] However, as seen on the clearest example, the BnF De Luynes specimen, it is actually a man with some bovine features, namely horns and ears, but the eyes and nose are clearly human.

On this bronze issue and the aforementioned silver issue with man-faced bull head, the figure is certainly Acheloios, whose cult was well known in Metapontion.[114] The local river was the Casuention, so he was probably worshipped as Acheloios Casuention.

194. AE Unit, Unrecorded Weight	3rd Cent. BC?
	OBV: Forepart of Acheloios Casuention as a man-faced bull to left, head in profile, METAP above. REV: Ear of barley and leaf. REF: Garrucci, p. 139, No. 7* (redrawn).

BnF De Luynes 466

[110] Personal correspondence, mid 2014.

[111] N.K. Rutter, *HN Italy*, 132, no. 1492.

[112] Cf. MSP I, 75. It is doubtful Garrucci confused the two, since this coin shows a forepart, not a head, and in the opposite direction (to left, not right). The inscription, too, is entirely different.

[113] Cf. Sophochles, *Trachiniae*, 1.10-14. 'Now ox-faced with human trunk,' –Sir Richard Jebb translation.

[114] See L. Lacroix, *Monnaies et colonization dans l'occident grec*, 82-3.

NEAPOLIS

Neapolis, like Gela in Sicily, issued man-faced bull coinage with great enthusiasm throughout the entire time the mint was in operation. Beginning as early as 470 to 450 BC,[115] the Neapolitans began issuing silver didrachms featuring a nymph on one side, and Acheloios Sebethos as a man-faced bull on the other.

Neapolis has always been an area of mixed populations, originally divided by the old city, Parthenope,[116] whose namesake is the daughter of Acheloios, and the re-founded 'New City,' Neapolis. Strabo confirms additional mixing in the city's early stages, claiming that it was founded by Cumaeans, but then re-colonized by people from Chalcis, Pithecusae, and Athens.[117] The ancient sources are very complex and often contradictory[118] when describing the re-foundation of Neapolis near the remains of Parthenope, the 'Old City' (also Palaepolis).

The mint of Neapolis began to issue bronze coinage of the man-faced bull around the mid 4th century BC. In this catalog we follow Marina Taliercio Mensitieri's layout, which is divided into chronological phases.[119] Phase I dates from 350 to 326 BC, and is divided into four groups based on the main reverse devices: a) protome, b) protome and star with 4 rays, c) protome and star with 8 rays, d) protome and dolphin. Taliercio describes Group Ib as consisting of half-units, whereas group a, c, and d are quarter-units.[120] According to Taliercio the full unit was not issued during Phase I, which utilized the silver obol instead.[121]

Taliercio also argues that the half-unit was not minted in the very earlier stages of bronze coinage at Neapolis. However, in this catalog we propose that the half-unit may indeed have appeared alongside the quarter-units. Our rationale is based on a specimen published by Taliercio, listed as 'Vienna 1595,' which weights 5.54g (see no. 195 below). The coin is actually listed twice by Taliercio: in both Group Ia (protome), and Ib (protome and star), as series Ia.1,[122] and Ib.1 (15th specimen cited),[123] respectively. Although the weight suggests the coin is a half-unit, Taliercio rejects the idea that half-units with no star on shoulder existed, and instead concludes Vienna 1595 is an error, and that a reverse die of the quarter-unit was mistakenly struck together with the obverse die of a half-unit, on a flan corresponding to the half-unit. This is the reason why the coin is inserted in both groups: in Ia for typology (no star), in Ib for metrology. During our research, however, we found a coin sold recently at auction (NAC 64, lot 1991), which demonstrates Taliercio Ia.1 was not a unique error, but might have been a distinct issue. The NAC specimen shows a reverse type without star on shoulder, and weighs 6.21g. It is also from a different reverse die than Vienna 1595. This suggests that at the onset of bronze coinage in Neapolis there were both half units and quarter units, and only later the mint adopted the practice of distinguishing half units and quarter units by employing stars with four or eight rays, at about the time it started issuing full units (featuring the full body of the man-faced bull) and stopped minting silver obols.

Further evidence to support our hypothesis of an early coinage of half-units without star symbol comes from Sambon. Under his no.560 he describes half-units with star, giving a list of specimens that from a metrological point of view are all half-units. However, under the description he illustrates two coins, one with star on shoulder and the other without star. On this starless coin the arrangement of letters corresponds to Taliercio Ia.1, an arrangement not found on any other quarter-units of Group Ia. It, too, is also from a different die than the other two specimens without star. Thus, it appears that there might have been an early series of half-units without star on the shoulder issued at Neapolis.

[115] Rutter suggests 450 BC, while other scholars suggest an earlier date, c. 470 BC. See page 160 above.

[116] According to Strabo, the ancient Parthenope was founded by Rhodian settlers (Strabo, *Geographica*, 14.2.10). For an interesting essay on the role of Rhodian sailors in the diffusion of the cult and image of Acheloios from the eastern to western Mediterranean, in particular to Gelas and Neapolis, see: E. Gabrici, *Problemi di Numismatica Greca della Sicilia e Magna Grecia* (Napoli: Macchiaroli, 1959), 85-88. Certainly, the Rhodians found a fertile cultural soil in the pre-existing Etruscan traditions of the man-faced bull in the area, and were not the sole source of diffusion of the cult and its most popular iconography (see above, Chapter 3 and 4, for extensive discussion). Gabrici's reference to Schol. *Il.* XXIV.616 in reference to a Rhodian origin is not accurate, since the passage refers to Akarnania, not Rhodes, and simply mentions that games were held in honor of Acheloios.

[117] Strabo stated: 'After Dicaearchia is Neapolis, [founded originally] by the Cumaei, but afterwards being peopled by Chalcidians, and certain Pithecussaeans and Athenians' (Strabo, *Geographica*, 5.4.7, English translation by H.C. Hamilton and W. Falconer, *The Geography of Strabo* (London: George Bell & Sons, 1903). The re-foundation of Neapolis is commonly dated to 470 BC, contemporaneous to the appearance of the first silver didrachms. However, after recent research and archaeological discoveries, the chronology of the re-foundation of Neapolis was revised to the final decades of the 6th century BC. For detailed archaeological reports and updated bibliography, see D. Giampaola and B. d'Agostino, 'Osservazioni storiche e archeologiche sulla fondazione di Napoli,' in *Noctes Campanae. Studi di storia antica ed archeologia dell'Italia preromana e romana in memoria di M. Frederiksen*, edited by A.V. Harris and E. Lo Cascio (Napoli, 2005), 49-80.

[118] For a complete bibliography of all the ancient sources citing the argument, see: N.V. Mele, 'Napoli,' in *Bibliografia Topografica della Colonizzazione Greca in Italia e nelle Isole Tirreniche*, Vol.XII (Roma, 1993), 166-9. For an extensive dissertation on the issue, see F. Raviola, *Napoli Origini* (Roma: Bretschneider, 1995).

[119] This book follows Taliercio Mensitieri's metrological framework. For an accurate study on the metrology of the bronze coinage of Neapolis, see M. Taliercio Mensitieri, 'Il bronzo di Neapolis,' Tab.1-5. For the definition of the absolute chronology see ibid., 236-7.

[120] For a more detailed discussion on the metrology and relative chronology of this phase, see Ibid., 221-4.

[121] As the silver-bronze exchange rate was 1:20 during these years, the theoretical unit for bronze would weigh about 12g (Ibid., 248).

[122] Ibid., 262.

[123] Ibid., 263.

Phase T.I-II (also known as Transitional Phase) dates from 326 to 317/310 BC, and is divided into three groups: a) full man-faced bull, b) protome and star with 4 rays, and c) protome and dolphin. Taliercio describes Group T.I-IIa as consisting of units, Group I-IIb as half-units, and Group I-IIc as quarter-units.[124] It is during this phase that the mint stopped issuing silver obols.[125]

Phase II shows a reduction of size and weight. This phase dates from 317/310 to 270 BC, and is divided into four groups: a) full man-faced bull, b) tripod,[126] c) protome, and d) protome and dolphin. Taliercio describes Group IIa as consisting of units, Group IIb as half-units, Group IIc as third-units, and Group IId as quarter-units.[127]

Phase III dates from 270 to 250 BC, and is divided into three groups: a) man-faced bull crowned by winged nymph,[128] b) same type, but reduced weight and size, and c) tripod.[129] Taliercio describes Group IIIa as consisting of units, Group IIIb as third-units, and Group IIIc as quarter-units. Taliercio noted that during this phase symbols (trident, grapes, owl, etc.) were replaced by letters which in the previous phase operated only as indicators of the workshops, while the symbols worked as signs of distinction of the series in chronological succession. Taliercio also points out that during this phase Neapolis stopped issuing any denominations of silver coinage, overstrikes became frequent, and the blanks and dies were of poor quality, all of which lead the scholar to place the coinage of this phase in relation to the economic and military needs of the First Punic War.[130]

Phase IV dates to after 250 BC, and is divided into six groups: a) lyre and omphalos, b) horseman, c) cornucopia, d) man-faced bull crowned by winged nymph, e) tripod, and f) protome.[131] Taliercio describes Group IVa as consisting of units, Group IVb as half-unit, Group IVc and IVd as third-units, and Group IVe and IVf as quarter-units. She also pointed out that this phase exhibits a further decline and 'barbarism' in style. During this phase the control system is again entrusted to symbols, not letters, re-employing the approach of Phase II.[132]

All bronze varieties issued in Neapolis appropriately pair Apollo on the obverse and Acheloios Sebethos on the reverse. The rationale for Apollo and his association with mercenaries, many of whom came from Campania, is discussed in Chapter 2. The use of Apollo finds further rationale when we consider his role as a god of colonization, given the early mixing of various groups in the area. Acheloios Sebethos as a man-faced bull is also fitting, insofar as he represents the synoecism experienced by the city's inhabitants, new and old, foreign and 'local.' In fact, the very notion of 'New City' recalls the man-faced bull's association with rebirth and renewal. The use of the IΣ control mark probably indicates the river is a sinew of Acheloios. The fact that this numismatic device was adopted by other cities whose coins were minted at (or in association with) Neapolis further reinforces this point.

---

124 For a more detailed discussion on the metrology and relative chronology for this phase, see M. Taliercio Mensitieri, 'Il bronzo di Neapolis,' 225-7.

125 Ibid., 249.

126 This type is not listed in this catalog because it does not feature a man-faced bull.

127 For a more detailed discussion on the metrology and relative chronology for this phase, see ibid., 228-38.

128 According to E. Gabrici the winged figure crowing the man-faced bull would not have originally indicated 'Nike,' because the iconographical codification of Nike as 'strategic victory' is later than its appearance on western coins (we suggest its earliest origins might be the First Punic War, but it is impossible to know for sure). Gabrici cites the coinage of Terina, and also the winged female that appears on the reverse of the silver coins from Neapolis whose obverse features a horned male labeled Sebethos (in both cases the winged female does not symbolize 'victory'). Ultimately, Gabrici proposed that the winged female is the personification of the spring of the local river (E. Gabrici, *Problemi di Numismatica Greca*, 111-120). Following his dissertation this catalog defines the flying figure above the man-faced bull as a 'winged nymph,' and not 'Nike,' as it is commonly described. For additional evidence for the winged nymph interpretation, see above, pg. 64ff.

129 This type is not listed in this catalog because it does not feature a man-faced bull.

130 For a more detailed discussion on the metrology and relative chronology for this phase, see M. Taliercio Mensitieri, 'Il bronzo di Neapolis,' 238-245.

131 Groups a, b and c of this phase are not listed in this catalog, because they do not feature man-faced bulls.

132 For a more detailed discussion on the metrology and relative chronology for this phase, see M. Taliercio Mensitieri, 'Il bronzo di Neapolis,' 245-8.

Coinage

TALIERCIO PHASE I

GROUP IA

195. AE Half Unit ?	350 to 326 BC
 * Taliercio = Vienna1595  ** NAC 64, 1991  ***Sambon 560	OBV: Head of Apollo facing right, wearing laurel wreath with leaves in triple clusters. REV: Forepart of Acheloios Sebethos as a man-faced bull to right, ΝΕΟΠ behind, ΟΛΙΤΕΩ above, N between legs. Linear border. REF: Vienna 1595 = Taliercio Ia.1 = Ib.1,15 (5.54g)*; NAC 64, lot 1991 (6.21g)**; Sambon 560***. *Size and weight of this allegedly unique specimen (Vienna 1595) led Taliercio to attribute the coin to her group Ib.1 (half unit). Meanwhile she listed the same specimen as Ia.1 (quarter unit), but from a typological point of view (with star). For Taliercio, this ambiguity results from a minting error, in which the reverse die of the quarter unit was accidentally struck on the blank for a half unit. However, we have found a second specimen of this series struck by different dies (NAC 64 lot 1991), so perhaps there was an early series of half-units without the star symbol. Moreover, Sambon depicted two specimens under no. 560 in his catalog, one with the star and the other, without, which adds additional evidence that this coin was not an error.*

196. AE Quarter Unit, 3.86g	350 to 326 BC
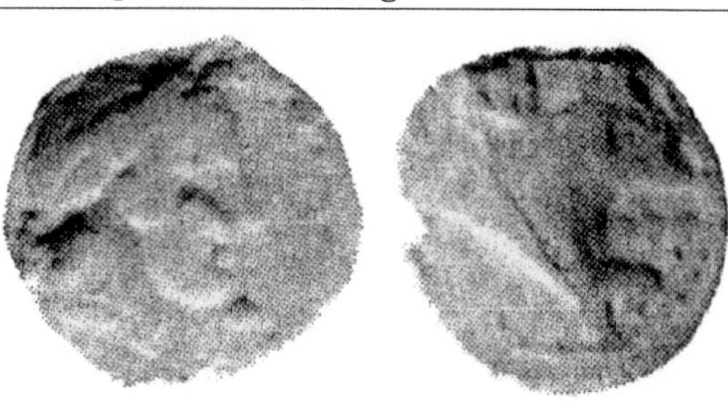	OBV: Head of Apollo facing right, wearing laurel wreath with leaves in opposing pairs. REV: Forepart of Acheloios Sebethos as a man-faced bull to right, ΝΕΟΠΟ–ΛΙ-___N. Dotted border. REF: Taliercio Ia.2*. *Taliercio cites 1 known example (Napoli 1121).*

197. AE Quarter Unit, 3.59g	**350 to 326 BC**
	OBV: Head of Apollo facing right, wearing laurel wreath with leaves in opposing pairs. REV: Forepart of Acheloios Sebethos as a man-faced bull to right, ΝΕΟΠ–ΟΛΕΤΕΩ–Ν. Dotted border. REF: Sambon 562; Taliercio Ia.3*. *Taliercio cites 4 known examples and 1 known die pair.*

198. AE Quarter Unit, 3.49g	**350 to 326 BC**
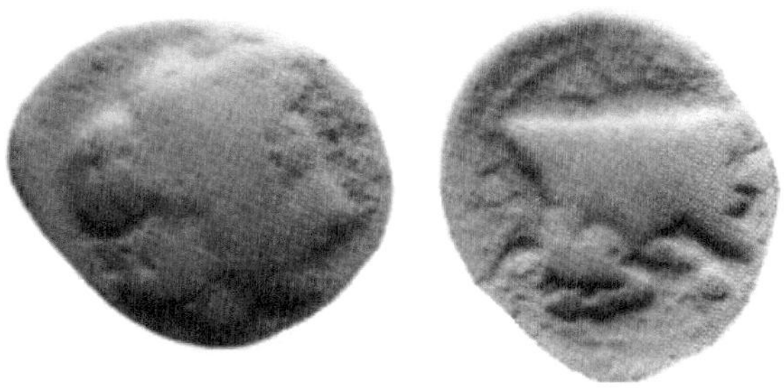	OBV: Head of Apollo facing right, wearing laurel wreath with leaves in opposing pairs(?). REV: Forepart of Acheloios Sebethos as a man-faced bull to right, ΝΕΟ–Π–ΟΛΕΙ. Dotted border. REF: Taliercio Ia.4* = BnF Fonds Général 372. *Taliercio cites 1 known specimen.*

199. AE Quarter Unit, 3.27g	**350 to 326 BC**
	OBV: Head of Apollo facing right, wearing laurel wreath with leaves in triple clusters. REV: Forepart of Acheloios Sebethos as a man-faced bull to right, ΝΕΟΠΟ–Λ–ΙΤΗΣ. Dotted border. REF: Taliercio Ia.5*. *Taliercio cites 2 examples and 1 known die pair.*

200. AE Quarter Unit, 2.48g, 15mm	**350 to 326 BC**
	OBV: Head of Apollo facing right, wearing laurel wreath with leaves in opposing pairs. REV: Forepart of Acheloios Sebethos as a man-faced bull to right, ΝΕΟΠΟ–ΛΙΤΗΣ. REF: Taliercio Ia.6; CNG, eAuction 233, lot 17*. *Taliercio cites 2 examples and 1 known die pair.*

Group Ib

201. AE Half Unit, 6.51g, 20mm	**350 to 326 BC**
	OBV: Head of Apollo facing right, wearing laurel wreath with leaves in opposing pairs, H in field. REV: Forepart of Acheloios Sebethos as a man-faced bull to right, star with four rays on shoulder, ΝΕΟΠ-ΟΛΙΤΕΩ-Ν. Linear border. REF: Sambon 560; Taliercio Ib.1; SNG France 867-8; CNG, eAuction 130, lot 25*. *Taliercio cites 16 examples with 7 obverse and 9 reverse dies.*

202. AE Half Unit, 5.74g	**350 to 326 BC**
	OBV: Head of Apollo facing right, wearing laurel wreath with leaves in triple clusters. REV: Forepart of Acheloios Sebethos as a man-faced bull to right, star with four rays on shoulder, ΝΕΟΠ-ΟΛ-ΕΙΤΕ. Linear border. REF: Sambon 561 var.; Taliercio Ib.2*. *Taliercio cites 3 known examples with 2 obverse dies and 1 reverse die.*

203. AE Half Unit, 6.67g	**350 to 326 BC**
	OBV: Head of Apollo facing right, wearing laurel wreath with leaves in opposing pairs. REV: Forepart of Acheloios Sebethos as a man-faced bull to right, star with four rays on shoulder, ΝΕΟΠ-Ο–ΛΙΤΕ. Linear border. REF: Taliercio - ; Sambon 561 = BMC 143; Gemini II, Lot 5*.

204. AE Half Unit, 5.57g	**350 to 326 BC**
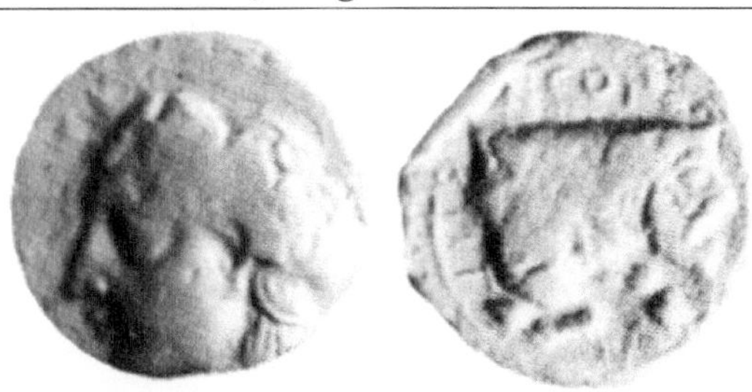	OBV: Head of Apollo facing right, wearing laurel wreath with leaves in triple clusters. REV: Forepart of Acheloios Sebethos as a man-faced bull to right, star with four rays on shoulder, ΝΕΟΡΟ–ΛΙ-ΤΗΣ. Linear border. REF: Sambon 563; Taliercio Ib, 3*. *Taliercio cites 6 known examples with 2 obverse dies and 2 reverse dies.* The line drawing in Sambon is incorrect, and shows a coin with Apollo facing right.

205. AE Half Unit, 5.18g	**350 to 326 BC**
	OBV: Head of Apollo facing right, wearing laurel wreath with leaves in opposing pairs. REV: Forepart of Acheloios Sebethos as a man-faced bull to right, star with four rays on shoulder, ΝΕΟΡΟ–ΛΙΤΗΣ. REF: Taliercio Ib, 4*. *Taliercio cites 14 known examples with 2 obverse dies and 2 reverse dies.*

206. AE Half Unit, 4.60g	**350 to 326 BC**
	OBV: Head of Apollo facing right, wearing laurel wreath with leaves in triple clusters. REV: Forepart of Acheloios Sebethos as a man-faced bull to right, star with four rays on shoulder, ΝΕΟΠΟΛΙΤΗΣ above. REF: Sambon 564; Taliercio Ib.5; Potamikon Collection*. *Taliercio cites 63 known examples with 14 obverse dies and over 15 reverse dies.*

207. AE Half Unit, 5.33g, 16mm | **350 to 326 BC**

OBV: Head of Apollo facing right, wearing laurel wreath with leaves in triple clusters.
REV: Forepart of Acheloios Sebethos as a man-faced bull to right, star with four rays on shoulder, ΝΕΟΠΟΛΙΤΗΣ written on tablet above.
REF: Sambon 567; Taliercio Ib.6; NAC 13, lot 46*.
Taliercio lists 21 examples with 4 obverse dies and 4 reverse dies.

208. AE Half Unit, 4.67g | **350 to 326 BC**

OBV: Head of Apollo facing right, wearing laurel wreath with leaves in triple clusters, A behind.
REV: Forepart of Acheloios Sebethos as a man-faced bull to right, star with four rays on shoulder, ΝΕΟΠΟΛΙΤΗΣ above.
REF: Sambon 571; Taliercio Ib.7*.
Taliercio cites 14 known examples with 3 obverse dies and 4 reverse dies.

209. AE Half Unit, 3.86g | **350 to 326 BC**

OBV: Head of Apollo facing right, wearing laurel wreath with leaves in triple clusters, E(?) in field.
REV: Forepart of Acheloios Sebethos as a man-faced bull to right, star with four rays on shoulder, ΝΕΟΠΟΛΙΤΗΣ above.
REF: Taliercio Ib.8*.
Taliercio cites 14 examples with 5 obverse dies and 5 reverse dies.

Group Ic

210. AE Quarter Unit, 3.20g | **350 to 326 BC**

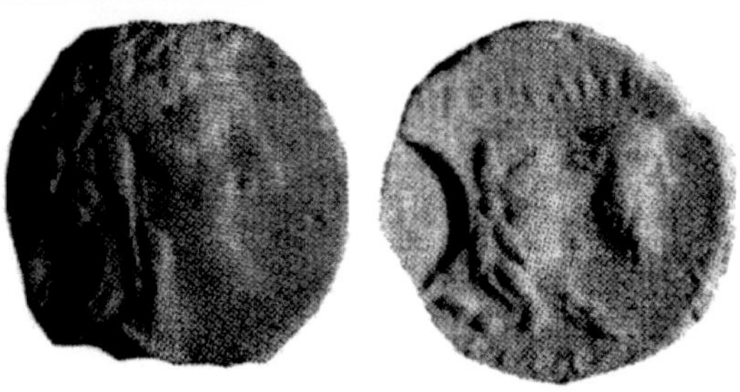

OBV: Head of Apollo facing right, wearing laurel wreath with leaves in triple clusters.
REV: Forepart of Acheloios Sebethos as a man-faced bull to right, star with eight rays on shoulder, lyre behind, waves below, ΝΕΟΠΟΛΙΤΗΣ above.
REF: Sambon 572; Taliercio Ic.1*.
Taliercio cites 6 examples with 1 obverse and 5 reverse dies. One of them shows no traces of lyre and star with eight rays, so we list it as a separate variety in the next entry.

211. AE Quarter (?) Unit, 3.71g	**350 to 326 BC**
	OBV: Head of Apollo facing right, wearing laurel wreath with leaves in triple clusters. REV: Forepart of Acheloios Sebethos as a man-faced bull to right, waves below, ΝΕΟΠΟΛΙΤΗΣ above (allegedly retrograde on one example). REF: Sambon 574-5: SNG France 872 = BnF Fonds Général 371*. *Sambon listed and drew his no.574, which is the same coin illustrated here (BnF 371), describing it 'without the star and lyre'. Sambon also described a coin from his collection (his no.575) with the same types but a retrograde ethnic on reverse. Taliercio ignored both Sambon 574 and 575, and listed this coin (BnF 371) under her series Ic.1 (n.6), which is our previous listing (204). However, even the compiler of SNG France described this coin as a different variant without star and lyre (SNG France, p.62, no.872). Therefore, we recognize this as a real variety described by Sambon and rejected by Taliercio.*

212. AE Quarter Unit, 1.51g	**350 to 326 BC**
	OBV: Head of Apollo facing right, wearing laurel wreath with leaves in triple clusters. REV: Forepart of Acheloios Sebethos as a man-faced bull to left, star with eight rays on shoulder, lyre (?) behind, ΝΕΟΠΟΛΙΤΗΝ (retro) above. REF: Taliercio Ic.2*. *Taliercio cites 2 examples with 1 obverse die and 1 reverse die.*

213. AE Quarter Unit, 2.75g	**350 to 326 BC**
	OBV: Head of Apollo facing right, wearing laurel wreath with leaves in triple clusters. REV: Forepart of Acheloios Sebethos as a man-faced bull to right, star with eight rays on shoulder, lyre behind, waves below, ΝΕΟΠΟΛΙΤΗИ above. REF: Sambon 573; Taliercio Ic.3 = SNG France 873 = BnF, Fonds Général 370*. *Incorrectly described by Taliercio as 'without lyre on reverse.' The author cites 2 examples with 1 obverse die and 1 reverse die.*

214. AE Quarter Unit, 3.57g	**350 to 326 BC**
	OBV: Head of Apollo facing right, wearing laurel wreath with leaves in triple clusters. REV: Forepart of Acheloios Sebethos as a man-faced bull to right, star with eight rays on shoulder, ΝΕΟΠΟΛΙΤΗΣ above. REF: Sambon 566; Taliercio Ic.4; SNG France 874; Kunker Fall Auction sale 2015, lot 8059*. *Taliercio cites 7 examples with 3 obverse dies and 3 reverse dies. This coin adds to this count, as does an example in the Ahala Collection.*

215. AE Quarter Unit, 4.20g	350 to 326 BC
	OBV: Head of Apollo facing right, wearing laurel wreath with leaves in triple clusters. REV: Forepart of Acheloios Sebethos as a man-faced bull to right, star with eight rays on shoulder, ΝΕΟΠΟΛΙΤΩΝ above. REF: Taliercio Ic, 5*. *Taliercio cites 2 examples with 2 obverse dies and 2 reverse dies.*

Group Id

216. AE Quarter Unit, 3.30g, 14mm	350 to 326 BC
	OBV: Head of Apollo facing right, wearing laurel wreath with leaves in opposing pairs. REV: Forepart of Acheloios Sebethos as a man-faced bull to right, ΝΕΟΠΟΛΙΤ–Η–Σ, dolphin to right above. Dotted border. REF: Sambon 576; Taliercio Id.1; ACR 7, lot 11*. *Taliercio cites 15 examples with 2 obverse dies and 3 reverse dies.*

217. AE Quarter Unit, 3.40g	350 to 326 BC
	OBV: Head of Apollo facing right, wearing laurel wreath with leaves in opposing pairs. REV: Forepart of Acheloios Sebethos as a man-faced bull to right, ΝΕΟΠΟ, dolphin to right above. Dotted border. REF: Taliercio Id.2*. *Taliercio cites 1 example and sol die pair.*

218. AE Quarter Unit, 4.27g, 15mm	350 to 326 BC
	OBV: Head of Apollo facing right, wearing laurel wreath with leaves in opposing pairs. REV: Forepart of Acheloios Sebethos as a man-faced bull to right, NEO (retro N, vertical E) behind, dolphin to right above. Dotted border. REF: CNG, eAuction 130, lot 26*.

219. AE Quarter Unit, 3.24g, 14mm	350 to 326 BC
	OBV: Head of Apollo facing right, wearing laurel wreath with leaves in triple clusters. REV: Forepart of Acheloios Sebethos as a man-faced bull to right, ΝΕΟΠΟ–ΛΙ–(ΤΗΣ), dolphin to right above. Dotted border. REF: Taliercio Id.3*. *Taliercio cites 4 examples with 1 die pair.*

220. AE Quarter Unit, 2.47g	**350 to 326 BC**
	OBV: Head of Apollo facing right, wearing laurel wreath with leaves in triple clusters. REV: Forepart of Acheloios Sebethos as a man-faced bull to right, ΝΕΟΠΟΛ–Ι–ΤΩΝ, dolphin to right above. Dotted border. REF: Taliercio Id.4 = SNG France 876 = BnF N3646* *Taliercio cites 2 examples, 1 obverse die and 1 reverse die. Taliercio incorrectly described the ethnic as ending in* ΤΗΣ.

221. AE Quarter Unit, 3.04g	**350 to 326 BC**
	OBV: Head of Apollo facing right, wearing laurel wreath with leaves in triple clusters. REV: Forepart of Acheloios Sebethos as a man-faced bull to right, ΝΕΟΠΟΛ–ΙΤ–ΗΣ, dolphin to right above. Dotted border. REV: Taliercio Id.5*. *Taliercio cites 2 examples with 1 die pair.*

222. AE Quarter Unit, 3.95g, 16mm	**350 to 326 BC**
	OBV: Head of Apollo facing right, wearing laurel wreath with leaves in opposing pairs. REV: Forepart of Acheloios Sebethos as a man-faced bull to left, head facing, dolphin to right above, ΝΕ–Ο–ΠΟΛΙΤΗΣ. Dotted border. REF: Taliercio Id.6; CNG eAuction 233, lot 18*. *Taliercio cites 5 examples with 1 die pair.*

223. AE Quarter Unit, 3.31g, 13mm	**350 to 326 BC**
	OBV: Head of Apollo facing right, wearing laurel wreath with leaves in opposing pairs. REV: Forepart of Acheloios Sebethos as a man-faced bull to right, head facing, Ν–Ε–Ο–ΠΟΛΙΤΗΣ, dolphin to left. REF: Taliercio Id, 7; SNG Cop 474; HN Italy 575; NAC 64, Lot 1992*. *Taliercio cites 3 examples with 1 die pair.*

TALIERCIO TRANSITIONAL PHASE I-II

Group I-IIa

224. AE Unit, 10.23g, 22mm	**326 to 317/310 BC**
	OBV: Head of Apollo facing right, wearing laurel wreath with leaves in triple clusters, ΝΕΟΠΟΛΙΤΗΣ before, Ε behind. Dotted border. REV: Acheloios Sebethos as a man-faced bull standing to right on single line, head facing, star with eight rays above, Μ below, Ε in ex. Dotted border. REF: Sambon 612; Taliercio t.I-IIa.1; Bode Museum, Objekt Nr: 18240884 (42393)*. *Taliercio cites 4 known examples with 1 die pair.*

225. AE Unit, 11.67g, 22mm	326 to 317/310 BC
	OBV: Head of Apollo facing right, wearing laurel wreath with leaves in triple clusters, ΝΕΟ(ΠΟΛΙΤΩΝ) before, Φ and ? behind. Dotted border. REV: Acheloios Sebethos as a man-faced bull standing to right on single line, head facing, dolphin to right above, ΔΙΟ in ex. REF: Sambon 615; Taliercio t.I-IIa.2; Bode Museum, Objekt Nr: 18240890 (42399) *. *Taliercio cites 2 known examples with 1 die pair.*

Group I-IIb

226. AE Half Unit, 5.66g	326 to 317/310 BC
	OBV: Head of Apollo facing right, wearing laurel wreath with leaves in triple clusters, M in field. REV: Forepart of Acheloios Sebethos as a man-faced bull to right, star with four rays on shoulder, ΝΕΟΡΟΛΙΤΗΣ above. REF: Taliercio t.I-IIb.1*. *Taliercio cites 24 examples with 6 obverse dies and 7 reverse dies.*

227. AE Half Unit, 6.00g	326 to 317/310 BC
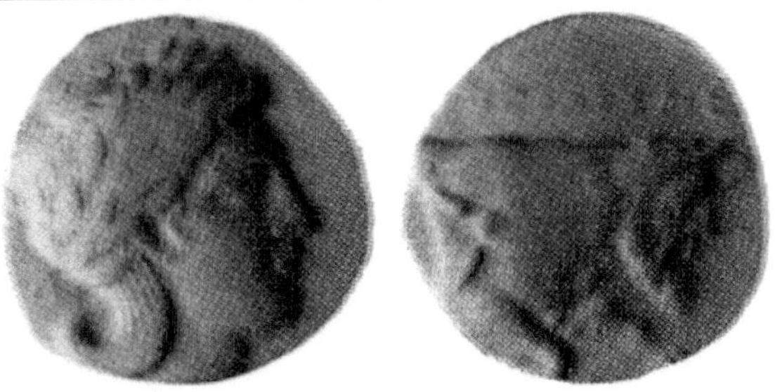	OBV: Head of Apollo facing right, wearing laurel wreath with leaves in triple clusters, Δ in field. REV: Forepart of Acheloios Sebethos as a man-faced bull to right, star with four rays on shoulder, ΝΕΟΡΟΛΙΤΗΣ above. REF: Sambon 568; Taliercio t. I-IIb.2*. *Taliercio cites 1 known example.*

Group I-IIc

228. AE Quarter Unit, 2-79-3.68g	326 to 317/310 BC
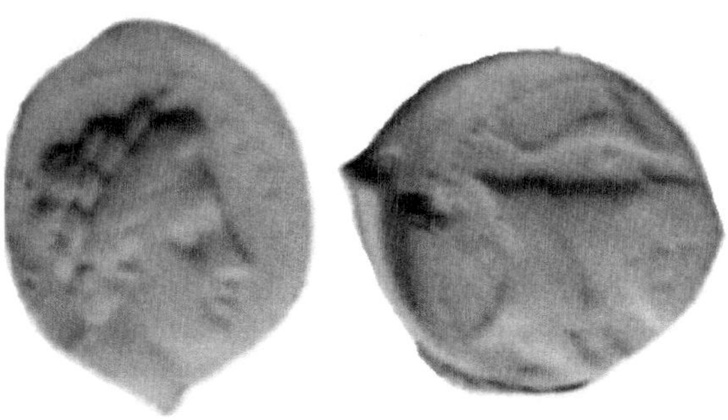	OBV: Head of Apollo facing right, wearing laurel wreath with leaves in triple clusters, E in field, ΝΕΟΠΟΛΙΤΩΝ before. REV: Forepart of Acheloios Sebethos as a man-faced bull to right, dolphin to right above, M in field. REF: Sambon 580+ (sometimes Γ in field?); Taliercio t.I-IIc.1*. *Taliercio cites 5 examples with 2 obverse dies and 3 reverse dies.*

229. AE Quarter Unit, 2.47g	326 to 317/310 BC
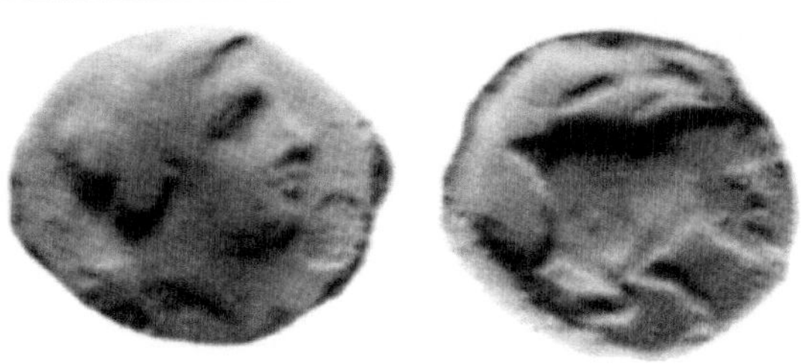	OBV: Head of Apollo facing right, wearing laurel wreath with leaves in triple clusters, Π(?)in field, ΝΕΟΠΟΛΙΤΩΝ before. REV: Forepart of Acheloios Sebethos as a man-faced bull to right, dolphin to right above, ? in field. REF: Taliercio t. I-IIc.2*. *Taliercio cites 2 known examples with 1 die pair.*

230. AE Quarter Unit, 2.75g	**326 to 317/310 BC**
	OBV: Head of Apollo facing right, wearing laurel wreath with leaves in triple clusters, N in field, (ΝΕΟΠΟΛΙΤΩΝ) before. REV: Forepart of Acheloios Sebethos as a man-faced bull to right, dolphin to right above, N in field. Dotted border. REF: Taliercio t.I-IIc.3; NAC P, lot 1009*. *Taliercio cites 5 known examples with 2 obverse dies and 1 reverse die.*

231. AE Quarter Unit, 3.70g	**326 to 317/310 BC**
	OBV: Head of Apollo facing right, wearing laurel wreath with leaves in triple clusters, ΝΕΟΠΟΛΙΤΩΝ before. REV: Forepart of Acheloios Sebethos as a man-faced bull to right, dolphin to right above, ΔΙΟ below. Dotted border. REF: Sambon 582; Taliercio t.I-IIc.4; Lindgren II, 11, 194 = M&M GmbH 21, lot 12*. *Taliercio cites 6 examples with 5 obverse dies and 5 reverse dies.*

TALIERCIO PHASE II

Group IIa

232. AE Unit, 5.46g, 16mm	**317/310 to 270 BC**
	OBV: Head of Apollo facing right, wearing laurel wreath with leaves in triple clusters, ΝΕΟΠΟΛΙΤΩΝ before. REV: Acheloios Sebethos as a man-faced bull standing to right on single line, head facing, star with 8 rays above. REF: Sambon 613; Taliercio IIa.1; SNG Milano 188-9 SNG France 883 = BnF Fonds Général 384*. *Taliercio cites 30 examples with 7 obverse dies and 8 reverse dies.*

233. AE Unit, 7.63g, 21mm	**317/310 to 270 BC**
	OBV: Head of Apollo facing right, wearing laurel wreath with leaves in triple clusters, ΝΕΟΠΟΛΙΤΩΝ before, astragalos in field. REV: Acheloios Sebethos as a man-faced bull standing to right on single line, head facing, star with 8 rays above. Dotted border. REF: Taliercio IIa.2; Artemide Live Auction 5, lot 10*. *Taliercio cites 1 example so 1 die pair, to which we add another.*

234. AE Unit, 6.87g	**317/310 to 270 BC**
	OBV: Head of Apollo facing right, wearing laurel wreath with leaves in triple clusters, ΝΕΟΠΟΛΙΤΩΝ before , M in field. Linear border. REV: Acheloios Sebethos as a man-faced bull standing to right on single line, head facing, star with 8 rays above, MA in ex. REF: Sambon 616; Taliercio IIa.3*. *Taliercio cites 5 examples with 1 die pair.*

235. AE Unit, 5.72g | **317/310 to 270 BC**

OBV: Head of Apollo facing right, wearing laurel wreath with leaves in triple clusters, ΝΕΟΠΟΛΙΤΩΝ before.
REV: Acheloios Sebethos as a man-faced bull standing to right on single line, head facing, crescent and star with 8 rays above (Sambon says sometimes M below, E in ex.). Linear border.
REF: Sambon 614;Taliercio IIa.4; Graziano 332*.
Taliercio cites 1 example and so 1 die pair, plus the example published by Graziano.

236. AE Unit, 6.35g | **317/310 to 270 BC**

OBV: Head of Apollo facing right, wearing laurel wreath with leaves in triple clusters, amphora behind. Dotted border.
REV: Acheloios Sebethos as a man-faced bull standing to right on single line, head facing, garland above, ΛΕ below. Dotted border.
REF: Sambon 623; Taliercio IIa.5; Pozzi 230 = NAC 64, Lot 616*.
Taliercio cites 18 examples with 2 obverse dies and 2 reverse dies.

237. AE Unit, 5.80g, 17mm | **317/310 to 270 BC**

OBV: Head of Apollo facing right, wearing laurel wreath with leaves in triple clusters, four dolphins surrounding. Dotted border.
REV: Acheloios Sebethos as a man-faced bull standing to right on single line, head in profile, trident above, ΝΕΟΠΟΛΙΤΩΝ in ex. Dotted border.
REF: Sambon 650; Taliercio IIa.6; SNG France 883-8; Private Collection*.
Taliercio cites 43 examples with 8 obverse dies and 11 reverse dies.

238. AE Unit, 4.69g, 16mm | **317/310 to 270 BC**

OBV: Head of Apollo facing right, wearing laurel wreath with leaves in triple clusters, ΑΡ in field.
REV: Acheloios Sebethos as a man-faced bull standing to right on single line, head facing, star with 8 rays in wreath above, Δ below, ΝΕΥΠΟΛΙΤΩΝ in ex. Dotted border.
REF: Sambon 629a; Taliercio IIa.7; SNG France 889 = BnF Fonds Général 390.
Taliercio cites 16 examples with 2 obverse dies and 3 reverse dies.

239. AE Unit, 3.94g | **317/310 to 270 BC**

OBV: Head of Apollo facing right, wearing laurel wreath with leaves in triple clusters, ΑΡ in field.
REV: Acheloios Sebethos as a man-faced bull standing to right on single line, head facing, mask in wreath above (Sambon says bunch of grapes in crown above), ΝΕΥΠΟΛΙΤΩΝ in ex.
REF: Taliercio IIa.8*.
Taliercio cites 6 examples with 1 die pair. She includes Sambon 628, but Sambon was correct that there is a distinct variety featuring a grape cluster within wreath (see next listing).

240. AE Unit,	**317/310 to 270 BC**
	OBV: Head of Apollo facing right, wearing laurel wreath with leaves in triple clusters, AP in field. REV: Acheloios Sebethos as a man-faced bull standing to right on single line, head facing, bunch of grapes in crown above, ΝΕΥΠΟΛΙΤΩΝ in ex. REF: Sambon 628, Potamikon Collection*.

241. AE Unit, 4.92g, 16mm	**317/310 to 270 BC**
	OBV: Head of Apollo facing right, wearing laurel wreath with leaves in opposing pairs. Dotted border. REV: Acheloios Sebethos as a man-faced bull standing to right on single line, head facing, above , bust of Helios facing between the letters Φ-I, M monogram and ΔE monogram below, ΝΕΟΠΟΛΙΤΩΝ in ex. REF: Sambon 630; Taliercio IIa.9; SNG France 894 = BnF Fonds Général 391*. *Taliercio cites 8 examples with 1 obverse die and 2 reverse dies.*

242. AE Unit, 3.90g	**317/310 to 270 BC**
	OBV: Head of Apollo facing right, wearing laurel wreath with leaves in triple clusters. REV: Acheloios Sebethos as a man-faced bull standing to right on single line, head facing, above, bust of Helios facing between the letters Φ-I, ΔE monogram below, ΝΕΟΠΟΛΙΤΩΝ in ex. Dotted border. REF: Sambon 631; Taliercio IIa.10*. *Taliercio cites 6 examples with 2 obverse dies and 2 reverse dies.*

243. AE Unit, 5.06g, 15mm	**317/310 to 270 BC**
	OBV: Head of Apollo facing right, wearing laurel wreath with leaves in triple clusters, BI (retro) behind REV: Acheloios Sebethos as a man-faced bull standing to right on single line, head facing, above, Cock right between letters Φ-I, ΝΕΟΠΟΛΙΤΩΝ in ex. Dotted border. REF: Sambon 632; Taliercio IIa.11; SNG France 895 = BnF 1966.453* *Taliercio cites 4 examples with 2 obverse dies and 2 reverse dies.*

244. AE Unit, 3.23g, 16mm	**317/310 to 270 BC**
	OBV: Head of Apollo facing left, wearing laurel wreath with leaves in triple clusters, ΝΕΟΠΟΛΙΤΩΝ before, CI behind. Dotted border. REV: Acheloios Sebethos as a man-faced bull standing to left on single line, head facing, eagle with head turning right, below, K (Taliercio says X). REF: Sambon 644; Taliercio IIa.12; SNG France 896 = BnF Fonds Général 398*. *Taliercio cites 13 examples with 2 obverse dies and 3 reverse dies.*

245. AE Unit, 5.03g	**317/310 to 270 BC**
	OBV: Head of Apollo facing right, wearing laurel wreath with leaves in opposing pairs, ΝΕΟΠΟΛΙΤΩΝ before. Dotted border. REV: Acheloios Sebethos as a man-faced bull standing to right on single line, head facing, club above, K below, star with 8 rays in ex. REF: Sambon 621; Taliercio IIa.13*. *Taliercio cites 10 examples with 1 obverse die and 2 reverse dies.*

246. AE Unit, 5.19g, 17mm	**317/310 to 270 BC**
	OBV: Head of Apollo facing right, wearing laurel wreath with leaves in opposing pairs, ΝΕΟΠΟΛΙΤΩΝ before, X in field (Sambon says retrograde K). Dotted border. REV: Acheloios Sebethos as a man-faced bull standing to right on single line, head facing, star with 7 rays above, ΛΕ (or XE) below. REF: Taliercio IIa.14; CNG eAuction 219, lot 160*. *Taliercio cites 3 examples with 1 obverse die and 1 reverse die.*

247. AE Unit, 4.82g, 18mm	**317/310 to 270 BC**
	OBV: Head of Apollo facing right, wearing laurel wreath with leaves in opposing pairs, ΝΕΟΠΟΛΙΤΩΝ, before, X or retro K behind. Dotted border. REV: Acheloios Sebethos as a man-faced bull standing to right on single line, head facing, corn-ear above to right. REF: Sambon 622; Taliercio IIa.15; CNG, eAuction 233, lot 39*. *Taliercio cites 21 examples with more than 3 obverses and more than 7 reverses.*

248. AE Unit, 3.36g, 15mm	**317/310 to 270 BC**
	OBV: Head of Apollo facing right, wearing laurel wreath with leaves in opposing pairs, ΝΕΟΠΟΛΙΤΩΝ, K behind. Dotted border. REV: Acheloios Sebethos as a man-faced bull standing to right on single line, head facing, kerykeion above. Dotted border. REF: Sambon 618.; Taliercio IIa.16; SNG France 900 = BnF Fonds Général 386*. *Taliercio cites 36 examples with more than 12 obverse dies and more than 12 reverse dies.*

249. AE Unit, 3.98g	**317/310 to 270 BC**
	OBV: Head of Apollo facing right, wearing laurel wreath with leaves in triple clusters, ΝΕΟΠΟΛΙΤΩΝ, E behind. Dotted border. REV: Acheloios Sebethos as a man-faced bull standing to right on single line, head facing, kerykeion above, AN monogram in ex. REF: Sambon 619; Graziano 350*.

250. AE Unit, 3.90g, 18mm	317/310 to 270 BC
	OBV: Head of Apollo facing right, wearing laurel wreath with leaves in triple clusters, ΝΕΟΠΟΛΙΤΩΝ before, K behind. Dotted border. REV: Acheloios Sebethos as a man-faced bull standing to right on single line, head facing, dolphin above to right, no letters. Dotted border. REF: Sambon 617; Taliercio IIa.17; Babelon-De Luynes 185*. *Taliercio records 15 examples with more than 3 obverse dies and more than 6 reverse dies.*

251. AE Unit, 4.50g, 16mm	317/310 to 270 BC
	OBV: Head of Apollo facing right, wearing laurel wreath with leaves in triple clusters, sometimes O behind (Taliercio says unclear), no legend. REV: Acheloios Sebethos as a man-faced bull standing to right on single line, head facing, fly above, EK monogram sometimes below, ΝΕΟΠΟΛΙΤΩΝ in ex. Dotted border. REF: Sambon 624+; Taliercio IIa.18; CNG 84, lot 53*. *Taliercio records 11 examples with 2 obverse dies and 2 reverse dies.*

252. AE Unit, 4.70g, 14mm	317/310 to 270 BC
	OBV: Head of Apollo facing right, wearing laurel wreath with leaves in triple clusters, Λ in field, ΝΕΟΠΟΛΙΤΩΝ. REV: Acheloios Sebethos as a man-faced bull standing to right on single line, head facing, dove in wreath above, M below. Linear border. REF: Sambon 627; Taliercio IIa.19; SNG France 906 = BnF Fonds Général 389*. *Taliercio records 6 examples with 1 die pair.*

253. AE Unit, 4.50g, 15mm	317/310 to 270 BC
	OBV: Head of Apollo facing right, wearing laurel wreath with leaves in opposing pairs, ΝΕΟΠΟΛΙΤΩΝ before, Λ behind. Dotted border. REV: Acheloios Sebethos as a man-faced bull standing to right on single line, head facing, torch above, ΟΛ below. Dotted border. REF: Sambon 620; Taliercio IIa.20; SNG München 267-8; SNG France 907 = BnF 1966.453*. *Taliercio records 8 examples with 4 obverse dies and 4 reverse dies.*

254. AE Unit, 3.77g	317/310 to 270 BC
	OBV: Head of Apollo facing left, wearing laurel wreath with leaves in opposing pairs, Λ behind, ΝΕΟΠΟΛΙΤΩΝ before. REV: Acheloios Sebethos as a man-faced bull standing to left on single line, head facing, kantharos above, Z-Ω (?) in field, MIA in ex. REF: Sambon 642-3; Taliercio IIa.21*. *Taliercio records 14 examples with 2 obverse dies and 1 reverse die. Sambon 642 describes ΔΙΩ in ex, but it was a misreading of this type.*

255. AE Unit, 3.37g | **317/310 to 270 BC**

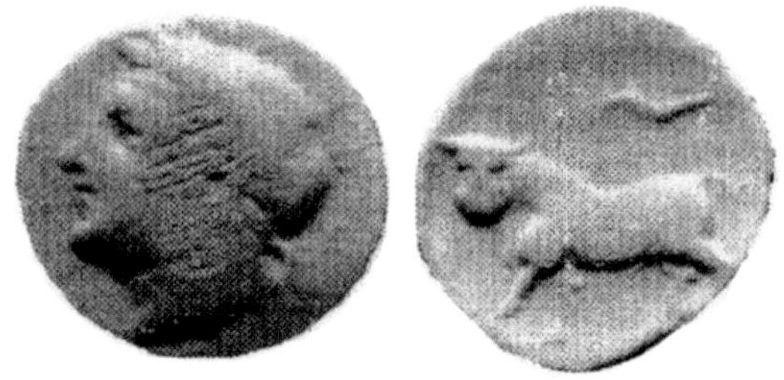

OBV: Head of Apollo facing left, wearing laurel wreath with leaves in opposing pairs, E behind.
REV: Acheloios Sebethos as a man-faced bull standing to left on single line, head facing, thrysos above, Δ in field, ΝΕΟΠΟΛΙΤΩΝ.
REF: Taliercio IIa.22*.
Taliercio records 6 examples with 2 obverse dies and 2 reverse dies.

256. AE Unit, 4.32g, 17mm | **317/310 to 270 BC**

OBV: Head of Apollo facing left, wearing laurel wreath with leaves in triple clusters, E behind.
REV: Acheloios Sebethos as a man-faced bull standing to left on single line, head facing, cornucopia above, [monogram] in field, ΝΕΟΠΟΛΙΤΩΝ in ex.
REF: Sambon 649; Taliercio IIa, 23; NAC 13, lot 47*.
Taliercio records 18 examples with 3 obverse dies and 4 reverse dies.

257. AE Unit, 4.45g | **317/310 to 270 BC**

OBV: Head of Apollo facing left, wearing laurel wreath with leaves in triple clusters, ΝΕΟΠΟΛΙΤΩΝ before, E behind. Dotted border.
REV: Acheloios Sebethos as a man-faced bull standing to right on single line, head facing, bunch of grapes on vine leaves above, [monogram] below, [monogram] in ex.
REF: Sambon 634a-b; Taliercio IIa.24*.
Taliercio records 23 examples with 2 obverse dies and 3 reverse dies.

258. AE Unit, 4.16g | **317/310 to 270 BC**

OBV: Head of Apollo facing left, wearing laurel wreath with leaves in triple clusters, ΝΕΟΠΟΛΙΤΩΝ before, E behind.
REV: Acheloios Sebethos as a man-faced bull standing to right on single line, head facing, bunch of grapes on vine leaves above, [monogram] below, [monogram] (retro)in ex.
REF: Sambon 634c; Taliercio IIa.25*.
Taliercio records 2 examples with 1 die pair.

259. AE Unit, 4.39g | **317/310 to 270 BC**

OBV: Head of Apollo facing right, wearing laurel wreath with leaves in opposing pairs, E behind. Dotted border.
REV: Acheloios Sebethos as a man-faced bull standing to right on single line, head facing, above, Phrygian helmet, [monogram] below, ΝΕΠΟΛΙΤΩΝ in ex.
REF: Sambon 625; Taliercio IIa.26; Potamikon Collection*.
Taliercio records 36 examples with more than 7 obverse dies and more than 7 reverse dies.

260. AE Unit, 2.82g, 15mm	317/310 to 270 BC
	OBV: Head of Apollo facing right, wearing laurel wreath with leaves in opposing pairs, ΝΕΟΠΟΛΙΤΩΝ before, E behind. REV: Acheloios Sebethos as a man-faced bull standing to right on single line, head facing, above, Tripod between letters Σ-A, below, E (Ξ for Taliercio). REF: Sambon 626a, Taliercio IIa.27; CNG 84, lot 54*. *Taliercio records 6 examples with 2 obverse dies and 2 reverse dies.*

261. AE Unit, 3.28g	317/310 to 270 BC
	OBV: Head of Apollo facing right, wearing laurel wreath with leaves in opposing pairs, ΝΕΟΠΟΛΙΤΩΝ before, E behind. REV: Acheloios Sebethos as a man-faced bull standing to right on single line, head facing, above, Tripod between the letters Ω-A, below. E (Ξ for Taliercio). REF: Sambon 626b, Taliercio IIa.28*. *Taliercio records 3 examples with 1 die pair.*

262. AE Unit,	317/310 to 270 BC
	OBV: Head of Apollo facing left, wearing laurel wreath with leaves in opposing pairs, ΝΕΟΠΟΛΙΤΩΝ before, Ξ behind. REV: Acheloios Sebethos as a man-faced bull standing to right on single line, head facing, above, Owl holding crayfish, E below, dolphin in ex. REF: Sambon 633+, Taliercio IIa.29; Agathodaimon Collection*. *Taliercio records 6 examples with 3 obverse dies and 3 reverse dies.*

263. AE Unit, 4.06g, 17mm	317/310 to 270 BC
	OBV: Head of Apollo facing left, wearing laurel wreath with leaves in triple clusters, ΝΕΟΠΟΛΙΤΩΝ before, Λ behind. Dotted border. REV: Acheloios Sebethos as a man-faced bull standing to right on single line, head facing, kantharos above, E below. REF: Sambon 635; Taliercio IIa.30; CNG 84, lot 55*. *Taliercio records 9 examples with 1 obverse die and 2 reverse dies.*

264. AE Unit, 3.78g	317/310 to 270 BC
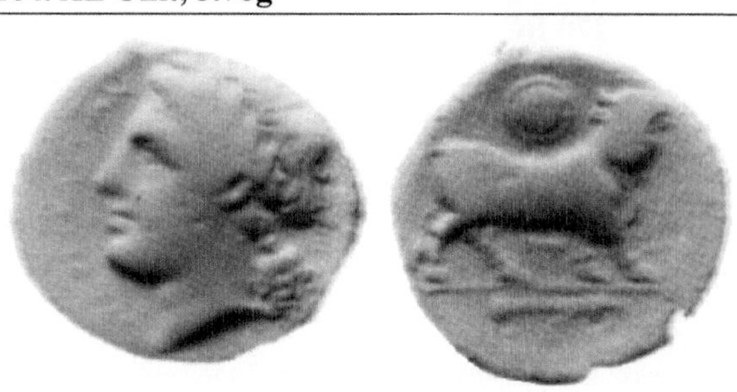	OBV: Head of Apollo facing left, wearing laurel wreath with leaves in triple clusters, ΝΕΟΠΟΛΙΤΩΝ before, E behind. Dotted border. REV: Acheloios Sebethos as a man-faced bull standing to right on single line, head facing, round shield above, ΑΦ below, sword in scabbard in ex. REF: Sambon 639; Taliercio IIa.31*. *Taliercio records 15 examples with 3 obverse dies and 6 reverse dies.*

265. AE Unit, 16mm | **317/310 to 270 BC**

OBV: Head of Apollo facing left, wearing laurel wreath with leaves in triple clusters, ΝΕΟΠΟΛΙΤΩΝ before, astragalos behind. Dotted border.
REV: Acheloios Sebethos as a man-faced bull standing to right on single line, head facing, round shield above, ΑΦ (?) below, sword in scabbard in ex. Linear border.
REF: Private Collection*

266. AE Unit, 4.60g, 15mm | **317/310 to 270 BC**

OBV: Head of Apollo facing left, wearing laurel wreath with leaves in opposing pairs (?), [monogram] behind.
REV: Acheloios Sebethos as a man-faced bull standing to right on single line, head facing, round shield above, (ΑΦ) in ex.
REF: Taliercio - ; Sambon 640, ACR e-Auction 7, lot 5*.
Sambon records a unique specimen, not reported by Taliercio. This is the second known specimen.

267. AE Unit, 17mm | **317/310 to 270 BC**

OBV: Head of Apollo facing left, wearing laurel wreath with leaves in opposing pairs, ΝΕΟΠΟΛΙΤΩΝ before, [monogram] behind. Dotted border.
REV: Acheloios Sebethos as a man-faced bull standing to right on single line, head facing, above, lightning bolt, E below, uncertain object in ex.
REF: Sambon 636; Taliercio IIa.32; Lanz eBay*.
Taliercio records 12 examples with 2 obverse dies and 2 reverse dies.

268. AE Unit, 4.57g, 16mm | **317/310 to 270 BC**

OBV: Head of Apollo facing left, wearing laurel wreath with leaves in triple clusters, ΝΕΟΠΟΛΙΤΩΝ before, [monogram] behind. Dotted border.
REV: Acheloios Sebethos as a man-faced bull standing to right on single line, head facing, lyre above, E below, uncertain symbol (sword or club?) in ex.
REF: Sambon 647; Taliercio IIa.33; SNG France 922 = BnF Fonds Général 404*.
Taliercio records 10 examples with 2 obverse dies and 3 reverse dies.

269. AE Unit 4.70g, 17mm | **317/310 to 270 BC**

OBV: Head of Apollo facing left, wearing laurel wreath with leaves in triple clusters, ΝΕΟΠΟΛΙΤΩΝ before. Dotted border.
REV: Acheloios Sebethos as a man-faced bull standing to right on single line, head facing, grasshopper above, ΕΩ in ex.
REF: Sambon 646; Taliercio IIa.34; SNG France 924 = BnF Y 20243.Seymour de Ricci 1233*.
Taliercio records 6 examples with 1 die pair.

270. AE Unit 4.55g, 18mm	**317/310 to 270 BC**
	OBV: Head of Apollo facing left, wearing laurel wreath with leaves in triple clusters, ΝΕΟΠΟΛΙΤΩΝ before. Dotted border. REV: Acheloios Sebethos as a man-faced bull standing to right on single line, head facing, above, grasshopper, below, ΣΑ. Linear border. REF: SNG Morcom 148 = BM no. 2013,4030.26*.

271. AE Unit, 3.59g	**317/310 to 270 BC**
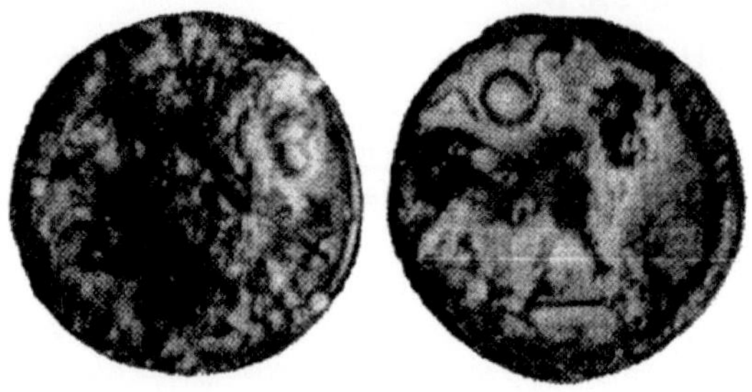	OBV: Head of Apollo facing left, wearing laurel wreath with leaves in triple clusters, ΝΕΟΠΟΛΙΤΩΝ before, X in field. REV: Acheloios Sebethos as a man-faced bull standing to right on single line, head facing, serpent above, uncertain symbol below. REF: Sambon 648; Taliercio IIa.35*. *Taliercio records 2 examples with 1 die pair.*

272. AE Unit, 2.92g, 15mmg	**317/310 to 270 BC**
	OBV: Head of Apollo facing left, wearing laurel wreath with leaves in triple clusters, ΝΕΟΠΟΛΙΤΩΝ before, I in field. REV: Acheloios Sebethos as a man-faced bull standing to right on single line, head facing, mask above, ΕΠ below, unclear device in ex. REF: Taliercio IIa.36; SNG France 925 = BnF Fonds Général 407*. *Taliercio records 5 examples with 1 obverse and 2 reverse dies.*

273. AE Unit, 4.92g, 15mm	**317/310 to 270 BC**
	OBV: Head of Apollo facing left, wearing laurel wreath with leaves in triple clusters, ΝΕΟΠΟΛΙΤΩΝ before, ΑΡ behind. Dotted border. REV: Acheloios Sebethos as a man-faced bull standing to right on single line, head facing, above, flower between letters Ε-Π, ΑΡ below, ΙΣ in ex. REF: Sambon 641; Taliercio IIa.37; Denant item n. 360876505527*. *Taliercio records 8 examples with 3 obverse and 3 reverse dies. She incorrectly listed this type as Sambon 640, which actually shows a round shield above, see our n. 258.*

274. AE Unit, 4.06g, 15mm	**317/310 to 270 BC**
	OBV: Head of Apollo facing left, wearing laurel wreath with leaves in triple clusters, ΝΕΟΠΟΛΙΤΩΝ before, BI monogram in field. REV: Acheloios Sebethos as a man-faced bull standing to right on single line, head facing, winged hippocampus above, nothing below, ΙΣ in ex. REF: Sambon 638; Taliercio IIa, 38; SNG France 927 = BnF Fonds Général 397*. *Taliercio records 12 examples with more than 3 obverse dies and 3 reverse dies.*

275. AE Unit, 3.49g, 15mm	**317/310 to 270 BC**
	OBV: Head of Apollo facing left, wearing laurel wreath with leaves in triple clusters, ΝΕΟΠΟΛΙΤΩΝ before, B in field. Dotted border. REV: Acheloios Sebethos as a man-faced bull standing to right on single line, head facing, above, astragalos, below, ΙΣ. REF: Taliercio IIa.39; Ancient Imports Classical Numismatics, VCoins SKU: 20367 *. *Taliercio records 1 example. The specimen illustrated here is the second known.*

276. AE Unit, 4.07g	**317/310 to 270 BC**
	OBV: Head of Apollo facing left, wearing laurel wreath with leaves in triple clusters, ΝΕΟΠΟΛΙΤΩΝ before, unclear (Sambon says /E) in field. Dotted border. REV: Acheloios Sebethos as a man-faced bull standing to right on single line, head facing, above, lyre, ΙΣ in ex. Linear border. REF: Sambon 637*; Taliercio IIa.40. *Taliercio records 2 examples with 2 obverse dies and 2 reverse dies.*

277. AE Unit, 4.08-4.35g	**317/310 to 270 BC**
	OBV: Head of Apollo facing left, wearing laurel wreath with leaves in opposing pairs, ΝΕΟΠΟΛΙΤΩΝ before. REV: Acheloios Sebethos as a man-faced bull standing to right on single line, head facing, bucrania above, ΙΣ in ex. REF: Sambon 645 var.; Taliercio - ; SNG München 286 (ΙΣ off flan and not recorded); Tintinna 53, lot 15=Potamikon Collection*.

Group IIc

278. AE Third Unit, 1.96g. 14mm	**317/310 to 270 BC**
	OBV: Head of Apollo facing right, wearing laurel wreath with leaves in opposing pairs. Dotted border. REV: Forepart of Acheloios Sebethos as a man-faced bull to right, ΝΕΟΠΟΛΙΤΩΝ above. Linear border. REF: Sambon 593; Taliercio Series IIc.1; LAC 19, lot 14*.

279. AE Third Unit, 2.29g	**317/310 to 270 BC**
	OBV: Head of Apollo facing right, wearing laurel wreath with leaves in triple clusters. REV: Forepart of Acheloios Sebethos as a man-faced bull to right, Δ in field, ΝΕΥΠΟΛΙΤΩΝ above. REF: Taliercio IIc, 2*. *Taliercio cites 6 examples with 1 die pair.* *Sambon 569 incorrectly lists the letter Δ on obverse instead of reverse field.*

280. AE Third Unit, 2.91g, 15mm	**317/310-270 BC**
	OBV: Head of Apollo facing right, wearing laurel wreath with leaves in triple clusters, ΑΡ in field. REV: Forepart of Acheloios Sebethos as a man-faced bull to right, Δ in field, ΝΕΟΠΟΛΙΤΩΝ above. REF: Taliercio - ; Artemide 24.2E, lot 1012*.

281. AE Third Unit, 1.43-3.08g	**317/310 to 270 BC**
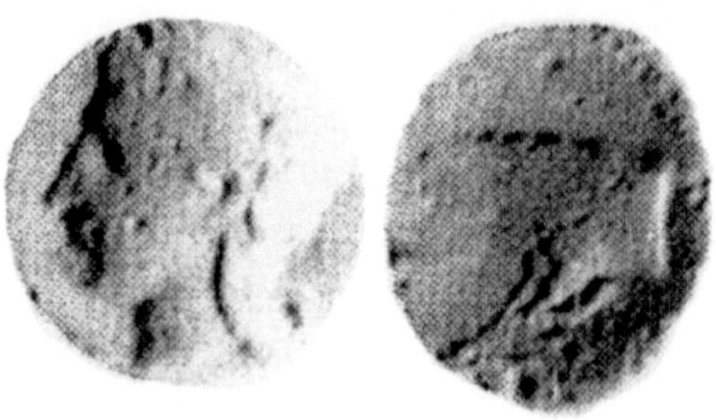	OBV: Head of Apollo facing left, wearing laurel wreath with leaves in opposing pairs, E in field. Dotted border. REV:Forepart of Acheloios Sebethos as a man-faced bull to left, (Δ in field), ΝΕΟΠΟΛΙΤΩΝ above. REF: Sambon 597-8; Taliercio IIc.3*. *Taliercio cites 11 examples with 3 die pairs.*

282. Third Unit 1.90g, 13mm	**317/310 to 270 BC**
	OBV: Head of Apollo facing right, wearing laurel wreath with leaves in opposing pairs, A in field. REV: Forepart of Acheloios Sebethos as a man-faced bull to right, E behind, ΝΕΟΠΟΛΙΤΩΝ above. REF: Taliercio - ; CNG 61, part of lot 12*.

283. AE Third Unit, 1.94g	**317/310 to 270 BC**
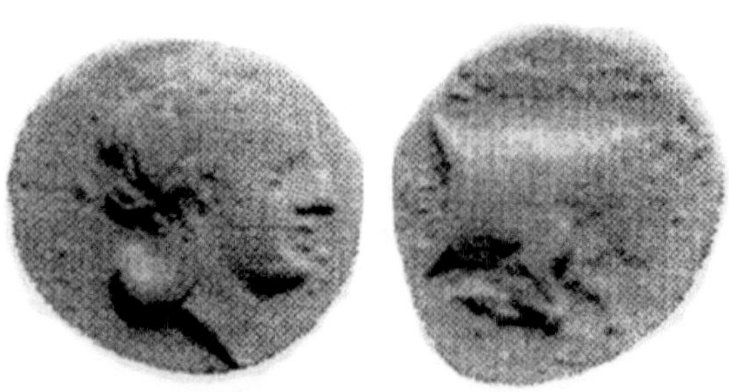	OBV: Head of Apollo facing right, wearing laurel wreath with leaves in triple clusters. REV:Forepart of Acheloios Sebethos as a man-faced bull to right, ME behind, E below, ΝΕΟΠΟΛΙΤΩΝ above. REF: Sambon 594; Taliercio IIc.4*. *Taliercio cites 1 known specimen.*

284. AE Third Unit, 1.80g	**317/310 to 270 BC**
	OBV: Head of Apollo facing right, wearing laurel wreath with leaves in triple clusters. REV: Forepart of Acheloios Sebethos as a man-faced bull to right, E below, (ΝΕΟΠΟΛΙΤΩΝ ?) above. REF: Sambon 595; Taliercio - ; SNG France 952 = BnF Y 20243, Seymour de Ricci 1224*.

285. AE Third Unit, 1.76g — **317/310 to 270 BC**

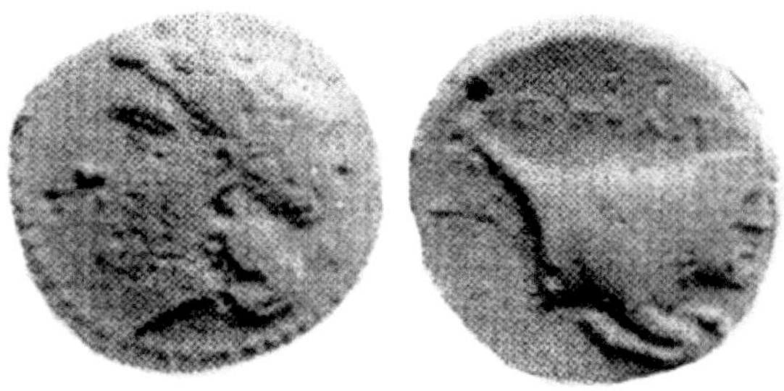

OBV: Head of Apollo facing left, wearing laurel wreath with leaves in opposing pairs, ΛΟ in field. Dotted border.
REV: Forepart of Acheloios Sebethos as a man-faced bull to right, ΝΕΟΠΟΛΙΤΩΝ above, ΜΕ over ΒΙ behind .
REF: Sambon 596; Taliercio IIc.5*.
Taliercio cites 4 examples with 1 die pair.
Sambon lists a variant with just Λ in obverse field.

286. AE Third Unit, 1.34g — **317/310 to 270 BC**

OBV: Head of Apollo facing left, wearing laurel wreath with leaves in opposing pairs, crescent in field.
REV: Forepart of Acheloios Sebethos as a man-faced bull to right, ΝΕΟΠΟΛΙΤΩΝ above, Π behind.
REF: Sambon 599; Taliercio IIc.6; InAsta 50, lot 16*.
Taliercio cites 20 known examples with 10 obverse dies and 5 reverse dies.

287. AE Third Unit, 1.92g, 12mm — **317/310 to 270 BC**

OBV: Head of Apollo facing left, wearing laurel wreath with leaves in opposing pairs, crescent in field.
REV: Forepart of Acheloios Sebethos as a man-faced bull to right, ΝΕΟΠΟΛΙΤΩΝ above, ΑΠ behind.
REF: Taliercio IIc.6 var.; SNG France 953 = BnF Fonds Général 378*.
Taliercio included the specimen stored at Paris under her series IIc.6, describing only Π in the reverse field, but it is actually a new variant with ΑΠ, cf. BnF AA. GR. 18322 (1.89g).

288. AE Third Unit, 2.33g — **317/310 to 270 BC**

OBV: Head of Apollo facing left, wearing laurel wreath with leaves in opposing pairs.
REV: Forepart of Acheloios Sebethos as a man-faced bull to right, ΝΕΟΠΟΛΙΤΩΝ above, Σ behind.
REF: Sambon 600; Taliercio IIc.7; H.D. Rauch GmbH 81, lot 25*.
Taliercio cites 3 examples with 1 die pair.

289. AE Third Unit, 2.05g — **317/310 to 270 BC**

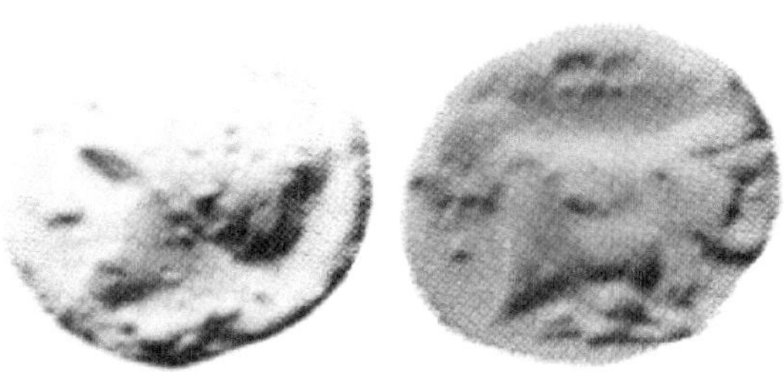

OBV: Head of Apollo facing left, wearing laurel wreath with leaves in opposing pairs, X in field.
REV: Forepart of Acheloios Sebethos as a man-faced bull to right, ΝΕΟΠΟΛΙΤΩΝ above, unclear symbol/ letter in field.
REF: Taliercio IIc.8*.
Taliercio cites 3 examples with 1 die pair.

290. AE Third Unit, 2.29g, 15mm	**317/310 to 270 BC**
	OBV: Head of Apollo facing left, wearing laurel wreath with leaves in opposing pairs, star with 8 rays behind, A in right field. REV: Forepart of Acheloios Sebethos as a man-faced bull to right, ΝΕΟΠΟΛΙΤΩΝ above, ΙΣ in field. REF: Taliercio IIc.9-10; SNG France 957 = BnF Y 20243.Seymour de Ricci 1225*. *Taliercio listed IIc.9 as a variant with Λ instead of ΙΣ, but the example she published (BnF Fonds Général 379) actually shows traces of Σ, not Λ. The same goes for SNG Cop. 482, which she included in IIc.9. Therefore, Taliercio IIc.9 is not a distinct variety.*

291. AE Third Unit, 2.17g	**317/310 to 270 BC**
	OBV: Head of Apollo facing left, wearing laurel wreath with leaves in opposing pairs, [monogram] before, A behind. Dotted border. REV: Forepart of Acheloios Sebethos as a man-faced bull to right, ΝΕΟΠΟΛΙΤΩΝ above, ΙΣ behind. REF: Sambon 601b; Taliercio IIc.11*. *Taliercio cites 4 known examples with 4 obverse dies and 4 reverse dies.*

292. AE Third Unit, 2.16g, 14mm	**317/310 to 270 BC**
	OBV: Head of Apollo facing left, wearing laurel wreath with leaves in opposing pairs, [monogram] before, A behind. Dotted border. REV: Forepart of Acheloios Sebethos as a man-faced bull to right, ΝΕΟΠΟΛΙΤΟΝ above. REF: Taliercio IIc.11 var ; SNG Morcom 149*. *This unique variant features an omicron instead of omega in the ethnic.*

293. AE Third Unit, 2.25g, 13mm	**317/310 to 270 BC**
	OBV: Head of Apollo facing left, wearing laurel wreath with leaves in triple clusters(?), [monogram] before, Λ behind. Dotted border. REV: Forepart of Acheloios Sebethos as a man-faced bull to right, ΝΕΟΠΟΛΙΤΩΝ above, ΙΣ behind. REF: Sambon 601var; Taliercio IIc.12; SNG France 959 = BnF Fonds Général 375*. *Taliercio cites 10 known examples with 3 obverse dies and 2 reverse dies.*

294. AE Third Unit, 12mm	**317/310 to 270 BC**
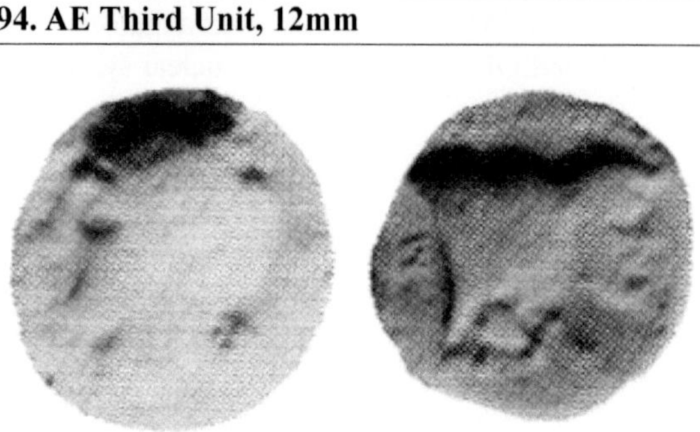	OBV: Head of Apollo facing left, wearing laurel wreath with leaves in opposing pairs, unclear symbol or letter before, uncertain letter behind (Π?). REV: Forepart of Acheloios Sebethos as a man-faced bull to right, ΝΕΟΠΟΛΙΤΩΝ above, ΙΣ behind. REF: Taliercio IIc.13*.

Group IId

295. AE Quarter Unit, 1.07g	**317/310 to 270 BC**
	OBV: Head of Apollo facing left, wearing laurel wreath with leaves in opposing pairs, ΝΕΟΠΟΛΙΤΩΝ before. Dotted border. REV: Forepart of Acheloios Sebethos as a man-faced bull to right, dolphin above swimming right. REF: Sambon 581; Taliercio IId.1; Dr. Busso Peus 384, lot 11*. *Taliercio cites 7 examples with 3 obverse dies and 3 reverse dies.*

296. AE Quarter Unit, 1.29-1.96g	**317/310 to 270 BC**
	OBV: Head of Apollo facing right, wearing laurel wreath with leaves in triple clusters, four dolphins surrounding, ΝΕΟΠΟΛΙΤΩΝ before. Dotted border. REV: Forepart of Acheloios Sebethos as a man-faced bull to right, dolphin above swimming right (Sambon: three globules behind). Dotted border. REF: Sambon 586*; Taliercio IId.2. *Taliercio cites 2 examples with 2 obverse dies and 2 reverse dies.*

297. AE Quarter Unit, 1.75g	**317/310 to 270 BC**
	OBV: Head of Apollo facing right, wearing laurel wreath with leaves in triple clusters, four dolphins surrounding, ΝΕΟΠΟΛΙΤΩΝ before. Dotted border. REV: Forepart of Acheloios Sebethos as a man-faced bull to right, dolphin above swimming right , ΔΙ in field . REF: Taliercio IId.3*. *Taliercio cites 2 examples with 1 obverse die and 2 reverse dies.*

298. AE Quarter Unit, 1.02g, 12mm	**317/310 to 270 BC**
	OBV: Head of Apollo facing right, wearing laurel wreath with leaves in triple clusters or opposing pairs, ΝΕΟΠΟΛΙΤΩΝ before, Δ in field. REV: Forepart of Acheloios Sebethos as a man-faced bull to right, dolphin above swimming right, star with 8 rays behind. REF: Sambon 583; Taliercio IId.4; SNG Fitzwilliam 180*.

299. AE Quarter Unit, 1.81g, 15mm	**317/310 to 270 BC**
	OBV: Head of Apollo facing right, wearing laurel wreath with leaves in opposing pairs, ΝΕΟΠΟΛΙΤΩΝ before. Dotted border. REV: Forepart of Acheloios Sebethos as a man-faced bull to right, dolphin above swimming right, ΦΙ behind, MA monogram below. Dotted border. REF: Taliercio IId.5; SNG France 964 = BnF N 3669*. *Taliercio cites 3 examples with 1 die pair.* *The coin illustrated here is the fourth known specimen.*

300. AE Quarter Unit, 1.71g	**317/310 to 270 BC**
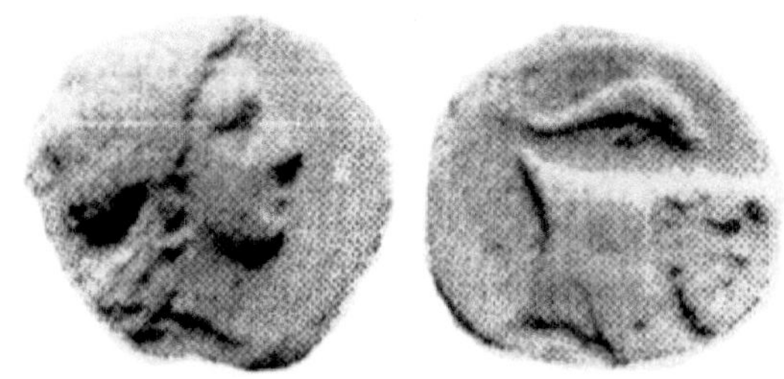	OBV: Head of Apollo facing right, wearing laurel wreath with leaves in opposing pairs, ΝΕΟΠΟΛΙΤΩΝ before, K in field. REV: Forepart of Acheloios Sebethos as a man-faced bull to right, dolphin above swimming right. REF: Sambon 584; Taliercio IId.6*. *Taliercio cites 6 examples with 2 obverse dies and 2 reverse dies.*

301. AE Quarter Unit, 1.52g	**317/310 to 270 BC**
	OBV: Head of Apollo facing right, wearing laurel wreath with leaves in triple clusters, K (retro) behind. REV: Forepart of Acheloios Sebethos as a man-faced bull to right, dolphin above swimming right, K (retro) behind. REF: Taliercio - (IId.6 var.); Künker 133, lot 7018*.

302. AE Quarter Unit, 1.91g, 11mm	**317/310 to 270 BC**
	OBV: Head of Apollo facing right, wearing laurel wreath with leaves in triple clusters, A in field, (ΝΕΟΠΟΛΙΤΩΝ) before. Dotted border. REV: Forepart of Acheloios Sebethos as a man-faced bull to right, dolphin above swimming right, A in field. Linear border. REF: Taliercio IId.7: SNG France 963 = BnF Armand Valton 20*. *Taliercio cites 2 examples with 1 die pair. The coin illustrated here is the third known specimen.*

303. AE Quarter Unit, 2.52g	**317/310 to 270 BC**
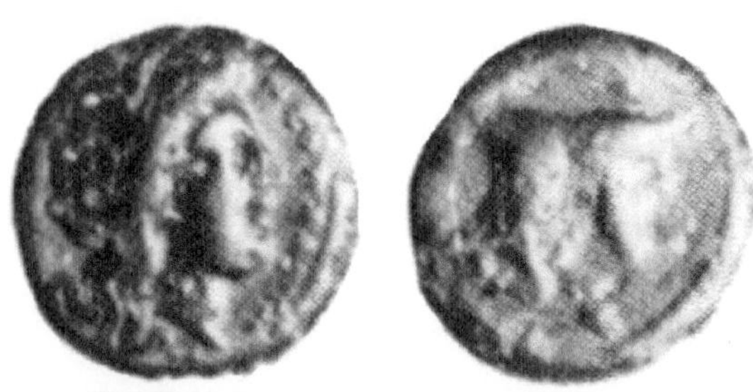	OBV: Head of Apollo facing right, wearing laurel wreath with leaves in opposing pairs, ΝΕΟΠΟΛΙΤΩΝ before. Dotted border (?). REV: Forepart of Acheloios Sebethos as a man-faced bull to right, dolphin above swimming right, Γ in field. Dotted border. REF: Taliercio IId.8*. *Taliercio cites 5 examples with 3 obverse dies and 3 reverse dies.*

304. AE Quarter Unit, 1.35g	**317/310 to 270 BC**
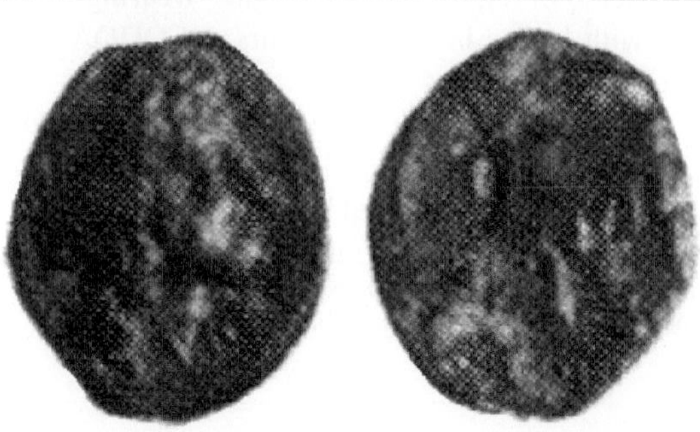	OBV: Head of Apollo facing right, wearing laurel wreath with leaves in opposing pairs. Dotted border. REV: Forepart of Acheloios Sebethos as a man-faced bull to right, dolphin above swimming right, Γ (retro) in field. Dotted border. REF: Taliercio IId.9*. *Taliercio cites 4 examples with 1 die pair.*

305. AE Quarter Unit, 0.97-1.54g | **317/310 to 270 BC**

OBV: Head of Apollo facing right, wearing laurel wreath with leaves in opposing pairs, Λ behind, ΝΕΟΠΟΛΙΤΩΝ before.
REV: Forepart of Acheloios Sebethos as a man-faced bull to right, dolphin above swimming right, Λ (Taliercio says ΟΛ (?)) behind.
REF: Sambon 585*; Taliercio IId.10.
Taliercio cites 6 known examples with 2 obverse dies and 2 reverse dies.

306. AE Quarter Unit, 1.37g | **317/310 to 270 BC**

OBV: Head of Apollo facing left, wearing laurel wreath with leaves in opposing pairs, Λ behind, ΝΕΟΠΟΛΙΤΩΝ before. Dotted border.
REV: Forepart of Acheloios Sebethos as a man-faced bull to left, dolphin above, Z and M in field.
REF: Sambon 587; Taliercio IId.11; Potamikon Collection*.
Taliercio cites 8 known examples with 2 obverse dies and 2 reverse dies.

307. AE Quarter Unit, 1.12g | **317/310 to 270 BC**

OBV: Head of Apollo facing left, wearing laurel wreath with leaves in opposing pairs, N behind, ΝΕΟΠΟΛΙΤΩΝ before. Dotted border.
REV: Forepart of Acheloios Sebethos as a man-faced bull to left, dolphin above, Z and M in field. Dotted border.
REF: Taliercio IId.12*.
Taliercio cites 7 examples with 1 die pair.

308. AE Quarter Unit, 0.94g | **317/310 to 270 BC**

OBV: Head of Apollo facing left, wearing laurel wreath with leaves in opposing pairs, ΑΡ in field, ΝΕΟΠΟΛΙΤΩΝ before.
REV: Forepart of Acheloios Sebethos as a man-faced bull to left, dolphin above, E in field.
REF: Taliercio IId.13*.
Taliercio cites 8 examples with 3 obverse dies and 2 reverse dies.

309. AE Quarter Unit, 1.34g | **317/310 to 270 BC**

OBV: Head of Apollo facing left, wearing laurel wreath with leaves in opposing pairs, EY in field, ΝΕΟΠΟΛΙΤΩΝ before. Dotted border.
REV: Forepart of Acheloios Sebethos as a man-faced bull to right, dolphin above, uncertain device in field behind and below. Dotted border.
REF: Taliercio IId.14*.
Taliercio cites 4 known examples with 2 obverse dies and 2 reverse dies.

310. AE Quarter Unit, unrecorded weight	317/310 to 270 BC
	OBV: Head of Apollo facing left, wearing laurel wreath with leaves in opposing pairs, ME monogram behind, ΝΕΟΠΟΛΙΤΩΝ before. Dotted border. REV: Forepart of Acheloios Sebethos as a man-faced bull to right, dolphin above, Σ behind. Dotted border. REF: Sambon 589; Taliercio IId.15; Private Collection*. *Taliercio cites 8 known examples with 4 obverse dies and 4 reverse dies.*

311. AE Quarter Unit, 1.19g	317/310 to 270 BC
	OBV: Head of Apollo facing left, wearing laurel wreath with leaves in opposing pairs, ME monogram behind, ΝΕΟΠΟΛΙΤΩΝ before. Dotted border. REV:Forepart of Acheloios Sebethos as a man-faced bull to right, dolphin above, BI behind. Dotted border. REF: Taliercio IId.16*. *Taliercio cites 1 known example.*

312. AE Quarter Unit, 1.06g	317/310 to 270 BC
	OBV: Head of Apollo facing left, wearing laurel wreath with leaves in opposing pairs, ME monogram behind, ΝΕΟΠΟΛΙΤΩΝ before. Dotted border. REV: Forepart of Acheloios Sebethos as a man-faced bull to right, dolphin above, ΛO over BI behind. Dotted border. REF: Sambon 590; Taliercio IId.17; SNG Morcom 151 = BM no. 2013,4030.27*. *Taliercio cites 1 known example.* *This one is the second known specimen.*

313. AE Quarter Unit, 0-96g	317/310 to 270 BC
	OBV: Head of Apollo facing left, wearing laurel wreath with leaves in opposing pairs, ME monogram behind, ΝΕΟΠΟΛΙΤΩΝ before. Dotted border. REV: Forepart of Acheloios Sebethos as a man-faced bull to right, dolphin above, NY over BI behind. Dotted border. REF: Sambon 591; Taliercio IId.18; InAsta 40, lot 42*. *Taliercio cites 3 known examples with 1 die pair.*

314. AE Quarter Unit, 1.18g	317/310 to 270 BC
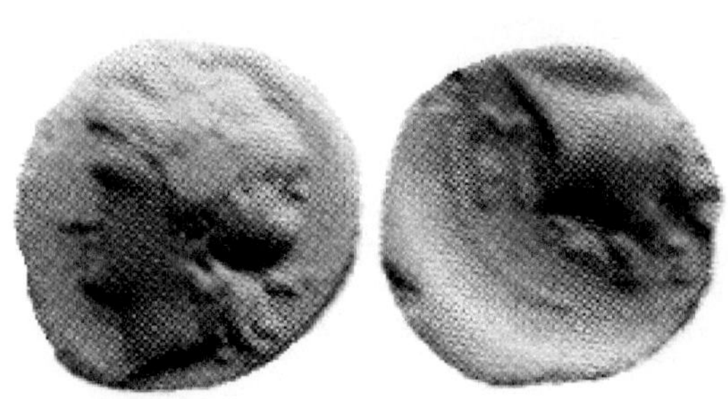	OBV: Head of Apollo facing left, wearing laurel wreath with leaves in opposing pairs, NU behind, ΝΕΟΠΟΛΙΤΩΝ before. Dotted border. REV: Forepart of Acheloios Sebethos as a man-faced bull to right, dolphin above, ΛO over BI behind. Dotted border. REF: SNG Morcom 151; Taliercio IId.19*. *Taliercio cites 5 examples with 1 die pair.*

315. AE Quarter Unit, 1.12g, 11mm	317/310 to 270 BC
	OBV: Head of Apollo facing left, wearing laurel wreath with leaves in opposing pairs, ΝΕΟΠΟΛΙΤΩΝ before. Dotted border. REV: Forepart of Acheloios Sebethos as a man-faced bull to right, dolphin above, BI behind. Dotted border. REF: Sambon 592; Taliercio IId.20; SNG France 966 = BnF Fonds Général 374*. *Taliercio cites 8 known examples with 7 obverse dies and 4 reverse dies.*

316. AE Quarter Unit, 1.45g	317/310 to 270 BC
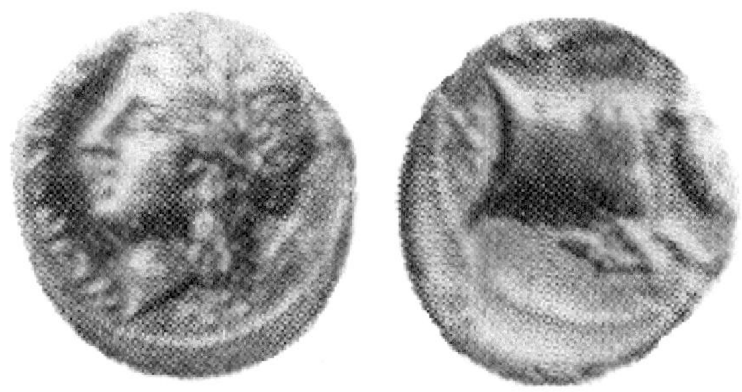	OBV: Head of Apollo facing left, wearing laurel wreath with leaves in opposing pairs, AP in field, ΝΕΟΠΟΛΙΤΩΝ before. Dotted border. REV: Forepart of Acheloios Sebethos as a man-faced bull to right, dolphin above, X behind. Dotted border. REF: Sambon 588+;Taliercio IId.21*. *Taliercio cites 11 known examples with 5 obverse dies and 4 reverse dies.*

317. AE Quarter Unit, 1.17g	317/310 to 270 BC
	OBV: Head of Apollo facing left, wearing laurel wreath with leaves in opposing pairs, behind, star with eight rays (over AP?), ΝΕΟΠΟΛΙΤΩΝ before. Dotted border. REV: Forepart of Acheloios Sebethos as a man-faced bull to right, dolphin above, A behind. Dotted border. REF: Potamikon Collection*. *Unique*

TALIERCIO PHASE III

Group IIIa

318. AE Unit, 4.36g, 18mm	270 to 250 BC
	OBV: Head of Apollo facing left, wearing laurel wreath with leaves in opposing pairs, ΝΕΟΠΟΛΙΤΩΝ before, lyre behind. Dotted border. REV: Acheloios Sebethos as a man-faced bull standing to right on single line, head facing, above, winged nymph crowns him. REF: Sambon 651; Taliercio IIIa.1; The New York Sale 5, lot 1*. *Taliercio records 11 examples with 3 obverse dies and 4 reverse dies.*

319. AE Unit 4.24g, 18mm	270 to 250 BC
	OBV: Head of Apollo facing left, wearing laurel wreath with leaves in opposing pairs, ΝΕΟΠΟΛΙΤΩΝ before, lyre behind. Dotted border. REV: Acheloios Sebethos as a man-faced bull standing to right on single line, head facing, above, winged nymph crowns him, trace of letter below. REF: CNG 84, lot 58*. *Unpublished. Taliercio does not list any variant with lyre behind Apollo and letters beneath the man-faced bull.*

320. AE Unit 5.35g	**270 to 250 BC**
	OBV: Head of Apollo facing left, wearing laurel wreath with leaves in opposing pairs, ΝΕΟΠΟΛΙΤΩΝ before, lyre behind. Dotted border. REV: Acheloios Sebethos as a man-faced bull standing to right on single line, head facing, above, winged nymph crowns him, O below. REF: Künker 94, lot 60*. *Unpublished. Taliercio does not list any variant with Lyre behind Apollo and letters beneath the man-faced bull.*

321. AE Unit, 6.91g	**270 to 250 BC**
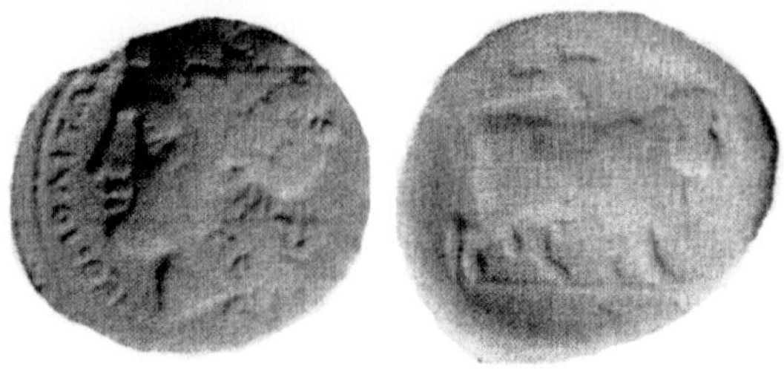	OBV: Head of Apollo facing left, wearing laurel wreath with leaves in opposing pairs, ΝΕΟΠΟΛΙΤΩΝ before. Dotted border. REV: Acheloios Sebethos as a man-faced bull standing to right on single line, head facing, above, winged nymph crowns him. REF: Taliercio IIIa.2*. *Taliercio records 4 examples with 3 obverse dies and 4 reverse dies.*

322. AE Unit	**270 to 250 BC**
	OBV: Head of Apollo facing left, wearing laurel wreath with leaves in opposing pairs, (ΝΕΟΠΟΛΙΤΩΝ) before, A in field. Dotted border. REV: Acheloios Sebethos as a man-faced bull standing to right on single line, head facing, above, winged nymph crowns him, uncertain below. REF: Taliercio - ; Torino 668; InAsta 29 lot 42*.

323. AE Unit, 5.40g	**270 to 250 BC**
	OBV: Head of Apollo facing left, wearing laurel wreath with leaves in opposing pairs, ΝΕΟΠΟΛΙΤΩΝ before, B in field. Dotted border. REV: Acheloios Sebethos as a man-faced bull standing to right on single line, head facing, above, winged nymph crowns him, ΙΣ below, M in ex. REF: Sambon 654; Taliercio IIIa.3; Artemide 5E lot 1027*. *Taliercio records 1 example, but the device in exergue was off flan and so she did not record that feature.*

324. AE Unit, 5.74g, 18mm	**270 to 250 BC**
	OBV: Head of Apollo facing left, wearing laurel wreath with leaves in opposing pairs, ΝΕΟΠΟΛΙΤΩΝ before, B in field. Dotted border. REV: Acheloios Sebethos as a man-faced bull standing to right on single line, head facing, above, winged nymph crowns him, E below, ΙΣ in ex. REF: Sambon 653; Taliercio IIIa.4; SNG France 969 = Delepierre BnF 1966.453*. *Taliercio records 19 examples with 7 obverse dies and 8 reverse dies.*

325. AE Unit, 6.55g	270 to 250 BC
	OBV: Head of Apollo facing left, wearing laurel wreath with leaves in opposing pairs, ΝΕΟΠΟΛΙΤΩΝ before, B in field. Dotted border. REV: Acheloios Sebethos as a man-faced bull standing to right on single line, head facing, above, winged nymph crowns him, ΛΟ (?) below. REF: Taliercio - ; Graziano 379 = Jencek H.I. n.596*.

326. AE Unit, 4.55g	270 to 250 BC
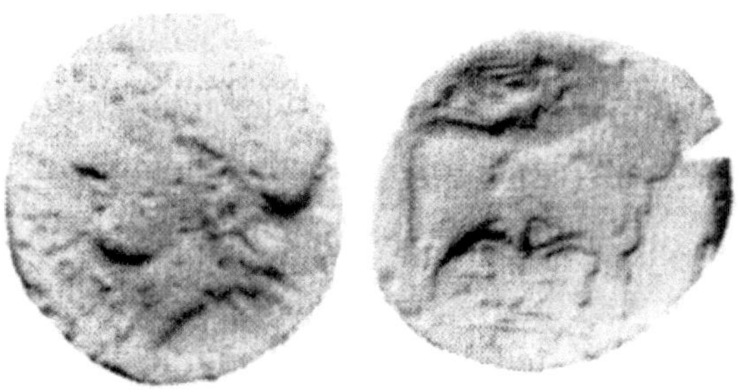	OBV: Head of Apollo facing left, wearing laurel wreath with leaves in opposing pairs, ΝΕΟΠΟΛΙΤΩΝ before, B in field. Dotted border. REV: Acheloios Sebethos as a man-faced bull standing to right on single line, head facing, above, winged nymph crowns him, ΟΣ below, I Σ in ex. REF: Sambon 652; Taliercio IIIa.5*. *Taliercio records 1 example.*

327. AE Unit, 6.48g, 21mm	270 to 250 BC
	OBV: Head of Apollo facing left, wearing laurel wreath with leaves in opposing pairs, ΝΕΟΠΟΛΙΤΩΝ before, B in field. Dotted border. REV: Acheloios Sebethos as a man-faced bull standing to right on single line, head facing, above, winged nymph crowns him, IΣ below, X in ex. REF: Sambon - ;Taliercio - ; SNG ANS 490; Forvm Ancient Coins item n.80455*.

328. AE Unit, 6.77g, 18mm	270 to 250 BC
	OBV: Head of Apollo facing left, wearing laurel wreath with leaves in opposing pairs, ΝΕΟΠΟΛΙΤΩΝ before, Γ in field. Dotted border. REV: Acheloios Sebethos as a man-faced bull standing to right on single line, head facing, above, winged nymph crowns him, IΣ below, X in ex. REF: Sambon 656; Taliercio IIIa.6; SNG France 986 = BnF Armand Valton 21*. *Taliercio records 13 examples with more than 4 obverse dies and more than 5 reverse dies.*

329. AE Unit, 5.77g	270 to 250 BC
	OBV: Head of Apollo facing left, wearing laurel wreath with leaves in opposing pairs, ΝΕΟΠΟΛΙΤΩΝ before, Γ in field. Dotted border. REV: Acheloios Sebethos as a man-faced bull standing to right on single line, head facing, above, winged nymph crowns him, ΟΣ below, IΣ in ex. REF: Sambon 655; Taliercio IIIa.7; InAsta 58, lot 19*. *Taliercio cites 2 examples with 1 obverse die and 2 reverse dies.*

330. AE Unit, 6.88g, 19mm

270 to 250 BC

OBV: Head of Apollo facing left, wearing laurel wreath with leaves in opposing pairs, ΝΕΟΠΟΛΙΤΩΝ before, Δ in field. Dotted border.
REV: Acheloios Sebethos as a man-faced bull standing to right on single line, head facing, above, winged nymph crowns him, ΙΣ below, ΒΩ in ex.
REF: Sambon 657; Taliercio IIIa.8; Artemide 13E, lot 13007*.
Taliercio cites 9 examples with 6 obverse dies and 5 reverse dies.

331. AE Unit, 4.93g

270 to 250 BC

OBV: Head of Apollo facing left, wearing laurel wreath with leaves in opposing pairs, ΝΕΟΠΟΛΙΤΩΝ before, Δ in field. Dotted border.
REV: Acheloios Sebethos as a man-faced bull standing to right on single line, head facing, above, winged nymph crowns him,ΟΣ below, ΙΣ in ex.
REF: Taliercio IIIa.9, n.3 = BnF Fonds Général 442*.
Taliercio cites 3 examples with 2 obverse dies and 2 reverse dies.

332. AE Unit, 5.20g

270 to 250 BC

OBV: Head of Apollo facing left, wearing laurel wreath with leaves in opposing pairs, ΝΕΟΠΟΛΙΤΩΝ before, Δ in field. Dotted border.
REV: Acheloios Sebethos as a man-faced bull standing to right on single line, head facing, above, winged nymph crowns him,ΙΣ below, ΟΣ in ex.
REF: Taliercio - ; Graziano 388*.

333. AE Unit, 6.46g

270 to 250 BC

OBV: Head of Apollo facing left, wearing laurel wreath with leaves in opposing pairs, ΝΕΟΠΟΛΙΤΩΝ before, E in field. Dotted border.
REV: Acheloios Sebethos as a man-faced bull standing to right on single line, head facing, above, winged nymph crowns him, MB monogram or ME below, ΙΣ in ex.
REF: Sambon 658; Taliercio IIIa.10; CNG 73, lot 11*.
Taliercio cites 20 examples with 10 obverse dies and 10 reverse dies.

334. AE Unit, 5.90g

270 to 250 BC

OBV: Head of Apollo facing left, wearing laurel wreath with leaves in opposing pairs, ΝΕΟΠΟΛΙΤΩΝ before, Z in field. Dotted border.
REV: Acheloios Sebethos as a man-faced bull standing to right on single line, head facing, above, winged nymph crowns him, ΙΣ below.
REF: Sambon 659; Taliercio IIIa.11; Brunetti Electronic Auction V, lot 29 *.
Taliercio cites 13 examples with 8 obverse dies and 9 reverse dies.

335. AE Unit, 5.01-6.53g	**270 to 250 BC**
	OBV: Head of Apollo facing left, wearing laurel wreath with leaves in opposing pairs, ΝΕΟΠΟΛΙΤΩΝ before, Z in field. Dotted border. REV: Acheloios Sebethos as a man-faced bull standing to right on single line, head facing, above, winged nymph crowns him, ΙΣ in ex. REF: Taliercio - ; SNG France 999 = BnF Luynes 184*. *This specimen is cataloged under variant IIIa.37 by Taliercio; we recognize it as a new variety.*

336. AE Unit, 6.06g	**270 to 250 BC**
	OBV: Head of Apollo facing left, wearing laurel wreath with leaves in opposing pairs, ΝΕΟΠΟΛΙΤΩΝ before, H in field. Dotted border. REV: Acheloios Sebethos as a man-faced bull standing to right on single line, head facing, above, winged nymph crowns him, ΙΣ below. REF: Sambon 662; Taliercio IIIa.12*. *Taliercio cites 5 examples with more than 3 obverse dies and more than 2 reverse dies.*

337. AE Unit, 6.32g	**270 to 250 BC**
	OBV: Head of Apollo facing left, wearing laurel wreath with leaves in opposing pairs, ΝΕΟΠΟΛΙΤΩΝ before, H behind. Dotted border. REV: Acheloios Sebethos as a man-faced bull standing to right on single line, head facing, above, winged nymph crowns him, ΙΣ below, Σ in ex. REF: Taliercio - ; SNG France 979 = BnF Seymour de Ricci 1238*.

338. AE Unit	**270 to 250 BC**
	OBV: Head of Apollo facing left, wearing laurel wreath with leaves in opposing pairs, ΝΕΟΠΟΛΙΤΩΝ before, H in field. Dotted border. REV: Acheloios Sebethos as a man-faced bull standing to right on single line, head facing, above, winged nymph crowns him, Σ below, ΙΣ in ex. REF: Sambon 661; Taliercio IIIa.13; ACR E8, lot 9*. *Taliercio cites 29 examples with more than 11 obverse dies and 11 reverse dies.*

339. AE Unit, 5.12g, 20mm	**270 to 250 BC**
	OBV: Head of Apollo facing left, wearing laurel wreath with leaves in opposing pairs, ΝΕΟΠΟΛΙΤΩΝ before, uncertain H or B in field. Dotted border. REV: Acheloios Sebethos as a man-faced bull standing to right on single line, head facing, above, winged nymph crowns him, Σ below, ΙΣ in ex. REF: SNG France 976 = BnF Fonds Général 413*. *This specimen is listed as IIIa.22 by Taliercio (our 329), but shows a Sigma instead of monogram below the man-faced bull.*

340. AE Unit, 4.73g, 20mm	**270 to 250 BC**
	OBV: Head of Apollo facing left, wearing laurel wreath with leaves in opposing pairs, ΝΕΟΠΟΛΙΤΩΝ before, H in field. Dotted border. REV: Acheloios Sebethos as a man-faced bull standing to right on single line, head facing, above, winged nymph crowns him, uncertain monogram (?) below, IΣ in ex. REF: Taliercio - ; LAC 8, lot 7*.

341. AE Unit, 6.45g	**270 to 250 BC**
	OBV: Head of Apollo facing left, wearing laurel wreath with leaves in opposing pairs, ΝΕΟΠΟΛΙΤΩΝ before, H in field. Dotted border. REV: Acheloios Sebethos as a man-faced bull standing to right on single line, head facing, above, winged nymph crowns him, ΟΣ below, IΣ in ex. REF: Sambon 660; Taliercio IIIa.14*. *Taliercio cites 4 examples with 3 obverse dies and 3 reverse dies.*

342. AE Unit, 4.47g	**270 to 250 BC**
	OBV: Head of Apollo facing left, wearing laurel wreath with leaves in opposing pairs, ΝΕΟΠΟΛΙΤΩΝ before, H in field. Dotted border. REV: Acheloios Sebethos as a man-faced bull standing to right on single line, head facing, above, winged nymph crowns him, IΣ below, ΟΣ in ex. REF: Taliercio IIIa.15*. *Taliercio cites 3 examples with 2 obverse dies and 2 reverse dies.*

343. AE Unit, 4.99g, 18mm	**270 to 250 BC**
	OBV: Head of Apollo facing left, wearing laurel wreath with leaves in opposing pairs, ΝΕΟΠΟΛΙΤΩΝ before, Θ in field. Dotted border. REV: Acheloios Sebethos as a man-faced bull standing to right on single line, head facing, above, winged nymph crowns him, IΣ below. REF: Sambon 663; Taliercio IIIa.16; ACR E-Auction 28 lot 12*. *Taliercio cites 3 examples with more than 1 obverse die and more than 1 reverse die.*

344. AE Unit, 4.69g, 18mm	**270 to 250 BC**
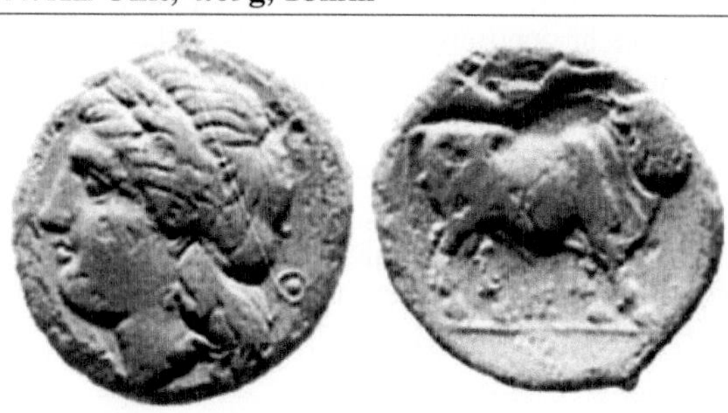	OBV: Head of Apollo facing left, wearing laurel wreath with leaves in opposing pairs, ΝΕΟΠΟΛΙΤΩΝ before, Θ in field. Dotted border. REV: Acheloios Sebethos as a man-faced bull standing to right on single line, head facing, above, winged nymph crowns him, IΣ below, [monogram] in ex. REF: Taliercio IIIa.17; SNG Morcom 157 = Graziano 398*. *Taliercio cites 2 examples with 2 obverse dies and 2 reverse dies.*

345. AE Unit, 5.65g	270 to 250 BC
	OBV: Head of Apollo facing left, wearing laurel wreath with leaves in opposing pairs, ΝΕΟΠΟΛΙΤΩΝ before, Θ in field. Dotted border. REV: Acheloios Sebethos as a man-faced bull standing to right on single line, head facing, above, winged nymph crowns him, ΟΣ below, ΙΣ in ex. REF: Taliercio IIIa.18; M&M GmbH 30 lot 3*. *Taliercio cites 22 examples with 12 obverse dies and 12 reverse dies.*

346. AE Unit, 4.92g, 18mm	270 to 250 BC
	OBV: Head of Apollo facing left, wearing laurel wreath with leaves in opposing pairs, ΝΕΟΠΟΛΙΤΩΝ before, Θ in field. Dotted border. REV: Acheloios Sebethos as a man-faced bull standing to right on single line, head facing, above, winged nymph crowns him, ΟΣ below, nothing in ex. REF: Taliercio - ; LAC A lot 1*.

347. AE Unit, 5.85g, 18mm	270 to 250 BC
	OBV: Head of Apollo facing left, wearing laurel wreath with leaves in opposing pairs, ΝΕΟΠΟΛΙΤΩΝ before, Θ in field. Dotted border. REV: Acheloios Sebethos as a man-faced bull standing to right on single line, head facing, above, winged nymph crowns him, ΙΣ below, ΟΣ in ex. REF: Sambon 679 ? (Θ misread as O) ; Taliercio IIIa.19; SNG France 982 = BnF Fonds Général 416*. *Taliercio cites 6 examples with 3 obverse dies and 3 reverse dies.*

348. AE Unit, 6.03g	270 to 250 BC
	OBV: Head of Apollo facing left, wearing laurel wreath with leaves in opposing pairs, ΝΕΟΠΟΛΙΤΩΝ before, I in field. Dotted border. REV: Acheloios Sebethos as a man-faced bull standing to right on single line, head facing, above, winged nymph crowns him, ΙΣ below, uncertain symbol in ex. REF: Sambon 665a/b; Taliercio IIIa.20*. *Taliercio cites 1 example and so 1 die pair.*

349. AE Unit, 5.18g	270 to 250 BC
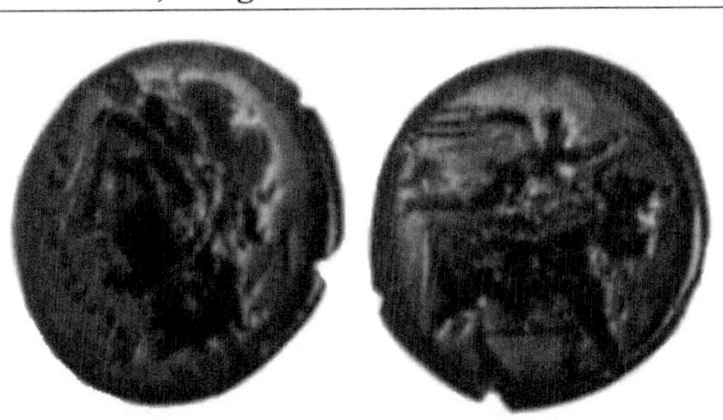	OBV: Head of Apollo facing left, wearing laurel wreath with leaves in opposing pairs, ΝΕΟΠΟΛΙΤΩΝ before, I in field. Dotted border. REV: Acheloios Sebethos as a man-faced bull standing to right on single line, head facing, above, winged nymph crowns him, ΙΣ in ex. REF: Taliercio IIIa.21*. *Taliercio cites 2 examples with 2 obverse dies and 2 reverse dies.*

350. AE Unit, 4.63g, 20mm	**270 to 250 BC**
	OBV: Head of Apollo facing left, wearing laurel wreath with leaves in opposing pairs, ΝΕΟΠΟΛΙΤΩΝ before, I in field. Dotted border. REV: Acheloios Sebethos as a man-faced bull standing to right on single line, head facing, above, winged nymph crowns him, ΙΣ below, X in ex. REF: Sambon 664; Taliercio IIIa.22; NAC P lot 1013*. *Taliercio cites 23 examples with 10 obverse dies and 11 reverse dies.*

351. AE Unit, 5.75g	**270 to 250 BC**
	OBV: Head of Apollo facing left, wearing laurel wreath with leaves in opposing pairs, ΝΕΟΠΟΛΙΤΩΝ before, I in field. Dotted border. REV: Acheloios Sebethos as a man-faced bull standing to right on single line, head facing, above, winged nymph crowns him, ΙΣ below, X in ex. REF: Taliercio IIIa.23*. *Taliercio cites 2 examples with 1 die pair.*

352. AE Unit, 5.08g	**270 to 250 BC**
	OBV: Head of Apollo facing left, wearing laurel wreath with leaves in opposing pairs, ΝΕΟΠΟΛΙΤΩΝ before, I in field. Dotted border. REV: Acheloios Sebethos as a man-faced bull standing to right on single line, head facing, above, winged nymph crowns him, Σ below, ΙΣ in ex. REF: Sambon 665a/b; Taliercio IIIa.24*. *Taliercio cites 2 examples with one die pair.*

353. AE Unit	**270 to 250 BC**
	OBV: Head of Apollo facing left, wearing laurel wreath with leaves in opposing pairs, ΝΕΟΠΟΛΙΤΩΝ before, I in field. Dotted border. REV: Acheloios Sebethos as a man-faced bull standing to right on single line, head facing, above, winged nymph crowns him, ΟΣ below, ΙΣ in ex. REF: Taliercio IIIa.25*. *Taliercio cites 4 examples with 2 obverse dies and 2 reverse dies.*

354. AE Unit, 5.68g, 16mm	**270 to 250 BC**
	OBV: Head of Apollo facing left, wearing laurel wreath with leaves in opposing pairs, ΝΕΟΠΟΛΙΤΩΝ before, I in field. Dotted border. REV: Acheloios Sebethos as a man-faced bull standing to right on single line, head facing, above, winged nymph crowns him, ΙΣ below, ΟΣ in ex. REF: Talierio IIIa.26, 6 = SNG France 985 = BnF Fonds Général 418*. *Taliercio cites 7 examples with 3 obverse dies and 3 reverse dies.*

355. AE Unit, 5.02g | **270 to 250 BC**

OBV: Head of Apollo facing left, wearing laurel wreath with leaves in opposing pairs, ΝΕΟΠΟΛΙΤΩΝ before, K in field. Dotted border.
REV: Acheloios Sebethos as a man-faced bull standing to right on single line, head facing, above, winged nymph crowns him, ΙΣ below.
REF: Sambon 667; Taliercio IIIa.27*.
Taliercio cites 6 examples with 4 obverse dies and 3 reverse dies.

356. AE Unit, 5.33g, 18mm | **270 to 250 BC**

OBV: Head of Apollo facing left, wearing laurel wreath with leaves in opposing pairs, ΝΕΟΠΟΛΙΤΩΝ before, K (retro) in field. Dotted border.
REV: Acheloios Sebethos as a man-faced bull standing to right on single line, head facing, above, winged nymph crowns him, ΙΣ below.
REF: Taliercio IIIa.28*.
Taliercio cites 2 examples with 2 obverse dies and 2 reverse dies.

357. AE Unit, 5.80g, 20mm | **270 to 250 BC**

OBV: Head of Apollo facing left, wearing laurel wreath with leaves in opposing pairs, ΝΕΟΠΟΛΙΤΩΝ before, K in field. Dotted border.
REV: Acheloios Sebethos as a man-faced bull standing to right on single line, head facing, above, winged nymph crowns him, ΒΞ below, ΙΣ in ex.
REF: Sambon 668; Taliercio IIIa.29; SNG France 988 = BnF Fonds Général 420*.
Taliercio cites 10 examples with 5 obverse dies and 5 reverse dies.

358. AE Unit, 3.1g | **270 to 250 BC**

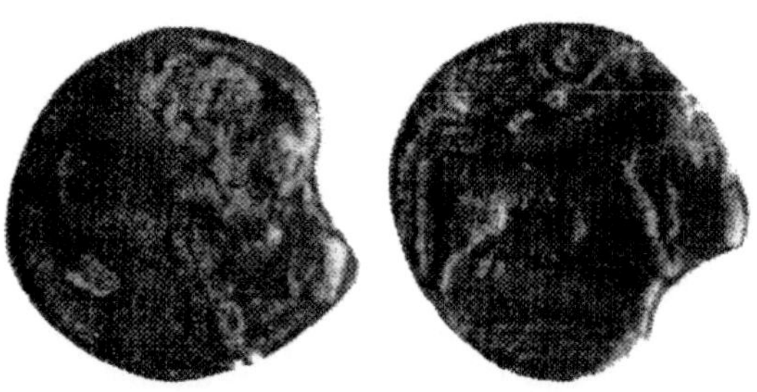

OBV: Head of Apollo facing left, wearing laurel wreath with leaves in opposing pairs, ΝΕΟΠΟΛΙΤΩΝ before, K in field. Dotted border.
REV: Acheloios Sebethos as a man-faced bull standing to right on single line, head facing, above, winged nymph crowns him, ΙΣ below, Ξ E in ex.
REF: Taliercio IIIa.30*.
Taliercio cites 1 example and so 1 die pair.

359. AE Unit , 5.68g, 20mm | **270 to 250 BC**

OBV: Head of Apollo facing left, wearing laurel wreath with leaves in opposing pairs, ΝΕΟΠΟΛΙΤΩΝ before, Λ in field. Dotted border.
REV: Acheloios Sebethos as a man-faced bull standing to right on single line, head facing, above, winged nymph crowns him, ΙΣ below.
REF: Taliercio IIIa, 31; SNG Morcom 159 = BM no.2013,4030.29*.
Taliercio cites 14 examples with 5 obverse dies and 6 reverse dies.

360. AE Unit, 5.31g | **270 to 250 BC**

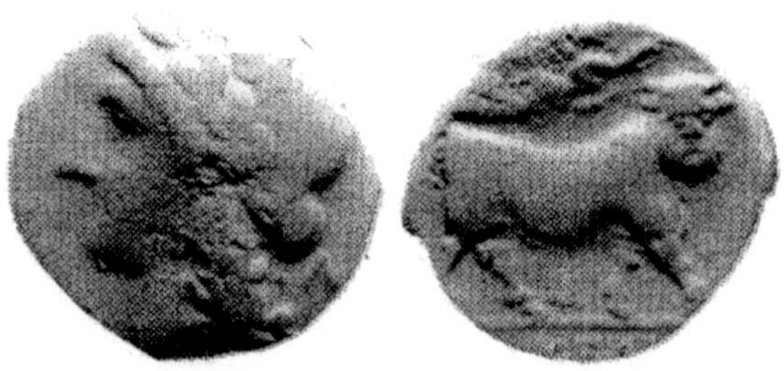

OBV: Head of Apollo facing left, wearing laurel wreath with leaves in opposing pairs, ΝΕΟΠΟΛΙΤΩΝ before, Λ in field. Dotted border.
REV: Acheloios Sebethos as a man-faced bull standing to right on single line, head facing, above, winged nymph crowns him, ΙΣ below, ΧΕ in ex.
REF: Sambon 669; Taliercio IIIa.32*.
Taliercio cites 18 examples with 5 obverse dies and 5 reverse dies.

361. AE Unit, 5.26g, 21mm | **270 to 250 BC**

OBV: Head of Apollo facing left, wearing laurel wreath with leaves in opposing pairs, ΝΕΟΠΟΛΙΤΩΝ before, Μ in field. Dotted border.
REV: Acheloios Sebethos as a man-faced bull standing to right on single line, head facing, above, winged nymph crowns him, ΙΣ below, ΧΕ in ex.
REF: Sambon 670; Taliercio IIIa, 33; Artemide 8E, lot 8014*.
Taliercio cites 45 examples with 15 obverse dies and 17 reverse dies.

362. AE Unit, 6.20g, 20mm | **270 to 250 BC**

OBV: Head of Apollo facing left, wearing laurel wreath with leaves in opposing pairs, ΝΕΟΠΟΛΙΤΩΝ before, Ν in field. Dotted border.
REV: Acheloios Sebethos as a man-faced bull standing to right on single line, head facing, above, winged nymph crowns him, Π below.
REF: Sambon 671; Taliercio - ; SNG France 1017 = BnF Fonds Général 430*.
This specimen is incorrectly listed by Taliercio under IIIa.50 (9th specimen listed.)

363. AE Unit, 6.67g | **270 to 250 BC**

OBV: Head of Apollo facing left, wearing laurel wreath with leaves in opposing pairs, ΝΕΟΠΟΛΙΤΩΝ before, Ν in field. Dotted border.
REV: Acheloios Sebethos as a man-faced bull standing to right on single line, head facing, above, winged nymph crowns him, ΙΣ below.
REF: Sambon 672; Taliercio IIIa.34; Brunetti Asta elettronica 7 lot 24*.
Taliercio cites 27 examples with 13 obverse dies and 14 reverse dies.

364. AE Unit, 6.33g | **270 to 250 BC**

OBV: Head of Apollo facing left, wearing laurel wreath with leaves in opposing pairs, ΝΕΟΠΟΛΙΤΩΝ before, Ν in field. Dotted border.
REV: Acheloios Sebethos as a man-faced bull standing to right on single line, head facing, above, winged nymph crowns him, ΙΣ in ex.
REF: Taliercio IIIa.35*.
Taliercio lists 4 examples with 3 obverse dies and 3 reverse dies. Sambon includes this type with 627.

365. AE Unit, 5.42g | **270 to 250 BC**

OBV: Head of Apollo facing left, wearing laurel wreath with leaves in opposing pairs, ΝΕΟΠΟΛΙΤΩΝ before, N in field. Dotted border.
REV: Acheloios Sebethos as a man-faced bull standing to right on single line, head facing, above, winged nymph crowns him, ΙΣ below, XE in ex.
REF: Taliercio IIIa.36*.
Taliercio lists 1 example and so 1 die pair.

366. AE Unit, 4.25g, 18mm | **270 to 250 BC**

OBV: Head of Apollo facing left, wearing laurel wreath with leaves in opposing pairs, ΝΕΟΠΟΛΙΤΩΝ before, Ξ in field. Dotted border.
REV: Acheloios Sebethos as a man-faced bull standing to right on single line, head facing, above, winged nymph crowns him, ΙΣ in ex.
REF: Sambon 675; Taliercio IIIa.37; SNG France 998 = BnF Fonds Général 439*.
Taliercio lists 27 examples with 13 obverse dies and 14 reverse dies.

367. AE Unit, 6.04g, 19mm | **270 to 250 BC**

OBV: Head of Apollo facing left, wearing laurel wreath with leaves in opposing pairs, ΝΕΟΠΟΛΙΤΩΝ before, Ξ in field. Dotted border.
REV: Acheloios Sebethos as a man-faced bull standing to right on single line, head facing, above, winged nymph crowns him, ΙΣ below, ⊠ in ex.
REF: Sambon 677 (+673); Taliercio IIIa.38; SNG France 1000 = BnF Fonds Général 412*.
Taliercio lists 17 examples with 6 obverse dies and 8 reverse dies. She also included Sambon 673 in this series.

368. AE Unit, 6.93g | **270 to 250 BC**

OBV: Head of Apollo facing left, wearing laurel wreath with leaves in opposing pairs, ΝΕΟΠΟΛΙΤΩΝ (Sambon says ΝΕΟΠΟΛΙΤΩΣ)before, Ξ in field. Dotted border.
REV: Acheloios Sebethos as a man-faced bull standing to right on single line, head facing, above, winged nymph crowns him, X below (Sambon lists monogram).
REF: Sambon 676; Taliercio IIIa.39*.
Taliercio lists 3 examples with 1 die pair.

369. AE Unit, 4.41g | **270 to 250 BC**

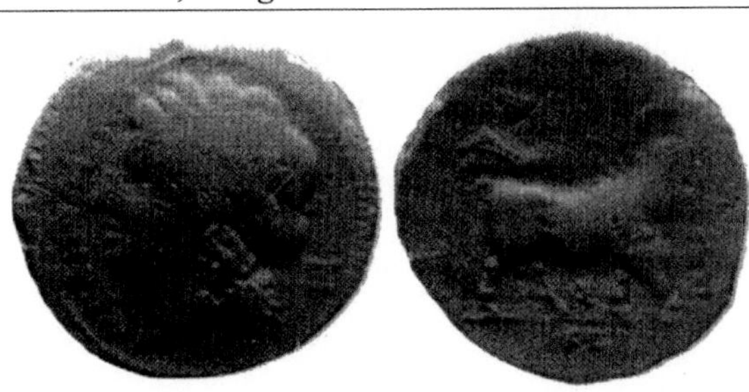

OBV: Head of Apollo facing left, wearing laurel wreath with leaves in opposing pairs, ΝΕΟΠΟΛΙΤΩΝ before, Ξ in field. Dotted border.
REV: Acheloios Sebethos as a man-faced bull standing to right on single line, head facing, above, winged nymph crowns him, ΙΣ below, XE in ex.
REF: Sambon 674, Taliercio IIIa.40*.
Taliercio cites 8 examples with 4 obverse dies and 4 reverse dies.

370. AE Unit, 5.38g	**270 to 250 BC**
	OBV: Head of Apollo facing left, wearing laurel wreath with leaves in opposing pairs, ΝΕΟΠΟΛΙΤΩΝ before, Ξ in field. Dotted border. REV: Acheloios Sebethos as a man-faced bull standing to right on single line, head facing, above, winged nymph crowns him, ΙΣ below, nothing in ex. REF: H.J. Berk n. 58282*.

371. AE Unit, 3.69g	**270 to 250 BC**
	OBV: Head of Apollo facing left, wearing laurel wreath with leaves in opposing pairs, ΝΕΟΠΟΛΙΤΩΝ before, O in field. Dotted border. REV: Acheloios Sebethos as a man-faced bull standing to right on single line, head facing, above, winged nymph crowns him, ΙΣ below. REF: Taliercio IIIa.41; Auctiones AG, 29, 55*. *Taliercio cites 62 examples with 6 obverse and 6 reverse dies.*

372. AE Unit, 4.73g	**270 to 250 BC**
	OBV: Head of Apollo facing left, wearing laurel wreath with leaves in opposing pairs, ΝΕΟΠΟΛΙΤΩΝ before, O in field. Dotted border. REV: Acheloios Sebethos as a man-faced bull standing to right on single line, head facing, above, winged nymph crowns him, ΙΣ in ex. REF: Taliercio IIIa.42*. *Taliercio cites 12 examples with 5 obverse dies and 6 reverse dies.*

373. AE Unit, 6.38g, 18mm	**270 to 250 BC**
	OBV: Head of Apollo facing left, wearing laurel wreath with leaves in opposing pairs, ΝΕΟΠΟΛΙΤΩΝ before, O in field. Dotted border. REV: Acheloios Sebethos as a man-faced bull standing to right on single line, head facing, above, winged nymph crowns him, ΙΣ below, X and ΣΠ in ex. REF: Sambon 678; Taliercio IIIa.43; SNG France 1007 = BnF Fonds Général 431*. *Taliercio cites 15 examples with 4 obverse dies and 5 reverse dies.*

374. AE Unit, 5.00g, 19mm	**270 to 250 BC**
	OBV: Head of Apollo facing left, wearing laurel wreath with leaves in opposing pairs, ΝΕΟΠΟΛΙΤΩΝ before, O in field. Dotted border. REV: Acheloios Sebethos as a man-faced bull standing to right on single line, head facing, above, winged nymph crowns him, ΙΣ below, ΧΕ in ex. REF: Taliercio IIIa.44; SNG France 1008 = BnF Fonds Général 432*. *Taliercio cites 3 examples with 1 obverse and 2 reverse dies.*

375. AE Unit, 6.75g	270-250 BC
	OBV: Head of Apollo facing left, wearing laurel wreath with leaves in opposing pairs, ΝΕΟΠΟΛΙΤΩΝ before, Π behind. Dotted border. REV: Acheloios Sebethos as a man-faced bull standing to right on single line, head facing, above, winged nymph crowns him, ΙΣ in ex. REF: Sambon 682-3; Taliercio IIIa.45; Künker 133, lot 7019*. *Taliercio cites 12 examples with 3 obverse dies and 3 reverse dies.*

376. AE Unit, 6.25g	270 to 250 BC
	OBV: Head of Apollo facing left, wearing laurel wreath with leaves in opposing pairs, ΝΕΟΠΟΛΙΤΩΝ before, Π behind behind. Dotted border. REV: Acheloios Sebethos as a man-faced bull standing to right on single line, head facing, above, winged nymph crowns him, MI below. REF: Sambon 691; Taliercio - ; LHS Numismatics 100, lot 8*.

377. AE Unit, 5.44g	270 to 250 BC
	OBV: Head of Apollo facing left, wearing laurel wreath with leaves in opposing pairs, ΝΕΟΠΟΛΙΤΩΝ before, P behind. Dotted border. REV: Acheloios Sebethos as a man-faced bull standing to right on single line, head facing, above, winged nymph crowns him, ΙΣ below. REF: Sambon 684; Taliercio IIIa.46*. *Taliercio cites 6 examples with 3 obverse dies and 3 reverse dies.*

378. AE Unit, 6.41g	270 to 250 BC
	OBV: Head of Apollo facing left, wearing laurel wreath with leaves in opposing pairs, ΝΕΟΠΟΛΙΤΩΝ before, P behind . Dotted border. REV: Acheloios Sebethos as a man-faced bull standing to right on single line, head facing, above, winged nymph crowns him, ΙΣ in ex. REF: Sambon 685-6; Taliercio IIIa.47; CNG 61, lot 11*. *Taliercio cites 28 examples with 13 obverse and 12 reverse dies.*

379. AE Unit, 3.71g	270 to 250 BC
	OBV: Head of Apollo facing left, wearing laurel wreath with leaves in opposing pairs, ΝΕΟΠΟΛΙΤΩΝ before, P behind. Dotted border. REV: Acheloios Sebethos as a man-faced bull standing to right on single line, head facing, above, winged nymph crowns him, ΣΙ in ex. REF: Graziano 464*.

380. AE Unit, unrecorded weight

270 to 250 BC

OBV: Head of Apollo facing left, wearing laurel wreath with leaves in opposing pairs, ΝΕΟΠΟΛΙΤΩΝ before, P retrograde behind. Dotted border.
REV: Acheloios Sebethos as a man-faced bull standing to right on single line, head facing, above, winged nymph crowns him, MI below.
REF: Taliercio -; Graziano 435*.

381. AE Unit, 6.46g, 20mm

270 to 250 BC

OBV: Head of Apollo facing left, wearing laurel wreath with leaves in opposing pairs, ΝΕΟΠΟΛΙΤΩΝ before, P behind. Dotted border.
REV: Acheloios Sebethos as a man-faced bull standing to right on single line, head facing, above, winged nymph crowns him, MI below.
REF: Taliercio IIIa.48; SNG France 1015 = BnF Fonds Général 436*.

Taliercio cites 16 examples with 2 obverse dies and more than 4 reverse dies.

382. AE Unit, 7.47g, 21mm

240 to 210 BC

OBV: Head of Apollo facing left, wearing laurel wreath with leaves in opposing pairs, ΝΕΟΠΟΛΙΤΩΝ before, P? behind. Dotted border.
REV: Acheloios Sebethos as a man-faced bull standing to right on single line, head facing, above, winged nymph crowns him, CALENO in ex.
REF: Sambon 696; SNG France 1024 = BnF Fonds Général 449*.

Some examples of Campanian bronze coinage bearing double ethnics exist, usually ΝΕΟΠΟΛΙΤΩΝ / CALENO and ΝΕΟΠΟΛΙΤΩΝ / SVESANO. However, they are just overstrikes and should not be considered as new variants with double ethnic, as pointed out by Sambon (p.268), when listing n.693-696 (citing Garrucci, Pl. LXXXV n. 32 e 33).

383. AE Unit, 7.72g

270 to 250 BC

OBV: Head of Apollo facing left, wearing laurel wreath with leaves in opposing pairs, ΝΕΟΠΟΛΙΤΩΝ before, P behind. Dotted border.
REV: Acheloios Sebethos as a man-faced bull standing to right on single line, head facing, above, winged nymph crowns him, M below.
REF: Taliercio IIIa.49*.

Taliercio cites 13 examples with 2 obverse dies and more than 4 reverse dies.

384. AE Unit, 5.41g, 18mm

270 to 250 BC

OBV: Head of Apollo facing left, wearing laurel wreath with leaves in opposing pairs, ΝΕΟΠΟΛΙΤΩΝ before, Σ behind (Sambon says Σ-like symbol or simply Σ). Dotted border.
REV: Acheloios Sebethos as a man-faced bull standing to right on single line, head facing, above, winged nymph crowns him, ΙΣ below.
REF: Sambon 687a/b; Taliercio IIIa.50/53; SNG France 1018 = BnF Fonds Général 438*.

Taliercio cites 16 examples with 8 obverse and 7 reverse dies.
She actually describes the same variants under two different listings, no. 50 and 53. According to Sambon the only difference is the epigraphic style of Σ behind Apollo.

385. AE Unit, 5.10g	**270 to 250 BC**
	OBV: Head of Apollo facing left, wearing laurel wreath with leaves in opposing pairs, ΝΕΟΠΟΛΙΤΩΝ before, Σ behind. Dotted border. REV: Acheloios Sebethos as a man-faced bull standing to right on single line, head facing, above, winged nymph crowns him, ΙΣ in ex. REF: Sambon 688; Taliercio IIIa.51-54; H.D. Rauch GmbH 12th live e-Auction, lot 23*. *Taliercio listed her series 51 and 54 as different variants, but with the same description.*

386. AE Unit, 3.62g, 18mm	**270 to 250 BC**
	OBV: Head of Apollo facing left, wearing laurel wreath with leaves in opposing pairs, ΝΕΟΠΟΛΙΤΩΝ before, retrograde Σ behind. Dotted border. REV: Acheloios Sebethos as a man-faced bull standing to right on single line, head facing, above, winged nymph crowns him, ΙΣ in ex. REF: Taliercio IIIa.52; SNG France 1019 = BnF Fonds Général 440*. *Taliercio cites 2 examples with 1 die pair.*

387. AE Unit, 5.38g	**270 to 250 BC**
	OBV: Head of Apollo facing left, wearing laurel wreath with leaves in opposing pairs, ΝΕΟΠΟΛΙΤΩΝ before, T behind. Dotted border. REV: Acheloios Sebethos as a man-faced bull standing to right on single line, head facing, above, winged nymph crowns him, ΙΣ below. REF: Sambon 689; Taliercio IIIa.55; Graziano 442*. *Taliercio cites 13 examples with 6 obverse dies and more than 8 reverse dies.*

388. AE Unit, 7.06g	**270 to 250 BC**
	OBV: Head of Apollo facing left, wearing laurel wreath with leaves in opposing pairs, ΝΕΟΠΟΛΙΤΩΝ before, T behind. Dotted border. REV: Acheloios Sebethos as a man-faced bull standing to right on single line, head facing, above, winged nymph crowns him, ΙΣ in ex. REF: Sambon 690; Taliercio IIIa.56; CNG Triton V, lot 30*. *Taliercio cites 27 examples with 6 obverse dies and more than 13 reverse dies.*

Group IIIb

389. AE 1/3 Unit, 1.36g	**270 to 250 BC**
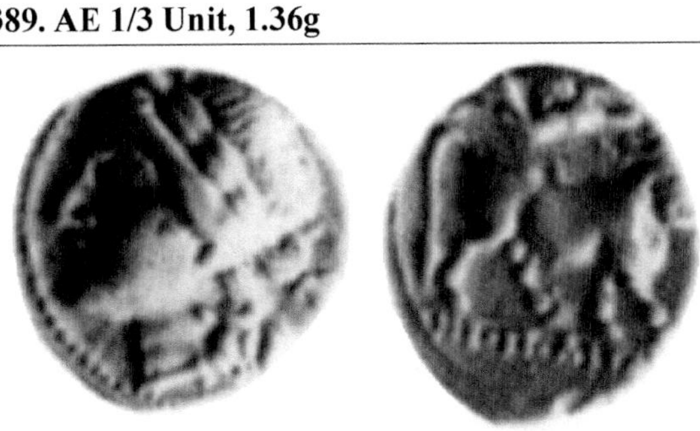	OBV: Head of Apollo facing left, wearing laurel wreath with leaves in opposing pairs, ΛΥ behind. Dotted border. REV: Acheloios Sebethos as a man-faced bull standing to right on single line, head facing, above, winged nymph crowns him, ΝΕΟΠΟΛΙΤΩΝ in ex. Linear border. REF: Sambon 698; Taliercio IIIb.1*. *Taliercio cites 1 examples and so 1 die pair.* *SNG ANS 504 shows a second specimen where the device behind Apollo is more clearly visible as LY instead of M.*

390. AE 1/3 Unit, 0.96g	**270 to 250 BC**
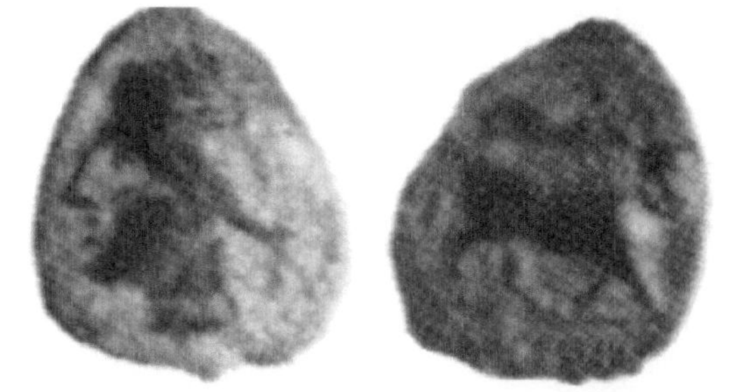	OBV: Head of Apollo facing left, wearing laurel wreath with leaves in opposing pairs, N behind. Dotted border. REV: Acheloios Sebethos as a man-faced bull standing to right on single line, head facing, above, winged nymph crowns him, ΝΕΟΠΟΛΙΤΩΝ in ex. Linear border. REF: Taliercio IIIb.2*. *Taliercio cites 4 examples with one die pair.*

391. AE 1/3 Unit, 3.14g, 17mm	**270 to 250 BC**
	OBV: Head of Apollo facing left, wearing laurel wreath with leaves in opposing pairs, Π behind. Dotted border. REV: Acheloios Sebethos as a man-faced bull standing to right on single line, head facing, above, winged nymph crowns him, Π in right field, ΝΕΟΠΟΛΙΤΩΝ in ex. Linear border. REF: Taliercio IIIb.3; ACR E-Auction 27, lot 29*. *Taliercio cites 2 examples with 2 obverse dies and 2 reverse dies.*

392. AE 1/3 Unit, 2.38g	**270 to 250 BC**
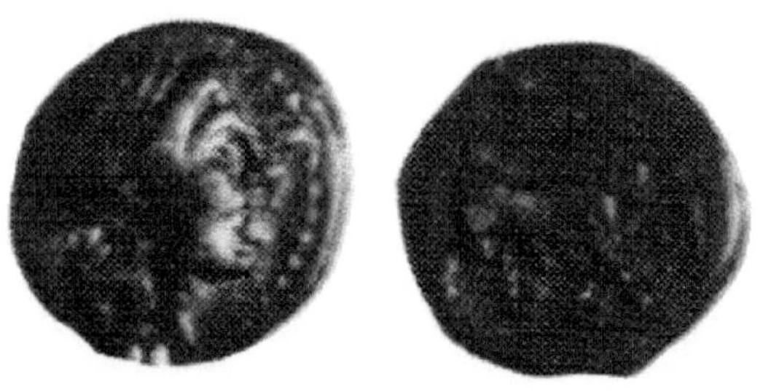	OBV: Head of Apollo facing right, wearing laurel wreath with leaves in opposing pairs. Dotted border. REV: Acheloios Sebethos as a man-faced bull standing to right on single line, head facing, above, winged nymph crowns him, Π in field. REF: Taliercio IIIb.4*. *Taliercio cites 1 example so 1 die pair.*

TALIERCIO PHASE IV

Group IVd

393. AE 1/3 Unit, 2.43g, 16mm	**After 250 BC**
	OBV: Head of Apollo facing left, wearing laurel wreath with leaves in opposing pairs, nothing behind. Dotted border. REV: Acheloios Sebethos as a man-faced bull standing to right on single line, head facing, above, winged nymph crowns him, ΝΕΟΠΟΛΙΤΩΝ in ex. Linear border. REF: Sambon 697; Taliercio IVd.1; CNG eAuction 106, lot 2*. *Taliercio cites 43 examples with 17 obverse and 18 reverse dies.*

394. AE 1/3 Unit, 2.24g	**After 250 BC**
	OBV: Head of Apollo facing right, wearing laurel wreath with leaves in opposing pairs, ΔΗ behind. Dotted border. REV: Acheloios Sebethos as a man-faced bull standing to right on single line, head facing, above, winged nymph crowns him, ΔΗ before, ΝΕΟΠΟΛΙΤΩΝ beginning behind man-faced bull and finishing in ex. Dotted border. REF: Sambon 702; Taliercio IVd, 2*. *Taliercio cites 1 example and so 1 die pair.*

395. AE 1/3 Unit, 2.56g, 14mm	**After 250 BC**
	OBV: Head of Apollo facing left, wearing laurel wreath with leaves in opposing pairs, ΔΗ behind. Dotted border. REV: Acheloios Sebethos as a man-faced bull standing to right on single line, head facing, above, winged nymph crowns him, ΣΟ before, ΝΕΟΠΟΛΙΤ over ΩΝ in two lines in ex. Dotted border. REF: Taliercio - ; Pegasi XXVI, lot 17*.

396. AE 1/3 Unit, 2.07g	**After 250 BC**
	OBV: Head of Apollo facing right, wearing laurel wreath with leaves in opposing pairs, ΔΗ behind. Dotted border. REV: Acheloios Sebethos as a man-faced bull standing to right on single line, head facing, above, winged nymph crowns him, ΝΕΟΠΟΛΙΤΩΝ in ex. Linear border. REF: Taliercio IVd.3*. *Taliercio cites 2 examples and 1 die pair.*

397. AE 1/3 Unit, 3.03g	**After 250 BC**
	OBV: Head of Apollo facing right, wearing laurel wreath with leaves in opposing pairs, ΠΥΙ in field. Dotted border. REV: Acheloios Sebethos as a man-faced bull standing to right on single line, head facing, above, winged nymph crowns him, ΝΕΟΠΟΛΙΤΩΝ beginning behind man-faced bull and finishing in ex. Dotted border. REF: Sambon 701; Taliercio IVd.4*. *Taliercio cites 3 examples with 1 die pair.*

398. AE 1/3 Unit, 1.15g	**After 250 BC**
	OBV: Head of Apollo facing right, wearing laurel wreath with leaves in opposing pairs. Dotted border. REV: Acheloios Sebethos as a man-faced bull standing to right on single line, head facing, above, winged nymph crowns him, ΝΕΟΠΟΛΙΤΩΝ in ex. REF: Sambon 704; Taliercio IVd.5. *Taliercio cites 1 examples and so 1 die pair.*

399. AE 1/3 Unit, 2.91g	**After 250 BC**
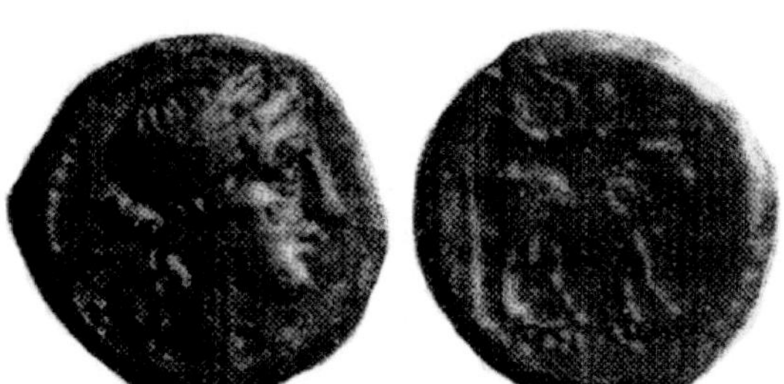	OBV: Head of Apollo facing right, wearing laurel wreath with leaves in opposing pairs. Dotted border. REV: Acheloios Sebethos as a man-faced bull standing to right on single line, head facing, above, winged nymph crowns him, ΦΙ in field, ΝΕΟΠΟΛΙΤΩΝ in ex. REF: Taliercio IVd.6*. *Taliercio cites 4 examples and 1 die pair.*

400. AE 1/3 Unit, 2.40g, 15mm	**After 250 BC**
	OBV: Head of Apollo facing left, wearing laurel wreath with leaves in opposing pairs. Dotted border. REV: Acheloios Sebethos as a man-faced bull standing to right on single line, head facing, above, winged nymph crowns him, ΦΙ before, ΝΕΟΠΟΛΙΤΩΝ in ex. Linear border. REF: Sambon 700; Taliercio IVd.7 = SNG France 1077 = Bnf Fonds Général 450*. *Taliercio cites 1 examples and so 1 die pair.*

401. AE 1/3 Unit, 2.81g	**After 250 BC**
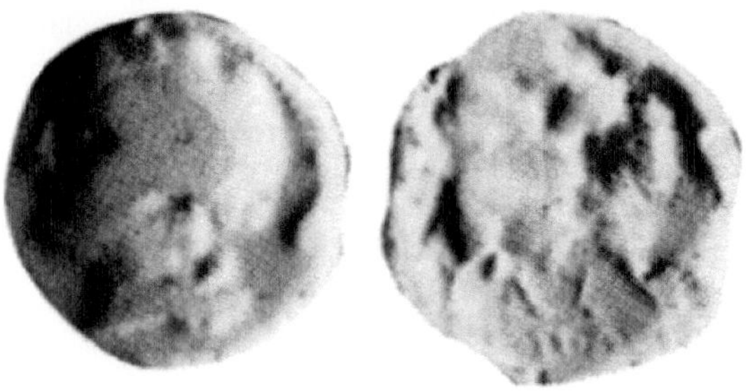	OBV: Head of Apollo facing left, wearing laurel wreath with leaves in opposing pairs, dolphin behind. Dotted border. REV: Acheloios Sebethos as a man-faced bull standing to right on single line, head facing, above, winged nymph crowns him,? in field, ΝΕΟΠΟΛΙΤΩΝ in ex. REF: Taliercio IVd.8*. *Taliercio cites 5 examples and 1 die pair.*

402. AE 1/3 Unit, 2.57g	**After 250 BC**
	OBV: Head of Apollo facing left, wearing laurel wreath with leaves in opposing pairs, dolphin and ΛΥ in field. Dotted border. REV: Acheloios Sebethos as a man-faced bull standing to left on single line, head facing, above, winged nymph crowns him, ΦΙ before, ΝΕΟΠΟΛΙΤΩΝ in ex. Linear border. REF: Sambon 699*; Taliercio IVd.9. *Taliercio cites 1 example and so 1 die pair.*

403. AE 1/3 Unit, 1.48g	**After 250 BC**
	OBV: Head of Apollo facing left, wearing laurel wreath with leaves in opposing pairs. Dotted border. REV: Acheloios Sebethos as a man-faced bull standing to right on single line, head facing, above, winged nymph crowns him, ΝΕΟΠΟΛΙΤΩΝ in ex. Linear border. REF: Taliercio IVd.10; CNG eAuction 306, lot 1*. *Taliercio cites 2 examples and 1 die pair.*

404. AE 1/3 Unit, 1.41g	**After 250 BC**
	OBV: Head of Apollo facing right, wearing laurel wreath with leaves in opposing pairs. Dotted border. REV: Acheloios Sebethos as a man-faced bull standing to right on single line, head facing, above, winged nymph crowns him, ΝΕΟΠΟΛΙΤ in ex., P before. Dotted border. REF: Sambon 703*.

Group IVf

405. AE Quarter Unit, 1.18-2.68g	After 250BC
	OBV: Head of Apollo facing right, wearing laurel wreath with leaves in opposing pairs. Dotted border. REV: Forepart of Acheloios Sebethos as a man-faced bull to right, ΝΕΟΠΟΛΙΤΩΝ above. Dotted border. REF: Taliercio IVf.1*. *Taliercio cites 7 examples with 2 obverse dies and 2 reverse dies.*

406. AE Quarter Unit, 1.65g	After 250BC
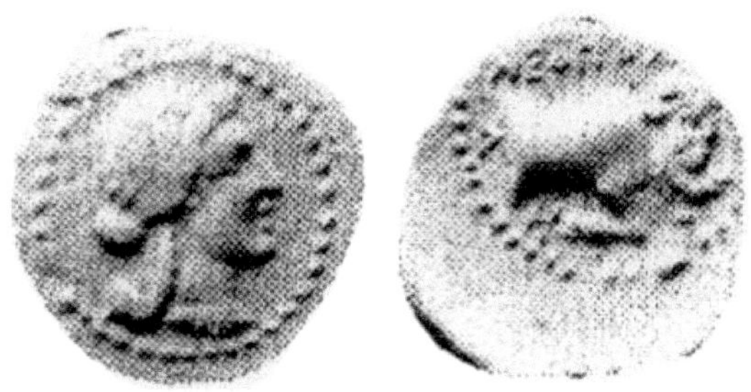	OBV: Head of Apollo facing right, wearing laurel wreath with leaves in opposing pairs. Dotted border. REV: Forepart of Acheloios Sebethos as a man-faced bull to right, ΔΗ in field, ΝΕΟΠΟΛΙΤΩΝ above. Dotted border. REF: Sambon 603; Taliercio IVf, 2*. *Taliercio cites 3 known examples with 2 obverse dies and 2 reverse dies.*

407. AE Quarter Unit, 1.00g	After 250BC
	OBV: Head of Apollo facing right, wearing laurel wreath with leaves in opposing pairs, Δ (?) behind. Dotted border. REV: Forepart of Acheloios Sebethos as a man-faced bull to right, ΝΕΟΠΟΛΙΤΩΝ above. Dotted border. REF: Sambon 604; Taliercio IVf.3*. *Taliercio cites 1 example so 1 die pair.*

408. AE Quarter Unit, 1.5g	After 250BC
	OBV: Head of Apollo facing right, wearing laurel wreath with leaves in opposing pairs, ΙΠ behind . Dotted border. REV: Forepart of Acheloios Sebethos as a man-faced bull to right, ΝΕΟΠΟΛΙΤΩΝ above. Dotted border(?). REF: Taliercio IVf.4. *Taliercio cites 1 example so 1 die pair.*

409. AE Quarter Unit, 0.99g, 11mm	After 250BC
	OBV: Head of Apollo facing right, wearing laurel wreath with leaves in opposing pairs, XT in field, surrounded by laurel wreath. REV: Forepart of Acheloios Sebethos as a man-faced bull to right, star on shoulder, ΝΕΟΠΟΛΙΤΩΝ with large A above. Dotted border. REF: Sambon 607; Taliercio IVf.5; SNG Morcom 172; SNG France 1078 = BnF Fonds Général 373*. *Taliercio cites 3 examples with 3 obverse dies and 3 reverse dies.*

410. AE Quarter Unit, 1.67g, 14mm	After 250BC
	OBV: Head of Apollo facing right, wearing laurel wreath with leaves in opposing pairs, unclear behind. Dotted border. REV: Forepart of Acheloios Sebethos as a man-faced bull to right, ΦΙ above, (ΝΕΟΠΟΛΙΤΩΝ above, says Taliercio, who does not illustrate the reverse die) REF: Sambon 605; Taliercio IVf.6; M&M GmbH 17, lot 20*. *Taliercio cites 5 examples with 2 obverse dies and 2 reverse dies.*

411. AE Quarter Unit, 1.06g	After 250BC
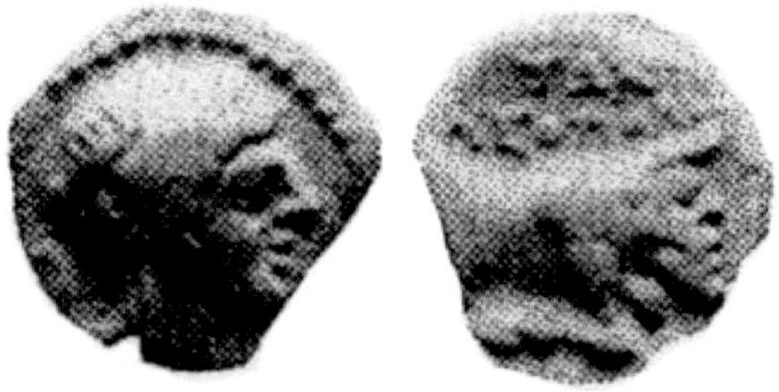	OBV: Head of Apollo facing right, wearing laurel wreath with leaves in opposing pairs. Dotted border. REV: Forepart of Acheloios Sebethos as a man-faced bull to right, ΙΤΩΝ over ΝΕΟΠΟΛ above. REF: Sambon 608; Taliercio IVf.7*. *Taliercio cites 1 example so 1 die pair.*

NOLA

Nola lies just northeast of Neapolis. Archaeological finds demonstrate that the site was inhabited since the Early Bronze Age.[133] Starting in the Iron Age there are clear signs of Villanovan (or proto-Etruscan) culture,[134] with an urban center dating to the end of the 8th century BC.[135] Starting in the 7th century the evidence suggests the development of Oscan culture. In fact, the name 'Nola' is Oscan, as the suffix *-la* means 'city,' Nola coming from *Nuv-la*, or the 'New-City,' which was raised on the remains of Hyria,[136] similar to the situation of Parthenope and Neapolis. Sambon was the first to propose the idea that Hyria was the Etruscan Palaeopolis of Nola,[137] but today not all scholars agree.[138] However, ancient sources report Nola was an Etruscan city,[139] and so it is reasonable to categorize Nola as an Oscan group heavily influenced by Etruscan culture.

Around 400 BC Nola began to issue silver coinage of the man-faced bull.[140] During the 4th century BC at the time of the Second Samnite War, Nola intervened in defense of Neapolis against Rome,[141] but in 313 BC Nola was finally defeated and conquered by the Romans.[142]

During the 3rd century BC the city was involved in the war against Hannibal in Campania.[143] It is at this point that they probably issued the two bronze varieties of man-faced bull coinage listed in this catalog.

The man-faced bull depicted on the coinage of Nola is probably the local embodiment of Acheloios, Acheloios Clanis, a river which, according to Virgil, was responsible for the fertility of the plains surrounding the city.[144]

Coinage

412. AE Unit, 6.60-7.45g	**275 to 250 BC**
	OBV: Head of Apollo facing left, wearing laurel wreath with leaves in opposing pairs, ΝΩΛΑΙ before, A behind. Dotted border. REV: Acheloios Clanis as a man-faced bull standing to right on single line, head facing, winged nymph above, MI below, nothing in ex. REF: Sambon 1019 ; SNG Cop 565; HN Italy 607; NAC 46, 779*.

413. AE Unit, 6.38g	**275 to 250 BC**
	OBV: Head of Apollo facing left, wearing laurel wreath with leaves in opposing pairs, ΝΩΛΑΙ before, A behind. Dotted border. REV: Acheloios Clanis as a man-faced bull standing to right on single line, head facing, winged nymph above, X below, MI in ex. REF: Sambon 1020*.

[133] F. Ruffo, *La Campania antica. Appunti di storia e di topografia. Parte I Dal Massico-Roccamonfina al Somma-Vesuvio* (Napoli: 2010), 142.

[134] Ibid., 19.

[135] Ibid., 145.

[136] G. Reccia, *Atella/Aderl: Confronti etimologici e riscontri geocartografici. Novissimae Editiones*, Vol.33 (Atella: I.S.A., 2014), 7.

[137] A. Sambon, *Les Monnaies Antiques de l'Italie*, 293ff.

[138] For the opposing viewpoint, see: R. Cantilena, 'La moneta in Penisola sorrentina tra IV e III secolo a.C.: dati acquisiti e problemi aperti,' in *Sorrento e la Penisola Sorrentina tra Italici, Etruschi e Greci nel contesto della Campania antica. Atti della giornata di studio in omaggio a Paola Zancani Montuoro*, edited by F. Senatore and M. Russo (Roma, 2010), 205.

[139] See for example Polybius, *Histories*, 2.17; 3.91, who states that the Etruscans lived in the plains between Capua and Nola. The earliest source mentioning Nola is very old, dating back to the 6th century BC, by Hecataeus of Miletus (Hecat, *FgrHist* 1, F.61), which states that Nola was a 'City of Ausones,' meaning people of proto-Etruscan ancestry, like the Oscans.

[140] Cf. SNG France 1079-1096.

[141] Livy, *Ab Urbe Condita Libri*, 8.23. To this same time period dates the fresco found in a tomb of Nola, showing an Oscan warrior wearing a horned helm, as discussed in Chapter 3.

[142] Livy, *Ab Urbe Condita Libri*, 9.28.

[143] Livy, *Ab Urbe Condita Libri*, 23.14-16, 39, 46; 24.13, 17.

[144] Virgil, *Georgics*, 2,.217-225.

Graziano 24, described as Sambon 1020

'ROME'

One popular opinion on the origin of man-faced bull coins with ΡΩΜΑΙΩΝ inscription, first advocated by M. Ch. Lenormant[145] and later Jean de Witte,[146] is that they were all struck at Neapolis on behalf of the Romans, who had seized the city in 327/326 BC, and formed an alliance, the *foedus Neapolitanum*, in the same year.[147] Although the Neapolitans basically surrendered to Rome, the actual treaty was considered a *foedus aequum*, in which the two parties were seen as equals.[148] In fact, the city was accorded the title *civitas foederata*, essentially recognizing a treaty between Rome and Neapolis.[149] Thus, it is upon this background that the first coinage of Rome was allegedly struck in c. 326 BC at Neapolis.[150] There are some alternatives to this view, however. Mommsen,[151] for instance, attributed the coins to Capua sometime after 338 BC, based primarily on the Greek script. Burnett, on the other hand, dates the issue to around 320 BC,[152] and Rutter uses that date in *HN Italy*.[153] Indeed, a date of around 320 is very appealing in light of the events of the Second Samnite War, especially in relation to the symbolism inherent in the iconography of the man-faced bull.[154]

In 321 BC Rome experienced a humiliating defeat to the Samnites at the Caudine Forks.[155] Livy's description of this situation claims the entire Roman army was trapped[156] and had to surrender on downright shameful terms, being stripped of their weapons and returned 'under the yoke' to Rome half-naked.[157] They agreed to this, rather than a more honorable death on the battlefield.[158] The rationale provided by L.C. Lentulus was that the surrender was for the sake of Rome itself, who would undoubtedly perish if its armies were obliterated.[159] Thus the Roman army sacrificed its honor for the sake of Roman citizens and their future. Even more symbolically, Spurius Postumius Albinus, once home, epitomized the notion of self-sacrifice in recommending that he, along with all the military leaders that agreed to the humiliating terms, should be handed over to the Samnites, and thereby free Rome of any obligation.[160] Thus they became the expiatory sacrifice (*piaculaque*) needed for the sake of

---

145 M.Ch. Lenormant, 'Recherches sur les époques et sure les causes d'émission de l'aes grave en Italie,' in *Revue Numismatique,* V. 9 (1844), 251.

146 J. de Witte, *Etudes sur les vases peints* (Gazette des Beaux-Arts, 1865), 103.

147 For a nice overview, see D. Vagi, 'Rome's First Didrachm in Light of the *foedus Neapolitanum* and the *equus October*,' in *Essays in Honor of Roberto Russo*, edited by P.G. van Alfen and R.B. Witschonke (Zürich: Numismatica Ars Classica, 2013), 73-94.

148 D. Vagi, 'Rome's First Didrachm,' footnote 34.

149 Ibid., 77.

150 L. Breglia (*La prima fase della coniazione romana dell'argento* (Roma: 1952), 25) also advocated the date of 326 BC. Her rationale, as summarized by Vagi ('Rome's First Didrachm,' footnote 47), is that it was 'a coin of occupation struck in Neapolis specifically to meet the needs of the Roman army, yet bearing designs that would allow it to circulate locally.' Crawford (*Roman Republican Coinage*, 29-30) suggested the coins were minted sometime after 326 BC, but acknowledges we do not know *why* (which is what we propose to explain, based on iconography). See also ibid., 36-37, 131, 713. He does not discuss the types: 'There is little that can be said about no. 1-2…Both issues are presumably isolated forerunners of the Roman Republican coinage proper; it is noticeable that there is nothing Roman whatever about their types' (ibid., 37). Crawford's comment is reminiscent of the issues in hellenocentric scholarship concerning the Etruscan man-faced bulls, in which a very old and rich tradition was reduced to 'copies' of Greek models. As we demonstrated in Chapter 3 & 4, nothing could be further from the truth. So, too, in the Roman tradition the man-faced bull is probably not a mere unintelligent copy of the Greeks, but takes on its own significance within a new context. For some Roman examples of Acheloios outside of these two coins (RRC 1/1 and 2/1), see: H.P. Isler, 'Acheloos,' in *LIMC*, no. 260-265; RIC I 319; RSC 432.

151 T. Mommsen, *Histoire de la monnaie romaine,* T.III (Paris: Rollin et Feuardent, 1865-75), 225. M. Caccamo Caltabiano also dates the issue to shortly after 338 BC (M. Caccamo Caltabiano, 'La serie ΡΩΜΑΙΩΝ e la cronologia delle prime emissioni bronzee di Neapolis,' in *RSA* (Bologna: Pàtron, 1981), 33-52.

152 A. Burnett, 'Early Roman Coinage and Its Italian Context,' in *The Oxford Handbook of Greek and Roman Coinage*, edited by W.E. Metcalf (Oxford: University Press, 2012), 297-314. For the technical analysis of dating see A.M. Burnett, 'The beginnings of Roman coinage,' in *AIIN*, 33 (1989), 33-64, specifically Appendix 1.

153 N.K.Rutter, *HN Italy*, 46; N.K.Rutter, 'The Coinage of Italy,' in *The Oxford Handbook of Greek and Roman Coinage*, 139.

154 The reader is advised to read the above section on mercenary involvement in the transference of man-faced bull iconography, located in Chapter 2.

155 See S.P. Oakley, *A Commentary on Livy Books VI-X. Volume III. Book IX* (Oxford: Clarendon Press, 2005), for a thorough commentary on Livy. He insists, 'It is wrong to minimize the importance of the events of 321-320: the Caudine Forks was remembered alongside the Allia, Trasimene, Cannae, and Arausio as one of the great Roman disasters….and the experience of Caudium probably strengthened her resolve to eliminate the threat of the Samnites' (Ibid., 38). Others, most notably Nissen, believe the episode is a fantasy invented after 136 BC, in which it must be understood strictly in terms of the Numantine War, after which Livy's account is allegedly modeled (Ibid., 29, and especially note 2). The main problems with accepting Livy's account, as explained by Oakley, are that (1) it consists of mostly speeches, (2) it appears as though he is trying to 'salvage' Roman honor, and (3) tribunes did not normally leave the city, especially on military campaigns (ibid., 26-7). Loreto, who believes Livy's account is mostly accurate, argues this constitutional impossibility results from Clausius Quadrigarius, who confused *tribunis plebis* with *tribunis militum* (ibid. 27, citing L. Loreto, 'Per una 'Quellenforschung' della pax Caudina,' in *BIDR*, XCII-XCIII (1990), 659-660).

156 Oakley believes Livy's description of the terrain of the Caudine Forks is imaginary (*A Commentary on Livy Books VI-X. Volume III. Book IX*, 16).

157 Livy, *Ab Urbe Condita Libri*, 9.1.1-19. Alternatively, Cicero (*off.* 3.109) claimed the Romans were defeated in battle.

158 The distinction between a *foedus* and *sponsio* in relation to this event is discussed by S.P. Oakley, *A Commentary on Livy Books VI-X. Volume III. Book IX*, 31-34. Here he makes the exceptional point that the two are not mutually exclusive, and the *sponsio* might have been the logical precursor to a *foedus* in military engagements (ibid., 33). Oakley himself seems to lean toward Nissen and the other skeptics who believe Livy's description is fictitious, but also cites the major proponents who advocate its legitimacy (ibid., 33, note 2).

159 Livy, *Ab Urbe Condita Libri*, 9.4.12.

160 Livy, *Ab Urbe Condita Libri*, 9.10.2-5. Zonaras describes Postumius similarly (Cf. S.P. Oakley, *A Commentary on Livy Books VI-X. Volume III. Book IX*, 6-11, for an overview of parallel narratives, in which Oakley concludes: 'Since all of our sources record versions of the story which are basically similar, L. probably did not make radical innovations. His originality lies in his mastery of structure and graphic detail, and in his ability to write a narrative highly charged with graphic detail.')

Rome, a notion at the very heart of the man-faced bull tradition.[161]

Ultimately, according to Livy, the humiliation of Rome was short-lived, and the Roman army experienced a rebirth[162] the next year, in 320 BC, after recruiting nine legions of soldiers from the dissolved army (they were not bound to the terms of surrender any longer).[163] The armies marched to Samnite territory and defeated the enemy, forcing the Samnites to undergo the same disgraceful surrender to which they themselves had been previously subjected. In fact, Livy informs us that, 'Hardly any victory that Rome ever won was more noteworthy for the sudden change that it wrought in the circumstances of the Republic.'[164] S.P. Oakley, in his monumental work, agrees with most scholars that Livy's account of Roman victories after the Caudine Forks episode are fictitious over-exaggerations to compensate for the humiliating defeat, and many probably did not occur.[165] However, he rejects the notion that there was uniform peace between the Romans and Samnites from 320 to 316/15 (he specifically argues there was fighting in 319 BC),[166] and upon this background it seems plausible that Rome might have issued its first coin: it symbolized the previous sacrifice of the army and later its generals for the sake of Rome, and also the promise of redemption from its previous humiliation (and thus rebirth into a life of honor).[167] In fact, there could not be a more appropriate means of payment for a previously disgraced soldier taking up arms again than a coin featuring the man-faced bull. Thus, based on the meaning of the iconography in relation to the events surrounding the Caudine Forks, it seems plausible to date Rome's first coins to 320/19 BC.

There appears to be four varieties of these ΡΩΜΑΙΩΝ, forepart of man-faced bull coins:[168] most have an eight-rayed star on the shoulder of the bull or no star at all, and one example has a six-rayed star.[169] There is a fourth quasi-variety in which the inscription is irregular looking.[170] The identification of a variety featuring a star with four rays is incorrect,[171] four-rayed stars only appear on the units with Neapolitan inscriptions. Ultimately, it is likely that the coins were struck at Neapolis (or at least in Campania) for the Romans c. 320 to 319 BC.[172] And who better to mint the coins than Campanians, the same people who (at Capua) clothed and adorned the disgraced Roman army with Campanian insignia before they returned home?[173] Ultimately, there might be more truth to Livy's account of the events surrounding the Caudine Forks than the scholarly tradition after Nissen chooses to recognize.[174]

[161] Livy (*Ab Urbe Condita Libri*, 9.10.4) actually describes Postumius as *piaculaque pro populo Romano dare*, or 'an expiatory victim for the people of Rome.' The notion of expiatory sacrifice is most clearly reflected in the forepart of man-faced bull types, in which the figure is kneeling in assent to being sacrificed (not swimming or charging). This notion is substantiated in Part I of this book. For a thorough analysis of expiatory sacrifice in relation to Greek and Roman river gods, see R. Taylor, 'River Raptures: Containment and Control of Water in Greek and Roman Constructions of Identity,' 31-36.

[162] The notion of rebirth is also intimately related to man-faced bull iconography, as discussed in depth above, but especially in relation to Sicilian coins issued by retired (mostly Campanian) mercenaries and other municipalities experiencing renewed freedom during the time of Timoleon.

[163] Livy, *Ab Urbe Condita Libri*, 9.10.6.

[164] Livy, *Ab Urbe Condita Libri*, 9.15.8.

[165] S.P. Oakley, *A Commentary on Livy Books VI-X. Volume III. Book IX*, 34. He argues: (1) that the Samnite 'Caudine legions' were included 'as much for literary as for historical reasons;' (2) the Romans, if indeed they were defeated in battle, would not have been able to march straight into the middle of Samnium shortly after; (3) if, as Livy says, the consuls were in eastern Italy, then Liri and Campania would have been 'denuded of troops;' (4) it is 'comic' to think the Tarentines attempted to arbitrate; (5) the capture of Pontius and marching of the Samnites 'under the yoke' is likely 'pure invention'; (6) if Rome did hand over 600 knights, they would not have risked their lives and if they did, the Samnites would have killed them; (7) it is odd that the hostages were kept at Luceria and not in a Samnite town (ibid., 34-5). He also rejects the capture of Luceria in 320, which he claims might have been inserted after the fictitious revenge in 320 was composed, in order to explain why the recapture in 315 BC was necessary. Oakley dismissed the Oxyrhynchus Chronicle, which records some of the campaigning described by Livy, because of its brevity, conflicts over chronology (it says 319 BC) and because it was likely derived from 'debased annalistic sources' (ibid., 36, note 1). We do not consider Livy's account of the Roman victories in 320 BC total fantasy. The rationale provided by other scholars, as outlined by Oakley, is certainly not conclusive. If we consider the numismatic (iconographic) evidence and, as Fredericksen did, the fact that Diodorus Siculus also never mentions a Caudine peace (Diodorus Siculus, *The Library of History*, XIX.10, 1), it becomes an appealing possibility (M.W. Frederiscksen, 'Review of E.T. Salmon, *Samnium and the Samnites* (1967),' in *JRS*, LVIII (1968), 224-9). Finally, even if the victories Livy describes in 320 are total fantasy (perhaps they were simply exaggerated), the coins still might have been struck that year and the next leading up to the recapture of Satricum in 319 BC. For an argument that the Romans did have a victory against the Samnites in 320 BC, see L. Loreto, 'Per una 'Quellenforschung' della pax Caudina,'653-4.

[166] S.P. Oakley, *A Commentary on Livy Books VI-X. Volume III. Book IX*, 36-38, who highlights the capture of Satricum and the campaign against the Frentani in 319 BC.

[167] Accepting, of course, that there is some truth to Livy's account.

[168] We count 15, but possibly as many as 18 examples: BMC (2.65g); BMC (3.07g); BnF (3.36g); Vienna (4.83g); Vienna (1.91g); Naples-Santangello 1150; Berlin (3.54g); Berlin (2.53g); Milan (Sambon 611/ disfigured legend); Bignami Coll. Capitoline (2.48g); Noble 62 (2.84g)?; Glasgow (3.14g); RBW (4.54g); Ahala Collection (2.72g); Dix-Noonan-Webb, Auction 9/29/2008, lot 5855 (3.46g); Specimen YGH? (3.07g); Additional Specimen 1, Roberto Russo Collection?; Additional Specimen 2 (3.70g); Artemide Aste 19.2E (2.22g)=Schottenstift Monastery example?(also 2.22g). In his work, Crawford noted 6 obverse dies and 7 reverse dies (M. Crawford, *Roman Republican Coinage*, 131, no. 1/1). We count 8 reverse dies, but possibly as many as 10.

[169] A. Sambon, *Les monnaies antiques de l'Italie*, no. 610.

[170] Ibid., no. 611.

[171] D. Vagi, in 'Rome's First Didrachm,' mentioned these issues had 4, sometimes 8-rayed stars, but has acknowledged that might have been in error (Personal correspondence, Summer 2015).

[172] The comparison below between a Neapolitan coin and a Roman coin might illustrate the phenomenon of a shared mint, insofar as the engravings were clearly done by the same individual. However, this is the only example of a near die match (if not an actual die match) we were able to find between the Neapolitan and Roman types.

[173] Livy, *Ab Urbe Condita Libri*, 9.6.4-7.

[174] H. Nissen, 'Der caudinische Friede,' in *RhM*, n.s. XXV (1870), 1-65, who is credited with revealing much about Roman history that had been shrouded by annalistic falsifications. However, as Oakley points out, 'not everything for which Nissen argued should be accepted' (S.P. Oakley, *A Commentary on Livy Books VI-X. Volume III. Book IX*, 25, note 2).

The other Roman coin likely minted at Neapolis that features a man-faced bull has the Latin legend ROMANO, which many have dated later than the RRC 1/1 type on account of the inscription. Some, such as Vagi, suggest it might have been contemporaneous or shortly after the emission of RRC 1/1, around 325 BC.[175] Rutter[176] and Crawford[177] both suggest c. 300 BC, and Russo dates it to before 320 BC.[178] The man-faced bull on this issue is shown full-body standing to right, with star above. This issue appears to show a helmeted Minerva on its obverse, although Burnett suggests it might be Roma,[179] and dates the coin to 310 BC.[180] We suggest a date of 297 BC, based on Livy's account of the beginning stages of the Third Samnite War. According to him, in 297 BC, faced with fighting multiple wars on multiple fronts, the Romans received word from Sutrium, Nepete, and Falerii[181] that the Etruscans were suing for peace (albeit short-lived, presumably like the coins).[182] This was extremely fortunate, since the Romans could focus on the Samnites. Thus, the coins, which combine man-faced bull and celestial iconography largely in accordance with the Etruscan tradition of Acheloios, were probably struck to pay troops in the early stages of the Third Samnite War and in recognition of the auspicious peace with the Etruscans. Moreover, MSP I, 237, minted at Neapolis c. 310 to 270 BC, uses the same iconographic scheme of the man-faced bull standing to right, with head in profile. It is the only such full-body man-faced bull coin from Neapolis and suggests the two issues were minted closely together, casting some doubt on Vagi's suggestion of a date around 325 BC, and also Russo's dating to 320 BC (See comparison below).

Finally, who is the man-faced bull on Rome's coinage? In terms of RRC 1/1, one might be tempted to think Acheloios Tiber, but since the coins were not minted in Rome and the Romans clearly adopted the iconography from Campania under special circumstances, that is unlikely. But Acheloios Sebethos, the figure probably depicted on the coins of Neapolis, would not make sense for the Romans either. Perhaps it is just Acheloios, a rare example on coinage (outside of Akarnania) in which a local manifestation is not the focus of worship. However, one appealing alternative is that it is Acheloios Isclero, since the battle at the Caudine Forks was presumably in the general area of that river (20 km south-east), and that is where the entire Roman Army was spared.[183] Thus, paying homage to Acheloios as he is embodied in the Isclero River would have been particularly important to the Romans. In terms of RRC 2/1, if indeed it was minted in recognition of the (shortlived) peace with Etruria, in 297 BC, it is probably Acheloios Tiber, since Falerii and Rome are both located on the Tiber.

[175] D. Vagi, 'Rome's First Didrachm,' 79.

[176] N.K.Rutter, *HN Italy,* 46.

[177] M. Crawford, *Roman Republican Coinage* (Cambridge: University Press, 1974), 131.

[178] R. Russo, 'Prima bozza preliminare di uno studio organico sulla monetazione del centro Italia e della Magna Grecia tra il 326 a.C. al 215 a.C.,' in *Numismatica Sottovoce* (London: Numismatica Ars Classica, 2009), 8.

[179] A.M. Burnett, 'Early Roman Coinage and Its Italian Context,' 300.

[180] A.M. Burnett, 'The beginnings of Roman coinage,' 61.

[181] Italy's first man-faced bull is from Falerii and dates to the 8th century BC, indicating a very old tradition (J.M. Eisenberg, 'The Art of the Italic Peoples. A Major Exhibition in Paris,' 4). Also from Falerii: an Ionian gem, dated to the 6th century BC, that was found in a grave (H.P. Isler, *Acheloos*, no.291), and an offering bowl from Etruscan Falerii (H.P. Isler, *Acheloos*, no.93), demonstrating the permanence of the iconography in that location.

[182] Livy, *Ab Urbe Condita Libri*, 10.14.1-3. Oakley confirms that the peace with the Etruscans is probably historically accurate (S.P. Oakley, *A Commentary on Livy, Books VI-X, Volume IV, Book X* (Oxford: Clarendon, 2005), 47: 'The reference to the two-year *indutiae* is the detail most likely to be sound.'

[183] As Postumius informs the Roman Senate, 'Nothing that happened at Caudium, senators, was dictated by human prudence; the gods deprived both the enemy's commanders and your own of their senses' (Livy, *Ab Urbe Condita Libri*, 9.9.10). In the past some scholars proposed that the site was in the actual valley of the Isclero River, near the modern town of Sant'agata dei Goti (cf. P. Mingazzini, 'Saticula' in *Enciclopedia Italiana* (Rome, 1936)). This hypothesis has been rejected by modern scholars for many reasons: (1) Livy never mentioned the Isclero River in his report, but only says that the location was '*campus herbidus aquosusque*' (*Ab Urbe Condita Libri*, 9.2), meaning there was vegetation and water, but not necessarily a river; (2) Cluver confused Caiatia and Calatia (the latter mentioned by ancient sources); (3) The Isclero River valley is narrow and steep, so it is very difficult to imagine Roman legions camping there;(4) Archaeological excavations in the valley of the Isclero revealed a large Samnite necropolis and the remains of a Samnite stronghold, indicating the Romans would not have chosen this site to camp (See P. Sommella, *Forche Caudine in Antichi campi di battaglia in Italia: Contributi all'identificazione topografica di alcune battaglie d'età repubblicana* (De Luca, 1967), 51-65; E.T. Salmon, *The Second Samnite War in Samnium and the Samnites* (Cambridge, 1967), 226). According to the most recent studies, the Caudine Fork is probably located in the Arienzo valley, between the modern towns of Forchia and Santa Maria a Vico, located about 20 km south-east of the site proposed by Cluver. Today there is no river flowing in the Arienzo valley, so perhaps the '*campus aquosus*' mentioned by Livy simply referred to a swampy site, consistent with the Arienzo valley. However, topographic changes might have occurred over the centuries, and there seems to be traces of a small stream at the site (P. Sommella, *Forche Caudine in Antichi campi di battaglia in Italia: Contributi all'identificazione topografica di alcune battaglie d'età repubblicana*, 53).

Coinage

414. AE Unit, 2.65g, 17mm, 9h	**320 to 319 BC**
	OBV: Head of Apollo to right, wearing laurel wreath with leaves in triple clusters(?). REV: Forepart of Acheloios (Isclero?) as a man-faced bull to right, no star on shoulder, ΡΩΜΑΙΩΝ above. REF: RRC 1/1; BM no. AN00624561_001* (description says star on flank but curator confirmed there is no star).

415. AE Unit, 2.53g, 15mm, 9h	**320 to 319 BC**
	OBV: Head of Apollo to right, wearing laurel wreath with leaves in triple clusters. REV: Forepart of Acheloios (Isclero?) as a man-faced bull to right, star with six rays on shoulder, ΡΩΜΑΙΩΝ above. REF: RRC 1/1; Sambon 610; Münzkabinett, Staatliche Museen zu Berlin, no. 18214343*.

416. AE Unit, 3.46g, 3h	**320 to 319 BC**
	OBV: Head of Apollo to right, wearing laurel wreath with leaves in triple clusters. REV: Forepart of Acheloios (Isclero?) as a man-faced bull to right, star with eight rays on shoulder, ΡΩΜΑΙΩΝ above. REF: RRC 1/1; Dix Noonan Webb, September 29th, 2008, lot 5855*.

417. AE Unit, 4.54g, 17mm	**320 to 319 BC**
	OBV: Head of Apollo to right, wearing laurel wreath with leaves in triple clusters. REV: Forepart of Acheloios (Isclero?) as a man-faced bull to right, star with eight rays on shoulder, ΡΩΜΑΙΩΝ (irregular inscription) above. REF: RRC 1/1; Sambon 611; RBW 1; CNG Triton IX, lot 1252*.

418. AE Unit, 6.14g, 19mm	**297 BC**
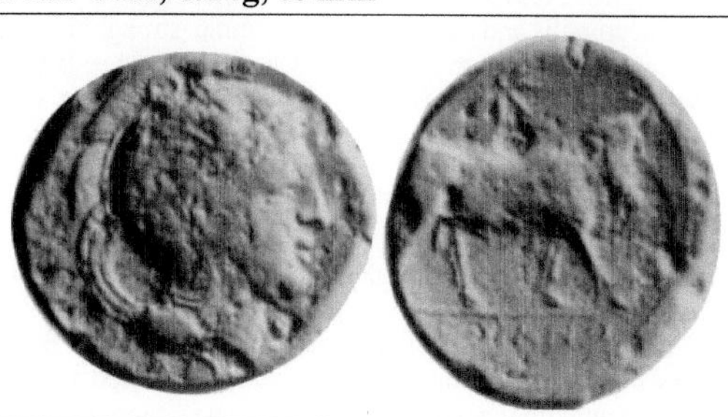	OBV: Head of Roma[184] to right, wearing Attic helm decorated with seahorse. REV: Acheloios Tiber as a man-faced bull standing to right, above, star with eight rays, ROMANO in ex. REF: RRC 2/1; HN Italy 252*. *Unique*

[184] A. Burnett, 'The Iconography of Roman Coin Types in the Third Century BC,' in NC, 146 (1986), 68 and note 11.

Comparison of Taliercio Type Ic 3 to RRC 1/1[185]

Comparison of Taliercio IIa 6 to RRC 2/1[186]

[185] Taliercio Ic 3 was minted c. 350 to 326 BC, but probably closer to 326 BC. Both coins from the Ahala collection.
[186] Taliercio IIa 6 was minted c. 317/310 to 270 BC. Image of RRC 2/1 courtesy of Keith Rutter.

SUESSA AURUNCA

Suessa Aurunca, the modern Sessa Aurunca, is a town in Campania located 60km north of Naples. It is situated on a rocky hill overlooking a vast plain crossed by the ancient Liris River (modern Garigliano). Archaeological evidence from the Archaic Age testifies to an Etruscan influence in the area.[187] The city itself was the site of an Italic settlement that ancient literary sources identify as the ancient Suessa, the main town of the Aurunci people, who occupied the territory since the 8th century BC.

Livy reports two different cities originally founded by the Aurunci: Aurunca and Suessa. During the second half of the 4th century BC a war broke out between the Sidicini of Teanum and the Aurunci. The Aurunci unsuccessfully asked for help from the Romans, and were forced to abandon Aurunca, moving to their colony called Suessa.[188]

Thus, the ancient metropolis Aurunca was taken and destroyed by the Sidicini in 337 BC, and since then Suessa was called Aurunca because it was the new capital of the Aurunci people.[189] The story of Suessa Aurunca as an independent city finally ended in 313 BC, with the destruction of the Italic site by Rome and the subsequent foundation of a Latin colony with the influx of about 3,000 settlers.[190] The new Roman colony had the same name as the previous settlement.

The bronze coinage of the man-faced bull issued at Suessa Aurunca copied the unit types of Taliercio Phase III (Neapolis), and are dated in accordance with those issues.

The man-faced bull depicted on the reverse is probably Acheloios Liris.

Coinage

419. AE Unit	**270 to 240 BC**
	OBV: Head of Apollo facing left, wearing laurel wreath with leaves in opposing pairs, SVESANO before, lightning bolt behind. REV: Acheloios Liris as a man-faced bull standing to right on single line, head facing, winged nymph above, N below. REF: Sambon 877; Carelli, LXV, 14* (does not show 'N' below) *Unconfirmed*
420. AE Unit, 6.21g	**270 to 240 BC**
	OBV: Head of Apollo facing left, wearing laurel wreath with leaves in opposing pairs, nothing before, lightning bolt behind. REV: Acheloios Liris as a man-faced bull standing to right on single line, head facing, winged nymph above, SVESANO in ex. REF: SNG Dreer 97*.

[187] E. Benelli, 'Materiali e tipi ceramici arcaici tra Abruzzo, Campania e Lazio,' in *Gli Etruschi e la Campania Settentrionale* (Roma, 2011), 111.
[188] Livy, *Ab Urbe Condita Libri*, 8.15.
[189] A. Sogliano, 'Disegno storico della Campania antica', in *Atti della Società italiana per il progresso delle scienze*, Vol. XIII (Roma, 1925), 262-270.
[190] Livy, *Ab Urbe Condita Libri*, 9.28.7.

421. AE Unit, 5.89g, 19mm | **270 to 240 BC**

OBV: Head of Apollo facing left, wearing laurel wreath with leaves in opposing pairs, SVESANO before, K behind. Dotted border.
REV: Acheloios Liris as a man-faced bull standing to right on single line, head facing, winged nymph above, IΣ below.
REF: Sambon 878; Weber 409; SNG France 1163 = BnF Fonds Général 539*.

422. AE Unit, 6.35g | **270 to 240 BC**

OBV: Head of Apollo facing left, wearing laurel wreath with leaves in opposing pairs, SVESANO before, K behind. Dotted border.
REV: Acheloios Liris as a man-faced bull standing to right on single line, head facing, winged nymph above, uncertain (N)? below.
REF: Sambon 878 var.; Private Collection*.

423. AE Unit, 7.50g, 22mm | **270 to 240 BC**

OBV: Head of Apollo facing left, wearing laurel wreath with leaves in opposing pairs, SVESANO before, uncertain (N) ? behind. Dotted border.
REV: Acheloios Liris as a man-faced bull standing to right on single line, head facing, winged nymph above, M below,
REF: Sambon 880-881/1; SNG ANS 604; Tintinna 21, lot 42*.

424. AE Unit, 6.21g | **270 to 240 BC**

OBV: Head of Apollo facing left, wearing laurel wreath with leaves in opposing pairs, SVESANO before, N behind. Dotted border.
REV: Acheloios Liris as a man-faced bull standing to right on single line, head facing, winged nymph above, N below.
REF: Sambon 881/2; BMC 10; H.D. Rauch GmbH, Summer Auction 2012, lot 104*.

425. AE Unit, 5.84g | **270 to 240 BC**

OBV: Head of Apollo facing left, wearing laurel wreath with leaves in opposing pairs, SVESANO before, N behind. Dotted border.
REV: Acheloios Liris as a man-faced bull standing to right on single line, head facing, winged nymph above, Π below.
REF:; Sambon 779, 881/3; BMC 9; SNG Gale 140; SNG Cop 585; SNG France 1164; Ancient Numismatic Enterprise, item 1728*.
Sambon incorrectly listed M instead of N for the BMC 9 specimen, listing it as a different variant (Sambon 879).

426. AE Unit, 7.21g, 19mm	270 to 240 BC
	OBV: Head of Apollo facing left, wearing laurel wreath with leaves in opposing pairs, SVESANO before, N behind. Dotted border. REV: Acheloios Liris as a man-faced bull standing to right on single line, head facing, winged nymph above, ΙΣ below. REF: Sambon 881/4; SNG Morcom 186; SNG Milano 283-284; SNG Budapest 503; SNG München 415; SNG Paris 1165 = BnF Fonds Général 541*.

427. AE Unit, 6.76g	270 to 240 BC
	OBV: Head of Apollo facing left, wearing laurel wreath with leaves in opposing pairs, SVESANO before, T behind. Dotted border. REV: Acheloios Liris as a man-faced bull standing to right on single line, head facing, winged nymph above, ΙΣ below. REF: Sambon 883; SNG Cop. 584*.

428. AE Unit, 6.99g	270 to 240 BC
	OBV: Head of Apollo facing left, wearing laurel wreath with leaves in opposing pairs, SVESANO before, T behind. Dotted border. REV: Acheloios Liris as a man-faced bull standing to right on single line, head facing, winged nymph above, M below, nothing in ex. REF: Sambon - ; Nomisma 48, lot 15*.

429. AE Unit, unrecorded weight	270 to 240 BC
	OBV: Head of Apollo facing left, wearing laurel wreath with leaves in opposing pairs, SVESANO before, Π behind. Dotted border. REV: Acheloios Liris as a man-faced bull standing to right on single line, head facing, winged nymph above, Π below, nothing in ex. REF: Sambon - ; Graziano 44*.

430. AE Unit, 6.94g, 20mm	270 to 240 BC
	OBV: Head of Apollo facing left, wearing laurel wreath with leaves in opposing pairs, no inscription before, O or hook behind. Dotted border. REV: Acheloios Liris as a man-faced bull standing to right on single line, head facing, winged nymph above, SVESANO in ex. REF: Sambon 884; CNG Triton XV, lot 1024*. *This is the most common variant for Suessa, with about 100 specimens known. Sambon 882 describes a variant with pentagram below the man-faced bull, but the type is unconfirmed, and probably a misreading of an issue from Teanum Sidicinum.*

431. AE Unit, 6.36g, 20mm	270 to 240 BC
	OBV: Head of Apollo facing left, wearing laurel wreath with leaves in opposing pairs, no inscription before, oval shield behind. REV: Acheloios Liris as a man-faced bull standing to right on single line, head facing, winged nymph above, SVESANO in ex. REF: Sambon - ; SNG Ashmolean 6; SNG Gale 142; ACR 6, lot 21*. *SNG Ashmolean 6 is incorrectly attributed to Cumae.*

432. AE Unit, 6.84g	270 to 240 BC
	OBV: Head of Apollo facing right, wearing laurel wreath with leaves in opposing pairs, SVESANO before, A(?) behind. Dotted border. REV: Acheloios Liris as a man-faced bull standing to left on single line (?), head facing, uncertain winged nymph or corn ear above, uncertain letter (retro K?) below. REF: BM no. 1920-7-25 6 = Weber 408*.

Uncertain (Samnite Imitation?)

433. AE Unit, 4.90g	270 to 240 BC
	OBV: Head of Apollo facing right, wearing laurel wreath with leaves in opposing pairs, uncertain inscription before. REV: Acheloios Liris as a man-faced bull standing to right on single line, head facing, uncertain winged nymph or corn ear above, I between back legs, Λ below bull with K between front legs and I before, _OVHN_ (?) in ex. REF: Potamikon Collection*.

TEANUM SIDICINUM

Ancient Teanum Sidicinum was located near the northern border of Campania. The site had been inhabited since prehistoric times and the earliest archaeological evidence in the area dates back to the Bronze Age. Many votive offerings from the Archaic Age have been found at a large shrine located near the Savone River.[191] However, the evidence available reveals that there was never an actual city during this time period, but instead the area consisted of several small centers scattered about, forming a network of communities and villages which today show themselves in the many necropolises, all located along the Savone.[192]

The city itself was founded in the 4th century BC, as the capital of the Italian people called the Sidicini, who were of Oscan lineage.[193] The archaeological evidence demonstrates strong Etruscan cultural influences on this population, mainly through Capua.[194]

Sometime between the late 4th and early 3rd century BC, Teanum allied with Rome[195] and in this same period began to mint coins.[196]

The bronze coinage of the man-faced bull issued in Teanum matches the general chronological framework of Cales and Neapolis, and the types, aside from a rare variety featuring Mercury instead of Apollo, are virtually identical. This catalog therefore arranges the coinage of Teanum Sidicinum into two phases: the very earliest coins of Phase I (317 to 272 BC) employed the head of Mercury (Group Ia) but were quickly changed to show Apollo (Group Ib). Both types feature a star above the man-faced bull. The variety with lyre above man-faced bull (Ic) probably appeared shortly after the star types, though we list all as contemporaneous under the general Phase I dates. The coins which compromise Phase II (272 to 250 BC) all feature a winged nymph crowning the man-faced bull and maintain the connection with the needs of the war against Hannibal.[197] This phase is divided into two groups: Group Ia features symbols behind Apollo whereas Group Ib features letters.

The man-faced bull depicted on the reverse is probably a representation of Acheloios Savo, just as in Cales.

Coinage

PHASE I: c. 317 to 272 BC

Group Ia

434. AE Unit, 5.63g, 18mm	317 to 272 BC
	OBV: Head of Mercury facing right, wearing petasos, caduceus on shoulder, star with eight rays behind, 𐌕𐌉𐌀𐌍𐌖𐌃 before. REV: Acheloios Savo as a man-faced bull standing to right on single line, head facing, star with 16 rays above, 𐌔𐌉𐌃𐌉𐌊𐌉𐌍𐌖𐌃 in ex. REF: Sambon 1003 ; SNG ANS 624; SNG France 1205 = BnF Fonds Général 558*.

[191] M. Pagano, 'L'Italia romana delle Regiones. Regio I Latium et Campania: Teano,' in *Enciclopedia Archeologica*, Vol.VI (Roma: Istit. Della Enciclopedia Italiana, 2004).

[192] L. Cerchiai, *Gli antichi Popoli della Campania. Archeologia e Storia* (Roma: Carocci, 2000), 84-5.

[193] Strabo, *Geographica*, 5.3.9.

[194] F. Sirano, 'Identità culturali nella Campania settentrionale: un aggiornamento,' in *Dalle sorgenti alla foce Il bacino del Liri-Garigliano nell'antichità, culture contatti scambi*, edited by Cristina Corsi, Eugenio Polito (Roma: Quasar, 2008), 48-9.

[195] The relationship between Teanum Sidicinum and Rome is unclear in the early stages from the foundation to the last quarter of the 4th century BC. In fact, in some cases the literary traditions report the Sidicini taking up arms against Rome, but then in other places allied to it, at least until 334 BC. It was assumed by scholars that in 334 BC Teanum received (from Rome) the title *civitas sine suffragio* (G. Coppola, G. Colamonico, D. Mustilli, and N. Nicolini, 'Teano,' in *Enciclopedia Italiana di scienze, lettere ed arti*, Vol. 33 (Roma, 1937). The only definitive evidence we have comes from numismatics, in which the bronze coins minted after 270 BC transition to the Latin inscription *Tiano* instead of the Oscan *Tianud Sidikinud* (cfr. SNG France 1206-1209). This proves at least that in the second half of the 3rd century BC Teanum received the right to use the Latin language on coinage.

[196] Cf. SNG France 1179-1209.

[197] We know from ancient sources that in 218 BC Sidicine troops were engaged in the battle of Lake Trasimeno against Hannibal (M. Pagano, 'L'Italia romana delle Regiones. Regio I Latium et Campania: Teano').

435. AE Unit	**317 to 272 BC**
	OBV: Head of Mercury facing right, wearing petasos, caduceus on shoulder, star with eight rays (or wreath?) behind, 𐌃𐌖𐌍𐌀𐌉𐌕 before. REV: Acheloios Savo as a man-faced bull standing to right on single line, head facing, star with 16 rays above, uncertain symbol (pentagram?) below, 𐌃𐌖𐌍𐌉𐌊𐌉𐌃𐌉𐌔 in ex. REF: Santangelo 1419 = M. Nassa, *Teanum Sidicinum, Rilettura sommaria, con raffronti, dei più significativi contributi sulla monetazione antica*, (Roma: 2012),44, n.6*.

Group Ib

436. AE Unit, 6.24g, 18mm	**317 to 272 BC**
	OBV: Head of Apollo facing right, wearing laurel wreath with leaves in opposing pairs, E behind, 𐌃𐌖𐌍𐌀𐌝𐌕 before. Dotted border. REV: Acheloios Savo as a man-faced bull standing to right on single line, head facing, star with 16 rays above, 𐌃𐌖𐌍𐌉𐌊𐌉𐌃𐌉𐌔 in ex. REF: Sambon 991; BMC 2; SNG France 1187 = BnF Fonds Général 548*. *Sambon described two unconfirmed variants without E behind (990) and with Γ behind (992), but they are both probably misreadings of this type, as the specimen illustrated here was listed by him as 990.*

437. AE Unit	**317 to 272 BC**
	OBV: Head of Apollo facing left, wearing laurel wreath with leaves in opposing pairs, 𐌃𐌖𐌍𐌀𐌉𐌕 before. REV: Acheloios Savo as a man-faced bull standing to right on single line, head facing, star with 16 rays above, 𐌃𐌖𐌍𐌉𐌊𐌉𐌃𐌉𐌔 in ex. REF: Sambon 995; Carelli, LXVI, 10* *Unconfirmed.*

Group Ic

438. AE Unit, 5.64g	**317 to 272 BC**
	OBV: Head of Apollo facing left, wearing laurel wreath with leaves in opposing pairs, 𐌃𐌖𐌍𐌀‖𐌕 before. REV: Acheloios Savo as a man-faced bull standing to right on single line, head facing, lyre above, 𐌃𐌖𐌍𐌉𐌊𐌉𐌃𐌉𐌔 in ex. REF: Sambon 993; SNG France 1188; SNG Cop 591; Graziano 20 = Numismatica Fiorentina item n.991*.

439. AE Unit, 5.50-6.12g	**317 to 272 BC**
	OBV: Head of Apollo facing left, wearing laurel wreath with leaves in opposing pairs, (𐌃𐌖𐌍𐌀𐌉𐌕) before. Dotted border. REV: Acheloios Savo as a man-faced bull standing to right on single line, head facing, lyre above, N below, 𐌃𐌖𐌍𐌉𐌊𐌉𐌃𐌉𐌔 or 𐌔𐌉𐌃𐌉𐌊𐌉𐌍𐌖𐌃 in ex. REF: Sambon 994; SNG ANS 616; BMC 3 = HN Italy 454*.

440. AE Unit, 19mm	**317 to 272 BC**
	OBV: Head of Apollo facing left, wearing laurel wreath with leaves in opposing pairs, 𐌃𐌖𐌍𐌀𐌉𐌕 before, dotted border REV: Acheloios Savo as a man-faced bull standing to right on single line, head facing, lyre above, K below, 𐌃𐌖𐌍𐌉𐌊𐌉𐌃𐌉𐌔 or 𐌔𐌉𐌃𐌉𐌊𐌉𐌍𐌖𐌃 in ex. REF: Pozzi 246*.

441. AE Unit	**317 to 272 BC**
	OBV: Head of Apollo facing right, wearing laurel wreath with leaves in opposing pairs, 𐌃𐌖𐌍𐌀𐌉𐌕 or 𐌃𐌖𐌍𐌀𐌉𐌉𐌕 before. Dotted border. REV: Acheloios Savo as a man-faced bull standing to right on single line, head facing, lyre above, 𐌃𐌖𐌍𐌉𐌊𐌉𐌃𐌉𐌔 in ex. REF: Sambon 989; Garrucci II, Pl.LXXXIII, n.7; J. Friedlaender, *Die osckischen münzen,* Pl.. I, n.3* (redrawn).

PHASE II: c. 272 to 250 BC

GROUP IIA

442. AE Unit, 5.22g, 18mm	**272 to 250 BC**
	OBV: Head of Apollo facing left, wearing laurel wreath with leaves in opposing pairs, lightning bolt behind, 𐌃𐌖𐌍𐌀𐌉𐌕 before. REV: Acheloios Savo as a man-faced bull standing to right on single line, head facing, winged nymph above, pentagram below. REF: Sambon 1000; BMC 15; SNG ANS 622-3; SNG Dreer 100; SNG München 421-2; SNG Milano 300; SNG Gale 143; SNG France 1201-1204, 1203 = BnF Armand Valton 37*.

443. AE Unit, 4.84g	**272 to 250 BC**
	OBV: Head of Apollo facing left, wearing laurel wreath with leaves in opposing pairs, hook behind, ꟼVИN⊦T before. REV: Acheloios Savo as a man-faced bull standing to right on single line, head facing, winged nymph above REF: Sambon - ; SNG Cop 593*. *Unique*

444. AE Unit, 6.00g, 20mm	**272 to 250 BC**
	OBV: Head of Apollo facing left, wearing laurel wreath with leaves in opposing pairs, oval shield behind. Dotted border. REV: Acheloios Savo as a man-faced bull standing to right on single line, winged nymph above, pentagram below, ꟼVИN⊦T in ex. REF: Sambon 1002; SNG France 1195; BMC 13; CNG, eAuction 205, lot 2*.

GROUP IIB

445. AE Unit, 4.27g	**272 to 250 BC**
	OBV: Head of Apollo facing left, wearing laurel wreath with leaves in opposing pairs, O behind, dotted border, ꟼVИN⊦T or ꟼVИNΛT before. Dotted border. REV: Acheloios Savo as a man-faced bull standing to right on single line, head facing, winged nymph above, pentagram below. REF: Sambon 997; SNG ANS 619; SNG Cop 592; SNG France 1197-1200; Dr. Busso Peus 384, lot 17*.

446. AE Unit, 4.40g, 20mm	**272 to 250 BC**
	OBV: Head of Apollo facing left, wearing laurel wreath with leaves in opposing pairs, O behind, ꟼVИN⊦T before. Dotted border (?). REV: Acheloios Savo as a man-faced bull standing to right on single line, head facing, winged nymph above, no pentagram. REF: Garrucci, II, Pl.LXXXIII, n.11; J. Friedlaender, *Die osckischen münzen,* Pl.I, n.6; Sambon 1001 = SNG France 1196 = BnF Fonds Général 537*. *This variant is unconfirmed, as the unique known specimen could simply be the last variant (n.435) with the pentagram missing due to wear on the die or a bad strike.*

447. AE Unit, 5.64g	**272 to 250 BC**
	OBV: Head of Apollo facing left, wearing laurel wreath with leaves in opposing pairs, O behind. REV: Acheloios Savo as a man-faced bull standing to right on single line, head facing, winged nymph above, pentagram below, ЯVИNꓘT in ex. REF: Sambon 1002; SNG Morcom 189; SNG France 1191-4; Weber 413; CNG, Triton V, lot 33*.

448. AE Unit, 5.13g	**272 to 250 BC**
	OBV: Head of Apollo facing left, wearing laurel wreath with leaves in opposing pairs, Ξ behind, ЯVИN⊦T before. Dotted border. REV: Acheloios Savo as a man-faced bull standing to right on single line, head facing, winged nymph above, pentagram below. REF: Sambon 998; SNG ANS 621; H.D. Rauch GmbH 86, lot 49*.

449. AE Unit, 5.02g	**272 to 250 BC**
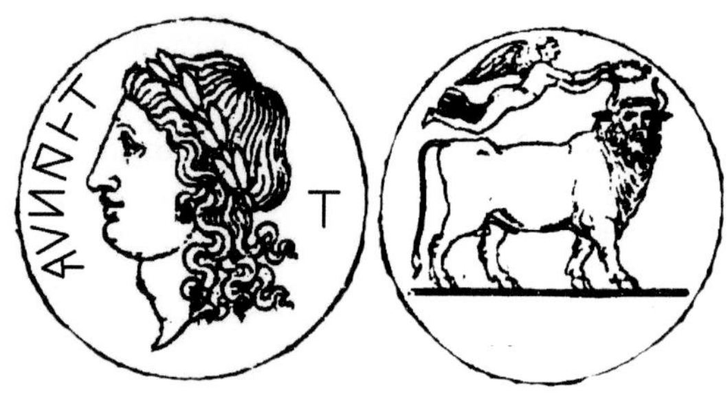	OBV: Head of Apollo facing left, wearing laurel wreath with leaves in opposing pairs, T behind, ЯVИN⊦T before. REV: Acheloios Savo as a man-faced bull standing to right on single line, head facing, winged nymph above. REF: Sambon 999. *Unconfirmed.*

TIATI APULORUM

Beyond Teanum Sidicinum there was a second ancient mint issuing man-faced bull coinage with an Oscan inscription, namely, TIIATIVM. The city was located in Daunia (northern Apulia), named Teanum Apulorum by Pliny, but also referred to as Tiati or Teate in ancient sources[198] not to be confused with the more northern Tiati, also known as Teate Marrucinorum, the modern day Chieti. The Apulian city of Teanum/Teate/Tiati, according to archaeologists, was located 4km north of the modern day town San Paolo di Civitate (FG),[199] on the right bank of the modern-day Fortore River, the ancient name of which is uncertain: Frento or Fertor.[200] In this catalog we refer to the mint as Tiati Apulorum, and the ancient river, the Frento.

The first signs of human settlements in the area date back to Neolithic times and continue on through the Bronze and Early Iron Age.[201] During the first half of the 1st millennium BC Tiati gradually became an organized settlement, in the form of a series of residential units scattered about a large area.[202] Because of the layout of the community the places of worship became the social, political, and economic centers. In fact, archaeological excavations demonstrate that in the Archaic Period there were three such sanctuaries in the area.[203] One of the sanctuaries even had features that archaeologists recognized as exhibiting Etruscan-Campanian style, dating back to the earliest phases of construction of the building.[204]

The proper attribution of the coins listed in this section has been hotly debated by numismatists for a long time. We report here a summary by Alberto Campana, published by Mario Nassa.[205] In the early antiquarian numismatic works from the 17th century, the coins had been attributed to Teate Marrucinorum. In the following century some antiquarians advocated the (seemingly) proper hypothesis that these coins belong to Tiati in Apulia. Nevertheless, during the first half of the 19th century the debate continued. Two schools of thought emerged: one for Teate Marrucinorum and the other for Tiati Apulorum. In the mid 19th century, thanks to the contributions of Mommsen, Friedlaender, and Cavedoni, the attribution to Tiati in Apulia was solidified, and, in our view, remains current. Incidentally, in 1885 Garrucci argued that the Oscan alphabet was unknown in Apulia, and suggested the coins were Campanian, without clearly specifying which mint.[206] Garrucci's hypothesis was not followed by any scholars and in fact later experts in linguistics have demonstrated that the original Oscan alphabet did indeed spread to northern Apulia as well as Campania, while in the area of Marrucini it assumed specific characteristics that diverged from the original Oscan.

Despite the now general acceptance of the attribution to Tiati in Apulia, there are still some who doubt it and suggest the coins were issued in Teanum Sidicinum,[207] while others still follow the obsolete attribution to Teate Marrucinorum.[208] However, there is little doubt that these coins are from Tiati Apulorum. In fact, Campana mentions that there is no record of discoveries of these types in the Campanian area, and not one example was present among the many coins found at the rich sanctuary of Fondo Ruozzo at Teanum Sidicinum.[209] Moreover, the use of Campanina types by an Apulian mint is not surprising, since Daunia had thriving economic exchanges with Campania between 325 and 275 BC and then until the final defeat of Pyrrhus, and this is also attested in neighboring Samnium.

The man-faced bull depicted on the coins of Tiati Apulorum is probably Acheloios Frento.

---

198 Ancient sources cite the name of the Apulian city in three different forms: the first, *Tiati*, is reported on the Oscan inscriptions of coins listed in this section; the variant *Teate* is reported by ancient literary sources (Livy, *Ab Urbe Condita Libri*, 9.20.7); and a third form, *Teanum Apulum*, appears in the first half of 1st century BC, both in literary sources (Cicero, *Pro Cluentio*, 9, 27; 69, 197) and on late Roman Republican inscriptions (P. Gentile, 'Centri della Daunia. Tiati-Teanum Apulum,' in *Archeologia delle Regioni d'Italia. Puglia*, edited by G. Ceraudo (Bologna, 2014), 122).

199 E. Antonacci Sanpaolo and L. Quilici, 'Tiati-Teanum Apulum-Civitate: Topografia Storica del territorio,' in *Atti del XV Convegno Nazionale sulla Preistoria-Protostoria-Storia della Daunia* (San Severo, 1995), 81ff.; P. Gentile, 'Centri della Daunia. Tiati-Teanum Apulum,' in *Archaeologia delle Regioni d'Italia.* Puglia, edited by G. Ceraudo (Bologna, 2014), 122f.

200 This ambiguity comes from early Pliny manuscripts, in which two different variants of his work *Naturalis Historia* have come down to us through the medieval transcripts, one naming the river *Frento* (*Flumen portuosum Frento, Teanum Apulorum*), the other calling it *Fertor* (*Flumen portuosum Fertor, Teanum Apulorum*). For *Frento*, see: Pliny, *Naturalis Historia*, 3.16, in the edition: M.L. Domenichini, *Della storia naturale di C. Plinio Secondo libri 37. traduzione di M. Lodovico Domenichi emendata per la prima volta secondo il testo latino con l'aggiunta di un nuovo indice generale*, Vol.1 (Venezia: Antonelli, 1844), 373. For *Fertor*, see: Pliny, *Naturalis Historia*, 3.103, in the edition: K.F.T. Mayhoff, *C. Plini Secundi naturalis historiae libri XXXVII. Recognovit atque indicibus instruxit Ludovicus Janus*, Vol.1 (Lipsiae: 1870), 143.

201 A. Gravina, 'Preistoria e Protostoria del basso Fortore,' in *Atti del I Convegno Nazionale sulla Preistoria-Protostoria-Storia della Daunia* (San Severo, 1980), 73-101.

202 E.M. De Juliis, *s.v.* 'Teano Apulo,' in *Enciclopedia dell'Arte Antica, Classica e Orientale*, II Suppl., V (Roma, 1997), 545-546.

203 P. Gentile, 'Centri della Daunia. Tiati-Teanum Apulum,' 123.

204 G. Mastronuzzi, *Repertorio dei contesti cultuali indigeni in Italia meridionale, 1. Età arcaica.* Beni archeologici Conoscenza e Tecnologie, Vol.4 (Bari-Lecce, 2005), 102-103, as cited in P. Gentile, 'Centri della Daunia. Tiati-Teanum Apulum,' 125.

205 M. Nassa and V. Nassa, *Teanum Sidicinum, Rilettura sommaria, con raffronti, dei più significativi contributi sulla monetazione antica* (Roma, 2012), 25-26. We express to both scholars our sincere gratitude for their assistance in preparing this section.

206 R. Garrucci, *Le monete dell'Italia antica* (Roma, 1885/Bologna: Forni reprint, 1967), 107-8.

207 See, for example: N. K. Rutter, *Historia Numorum Italy*, 81, n. 698; M.H. Crawford, 'Provenances, attributions and chronology of some early Italian coinages,' in *Coin Hoards*, Vol. IX (London, 2002), 273ff.

208 See, for example, A. D'andrea, 'Tiati: la monetazione,' in *La monetazione pugliese dall'età classica al medioevo. Atti del I° Congresso di Numismatica. Bari 21-22 Novembre 2008* (Bari, 2009), 71ff.

209 T. Giove, 'Le monete dal santuario di Fondo Ruozzo a Teano (CE),' in *Annali dell'Istituto Italiano di Numismatica*, N. 48 (Roma, 2001), 209-247.

Coinage

450. AE Unit, 6.38g, 17mm	**320 to 275 BC**
	OBV: Head of Apollo facing left, wearing laurel wreath with leaves in triple clusters(?), TIIRTIVM (retro) before. REV: Acheloios Frento as a man-faced bull standing to right on single line, head facing, thunderbolt above, club below. REF: J. Friedlaender, *Die osckischen münzen*, Pl. VI, n.1; SNG France 1415 = BnF Fonds Général 675*.

451. AE Unit, 5.67-6.05g, 16mm	**320 to 275 BC**
 *  **	OBV: Head of Apollo facing left, wearing laurel wreath with leaves in triple clusters, TIIRTIVM (retro) before. Dotted border. REV: Acheloios Frento as a man-faced bull standing to right on single line, head facing, И above, uncertain letter or symbol in exergue. REF: Sambon 996 = SNG France 1189 = BnF Fonds Général 549*. *This coin was incorrectly listed under Teanum Sidicinum by Sambon and SNG France, both considering it as a unique type (and specimen) for the Campanian mint. However, this coin should be re-attributed to Tiati, as a second specimen from the same dies clearly shows the legend* TIIRTIVM (British Museum n. 1884,0707.2**)

452. AE Unit, 7.67g, 19mm	**320 to 275 BC**
	OBV: Head of Apollo facing left, wearing laurel wreath with leaves in triple clusters (?), TIIRTIVM (retro) before. REV: Acheloios Frento as a man-faced bull standing to right on single line, head facing, lyre above, club below. REF: Münzkabinett, Staatliche Museen zu Berlin, object n. 18235401* .

453. AE Unit, 5.77g, 18mm	**320 to 275 BC**
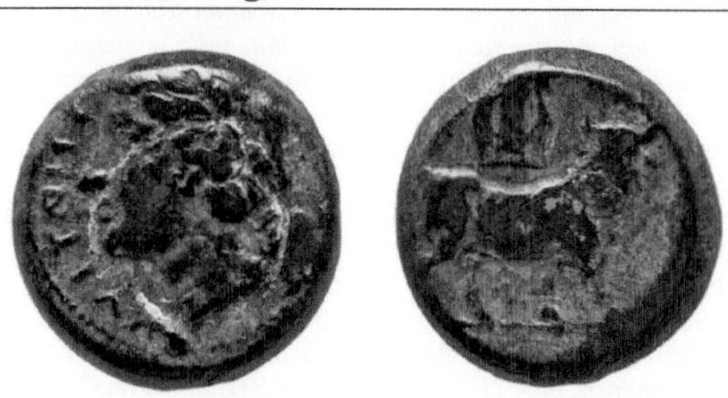	OBV: Head of Apollo facing left, wearing laurel wreath with leaves in triple clusters (?), TIIRTIVM (retro) before. Dotted border. REV: Acheloios Frento as a man-faced bull standing to right on single line, head facing, lyre above, nothing below. REF: BM no. 1907,0501.102*.

VENAFRUM

Venafrum (the modern-day Venafro) was located on the northern border of Campania. It was a Samnite city[210] situated on a high hill by the foot of which flowed the Volturnus River.[211] After the Third Samnite War Venafrum became a Roman *praefectura*, operating as a military outpost at the border of Campania and Samnium.[212]

The existence of a bronze coin from Venafrum featuring the man-faced bull has been questioned over time by numismatists, because the unique specimen is lost, and all that survives is a drawing by Garrucci, which he published in his famous work on the coinage of ancient Italy, stating that the coin was from his own collection. He claims it was found at Frosolone, near Aesernia, in Samnium.[213]

The coin described by Garrucci shows the typical Campanian obverse featuring Apollo, paired with a reverse depicting a winged nymph crowning the man-faced bull. The inscription on the obverse is Oscan: 𐌌𐌖𐌓𐌚𐌀𐌍𐌄, a retrograde legend that should be read as ENAVRUM.[214] The obverse appears to show two 'dots' in the area between the ear and neck of Apollo, which is probably just large curls of hair that have been worn flat. The reverse features the letter K below the man-faced bull.

Confirmation that man-faced bull coins were struck in Venafrum is demonstrated by a new variety that emerged on the market in 2015, described as an uncertain variety from Neapolis. The retrograde inscription on 455 appears to match Garrucci's drawing, in particular the last three Oscan letters, 𐌌𐌖𐌓. The shield on 455 indicates a new obverse die, just like that used in nearby Aesernia, and also Cales, Compulteria, Suessa, and Teanum. There are also traces of a letter below the man-faced bull and no inscription in exergue, just like 454. Moreover, large curls similar to those on the Garrucci coin and not present in the style of engraving at other mints issuing this type, are exhibited on coin 455, on the lock of Apollo's hair just left of the shield, where it too resembles a rather large dot.

According to Campana, the coinage of the man faced-bull issued in Venafrum dates between 265 and 240 BC.[215] The identity of this man-faced bull is undoubtedly Acheloios Volturnus, given the close proximity of the river. Volturnus is a name of Etruscan origin, and according to Livy it was the original Etruscan name of Capua before the Samnites conquered and re-named the city.[216]

Coinage

454. AE Unit, unrecorded weight	**265 to 240 BC**
	OBV: Head of Apollo facing left, wearing laurel wreath with leaves in opposing pairs, 𐌌𐌖𐌓𐌚𐌀𐌍𐌄 before. Dotted border? REV: Acheloios Volturnus as a man-faced bull standing to right on single line, head facing, winged nymph above, K below, nothing in ex. Dotted border? REF: Garrucci Pl.LXXXVIII, n.17*.

455. AE Unit, 5.65g, 20mm	**265 to 240 BC**
	OBV: Head of Apollo facing left, wearing laurel wreath with leaves in opposing pairs, 𐌌𐌖𐌓𐌚𐌀𐌍𐌄 before, oval shield behind. Dotted border. REV: Acheloios Volturnus as a man-faced bull standing to right on single line, head facing, winged nymph above, traces of letter below, nothing in ex. Dotted border? REF: ACR E-auction 28, lot 15*. *Unpublished*

210 Strabo, *Geographica*, 5.4.11.
211 Strabo, *Geographica*, 5.3.10.
212 A. Campana, 'Samnium. Venafrum (265-240 a.C.),' in *Panorama Numismatico*, n.85 (Serravalle: Nomisma, 1995), 301.
213 R. Garrucci, *Le Monete dell'Italia Antica*, 91.
214 Ibid., 302.
215 Ibid.
216 Livy, *Ab Urbe Condita Libri*, 4.37.

Enlargment

Section Five

AKARNANIA

According to tradition, Akarnania[1] was founded by Alkmaeon, who, after murdering his mother and seeking redemption for his transgression, came to the area of the Acheloios River and married the river god Acheloios' daughter, Kallirhoe.[2] They had two sons, one named Akarnan, from whom Akarnania gets its name.[3] Before that episode, according to Pausianus, the land was called Kuretes.[4]

Throughout its quarrelsome history there are a few defining moments: The Akarnanian Federation[5] probably emerged in the 5th century BC with its capital at Stratos, although this was lost when the Aetolians assumed control of it along with Oiniadai, in 270 BC (after the death of Pyrrhos). The division of Akarnania between Epeiros and Aetolia in the mid 250s BC[6] is also important insofar as it prompts important questions about Akarnanian identity in its relation to a formal federal state, or lack thereof. Here we see the western area operate as a new Akarnanian League, with Alexander II as its *hegemon*,[7] at least until his death in the 240s BC. From 232 to 189 BC the capital of the League was formally moved to Leukas, and thereafter Thyrreion, until the establishment of Nicopolis Actia by Augustus.[8]

The image of Acheloios as a man-faced bull appears on many of the coins issued in Akarnania. This makes perfect sense since the mighty Acheloios River, the greatest river in all of Greece, formed a natural barrier between the Akarnanians and their usually belligerent neighbors to the east, the Aetolians. It was also an image that could help unify, under the Akarnanian Federation, the entire area because the river and its god were such an integral part of the region's civic identity, insofar as the Akarnanians allegedly descended from Acheloios himself.

The Federation probably formalized its coinage in the early 3rd century BC.[9] The earliest bronze coinage of the man-faced bull, a civic issue, comes from Stratos, c. 350 BC. Another early civic issue comes from Leukas, minted sometime after 338 BC, and these are overstruck on bronze coinage of Phillip II of Macedon, who expelled various Akarnanian leaders that did not side with him in his struggles with the Athenians.[10]

It is difficult to identify the mint location and dates for the federal issues, due to the highly complex, often disorderly history of the area. This catalog's main function is to list all the varieties of man-faced bull coinage, and the dating of such issues is therefore only tentative.[11] The date ranges assigned by some numismatists are broad, c. 320 to 167 BC,[12] and we attempt to narrow those dates as best as possible. To assist us in this purpose, the federal coinage is cataloged separately from the civic coinage issued at individual mints, even when the latter incorporate an Akarnanian monogram.

---

1 The name Akarnania in reference to the mainland is attested as early as Hecataeus (*Fr.* 110-1) and Herodotus (*The Histories*, 2.10.3). For a thorough overview, see H.J. Gehrke, and E. Wirbelauer, 'Akarnania and Adjacent Areas,' in *An Inventory of Archaic and Classical Poleis*, edited by M. H. Hansen and T. H. Nielsen (Oxford: University Press, 2004), 351.

2 For a general history of Akarnania and the surrounding area, see E. Oberhummer, *Akarnanien... im Altertum* (Munich, 1887). For the most recent history focused mostly on Akarnania in Hellenistic times, see O. Dany, *Akarnanien in Hellenismus. Geschichte und Völkerrecht in Nordwestgriechenland* (Munich: Verlag C.H. Beck, 1999).

3 Pausanias, *Hellados Periegesis*, 8.24.9.

4 Ibid.

5 Akarnanian Federation, Akarnanian Confederacy, and Akarnanian League are all synonymous terms used to describe the political unit τὸ κοινὸν τῶν Ἀκαρνάνων (Xenophon, *Hellenica*, 4.6.4). O. Dany argues that the 'league' was a true '*Bundesstaat*,' not a '*Stammstaat*,' and so perhaps 'Akarnanian Federation' is best (*Akarnanien in Hellenismus*, 251).

6 J.D. Grainger, *The League of the Aitolians* (Brill, 1999),134-5.

7 Ibid., 136-7.

8 For an overview of the Akarnanian Federation, see O. Dany, *Akarnanien in Hellenismus*, 240-75.

9 O. Dany's dating (*Akarnanien in Hellenismus*, 276ff, catalog 311ff). For an overview of the 'federal' coinage in classical times, and an earlier dating scheme, see S. Psôma, 'Le monnayage fédéral acarnanien de l'époque classique,' in *KLIO* 89 (2007), 7-23.

10 J.B. Bury, S.A. Cook, and F.E. Adcock, *The Cambridge Ancient History, Vol. VI, Macedon 401-301 BC* (Cambridge: University Press, 1975), 266b.

11 For an overview of the coinage of Akarnania, see F. Imhoof-Blumer, *Die Münzen Akarnaniens* (Wien: Manz, 1878); Münzen & Medaillen GmbH (DE), *Sammlung BCD Griechische Münzen Akarnaniens und Aitoliens* (Auction 23, 2007); O. Dany, *Akarnanien in Hellenismus*, 276-339.

12 For Leukas especially, cf. Münzen & Medaillen GmbH (DE), *Sammlung BCD Griechische Münzen Akarnaniens und Aitoliens.* Imhoof-Blumer is at one extreme dating the bronze federal man-faced bull types to the late 4th century (*Die Münzen Akarnaniens*, 45).

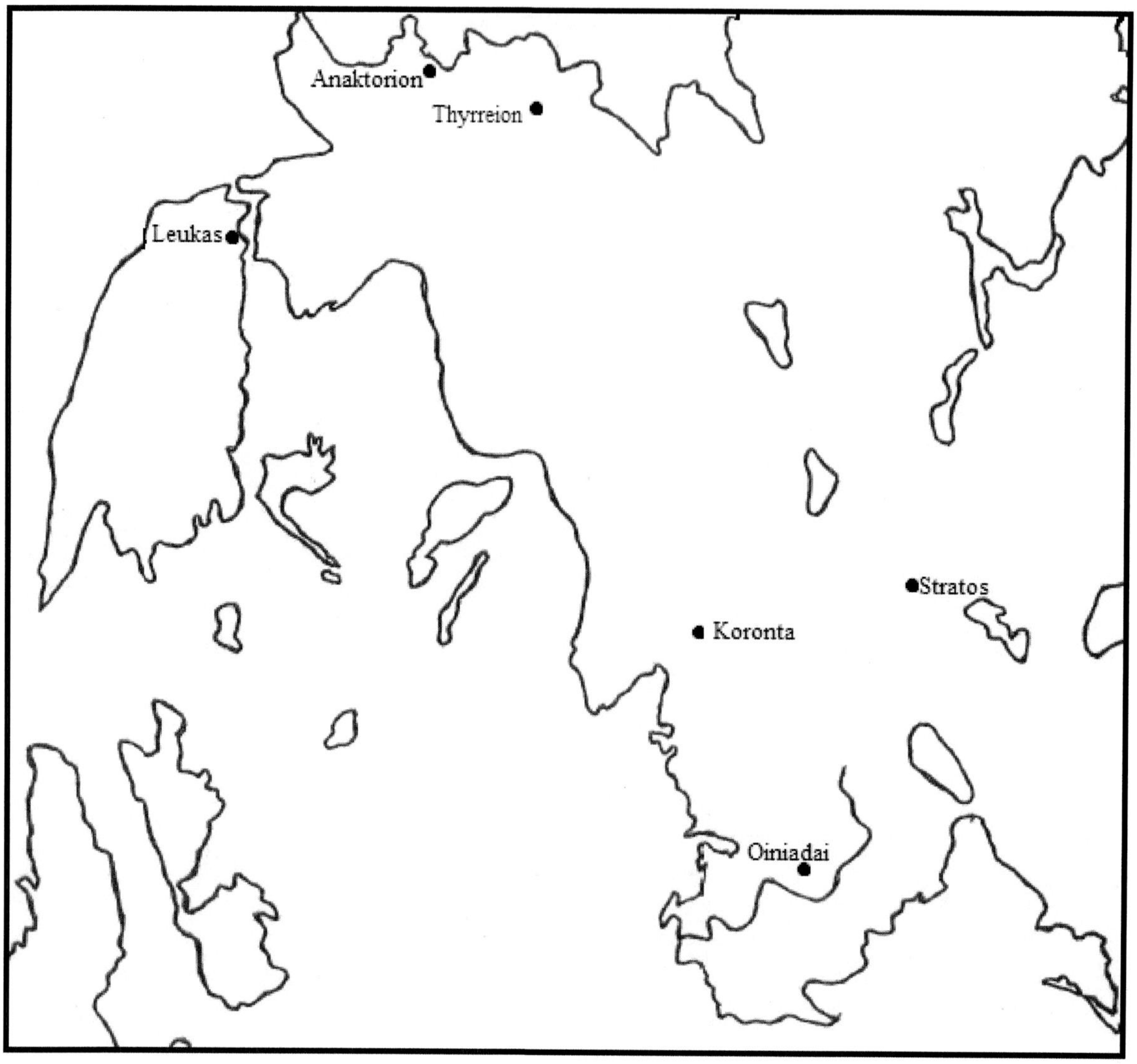

Map excludes Torhybeion, which is located north of the Ambrakian Gulf.

AKARNANIAN FEDERATION

The bronze coinage of the Akarnanian Federation presents many problems to the interpreter in terms of dating and mint location. The Athena/Acheloios type, for instance, does not feature an ethnic or even the federal monogram, yet it is essentially a federal issue minted in Akarnania. Other types, such as Herakles/Acheloios or Zeus/Acheloios, carry the federal monogram but provide no indication as to the mint. In this catalog, rather than a division by mint, since many times it is uncertain, we have grouped all apparent federal coins together.[13]

Phase I coinage probably began in the early 3rd century and lasted until about 220 BC. If they were minted at Leukas, there was probably a pause from the mid 3rd century until about 232 BC (hence Group Ia and Group Ib). The dating of Phase I should not be overly controversial. Imhoof-Blumer attributed these coins as well as the Zeus/Acheloios types to Stratos in the late 4th century.[14] Gardner, however, believed that was far too early. In writing the BMC catalog he advocated late 3rd century, settling on the date of c. 230 to 168 BC, though recognizing 'We cannot decided at what time [Akarnanian Federal Coinage] recommenced.'[15] However, the presumably earliest examples of these coins are undeniably similar to royal Macedonian bronzes of the mid to late 4th century, and it is therefore difficult to reconcile Gardner's rationale with the appearance of the coins themselves (no. 456-458 below). Thus, our dating for Phase I stretches from the end of Imhoof-Blumer's range to the beginning of Gardner's, a time when it was previously believed that the Akarnanians issued no coins at all.[16] This explanation also helps interpret the change in style observable on the (presumably) later variety, coin no. 459, which does not look anything like the aforementioned royal Macedonian bronzes of the 4th century.

Phase II is made up of the enigmatic Athena/Acheloios type, and probably dates from c. 250 to 220 BC. These are placed here for several reasons. In the first case, they are completely anepigraphic, which probably indicates that they emerged around the chaotic time of Akarnania's division between Epeiros and Aetolia. The western areas, including Thyrreion, existed in some ways as a new Akarnanian Federation with Alexander as its *hegemon*, and thus these coins were probably issued as quasi-federal issues (quasi because they lack a monogram). In fact, Dany notes that coins featuring Acheloios issued during this tumultuous time were possible expressions of Akarnanian identity.[17] The clear similarity to slightly earlier types (late 4th to mid 3rd century BC) from Thyrreion featuring the same helmeted Athena on the obverse suggests the obverse design was borrowed from them, and that the coins were minted there.[18] In fact, although Thyrreion was probably already part of the Federation in the 4th century, it is not attested until 263 BC, just before these coins were probably being struck.[19]

Phase III coinage features Zeus/Acheloios and was probably minted at Leukas from 219 to 211 BC. Because Oiniadai was part of the Federation during this short period, the Leukas types are easy to date in relation to the Oiniadai types, since they are nearly identical. In fact, of the two published hoards containing Akarnanian bronze coinage, both consist of a mix of federal issues and coins of the Oiniadai.[20] Group IIIb consists of one unconfirmed variety featuring a female head on its obverse and Acheloios on its reverse. Because of the control marks it is grouped in Phase III.

Phase IV coins share the same type as Phase I, but the magistrate name, ΑΓΗΤΩΡ,[21] appears on a reduced silver stater (Attic standard) attributed by B. Demetriadi to Thyrreion, and therefore suggests a date of after 167 BC, when the capital moved there.[22]

[13] Coins featuring both an Akarnanian monogram and local ethnic are featured in the subsequent sections.

[14] F. Imhoof-Blumer, *Die Münzen Akarnaniens*, 45.

[15] P. Gardner, *Catalog of Greek Coins: Thessaly to Aitolia* (London: Trustees of the British Museum, 1883), lii.

[16] P. Gardner, *Catalog of Greek Coins: Thessaly to Aitolia*, lii. O. Dany dates the formalization of the federal coinage to 272 BC, but recognizes there was some experimentation with federal designs before this date (*Akarnanien in Hellenismus*, 276ff). See J. Roy, 'Review: Oliver Dany, *Akarnanien im Hellenismus. Geschichte und Völkerrecht in Nordwestgriechenland. Münchener Beiträge zur Papyrusforschung und antiken Rechtsgeschichte, Heft 89,*' in *Bryn Mawr Classical Review* (2000.02.21), for a convenient overview of Dany's work.

[17] See J. Roy, 'Review: Oliver Dany, *Akarnanien im Hellenismus. Geschichte und Völkerrecht in Nordwestgriechenland. Münchener Beiträge zur Papyrusforschung und antiken Rechtsgeschichte, Heft 89,*' paragraph 5.

[18] H.J. Gehrke, and E. Wirbelauer, 'Akarnania and Adjacent Areas,' 373. For slightly later dating see BCD Akarnania 378a-b, c. 300 to 250 BC.

[19] H.J. Gehrke, and E. Wirbelauer, 'Akarnania and Adjacent Areas,' 373, citing *IG* IX^{2}.1 3A.23.

[20] *IGCH* 145, containing 5 bronzes of the Akarnanian Federation and 18 bronzes of the Oiniadai. *IGCH* 312, containing 73 bronzes of the Akarnanian Federation and 61 bronzes of the Oiniadai (all types).

[21] For the role of magistrates and in particular how their functions and titles changed, see K. Frietag, 'Akarnania and the Akarnanian League,' in *Federalism in Greek Antiquity*, edited by H. Beck and P. Funke (Cambridge: University Press, 2015), 79-81.

[22] O. Hoover (*HGC* 4, 739) dates these to the 1st century BC, along with a silver stater of the reduced Attic standard, cf. BCD Akarnania 54-5 (*HGC* 4, 733). However, BCD attributed both these issues to Leukas, c. 320 to 167 BC. S. Grose (McCLean 5394) dated these to after 167 BC and attributed them to Leukas.

Coinage

PHASE I: c. 300 to 220 BC

Leukas

GROUP IA

456. AE Unit, 6.10g, 21mm	c. 300 to 250 BC
	OBV: Head of Herakles wearing Nemean Lion headdress to right, [monogram](?)below. Dotted border. REV: Head of Acheloios as a man-faced bull to right, behind, trident above. Linear border. REF: BMC Thessaly, p. 169, no. 19 (no reverse monogram listed for that specimen but it appears to be visible on the plate); M&M GmbH 23, lot 36=BCD Akarnania 36*. *BMC Thessaly lists A below Herakles' head, but McClean 5394 gives the monogram [monogram]. On some examples, it appears to have a line below, too, and on others it looks like [monogram], which is how Imhoof-Blumer describes it (Die Münzen Akarnanien, no.5). All varieties are probably the result of differentiations in strike and/or wear of the same monogram, [monogram].*

457. AE Unit, 5.77g	c. 300 to 250 BC
	OBV: Head of Herakles wearing Nemean Lion headdress to right, [monogram](?) below. Dotted border. REV: Head of Acheloios as a man-faced bull to right, [monogram] (or [monogram]?) behind, trident above. Linear border. REF: Grose-McClean 5393; BnF Fond Général 97*.

458. AE Unit, 5.88g, 22mm	c. 300 to 250 BC
	OBV: Head of Herakles wearing Nemean Lion headdress to right, nothing below. Dotted border. REV: Head of Acheloios as a man-faced bull to right, [monogram] (or [monogram]?) behind, trident above. Linear border. REF: M&M GmbH 23, lot 34=BCD Akarnania 34*.

GROUP IB

459. AE Unit, 7.14g, 23mm	c. 232 to 220 BC
	OBV: Head of Herakles wearing Nemean Lion headdress to right. REV: Head of Acheloios as a man-faced bull to right, A behind, trident above. REF: BMC Thessaly, p. 169, n. 16-18; BCD Akarnania 35=CNG 803267*. *Probably issued closer to 220 BC*

PHASE II: c. 250 to 220 BC

Thyrreion

460. AE Unit, 6.12g, 20mm	**c. 250 to 220 BC**
	OBV: Helmeted head of Athena facing left. REV: Head of Acheloios as a man-faced bull to left, trident above. Linear border. REF: SNG Cop 423; BMC Thessaly p. 170, no. 21-4; BCD Akarnania 41-43; CNG 733572*. *Sometimes countermarked with trophy, Cf. BMC Thessaly p. 170, no.24. One example has a monogram of the Federation (Private Collection, 5.7g), which further supports the earlier dating of this Phase, before the Federation had official re-emerged with its new capital at Leukas.*

PHASE III: c. 219 to 211 BC

Leukas

GROUP IIIA

461. AE Unit, 6.71g, 21mm	**c. 219 to 211 BC**
	OBV: Laureate head of Zeus facing right, bird behind, API below . Dotted border. REV: Head of Acheloios as a man-faced bull to right, trident above, [monogram] behind. Linear border. REF: Imhoof-Blumer 3; BMC Thessaly, p. 169, n. 15; M&M GmbH 23, lot 33c=BCD Akarnania 33c*. *The API magistrate inscription appears also at Anaktorion.*

462. AE Unit, 7.32g	**c. 219 to 211 BC**
	OBV: Laureate head of Zeus facing right, behind, bird looking back, API below. Dotted border. REV: Head of Acheloios as a man-faced bull to right, trident above, [monogram] behind. Linear border. REF: BMC Thessaly, p. 169, n. 15 var.; BCD Akarnania 32; Potamikon Collection*.

463. AE Unit, 7.02g	**c. 219 to 211 BC**
	OBV: Laureate head of Zeus facing right, behind, bird looking back, API below. Dotted border. REV: Head of Acheloios as a man-faced bull to right, trident above, [monogram] behind. Linear border. REF: Imhoof-Blumer 3; BnF Fonds général 17*.

GROUP IIIB

Leukas?

464. AE Half Unit?, 3.20g, 16mm	Late 3rd century
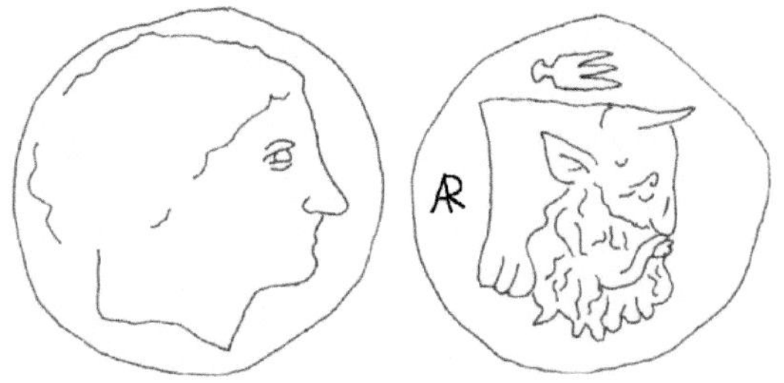	OBV: Kallirhoe facing right. REV: Head of Acheloios as a man-faced bull to right, monogram behind, trident above. REF: Imhoof-Blumer 4* (redrawn). *Unconfirmed. Imhoof-Blumer lists this type with the coins of Oiniadai based on the reverse type.*

PHASE IV: After 167 BC?

Thyrreion or Leukas

465. AE Unit, 4.33g, 20mm	After 167 BC?
	OBV: Head of Herakles wearing Nemean Lion headdress to right, nothing below. REV: Head of Acheloios as a man-faced bull to right, ΑΓΗΤΩΡ behind. REF: Grose-McClean 5394; M&M GmbH 23, 38= BCD Akarnania 38*.

466. AE Unit, 4.70g, 20mm	After 167 BC?
	OBV: Head of Herakles wearing Nemean Lion headdress to right, nothing below. Crude style. REV: Head of Acheloios as a man-faced bull to right, ΑΓΗΤΩΡ behind. Crude style. REF: BCD Akarnania 39.8; CNG eAuction 203, lot 80*.

LEUKAS

Leukas was located on the far western side of Akarnania, connected only by a very narrow strip of land, and served as the capital of the revived Akarnanian Federation until Rome overtook Macedonian rule (232 to 167 BC).[23] The name comes from the Greek word for 'white,' which serves as the basis for words involving the notion of cleansing, e.g. λευκαίνω,[24] 'to make white,' and 'to be clarified.' Apparently, the *Alkmaionis* records that it received this name from Leukadios.[25] The area itself has been inhabited since Paleolithic times, albeit sparsely.[26] In historical times, it was originally a Corinthian colony,[27] and Strabo claims the entire western coast of Akarnania was once called Leukas (this is also interesting given that Alkmaeon came to the area seeking purification).[28]

The archaeologist Wilhelm Dörpfeld identified Leukas with Homer's Ithaca, to much controversy.[29] It sided with Sparta throughout the Peloponnesian War and was never captured by the Athenians,[30] despite Athens' allegiance with the rest of the Akarnanian cities. It joined the Akarnanian Federation in 280/265 BC.[31]

Most of the bronze man-faced bull coins minted at Leukas are federal issues and cataloged in that section. However, two enigmatic early types appear to be civic coins issued in the second half of the 4th century BC, all of which are overstruck on bronze units of Philip II of Macedon. There are two main types, Chimera/Acheloios and Acheloios/Trident. They likely pre-date Leukas' official joining with the Akarnanian Federation (280 BC), but oddly all varieties except one feature the AK monogram, which suggests a later date. However, the monogram probably refers to the ethnic community[32] rather than the federal state, and therefore the general date of 338 to 280 BC is adopted here, earlier than Imhoof-Blumers attribution to the early to mid 3rd century and slightly later than Gardner (thus we find ourselves between the two great scholars once again).[33]

Ultimately, these coins probably date after the Battle of Chaeronea when Leukas became part of Akarnania,[34] but before Leukas' enrollment as a formal member of the Akarnanian Federation. The AG monogram on the new variety listed below (no. 470) also attest to this early date, as it appears on the Corinthian type staters of the late 4th century minted at Leukas.[35]

Coinage

467. AE Unit, 5.99g, 21mm	**338 to 280 BC**
	OBV: Chimera standing to left on single line, AK below. Dotted border. REV: Head of Acheloios as a man-faced bull to left, AK behind. REF: Imhoof-Blumer 10 var (AK monogram); BCD Akarnania 236; BMC Thessaly, p. 175, no. 19; Pecunem 16, lot 205=Potamikon Collection*.

[23] *Britannica Academic Online*, 'Acarnania' (Britanica Online 2015).

[24] H.G. Liddell and R.Scott, *Greek-English Lexicon* (Oxford: Clarendon, 1996), 1041.

[25] H.J. Gehrke, and E. Wirbelauer, 'Akarnania and Adjacent Areas,' 365, citing *Fr.* 5.

[26] A. Dousougli, 'Palaeolithic Leukas,' in *British School of Athens, Vol. 3: The Palaeolithic Archaeology of Greece and Adjacent Areas* (British School at Athens, 1999), 288-92.

[27] J.B. Bury, *Cambridge Ancient History, Vol. VI, Macedon 401-301 BC*, 249.

[28] Strabo, *Geographica*, 10.452.

[29] W. Dörpfeld, *Alt-Ithaka: Ein Beitrag zur Homer-Frage, Studien und Ausgrabungen aus der insel Leukas-Ithaka* (München: R. Uhde, 1927).

[30] J.B. Bury, *A History of Greece to the Death of Alexander the Great* (MacMillan, 1967), 418.

[31] H.J. Gehrke, and E. Wirbelauer, 'Akarnania and Adjacent Areas,' 365, citing, cf. *IG* IX^2.1 3A.24. (263?).

[32] The community of Akarnania is attested as τὸ πλῆθος τῶν Ἀκαρνάνων (cf. H.-J. Gehrke, and E. Wirbelauer, 'Akarnania and Adjacent Areas,' 351, citing *IG* IX^2.1 583.11-12, 56).

[33] F. Imhoof-Blumner (*Die Münzen Akarnaniens*, 45) dates these to 300 to 250 BC, but Gardner suggests 4th century (*BMC Thessaly*, 175, no. 15-25).

[34] S. P. Morris, 'The Towers of Ancient Leukas: Results of a Topographic Survey, 1991-1992,' in *Hesperia* 70 (2001), 287.

[35] Cf. SNG Copenhagen 357.

468. AE Unit, Unrecorded Weight, 20mm	**338 to 280 BC**
	OBV: Chimera standing to left on single line, lyre below. Dotted border. REV: Head of Acheloios as a man-faced bull to left, AK (retro) behind. Dotted border. REF: Imhoof-Blumer 10; Sestini, *Mus. Fontana III, Pl. IV, 9** (redrawn). *Unconfirmed. Imhoof-Blumer indicates the lyre is in the spot usually reserved for ΛE.*

469. AE Unit, 4.52g, 19mm	**338 to 280 BC**
	OBV: Chimera standing to left on single line, ΛE below. Dotted border. REV: Head of Acheloios as a man-faced bull to right, AK monogram behind. Dotted border. REF: Imhoof-Blumer 9; BCD Akarnania 237; BMC Thessaly, p. 175, no. 15-18; M&M GmbH 23, lot 237=BCD Akarnania 237*.

470. AE Unit, 5.44g, 19mm	**338 to 280 BC**
	OBV: Chimera standing to left on single line, ΛE below. Dotted border. REV: Head of Acheloios as a man-faced bull to right, AG monogram behind. Dotted border. REF: Obolos 4, lot 220*.

471. AE Half Unit (?), 2.92g , 16mm	**338 to 280 BC**
	OBV: Head of Acheloios as a man-faced bull to left, AK behind. Dotted border. REV: Trident oriented downward, ΛE to left, dolphin to right. REF: Imhoof-Blumer 7 (4.25g); BMC Thessaly, p. 175, no. 3; M&M GmbH 23, lot 239=BCD Akarnania 239*.

472. AE Half Unit (?), 3.33g , 17mm	**338 to 280 BC**
	OBV: Head of Acheloios as a man-faced bull to right, AK behind. REV: Trident oriented downward, ΛE to left, dolphin to right. REF: Imhoof-Blumer 8; BMC Thessaly, p. 175, no. 21; M&M GmbH 23, lot 240=BCD Akarnania 240*.

THE OINIADAI

Oiniadai was located in the southern part of Akarnania, near the mouth of the Acheloios River. Not much is written about Oiniadai in antiquity, and we hear about it mostly through stories of its aggressors.[36] The great physician Hippocrates is said to have practiced there, but no actual citizens are mentioned by name.[37] It was allegedly founded by Alkmaion who named it after his son, Oineus.[38] Neither Tolmides nor the great Perikles were able to capture the city in antiquity;[39] however, it joined the Athenians in 424 BC, having originally sided with Sparta.[40]

Around 330 BC it was taken by the Aetolians, then returned in 324 BC after Alexander the Great personally demanded it.[41] However, the history of the city thereafter reflects a struggle between the Akarnanias and Aetolians, and the city changes hands several times in the following century: In 313 BC the Aetolians ravaged Akarnania and Oiniadai with it, briefly controlling the city.[42] In 272 BC it came under Aetolian influence again and remained so until 219 BC, when Philip V returned it to the Akarnanians.[43] Slightly later, in 211 BC, the Romans returned control of Oiniadai to the Aetolians, and it was not until 189 BC, seven years after the Isthmian Games and the proclamation of the freedom of Greek states, that Oiniadai became Akarnanian again.[44]

The Oiniadai issued federal bronze coinage of the man-faced bull[45] just after Philip V gave the city back to the Akarnanians in 219 BC, up until it was given back to the Aetolians by the Romans in 211 BC (Group Ib). It also issued a series of coins that do not feature the Akarnanian monogram, but these coins must date to about the same time period. In fact, the birds on the obverse of these coins, behind Zeus' head, match those of the federal issues minted at Leukas, in which the bird faces forward on one issue and back on the next, indicating they were all minted in the same time period. However, Group Ia is differentiated here with 'circa 219 to 211 BC,' since we cannot be entirely sure of the dates, and these might have been minted at Oiniadai slightly before Phillip V returned the city to the Akarnanians in 219 BC.

Coinage

GROUP IA

473. AE Unit, 6.56g, 26mm	c. 219 to 211 BC
	OBV: Laureate head of Zeus facing right, bird behind, Λ (or A?) below. Dotted border. REV: Head of Acheloios as a man-faced bull to right, trident above, OINIAΔAN behind. Linear border. REF: BMC Thessaly, 190, no. 12; M&M GmbH 23, 349= BCD Akarnania 349*.

[36] B. Powell, 'Oeniadae: I. History and Topography,' in *American Journal of Archaeology*, Vol. 8, No.2 (New York, 1904), 137-73.
[37] Ibid., 141-142.
[38] C. Runnels, 'Acarnania,' in *Perseus Encyclopedia*, available from the Perseus Digital Library at Tufts University.
[39] J.B. Bury, *A History of Greece to the Death of Alexander the Great*, 358.
[40] B. Powell, 'Oeniadae,' 140.
[41] Diodorus Siculus, *The Library of History*, 18.8.6; Plutarch, *Alexander*, 49.
[42] B. Powell, 'Oeniadae,' 142.
[43] Ibid., 143.
[44] Ibid., 144.
[45] D. Sestini reports the existence of a coin featuring Herakles on its obverse and Acheloios on its reverse with the ethnic for Oiniadai (D. Sestini, *Descrizione d'alcune medaglie greche del museo del Signore Carlo d'Ottavio Fontana di Trieste, Parte Terza* (Firenze: G. Piatti, 1829), Taf. X, 12). However, F. Imhoof-Blumer doubts the existence of this coin, and we found no evidence to support its existence (F. Imhoof-Blumer, *Die Münzen Akarnaniens*, 17, note 16). See Sestini's line drawing at the end of this section of the catalog.

474. AE Unit, 6.34g	c. 219 to 211 BC
	OBV: Laureate head of Zeus facing right, behind, bird (eagle?) looking back, A below. No border. REV: Head of Acheloios as a man-faced bull to right, trident above, ΟΙΝΙΑΔΑΝ behind. Linear border. REF: BMC Thessaly, 190, no. 12 (incorrectly described as Λ below Zeus); BnF N 5320*.

475. AE Unit, 6.20g, 22mm	c. 219 to 211 BC
	OBV: Laureate head of Zeus facing right, nothing behind, nothing below. No border. REV: Head of Acheloios as a man-faced bull to right, trident above, ΟΙΝΙΑΔΑΝ behind. Linear border. REF: CNG eAuction 182, lot 44*.

GROUP IB

476. AE Unit, 7.21g	219 to 211 BC
	OBV: Laureate head of Zeus facing right, lightning bolt behind, PPI below. Dotted border. REV: Head of Acheloios as a man-faced bull to right, AR behind, ΟΙΝΙΑΔΑΝ above. Linear border. REF: Mionnet, Suppl. III, 471, 124; BMC 10; BCD Akarnania 347; BnF FG 94*.

477. AE Unit, 8.28g	219 to 211 BC
	OBV: Laureate head of Zeus facing right, lightning bolt behind, PPI below. Dotted border. REV: Head of Acheloios as a man-faced bull to right, AK behind, ΟΙΝΙΑΔΑΝ above. Linear border. REF: BMC Thessaly, p. 189, no.8; BnF 1966.453*.

478. AE Unit, 6.05g, 23mm	219 to 211 BC
	OBV: Laureate head of Zeus facing right, star behind, AR below. Dotted border. REV: Head of Acheloios as a man-faced bull to right, AR behind, ΟΙΝΙΑΔΑΝ above. Linear border. REF: BMC Thessaly, p. 189, n. 6; BCD Akarnania 345; BCD Akarnania 348 (described as M? below Zeus); CNG 76, 435*. *BCD/Hoover's description of a coin of this type but featuring M below Zeus is probably a misreading of this variety, which when worn, the monogram resembles an M.*

D. Sestini, *Descrizione d'alcune medaglie greche del museo del Signore Carlo d'Ottavio Fontana di Trieste,* Pars II, Taf. X, No. 12, fantasy issue

STRATOS

Stratos was located on the eastern side of Akarnania and was its capital (c. 5th century to c. 272 BC) and most important city throughout much of antiquity. It was situated next to the Acheloios River and served as a stronghold against attacks from the Aetolians, with whom the Akarnanians constantly struggled. Its importance for military engagements in the area is reflected in the name, which comes from the Greek στρᾰτός, meaning 'army'.[46] Thus, it should be no surprise that a group with strong military associations residing close to the Acheloios River adopted the image of the man-faced bull for its coinage. The walls of the city itself were built before 429 BC,[47] and helped the city fend off Cnemus and his 1,000 hoplite troops after the Ambrakians persuaded Sparta to attack.[48] The nearby Oiniadai, with their early allegiance to Sparta, helped Cnemus flee after his loss at Stratos,[49] which helps reinforce to the reader the unstable, often divided nature of the various groups inhabiting Akarnania in the 5th to 4th century BC.

After the death of Pyrrhos, in 272 BC, both Stratos and Oiniadai were assigned to Aetolia, and Stratos ceased its role as the capital of the Akarnanian Federation, since it was more-or-less dissolved and would not be formally reestablished for some forty years.[50]

The earliest coins of Akarnania featuring a man-faced bull are often attributed to Stratos and Oiniadai, silver fractionals dating to c. 430 BC and depicting the head of Acheloios paired with various letters.[51] However, Dany argues that these types were not true federal coinage.[52] Bronze coinage of the man-faced bull is scarce, with only four varieties known. The dating of these coins is also difficult to determine, but the second half of the 4th century BC, coinciding with the early bronze man-faced bull issues from Leukas, seems reasonable. Imhoof-Blumer argued that all early federal bronze issues were minted at Stratos and Oiniadai, essentially complementing these civic types.[53]

Coinage

479. AE Chalkous, 2.51g, 13mm	**350 to 300 BC**
	OBV: Head of Acheloios as a man-faced bull to right. REV: Tripod, ΣΤΡΑΤΙΩΝ to left, E to right. REF: Roma 4, lot 122*.

480. AE Dichalkon, 5.60g, 18mm	**350 to 300 BC**
	OBV: Head of Kallirhoe to right. REV: Head of Acheloios as a man-faced bull to right, ΣΤΡΑΤΙΩΝ before, E (retrograde) behind. REF: Imhoof-Blumer, A., 163, 9 Anm.; BMC Thessaly, Plate 29, no. 16; M&M GmbH 23, 362=BCD Akarnania 362*.

46 H.G. Liddell and R.Scott, *Greek-English Lexicon*, 1653.

47 C. Runnels, 'Acarnania,' in *Perseus Encyclopedia*, available from the Perseus Digital Library at Tufts University.

48 J.B .Bury, *A History of Greece to the Death of Alexander the Great*, 417.

49 B. Powell, 'Oeniadae,' 141.

50 R. Stillwell, W. L. MacDonald, and M. H. McAllister, *The Princeton Encyclopedia of Classical Sites* (Princeton, N.J.: Princeton University Press, 1976). See also J.D. Grainger, *The League of the Aitolians* (Brill, 1999),136-7, and especial O. Dany, *Akarnanien im Hellenismus*,, 250-65, for the period in question.

51 S. Psôma, 'Le monnayage fédéral acarnanien de l'époque classique,' 12-3.

52 O. Dany, *Akarnanien im Hellenismus*, 276-310.

53 F. Imhoof-Blumer, *Die Münzen Akarnaniens*, 15-16.

481. AE Dichalkon, 6.30g, 18mm	**350 to 300 BC**
	OBV: Head of Kallirhoe to right. REV: Head of Acheloios as a man-faced bull to right, ΣΤΡΑΤΙΩ(Ν) before, Serpent (?) behind. REF: Obolos 4, lot 222*. *Apparently Unique.*

482. AE Dichalkon, 5.60g, 18mm	**350 to 300 BC**
	OBV: Head of Kallirhoe to right. REV: Head of Acheloios as a man-faced bull to left. REF: Roma E-Sale 17, lot 129*. *Apparently Unique.*

THYRREION

Thyrreion,[54] located in the northern part of Akarnania just east of Leukas and south of the Ambrakian Gulf, lies between Echinos and Euripos.[55] It was an important town in Akarnania and around 167 BC, after the fall of Leukas, it became the capital of the Akarnanian Federation, which it had originally joined sometime in the 4th century BC, perhaps earlier.[56] According to Xenophon, the warriors of Thyrreion were noteworthy for their bravery.[57]

Aside from the Athena/Acheloios and later Herakles/Acheloios federal issues, two other bronze man-faced bull types were probably minted in Thyrreion. They both feature the head of Acheloios on the obverse and on the reverse, a wreath, sometimes surrounding Θ.

Many dealers have attributed the coins lacking the Θ to an uncertain Sicilian mint because they were allegedly discovered there. However, both coins probably come from Thyrreion. The type without Θ (no. 483) was probably issued around the time of the anepigraphic Athena/Acheloios type (MSP I, 460), in the mid 3rd century. The type with Θ was most likely minted after 232 BC, when the Akarnanian Federation was formally reestablished and differentiation between federal and civic issues would have been warranted. It is important to note that many Thyrreion coins are found in Sicily,[58] and therefore the alleged find spots of type 483 do not necessarily mean they were minted there.

Coinage

Uncertain

483. AE Quarter Unit, 1.15g	c. 250 BC
	OBV: Head of Acheloios as a man-faced bull to right. REV: Wreath. REF: Gorny & Mosch (1.46g); Künker, 133, 7119*.

484. AE Quarter Unit, 1.39g	After 232 BC
	OBV: Head of Acheloios as a man-faced bull to right. REV: Θ in wreath. REF: Isler 369; BMC Thessaly 193, n. 12-13, Taf. 30,1. Head 332; Dr. Busso Peus 399, 116*.

[54] There are many variations in the orthographic tradition, including: θυρίον (Stephanus Byzantius, *Ethnika*, 320, 1. 20-1 M.), θύριον (Polybius, *Histories*, 4.6.2), and also θουρίου (Polybius, *Histories*, 18.10.10), as cited in D. Marcotte, 'Le Premier Koinon Acarnanien et la Fin de la Seconde Ligue Délienne,' in *L'Antiquité Classique*, 54 (1985), 255, note 12. See H.J. Gehrke, and E. Wirbelauer, 'Akarnania and Adjacent Areas,' 372-3 for additional variants.

[55] P.J. Perlman, *City and Sanctuary in Ancient Greece: The Theorodokia in the Peloponnese* (Vandenhoeck & Ruprecht, 2000), 121; H.J. Gehrke, and E. Wirbelauer, 'Akarnania and Adjacent Areas,' 372-3.

[56] H.J. Gehrke, and E. Wirbelauer, 'Akarnania and Adjacent Areas,' 373.

[57] Xenophon, *Hellenica*, 6.2.37.

[58] For references specifically relating to Thyrreion coinage found in Italy and Sicily, see H.J. Gehrke, and E. Wirbelauer, 'Akarnania and Adjacent Areas,' 373.

Section Six
REMAINING MINTS

The remaining mints to issue bronze coinage of the man-faced bull are Ambrakia, Metropolis, Methylion, Istros, Tarsos, Ai Khanoum, and an uncertain mint probably located on the Meander River, near Magnesia.

The map below highlights most of the remaining mints, with the exception of Tarsos and Ai Khanoum, and identifies the surrounding locations where man-faced bull coinage was issued in other metals.

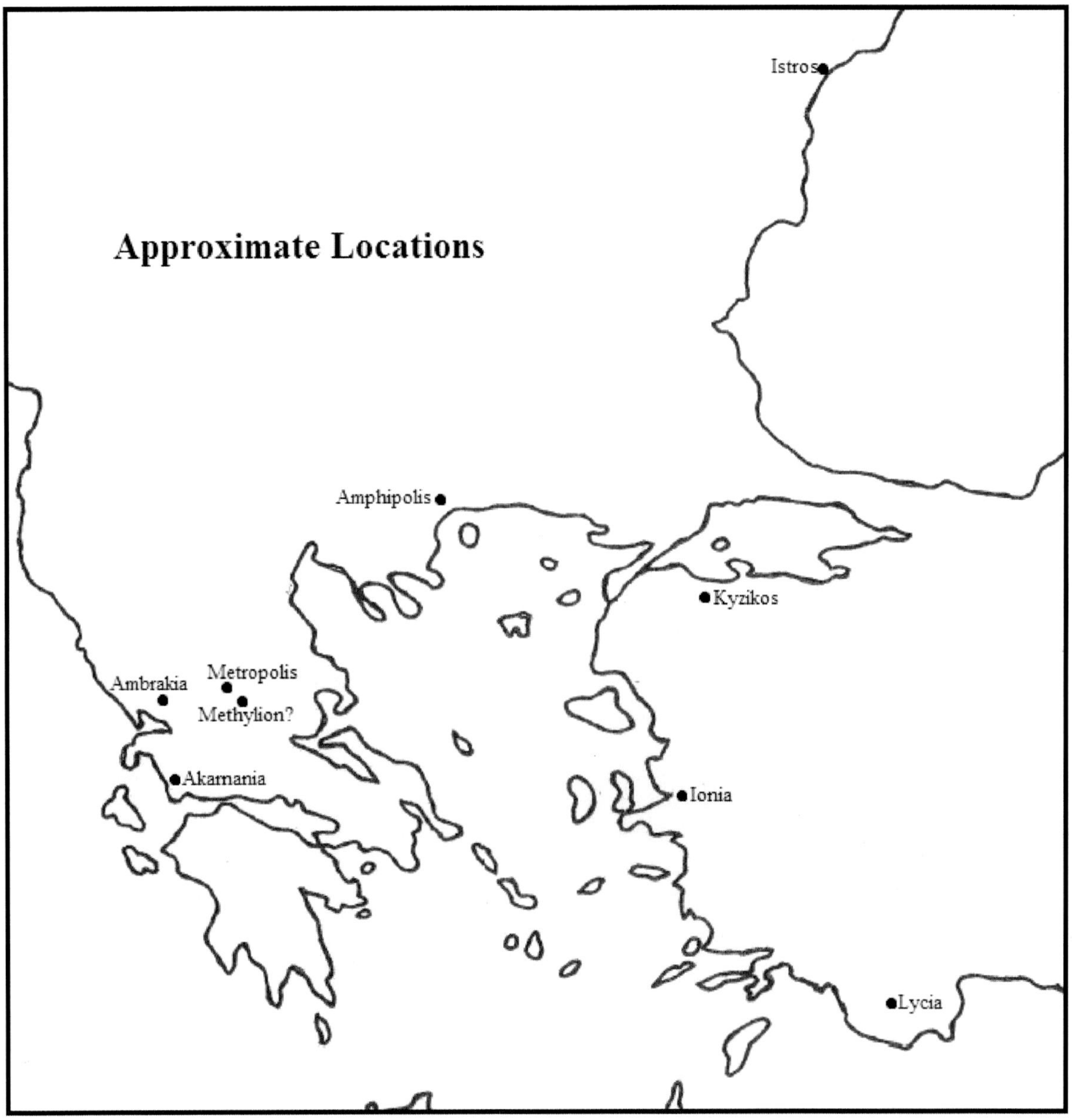

AMBRAKIA

Ambrakia lies in the southern portion of Epeiros on the eastern side of the Aracthos River, and it even had a fort named Ἀμβρακος located within the river's lagoons.[1] The area has been inhabited since the Bronze Age, and early Dorian influence has been well established.[2] According to legend, it was a Thesprotian town later colonized by Corinthians in the mid 7th Century BC (Leukas, in Akarnania, was colonized by Corinthians at the same time).[3] It sided with Sparta during the Peloponnesian War and was at times in conflict with the Akarnanians to the south, most of whom supported Athens. Throughout its long and reasonably well documented history it came under both Akarnanian and Aetolian domination. It was besieged in 189 BC by Rome and all of its valuable artworks removed,[4] and the city was finally completely uninhabited after Augustus moved its residents to Nicopolis.[5]

The Ambrakians issued a few varieties of bronze coinage featuring the man-faced bull in the late 3rd, early 2nd century BC, probably starting sometime during the wars between Philip V and the Epirotes vs. the Aetolians (220 BC), and ending before the time of Roman occupation (189 BC).[6] Due to the fact that the Abrakians were constantly shifting sides during this dispute, these coins would have helped facilitate local trade during a tumultuous period.[7]

In terms of the identity of the man-faced bull of Ambrakia, it should be mentioned that Acheloios is well known in the area, since at nearby Dodona the oracle would instruct all patrons to offer sacrifices to him.[8] Thus, although the Ambrakians and Akarnanians were often times on opposing sides of the battle field, it makes perfect sense for Acheloios to be featured on Ambrakian coinage.[9] As a result, this man-faced bull is probably Acheloios Arachthos.

It is curious that the man-faced bull is depicted both with and without beard. The same phenomenon can be seen on the coinage of the Akarnanians, but does not occur anywhere else in the Greek world on coinage. Perhaps the explanation involves the states of the river (wild vs. tame, etc.) at different parts of its course or even different times of the year, as some have hypothesized about the youthful horned river gods vs. bearded man-faced bulls of Sicily.[10] Of course, there is also the chance that the bearded man-faced bull is Acheloios and the beardless man-faced bull is Arachthos, since these issues are so late in the general scheme of man-faced bull iconography. Ultimately, we opt for Acheloios Arachthos in both cases.

Coinage

485. AE Unit, 5.20g, 19mm	**c. 220 to 189 BC**
	OBV: Head of bearded Acheloios Arachthos as a man-faced bull to right. REV: Crab, AXP monogram above, AMBPA below. REF: BMC Thessaly pg. 95, 18; CNG, eAuction 98, 27*.

[1] For an overview, see H.J. Gehrke and E. Wirbelauer, 'Akarnania and Adjacent Areas,' 354-6.

[2] N.G.L. Hammond, 'Prehistoric Epirus and the Dorian Invasion,' in *The Annual of the British School at Athens,* Vol. 32 (1933), 131-79.

[3] N.G.L. Hammond, 'Ambracia,' in *Oxford Classical Dictionary* (Oxford: University Press, 1996).

[4] Polybius, *Histories*, 22. 9-13; Livy, *Ab Urbe condita Libri*, 38. 3-9.

[5] Pausanius, *Hellados Periegesis*, 5.23.3.

[6] Cf. N.G.L. Hammond, 'Ambracia,' for dating of significant events in Ambrakian history.

[7] Ibid. For ancient accounts, see in particular Polybius, *Histories*, 4.61ff.

[8] For an overview of practices at Dodona, see D.M. Nicol, 'The Oracle of Dodona,' in *Greece and Rome,* Vol. 5, No. 2 (1958), 128-43.

[9] It should also be mentioned that Herakles, the natural counterpart of Acheloios, was a patron god of Ambrakia (H.J. Gehrke, and E.Wirbelauer, 'Akarnania and Adjacent Areas,'355).

[10] See Chapter 7 for specific examples.

486. AE Half Unit, 2.55g, 14mm	**c. 220 to 189 BC**
	OBV: Head of beardless Acheloios Arachthos as a man-faced bull to right. REV: Crab, AMB below. REF: SNG Cop 29; CNG 61, 204*.

487. AE Unit, 6.12g	**c. 220 to 189 BC**
	OBV: Head of Acheloios Arachthos as a man-faced bull to left. REV: Bull butting left on single line, AMBPA above. REF: M&M GmbH, 30, 269*.

488. AE Unit, Unrecorded Weight	**c. 220 to 189 BC**
	Obv: Head of Acheloios Arachthos as a man-faced bull to right. Rev: Bull to left, head down, AM in ex. REF: Cf. SNG Evelpidis, 1771. As published in Oliver Picard, 'Le tresor de Senitsa et le monnayage des Chaones en Epire' in Revue Numismatique, Vol. 6 (2005), 51-58. *Hypothetical line drawing based on style of other varieties from the mint and Picard's description.*

489. AE Unit, 4.56g, 17mm	**c. 220 to 189 BC**
	OBV: Head of beardless Acheloios Arachthos as a man-faced bull to right. REV: Bull butting left on single line, ΣΩ above, [A] MBPAKI[...] in exergue. REF: Cf. SNG Cop 26-8; cf. SNG Evelpidis 1771; CNG, 76, 347*.

490. AE Unit, 4.34g	**c. 220 to 189 BC**
	OBV: Head of beardless Acheloios Arachthos as a man-faced bull to right. REV: Bull butting left on single line, AMB ___ above, uncertain letters below. REF: BnF Fonds général 122*.

ISTROS (Black Sea)

Located on the western shore of the Black Sea near the mouth of the Ister River (modern Danube), Istros, or Histria,[11] is the only city in the general area to mint coinage depicting the man-faced bull.[12] The general area has been inhabited since Paleolithic times, and from this side of the Black Sea emerged one of our very first man-faced bulls, from Karanovo VI culture of Old Europe, during the Bronze Age.[13]

Like many other cities in the Black Sea circuit, Istros was founded by Milesians sometime in the 7th century BC,[14] and it might be from these early roots that the man-faced bull tradition of Istros originated[15].

From the 7th to 4th century the town was destroyed and rebuilt many times. The man-faced bull probably appeared on the earliest issues of bronze coinage, in the late 4th century BC. We tentatively place the date here because we know that Istros was sacked at the end of the 4th century,[16] and the man-faced bull probably operated as a symbol of rebirth once Istros reestablished itself thereafter.

An examination of the city's bronze coinage might also provide insight into the changes in river god iconography over time.[17] The presumably earliest issues of Istros, catalogued here, probably depict the local embodiment of Acheloios, Acheloios Istros, with the head or mask of a man-faced bull. The presumably later series depicts a bearded and horned Istros with a distinctly human neck.[18] No. 482 is uncertain, but probably a man-faced bull head.

Coinage

491. AE Unit, 3.35g, 16mm	**Late 4th to 3rd century BC**
	OBV: Three-quarter facing head of Acheloios Istros as a man-faced bull, eyes looking to left. Bull neck extending horizontally from head. REV: Eagle grasping Dolphin (both oriented to left), ΙΣΤΡΙ above. REF: AMNG I, 468; CNG, eAuction 288, 99*.

492. AE Unit, 4.10g, 15mm	**Late 4th to 3rd century BC**
	OBV: Three-quarter facing head of Acheloios Istros as a man-faced bull, eyes looking to left. Bull neck extending diagonally downward from head. Dotted border. REV: Eagle grasping Dolphin (both oriented to left), ΙΣΤΡΙ above. REF: AMNG I, 468; CNG 161017*.

[11] Greek Ἴστρος, cf. Hesiod, *Theogony*, 339.

[12] For an overview of the coinage of Istros, see BB. Pick, *Die antiken Münzen Nord-Griechenlands*. Vol. I/1: *Die antiken Münzen von Dacien und Moesien*; edited by Friedrich Imhoof-Blumer (Berlin: Reimer, 1898) 139-179.

[13] See above, pg. 3-5.

[14] J.B. Bury, *A History of Greece to the Death of Alexander the Great*, 91-92.

[15] The very first man-faced bull on coinage was minted at Miletos, and many of the Iron Age Greek mercenaries responsible for the transmission of man-faced bull iconography from East to West were Ionian. See above, pg. 25-9 for discussion.

[16] S.v. 'ISTROS (Histria) Romania,' in R. Stillwell, W. L. MacDonald, and M. H. McAllister, *The Princeton Encyclopedia of Classical Sites*.

[17] B. Pick and K. Regling do not differentiate between obverse types (*Die antiken Münzen von Dacien und Moesien*, AMNG I, 468).

[18] The human neck also appears on the coins of Olbia, which led Jenkins to incorrectly identify the image on the obverse of such coins as the head of a man-faced bull, or 'Achelous bull,' as he calls it. See G.K. Jenkins, *The Coinage of Gela*, 170.

493. AE Half Unit(?), 1.54g, 12mm	**Late 4th to 3rd century BC**
	OBV: Mask of Acheloios Istros as a man-faced bull. REV: Eagle grasping Dolphin (both oriented to left), IΣ[TPI] above, ΔIO below. REF: AMNG I, 468; CNG, eAuction 161, 15*.

494. AE Unit, 2.19g, 13mm	**3rd century BC**
	OBV: Mostly facing head of Acheloios Istros as a man-faced bull. REV: Eagle grasping Dolphin (both oriented to left), IΣTPI above. REF: AMNG I, 468; CNG eAuction 258, lot 12*. *Unconfirmed. The slight trace of a neck to the left might be human or bovine. For a specifically human neck on this general type, see CNG 185, lot 20.*

METHYLION? (Thessaly)

Methylion is one of those places we know hardly anything about. It was certainly located in Thessaly in central Greece.[19] Several theories abound about its location, the earliest coming from Livy, who identified the site with ancient Euhedrion of the Enipeus Valley.[20] Phillipson identified Methylion with Seklista, whereas Stählin remained uncertain.[21]

One extremely rare type of bronze coin depicting the man-faced bull exists, with two known specimens.[22] The obverse is clearly Herakles wrestling Acheloios, and the reverse depicts Herakles' club and bow with the city's ethnic.

In his *Handbook of Coins of Northern and Central Greece*, Oliver Hoover remarks that the mint is probably not Methylion, and instead an unknown Akarnanian mint (though he lists it under Methylion for convenience).[23] However, the coins were found in Thessaly, so we opt for Methylion in this catalog, especially since the man-faced bull of Akarnania is always portrayed with head and neck only, and never in the form of a protome or full body.

Coinage

495. AE Unit, 0.83-1.50g, 11mm	**4th Century BC**
	OBV: Herakles standing left, holding Acheloios by the horns in psychopompic display. Dotted border. REV: Club with bow resting on top, M-E below (retrograde), X-E above (retrograde). All in incuse square. REF: CNG eAuction 251, 18; CNG Triton XV, 469*.

[19] D. Sear, *Greek Coins and Their Values. Volume I: Europe,* 206.
[20] Livy, *Ab Urbe Condita Libri*, 32.13. See also, P.J. Pearlman, *City and Sanctuary in Ancient Greece: The Theorodokia in the Peloponnese* (Vandenhoeck & Ruprecht, 2000), 75, footnote 44.
[21] See P. J. Pearlman, *City and Sanctuary in Ancient Greece,* 75, footnote 44, citing Philippson, 1950, 60-61, 305 no. 59, and Stählin 1924, 143 n.6.
[22] For an overview of other types from Methylion, see C. Heyman, 'Les types de monnaies de Méthylion en Thessalie,' in *Anc. Soc.* I, 1970.
[23] O. Hoover, *Handbook of Greek Coinage*, Vol. 4, 199.

METROPOLIS (Thessaly)

etropolis, a member of the Thessalian League during the 2nd century BC, consisted of a group of small towns of Hestiaiotis[24] in central-western Thessaly that minted a common coinage in the 5th to 3rd century BC.[25] Like the nearby Akarnanians, Metropolis was subjected to invasion by the belligerent Aetolians. The most devastating attack, in which the surrounding farmland was destroyed, took place in 198 BC, the same year Metropolis surrendered to Rome.[26]

There are two main types of bronze coinage of the man-faced bull from Metropolis, as Rogers outlined in *The Copper Coinage of Thessaly*.[27] The iconographic style of these man-faced bulls is unique to the mint and finds no true parallel in this catalog, nor on the silver or gold coinage of the man-faced bull. Rogers dated them to the 3rd century BC during the time of Demetrios Poliokretes (king of Macedon from 294 to 288 BC),[28] and we see no reason to revise that dating.

The pairing of Apollo and the man-faced bull is especially appropriate at Metropolis. In the city's temple to Apollo, dating back to the mid 5th century BC, he is shown in full hoplite armor, which Catherine Morgan[29] rightly suggests is in reverence to the god's role in protecting mercenaries. This is an attribute he has in common with the man-faced bull, as we discussed at length in Chapter 2. Moreover, Rogers reports that an Asiatic cult of Aphrodite was operative at the site, Aphrodite Kastnia (the chief deity, in fact),[30] and so it is likely the man-faced bull of Metropolis migrated west along with this cult, no doubt carried by itinerant mercenaries and seer-healers.

The man-faced bull on the coinage of Metropolis is probably Acheloios Pamisos, since Metropolis (modern Karditza) is located near the source of the Pamisos River.[31]

Coinage

496. AE Trichalkon, 6.98g	**Early 3rd century BC**
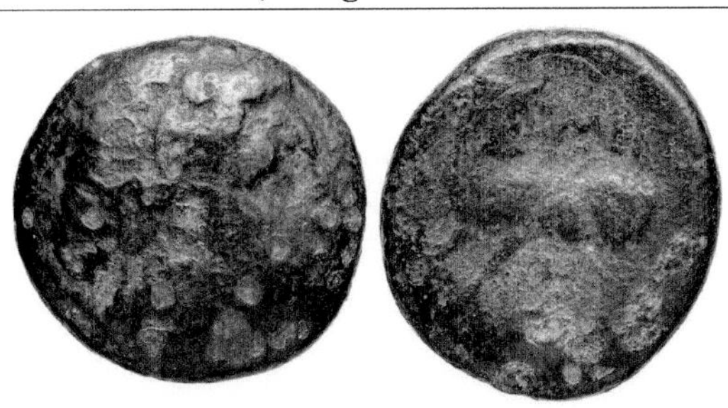	OBV: Head of Apollo facing right, wearing laurel wreath with leaves in opposing pairs. REV: Forepart of Acheloios Pamisos as a man-faced bull to left, head turned back so face is in profile, MET in upper-right field. REF: Rogers 410; BnF FG 364*.

497. AE Trichalkon, 8.44g, 19mm	**Early 3rd century BC**
	OBV: Head of Apollo facing right, wearing laurel wreath with leaves in opposing pairs. REV: ΜΗΤ-ΡΟΠΟΛΙΤΩΝ (inscription ending at base of forepart) surrounding forepart of Acheloios Pamisos as a man-faced bull to left, head facing, monogram below, ribbons hanging from head. REF: Rogers 411; CNG eAuction 311, lot 212*.

[24] T.S. Mackay, 'Metropolis: Thessaly,' in *The Princeton Encyclopedia of Classical Sites*.
[25] D. Sear, *Greek Coins*, Vol. 1, 206.
[26] Livy, *Ab Urbe Condita Libri*, 32.13.11 and 32.15.3.
[27] E. Rogers, *The Copper Coinage of Thessaly* (London: Spink, 1932).
[28] Ibid., 132.
[29] C. Morgan, *Early Greek States Beyond the Polis* (New York: Routeldge, 2003), 141-142.
[30] E. Rogers, *The Copper Coinage of Thessaly*, 133.
[31] Ibid.

498. AE Trichalkon, 7.12g, 20mm	**Early 3rd century BC**
	OBV: Head of Apollo facing right, wearing laurel wreath with leaves in opposing pairs. REV: ΜΗΤ-ΡΟΠΟΛΙΤΩΝ surrounding forepart of Acheloios Pamisos as a man-faced bull to left, head facing, monogram below, ribbons hanging from head. REF: CNG 733499*.

499. AE Trichalkon, 7.37g, 19.5mm	**Early 3rd century BC**
	OBV: Head of Apollo facing right, wearing laurel wreath with leaves in opposing pairs. REV: ΜΗΤΡΟΠΟΛΙΤΩΝ surrounding forepart of Acheloios Pamisos as a man-faced bull to left, head facing, monogram to left, ribbons hanging from head. REF: CNG Triton XV, 482.1*.

500. AE Trichalkon, 7.02g, 19.5mm	**Early 3rd century BC**
	OBV: Head of Apollo facing right, wearing laurel wreath with leaves in opposing pairs. REV: ΜΗΤΡΟΠΟΛΙΤΩΝ surrounding forepart of Acheloios Pamisos as a man-faced bull right, head facing, monogram directly behind bull and oriented 45 degrees clockwise, two ribbons hanging from neck. REF: CNG Triton XV, 483.4*.

TARSOS

These rare coins from Tarsos in Cilicia are extremely interesting. All varieties examined except the one pictured below[32] show a horned, winged animal (when exhibiting any defining characteristics at all). However, on this variety it is a winged man-faced bull. The figure standing on top of the bull is Sandan-Herakles.[33] In fact, it is believed that Sandan is a remnant of earlier Hittite occupation in Cilicia, where Teshub/Tarhun was worshipped.[34] Teshub, in turn, is associated with the even earlier Mesopotamian god Adad, often depicted on a bull.[35] All figures share many iconographic devices: they are always depicted standing on mythical creatures (usually a bull for Teshub and Adad, but in some cases a lion and bull), wings or birds are often depicted above the latter figures, and they often hold flowers. In later, 2nd century BC depictions, the figure beneath Sandan-Herakles is almost always a horned lion, sometimes winged. [36]

We know man-faced bulls, with or without wings, played an important part in the earlier cultural practices of Cilicia. On coinage alone, there are winged man-headed bulls with lion paws depicted beneath thrones on earlier issues (c. 380 BC) from Tarsos,[37] and regular man-faced bulls appear as countermarks on some coins as well (c. 380 to 374 BC).[38] In nearby Mallos, the man-faced bull is featured on many coins, and on one variety, a winged man (presumably Sandan-Herakles) holding a solar disc appears above a man-faced bull.[39] On the variety listed below, we see the pyre on which an effigy of Sandan-Herakles was burned each year, indicating the withering heat of summer and eventual rebirth,[40] linked here to the man-faced bull. The man-faced bull was presumably replaced by the horned, winged lion as the iconography went out of style in the 2nd century. The man-faced bull featured on this coin is probably Acheloios Kalykadnos.

Coinage

501. AE Unit, 14.82g, 21mm	**After 164 BC?**
	OBV:Draped, veiled and turreted bust of Tyche facing right. Dotted border. REV:ΤΑΡΣΕΩΝ to right of pyramidal pyre, within, Sandan-Herakles standing on Acheloios Kalykadnos as a winged man-faced bull to right, its head in profile. Eagle atop structure, monograms in left field. REF: CNG, Triton VII, lot 329*.

[32] The winged man-faced bull only appears on the examples with these monograms. These dies, presumably the first in the series, were probably carved by a master engraver and subsequent issues by normal mint workers, hence the evolution from winged man-faced bull, to winged, horned creature, to barely identifiable creature.

[33] D.A. Mackenzie, *Mythology of the Babylonian People* (Braken Books, 1915), 261.

[34] *Encyclopedia Britannica Online*, s. v. 'Teshub,' accessed July 15, 2015.

[35] A. R.W. Green, *The Storm-god in the Ancient Near East* (Eisenbrauns, 2003), 170.

[36] In fact, on some contemporaneous bronze issues we see Sandan standing on a winged, horned lion, and sometimes the figure has a man's face (Cf. SNG France 2, 1305; SNG Levante 962).

[37] R.A. Moysey, 'The silver stater issues of Pharnabazos and Datames from the mint of Tarsus in Cilicia,' in *ANSMN* 31 (New York, 1986),60 Nr. 17a Taf. 5.

[38] Cf. SNG France 268–9.

[39] CNG eAuction 299, lot 192.

[40] J. Civan, Excerpt from Lecture Series on *Abraham's Knife: The Mythology of the Deicide in Anti-Semitism* (XLibris, 2004), reproduced on Forvm Ancient Coins' website.

AI KHANOUM? (Seleukid Kings)

A Seleukid bronze type known from three extant specimens, some found in Bactra,[41] features an Indian humped man-faced bull to right, probably kneeling in assent to being sacrificed.[42] The coin probably comes from Ai Khanoum and represents the only man-faced bull ever used on official Seleukid coinage.

Lloyd Taylor's essay in the appendix sheds some light on this enigmatic coin and the attribution to Ai Khanoum instead of Bactra. The figure likely represents Acheloios Oxus, fitting indeed as a synoecistic image in a distant land.

Coinage

502. AE Unit, 5.16g, 19mm	**294 to 281BC**
	OBV: Acheloios Oxus in the form of an Indian humped man-faced bull to right on single line, probably kneeling in assent to being sacrificed. Dotted border. REV: Anchor oriented upwards, ΒΑΣΙΛΕΩΣ ΣΕΛΕΥΚΟΥ reading downward in two lines on right, ΑΝΤΙΟΧΟΥ reading downward on left, circled Δ in outer left field, Brahmi (?) letter (pa?) in outer right field. REF: SC 283A; Image courtesy of Brian Kritt*.

[41] For an attribution to Bactra, see O. Bopearachchi, 'The Seleukid Coins of Central Asia and the Bactra Mint,' *Travaux de Numismatique Grecques Offerts à Georges Le Rider*, edited by M. Amandry and S. Hurter (London: Spink, 1999), 17-37; O. Bopearachchi, 'The Monetary Policy of Bactria under the Seleukids,' *Topoi, Suppl.* 6 (2004), 43-60. For the alternative view, cf. B. Kritt, *New Discoveries in Bactrian Numismatics* (Lancaster, PA: CNG, 2015).

[42] For an extensive essay on the type see Appendix 4, by L.W. Taylor. See also pg. 28-9 and 92-3 above.

IONIA: UNCERTAIN MINT ON THE MEANDER RIVER

An interesting and apparently unique countermark found on a coin of Antiochos II, Theos, provides evidence of the migrations of man-faced bull iconography from east to west at a much later date. Here we see an iconography that was used during the reign of Seleukos I and Antiochos I at Ai Khanoum making its way back to the western coast of Asia Minor. Presumably, a group of mercenaries who served under one of the aforementioned kings were allotted some land back home upon retirement and decided to pay homage to the god that protected them while away, and made special arrangements to honor that god by incorporating it into the mythos of the local river, hence the meander symbol above the humped man-faced bull in the countermark.[43]

The reason for attributing this countermark to a group in Asia Minor and not Ai Khanoum (or Bacrta) is straightforward: the coin was very likely found in Asia Minor because it emerged with a large group of other coins from the region; the undertype was minted at an unknown location, possibly Tralles, at a later date than the Ai Khanoum humped man-faced bull; finally, the meander symbol indicates a mint near the Meander River. Moreover, this particular elongated meander symbol is remarkably similar to those on issues of the 4th century BC from Magnesia.[44] Thus, on this coin, we see Acheloios Oxus Meander, a figure encompassing, first, the god of all water, second, the river that nourished them while away, and finally, the local river on which they likely established their new home.

Coinage

503. AE Unit, 4.09g, 18mm	**261 to 246 BC**
	OBV: Head of Apollo to right, wearing laurel wreath with leaves in opposing pairs. REV: Tripod, ANTIOXOY to left (with abnormal N), ΒΑΣΛΙΕΩΣ to right. Countermark: Acheloios Oxus Meander as a humped man-faced bull standing to right, head in profile, elongated meander symbol above. REF: SC 537 (Uncertain mint, possibly Tralles in Mysia), Countermark Unpublished, Potamikon Collection*. *Unique*

Countermark Enlargement and Line Drawing:

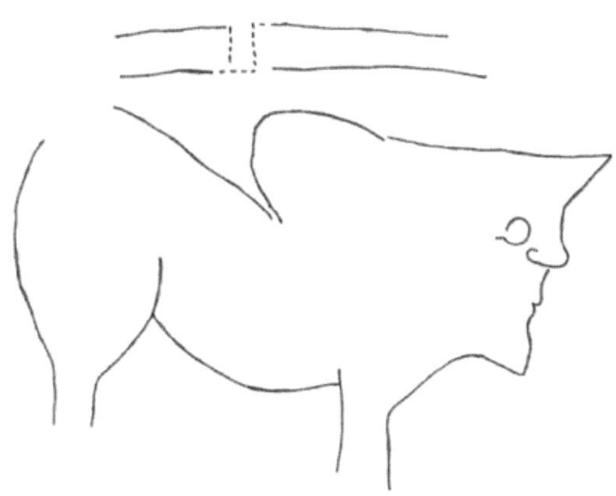

[43] For additional discussion specifically in the context or itinerant mercenaries, see above, Chapter 2 and Chapter 7.

[44] Cf. SNG von Aulock 2036.

Appendix 1

Joseph Eckhel, 'De tauro cum facie humana,' in *Doctrina Numorum Veterum*, Vol. 1 (Wien: Ignatius Alberti, 1792). Translated by Curtis Clay, 2013.

Dissertation III: Concerning the Man-Faced Bull

The geographical spread of monsters of this sort was restricted, for they are attested only in Campania and Sicily for the most part, to which Arcanania in Greece must be added, where the river god Achelous was depicted in this guise. Within this limited area, however, the motif was very common, appearing on the coins of many of the cities of the two regions, namely in Campania on the coins of Campania herself, or rather Capua, and on those of Callatia, Calles, Cumae and Liternum, Neapolis, Nola, Stabiae, Suessa, and Teanum, then in Samnium on the coins of Aesernia and Murgantia, in Lucania on those of Larinum Frentanorum, Laium, Posidonia, and Sybaris, Hyrium whose location is uncertain, finally in Sicily on the coins of Agyrium, Aluntium, Catana, Entella, Gelas, Himera, Megara, Selinus, Tauromenium, and possibly Syracuse, if a coin published by Paruti can be trusted. It was above all Neapolis and Gelas, however, that depicted this monster on their coins. Yet given that the coins prove that this monster must have been well known to the inhabitants of so many cities, it seems extraordinary that there is no explanation of the man-headed bull in any surviving ancient author, not in the historians, the mythologists, or the poets, though the same authors do inform us of hippocentaurs, minotaurs, tritons, giants, sphinxes, Pegasi, chimaeras, and several other monsters combining the parts of more than one beast. Since no help could be derived from the literary sources, modern authors have had to come up with their own ideas to explain this coin type.

The earliest modern commentators on ancient coins confidently identified this man-headed bull as the Minotaur, despite the contrary testimony of all ancient authors and of the genuine surviving artefacts. According to that testimony, the Minotaur was indeed a monster of mixed parts, but he had the head of a bull and the body of a man. Diodorus,[1] for example, states that 'τουτον δε φασι διφυη γεγονεναι, χαι τα μεν άνωτερα μερη του σωματος ἀχρι των ώμων ἐχειν ταυρου, τα δε λοιπα ἀνζρωπον; the Minotaur is said to have had a combined nature, with the head of a bull down to his shoulders, but the body of a man from his shoulders down.' Apollodorus[2] is succinct: 'οὑτος εἰχε ταυρου προσωπον, τα δε λοιπα ἀνδρος ;This monster had the face of a bull, but the body of a man.'

[1] L. IV. c. 77.

[2] L. III. § 8.

Tzetzes,[3] Hyginus,[4] and Palaephatus[5] confirm the same description. The artifacts are in full agreement with the authors, for they too show the Minotaur as having the head of a bull joined to the body of a man, for example an elegant gem in the imperial collection in Vienna,[6] an Athenian[7] coin type, a painting at Herculaneum,[8] and a vase painting published by Winkelmann,[9] all of which depict Theseus fighting with the Minotaur. A gem in the French royal collection published by Mariettus[10] and a marble urn published by Gorius[11] show the same motif, which the authors have however erroneously identified as showing Hercules fighting with Achelous, when in fact it is the same struggle between Theseus and the Minotaur. Since in these cases Theseus has a lionskin and club, Mariettus and Gorius wrongly identified him as Hercules. But Plutarch[12] and Aristides[13] state that Theseus wanted to imitate Hercules in every way, and on coins of Commodus and Caracalla struck at Nicaea, Theseus,[14] with his name written beside him, is depicted with all of the attributes of Hercules. I may note that antiquarians have often misidentified the fight of Theseus with the Minotaur as being that of Hercules with Achelous. Apart from Mariettus and Gorius whom I have just mentioned, Joseph Allegranza made the same mistake in his explication of an ancient mosaic that depicts a naked man wrestling with another naked man who however has the head of a bull. From a raised location nearby, six astonished girls observe the outcome of the fight, while human bones are scattered about on the ground. Allegranza explains the scene as depicting the fight between Hercules and Achelous.[15] But every motif in this scene argues for its identification with the fight between Theseus and the Minotaur, firstly the man with the bull's head, the attested form of the Minotaur, as I have just argued; then the group of girls looking on, clearly the Athenian girls who were destined to be the monster's next meal, according to the well-known myth;

[3] in Cassandr. v. 653

[4] Fab. 40.

[5] de Incredib. c. 2.

[6] Choix de pier. grav. tab. XXXII.

[7] Pellerin. Rec. I. tab. 22.

[8] Tom. I. tab. 5.

[9] Mon. ined. Tav. 100.

[10] Tom. II, tab. 76.

[11] Mus. Etr. T. II. p. 214.

[12] in Thes.

[13] T. I. p. 486.

[14] Vaillant

[15] Opusculi erud. P. 232.

and finally the bones scattered on the ground, obviously the gruesome remainders of recent meals. Whether the same motifs can be applied with equal aptness to the fable of Achelous, I would greatly doubt! As a final proof for the configuration of the Minotaur, I may cite an excellent coin of Pellerin's,[16] showing on one side the Minotaur with bull's head and human body as described above, and on the other side the labyrinth in which the Minotaur was confined. In the face of so much contrary evidence, it is clear that we must doubt the authenticity of a gem published by Gorius from the Strozzi Collection,[17] showing a purported Minotaur with a human head and the body of a bull, enclosed in the labyrinth. Therefore the man-headed bull that appears on the Campanian and Sicilian coins in question cannot be the Minotaur, and all the theories about possible Cretan colonies in Sicily and Campania and the like, which scholars have invented with more ingenuity than wisdom, fall to the ground. Spanheim[18] and Beger[19] were not unaware of this contradiction between the alleged Minotaur on the coins and the Minotaur described by the written sources, yet they could not summon the courage to throw off the yoke that the traditional identification had imposed on them. There is a difference, then, between a man-headed bull and a man with the head of a bull, as is also stated in the following lines of Empedocles as quoted by Aelianus[20]: 'Πολλα μεν ἀμφιπροσωπα χαι ἀμφιςιρνα φυεσζαι, Βουγενη ἀνδροπρωρα, τα δ ἐμπαλιν ἐξανατελλειν Ανδροφυν Βουχρανα, χ. τ. λ. ; Many animals are born with a head and body of different kinds, for example offspring of cattle but with a human head, or human offspring but with the head of a bull, etc.' The monster that we are discussing was of the first sort mentioned by Empedocles, while the Minotaur, in contrast, was of the second sort.

A second old interpretation of the man-headed bull proposed that it was an allegorical type, referring to agricultural production, for which the bull was a traditional symbol. This interpretation was espoused by Carrera,[21] Pighius,[22] and Hardouin,[23] though Hardouin, with his customary inconstancy, also accepted the Minotaur identification elsewhere in his writings.[24] More recently Wachterus[25] took up the 'agricultural production' explanation once more, and was followed therein by the French scholars la Chau and le Blond.[26]

[16] Rec. III. Tab. 98.

[17] Mus. Flor. T. II. tab. 35.

[18] Tom. I. p. 284.

[19] Thes. Br. T. I. p. 349.

[20] de Nat. anim. L. XVI. E. 29.

[21] Monum. hist. Catan.

[22] Annal. T. I. p. 423.

[23] Plin. T. I. p. 162.

[24] Num. illustr. in *Gela et Neap.*

[25] Archaeol. num. p. 95

[26] Pierr. Grav. du Duc. d'Orl. T. I. p. 123.

There have been more recent interpretations of this coin type too, for example that of Mazochius,[27] who saw in the man-headed bull a representation of Neptune, though without convincing any other scholars, as far as I am aware. Equally unconvincing was the theory advanced by Ignarra, who upon observing that the river Achelous was shown as a man-headed bull on the coins of several cities in Acarnania, went on to propose that the ancients applied the name Achelous to every river in every land, so that the rivers of Campania and Sicily would also have borne that name, and the nickname 'Acheloici'[28] could be applied to all coins bearing the type of the man-headed bull.

A decade later, in his work Delle antiche Colonie venute in Napoli,[29] Martorellus interpreted the man-headed bull as a god, suggesting that the type represented Liber Pater, or Bacchus, who according to Macrobius[30] was worshipped at Neapolis in Campania under the name Hebo, an idea that I note had already earlier been expressed by Matthaeus Aegyptius.[31]

In the same year Petrus Burmannus in Bavaria proposed yet another interpretation of the man-headed bull, writing that he did not doubt 'that the horned heads of this kind should instead be referred to the rivers adjacent to the cities that struck the coins.'[32] Burmannus advanced this idea as a conjecture only, and made no attempt to formulate arguments to support it. The Prince of Turris Mucia, however, who had until then accepted the old 'Minotaur' explanation of the man-headed bull type, changed his mind upon reading Burmannus' idea, and afterwards interpreted the type as undoubtedly representing rivers. He argued so persistently for this idea first in the prologue of his work *Siciliae inscriptiones*, p. 26, and then in all of his later works, that one could legitimately consider the theory to be his rather than Burmannus'. And since I observe that the Prince's authority has moved many current scholars to accept this explanation, although there are powerful arguments that lead me on the other hand to reject it, we must start by recording the reasons which have persuaded the Prince to think that the man-headed bull types on coins must represent rivers.

The Prince argues 1. That the ancients, particularly the Sicilians, accorded divine honors to rivers. 2. It is also certain that the ancients often depicted rivers as bulls, as attested by Aelianus, Strabo, and other ancient sources. 3. Rivers could also be depicted by the type of a human face with one or two horns. Such types occur frequently on Sicilian coins. 4. The conclusive argument, finally,

[27] Tab. Heracl. p. 518.

[28] de Pal. Neap. p. 232.

[29] Tom. I. p. 229.

[30] L. I. c. 18.

[31] S. C. de Bacch. p. 232.

[32] D'orville Sic. p. 390.

is supplied by the man-headed bull that is depicted on the coins of several cities in Ambracia and Acarnania. Since that man-headed bull certainly represents the river Achelous, it follows that the same type appearing on the coins of other cities must represent the local river adjacent to the city in each case. So argues the Prince, with erudition and apparent probability. But I think that a different explanation of the man-headed bull type is much to be preferred. Whether my explanation is correct or erroneous the reader will be able to judge from the two sections that I have appended below.

Section I

The man-headed bull types on the coins of Campania and Sicily probably do not represent rivers

The ancients, then, the learned Prince says, represented rivers in the form of bulls. That is true according to the literary sources. Strabo[33] states that 'Achelous is said to have had the form of a bull, like other rivers too, because of the noise they make and the frequent bends in their courses, which are called 'horns.' Cornutus[34] is even more explicit: 'τουτου δ ένεχεν χαι τουςποταμουσ χερασφορουσ χαι ταυρωπας ἀναπλαττουσιν, ὡσανει βιαιον τι της φρρας αὐτων χαι μυχητιχον ἐχουσης'. They accordingly represent rivers as horned and having the face of a bull, because their flow is so violent and the sound they make is like that of a bellowing animal.' Festus[35]: 'Images of rivers are given the form of bulls, that is with horns, because they are fierce, like bulls.' Aelianus too, whom I cite often in this essay, states that rivers were depicted in the form of bulls. It would be superfluous to give exact references to the ancient poets, who often call rivers 'tauriform' or the like. The surviving artifacts, however, do not agree with these statements of the authors. According to the monuments, the Romans used the type of a reclining man with an urn below his elbow for all rivers, the Tiber, the Danube, the Rhine, the Savus, the Colapis, the Nile, the Euphrates, the Tigris, and so on. The cities of European Greece and some of the regions of Asia Minor did the same. But the Sicilians depicted rivers as young men, and the Cilicians and Syrians represented them as boys swimming in waves. The Egyptians used the type of an eagle to represent the Nile. As far as I am aware there is no surviving monument that shows clearly, without reliance on conjecture, that the type of a bull was ever used to represent a river, except in the case of Achelous, whose depiction as a bull was however dependent on particular reasons, as I shall argue below.

I am reluctant to suppose, however, that so many serious authors either were ignorant of their subject matter or intentionally misrepresented the facts. We have to consider that far more ancient monuments have perished than have come down to us, and that some of the surviving images of bulls might have been intended by their artists to represent rivers, but we have no means of discovering that fact. The conventions of ancient art changed over time, so perhaps the bull as a depiction of rivers went out of use precisely during that era that produced most of the artifacts that have come down to us. Yet whatever conventions for depicting rivers prevailed in the different regions of the Greek world, it appears certain that in Sicily rivers were not rendered as bulls. Aelianus devotes the entire 37th chapter of the second book of his Var. hist. to a discussion of which cities were accustomed to depict rivers as human figures, and which cites on the other hand depicted them as bulls. He names six Sicilian rivers, Anapios, Cyanis, Porpax, Crinisos, Telmissos, and Akragas, and asserts that they were all depicted in human form. And the surviving coins of Sicily concur perfectly with this testimony, for they depict all rivers that can certainly be identified as such, because they have their names written beside them, Amenanos, Hypsas, Crysas, and so on, as human heads, though with one or two small horns protruding from their foreheads, clearly to indicate what the ancients understood to be the nature of a river. Is it credible, when we have so many Sicilian coins showing the type of the man-headed bull, proving that this method of rendering rivers, if that is indeed the correct meaning of the type, must have been widespread in Sicily, is it credible, I repeat, that this fact could have remained unknown to Aelianus, in a passage where he is specifically explaining how various cities, including cities on Sicily, depicted their rivers? Could Aelianus, who tells us how the Porpax and the Telmissos were depicted, rivers so unimportant that they are not even named by any other author, nevertheless have remained silent about the fact that the Himeras, Sicily's largest river, was regularly depicted as a bull by the people of Himera, if that was in fact the truth, as the learned Prince contends?

The Prince overlooked a noteworthy passage of an ancient scholiast on Pindar which might seem to prove that in Sicily rivers were indeed depicted as bulls. The scholiast states[36]: 'τον δε του Φαλαριδος ταυρον οι Αχραγαντινοι χατεποντωσαν, ὡς φησι Τιμαιος τον γαρ ἐν τη πολει δειχνυμενον μη εἰναι του Φαλαριδος, χαιζαπερ ἡ πολλη ἐχει δοξα, ἀλλ εἰχων ἐςι Γελωνοσ του ποταμου ;The Agrigentines hurled the bull of Phalaris into the sea, as Timaeus relates. So the bull that can be seen in the city today is not Phalaris', as popular opinion holds, but is a representation of the river Gelon.' We may ignore the scholiast's obvious mistake in calling the river Gelon when Gelas was

33 L.X. (?)

34 de Nat. deor. C. 22.

35 in *Taurorum*

36 Pyth. A. v. 185

what he meant. But why an image of the river Gelas at Agrigentum, which had its own river, the Akragas, unless we suppose that the Agrigentines looted the statue from Gela and set it up in their own city as booty? Moreover how reliable is the scholiast's attribution to Timaeus of the statement that the Agrigentines hurled Phalaris' bull into the sea, when according to Polybius Timaeus denied that there ever had been such a bull at Agrigentum?[37] In any case the scholiast's statement can be directly refuted by a much weightier authority. Cicero[38] relates that among the artworks confiscated from Agrigentum and transported to Carthage by the Carthaginians, but later restored to their original owners by P. Scipio, was 'that noble bull which is said to have belonged to that cruelest of tyrants, Phalaris, who would enclose men in it and scorch them to death over a fire as punishment. And when Scipio restored the bull to the Agrigentines, he is reported to have recommended that they should consider whether it was more advantageous to the Sicilians to be subject to their own princes or to be under the dominion of the Roman people, now that they had a single monument commemorating both the cruelty of their domestic masters and our liberality.' What belief does the scholiast deserve when contradicted by this much weightier testimony of Scipio and Cicero? Were these two eminent men just following the erroneous 'popular opinion' mentioned by the scholiast, when the first of them publicly restored that monument to the Agrigentines and called it the bull of Phalaris, and when the second stated in a public speech that Scipio had returned the bull of Phalaris to Agrigentum? Couldn't Scipio and Cicero too have learned from Timaeus, as the scholiast claims to have done, that the bull in question actually represented a river? And even if we accepted that the bull represented a river, the fact that many considered it to be the bull of Phalaris would suggest that it could not have had a human head, since the tyrant had decreed that his scorched victims should be lamented not in the normal human way, but by mooing! But the point of the present examination is to discover not just whether Sicilian rivers could be portrayed as bulls, but whether they could be portrayed as man-headed bulls.

There are other strong arguments too that contradict the Prince's theory. The names of eight rivers occur on Sicilian coins, Akragas on the coins of Agrigentum, Amenanos on those of Catana, Arethusa on those of Syracuse, Assinos on those of Naxus, Chrysas on those of Assorus, Gelas on those of Gela, Hipparis on those of Camarina, and Hypsas on those of Selinus, in every case written alongside a male or female bust representing the river. But if the man-headed bulls too represented Sicilian rivers, why were the names of the rivers not added to these types too, as in those eight other cases? I will immediately end all opposition to my noble adversary if he can show me just one example of the man-headed bull type labeled with the name of a river, provided, however, that that name is unambiguous. For the examples the Prince cites, ΓΕΛΑΣ and ΣΕΛΙΝΟΕΣ, cannot pass the test, since these are the names not only of rivers but of the cities located on the rivers, to which the names doubtless actually apply. If I ever see the man-headed bull type labeled not with these ambiguous names, but with a name such as Amenanos, Hypsas, or Hipparis that can apply only to a river, I will become an immediate convert to the theory of the learned Prince.

The Prince's theory leads to a number of other improbable consequences. It is clear from their coins that the people of Agyrium, Catana, Gela, and Selinus depicted their rivers in human form. Yet the coins of these cities also used the type of the man-headed bull. So if that type too represented the local river in each case, it follows that these cities sometimes depicted their rivers as humans and sometimes as man-headed bulls. Moreover on Plate XXXIII of his excellent *Sicilia numismatica* the Prince himself illustrates several coins combining the obverse ΓΕΛΑΣ, youthful horned head, with a reverse showing the man-headed bull. A similar combination of types also occurs on the coins of Agyrium. The Prince himself does not doubt that the youthful head on the obverse depicts the river Gelas, yet on his theory the reverse type too depicts the same river. So one and the same coin depicts the same river in two such different guises? The reader may decide for himself whether that seems probable. Finally if the man-headed bull represented a river, why do the coins of Neapolis almost always show a Victory flying above the bull and crowning it? Victory should only crown winners in a contest of some sort, so the sculptor Myron was right to show a Victory crowning his heifer, because it was in the guise of a heifer that Jupiter won the prize of adultery by carrying off Europa, as Tatianus[39] explains. But what victory had the Sebathos won? It seems unlikely that the Sebathos might have overflowed on behalf of Neapolis during a war, as the Xanthos once overflowed and chased away Achilles on behalf of Troy! I do not deny that the image of a river could be crowned, but it bothers me that a Victory should carry out that task. According to the learned Ignarra the added Victory was intended to indicate that the Campanian rivers surpassed all others in the fertility of their soil.[40]

We now proceed to the Prince's final argument, which he regards as his most powerful: the case of Achelous, who was definitely a river, and who was depicted on the coins of Acarnania and the neighboring district in the same manner, with a human head and the body of a bull. I do not believe that the Prince intends to argue that since that type represented a river on the coins of the Acarnanians,

[37] de Virt. et vit. L. XII sub fin.

[38] in Verr. L. IV. c. 33.

[39] Orat. c. 54.

[40] de Pal. Neap. p. 215.

therefore whenever the same type appeared on the coins of other cities it must also represent a river. Accepting that logic we could also argue as follows: the Egyptians used the type of an eagle to represent the Nile, therefore the same eagle on the coins of Rome and Antioch must indicate the Tiber and the Orontes respectively. The club and the lionskin are attributes of Hercules and the winged cap is an attribute of Mercury, so whenever you see a bust with those attributes, it must be Hercules in the one case and Mercury in the other, never Theseus or Perseus. Since in some depictions of the Rape of Europa, as I will show in the following section, the bull that is Jupiter was given a human head like Achelous on the coins, one could boldly declare that Europa must have been carried off by a river! The Prince himself would certainly not want to draw that conclusion. But upon consideration we will be forced to concede that one and the same image could sometimes designate quite different things. And it is not hard to understand why Achelous was depicted as a man-headed bull. Achelous played an important role in mythology, and since his rival Hercules was said to have broken off a bull's horn from Achelous' head, it made sense to depict Achelous as a bull. But since Achelous also associated and conversed with humans, even soliciting the hand of Deianira in marriage, his head at least had to be made human. He would have made a sorry suitor if he had had to moo out his love to the royal maiden, or if, like Io, he had had to inscribe his entreaties in the dirt with his hoof, because he lacked a human voice! Since these same considerations did not apply to other rivers, it is not surprising that while Achelous was depicted as a man-headed bull, they were represented in other ways. For the same reason Lysippe, the mother of Teuthrans, dedicated to Diana a gold statue of a boar with a human face, so that it would be understood that the boar depicted was the sacred boar of Diana that, upon being chased down by Teuthrans in a hunt, had entreated him in a human voice not to take its life.[41]

Section II

The man-headed bull types on the coins of Campania and Sicily probably represent Bacchus

The Prince cites ancient authors to prove that rivers could be depicted as bulls; but the ancient authors also demonstrate that Bacchus could take the form of a bull. Greek authors call Bacchus 'tauromorfoς/bull-shaped', 'ταυροχεφαλος/bull-headed', 'ταυρωποϛ/bull-faced', and 'ταυροχερως/bull-horned'; see the numerous texts cited by Gyraldus[42] and Spanheim.[43] Lycophron[44] calls Bacchus a bull; and on a Boeotian coin published by Pellerin, a bull's horn is added to what is clearly the bearded head of Bacchus.[45] But the best testimony comes from two passages in Plutarch, which I shall accordingly cite in full. In the first passage, Plutarch asks, 'δια τι τον Διονυσον αἱ των Ηλειων γυναιχες ὑμνουσαι παραχαλουσι βοεω ποδι παραγινεσζαι προσ αὐτασ; ἐχει δ οὑτως ὁ ὑμνος: 'Ελζειν ἡρω Διονυσε ἁλιον ἐς ναον ἁγνον συν Χαριτεσσιν ἐς ναον τῳ βοεῳ ποδι ζυων, εἰτα δις ἐπᾳδουσιν: Αξιε Ταυρε ποτερον ὁτι χαι βουγενη προσαγορευουσιν χαιταυρον ἐνιοι τον ζεον; χ. τ. λ.; Why do the women of Elis urge Bacchus in a hymn to approach them 'with the foot of a bull'? The words of the hymn are as follows[46]: 'Come, hero Bacchus, to the holy temple by the sea, hurrying with the foot of a bull to the temple with the Graces.' And then they twice cry out, 'Worthy bull!' Is it because some people call Bacchus 'born of cattle' and a 'bull', etc.?' And similarly in the second passage[47]: 'διο χαι ταυρομορφον Διονυσον ποιουσιν ἀγαλματα πολλοιτων Ελληνων αἱ δε Ηλειων γυναιχες χαι παραχαλουσιν εὑχομεναι, ποδι βοειῳ τον ζεον ἐλζειν προς αὑτασ'; For that reason many Greeks depict Bacchus as a bull; while the women of Elis evoke the god with the prayer that he should come to them with the foot of a bull.' This evidence is highly relevant to our present inquiry, since it confirms not only that Bacchus was designated as a bull ('ἀξιε ταυρε/Worthy bull'), but also, lest anyone should claim that that designation just depended on the fact that he was depicted with horns on his head, that he had the body of a bull ('ποδι βοειῳ/with the foot of a bull'). And indeed a coin of Gela, first published by Burmannus[48] and then included by the Prince in two of his works,[49] seems to illustrate Plutarch's account wonderfully, for I think it shows a woman like the ones mentioned by Plutarch, summoning Bacchus who approaches her 'with the foot of a bull', and offering him a wreath. This coin will make a deeper impression if the reader can see it with his own eyes, so I have appended an illustration of it on Pl. III, 1.

There is satisfactory evidence, then, that Bacchus could be represented as a bull. But why was the bull given a human head? Doubtless for the same reason that the bull who is Jupiter shown in the act of carrying off Europa was depicted with a human head on two ancient gems, one in the Florence cabinet,[50] the other published by Gravellius,[51] both of which I also illustrate on Pl. III, 2- 3. The man-headed bull on these gems is so similar in every detail to those on the Campanian and Sicilian coins that you would not be able to tell them apart, and might even be tempted to think, as Count Caylus[52] once cautiously suggested, that since the gems

[41] Plut. de'flum. in Caieo.
[42] Synt. p. 280.
[43] T. I. p. 392.
[44] in Alex. v. 209.
[45] Rec. I. tab. XXIV. n. 8.
[46] Quaest. Graec. p. 299.
[47] de Is. et Osir. p. 364. E.
[48] D'Orville Sicula tab. X. n. [?]
[49] Aggiunt. tab. III. n. 23. et Sicil. numism. tab. XXXII. n. 1.
[50] Tom. I. tab. 57. n. 2.
[51] Rec. des pier. grav. T. II. n. 45.
[52] Rec, d'Ant. T. IV. p. 164.

definitely represent Jupiter, the coins must represent Jupiter too, were it not for the consideration that so many illustrious cities would probably not all have based their cult of the highest god on such a disreputable episode of his myth, his violation of a maiden, when so many other respectable aspects of his divinity might have been chosen instead. It would appear, then, that in both of these cases the purpose of adding a human head, which is the principle part of the body in which intellect and wisdom reside, was to make it clear that there was a god within the animal in question, which might otherwise have been considered to be just an ordinary bull. In the same way the ancients did not depict Agathodaimon as a simple serpent, but added a human head to the serpent's body, a convention that was later imitated by Alexander the False Prophet in order to convince his astonished onlookers that his serpent was divine, as Lucan relates and as I shall explain below in connection with the coins of Abonuteichus in Paphlagonia. I think it was for the same reason that Aeschylus described the heifer Io as having mixed parts, when he says that people were disturbed by her extraordinary appearance[53]: 'Βοτον ἐσορωντες δυσχερες μιξομβροτον, Ταν μεν βοος, Ταν δ αὐ γυναιχοσ τερας δ ἐζαμβουν; Seeing an unruly heifer that was partly human, one part bovine, one part a woman; they were astonished at the prodigy.'

Another coin too, in the Imperial collection in Vienna, illustrated on pl. III, 4, strongly supports my argument. It is a coin of Selinuntum in Sicily. Havercamp and the Prince called the seated woman on the obverse Salus, because of the serpent that she grasps with her right hand. But a more convincing explanation of this coin type can be derived from the ancient fable recounting that Jupiter, assuming the form of a bull, ravished Ceres, who then gave birth to Proserpina, also called Pherephatta, and that when Proserpina grew up Jupiter desired her too, though she was his daughter, and assumed the form of a serpent to ravish her, whence she bore him a son in the form of a bull, a course of events that was commemorated in a Greek hexameter, 'Ταυροσ δραχοντοσ, χαι δραχων ταυρου πατηρ'; As a bull he was father of a serpent, and as a serpent he was father of a bull.' This unedifying tale is recounted by Clemens of Alexandria,[54] Eusebius,[55] Arnobius,[56] Nonnus of Panopolis,[57] and Athenagoras,[58] the last of whom also states that the bull that Proserpina bore to Jupiter was Bacchus. In the light of this story it seems clear that the coin in question must show Jupiter as a serpent seducing Proserpina on the obverse, and on the reverse Bacchus as a bull who was the offspring of that seduction, and who thus joins his parents on the same coin. The fact that the coin comes from Silicly, where Ceres and Proserpina were frequently depicted on monuments of every sort, supports this interpretation. And I think this is not the only coin type that refers to this absurd fable. There are Roman quadrantes in the Imperial collection and elsewhere whose reverse type shows a running bull, with a serpent slithering below and the legend ROMA in the exergue, a type that it will be difficult to explain in any other way than as a reference to the hexameter that I quoted above.

That Bacchus was highly honored in Campania because of the abundance and excellence of the wine that was produced there on the slopes of Mount Gaurus is not only inherently probable, but is attested by Sophocles, who addresses Bacchus as[59] 'χλυταν ὁς ἀμφεπεις Ιταλιαν; ψου ωηο ωατχη οϖερ ρενοωνεδ Ιταλψ', το ωηιχη τηε ανχιεντ σχηολιαστ χομμεντσ, 'δια το πολυαμπελον τησ χωρασ; because of the abundant production of wine in that region'. Therefore since the man-headed bull clearly represents a divinity, probably Bacchus as I have said, it is not at all strange that Victory can offer him a crown, either with reference to Bacchus' old victories over the Titans and in India or because the Campanian cities had attributed to Bacchus their own victories over their enemies. This theory also readily explains the archaic tetradrachms of Catana that show a man-headed bull on one side and Victory advancing and holding out one or two untied diadems on the other side: the two types together show Victory offering a diadem to Bacchus, who was reputed to be the inventor of the diadem, as I have demonstrated elsewhere with full citation of the relevant ancient authors.[60]

From what I have written so far it should be obvious that I will not oppose those who, as stated above, interpret the man-headed bull as representing the god Hebo, an idea advanced by Matthaeus Aegyptius and followed by several other Neapolitan scholars. For according to Macrobius, who is the only ancient author to mention this god, Hebo was merely another name for Bacchus, a god whom Sophocles[61] rightly calls 'polynominal', because he had so many different names. And just as the man-headed bull appeared on the coins of a number of Campanian cities, so we find that Hebo too was worshipped at several Campanian cities, for though Macrobius mentions only Neapolis, an inscription published by Matthaeus Aegyptius[62] adds Callatia, another Campanian city, since it is a dedication reading 'ΗΒΩΝΙ. ΕΠΙΦΑΝΕΣΤΑΤΩΙ. ΘΕΩΙ. ΤΑΓΜΑ. ΚΑΙ. ΛΕΩΣ. ΚΑΛΑΤΙΝΟΣ; To Hebo , the most manifest god, the soldiers and people of Callatia'. The only difficulty for this theory might be that according to Macrobius Hebo was depicted in the form of a bearded old man, not of a bull.

[53] Supplie. v. 576.
[54] Protrept. p. 14. edit. Oxon.
[55] Praepar. Ev.
[56] advers. gent. L. V.
[57] Dionys. L. V. sub fin. et I., VI. v. 157.
[58] Legat. p. 71. edit. Oxon.
[59] Antigone v. 1130.
[60] Num. vet. p. 22.
[61] l. c.
[62] S.C. de Bacch. p. 33.

I also have no strong objections to the eminent authors who, as I stated above, have interpreted the man-headed bull type as a symbol of agriculture. This explanation would not exclude Bacchus, who according to Plutarch was believed by many to be the inventor of plowing and sowing.[63] According to Diodorus Bacchus was believed to have been the first to submit bulls to the yoke and to undertake sowing, whence, Diodorus adds, Bacchus' head is shown with horns.[64] According to Arrian[65] Liber was held to have been the first to fasten bulls to a plow and to convert some Indian nomads into farmers. Might the man-headed bull type even indicate the harmony between Ceres and Bacchus, the two principle deities of agriculture, since grain and wine are agriculture's two chief products? The horned male head could indicate Bacchus, who we know was depicted with horns, while the bull was Ceres' favorite animal, because it plowed the fields, and thus could stand for Ceres herself. For the same reason Vergil linked Bacchus and Ceres in his poem on agriculture[66]: 'O you brightest lights of the universe that lead the passing year through the skies, Liber and kindly Ceres'[67] (translation by A.S. Kline, online, ©2002). Similarly Pindar calls Bacchus 'χαλυοχροτουπαρεδρον Δαματέρος; χομπανιον οφ Χερεσ, ωηο ισ ωορσηιππεδ ωιτη χλαση οφ βρονζε', ον ωηιχη τηε σχηολιαστ χομμεντσ; 'παρεδρον Δημητροσ εἰπεν τον Διονυσον, ἐπειδη τη ξηρφ τροφῃ, ἡ ἀναχειται τῃ Δημητρι, παρεπεται ἡ του οἰνου χρησις; He calls Bacchus the companion of Ceres because the consumption of dry food, which Ceres provides, is accompanied by the drinking of wine.' Florus[68] mentions Bacchus and Ceres together with particular reference to Campania: 'The district of Campania is the fairest of all regions not only in Italy but in the whole world. Nothing can be gentler than its climate: indeed it has spring and its flowers twice a year. Nowhere is the soil more fertile; for which reason it is said to have been an object of contention between Liber and Ceres' (Loeb translation by E. S. Forster, online at Bill Thayer's Lacus Curtius website). In the same way the dual nature of the sphinx had a definite allegorical meaning, for as Synesius[69] relates the Egyptians 'placed an image of the sphinx in the vestibules of their temples, as an abstruse symbol of the joining of two sorts of virtues, the animal parts of the creature designating strength, but its human parts designating intelligence.'

So I would not argue against anyone who wanted to propose a similar allegorical interpretation (ζηρια συνζετα χαι ἀλλοχοτα) of the type of the man-headed bull. For as I have said, my primary purpose in this disputation has just been to refute the idea that the ancients used this type to represent rivers.

[63] Quaest. Graec. p. 299.
[64] L. IV. c. 4.
[65] Hist. Ind. c. 7.
[66] Georg. I. 5.
[67] Isth,. Z. v. 3.
[68] L. I. c. 16.
[69] de Regno p. 7. et de Provid. p. 101.

Appendix 2
'The Oxus River God: a man-faced Indian humped bull'

Dr. Lloyd W. H. Taylor

This remarkable coin type is known from a single example, first documented by Houghton and Lorber in *Seleucid Coins*.[70] Apparently it was acquired from a source in Pakistan shortly before the publication of *Seleucid Coins*. For the reasons detailed below the coin is attributed to the Baktrian Mint at Ai Khanoum, during the co-regency of Seleukos I Nikator and his son Antiochos I Soter in the period 292-281 BC. The co-regency dating is unequivocally indicated by the legend in the names of both kings.

Within the man-faced bull typology the coin is notable for three reasons. Firstly, it is the sole example of the man faced bull iconography bearing the body of the Indian humped bull, a reflection of its association with one of the easternmost river systems known to the Greeks, the mighty Oxus River (the present day Amu Darya). Secondly, despite its essentially Greek nature, the coin bears a mint control in the left field that appears to be in local Indian script, possibly a local variation of the Brahmi letter *pa*. This is the earliest known occurrence of an Indian script mint control accompanied by what appears to be a Greek control, a circled Δ, on an essentially Greek coin. A final notable point is that not only is this the easternmost example of the man-faced bull typology on a Greek coin, it is the only known example on a Seleukid coin. To the west, the closest occurrence of the man-faced bull typology is on some rare civic issues in Asia Minor, some 3,200 kilometres distant from Ai Khanoum.

This unique coin (*SC* 283A) appears to be amongst the first and the largest denomination in a series of co-regency bronze issues from Ai Khanoum. The others (*SC* 284-SC 288) all carry a right charging Indian humped bull, but for the smallest denomination (*SC* 288), which bears a standing humped bull. No man-faced bull is present on the smaller denominations, although within the iconographic association it might be that the Indian humped bull is to be considered yet another portrayal of the Oxus river god.

Associated with this coin is an anepigraphic issue (*SC* 284) of the same large denomination, bearing a charging Indian humped bull. This associated anepigraphic coin suggests that the coinage was inaugurated in the earliest period of the co-regency, perhaps as early as 290 BC, when there was some uncertainty as to the appropriate legend to accompany the co-regency, at the time a novel experiment for a Macedonian ruler. Antiochos I took up his role as viceroy in the east and was resident in Ai Khanoum from around 293/2 BC.[71] Amongst his works was the development of Ai Khanoum into a Seleukid administrative centre, plus the establishment of an associated mint.

A remarkable aspect of this coin series is that it marked the first appearance of the Indian humped bull in Greek numismatic iconography. The Ai Khanoum charging Indian bull series of bronze coins may have provided the inspiration for the transfer of the Indian humped bull typology to the west. The Indian humped bull appears on the reverse of some of the bronze coinage of Seleukos I that was a standard through Seleukos' realm from the late 280's i.e. post-dating the inauguration of the Ai Khanoum co-regency issues. On this bronze coinage of Seleukos I, the humped bull typology is often co-mingled with the European bull typology that existed in the Greek world before knowledge of the existence of the humped bull of the Indus Valley returned with the army of Alexander III the Great.

Newell[72] attributed the charging bull motif on the coinage of Seleukos I Nikator to propaganda making by the latter. This interpretation was based on Appian's history whereby Seleukos personally restrained a sacrificial bull that had broken free before Alexander III the Great. This event purportedly occurred while Alexander was in the east. With little doubt it was part of the personal myth making of Seleukos I Nikator, but the typology of the exotic Indian humped bull added to the myth and the heroic status of Seleukos, who through his own eastern anabasis (307-303 BC) ranked with Dionysos and Alexander in the mythology of the day, another validation of his right to kingship. In this coin and the related co-regency issues from Ai Khanoum we appear to have the first numismatic evidence of the Seleukos' bull myth making and propaganda that surrounded the king.

It is noteworthy that the co-incident appearance of the Indian humped bull and the Brahmi mint control on

[70] A. Houghton and C. Lorber, *Seleucid Coins* (New York, ANS, 2002). EDITOR'S NOTE: There are actually three known examples that were discovered by Dr. Taylor after this essay was written. See Chapter 2, pg. 29, note 198.

[71] J. D. Grainger, *Seleukos Nikator Constructing a Hellenistic Kingdom* (Abingdon: Routledge, 1990).

[72] E. T. Newell, *The Coinage of the Eastern Seleucid Mints From Seleucus I to Antiochus III* (New York: ANS, 1938).

this coin is one of the earliest numismatic examples of Graeco-Bactrian cultural fusion, a process that began with Antiochos I, who himself was the product of a marriage between Seleukos, a Macedonian officer in the army of Alexander III the Great and Apama, the daughter of Spitamenes, the greatest Baktrian warrior to confront Alexander the Great. The representation of the Greek man-faced bull river god amongst the co-regency issues appears to be another aspect of this process of cultural fusion, overlaying as it does Greek religious belief and iconography on local history as detailed below.

Some influential scholars remain steadfast in the opinion that this and associated coins originated from the Baktrian mint at Baktra/Balkh. Yet the evidence for an Ai Khanoum origin is persuasive, as detailed by Kritt in *Seleucid Coins of Bactria.*[73] The circled delta mint control and the thick, beveled edge fabric of this coin place it as a product of the mint at Ai Khanoum. The find locations of associated bronze issues, dominated as they are by Ai Khanoum and the immediately adjacent plain, further substantiate this attribution, as does the analysis of the diffusion of Seleukid bronze issues detailed by Kritt in *Dynastic Transitions in the Coinage of Bactria.*[74]

Additional support for the Ai Khanoum origin of this coin is to be found in this coin's iconography of a river god, or man-faced bull, bearing the body of an Indian humped bull. Ai Khanoum sits directly at the confluence of the Amu Darya (the ancient Oxus) and Kokcha Rivers (Figures 1 & 2). Respectively these rivers form the immediate western and southern boundaries of the ancient city. Baktra/Balkh on the other hand sits about 75 km to the south of the Oxus (Amu Darya), located on a drainage outwash fan delta adjacent to the northern foothills of the Hindu Kush, on the edge of the desert which separates it from the Oxus. The outwash fan is fed by the seasonal melt water of Balkh River, the course of which is located 12 km west of the location of ancient Bactra/Balkh. This seasonal river feeds irrigation canals in the area around Baktra/Balkh before it disappears into the desert sands that loop around the outwash fan, 25 km north of the ancient city. In contrast, Ai Khanoum sits at the confluence of two major permanent rivers that are both subject to major flood each spring, due to melt water influx from the eastern Himalayas (Oxus River/Amu Darya) and the Hindu Kush (Kokcha River) respectively.

Why should the charging man-faced Indian humped bull, or Oxus River God, be placed on an inaugural issue of bronze co-regency coinage issued by Antiochos I from his newly established mint at Ai Khanoum? The most plausible answer is to be found in the setting of the ancient city.

The city is adjacent to an extensive fertile plain that was a site of irrigation based agriculture from the Bronze Age[75]. One and a half kilometres to the north of Ai Khanoum is the site of the circular Achaemenid citadel and fortress of ancient Kohna Qala[76] (Figure 1 & 3) that was partially destroyed by a massive Oxus River flood some time in the centuries preceding Greek occupation of the area. The remaining site of ancient Kohna Qala has a double encircling rampart to the south and east with a high citadel on its NW quadrant. The northern most portions of the ancient citadel and fortified city appear to have been washed away by the Oxus in pre-history, leaving a prominent erosional escarpment transecting the citadel and outlying ramparts, below and to the north of which now extend an abandoned river channel. The remains and physical relationship of this ancient city to the later foundation of Ai Khanoum and the Oxus river course are clearly visible on satellite imagery (Figures 1-3).

From Kohna Qala, south to Ai Kahnoum over a distance of 3.5 km, the course of the Oxus River is at its most tightly constricted, the river flowing along a geological fault line, bounded by a mountains range on the right bank and the elevated plain of Ai Khanoum on the left bank. The abrupt constriction of the Oxus River valley at Kohna Qala makes this location amongst the most exposed to the effects of elevated river levels in times of extreme flood and the northern extent of ancient Kohna Qala was eroded by the changing course of the Oxus. A catastrophic ancient re-alignment of the river is evident in the geometries of the riverbank, flood plain and archaeological remains at this point. Unfortunately our knowledge of this site remains largely based on the interpretation satellite imagery. The French Archaeological Mission in Afghanistan surveyed, but did not excavate the ancient site at Kohna Qala prior to the Soviet invasion in 1979, so that its origins, history and significance remain underappreciated, if not almost completely unknown.

The river flood which partially destroyed ancient Kohna Qala was possibly associated with a major glacial melt dam burst at the upstream river source that caused the Oxus to excavate a new broader channel through the northern portion of the citadel as the river channel expanded toward the east. Later reduced flow and sedimentation saw the river channel migrate back to the west, leaving exposed an extensive riverine plain extending to the north east of Kohna Qala. The remains of ancient Kohna Qala were occupied in Achaemenid times. This small fortress and with its strategic location

[73] B. Kritt, *Seleucid Coins of Bactria* (Lancaster, PA: CNG,1996).
[74] B. Kritt, *Dynastic Transitions in the Coinage of Bactria: Antiochos-Diodotos-Euthydemos* (Lancaster: CNG, 2001).

[75] R. Mairs, *The Founder's Shrine and the Foundation of Ai Khanoum* in *Foundation Myths in Ancient Societies Dialogue and Discourses*, edited by N Mac Sweeney (Philadelphia: University of Pennsylvania Press, 2014).
[76] L. Martineze-Seve, 'The Spatial Organization of Ai Khanoum, a Greek City in Afghanistan,' in *AJA* 118 (2014), 267-283.

may have provided the inspiration for the foundation of the much larger Ai Khanoum, initially as a garrison site by Alexander the Great, then to be greatly expanded to become the Seleukid satrapal capital of Baktria by Antiochos I between 292-281 in his role as viceroy of the east.

In the geographical setting of Ai Khanoum there is more than ample archaeological and historical context for the presence of a sometimes angry and enraged Oxus river god. Thus the portrayal on this coin of a vigorously charging Indian humped man-faced bull, or river god. It is possible that at the time of the Greeks in Baktria the oral tradition of the region included reference to the partial destruction of ancient Kohna Qala by the Oxus. Even if not the case, the physical evidence remained for the Greeks to see, less than a couple of kilometres from the Ai Khanoum city gate, across the fertile irrigated fields of the elevated plain adjacent to the mighty Oxus. Any wonder then that when Antiochos I arrived to take up his role as viceroy in the east he paid attention to the mood of the river god and chose to pay homage to that god on his inaugural coinage in the city?.[77]

[77] Since the above was written Brian Kitt's book *New Discoveries in Bactrian Numismatics*(Lancaster, PA: CNG) was published in June 2015. His work, particularly Chapters 6 and 7 shed additional insights on this enigmatic coin, its iconography, epigraphy and numismatic significance. The inquiring reader is referred to this publication for a more expansive numismatic analysis.

Figure 1: The ancient Graeco-Baktrian city of Ai Khanoum at the confluence of the Amu Darya (Oxus) and Kokcha Rivers, with the remains of the semi-circular citadel and fortification of ancient Kohna Qala 1.5 kilometres to the north of the Ai Khanoum. The fertile irrigated plain, a site of agriculture from the Bronze Age, extends from the Oxus between and to the east of the two cities. In this image the Oxus (Amu Darya) River flows from top centre of the image, while the Kokcha River flows from the lower left of centre, to converge with the Oxus. Immediately to the left (east) of the confluence of the two rivers is Ai Khanoum, outlined by the uncultivated triangular area. Kohna Qala is outlined by the remnant semi-circular walls immediately to the left of the Oxus, just above the middle of the image.

Figure 2: Ai Khanoum bounded by the Oxus (Amu Darya) to the west and the Kokcha River to the south. Part of the irrigated fertile plain that supported the city abuts the city walls and the elevated acropolis that jointly define the northern and eastern limits of the ancient city.

FIGURE 3: KOHNA QALA DEFINED BY TWIN SEMI-CIRCULAR RAMPARTS WITH THE NORTHERNMOST PORTION OF THE CITADEL TRUNCATED BY THE EROSIONAL VALLEY OF THE OXUS.

Bibliography

Abramzon, Mikhail G., and Nina A. Frolova. 2007. 'Le trésor de Myrmekion de statères cyzicènes.' *Revue Numismatique*, 6e série, tome 163. Paris: Blois. 15-44.

Achaeus of Eretria, and August Nauck. 1889. 'Athens.' *Tragicorum Graecorum Fragmenta*. Lipsiae: Teubner.

Adamo, Ornella, and Domenica Gullì. 2014. 'Cracks, crevices and caves in the Serraferlicchio hill.' *From Cave to Dolmen: ritual and symbolic aspects in the prehistory between Sciacca, Sicily and the central Mediterranean*; edited by Domenica Gullì. Oxford: Archaeopress. 69-72.

Aegyptius, Matthaeus. 1729. *Senatusconsulti de Bacchanalibus; sive, aeneae vetustae tabulae Musei Caesarei Vindobonensis explicatio*. Neapoli: apud F. Muscam.

Aeschylus, and Herbert Weir Smyth. 1926. *Prometheus Bound*. Cambridge: Harvard University Press.

Agostiniani, Luciano. 1987. 'Epigrafia e linguistica anelleniche in Sicilia: bilancio di un quadriennio.' *Atti del VI Congresso Internazionale di studi sulla Sicilia antica. Kokalos*, Vol. XXX-XXXI (1984-1985), Tomo I. Roma: Bretschneider. 193-220.

Agustínus, Antonio. 1592. *Discorsi del S. Don Antonio Agostini sopra le medaglie et altre anticaglie divisi in XI dialoghi. Tradotti dalla lingua Spagnuola nell' Italiana, con l'aggiunta di molti ritratti di belle, e rare medaglie*. Roma: Presso Ascanio et Girolamo Donangeli.

Aharoni, Yohanan, Joseph Naveh, and Anson F. Rainey. 1981. *Arad Inscriptions*. Jerusalem: Israel Exploration Society.

Akkermans, Peter M., and Glenn M. Schwartz. 2003. *The Archaeology of Syria: from Complex Hunter-Gatherers to Early Urban Societies (c. 16,000-300 BC)*. Cambridge: University Press.

Aksu, Ali E., Richard N. Hiscott, Peta J. Mundie, Andre Rochon, Michael A. Kaminski, Teofilo Abrajano, and Dogan Yasar. 2002. 'Persistent Holocene outflow from the Black Sea to the Eastern Mediterranean contradicts Noah's flood hypothesis.' *GSA Today*, 12 (5). Boulder, CO: Geological Society of America. 4-10.

Alba, Elisabetta. 2000. 'L'Ipogeo della Nurra.' *L'ipogeismo nel Mediterraneo: origini, sviluppo, quadri culturali: atti del Congresso internazionale, 23- 28 maggio 1994, Sassari-Oristano*. Università degli studi di Sassari, Facoltà di Lettere e filosofia, Istituto di Antichità, Arte e Discipline Etnodemologiche e Dipartimento di Scienze Umanistiche e dell'Antichità. Vol. II. Sassari: Stampacolor. 761-778.

Albanese Procelli, Rosa Maria 2003. *Sicani, Siculi, Elimi: forme di identità, modi di contatto e processi di trasformazione*. Milano: Longanesi.

Albenda, Pauline. 1983. *A Mediterranean Seascape from Khorsabad*. Malibu: Undena Publications.

Alberti, Gianmarco. Forthcoming. 'Brocche Base Ring II da contesti del Bronzo Medio in Sicilia: produzione levantina, cipriota, o locale? Alcune considerazioni.'

Albright, William Foxwell. 1969. 'Palestinian Inscriptions.' *Ancient Near Eastern Texts Relating to the Old Testament*; edited by J.B. Pritchard. 3rd ed. Princeton: University Press. 320-322

Alcaeus, of Mytilene, and Theodorus Fredericus Strange. 1810. *Alcaei Poetae Lyrici Fragmenta*. Halae: Offic. Libraria Io. Chr. Hendelii.

Alfieri Tonini, Teresa. 2012. 'Riflessi del sincretismo religioso della Sicilia orientale nelle testimonianze scritte.' *Convivenze etniche, scontri e contatti di culture in Sicilia e Magna Grecia. Aristonothos. Scritti per il Mediterraneo antico*. Vol. 7. Trento: Tangram. 195-207.

Alföldi, Andreas. 1952. 'Zu den römischen Reiterscheiben.' *Germania*, 30. Berlin: C. Plahn. 187-190.

Alteri, Giancarlo. 2000. *Le antiche monete di Neapolis*. Napoli: Banco di Napoli.

Alvarez Burgos, Fernando. 1982. *Catálogo general de la moneda hispánica: desde sus orígenes hasta el sig V*. Madrid: J. Vico.

Amandry, Pierre. 1994. 'Astragalo.' *Enciclopedia dell'Arte Antica*. Secondo Supplemento 1971-1994. Roma: Istituto della Enciclopedia Italiana. 492-494.

Amata, Sandro. 2002. 'Cozzo Scavo. I rinvenimenti numismatici dalle campagne di scavo 1993-1996.' *Atti del IX Congresso Internazionale sulla Sicilia antica. Kokalos* Vol. XLIII-XLIV (1997-1998) Tomo II, 1. Roma: Bretschneider. 41-54.

Ambrosini, Laura. 2002. *Thymiateria etruschi in bronzo: di età tardo classica, alto e medio ellenistica*. Roma: Bretschneider.

------, and Laura Maria Michetti. 2013. 'L'ultima frequentazione del santuario meridionale: Testimonianze dai contesti.' *Riflessioni su Pyrgi. Scavi e Ricerche Nelle Aree Del Santuario*; edited by Maria Paola Baglione and Maria Donatella Gentili. Roma: Bretschneider. 123-166.

Amiet, Pierre. 1961. *La glyptique mésopotamienne archaïque*. Paris: Éditions du Centre national de la recherche scientifique.

Anakreon, and Eduard Mörike. 1913. *Anakreon*. Leipzig: Insel-Verlag.

André-Salvini, Béatrice. 2003. *Art of the First Cities : The Third Millenium B.C. from the Mediterranean to the Indus*. New York: The Metropolitan Museum of Art.

Annus, Amar. 2002. *The God Ninurta: in the Mythology and Royal Ideology of Ancient Mesopotamia*. Helsinki, Finland: Neo-Assyrian Text Corpus Project.

Antiphanes Comicus, and Theodor Kock. 1884. 'Fragmenta.' *Comicorum Atticorum Fragmenta*. Volume II. Lipsiae: Teubner.

Antona, Angela. 1994. 'Monumenti nuragici nel territorio di Olbia.' *Omaggio a Doro Levi*. Quaderni della Soprintendenza Archeologica di Sassari e Nuoro, Vol.19. Ozieri: Il Torchietto. 23-36.

Antonacci Sanpaolo, Elena, and Lorenzo Quilici. 1995. 'Tiati-Teanum Apulum-Civitate: Topografia Storica del territorio.' *Tiati-Teanum Apulum-Civitate ed il suo territorio. Atti del 15° Convegno Nazionale sulla Preistoria-Protostoria-Storia della Daunia;* edited by G. Pittaluga. San Severo: Bpd. 81-99.

Antonaccio, Carla M. 1999. 'Kupara, a Sikel Nymph?.' *Zeitschrift für Papyrologie und Epigraphik*. Volume 126. Bonn: Habelt. 177–185.

Antonetti, Claudia, Stefania De Vido, and Luciana Drago Troccoli. 2013. 'Lithoi, Semata, Anathemata. Connotare lo spazio Sacro: contesti esemplari tra Grecia ed Etruria.' *Epigrammata 2. Definire, descrivere, proteggere lo spazio. In ricordo di André Laronde. Atti del convegno di Roma, 26-27 Ottobre 2012;* edited by Alessandra Inglese. Tivoli: Tored. 1-37.

Antonini, Rosalba. 1989. 'Materiali per un'indagine preliminare sull'alfabeto osco. Documenti, problemi, prospettive concernenti la riforma.' *Quaderni dell'Istituto di Linguistica dell'Università di Urbino*. Vol. 6. Urbino. 33-91.

Anonymous. *A Classical Manual, Being a Mythological, Historical, and Geographical Commentary on Pope's Homer and Dryden's Aeneid of Virgil*. 1833. London: J. Murray.

Apte, Vaman Shivram. 2000. *The Student's Sanskrit-English Dictionary*. Delhi: Motilal Banarsidass.

Archilochus, and Theodor Bergk. 1853. 'Fragmenta.' *Poetae Lyrici Graeci*. Lipsiae: Teubner.

Arena, Emiliano. 2008. 'La fondazione di Tauromenion fra i Dionisi ed Andromaco.' *Sicilia Antiqua*, Vol.V. Pisa-Roma: Fabrizio Serra. 93-114.

Aristophones, William Martin Geldart, and Frederick William Hall. 1951. 'Fragmenta.' *Aristophanis Comoediae, Tomus II: Lysistratam, Thesmophoriazusas, Ranas, Ecclesiazusas, Plutum, Fragmenta, Indicem nominum cont.* Oxford: Clarendon.

Aristotle, and Hippocrates G. Apostle. 1979. *Aristotle's Metaphysics*. Grinnell, IA: The Peripatetic Press.

Arnold Biucchi, Carmen. 1981. 'Alaisos.' *Lexicon Iconographicum Mythologiae Classicae*, Vol. I. Zürich: Artemis Verlag. 478-9.

------. 1990. *The Randazzo Hoard 1980 and Sicilian Chronology in the Early Fifth Century B.C.* New York: American Numismatic Society.

Arslan, Ermanno. 2008. 'Spiriti delle acque.' *Anima dell'Acqua. Da Talete a Caravaggio da Segantini a Bill Viola, Catalogo della Mostra, Milano, Palazzo Reale*; edited by C.D. Fonseca and E. Fontanella. Roma: Bretschneider 100-106.

Aruz, Joan, and Ronald Wallenfels. 2003. *Art of the First Cities: the Third Millennium B.C. from the Mediterranean to the Indus*. New York: Metropolitan Museum of Art.

------, Kim Benzel, and Jean M. Evans. 2008. *Beyond Babylon: Art, Trade, and Diplomacy in the Second Millennium B.C.* New York: Metropolitan Museum of Art.

Ascalone, Enrico. 2005. *Mesopotamia*. Milano: Electa.

Aston, Emma. 2011. *Mixanthropoi. Animal-human hybrid deities in Greek religion*. Kernos, Suppl. 23, Liège: Centre International d'Étude de la Religion Grecque Antique.

Astone, Fabio. 2013. 'Poseidon e Poseidonia: le acque, il paesaggio, gli insediamenti, il culto, il nome della città.' *Annali Storici di Principato Citra*, a.XI, No.1. Acciaroli: Centro di Promozione Culturale per il Cilento. 34-61.

Åström, Paul 1969. 'Cocci ciprioti provenienti da Gela.' *Atti del II Congresso Internazionale di Studi sulla Sicilia antica. Kokalos*, Vol. XIV-XV (1968-1969). Palermo: Banco di Sicilia. 332-333.

Ataç, Mehmet-Ali. 2010. *The Mythology of Kingship in Neo-Assyrian Art*. Cambridge: University Press.

Atsma, Aaron J. 2014. 'Asclepius Cult.' *The Theoi Project*. Available at: www.theoi.com.

Attianese, Pasquale. 1996. 'Una nuova zecca brettia?.' *Panorama Numismatico*, No. 96. Serravalle: Nomisma. 11-16.

Avellino, Francesco Maria. 1826. 'Osservazioni sul toro dal volto umano, tipo di talune medaglie della Italia e della Sicilia.' *Opuscoli Diversi*, Tomo I. Napoli: Tramater. 81-153.

------. 1836. 'Secondo saggio di osservazioni numismatiche, Hyrium.' *Opuscoli Diversi*. Tomo III. Napoli : Tramater. 109-114.

Babbi, Andrea and Uwe Peltz. 2013. *La tomba del guerriero di Tarquinia, Das Kriegergrab von Tarquinia*. Römisch-Germanisches Zentralmuseum, Monographien, Vol. 109. Mainz: Schnell & Steiner.

Babelon, Ernest, and Jacques Jean Marie de Morgan. 1901. *Traité des monnaies grecques et romaines*. Paris: E. Leroux.

Bacci, Giovanni Maria. 1987. 'Scavi e ricerche ad Avola, Grammichele, Portopalo, Taormina.' *Atti del VI Congresso Internazionale di studi sulla Sicilia antica. Kokalos*, Vol. XXX-XXXI (1984-1985), Tomo II, 2. Roma: Bretschneider. 711-725.

Bacco, Ginetto. 2000. 'La necropoli ipogeica di Campumajore-Busachi (OR).' *L'ipogeismo nel Mediterraneo: origini, sviluppo, quadri culturali: atti del Congresso internazionale, 23- 28 maggio 1994, Sassari-Oristano*. Università degli studi di Sassari,

Facoltà di Lettere e filosofia, Istituto di Antichità, Arte e Discipline Etnodemologiche e Dipartimento di Scienze Umanistiche e dell'Antichità, Vol. II. Sassari: Stampacolor. 971-8.

Baglione, Maria Paola. 1991. 'Considerazioni sui santuari di Pyrgi e di Veio-Portonaccio.' *Anathema: regime delle offerte e vita dei santuari nel Mediterraneo antico. Atti del Convegno Internazionale.* Scienze dell'Antichità Vol. 3-4 (1989-90); edited by Gilda Bartoloni, G. Colonna and C. Grottarelli. Roma: La Sapienza 651-667.

Bailey, Douglass W. 2007. 'Holocene Changes in the Level of the Black Sea: Consequences at a Human Scale'. *The Black Sea Flood Question: Changes in Coastline, Climate, and Human Settlement,* edited by Valentina Yanko-Hombach, Allan S. Gilbert, Nicolae Panin, Pavel M. Dolukhanov. Springer. 515-36.

Bailo Modesti, Gianni, Annamaria Frezza, Aurora Lupia, and Marcella Mancusi. 2005. 'Le acque intorno agli dei: rituali e offerte votive nel santuario settentrionale di Pontecagnano.' *Offerte dal regno vegetale e dal regno animale nelle manifestazioni del sacro, Atti Incontro di Studio (Milano 2003),* Tarchna. Supplement 1; edited by M. Bonghi Jovino and F. Chiesa. Roma: Bretschneider. 37-64.

Baldelli, Gabriele. 1997. 'Deposito votivo da Cupra Marittima, località Sant'Andrea.' *Acque, grotte e Dei. 3000 anni di culti preromani in Romagna, Marche e Abruzzo. Imola, Chiostri di San Domenico, 5 aprile-13 luglio 1997*; edited by Marco Pacciarelli. Imola: Musei Civici. 161-171.

------, and Vincenzo D'Ercole. 2001. 'I luoghi di culto. Marche.' *Eroi e Regine. Piceni popolo d'Europa. Catalogo della Mostra. Roma – Galleria Nazionale d'Arte Antica, Palazzo Barberini 12/4/2001 – 1/7/ 2001.* Roma: De Luca. 86-88.

Banti, Luisa. 1966. 'Tolosa, Pittore di.' *Enciclopedia dell'Arte antica classica e orientale.* Volume VII. Roma: Istituto della Enciclopedia italiana.

Barbanera, Marcello. 2006. 'Altre presenze. 'Stranieri' nei luoghi di culto in Magna Grecia.' *Stranieri e non cittadini nei santuari greci. Atti del Convegno Internazionale*; edited by Alessandro Naso. Firenze: Le Monnier. 364-375.

Barnett, Richard D. 1977. 'The Amathus Shield-Boss Rediscovered and the Amathus Bowl Reconsidered.' *Report of the Department of Antiquities, Cyprus.* Nicosia: Government Print Office. 157-169

Barra Bagnasco, Marcella. 1999. 'Il culto delle acque in Magna Grecia dall'età arcaica alla romanizzazione. Documenti archeologici e fonti letterarie.' *Archeologia dell'acqua in Basilicata*; edited by Maria Luisa Nava. Lavello: Soprintendenza Archeologia della Basilicata. 25-52.

------. 2001. 'Il culto delle acque a Locri Epizefiri. Contesti e documenti.' *Zona Archeologica: Festschrift für H.P. Isler zum 60. Geburtstag*; edited by Sabrina Buzzi and Hans Peter Isler. Bonn: Habelt. 27-40.

Bartoloni, Gilda. 1997. 'Bronzetti nuragici importati nell'Italia peninsulare.' *Dal Bronzo al Ferro. Il II millennio a.C. nella Toscana centro-occidentale, Catalogo della mostra (Livorno, 1997)*; edited by A. Zanini. Pisa: Pacini. 27-31.

------. 2010. 'Le città etrusche e gli altri: l'esempio di Veio.' *Meetings between cultures in the ancient Mediterranean, 17th International Congress of Classical Archaeology (Rome, 22-26 September 2008).* Bollettino di Archeologia Online, I, 2010, Volume speciale F/F7/1. Roma: Direzione Generale per le Antichità. 1-4.

Baṣmah'jī (Basmachi), Faraj. 1975. *Treasures of the Iraq Museum.* Baghdad: Al-Jumhuriya Press.

Basoli, Paola, and Alba Foschi Nieddu. 1988. 'La Tomba delle Protomi Taurine in località Montalé (Sassari).' *Rivista di Studi Pompeiani,* Vol. XL. Roma: Bretschneider. 317-325.

Bayerischen Numismatischen Gesellschaft. 1882. *Jahrbuch für Numismatik und Geldgeschichte.* München: Im Eigenverlag der Bayerischen Numismatischen Gesellschaft.

Bates, William N. 1911. 'Archaeological Discussions.' *American Journal of Archaeology,* Vol. 15, No. 4. New York: Macmillan. 533-593.

Bayet, Jean. 1923. 'Hercule funéraire.' *Mélanges de l'École française de Rome,* Vol. XL. Paris: De Boccard. 19-102.

Beal, Rebecca. 2000. 'Minotaur.' *The Dante Encyclopedia*; edited by R. Lansing. New York: Garland. 615-616.

Beaulieu, Marie-Claire Anne. 2008. *The Sea as a Two-Way Passage between Life and Death in Greek Mythology.* Doctoral Dissertation. Austin: The University of Texas.

Beazley, John D. 1956. *Attic Black-Figure Vase-Painters.* Oxford: Clarendon.

Beger, Lorenz. 1696. *Thesaurus Brandenburgicus Selectus : sive gemmarum, et numismatum Græcorum, in cimeliarchio electorali Brandenburgico, elegantiorum series, commentario illustratæ.* Coloniae Marchicae.

Behm Blancke, Manfred R. 1979. *Das Tierbild in der altmesopotamischen rundplastik.* Baghdader Forschungen Band 1. Mainz am Rhein: Philip von Zabern.

Beinhauer, Karl.W. 1985. *Untersuchungen zu den eisenzeitlichen Bestattungsplätzen von Novilara (Provinz Pesaro und Urbino, Italien). Archäologie, Anthropologie, Demographie. Methoden und Modelle.* Band 1. Frankfurt am Main: Haag und Herchen.

Belelli Marchesini, Barbara. 2013. 'Le linee di sviluppo topografico del Santuario Meridionale.' *Riflessioni su Pyrgi. Scavi E Ricerche Nelle Aree Del Santuario. Archeologia Classica Suppl. 11, n.s. 8*; edited by

Maria Paola Baglione and Maria Donatella Gentili. Roma: Bretschneider. 11-39.

Belleli, Vincenzo. 2012. 'Caere e il Mondo Greco. Appunti di Archeologia e di Storia.' *Incidenza dell'Antico. Dialoghi di storia greca,* 10. Napoli: Luciano. 137-166.

------. 2011. 'Ceramiche e bronzi laconici nel Mediterraneo arcaico: osservazioni su un libro recente da una prospettiva occidentale.' *Archeologia Classica.* Vol. LXII. Roma: Bretschneider. 357-412.

Bellini, Giovanna Rita. 2004. 'Il santuario di Casale Pescarolo in Valle di Comino.' *Religio: santuari ed ex voto nel Lazio meridionale*; edited by Anna Maria Reggiani, Lorenzo Quilici, Stanislao Nievo and Giovanni Papi. Terracina: Comune de Terracina. 95-107.

Beloch, Karl Julius. 1877. 'Sulla confederazione nocerina.' *Archivio storico per le province napoletane.* Napoli. 285-298.

Benedettini, Gilda, Fiorenzo Catalli and Maria Anna de Lucia Broll. 1999. 'Rinvenimenti monetali nel territorio dell'antica Narce: il santuario suburbano in località Monte Li Santi-Le Rote.' *Bollettino di Numismatica,* No. 32-33. Roma: Istituto Poligrafico e Zecca dello Stato. 47-102.

Benelli, Enrico and Francesco Maria Cifarelli. 2011. 'Materiali e tipi ceramici arcaici tra Abruzzo, Campania Settentrionale e Lazio Meridionale Interno. Tradizioni Locali e Circolazione di Modelli' *Gli Etruschi e la Campania Settentrionale. Atti del XXVI Convegno di Studi Etruschi ed Italici, 11-15 Novembre 2007.* Pisa-Roma: Fabrizio Serra. 105-114.

Benson, Jack Leonard. 1989. *Earlier Corinthian Workshops. A Study of Corinthian Geometric and Protocorinthian Stylistic Groups.* Amsterdam: Allard Pierson Museum.

Bérend, Denise. 1984. 'Réflexions sur les fractions du monnayage grècques.' *Studies in Honor of Leo Mildenberg*; edited by Arthur Houghton and al. Wetteren: Editions NR. 7-30.

Bergoffen, Celia J. 2003. 'The Cypriote pottery from Alalakh: Chronological Considerations.' *The Synchronisation of Civilisations in the Eastern Mediterranean in the Second Millennium BC*; edited by Manfred Bietak. Vol. II. Wien: Verlag der Österreichischen Akademie der Wissenschaften. 395-410.

Bernabei, Marco, and Renata Grifoni Cremonesi. 1996. 'I culti delle acque nella Preistoria dell'Italia peninsulare.' *Rivista di Scienze Preistoriche.* Vol. XLVII (1995-96). Firenze: Istituto Italiano di Preistoria e Protostoria. 331-366.

Bernabò Brea, Luigi. 1965. 'Leggenda e Archeologia nella protostoria siciliana.' *Atti del I Congresso Internazionale di studi sulla Sicilia antica. Kokalos,* Vol. X-XI (1964-1965). Palermo: Banco di Sicilia. 1-33.

------. 1978. 'Eolie, Sicilia, e Malta nell'età del Bronzo.' *Atti del IV Congresso Internazionale di studi sulla Sicilia antica. Kokalos,* Vol. XXII-XXIII (1976-1977), Tomo I. Roma: Bretschneider. 33-110.

------, and Madeleine Cavalier (eds.) 1980. *Meligunìs-Lipára, IV. L'acropoli di Lipari nella Preistoria.* Palermo: Regione siciliana, Assessorato ai Beni Culturali ed Ambientali e della Pubblica Istruzione.

Bernard, Paul. 1982. 'An Ancient Greek City in Central Asia.' *Scientific American,* No. 246. New York. 148-159

------. 1994. 'L'Asie centrale et l'Empire séleucide.' *Topoi,* Vol. 4/2. Dordrecht: Kluwer Academic Publishers Dordrecht. 473-511.

Bernardini, Paolo. 1993. 'Considerazioni sui rapporti tra la Sardegna, Cipro e l'area egeo-orientale nell'età del Bronzo.' *Quaderni della Soprintendenza Archeologica per le Province di Cagliari e Oristano,* 10. Cagliari: STEF. 29–67.

------, and Rubens D'Oriano. (eds.) 2001. *Argyròphleps nesos. L'isola dalle vene d'argento. Esploratori, mercanti e coloni in Sardegna tra il XIV e il VI sec. a.C.* Fiorano Modenese.

------, and Massimo Botto. 2011. 'I bronzi 'fenici' della Penisola Italiana e della Sardegna.' *Rivista di Studi Fenici.* Vol. XXXVIII, 1. Pisa-Roma: Fabrizio Serra. 17-117.

Bertelli, Massimiliano, and Romolo Calciati. 2011. 'Considerazioni sulla serie bronzea Zeus Eleuterio/ Flumine
di Siracusa e della symachia. ' *Numismatica e Antichà Classiche.* Quaderni ticinesi, XL. Lugano: Arti Grafiche Gaggini-Bizzozero. 1-12.

Bettalli, Marco. 1995. *I mercenari nel mondo greco, Vol. 1: Dalle origine alla fine del V. secolo a.C.* Studi e testi di storia antica, Part 5. Pisa: Edizioni ETS.

------. 2004. "Divinità migranti'? Possibili influssi dal Mediterraneo orientale nell'iconografia dell'età del Bronzo italiana.' *Miti simboli decorazioni. Ricerche e scavi, Atti del Secondo Incontro di Studi. Pitignano - Valentano, 13-15 settembre 2002*; edited by N. Negroni Catacchio. Milano: Centro Studi di Preistoria e Archeologia. 247-260.

Bianco, Fausto. 1988. 'Il territorio di S. Agata Militello (ME) nell'antichità.' *Archivio Storico Messinese,* XLIII. Messina: Università degli Studi. 161-183.

Bianco, Salvatore. 1999. 'Il culto delle acque nella preistoria.' *Archeologia dell'acqua in Basilicata*; edited by Giovanni Bulfaro et al. Potenza: Soprintendenza Archeologica della Basilicata. 13-24.

Bietti Sestieri, Anna Maria, Isabella Damiani, Jacopo De Grossi Mazzorin, Anna De Santis, Giulia Recchia, and E. Remotti. 1996. 'Un edificio della I età del Ferro nell'abitato di Fidene (Roma): posizione stratigrafica, caratteristiche strutturali, materiali.' *The Colloquia of the XIII International Congress of Prehistoric and Protohistoric Sciences.* Forlì: A.B.A.C.O. 595-604.

Bignasca, Andrea. 2000. *I kernoi circolari in Oriente e in Occidente. Strumenti di culto e immagini cosmiche.* Orbis Biblicus et Orientalis. Series Archaeologica. Vol.19. Freiburg: Universitätsverlag Freiburg.

Bikai, Patricia Maynor. 1978. *The Pottery of Tyre.* Warminster: Aris and Phillips.

Black, Jeremy A., Anthony Green, and Tessa Rickards (ill.). 1992. *Gods, demons, and symbols of ancient Mesopotamia: an illustrated dictionary.* Austin: University of Texas Press.

------, Andrew George, and Nicholas Postgate. 2000. *A Concise Dictionary of Akkadian.* Wiesbaden: Harrassowitz Verlag.

Blake, Emma. 2005. 'The Material Expression of Cult, Ritual, and Feasting.' *The Archaeology of Mediterranean Prehistory*; edited by Emma Blake and Arthur Bernard Knapp. Oxford: Blackwell. 102-129.

Bloch, Raymond, and James Hogarth. 1969. *The Etruscans.* London: Cresset Press.

Boardman, John. 1980. *The Greeks Overseas: Their Early Colonies and Trade.* New York: Thames and Hudson.

------. 1982. 'Herakles, Theseus and Amazons.' *The Eye of Greece. Studies in the Art of Athens.* Cambridge: University Press. 1-28.

------. 1988. 'Herakles.' *Lexicon Iconographicum Mythologiae Classicae.* Vol. IV/1. Zürich: Artemis & Winkler. 728-838.

------. 1990. 'Al Mina and history.' *Oxford Journal of Archaeology.* Oxford: Blackwell. 169-190.

------. 1990. 'Herakles.' *Lexicon Iconographicum Mythologiae Classicae.* Vol. V/1. Zürich: Artemis & Winkler. 1-192.

------. 1999. 'The excavated history of Al Mina.' *Ancient Greeks West and East*; edited by G.R. Tsetskhladze. Leiden: Brill. 135-161.

------. 2004. 'Copies of Pottery: by and for Whom?.' *Greek identity in the Western Mediterranean. Papers in honour of Brian Shefton,* suppl. *'Mnemosyne'*; edited by C. Lomas. Leiden: Brill. 149-162.

------. 2006. 'Greeks in the East Mediterranean (South Anatolia, Syria, Egypt).' *Greek Colonisation – An Account of Greek Colonies and Other Settlements Overseas*; edited by G.R. Tsetskhladze. Vol. I. Leiden: Brill. 507-534.

Bodenstedt, Friedrich. 1981. *Die Elektronmünzen von Phokaia und Mytilene.* Tübingen: Wasmuth.

Boehringer, Christof. 1975. 'Die Barbarisierten muenzen von Akragas, Gela, Leontinoi und Syrakus im 5. Jahrhundert v. Chr.' *Le emissioni dei centri Siculi fina all'epoca di Timoleonte e i loro rapporti con la monetazione delle colonie Greche di Sicilia. Atti del IV Convegno del centro internazionale di studi numismatici - Napoli 9-14 Aprile 1973.* Supplemento al Vol. 20 degli Annali. Roma: Istituto Italiano di Numismatica. 157-190.

------. 1979. 'Die fruhen Bronzemunzen von Leontinoi und Katane.' *Le origini della monetazione di bronzo in Sicilia e Magna Grecia. Atti del VI Convegno del Centro Internazionale di Studi numismatici, Napoli 1977.* Suppl. Annali Istituto Numismatica Vol.25. Roma. 145-179.

Bologa, Valeriu L. 1960. 'Gutti (biberoane) romane din sticlă.' *Omagiu lui Constantin Daicoviciu cu prilejul împlinirii a 60 de ani*; edited by Constantin Daicoviciu. Bucureşti: Academia Republicii Populare Romîne. 55-61.

Bonghi Jovino, Maria and Giovanna Bagnasco Gianni. 2001. *Tarquinia. Testimonianze archeologiche e ricostruzione storica. Scavi sistematici nell'abitato. Campagne 1982-1988.* Roma: Bretschneider.

------. 1999. 'Tantum ratio sacrorum gerebatur. l'edificio beta di Tarquinia in epoca orientalizzante e alto arcaica. Ancora in merito alle tecniche edilizie, agli aspetti architettonici, sacri e culturali con comparanda mediterranei.' *Koina. Miscellanea di studi archeologici in onore di Piero Orlandini*; edited by Marina Castoldi. Milano: E.T. 87-103.

Bopearachchi, Osmund. 1999. 'The Seleukid Coins of Central Asia and the Bactra Mint.' *Travaux de Numismatique Grecques Offerts à Georges Le Rider*; edited by Michel Amandry and Silvia Hurter. London: Spink. 17-37.

------. 2004. 'The Monetary Policy of Bactria under the Seleukids.' *Topoi.* Suppl. 6. Dordrecht: Kluwer Academic Publishers Dordrecht. 43-60.

Borrelli, Nicola. 1920. 'La moneta dell'antica Cales.' *Bollettino del Circolo Numismatico Napoletano.* Napoli. 1-8.

------. 1935. 'Le monete di Malies.' *Numismatica e Scienze affini.* Perugia : Grafica Soc. an. per le arti grafiche. 5-7.

Bottéro, Jean. 1976. 'Antiquités assyro-babyloniennes.' *École pratique des hautes études. 4E section. Sciences historiques et philologiques.* Vol. 108, No. 1. Paris: à la Sorbonne. 77-126.

------. 1977. 'Les noms de Marduk, l'écriture et la 'logique' en Mésopotamie ancienne.' *Essays on the Ancient Near East in Memory of Jacob Joel Finkelstein*; edited by J.J. Finkelstein and Maria de Jong Ellis. Hamden, CT: Archon Books. 5-28.

------. 1991. 'L'anthropogonie mésopotamienne et l'élément divin en l'homme.' *Orphisme et Orphée en l'honneur de Jean Rudhardt*; edited by Jean Rudhardt and Philippe Borgeaud. Genève: Droz. 211-225.

Botto, Massimo. 1993. 'I bronzi di produzione orientale del tumulo F di Satricum.' *Annali di Archeologia e Storia Antica.* Napoli: Istituto Universitario Orientale. 9-22.

------. 2004. 'Artigiani al seguito di mercanti: considerazioni su un aspetto del commercio fenicio nel Mediterraneo.' *Archaeologica Pisana. Scritti per Orlanda Pancrazzi*; edited by S. Bruni, T. Caruso, and M. Massa. Pisa: Giardini. 31-38.

------. 2007. 'I rapporti fra la Sardegna e le coste medio-tirreniche della Penisola Italiana nella prima metà del I millennio a.C.' *Etruschi, Greci, Fenici e Cartaginesi nel Mediterraneo centrale. Atti del XIV Convegno Internazionale di Studi sulla Storia e l'Archeologia dell'Etruria*; edited by Giuseppe M. Della Fina. Roma: Quasar. 75-136.

------. 2011. 'Le più antiche presenze fenicie nell'Italia meridionale.' *Fenici e Italici, Cartagine e la Magna Grecia. Popoli a contatto, culture a confronto. Atti del Convegno Internazionale, Rivista di Studi Fenici, (Cosenza, 27-28 maggio 2008)*; edited by M. Intrieri and S. Ribichini. Volume 36. Pisa-Roma: Fabrizio Serra. 157-179.

Bourogiannis, Giorgos. 2013. 'The Sanctuary of Ayia Irini: looking beyond the figurines.' *Pasiphae*. Vol. VII. Pisa-Roma: Fabrizio Serra. 35-45.

Bowersock, Glen W. 1995. 'The Barbarism of the Greeks.' *Harvard Studies in Classical Philology*, Vol. 97. Cambridge: Harvard University Press. 3-14.

Braccesi, Lorenzo, and Giovanni Millino. 2000. *La Sicilia greca*. Roma: Carocci.

Bracci, Domenico A. 1786. *Memorie degli antichi incisori che scolpirono i loro nomi in gemme e cammei con molti monumenti inediti.* Firenze: Gaetano Cambiagi.

Brandimarte, Antonio and Giovanni Battista Cipriani. 1815. *Plinio seniore illustrato nella descrizione del Piceno.* Roma: Mordacchini.

Braun, Thomas F. R. G. 1982. 'The Greeks in the Near East.' *The Cambridge Ancient History. Vol. III, Part 3. The Expansion of the Greek World, Eighth to Sixth Centuries BC*; edited by John Boardman and N. G. L. Hammond. Cambridge: University Press. 1-31.

Breglia, Laura. 1952. *La prima fase della coniazione romana dell'argento.* Roma: Santamaria.

------. 1966. *Le antiche rotte del mediterraneo documentate da monete e pesi.* Studia Archaeologica. Vol. 8. Roma: Bretschneider. (reprint of the essay from the original 1955 edition)

Brelich, Angelo. 1965. 'La religione greca in Sicilia.' *Atti del I Congresso Internazionale di studi sulla Sicilia antica. Kokalos*, Vol. X-XI (1964-1965). Palermo: Banco di Sicilia. 35-62.

Brendel, Otto. 1995. *Etruscan Art*. 2nd edition. New Haven: Yale University Press.

Bresciani, Edda (ed.) 2005. *Grande enciclopedia illustrata dell'antico Egitto*. Novara: De Agostini.

Brewster, Harry. 1997. *The River Gods of Greece: Myths and Mountain Waters in the Hellenic World*. London: I.B. Tauris.

Brommer, Frank. 1982. *Theseus. Die Taten des griechischen Helden in der antiken Kunst und Literatur.* Darmstadt: Wissenschaftliche Buchgesellschaft.

Brotherton, Paul et al. 2013. 'Neolithic mitochondrial haplogroup H genomes and the genetic origins of Europeans.' in *Nature Communications*, 4, Article 1764. United Kingdom: Nature Publishing Group. 1-11.

Brulé, Pierre. 1998. 'Le lange des épiclèses dans le polythéisme hellénique.' *Kernos, 11. Actes du VIe Colloque international du C.I.E.R.G.A. Les Panthéons des cités. Origines et développements*. Liege. 13-34.

Buceti, Giuseppe. 2008. *Alcune monete di bronzo inedite della Sicilia Greca.* Cassino: Diana.

------. 2010. *Monete, storia e topografia della Sicilia greca*. Messina: Effegieffe.

Budin, Stephane L. 2009. *The Ancient Greeks: An Introduction.* Oxford: University Press.

Burgess, E. Martin, and Anthony J. Arkell. 1958. 'The Reconstruction of the Hathor Bowl.' *The Journal of Egyptian Archaeology*, 44. London. 5-11.

Burkert, Walter. 1992. *The Orientalizing Revolution: Near Eastern Influence on Greek Culture in the Early Archaic Age*. Cambridge: Harvard University Press.

------. 2004. *Babylon, Memphis, Persepolis: Eastern Contexts of Greek Culture.* Cambridge: Harvard University Press.

Burnett, Andrew M. 1986. 'The Iconography of Roman Coin Types in the Third Century BC.' *The Numismatic Chronicle*, Vol. 146. London: Royal Numismatic Society. 67-75.

------. 1989. 'The beginnings of Roman coinage.' *Annali dell'Istituto Italiano di Numismatica*, 33. Roma: Istituto Italiano di numismatica. 33-64.

------, and Michael H. Crawford. 1998. 'Overstrikes at Neapolis and Coinage at Poseidonia-Paestum.' *Studies in Greek Numismatics in memory of Martin Jessop Price*, edited by Richard Ashton and S. Hurter. London: Spink. 55-57.

------. 2012. 'Early Roman Coinage and its Italian Context.' *The Oxford Handbook of Greek and Roman Coinage*; edited by William E. Metcalf. Oxford: University Press. 297-314.

Bury, John Bagnell. 1967. *A History of Greece to the Death of Alexander the Great*. London: Macmillan.

------ , Stanley Arthur Cook, and Franz Erza Adcock (eds.). 1953. *The Cambridge Ancient History, Vol. VI, Macedon 401-301 BC.* Cambridge: University Press (1975 reprint).

Byzantius, Stephanus, M. Billerbeck, et al. 2006. *Ethnica*. 5 volumes. Berlin: de Gruyter.

Caiazza, Domenico. 2007. 'Contributo per l'identificazione dei siti di Phistelia e Malies.' *Popoli dell'Italia antica. Gentes Fortissimae Italiae. Samnium, Latium et Campania. Le antiche città scomparse*. Atti del II Convegno San Vittore del Lazio, 28 ottobre, 2007. Quaderni di Studi II dell'Associazione Culturale Italia Numismatica. Cassino. 185-231.

Cain, Hans-Ulrich. 1994. 'Candelabro.' *Enciclopedia dell'Arte Antica Treccani*. Volume II. Roma: Istituto della Enciclopedia Italiana. 304.

Calciati, Romolo. 1983-1987. *Corpus nummorum siculorum. La monetazione di bronzo. The bronze coinage*. 3 Volumes. Milano: Edizioni G.M.

------. 1990. *Pegasi*. Mortara: Edizioni I.P.

Calderone, Anna (ed.) 2012. *Cultura e religione delle acque Atti del Convegno interdisciplinare, Qui fresca l'acqua mormora... (S. Quasimodo, Sapph. fr. 2,5) Messina 29-30 marzo 2012*. Roma: Bretschneider.

Calogero, Guido. 1929. 'Acheronte'. *Enciclopedia Italiana Treccani*, Vol. I. Roma.

Caltabiano, Maria Caccamo. 1981. 'La serie ΡΩΜΑΙΩΝ e la cronologia delle prime emissioni bronzee di Neapolis.' *Rivista Storica Dell'Antichità*, XI. Bologna: Pàtron Editore. 33-52.

------. 1993. *La monetazione di Messana, Antike Münzen und Geschnittene Steine*. Bd.13. Berlin: de Gruyter.

------. 1994. 'Palankaios.' *Lexicon Iconographicum Mythologiae Classicae*, Vol. VII. Zürich: Artemis Verlag. 149-150.

------. 1996. 'Tipi monetali siracusani in Asia Minore.' in *Sicilia e Anatolia dalla preistoria all'età ellenistica*, (Palermo, 1996), 103-114.

------. 1999. 'Identità e peculiarità dell'esperienza monetale siciliana.' *Magna Grecia e Sicilia. Stato degli studi e prospettive di ricerca, Atti dell'Incontro di Studi Messina 2-4 dicembre 1996*; edited by M. Barra Bagnasco, E. DeMiro, and A. Pinzone. Messina: Di. Sc. A.M. 295-311.

------. 2003. 'Il Pansicilianesimo e l'annuncio di un'era nuova. Su alcuni tipi monetali di Siracusa ed Erice dell'epoca dei maestri firmanti.' *Quarte Giornate Internazionali Di Studi Sull'area Elima, Erice 1-4 dicembre 2000*, Atti Vol. I. Pisa. 103-125.

------. 2000. 'Monetazione e circolazione monetaria.' *Magna Grecia e Oriente Mediterraneo prima dell'età Ellenistica. Atti del trentanovesimo convegno di studi sulla Magna Grecia*. Taranto, 1-5 Ottobre 1999. Napoli: Arte Tipografica. 291-328.

------. 2011. 'La moneta dei Bretii e l'identità di Nika.' *Enotri e Brettii in Magna Grecia. Modi e forme di interazione culturale*; edited by Giovanna De Sensi Sestito and Stefania Mancuso. Soveria Mannelli: Rubbettino. 445-476.

Cammarata, Enzo. 1971. 'L'importanza della numismatica per l'identificazione di Erbessos.' *Bollettino Nusmismatico*, Anno VIII, n.2. Roma: Ministero per i beni Culturali e Ambientali.

------. 1984. *Da Dionisio a Timoleonte. Problemi di Numismatica della Sicilia Antica.* Modica: La Grafica.

Campana, Alberto. 1992-2003. 'Corpus Nummorum Antiquae Italiae (Zecche minori).' *Panorama numismatico*. Nos. 57-178. Serravalle: Nomisma.

------. 2007. 'Aggiornamento al Corpus Nummorum Antiquae Italiae. Sicilia: Kersini.' *Monete Antiche*, No. 36. Cassino: Diana. 5-9.

------. 2007. 'Aggiornamento al Corpus Nummorum Antiquae Italiae. Samnium: Malies (300-275 a.C.).' *Popoli dell'Italia antica. Gentes Fortissimae Italiae. Samnium, Latium et Campania. Le antiche città scomparse. Atti del II Convegno San Vittore del Lazio, 28 ottobre, 2007*. Quaderni di Studi II dell'Associazione Culturale Italia Numismatica. Cassino. 267-271.

------. 2010. 'Campania: Kampanos.' *Kampanos*. Centro di Studi Storici Saturnia. Associazione Culturale Italia Numismatica. Cassino: Editrice Diana. 33-55.

Campbell Gagné, Laura A. 2012. *Middle Cypriot White Painted Ware: A study of ceramic production and distribution in Middle Bronze Age Cyprus*. Unpublished Doctoral Thesis. University of Toronto.

Campo, Marta. 2002. 'Las Emisiones des Emporion y su Difusión en el Entorno Iberico.' *La monetazione dei Focei in Occidente. Atti dell'IX convengno del centro internazionale di studi numismatici – Napoli 25-27 Ottobre 1996*. Roma: Istituto Italiano di Numismatica. 139-166.

Camporeale, Giovannangelo. 2013. 'Artigiani e mercanti stranieri in Etruria ed Etruschi fuori d'Etruria.' *Mobilità geografica e mercenariato nell'Italia Preromana. Atti del XX convegno internazionale di Studi sulla Storia e l'Archeologia dell'Etruria. Orvieto, Palazzo dei Congressi, Sala dei Quattrocento, 14-16 dicembre 2012*; edited by Giuseppe M. Della Fina. Roma: Quasar. 25-57.

Campus, Franco, Valentina Leonelli, and Fulvia Lo Schiavo. 2010. 'La transizione culturale dall'età del bronzo all'età del ferro nella Sardegna nuragica in relazione con l'Italia tirrenica.' *Meetings between cultures in the ancient Mediterranean, 17th International Congress of Classical Archaeology (Rome, 22-26 September 2008)*. Bollettino di Archeologia Online, I, 2010, Volume speciale F/F2/6. Roma: Direzione Generale per le Antichità. 62-76.

------, and Giovanni Pitzalis. 2012. 'Il complesso cultuale di Predio Canopoli.' *Simbolo di un simbolo: i modelli di nuraghe*; edited by Franco Campus & Valentina Leonelli. Monteriggioni: ARA edizioni. 157–160.

Canby, Jeanny V. 1995. 'Jewelry and Personal Arts in Anatolia.' *Civilizations of the Ancient Near East*; edited by J.M. Sasson. New York: Scribner. 1673-1682.

Cantilena, Renata. 1988. *Monete della Campania antica*. Napoli: Banco di Napoli.

------. 1991. 'Le emissioni monetali di Larino e dei Frentani.' *Samnium. Archaeologia del Molise*; edited by S. Capini and A. Di Niro. Roma. 141-148.

------. 2001. 'Le prime monete di Roma e le colonie latine.' *La collezione numismatica. Per una storia monetaria del Mezzogiorno*. Napoli: Electa. 47-50.

------. 2004. 'Presenza e funzioni della moneta nelle Chorai delle colonie greche della Campania.' *Presenza e funzioni della moneta nelle chorai delle colonie greche dall'Iberia al Mar Nero, Atti del XII Convegno organizzato dall'Università 'Federico II' e dal Centro Internazionale di Studi Numismatici*. Roma : Istituto Italiano di Numismatica. 171-193.

------. 2010. 'La moneta in Penisola sorrentina tra IV e III sec. a.C.: dati acquisiti e problemi aperti.' *Sorrento e la Penisola Sorrentina tra Italici, etruschi e Greci nel contesto della Campania antica*, edited by F. Senatore and M. Russo. Roma: Scienze e Lettere. 201-222.

------. 2008. 'Un gruzzolo di monete d'argento da Pontecagnano: l'offerta votiva di un mercenario?.' *Incidenza dell'Antico,* Vol.6. Napoli: Luciano Editore 183-203.

Cardella, Domenico. 1894. *Lotta di Ercole con Acheloo incisa sopra uno scarabeo arcaico*. Orvieto: Marsili.

Caré, Barbara. 2006. 'Alcune osservazioni sulle sepolture di defunti in età pre-adulta nelle necropoli greche d'Occidente: la diffusione dell'astragalo.' *Orizzonti. Rassegna di Archeologia*. Vol. VII. Pisa: Istituti Editoriali e Poligrafici Internazionali, 143-151.

------. 2010. 'L'astragalo nel sepolcro 'μειρακίων τε και παρθένων παίγνιον'? riflessioni per la rilettura di un costume funerario: i casi di Locri e Caulonia.' *Caulonia tra Crotone e Locri. Tomo 2. Atti del Convegno Internazionale, Firenze, 30 maggio – 1 giugno 2007*. Firenze: University Press. 459-467.

------. 2012. 'L'astragalo in tomba nel mondo greco: un indicatore infantile? Vecchi problemi e nuove osservazioni a proposito di un aspetto del costume funerario.' *L'Enfant et la Mort dans l'Antiquité. III. Le matériel associé aux tombes d'enfants. Actes de la table ronde international. Aix-en-Provence, 2012;* edited by Céline Dubois and Antoine Hermary. Paris: Errance. 403-416.

------. 2013. 'Knucklebones from the Greek Necropolis of Locri Epifiziri, Southern Italy (VI-III century BC). Typological and Functional Analysis.' *The Sound of Bones. Proceedings of the 8th Meeting of the ICAZ Worked Bone Research Group in Salzburg 2011. ARCHAEOPlus. Schriften zur Archäologie und Archäometrie an der Paris Lodron-Universität Salzburg*, Band 5. Salzburg: Felix Lang. 87-99.

Carratelli, Giovanni Pugliese. 1988. 'I santuari extramurani.' *Magna Grecia, III. Vita religiosa e cultura letteraria, filosofica e scientifica*; edited by Giovanni Pugliese Carratelli. Milano: Electa. 149-158.

Carreræ, D. Petri, and Diodorus Siculus. 1723. *Monumentorum historicorum urbis Catanaœ libri quatuor. Adjunguntur Epistolaœ Diodori cum annotationibus ejusdem Petri Carraraœ. Ex Ital. Lat. vertit, recens. & illustr*; edited by Abrahamus Preigerus. Oxford: University Press.

Carroccio, Benedetto 1996. 'A proposito di due nuove emissioni del koinon Brettio.' *Panorama Numismatico*, No. 101. Serravalle: Nomisma. 8-9.

------. 2000. 'Il toro androprosopo, la cicala e l'incuso reggino.' *Numismatica e Antichità classiche.* Quaderni ticinesi. Vol. XXIX. Lugano: Arti Grafiche Gaggini-Bizzozero. 47-68.

------. 2013. 'Il dio fluviale giovane in Magna Grecia e Sicilia.' *Polis, urbs, civitas: moneta e identità. Atti del convegno di studio del Lexicon Iconographicum Numismaticae (Milano 25 ottobre 2012)* edited by L. Travaini and G. Arrigoni. Rome: Quasar. 65-75.

Casagrandi Orsini, Vincenzo. 1898. *Il fiume Taurominius in Vibo Sequestre*. Catania.

Casoria, Giuseppe. 1988. 'La flora e le risorse agricole.' *Etruria meridionale: conoscenza, conservazione, fruizione*. Roma: Quasar. 43-50.

Cassieri, Nicoletta. 2004. 'Il deposito votivo di Tratturo Caniò a Sezze.' *Religio. Santuari ed ex voto nel Lazio meridionale*; edited by A.M. Reggiani et al. Terracina: Comune de Terracina. 163-181.

Castellana, Giuseppe. 1995. 'Le fosse votive della necropoli e credenze religiose.' *La necropoli protoeneolitica di Piano Vento nel territorio di Palma di Montechiaro*. Palermo: Assessorato Beni Culturali ed Ambientali. 67-80.

------. 1996. *La stipe votiva del Ciavolaro nel quadro del Bronzo Antico siciliano*. Palermo: Assessorato Beni Culturali ed Ambientali.

Castello, Gabriele Lancilotto (principe di Torremuzza). 1769. *Siciliae et objacentium insularum veterum inscriptionum nova collectio, prolegomenis et notis illustrata*. Panormi: Ex Bentivenga.

Castrizio, Daniele. 2000. *La monetazione mercenariale in Sicilia: strategie economiche e territoriali fra Dione e Timoleonte*. Soveria Mannelli: Rubbettino.

------. 2011. 'Considerazioni sul pagamento del sîtos ai mercenari nella Sicilia tra Dionisio I e Timoleonte,' in *Polifemo. Rassegna bibliografica di storia delle religioni e storia antica*; edited by Fabio Mora. Vol. XI. Roma: Aracne. 209-232.

Carter, R. A., and G. Philip. 2010. 'Deconstructing the Ubaid.' *Beyond the Ubaid: Transformation and Integration in the Late Prehistoric Societies of the Middle East* edited by R.A. Carter and G. Philip. Chicago: The Oriental Institute of the University of Chicago. 1-22.

Catacchio, Nuccia Negroni. 2012. 'L'alba dell'Etruria nel territorio di Vulci dal bronzo medio alla prima età del ferro.' *Interpretando l'antico: scritti di archeologia offerti a Maria Bonghi Jovino;* edited by C. Chiaromonte Trere, G. Bagnasco Gianni, F. Chiesa. Quaderni di Acme, Vol. 134. Milano: Cisalpino. 111-138.

------, Massimo Cardosa, and Marco Romeo Pitone. 2012. 'Dalla grotta naturale al tempio, tra natura e artificio: forma ed essenza del luogo sacro in Etruria durante l'età dei metalli.' *Antropologia e Archeologia a confronto: rappresentazioni e pratiche del sacro. Atti dell'incontro internazionale di studi Roma, Museo Nazionale Preistorico Etnografico 'Luigi Pigorini' 20-21 maggio 2011;* edited by Valentino Nizzo and

Luigi La Rocca. Roma: Editriale Service System. 595-607.

Catalli, Fiorenzo. 1982. 'Note sulla produzione e circolazione monetaria dell'Etruria meridionale in età Romana.' *Il Lazio nell'antichità romana.* Roma: Gruppo culturale di Roma e del Lazio. 129-136.

------. 1998. *Monete Etrusche.* Roma: Istituto Poligrafico e Zecca dello Stato.

------. 2010. *Le monete di Talamone (Orbetello, GR), 1801-1892. Collezioni numismatiche in Italia, Documentazione dei complessi.* Firenze: Soprintendenza per i Beni Archeologici della Toscana.

Cattani, Maurizio. 1997. 'Una fornace per ceramica delle terramare.' *Le terramare: la più antica civiltà padana.* Milano: Electa. 507-515.

------. 2010. 'La Terramara di Rastellino.' *Paesaggio ed economia nell'età del Bronzo. La pianura bolognese tra Samoggia e Panaro*; edited by Maurizio Cattani, M. Marchesini and S. Marvelli. Bologna: Museo Archeologico Ambientale, Centro Stampa della Regione Emilia-Romagna. 159-170.

Caubet, Annie, and Marthe Bernus-Taylor. 1991. *The Louvre.* London: Scala Books.

------. 2000. *Exposition des quatre grandes civilisations mondiales: La Mésopotamie entre le Tigre e l'Euphrate. Exposition itinérante, Setagaya, Musée d'art de Setagaya, 5 août 2000-3 décembre 2000, Fukuoka, Musée d'art asiatique de Fukuokua, 16 décembre 2000- 4 mars 2001.* Tokyo: NKH.

Cauvin, Jacques. 1994. *Naissance des divinités. Naissance del'agriculture. La Révolution des Symboles au Néolithique.* Paris: CNRS.

------, and Trevor Watkins. 2000. *The Birth of the Gods and the Origins of Agriculture.* Cambridge: University Press.

Cazzella, Alberto, Massimo Cultraro, and Giulia Recchia. 2011. 'Relazioni tra l'Italia centro-meridionale, la Sicilia e l'area egeo-balcanica durante l'Eneolitico.' *Atti della XLIII Riunione scientifica: l'età del rame in Italia. dedicata a Gianni Bailo Modesti. Bologna, 26-29 novembre 2008.* Firenze: Istituto Italiano di Preistoria e Protostoria. 157-164.

Ceccarelli, Letizia, and Elisa Marroni. 2011. *Repertorio dei Santuari del Lazio.* Roma: Bretschneider.

Cecchelin, Riccardo. 1987. *Guida Al Museo Nazionale Etrusco Di Tarquinia.* Roma: Edizioni Mediterranee.

Celestino Perez, Sebastiàn, Nùria Rafel, and Xosé-Lois Armada (eds.) 2008. *Contacto cultural entre el Mediterraneo y el Atlantico (siglos XII-VIII ane: la precolonizacion a debate).* Madrid: Consejo Superior de Investigaciones Científicas.

Cera, Giovanna. 2004. 'Il territorio di Cubulteria.' *Carta archeologica e ricerche in Campania*, Suppl. XV, Fasc. 1. Roma: Bretschneider. 21-235

Cerchiai, Luca. 2008. 'Euphronios, Kleophrades, Brygos: circolazione e committenza della ceramica attica a figure rosse in Occidente.' *Workshop di Archeologia classica. Paesaggi, costruzioni, reperti.* Pisa-Roma: Fabrizio Serra. 9-28.

------. 2010. *Gli antichi Popoli della Campania. Archeologia e Storia.* Roma: Carocci.

Chapa Brunet, Teresa. 1981. 'El Toro Androcefalo de Balazote: Nueva Puesta a Punto de su Problematica.' *Revista de Estudios Albacetenses*, No. 10. Albacete: Instituto de Estudios Albacetenses. 145-158.

Cherif, Zohra. 2006. 'Le pectoral à Carthage à l'époque punique: origine et diffusion.' *L'Africa Romana.* Vol. III. Roma: Carocci. 1489-1507.

Chiesa, Federica. 1993. *Aspetti dell'Orientalizzante recente in Campania. La tomba 1 di Cales*, Quaderni di Acme Vol. 19. Milano: Cisalpino.

Champion, Jeff. 2010. *The Tyrants of Syracuse. War in Ancient Sicily. Volume I: 480-367 BC.* England: Pen & Sword.

Charpin, Dominique. 1986. *Le Clergé d'Ur au siècle d'Hammurapi.* Genève: Droz. 357-366.

Chevillon, Jean-Albert, and Pere Pau Ripollès Alegre. 2014. 'The Greek Far West: An Exceptional Adaptation of a Design from Asia Minor with Bull and Lion Foreparts.' *Journal of the Numismatic Association of Australia*, Vol. 25. Sydney: Numismatic Association of Australia. 41-46.

Chiaramonte Treré, Cristina. 2003. 'Simboli nella necropoli orientalizzante ed arcaica di Campovalano. Ornamenti rituali e propiziatori nei corredi femminili.' *I Piceni e l'Italia medioadriatica, Atti del XXII Convegno di Studi Etruschi ed Italici. Ascoli Piceno, Teramo, Ancona, 9-13 aprile 2000.* Pisa-Roma: Istituti Editoriali e Poligrafici Internazionali. 471-490.

Chierici, Armando. 2008. 'Armati e tombe con armi nella società dell'Etruria padana: analisi di alcuni documenti.' *La Colonizzazione Etrusca in Italia. Atti del XV Convegno Internazionale di Studi sulla Storia e l'Archeologia dell'Etruria*; edited by Giuseppe M. Della Fina. Annali della Fondazione per il Museo Claudio Faina. Vol. XV. Roma: Quasar. 187-246.

Chlup, Radek. 2007. 'The Ritualization of Language in the Hermetica.' *Aries*, Volume 7, Issue 2. Paris: La Table d'Emeraude. 133–159.

Cianfaloni, Davide. 2006. 'Nota sulle tipologie architettoniche e murarie tarquiniesi. Ulteriori corrispondenze con il Vicino Oriente antico.' *Tarquinia e le civiltà del Mediterraneo. Convegno Internazionale, Milano 22-24 giugno 2004*; edited by M. Bonghi Jovino. Milano: Cisalpino. 145-161.

Ciaceri, Emanuele. 1927. *Storia della Magna Grecia, Vol. II. La grande civiltà del Mezzogiorno d'Italia.* Roma

Ciasca, Antonia. 1988. 'Le Protomi e le Maschere.' *I Fenici.* Milano: Bompiani. 354-369.

Cicero, and W.A. Falconer. 1923. *De Divinatione.* Cambridge: Harvard University Press.

Cintas, Pierre. 1946. *Amulettes puniques.* Tunis: Institut des hautes études de Tunis.

Ciuccarelli, Maria Raffaella. 2007. 'Acheloo Ctonio dalla Magna Grecia all'Etruria?.' *Mediterranea. Quaderni annuali dell'Istituto di Studi sulle Civiltà Italiche e del Mediterraneo Antico del Consiglio Nazionale delle Ricerche*, Vol.III (2006). Pisa-Roma: Fabrizio Serra. 121-140.

------. 2010. 'Due nuovi balsamari greco-orientali da Cerveteri.' *Agoge. Atti della Scuola di specializzazione in archeologia*, Vol. IV-V (2007-2008). Pisa: University Press. 163-185.

Civan, Judith. 2004. *Abraham's Knife: The Mythology of the Deicide in Anti-Semitism*. XLibris.

Clarke, Michael. 2004. 'An Ox-Fronted River-God Sophocles, 'Trachiniae' 12-13.' *Harvard Studies in Classical Philology*, Vol. 102. Cambridge: Harvard University Press. 97-112.

Clerc, Gisèle. 1991. 'Démons Cornus.' *La Necropole d'Amathonte. Tombes 110-385. Études Chypriotes*, Vol.XIII; edited by K. Karageorghis and O. Picard. Nicosia: Nicolaou. 100-102.

Clottes, Jean. 2003. *Return To Chauvet Cave, Excavating the Birthplace of Art: The First Full Report.* London: Thames & Hudson.

Clüver, Philipp. 1619. *Sicilia Antiqua: cum minoribus insulis, ei adjacentibus, item, Sardinia et Corsica.* Lugduni Batavorum: Officina Elseviriana.

------. 1624. *Italia antiqua; opus post omnium curas elaboratissimum; tabulis gegraphicis aere expressis illustratum. Ejusdem Sicilia Sardinia et Corsica. Cum indice locupletissimo.* Lugduni Batavorum: Officina Elseviriana.

Coacci Polselli, Gianna. 1983. 'L'epigrafia punica in Sicilia.' *Atti del V Congresso Internazionale di studi sulla Sicilia antica. Kokalos*, Vol. XXVI-XXVII (1980-1981), Tomo I. Roma: Bretschneider. 468-479.

Coldstream, John N. 1982. 'Greeks and Phoenicians in the Aegean.' *Phönizier im Westen: die Beiträge des Internationalen Symposiums über 'Die Phönizische Expansion im Westlichen Mittelmeerraum in Köln vom 24. bis 27. April, 1979*; edited by Hans Georg Niemeyer. Mainz am Rhein: Zabern. 261-275.

------. 1998. 'The first exchanges between Euboeans and Phoenicians: who took the initiative?.' *Mediterranean Peoples in Transition: Thirteenth to Early Tenth Centuries BCE. In Honor of Prof. Trude Dothan*; edited by Gitin Seymour, Amihay Mazar, and Ephraim Stern. Jerusalem: Israel Exploration Society. 353-360.

Cole, S. Guettel. 1988. 'The Uses of Water in Greek Sanctuaries.' *Early Greek Cult Practice. Proceedings of the Fifth International Symposium at Swedish Institute at Athens, 26-29 June 1986*; edited by R. Hagg, N. Marinatos, G. Z. Nordquist. Stockholm. 161-165.

Colletta, Teresa. 1989. *La Struttura antica del territorio di Sessa Aurunca: il ponte Ronaco e le vie per Suessa.* Napoli: Edizioni Scientifiche italiane.

Collin Bouffier, Sophie. 2013. 'Il culto delle acque nella Sicilia greca: mito o realtà?.' *Storia dell'acqua. Mondi materiali e universi simbolici*; edited by Vito Teti. Roma: Donzelli. 43-66.

Collon, Dominique. 1995. 'Clothing and Grooming in Ancient Western Asia.' *Civilizations of the Ancient Near East*; edited by Jack M. Sasson. New York: Scribner. 503-515.

------. 2005. *First Impressions: Cylinder Seals in the Ancient Near East.* London: British Museum Press.

Colonna, Giovanni. 1970. 'Il giacimento preistorico della zona del Templio A.' *Notizie degli Scavi di Antichità.* Serie 8, Vol. XXIV, Supplemento II. Roma: Accademia Nazionale dei Lincei. 267-274.

------. 1970. *Bronzi votivi umbro-sabellici a figura umana, I, Periodo arcaico.* Firenze: Sansoni.

------. 1975. 'Nuovi dati epigrafici sulla protostoria della Campania.' *Atti della XVII Riunione Scientifica Dell'Istituto Italiano di Preistoria e Protostoria (13-16 Ottobre 1974).* Firenze. 151-169.

------, and F.W.Von Hase. 1984. 'Alle origini della statuaria etrusca: la tomba delle statue presso Ceri.' *Studi Etruschi*, Vol. LII, Serie III. Roma : Bretshneider. 13-59.

------. 1987. 'Note preliminari sui culti del santuario di Portonaccio a Veio.' *Scienze dell'Antichità. Storia Archeologia Antropologia.* Vol. I. Firenze: Rinascimento del libro. 419-46.

------. 1991. 'Le civiltà anelleniche.' *Storia e Civiltà della Campania. L'evo Antico*; edited by Giovanni Pugliese Carratelli. Napoli: Electa. 25-67.

------. 1992. 'I due pozzi antistanti il tempio A; La struttura e i dati stratigrafici.' *Pyrgi. Scavi del santuario etrusco. Notizie degli Scavi di Antichità,* Serie 8, Vol.XLII-XLIII, Suppl. II. Roma: Accademia Nazionale dei Lincei. 11-138.

------. 1994. 'Altari e sacelli. L'area sud di Pyrgi dopo otto anni di ricerche.' *Rendiconti della Pontificia Accademia Romana di Archeologia.* Vol. LXIV. (1991-1992) Roma: Tipografia Vaticana. 63-115.

------, and Luisa Franchi dell'Orto. 2001. 'Le forme della devozione.' *Eroi e Regine. Piceni popolo d'Europa. Catalogo della Mostra. Roma – Galleria Nazionale d'Arte Antica, Palazzo Barberini 12/4/2001 – 1/7/ 2001.* Roma: De Luca. 89-92.

------. 2001. 'Divinazione e culto di Rath/Apollo a Caere (a proposito del santuario in località S. Antonio).' *Archeologia Classica.* Vol. LII. Roma: Bretschneider. 151-173.

------. 2002. 'Il santuario di Pyrgi dalle origini mitistoriche agli altorilievi frontonali dei Sette e di Leucotea.' *Scienze dell'Antichità.* Vol. 10. Roma: Quasar. 251-336.

------. 2005. 'Discussione e interventi.' *Oriente e Occidente: metodi e discipline a confronto. Riflessioni sulla cronologia dell'età del ferro in Italia, Atti dell'Incontro di Studi, Roma, 30-31 ottobre 2003;* edited by Gilda Bartoloni e Filippo

Delpino. Mediterranea. I (2004). Pisa-Roma: Istituti Editoriali e Poligrafici Internazionali. 478-483.

------. 2009. 'L'Apollo di Pyrgi, Sur/Suri (il 'nero') e l'Apollo Sourios.' *Studi Etruschi*, Vol.LXXIII. Roma: Bretschneider. 101-134.

------. 2012. 'Il pantheon degli Etruschi 'i più religiosi degli uomini' alla luce delle scoperte di Pyrgi.' *Atti della Accademia Nazionale dei Lincei, anno CDIX – 2012, Classe di Scienze Morali, Storiche e Filologiche, Memorie*. Ser. IX, Vol. XXIX, Fasc. 3. Roma: Accademia Nazionale dei Lincei. 557-595.

Coltorti, Mauro, Mauro Cremaschi, Antonio Guerreschi, Carlo Peretto, and Benedetto Sala. 1982. 'L'accampamento preistorico di Isernia La Pineta.' *Atti della XXIII Riunione Scientifica I.I.P.P., Firenze 7-9 Maggio 1980*. Firenze: Istituto Italiano di Preistoria e Protostoria. 577-587.

Comella, Annamaria 1986. *I materiali votivi di Falerii*. Roma: Bretschneider.

Consolo Langher, Sebastiana Nerina 1967. 'Numismatica tauromenitana (357-306).' *Ricerche di numismatica*. Roma. 63-165.

------. 1983. 'Tauromenio e le vicende siciliane tra Dionisio e Agatocle.' *Archivio Storico Messinese*, Vol. XXXIII. Messina: Università degli Studi. 189-214.

------. 1996. 'Andromaco e Tauromenio. Dalla indipendenza politica ed economica di età timoleontea alla sottomissione ad Agatocle.' *Siracusa e la Sicilia greca tra età arcaica ed alto ellenismo*. Messina. 534-573.

------. 2000. 'Erice e il koinon degli Elimi nella storia della Sicilia occidentale tra VI e IV sec. a. C.' *Atti delle Terze Giornate Internazionali di Studi sull'Area Elima, Gibellina-Erice-Contessa Entellina 1997*. Pisa. 287-310.

Constans, Léopold-Albert.1921. 'Récentes découvertes archéologiques en Italie. Deuxième et dernier article.' in *Journal des savants*, Vol. 19, No. 5. Paris: De Boccard. 214-223.

Cook, Arthur Bernard. 1925. *Zeus: A Study in Ancient Religion, Vol. II, Zeus: God of the Dark Sky*. Cambridge: University Press.

Cope, Edward Meredith. 1970. *Commentary on the Rhetoric of Aristotle*, Vol.III . New York: Olms.

Coppola, Goffredo, Carmelo Colamonico, Domenico Mustilli, and Nicola Nicolini. 1937. 'Teano.' *Enciclopedia Italiana di Scienze, Lettere ed Arti*, Vol. 33. Roma.

Costabile, Felice. (ed.) 1991. *I ninfei di Locri Epizefiri. Architettura, culti erotici, sacralità delle acque*. Soveria Mannelli: Rubbettino.

Costantini, Sara. 1995. *Il deposito votivo del santuario campestre di Tessennano*. Corpus delle stipi votive in Italia, 8, Regio VII, 4. Roma: Bretschneider.

Crawford, Michael H. 1974. *Roman Republican Coinage*. Cambridge: University Press.

------. 1985. *Coinage and Money under the Roman Republic: Italy and the Mediterranean Economy*. Berkeley: University of California Press.

------. 2002. 'Provenances, attributions and chronology of some early Italian coinages.' *Coin Hoards*, Vol. IX. London: The Royal Numismatic Society. 269-274.

------. 2011. *Imagines Italicae: a Corpus of Italic Inscriptions*. London: Institute of Classical Studies, University of London.

Cremaschi, Mauro, and Carlo Peretto. 1988. 'Les sols d'habitat du site paleolithique d'Isernia La Pineta (Molise, Italie centrale).' *L'Anthropologie*, Vol.92. Paris. 107-140.

Crisà, Antonino. 2009. 'G. L. Castelli, principe di Torremuzza, numismatico ed antichista ad Halaesa Archonidea.' *LANX*, No. 2. Milano: Università degli Studi. 116-149.

------. 2011. 'Heroic Cults in northern Sicily between Numismatics and Archaeology.' *Proceedings of the XIV International Numismatic Congress, Glasgow 2009*, edited by Nicholas Holmes. Vol. I Glasgow: International Numismatic Council. 114-120.

Crispino, Anita, and Massimo Cultraro. 2014. 'Exploring underground paths. Caves and human landscape in the Siracusa district during prehistory.' *From Cave to Dolmen: ritual and symbolic aspects in the prehistory between Sciacca, Sicily and the central Mediterranean*; edited by Domenica Gullì. Oxford: Archaeopress. 179-194.

------, and Massimo Cultraro. Forthcoming. 'Il deposito votivo di Ferla (Sr) e il culto delle acque nella Sicilia protostorica.' *Santuari indigeni di Sicilia e Magna Grecia. Modelli di organizzaione e regime delle offerte a confronto, Atti del convegno (aprile 2011).*

Cristofani, Mauro. 1976. 'Storia dell'arte e acculturazione: le pitture tombali arcaiche di Tarquinia.' *Prospettiva*. Vol. VII. Firenze: Centro Di. 2-10.

------, and Marina Martelli. 1983. *L'oro degli Etruschi*. Novara: Istituto Geografico de Agostini.

Cultraro, Massimo. 2009. 'Prima di Cartagine. Forme di contatto tra Sicilia, Nord Africa e Mediterraneo orientale nella Protostoria recente.' *Traffici, commerci e vie di distribuzione nel Mediterraneo tra Protostoria e V secolo a.C. Atti del Convegno Internazionale Gela, maggio 2009*. Palermo: Regione Siciliana, Assessorato ai Beni Culturali, Ambientali e della Pubblica Istruzione. 55-66.

------. 2012. 'Ex Parte Orientis: i Teresh e la questione dell'origine anatolica degli Etruschi.' *Le origini degli Etruschi. Storia, archeologia, antropologia;* edited by Vincenzo Bellelli. Roma: Bretschneider. 105-141.

------. 2012. 'Quis Deus? Su alcune rappresentazioni di carattere cultuale nella Sicilia dell'età del ferro.' *Antropologia e Archeologia a confronto: rappresentazioni e pratiche del sacro. Atti dell'incontro internazionale di studi Roma, Museo Nazionale Preistorico Etnografico 'Luigi Pigorini'*

20-21 maggio 2011; edited by Valentino Nizzo et Luigi La Rocca. Roma: E.S.S. 387-902.

------. 2012. 'I Siculi all'ombra del vulcano: per una proposta di definizione dell'età del Bronzo recente e finale nella media valle del Simeto.' *Dal mito alla storia. La Sicilia nell'Archaiologhia di Tucidide. Atti del VIII Congresso di Studi;* edited by Marina Congiu, Calogero Micciché and simona Modeo. Caltanissetta-Roma: Sciascia Editore. 181-203.

------. 2014. 'Catania Prima di Evarco. Per una carta archeologica delle evidenze preistoriche nell'area urbana.' *Tradizione, Tecnologia e Territorio 2. Topografia Antica*. Vol. 3. Acireale-Roma: Bonanno. 39-74.

------. 2014. 'The Grotta del Vecchiuzzo (Petralia Sottana, Palermo): a multi-purpose cave in a karst system.' *From Cave to Dolmen: ritual and symbolic aspects in the prehistory between Sciacca, Sicily and the central Mediterranean*; edited by Domenica Gullì. Oxford: Archaeopress. 137-150.

-----. Forthcoming. 'Giovani operatori del sacro: infanzia e divinazione a Cipro nella tarda età del Bronzo.' Paper presented during the conference: *Gli operatori cultuali. Secondo Incontro di studio del Gruppo di Contatto CNR per lo studio delle religioni mediterranee. Rome, 2005.*

Cuozzo, Mariassunta, Bruno d'Agostino, and Laura Del Verme (eds.) 2006. '*Cuma. Le fortificazioni. 2. I materiali dai terrapieni arcaici*; edited by Bruno D'Agostino and Mariassunta Cuozzo. Napoli: Istituto Universitario Orientale.

------. 2010. 'Pontecagnano e i centri greci della Campania: osservazioni sulle produzioni ceramiche di età orientalizzante.' *Meetings between cultures in the ancient Mediterranean, 17th International Congress of Classical Archaeology (Rome, 22-26 September 2008).* Bollettino di Archeologia Online, I, 2010, Volume speciale F/F3/6. Roma: Direzione Generale per le Antichità. 59-65.

------. 2013. 'Etruscans in Campania.' *The Etruscan World*; edited by Jean MacIntosh Turfa. London: Routledge, 301-318.

Currie, Bruno. 2002. 'Euthymos of Locri: a case study in heroization in the classical period.' *Journal of Hellenic Studies*, No. 122. London: The Council for the Society for the Promotion of Hellenic Studies. 24-44.

Curtin, Philip D. 1984. *Cross-Cultural Trade in World History*. Cambridge: University Press.

Curtius, Ernst. 1894. *Gesammelte Abhandlungen*. Vol. 2. Berlin: W. Hertz.

Cutroni Tusa, Aldina. 1968. 'Sopravvivenza di un motivo miceneo su monete siceliote.' *Atti e Memorie del I Congresso Internazionale di Micenologia*. Roma, 27 Settembre – 3 Ottobre 1967. Roma: Edizioni dell'Ateneo. 266-274.

------. 1968. 'La riconiazione della litra siracusana nel IV a.C.' *Sicilia Archeologica* No.4. Trapani: STET. 44-49.

Dági, Marianna. 2013. 'A Sicilian askos. Highlighted Works of Art - Spring 2013.' Exhibit. Museum of Fine Arts at Budapest.

D'Agostino, Bruno. 1974. 'Il mondo periferico della Magna Grecia.' *Popoli e Civiltà dell'Italia Antica*. Vol. II. Roma: Biblioteca di Storia Patria. 177-271.

D'Alessio, Giovan Battista. 2004. 'Textual Fluctuations and Cosmic Streams: Ocean and Acheloios.' *Journal of Hellenic Studies*, No. 124. London: The Council for the Society for the Promotion of Hellenic Studies. 16-37.

Dalley, Stephanie. 1989. *Myths from Mesopotamia: Creation, the Flood, Gilgamesh, and Others*. Oxford: University Press.

------. 1998. 'The Influence of Mesopotamia upon Israel and the Bible.' *The Legacy of Mesopotamia*; edited by S. Dalley. Oxford: University Press. 57-83.

------. 2008. *Esther's revenge at Susa: from Sennacherib to Ahasuerus*. Oxford: University Press.

------, and John Peter Oleson. 2003. 'Sennacherib, Archimedes, and the Water Screw: The Context of Invention in the Ancient World.' *Technology and Culture*, Vol. 44, No. 1. Chicago: University Press. 1-26.

D'andrea, Alberto. 2009. 'Tiati: la monetazione.' *La monetazione pugliese dall'età classica al medioevo. (1) La monetazione della Daunia. Le monete Normanne dell'Italia Meridionale. Atti del 1° Congresso di Numismatica. Bari 21-22 Novembre 2008*. Bari: Circolo Numismatico Pugliese.71-90.

Danrey, Virginie. 2004. 'Winged Human-Headed Bulls of Nineveh: Genesis of an Iconographic Motif.' *Nineveh. Papers of the 49th Rencontre Assyriologique Internationale, Part One*. Iraq, Vol. LXVI. London: British Institute for the Study of Iraq. 133-139.

Dany, Oliver. 1999. *Akarnanien in Hellenismus. Geschichte und Völkerrecht in Nordwestgriechenland.* Munich: Verlag C.H. Beck.

De Angelis, Maria Cristina, Enrico Pellegrini and Simona Rafanelli. 2015. 'Circoli di Pietre. Gli Etruschi e l'ideologia della Casta.' *Archelogia Viva,* XXXIV, n.169. Firenze: Giunti. 16-27.

De Caro, Stefano. 2012. *La terra nera degli antichi Campani*. Napoli.

De Cazanove, Olivier. 1986. 'Plastique votive et imagerie Dionysiaque: à propos de deux ex-voto de Vulci.' *Mélanges de l'École française de Rome*, Vol. XCVIII. Paris: De Boccard. 7-36.

De Cesare, Monica. 2012. 'Pittura vascolare e politica ad Atene e in Occidente: vecchie teorie e nuove riflessioni.' *Arte-Potere. Forme artistiche, istituzioni, paradigmi interpretativi. Atti del convegno di studio, Pisa, 25-27 Novembre 2010*; edited by M. Castiglione and A. Poggio. Milano: LED. 97-127.

Decharme, Paul. 1886. *Mythologie de la Grèce antique*. Paris: Garnier.

De Felice, Eugenio. 1994. *Larinum*. Firenze: L.S. Olschki.

De Grummond, Nancy T. 2013. 'Haruspicy and Augury: Sources and Procedures.' *The Etruscan World*; edited by Jean MacIntosh Turfa. London: Routledge. 539-556.

De Juliis, Ettore M. 1997. 'Teano Apulo.' *Enciclopedia dell'Arte Antica, Classica e Orientale*, Suppl., V. Roma. 545-546.

------. 2000. *I fondamenti dell'arte italica*. Bari: Laterza.

Delattre, Alfred Louis. 1894. 'Notes sur la nécropole punique voisine du Serapeum, à Carthage, communiquées par M. Héron de Villefosse.' *Comptes rendus des séances de l'Académie des Inscriptions et Belles-Lettres*. 38e année, No. 6. Paris: Klincksieck. 430-442.

Della Fina, Giuseppe Maria (ed.) 2014. *Artisti, committenti e fruitori in etruria tra VIII e V secolo a.C. Atti del XXI Convegno Internazionale di Studi sulla Storia e l'Archeologia dell'Etruria*. Roma: Quasar.

Della Seta, Alessandro.1922. *Italia Antica*. Bergamo: Istituto Italiano d'Arti Grafiche.

De Miro, Ernesto. 1991. 'Eredità Egeo-Micenee e alto arcaismo in Sicilia.' *La transizione dal miceneo all'alto arcaismo. Atti convegno Roma 1988*. Roma: Consiglio nazionale delle ricerche. 593-617.

De Monaco, Arminio, and Matteo G. Sperandeo. 1960. *Teano osco e romano: Presentazione di Matteo G. Sperandeo*. Teano: tip. D'Amico.

Demosthenes, and Samuel H. Butcher. 1903. *Orationes*. Oxford: Clarendon.

Depalmas, Anna. 2005. *Le navicelle di bronzo della Sardegna nuragica*. Cagliari: Gasperini.

De Puma, Richard Daniel. 2013. *Etruscan Art in the Metropolitan Museum of Art*. New Haven and London: The Metropolitan Museum of Art.

De Ridder, André. 1896. *Catalogue des bronzes trouvés sur l'Acropole d'Athènes*. Cambridge: Harvard University Press.

De Sarzec, Ernest. 1884-1912. *Découvertes en Chaldéée. Publié par les soins de L. Heuzey. Avec le concours de A. Amiaud et F. Thureau-Dangin*. Paris: E. Leroux.

De Sensi Sestito. 1999. *Tra l'Amato e il Savuto. Tomo I. Terina e il Lametino nel contesto dell'Italia antica*. Soveria Mannelli: Rubbettino.

De Simone, Carlo. 1966. 'Per una cronologia delle iscrizioni messapiche.' *Studi Salentini*, Vol. 23. Lecce: I.T.E.S. 321-356.

Deutsche Akademie der Wissenschaften zu Berlin. 1862. *Corpus Inscriptionum Latinarum*. Berlin: Reimer.

Deutsche Akademie der Wissenschaften zu Berlin. 1908. *Inscriptiones Graecae, Volume 9, Part 2, Inscriptiones Thessaliae*. Berlin: Reimer.

De Villefosse, Antoine Héron. 1888. 'Une tête de bronze récemment découverte à Lezoux (Puy-de-Dôme) par M. le Dr Plicque.' *Comptes rendus des séances de l'Académie des Inscriptions et Belles Lettres*, 32e année, No. 4. Paris: de Boccard. 308.

De Witte, Jean. 1865. *Etudes sur les vases peints*. Paris: Gazette des Beaux-Arts.

Diels, Hermann, and Walther Kranz. 1952. *Die Fragmente der Vorsokratiker*. Band 3. Berlin: Weidmann.

Dietrich, Bernard Clive. 1997. 'Death and Afterlife in Minoan Religion.' *Kernos*, 10. Liège. 19-38.

Di Fraia, Tommaso, and Renata Grifoni Cremonesi (eds.). 1996. *La Grotta S. Angelo sulla Montagna dei Fiori e il problema delle frequentazioni cultuali in grotta*. Pisa-Roma: Istituti Editoriali e Poligrafici Internazionali.

Di Gennaro, Francesco, and Letizia Ceccarelli. 2012. 'Fidene. Santuari urbani e del territorio.' *Sacra Nominis Latini. I santuari del Lazio arcaico e repubblicano, Atti del Convegno Internazionale, Roma, Palazzo Massimo, 19-21 febbraio 2009*; edited by Elisa Marroni. Ostraka volume speciale, Tomo I. Napoli: Loffredo. 211-226.

Di Giuseppe, Helga. 2006. 'L'Acheloo e gli altri indicatori religiosi della villa.' *La fattoria e la villa dell'Auditorium nel quartiere Flaminio di Roma*. Roma: Bretschneider. 465-470.

------. 2010. 'Acheloo e le acque deviate.' *I riti del costruire nelle acque violate. Atti del Convegno Internazionale. Roma 12-14 giugno 2008*; edited by H. Di Giuseppe and M. Serlorenzi. Roma: Scienze e Lettere. 69-90.

Di Mario, Francesco. 2011 'Sito archeologico del Fosso dell'Incastro 'Castrum Inui',' Excavation Report M.I.B.A.C. Rome: Direzione Generale Archeologia, 2011. http://www.archeologia.beniculturali.it/ index.php?it/142/scavi/scaviarcheologici_4e048966cfa3a/96.

Dimitrov, Petko and Dimitar Dimitrov. 2004. *The Black Sea, the Flood, and the Ancient Myths*. Varna: Slavena.

Diodorus Siculus, and Charles H. Oldfather. 1935. *Library of History*. Cambridge: Harvard University Press.

Diogenes Laertius, and R.D. Hicks. 1972. *Lives of Eminent Philosophers*. Cambridge: Harvard University
Press.

Dionysius of Halicarnassus, and Earnest Cary. 1937. *The Roman antiquities of Dionysius of Halicarnassus*, Vol. I . Cambridge: Harvard University Press.

Dohrn, Tobias. 1937. *Die schwarzfigurigen etruskischen vasen aus der 2. Halfte des 6. Jh*. Berlin: Triltsch & Huther.

Domenichini, Lodovico. 1844. *Della storia naturale di C. Plinio Secondo libri 37. traduzione di M. Lodovico Domenichi emendata per la prima volta secondo il testo latino con l'aggiunta di un nuovo indice generale*, Vol.1. Venezia: Antonelli.

D'Oriano, Rubens, and Antonio Sanciu. 2013. 'Phoenician and Punic Sardinia and the Etruscans.' *The Etruscan World*; edited by Jean MacIntosh Turfa. London: Routledge. 231-243.

Dörpfeld, Wilhelm. 1927. *Alt-Ithaka: Ein Beitrag zur Homer-Frage, Studien und Ausgrabungen aus der insel Leukas-Ithaka.* München: R. Uhde.

Dothan, Trude, Gitin Seymour, Amihay Mazar, and Ephraim Stern. 1998. *Mediterranean Peoples in Transition: Thirteenth to Early Tenth Centuries BCE.* Jerusalem: Israel Exploration Society.

Dousougli, Angelika. 1999. 'Palaeolithic Leukas.' *British School of Athens, Vol. 3: The Palaeolithic Archaeology of Greece and Adjacent Areas.* British School at Athens. 288-92.

Dowden, Ken. 1989. *Death and the Maiden: Girls' Initiation Rites in Greek Mythology.* London: Routledge.

Downey, Susan B. 1995. *Architectural Terracottas from the Regia.* Ann Arbor: University of Michigan Press.

Dougherty, Carol. 1993. 'It's Murder to Found a Colony.' *Cultural Poetics in Archaic Greece: Cult, Performance, Politics*; edited by Carol Dougherty and Leslie Kurke. Oxford : University Press. 178-198.

Drago Troccoli, Luciana. 2009. 'Veio tra villanoviano e tardo arcaismo. Appunti sulla necropoli di Casale del Fosso.' *Etruria e Italia preromana. Studi in onore di Giovannangelo Camporeale*; edited by S. Bruni. Studia Erudita 4. Pisa-Roma: Fabrizio Serra. 327-370.

------. 2012. 'Ricerche sul tema del bestiario fantastico di età orientalizzante. I precedenti della prima età del Ferro: continuità o discontinuità?.' *Il bestiario fantastico di età orientalizzante nella penisola italiana. Aristonothos. Scritti per il Mediterraneo antico. Quaderni*, No. 1; edited by Maria Cristina Biella, Lucio Giuseppe Perego, and Enrico Giovannelli. Trento: Tangram. 15-34.

------. 2012. 'Rapporti tra Sardegna e Italia medio-tirrenica nell'età del Ferro: aspetti inediti del ruolo e delle interrelazioni tra aristocrazie, mercanti e artigiani.' *La preistoria e la protostoria della Sardegna. Atti della XLIV riunione scientifica. Cagliari, Barumini, Sassari 23-28 novembre 2009.* Firenze: I.I.P.P. 1087-1093.

Dressel, Heinrich, and Kurt Regling. 1927. 'Zwei ägyptische Funde altgriechischer Silbermünzen.' *Zeitschrift für Numismatik der Numismatischen Gesellschaft Berlin.* Berlin: Weidmann. 1-138.

------. 1894. *Konigliche Museen zu Berlin. Beschreibung der Antiken Munzen. Italien.* Berlin: Spemann.

Drews, Robert. 1995. *The End of the Bronze Age: Changes in Warfare and the Catastrophe Ca. 1200 B.C.* Princeton: University Press.

Ducat, Jean. 1963. 'Les vases plastiques corinthiens.' *Bulletin de correspondance hellénique,* Vol. 87, Livraison 2. Paris: De Boccard. 431-458.

------. 1966. *Les vases plastiques rhodiens archaiques en terre cuite.* Paris: de Boccard.

Dunbabin, Thomas James. 1948. *The Western Greeks: the History of Sicily and South Italy from the Foundation of the Greek Colonies to 480 B.C.* Oxford: Clarendon.

Dumas-Reungoat, Christine. 2009. 'Créatures composite de Mésopotamie et de Grèce: Classification et comparaison.' *Schedae.* Prépublication No.2, Fascicule No.1. Kraków: Jagiellonian University Press. 15-32

Durandm, Jean-Marie. 1993. 'Le mythologème du combat entre le dieu de l'orage et la mer en Mésopotamie.' *Mari: Annales de recherches interdisciplinaires*, 7. Paris: Editions Recherche sur les civilisations. 41-61.

Du Ry, Carel J. 1970. *Art of the Ancient Near and Middle East.* New York: Harry N. Abrams.

Eckhel, Joseph. 1792. 'De tauro cum facie humana.' *Doctrina Numorum Veterum*, Part 1,Vol. I. Wien: Ignatius Alberti. 129-140.

Eisen, Gustavus. 1940. *Ancient Oriental Seals and Other Seals, with a Description of the Collection of Mrs. William H. Moore.* Chicago: University Press.

Eisenberg, Jerome M. 1994. 'The Art of the Italic Peoples. A Major Exhibition in Paris.' *Minerva*, Vol.5, No.2. London: Aurora. 4-12.

Elia, Diego, and Barbara Caré. 2004. 'Ancora sull''astragalomania' a Locri Epizefiri. La documentazione dalla necropoli in contrada Lucifero.' *Orizzonti. Rassegna di Archeologia.* Vol. V. Pisa: Istituti Editoriali e Poligrafici Internazionali. 77-90.

Emery, Walter B., and Zaki Yusef Saad. 1938. *The Tomb of Hemaka.* Cairo: Government Press.

Empedocles, and Brad Inwood. 2001. *The Poem of Empedocles.* Toronto: UP.

Ephorius Historicus, Carl Müller, and Theodor Müller. 2010. 'Fragmenta.' *Fragmenta Historicorum Graecorum.* Volume 1. Cambridge: University Press.

Epifanio Vanni, Elena. 1993. 'Terravecchia di Cuti. Campagne di scavo 1984, 1986, 1987.' *Atti del VII Congresso Internazionale sulla Sicilia antica. Kokalos* Vol. XXXIV-XXXV (1988-1989) Tomo II. Roma: Bretschneider. 669-678.

Epstein, Hellmut, and Ian L. Mason. 1971. *The Origin of the Domestic Animals of Africa.* New York: Africana.

Eriksson, Kathryn O. 2001. 'Cypriote Proto White Slip and White Slip I: Chronological Beacons on Relations between Late Cypriote I Cyprus and Contemporary Societies of the Eastern Mediterranean.' *The White Slip Ware of Late Bronze Age Cyprus*; edited by Vassos Karageorghis. Wien: Verlag der Österreichischen Akademie der Wissenschaften. 51-64.

------. 2003. 'A Preliminary Synthesis of Recent Chronological Observations on the Relations Between

Cyprus and Other Eastern Mediterranean Societies During the Late Middle Bronze - Late Bronze II Periods.' *The Synchronisation of Civilisations in the Second Millennium BC*, Volume II; edited by M. Bietak. Wien: Verlag der Österreichischen Akademie der Wissenschaften. 411-430.

Euripides, and Paul Woodruff. 1998. *Euripides' Bacchae*. Indianapolis: Hackett.

Evershed, Emily, et al. 1962. *Larousse Encyclopedia of Prehistoric and Ancient Art;* edited by René Huyghe. London: Hamlyn.

Fabbricotti, Emanuela. 1968. 'Considerazioni su di un tesoretto di monete proveniente da S. Marco d'Alunzio.' *Annali Istituto Italiano di Numismatica*, Vol. XV. Roma: Istituto Italiano di Numismatica. 83-90.

Fàbry, Nicola Bianca, and Daniele Vitali. 2015. 'Il Principe Celtico di Lavau. Dentro lo scavo.' *Archeologia Viva*, No.171. Milano: Giunti. 58-61.

Facchinetti, Grazia. 2003. 'Iactae stipes: l'offerta di monete nelle acque nella penisola italiana.' *Rivista Italiana di Numismatica e scienze affini*, Vol. CIV. Milano. 13-55.

------. 2004. 'L'offerta di monete nelle acque in Età Romana e Tardo-Antica: alcune riflessioni.' *Acque per l'Utilitas, per la Salubritas, per l'Amoenitas;* edited by Mariavittoria Antico Gallina. Milano: Et. 273-298.

Facella, Antonino. 2010. 'San Marco d'Alunzio.' *Bibliografia Topografica della Colonizzazione Greca in Italia e nelle Isole Tirreniche*, Vol.XVIII. Pisa-Roma: Scuola Normale Superiore. 44-57.

Fadda, Maria Ausilia. 2006. *Il Museo Archeologico Nazionale di Nuoro.* Collana 'Sardegna Archeologica', Serie Guide e Itinerari. Sassari: Delfino

------. 2013. *Nel segno dell'acqua. Santuari e bronzi votivi della Sardegna nuragica.* Sassari: Delfino.

------. 2014. 'Il Sacro monte di Nurdole.' *Archeologia Viva*, XXXIII, n.167. Firenze: Giunti. 28-45.

Falsone, Gioacchino. 1980. 'Per salvare Entella.' *Sicilia Archeologica*, 43. Trapani: Ente provinciale per il turismo di Trapani. 21-26.

Fantalkin, Alexander. 2006. 'Identity in the making: Greeks in the eastern Mediterranean during the Iron Age.' *Naukratis: Greek Diversity in Egypt: Studies on East Greek Pottery and Exchange in the Eastern Mediterranean*; edited by Alexandra Villing and Udo Schlotzhauer. London: British Museum. 199-208.

Farber, Walter. 1981. 'Zur älteren akkadischen Beschwörungsliteratur.' *Zeitschrift für Assyriologie und vorderasiatische Archäologie*, 71. Berlin: de Gruyter. 51-72.

Felli, Candida. 2001. 'Some notes on the Akkadian Glyptic from Tell Brak.' *Excavations at Tell Brak Vol. 2: Nagar in the Third Millennium BC*; edited by D. Oates, J. Oates and H. McDonald. Cambridge, McDonald Institute for Archaeological Research. 141-50.

Fields, Nicholas. 1994. 'Apollo: God of War, Protector of Mercenaries.' *Archaeology in the Peloponnese, New Excavations and Research*; edited by Kenneth Sheedy. Oxford: Oxbow Books. 95-113.

Fiorelli, Giuseppe. 1845. *Monete inedite dell'Italia antica.* Napoli: Virgilio.

Fischer-Bossert, Wolfgang. 2012. 'A Brief Numismatic History of Sicily.' *Handbook of Coins of Sicily*, edited by Oliver D. Hoover. Lancaster, PA: Classical Numismatic Group. liii-lxv.

Flower, Michael A. 2008. *The Seer in Ancient Greece.* Oakland: University of California Press.

Fontan, Elisabeth. 2001. 'La Frise du Transport du Bois, Décor du Palais de Sargon II à Khorsabad.' *Cedrus Libani, Archaeology and History in Lebanon.* No. 14; edited by C. Doumet-Serhal. London. 58-63.

Forsythe, Gary. 1999. *Livy and Early Rome: A Study in Historical Method and Judgment.* Stuttgart: Franz Steiner Verlag.

Fortunelli, Simona. 2007. *Gravisca. Scavi nel santuario greco. I.2* Bari: Edipuglia.

Fowler, Robert L. 2013. *Early Greek Mythography*. Vol. II. Oxford: University Press.

Franke, Peter Robert, and Max Hirmer. 1964. Die griechische Münze. München: Hirmer Verlag.

Frankfort, Henri. 1939. *Cylinder Seals. A Documentary Essay on the Art and Religion of the Ancient Near East.* London: Macmillan.

------. 1943. *More Sculpture from the Diyala Region.* Chicago: University Press.

------. 1951. *The Birth of Civilization in the Near East.* Bloomington: Indiana University Press.

------. 1996. *The Art and Architecture of the Ancient Orient.* New Haven: Yale University Press.

Frazer, James G. 2003. *Adonis Attis Osiris: Studies in the History of Oriental Religion.* London: Macmillan.

Frederisckson, M. W. 1968. 'Review of E.T. Salmon, *Samnium and the Samnites* (1967).' *Journal of Roman Studies*, LVIII. Cambridge: University Press. 224-9.

Frel, Jiří. 1980. 'Preface.' *Stamnoi: An Exhibition at the J. Paul Getty Museum*; edited by Cornelia Isler-Kerényi and Jiří Frel. Malibu: The J. Paul Getty Museum.

Frenez, Dennys, and Massimo Vidale. 2012. 'Harappan Chimaeras as 'Symbolic Hypertexts'. Some Thoughts on Plato, Chimaera and the Indus Civilization.' *South Asian Studies*, Vol. 28, No. 2. Lahore: Centre for South Asian Studies, University of the Punjab. 107-130.

Frey Kupper, Susanne. 2001. 'Ein 'neuer' Acheloos der Iaitiner. Ein Beitrag zur Erforschung der frühen Münzprägung von Iaitas.' *Zona Archeologica: Festschrift für Hans Peter Isler zum 60. Geburtstag.* Bonn: Dr. Rudolf Habelt GMBH. 159-173.

------. 2013. *Die antiken Fundmünzen vom Monte Iato 1971-1990. Ein Beitrag zur Geldgeschichte Westsizilien.* Studia Ietina X, 1-2. Lausanne: Éditions di Zèbre.

Friedläender, Julius. 1850. *Die Oskischen Münzen.* Leipzig: Wigand.

Frietag, Klaus. 2015. 'Akarnania and the Akarnanian League.' *Federalism in Greek Antiquity*, edited by Hans Beck and Peter Funke. Cambridge: University Press. 66-85.

Fuentes, Oscar. 2013. 'The depiction of the individual in prehistory: human representations in Magdalenian societies.' *Antiquity*, Vol. 87, No. 228. Oxford: University Press. 985-1000.

Fugazzola Delfino, Maria Antonietta. 1988. 'Le acque interne: appunti di archeologia preistorica.' *Etruria Meridionale. Conoscenza, conservazione, fruizione. Atti del Convegno Viterbo. 29 Novembre – 1 Dicembre 1985.* Roma: Quasar. 17-25.

Funghi, Maria Serena. 1997. 'The Derveni Papyrus.' *Studies on the Derveni Papyrus*; edited by André Laks and Glenn W. Most. Oxford: Clarendon. 25-37.

Gabrici, Ettore. 1925. 'Polizzello. Abitato preistorico presso Mussomeli.' *Atti della Accademia di Scienze, Lettere e Arti di Palermo*, Vol. XIV. Palermo: Presso L'Accademia. 3-11.

------. 1927. *La monetazione del bronzo nella Sicila antica.* Bologna: Forni.

------. 1959. *Problemi di numismatica greca della Sicilia e Magna Grecia.* Napoli: G. Macchiaroli.

Gais, Ruth M. 1978. 'Some Problems of River God Iconography.' *American Journal of Archaeology, No.* 82. New York: Macmillan. 355-77.

Gallou, Chrysanthi. 2002. *The Cult of the Dead in Central Greece during the Mycenaean Period.* Doctoral Thesis. University of Nottingham.

Galvagno, Emilio. 2006. 'I Siculi: fine di un ethnos.' *Diodoro Siculo e la Sicilia indigena. Atti del convegno di studi, Caltanissetta 21-22 maggio 2005*; edited by Calogero Miccichè, Simona Modeo, Luigi Santagati. Palermo: Regione siciliana, Assessorato dei Beni Culturali, Ambientali e della Pubblica Istruzione. 34-50.

Gandolfo, Lucina. 1998. 'Monete.' *Palermo Punica. Museo Archeologico Regionale Antonino Salinas.* Palermo: Sellerio. 348-359.

------. 2005. 'Note su due monete inedite del Museo Archeologico Regionale 'Antonino Salinas'.' *Atti del V Congresso Internazionale di Studi Fenici e Punici, Marsala-Palermo, October 8th-9th, 2000*; Edited by A. Giammellaro. Vol. 2. Palermo: Università degli Studi. 889-893.

Garbati, Giuseppe, and Chiara Peri. 2008. 'Considerazioni sul 'culto delle acque' nella Sardegna punica e tardo punica: l'esempio di Mitza Salamu (Dolianova -Ca).' *Saturnia Tellus: definizioni dello spazio consacrato in ambiente etrusco, italico, fenicio-punico, iberico e celtico. Conference proceedings.* Roma: Consiglio nazionale delle ricerche. 385-395.

Garbini, Giovanni. 1990. 'Sys 'campo salato' in ebraico.' *Egitto e Vicino Oriente,* Vol. 13. Pisa. 139-141.

Garraffo, Salvatore. 1993. 'La monetazione dell'età dionigiana. Contromarche e riconiazioni.' *La monetazione dell'età dionigiana. Atti dell'VIII Convegno del Centro Internazionale di Studi Numismatici Napoli 29 maggio – 1 giugno 1983.* Roma. 191-242.

Garrucci, Raffaele. 1885. *Le monete della Italia Antica, raccolta generale del P. Raffaele Garrucci. Parte seconda: monete coniate.* Roma: Salviucci. (Bologna: Forni, 1967 reprint).

Gardner, Percy. 1876. *Greek River Worship.* London: Royal Society of Literature.

------. 1883. *The Types of Greek Coins; an Archaeological Essay.* Cambridge: University Press.

------. 1883. *Catalog of Greek Coins: Thessaly to Aitolia.* London: Trustees of the British Museum.

Gatti Lo Guzzo, Laura. 1978. *Il deposito votivo dell'Esquilino detto di Minerva Medica.* Firenze: Sansoni.

Gehrke, Hans Joachim, and Eckhard Wirbelauer. 2004. 'Akarnania and Adjacent Areas.' *An Inventory of Archaic and Classical Poleis*, edited by Mogens Herman Hansen and Thomas Heine Nielsen. Oxford: University Press. 351-378.

Geller, Mark J. 1985. *Forerunners to Udug-hul. Sumerian Exorcistic Incantations.* Freiburger Altorientalische Studien, 12. Stuttgart.

------. 2001-2. 'West Meets East: Early Greek and Babylonian Diagnostics.' *Archiv für Orientforschung*, Bd. 48/49. Berlin: Ernst Weidner. 50-75.

Genick, Daniela Cocchi. 2002. 'Dati relativi ai culti delle acque in età protostorica nell'Italia centrale tirrenica.' *Paesaggi d'acque. Atti del quinto incontro di Studi, Preistoria e Protostoria in Etruria;* edited by Nuccia Negroni Catacchio. Vol. II. Milano: Centro Studi Preistoria e Archeologia. 405- 416.

------. 2014. 'Le evidenze di contrada Scintilia nell'ambito dei rituali funerari dell'eta` del rame.' *Storie Sepolte. Riti, culti e vita quotidiana all'alba del IV millennio a.C. La necropoli dell'età del rame di contrada Scintilia di Favara*; edited by Domenica Gullì. Palermo: Assessorato Regionale dei Beni culturali e dell'Identità Siciliana. 45-54.

Genovese, Guglielmo. 1999. *I santuari rurali della Calabria Greca.* Rome: Bretschneider.

Gentile, Patrizia. 2014. 'Centri della Daunia. Tiati-Teanum Apulum.' *Archeologia delle Regioni d'Italia. Puglia*, edited by G. Ceraudo. Bologna: BraDypUS. 122-124.

Gentili, Gino Vinicio. 1963. 'Milazzo.' *Enciclopedia dell'Arte Antica.* Treccani.

Georgiev, Georgi. J. 1961. 'Kulturgruppen der Jungstein-und der Kupferzeit in der Ebene von Thrazien (Südbulgarien).' *L'Europe à la fin de l'âge de lapierre*. Prague: L'Académie tchécoslovaque des Sciences. 45-100.

Gerhard, Eduard. 1867. *Etruskische Spiegel*. Volume IV. Berlin: G. Reimer.

Gernet, Louis. 1981. *The Anthropology of Ancient Greece*; trans. Johan Hamilton and Blaise Nagy. Baltimore, MD: Johns Hopkins University Press.

Ghirotto, Silvia, Francesca Tassi, Erica Fumagalli, Vincenza Colonna, Anna Sandionigi, Martina Lari, Stefania Vai, Emmanuele Petiti, Giorgio Corti, Ermanno Rizzi, Gianluca De Bellis, David Caramelli, and Guido Barbujani. 2013. 'Origins and Evolution of the Etruscans' mtDNA.' *PLoS ONE* 8(2): e55519. doi: 10.1371/journal.pone.0055519. Accessed March 2016.

Giammatteo, Tonia. 2005. 'Il ruolo dell'acqua nelle dinamiche del sacro.' *Torre di Satriano I. Il santuario Lucano*. Roma: Osanna. 443-447.

Giampaola, Daniela, and Bruno d'Agostino. 2005. 'Osservazioni storiche e archeologiche sulla fondazione di Napoli.' *Noctes Campanae. Studi di storia antica ed archeologia dell'Italia preromana e romana in memoria di M. Frederiksen*, edited by A.V. Harris and E. Lo Cascio. Napoli. 49-80.

Giannelli, Giulio. 1920. 'La figura taurina sulle monete della Magna Graecia.' *Rivista italiana di Numismatica*. Vol. XXXIII. Milano: Società Numismatica Italiana. 105-140.

Gilmour, Garth H. 1997. 'The nature and function of astragalus bones from archaeological contexts in the Levant and Eastern Mediterranean.' *Oxford Journal of Archaeology*, 16, 2. Oxford: Blackwell. 167-175.

Gilotta, Fernando. 1985. *Gutti e Askoi a rilievo Italioti ed Etruschi*. Roma: Bretschneider.

Gimbutas, Marija. 1982. *The Goddesses and Gods of Old Europe, 6500-3500 BC, Myths and Cult Images*. Berkeley: University of California.

------. 1989. *The Language of the Goddess: Unearthing the Hidden Symbols of Western Civilization*. San Francisco: Harper & Row.

------, Miriam Robbins Dexter, and Karlene Jones-Bley (eds.). 1997. *The Kurgan culture and the Indo-Europeanization of Europe*. Journal of Indo-European Studies Monograph, No.18. Washington, DC: Institute for the Study of Man.

------. 2001. *The Living Goddess*. Oakland: University of California Press.

Giontella, Claudia. 2006. *I luoghi dell'acqua 'divina'. Complessi santuariali e forme devozionali in Etruria e Umbria fra epoca arcaica ed età romana*. Roma: Aracne.

Giorgetti, Dario. 2004. 'La Stipe Votiva del Titano.' *Romanizzazione e Moneta. La testimonianza dei Rinvenimenti dall'Emilia Romagna*; edited by E. Ercolani Cocchi, A.L. Morelli, and D. Neri. Firenze: All'insegna del Giglio. 43-45.

Giosan, Liviu, Florin Filip and Stefan Constantinescu. 2009. 'Was the Black Sea catastrophically flooded in the early Holocene?.' *Quaternary Science Reviews*, 26. United Kingdom: Elsevier. 1–6.

Giove, Teresa. 2001. 'Le monete dal santuario di Fondo Ruozzo a Teano (CE).' *Annali dell'Istituto Italiano di Numismatica*, N. 48. Roma. 209-247.

Giudice, Filippo. 1996. 'Il ruolo di Catania nella rete dei traffici commerciali del Mediterraneo.' *Catania Antica. Atti del convegno della Società italiana per lo studio dell'antichità classica, Catania 23 - 24 maggio 1992;* edited by Bruno Gentili. Pisa-Roma: Istituti Editoriali e Poligrafici Internazionali. 97-148.

------, Enrico Procelli, Rosa Maria Albanese, and Massimo Frasca. 1979. 'Catania. Scavo all'interno del muro di cinta del Monastero dei Benedettini.' *Cronache di Archeologia*, Vol. XVIII. Catania: Università di Catania. 129-141.

Giuffrida, M. 1990. 'Rapporti tra l'area elima e il Mediterraneo orientale.' *Gli Elimi e l' area Elima fino all' inizio della prima guerra punica. Atti del Seminario di Studi. Palermo - Contessa Entellina 25-28 maggio 1989*. Archivio Storico Siciliano Vol. XIV-XV (1988-1989). Palermo, Società Siciliana per la Storia Patria. 115-131.

Giuliano, Antonio. 1969. 'Osservazioni sulle pitture della 'Tomba dei tori' a Tarquinia.' *Studi Etruschi*, Vol. XXXVII. Firenze: Olschki. 3-26.

Gjerstad, Einar. 1926. *Studies on Prehistoric Cyprus*. Uppsala: P. Åström.

------. 1934-1937. *The Swedish Cyprus Expedition. Finds and Results of the Excavations in Cyprus 1927-1931*. Volume I-III. Stockholm: The Swedish Cyprus Expedition.

Goblot, Henri. 1979. *Les Qanat. Une technique d'acquisition de l'eau*. Paris: Mouton.

Goldwasser, Orli, and Joseph Naveh. 1976. 'The origin of the Tet-Symbol.' *Israel Exploration Journal*, 26. Jerusalem. 15-19.

Golovinski, Evgeni. 2002. 'Ахелой.' Българска енциклопедия А-Я, БАН. Sophia: Сирма.

Goltzius, Hubert. 1576. *Graecia sive historia urbium et populorum Graeciae ex antiquis numismatibus restituta*. Brugis Flandrorum: Goltz.

Gori, Antonio Francesco. 1731. *Gemmae Antiquae Ex Thesauro Mediceo Et Privatorum Dactyliothecis Florentiae: exhibentes tabulis C imagines virorum illustrium et deorum*. Florence: Moücke.

Gorini, Giovanni. 1975. *La monetazione incusa della Magna Grecia*. Milano: Edizioni Arte e Moneta.

Gornés, Hachero, J. S. 2000. 'Ipogei del Talaiotico finale: analisi e interpretazione della necropoli di Cales Coves, Minorca.' *L'ipogeismo nel Mediterraneo: origini, sviluppo, quadri culturali: atti del Congresso internazionale, 23- 28 maggio 1994, Sassari-Oristano*. Università degli studi di Sassari, Facoltà di Lettere e filosofia, Istituto di Antichità, Arte e Discipline Etnodemologiche e Dipartimento di Scienze Umanistiche e dell'Antichità, Vol. II. Sassari: Stampacolor. 553-571.

Grainger, John D. 1990. *Seleukos Nikator: Constructing a Hellenistic Kingdom*. London: Routledge.

------. 1999. *The League of the Aitolians*. Leiden: Brill.

Gran-Aymerich, Jean. 2013. 'Etruria Marittima: Massalia and Gaul, Carthage and Iberia.' *The Etruscan World*; edited by Jean MacIntosh Turfa. London: Routledge. 319-348.

Grant, Michael. 1969. *From imperium to auctoritas. A historical study of aes coinage in the Roman Empire, 49 B.C. - A.D. 14*. Cambridge: University Press.

Gravina, Armando. 1980. 'Preistoria e Protostoria del basso Fortore.' *Atti del I Convegno Nazionale sulla Preistoria-Protostoria-Storia della Daunia.* San Severo. 73-101.

Graziadio, Giampaolo. 1997. 'Le presenze cipriote in Italia nel quadro del commercio mediterraneo dei secoli XIV e XIII a.C.' *Studi Classici e Orientali*, Vol. XLVI. Pisa: Libreria Goliardica Editrice. 681-719.

------, and Riccardo Guglielmino. 2011. 'The Aegean and Cypriot Imports to Italy as Evidence for Direct and Indirect Trade in the 14th and 13th Centuries BC.' *Intercultural Contacts In The Ancient Mediterranean. Proceedings of The International Conference At the Netherlands-Flemish Institute in Cairo. 25th to 29th October 2008*. Leuven: Peeters. 309-326.

Green, Alberto Ravinell Whitney. 2003. *The Storm-god in the Ancient Near East*. Winona Lake: Eisenbrauns.

Green, Antony. 2000. 'Ancient Mesopotamian Religious Iconography.' *Civilizations of the Ancient Near East;* edited by Jack M. Sasson. Peabody: Hendrickson Publishers (reprint of New York: Scribner, 1995 edition). 1837-1855.

Greene, Andrew. 2000. 'Theseus, Hero of Athens.' *Heilbrunn Timeline of Art History.* New York: The Metropolitan Museum of Art, online publication.

Grenfell, Bernard Pyne, and Arthur Surridge Hunt. 1899. *P.Oxy.II 0221. Scholia on Iliad XXI.* London.

Greenwell, William. 1887. 'The electrum coinage of Cyzicus.' *Numismatic Chronicle*, Ser. 4, Vol. VII. London: Rollin and Feuardent. 1-124.

Grifoni Cremonesi, Renata. 1986. 'Alcuni dati relativi a fenomeni funerari con implicazioni cultuali nella Preistoria e problemi di interpretazione.' *Prospettive storico-antropologiche in archeologia preistorica.* Part II, Dialoghi di Archeologia Vol. 4, No. 2. Roma: Quasar. 265-269.

------. 1987. 'Témoignages de cultes dans le néolithique ancienne des Abruzzes.' *Prémières communautés paysannes de la Méditerranée occidentale.* Paris: Centre national de la recherche scientifique. 413-418.

------. 1994. 'Observations on the Problems Related to Certain Cult Phenomena during the Neolithic in the Italian Peninsula.' *Journal of European Archaeology*, 2, 2. Aldershot: Avebury. 179–197.

------. 2007. 'Notes on some cultic aspects of Italian Prehistory.' *Documenta Praehistorica*, Vol. XXXIV. Ljubljana: University Press. 221-230.

Grinsell, Leslie Valentine 1941. 'The Boat of the Dead in the Bronze Age.' *Antiquity*, Vol. 15, Issue 60. Oxford: University Press. 360-369.

Groenewoud, Elvira. 2001. 'Use of Water in Phoenician Sanctuaries.' *Ancient Near Eastern Studies*, Vol. 38. Louvain: Peeters. 139-159.

Gruzinski, Serge. 1999. *La pensée métisse*. Paris: Fayard.

Guerrero Ayuso, Víctor M. 1986. *Una aportación al estudio de las ánforas púnicas Maña C*. Paris: CNRS. 163-78.

------. 1987. 'Los sarcofagos tauromorfos de 'La Punta'. Un caso de aculturacion indigena en la Protohistoria de Mallorca.' *Rivista di Studi Fenici*, XV, 2. Roma: Consiglio Nazionale delle Ricerche. 163-78.

Guglielmino, Riccardo. 2011. 'The Aegean and Cypriot Imports to Italy as Evidence for Direct and Indirect Trade in the 14th and 13th Centuries BC.' *Intercultural Contacts in the Ancient Mediterranean Proceedings of The International Conference at the Netherlands-Flemish Institute in Cairo, 25th to 29th October 2008*. Leuven: Peeters. 309-326.

Guidetti, Massimo. 2004. *Storia del Mediterraneo nell'antichità: 9.-1. secolo a.C.* Milano: Jaca Book.

Guidi, Alessandro. 1980. 'Luoghi di culto dell'età del Bronzo finale e della Prima età del Ferro nel Lazio meridionale.' *Archeologia Laziale*. Vol. 3. Quaderni del Centro di studio per l'Archeologia etrusco-italica. Roma: Consiglio Nazionale delle Ricerche. 148-155.

------. 1990. 'Alcune ossevazioni sulla problematica delle offerte nella protostoria dell'Italia centrale.' *Scienze dell'Antichità*, Vol. III-IV. Roma: Università degli studi di Roma La Sapienza. 403-414.

------. 1992. 'Recenti ritrovamenti in grotta nel Lazio: un riesame critico del problema dell'utilizzazione delle cavità naturali.' *Rassegna di Archeologia*. Vol. 10. Firenze : All'Insegna del Giglio. 427-437.

------. 2009. 'Aspetti della religione tra la fine dell'età del bronzo e la I età del ferro.' *Il Lazio dai Colli Albani ai Monti Lepini tra preistoria ed età moderna*. Roma: Quasar. 143-151.

Gulletta, Maria Ida. 2006. 'Kamisos/Lykos/Halykos. Da 'via del sale' a 'confine' tra le due eparchie (note di geografia storica nella Sicilia centro-occidentale).' *Troianer sind wir gewesen - Migrationen in der antiken Welt*; edited by Olshausen E. and Sonnabend H. Geographica Historica, Vol. 21. Stuttgart: Steiner. 402-419.

------. 2011. 'Taormina.' *Bibliografia Topografica della Colonizzazione Greca in Italia e nelle Isole Tirreniche*, Vol. XX. Pisa-Roma: Scuola Normale Superiore.

Gullì, Domenica. 2014. 'The meanings of caves in the prehistory and protohistory of the Agrigento territory.' *From Cave to Dolmen: ritual and symbolic aspects in the prehistory between Sciacca, Sicily and the central Mediterranean*; edited by Domenica Gullì. Oxford: Archaeopress. 73-80.

Guzzo, Pietro Giovanni. 2003. 'Fonti divine. Miti dell'acqua in Magna Grecia.' *Storia dell'acqua. Mondi materiali e universi simbolici*; edited by V. Teti. Roma: Donzelli. 35-42.

Haider, Peter W. 1996. ‚Griechen im Vorderen Orient und in Ägypten bis ca. 590 v. Chr.' *Wege zur Genese griechischer Identität – Die Bedeutung der früharchaischen Zeit*; edited by C. Ulf. Berlin: Akademie Verlag. 59-115.

------. 2004. ‚Kontakte zwischen Griechen und Ägyptern und ihre Auswirkungen auf die archaisch-griechische Welt.' *Griechische Archaik: Interne Entwicklungen – Externe Impulse*; edited by R.Rollinger and C. Ulf. Berlin: Akademie Verlag. 447-474.

Håland, Evy J. 2009. ‚Take, Skamandros, My Virginity.' *The Nature and Function of Water, Baths, Bathing, and Hygiene from Antiquity through the Renaissance*; edited by Cynthia Kosso and Anne Scott. Leiden: Brill. 109-148.

Haldon, John. 1999. *Warfare, State and Society in the Byzantine World*. London: Routledge.

Hale, John R. 2013. 'Not Patriots, Not Farmers, Not Amateurs: Greek Soldiers of Fortune and the Origins of Hoplite Warfare.' *Men of Bronze: Hoplite Warfare in Ancient Greece*; edited by Donald Kagan and Gregory F. Viggiano. Princeton: University Press. 176-193.

Hallo, William H. 1999. 'More Incantations and Rituals from the Yale Babylonian Collection.' *Mesopotamian Magic: Textual, Historical, and Interpretative Perspectives*, vol.1; edited by I. Tzvi Abusch, Karel Van Der Toorn. Groningen: Styx. 275-289.

Hammond, Nicholas Geoffrey Lemprière. 1933. 'Prehistoric Epirus and the Dorian Invasion.' *The Annual of the British School at Athens*, Vol. 32. 131-79.

------. 1996. 'Ambracia.' *Oxford Classical Dictionary*. Oxford: University Press.

Hansen, Donald P. 2001. 'The Reclining Human-faced Bison Sculpture from Area SS.' *Excavations at Tell Brak Vol. 2: Nagar in the Third Millennium BC*; edited by D. Oates, J. Oates and H. McDonald. Cambridge, McDonald Institute for Archaeological Research. 257-263.

Harari, Maurizio. 2010. 'The Imagery of the Etrusco-Faliscan Pantheon Between Architectural Sculpture and Vase-painting.' *Material Aspects of Etruscan Religion: Proceedings of the International Colloquium in Leiden, May 29 and 30, 2008*. Bulletin Antieke Beschaving: Annual Papers on Classical Archaeology, Suppl. 16; edited by L.B. van der Meer. Leuven: Peeters. 83-103.

Harlan, Michael. 1995. *Roman Republican Moneyers and Their Coins 63 BC-49 BC*. London: Seaby.

Harper, Robert F. 1888. 'Transliteration and Translation of Cylinder a of the Esarhaddon Inscriptions.' *Hebraica*, 4, 2. Chicago: American Publication Society of Hebrew. 99-117.

Hassan, Fekri. 1988. 'The Predynastic Egypt.' *Journal of World Prehistory*, Vol. 2. Berlin: Springer. 136-85.

Haynes, Sybille. 2000. *Etruscan Civilization: A Cultural History*. Los Angeles: Getty Publications.

Head, Barclay Vincent. 1911. *Historia Numorum: A Manual of Greek Numismatics*. Oxford: Clarendon.

Hecataeus, and Rud. Henr Klausen. 1831. *Hecataei Milesii Fragmenta*. Berolini: Reimer.

Hendrickx, Stan. 2002. 'Bovines in Egyptian Predynastic and Early Dynastic Iconography.' *Drought, Food and Culture: Ecological Change and Food Security in Africa's Later Prehistory*; edited by Fekri Hassan. New York: Kluwer Academic - Plenum Publishers. 275-318.

Hermary, Antoine. 1979. 'Statuette d'un 'pretre' masqué.' *Bulletin de correspondance hellénique*, Vol. 103, No. 2. Paris: De Boccard. 734-741.

Herring, Edward. 1996. 'Using your Religion. Native Ritual and Belief in Southern Italy in the 5th and 4th Centuries BC.' *Approaches to the Study of Ritual (Italy and the Ancient Mediterranean)*. Vol. II; edited by J. B. Wilkins. London: Accordia Research Centre. 142-183.

Herzog, Werner, dir. 2010. *Cave of Forgotten Dreams*. Los Angeles: Creative Differences Production Company.

Hesiod, and Friedrich Solmsen. 1970. *Hesiodi Theogonia*. Oxford: Clarendon.

Hesiod, Friedrich Solmsen, Reinhold Merkelbach, and M. L. West. 1990. *Hesiodi Theogonia; Opera et dies; Scvtvm*. Oxford: Clarendon.

Hesiod, and M.L. West. 1978. *Hesiod: Theogony: with Prolegomena and Commentary*. Oxford: Clarendon.

Heuzey, Léon. 1899. 'Le taureau chaldéen à tête humaine et ses dérivés.' *Monuments et mémoires de la Fondation Eugène Piot*, Tome 6. Paris: Académie des inscriptions et belles-lettres. 115-132.

Heyman, Carlo. 1970. 'Les types de monnaies de Méthylion en Thessalie.' *Ancient Society*, Vol. I. 115-128. Leuven: Peeters.

Higgins, Reynold Alleyne. 1954. *Catalogue of the Terracottas in the Department of Greek and Roman Antiquities, British Museum*. Vol. I London: British Museum.

Hill George F. 2010. *A History of Cyprus*, Vol.1. Cambridge: University Press.

Hirth, Kenneth G. 1978. 'Interregional trade and the formation of prehistoric gateway communities.' *American Antiquity*, Vol. 43, No.1. Washington: S.A.A. 25-45.

Hodder, Ian. 1990. *The Domestication of Europe*. Oxford: Blackwell.

Hoffmann, Herbert. 1997. *Sotades. Symbols of Immortality on Greek Vases*. Oxford: University Press.

Hogart, David George. 1920. *Hittite Seals, with particular reference to the Ashmolean Collection*. Oxford.

Hole, Frank. 1983. 'Symbols of Religion and Social Organization at Susa.' *The Hilly Flanks and Beyond: Essays on the Prehistory of Southwestern Asia Presented to Robert J. Braidwood*; edited by T.C. Young, P.E.L. Smith, and P. Mortensen. SAOC Vol. 36. Chicago: The Oriental Institute. 315-331.

------. 2010. 'A Monumental Failure: the Collapse of Susa.' *Beyond the Ubaid: Transformation and Integration in the Late Prehistoric Societies of the Middle East*; edited by R.A. Carter and G. Philip. SAOC Vol. 63. Chicago: The Oriental Institute. 227-243.

Hollander, Robert, and Jean Hollander. 2000. *Dante, the Inferno*. New York: Random House.

Holloway, R. Ross. 1975. 'Le monetazioni di Agyrion, Aluntion, Entella, Hipana, Nakone, Stiela.' *Le emissioni dei centri siculi fino all'epoca di Timoleonte e i loro rapporti con la monetazione delle colonie greche di Sicilia : atti del IV Convegno del Centro internazionale di studi numismatici, Napoli, 9-14 aprile 1973 (CCISN*, 4). Roma: Istituto Italiano di Numismatica. 133-155.

------. 1986. 'The Bulls in the 'Tomb of the Bulls' at Tarquinia.' *American Journal of Archaeology*, Vol. 90, No. 4. New York: Macmillan. 447-452.

Holm, Adolf. 1906. *Storia della Sicilia nell'antichità*, Vol. 3.2, edited by G. Kirner. Torino: Clausen.

Holton, Robert. 2012. 'Some comments on Cosmopolitanism and Europe.' *European Cosmopolitanism in Question;* edited by Roland Robertson and Anne Sophie Krossa. New York: Macmillan. 25-43.

Homer, and Robert Fagles. 1990. *The Iliad*. New York: Penguin.

Honeyman, Alexander Mackie. 1947. 'Varia Punica.' *American Journal of Philology*, Vol. 68. Baltimore, MD: Johns Hopkins University Press. 77-82.

Hoover, Oliver. 2012. *Handbook of Coins of Sicily (Including Lipara)*. Lancaster, PA: Classical Numismatic Group.

------. 2015. *Handbook of the Coinage of Northern and Central Greece*. Lancaster, PA: Classical Numismatic Group.

Houghton, Arthur, Catharine C. Lorber, and Oliver D. Hoover. 2002. *Seleucid Coins: A Comprehensive Catalogue*. New York: The American Numismatic Society.

Houseman, Laura Alexander. 2014. *Fluid Metaphors: Exploring the Management, Meaning and Perception of Fresh Water in Minoan Crete*. Doctoral Thesis, The University of Manchester.

Hult, Gunnel. 1983. *Bronze Age ashlar masonry in the eastern Mediterranean. Cyprus, Ugarit, and neighbouring regions*. Göteborg: P. Åström.

Huot, Jean Lonis. 1978. 'The Man-Faced Bull L.76.17 of Larsa.' *Sumer: A Journal of Archaeology and History in Iraq*, 34. Bagdad: State Organization of Antiquities and Heritage. 104-110.

Hurter, S. Mani, and Hans-Joachim Liewald. 2002. 'Neue münztypen der Kyzikener Elektronprägung.' *Schweizerische numismatische Rundschau*, Band 81. Bern: Schweizerische Numismatische Gesellschaft. 21-38.

------, and Hans Joachim Liewald. 2004. 'Neue Nominale in der Elektronprägung von Kyzikos.' *Schweizerische numismatische Rundschau*, Band 83. Bern: Schweizerische Numismatische Gesellschaft. 27-43.

Hyginus, Gaius Julius and Peter K. Marshall. 1993. *Hygini Fabulae*. Stutgardiae: Teubner.

Iaia, Cristiano. 2001. 'Gli oggetti di uso cerimoniale.' *Tarquinia Etrusca. Una nuova storia. Catalogo della Mostra*; edited by A.M. Moretti Sgubini. Roma: Bretschneider. 81-93.

Ignarra, Nicola. 1770. *De palaestra Neapolitana: commentarius inscriptionem athleticam Neapoli anno 1754 detectam ... ; ad calcem operis adnectitur de Buthysiae agone Puteolano dissertatio*. Neapoli: Donati Campi.

Illingworth, Nicholas J. 1988. 'Inscriptions from Tell Brak 1986.' *Iraq*, Vol. 50. London: British Institute for the Study of Iraq. 87-108.

Imhoof-Blumer, Friedrich. 1878. *Die Münzen Akarnaniens*. Wien: Manz.

------. 1883. *Monnaies grecques*. Amsterdam: J. Müller.

------. 1915. 'Di alcune monete italiche e sicule.' *Atti e Memorie dell'Istituto Italiano di Numismatica*, Vol. 2. Roma. 13-19.

------. 1924. 'Fluß- und Meergötter auf griechischen und römischen Münzen. (Personifikationen der Gewässer).' *Schweizerische Numismatische Rundschau*, Band 23. Bern: Schweizerische Numismatische Gesellschaft. 173-421.

Ingoglia, Caterina. 2007. 'La più antica ceramica in Wild Goat Style da Gela.' *Sicilia Antiqua. An International Journal of Archaeology*, Vol. III (2006). Pisa-Roma: Fabrizio Serra. 19-37.

Isaac, Eric. 1962. 'On the Domestication of Cattle.' *Science*, New Series, Vol. 137, No. 3525. Washington, DC: American Association for the Advancement of Science. 195-204.

Isidore of Seville. *Isidori Hispalensis Episcopi Etymologiarum Sive Originum*. Liber XIV (Accessed online via thelatinlibrary in April 2016, http://www.thelatinlibrary.com/isidore/14.shtml).

Isler, Hans Peter. 1970. *Acheloos: Eine Monographie*. Bern: Verlag.

------. 1981. 'Acheloos.' *Lexicon Iconographicum Mythologiae Classicae*. Vol. I. Zürich: Artemis & Verlag. 12-36.

------. 2006. 'Monte Iato. Indigène et Grecs à l'époque archaïque.' *Des Grecs en Sicile... Grecs et indigènes en Sicile occidentale d'après les fouilles archèologiques*, edited by F. Spatafora and S. Vassallo. Caltanissetta. 77-80.

Isocrates, and George Norlin. 1928. *Isocrates*. London: W. Heinemann, Ltd.

Ivanov, Totju. 1981. 'Two Religious Courts of Razgrad.' *Art*, 9-10. Bulgaria. 72.

Jakobsen, Thorvild. 1934. 'The Water Supplies of Nineveh.' *Sennacherib's Aqueduct at Jerwan*; edited by Thorvild Jakobsen and Seton Lloyd. Chicago: University Press. 36-41.

Jameson, Robert. 1980. *Collection R. Jameson*. Volume 3. Chicago: OBOL International.

Jameson, Michael H. 1991. 'Sacrifice before Battle.' *Hoplites: The Classical Greek Battle Experience*; edited by V.D. Hanson. London: Routledge. 197-228.

Janko, Richard. 2002. 'The Derveni Papyrus: an interim text.' *Zeitschrift für Papyrologie und Epigraphik*, 141. Bonn: Habelt. 1-62.

Jannot, Jean-René. 1974. 'Acheloos, le taureau androcéphale et les masques cornus dans l'Etrurie archaique.'
Latomus, 33, 4. Bruxelles: Latomus. 765-789.

------. 1984. 'Sur les fausses portes étrusques.' *Latomus*, 43, 2. Bruxelles: Latomus. 273-283.

------. 1984. *Les reliefs archaïques de Chiusi*. Rome: École Française de Rome.

------. 2005. *Religion in Ancient Etruria*. Wisconsin: University Press.

Jenkins, Gilbert Kenneth. 1970. *The Coinage of Gela*. Berlin: De Gruyter.

------, and Mário de Castro Hipólito. 1989. *A Catalogue of the Calouste Gulbenkian Collection of Greek Coins: Greece to East*. Part 2. Lisbon: Fundação Calouste Gulbenkian.

------. 1997. *Coins of Punic Sicily*. Zürich. Combined reprint of the original article published in four parts in *Schweizerische Numismatische Rundschau*. Bern. [Vol. 50 (1971), 25-78; Vol. 53 (1974), 23-41; Vol. 56 (1977), 5-65; Vol. 57 (1978), 5-68].

Johannowsky, Werner. 1989. *Capua antica*. Napoli: Banco di Napoli, 1989.

Johnson, Mats. 1996. 'Water, animals and agricultural technology: a study of settlement patterns and economic change in Neolithic southern Greece.' *Oxford Journal of Archaeology*. 15, 3. Oxford: Blackwell. 267-295.

Johnston, Sarah Iles. 2004. *Religions of the Ancient World: A Guide*. Cambridge: Belknap Press of Harvard University Press.

Julian the Emperor, and Wilmer Wright. 1913. 'Hymn to the Mother of the Gods.' *The Works of the Emperor Julian*. Vol. I. London: Heinemann. 462-3.

Jung, Reinhard and Mathias Mehofer. 2008. 'A Sword of Naue II Type from Ugarit and the Historical Significance of Italian type Weaponry in the Eastern Mediterranean.' *Aegean Archaeology*, Vol.8. Warsaw: Art and Archaeology. 111-136.

Kagan, Donald. 1991. *Pericles of Athens and the Birth of Democracy*. New York: Simon & Schuster.

------, and Gregory F. Viggiano. 2013. *Men of Bronze: Hoplite Warfare in Ancient Greece*. Princeton: University Press.

Kähler, Heinz. 1949. *Das griechische Metopenbild*. München: Münchner Verlag.

Kahn, Jeff. 2011. 'Acheloös: A Link Between the Indus and Achaean Civilizations.' *The Celator*, Vol. 25, No. 4. Lancaster, PA: Kerry Wetterstrom.

Kaltchev, Peter. 2005. *Neolithic Dwelling of Stara Zagora*. Exposition Catalog. Stara Zagora: Regionalen istoricheski muzeĭ.

Kanta, Athanassia. 2003. 'The Aegean World Between the East and the West. Aspects of Common Cultural Elements, 16th - 6th c. BC.' *Πλοες. Sea routes. Interconnections in the Mediterranean, 16th - 6th c. B.C. Proceedings of the international symposium held at Rethymnon, Crete September 29th - October 2nd, 2002*; edited by N.C. Stampolidis and V. Karageorghis. Athens: Museum of Cycladic Art. 27-40.

Kaplan, Philip. 2002. 'The Social Status of the Mercenary in Archaic Greece.' *Oikistes: Studies in Constitutions, Colonies, and Military Power in the Ancient World. Offered in Honor of A.J. Graham*; edited by V. Gorman and E.W. Robinson. Leiden: Brill. 229-243.

Karageorghis, Vassos. 1962. 'Chronique des fouilles et découvertes archéologiques à Chypre en 1961.' *Bulletin de correspondance hellénique*, Vol. 86, livraison 1. Paris: De Boccard. 327-414.

------. 1964. 'Notes on some Centaurs from Cyprus.' *Χαριστήριον εις*; edited by Anastasion K. Orlandon,Vol. II. Athens: Hē en Athēnais Archaiologikēs Hetaireias. 160-169.

------. 1970. 'Two religious Documents of the Early Cypriote Bronze Age.' *Report of the Department of Antiquities, Cyprus*. Nicosia: Government Print Office. 10-13.

------. 1971. 'Notes on Some Cypriote Priests Wearing Bull-Masks.' *The Harvard Theological Review*, Vol. 64, No.2-3. Cambridge: Harvard University Press. 261-270.

------. 1991. *The Coroplastic Art of Ancient Cyprus*. Vol. III. Nicosia: A.G. Leventis Foundation.

------. 1999. 'Aspects of trade Between Cyprus and the West During the 14th- 13th Centuries BC.' *The Point Iria Wreck: Interconnections in the Mediterranean ca. 1200 BC: Proceedings of the International conference, Island of Spetses, 19 September 1998*; edited by W. Phelps, Y. Lolos and Y. Vichos. Athens: Hellenic Institute of Marine Archaeology. 121-130.

------. 2002. *Cipro. Crocevia del Mediterraneo Orientale 1600 – 500 a.C.* Milano: Electa.

------, and Jean Des Gagniers. 1974. *La céramique chypriote de style figuré, Âge du Fer (1050-500 Av. J. C.)*. 2 vols. Roma: Edizioni dell'Ateneo.

------, Sophocles Hadjisavvas, and Franz Georg Maier. 2005. 'L'archeologia del Vicino Oriente antico. Cipro.' *Il mondo dell'archeologia*. Roma: Istituto della Enciclopedia italiana.

------, and Jacqueline Karageorghis .2013. 'Sull'isola di Afrodite. Cipro fra Oriente e Occidente.' *Archeologia Viva,* XXXII, n.159. Firenze: Giunti. 40-53.

Kearsley, Rosalinde A. 1999. 'Greeks overseas in the 8th century B.C.: Euboeans, Al Mina and Assyrian imperialism.' *Ancient Greeks West and East*; edited by G.R. Tsetskhladze. Leiden: Brill. 109-134.

Kenna, Victor G.E. 1967. 'The seal use of Cyprus in the Bronze Age.' *Bulletin de correspondance hellénique*, Vol. 91, livraison 1. Paris: De Boccard. 255-268.

------. 1967. 'The seal use of Cyprus in the Bronze Age, II.' *Bulletin de correspondance hellénique*, Vol. 91, livraison 2. Paris: De Boccard. 552-577.

------. 1968. 'The seal use of Cyprus in the Bronze Age, III.' *Bulletin de correspondance hellénique*, Vol. 92, livraison 1. Paris: De Boccard. 142-156.

Kenoyer, Jonathan M. 2010. 'Master of Animals and Animal Masters in the Iconography of the Indus Tradition.' *The Master of Animals in Old World Iconography*; edited by Derek B. Counts and Bettina Arnold. Budapest: Archaeolingua. 37-58.

Kern, Hermann. 2000. *Through the Labyrinth: Designs and Meanings Over 5,000 Years*. New York: Prestel.

Kerschner, Michael, and Hans Mommsen. 2009. 'Imports of East Greek pottery to Sicily and Sicilian production of East Greek type. Archaeometrical analyses of finds from the votive deposit in Katane.' *Stipe votiva del santuario di Demetra a Catania. La ceramica Greco-Orientale*; edited by Antonella Pautasso. Catania: IBAM. 125-154.

King, R. J., and P.A. Underhill. 2002. 'Congruent Distribution of Neolithic Painted Pottery and Ceramic Figurines with Y-chromosome Lineages.' *Antiquity, Vol.* 76. Oxford: University Press. 707-14.

------, S.S. Ozcan, et al. 2008. 'Differential Y-chromosome Anatolian influences on the Greek and Cretan Neolithic.' *Annals of Human Genetics,* Vol.72. London: University Press. 205-214.

Klementa, Sylvia. 1993. *Gelagerte Flussgötter des Späthellenismus und der römischen Kaiserzeit.* Köln: Böhlau.

Knapp, Arthur Bernard. 2013. *The Archaeology of Cyprus: From Earliest Prehistory through the Bronze Age.* Cambridge: University Press.

Kohlmeyer, Kay. 1995. 'Anatolian Architectural Decorations, Statuary, and Stelae.' *Civilizations of the Ancient Near East*; edited by J.M. Sasson. Peabody: Hendrickson. 2639-60.

Konuk, Koray. 2007. 'Orou, dynaste de Carie.' *Scripta Anatolica, Mélanges en l'honneur de Pierre Debord*; edited by Patrice Brun. Bordeaux: Ausonius. 103-111.

Kotz, Suzanne. 2012. *Dallas Museum of Art: A Guide to the Collection.* New Haven: Yale University Press.

Kourou, Nota. 1989. 'Aegean Orientalizing versus Oriental Art: the Evidence of the Monsters.' *The Civilizations of the Aegean and Their Diffusion in Cyprus and in the Eastern Mediterranean, 2000-600 BC. Proceedings of the International Symposium at Larnaka 18-24 September 1989.* Larnaca: Pierides Foundation. 110-122.

Kraay, Colin M. 1976. *Archaic and Classical Greek Coins*. Berkeley: University of California Press.

------, and Max Hirmer. 1966. *Greek Coins*. New York: H.N. Abrams.

Kramer, Samuel Noah. 1948. 'New Light on the Early History of the Ancient Near East.' *American Journal of Archaeology*, Vol. 52, No. 1. New York: Macmillan. 156-164.

Kratinus, and Theodor Kock. 1880. 'Fragmenta.' *Comicorum Atticorum Fragmenta.* Volume 1. Lipsiae: Teubner.

Krebernik, Manfred. 1984. *Die Beschworungen aus Fara und Ebla: Untersuchungen zur altesten keilschriftlichen Beschworungsliteratur*. Hildesheim: G. Olms.

Kritt, Brian. 1996. *Seleucid Coins of Bactria.* Classical Numismatic Studies, No 1. Lancaster, PA: Classical Numismatic Group.

------. 2015. *New Discoveries in Baktrian Numismatics.* Classical Numismatic Studies, No 8. Lancaster, PA: Classical Numismatic Group.

Kunze, Emil. 1956. 'Schildbeschläge.' *Bericht über die Ausgrabungen in Olympia*; edited by Emil Kunze and Helmut Kyrieleis. Berlin: de Gruyter. 35-68.

------. *Olympische Forschungen XXI: Beinschienen.* Berlin: de Gruyter.

Kyrieleis, Helmut. 1996. *Samos X: Der grosse Kuros von Samos*. Bonn: R. Habelt.

------, Hermann J. Kienast, and Günter Neumann. 1996. *Der grosse Kuros von Samos*. Bonn: R. Habelt.

La Chau, Géraud de, Le Blond, and François Thomas Marie de Baculard d'Arnaud. 1780. *Description des principales pierres gravées du cabinet de S.A.S. Monseigneur le duc d'Orleans.* Paris: Pissot.

La Delfa Orazio. 2010. *Nuovi dati per lo studio della monetazione di Agyrion.* Unpublished dissertation.

Lacroix, Léon. 1953. 'Flueves et nymphes eponyms sur les monaies grecques.' *Revue belge de numismatique et de sigillographie*, 99. Bruxelles: Société Royale de Numismatique. 5-21.

------. 1965. *Monnaies et colonization dans l'occident grec.* Bruxelles: Académie royale de Belgique.

Lajard, Félix Jean Baptiste. 1847. *Introduction a l'*étude du culte public et des mystères de Mithra en Orient et en Occident. Vol.2. Paris: Imprimiere Royale.

Laks, André, and Glenn W. Most (eds.). 1997. *Studies on the Derveni papyrus*. Oxford: Clarendon Press.

Lagona, Sebastiana. 1968. 'Il tipo del toro androprosopo a Gela.' *Cronache di Archeologia e Storia dell'Arte.* Vol. 7. Catania: Università di Catania. 137-142.

Lambert, Wilfred George. 1985. 'Trees, snakes and Gods in ancient Syria and Anatolia.' *Bulletin of the School of Oriental and African Studies*, Vol 48, No. 3. Oxford: University Pess. 435-51.

Landolfi, Maurizio, and Gabriele Baldelli. 1997. 'San Vittore di Cingoli.' *Acque, grotte e dei, 3000 anni di culti preromani in Romagna, Marche e Abruzzo. Imola, Chiostri di San Domenico, 5 aprile-13 luglio 1997*; edited by Marco Pacciarelli. Imola: Musei Civici. 180-183.

------. 1997. 'Montefortino di Arcevia.' *Acque, grotte e Dei. 3000 anni di culti preromani in Romagna, Marche e Abruzzo. Imola, Chiostri di San Domenico, 5 aprile-13 luglio 1997*; edited by Marco Pacciarelli. Imola: Musei Civici. 172-179.

La Regina, Adriano. 1971. 'Contributo dell'Archaeologia alla Storia Sociale: I Territori Sabellici e Sannitici.' *Dialoghi di Archeologia*, Vol. IV-V (1970-1971). Milano: Il Saggiatore. 443-459.

Larizza, Pietro. 1905. *Rhegium Chalcidense (Reggio di Calabria). La storia e la numismatica dai tempi preistorici fino alla cittadinanza romana*. Roma: Forzani.

La Rosa, Vincenzo. 1969. 'Un frammento fittile da Capodarso e il problema delle sopravvivenze micenee in Sicilia.' *Cronache di Archeologia e Storia dell'Arte*, Vol.8. Catania: Università di Catania. 33-46.

------. 1977. 'Considerazioni sul problema siculo.' *Sileno*, Vol. III. Catania: Sileno. 65-81.

------. 1995. 'Ultra Mortem: Nuove Testimonianze di Età Preistorica dalla Sicilia.' *SICVLORVM GYMNASIVM: Studi in ricordo di Rosario Contarino*; edited by Nicolò Mineo and Rosario Contarino. Catania: Università di Catania. 193-204.

------. 1997. 'A proposito di una recente pubblicazione di preistoria siciliana.' *Archivio Storico per la Sicilia Orientale,* Anno XCIII, Fasc I-III. Catania: Società di Storia Patria per la Sicilia Orientale. 283-289.

Larson, Jennifer. 2001. *Greek Nymphs Myth, Cult, Lore*. Oxford: University Press.

------. 2007. *Ancient Greek Cults: A Guide.* London: Routledge.

Lazzarini, Lorenzo. 2005. 'La Monetazione e il sito di Halykiai (Alicie).' *Schweizerische numismatische Rundschau*, Band 84. Bern: Schweizerische Numismatische Gesellschaft. 15-24.

Lee, Mireille M. 2006. 'Acheloos Peplophoros: A Lost Statuette of a River God in Feminine Dress.' *Hesperia,* Vol. 75, No. 3. Cambridge: Harvard University Press. 317-325.

Legrain, Leon, and Leonard Woolley. 1936. *Archaic Seal-Impressions*. Oxford: University Press.

Lehmann, Gunnar. 2005. 'Al Mina and the East - A report on research in progress.' *The Greeks in the East*; edited by A. Villing. London: The British Museum Press. 61-92.

Lehnerdt, Maximilian. 1885. 'Herakles and Acheloos.' *Archäologische Zeitung*, Vol. XLIII. Berlin: Reimer. 105-120.

Leighton, Robert. 1999. *Sicily Before History: an archaeological survey from the Palaeolithic to the Iron Age*.
Ithaca, N.Y.: Cornell University Press.

Lemos, Irene S. 2005. 'The changing relationship of the Euboeans and the East.' *The Greeks in the East*; edited by A. Villing. London: The British Museum Press. 53-60.

Lenormant, Charles. 1844. 'Recherches sur les époques et sure les causes d'émission de l'aes grave en Italie.' *Revue Numismatique*, Vol. 9. Paris: Rollin. 245-270.

Le Rider, Georges. 1977. *Le Monnayage d'argent et d'or de Philippe II frappé en Macédoine de 359 à 294*. Paris: Bourgey.

Lévesque de Gravelle, Michel Philippe, and Pierre-Jean Mariette. 1732. *Recueil de pierres gravées antiques*. Paris: De l'imprimerie de P.J. Mariette, ruë S. Jacques, aux Colonnes d'Hercule.

Levi, Doro. 1937. 'Nule. Bronzi protosardi rinvenuti fortuitamente in località Santu Lisei presso Nule.' *Notizie degli Scavi di Antichità*. Roma: Tip. della R. Accademia dei Lincei. 83-90.

Levi, Sara, Tiziana Benedetta Prosdocimi, Gabriella Tigano, and Alessandro Vanzetti. 2009. 'Il villaggio protostorico di Viale dei Cipressi e la facies Capo Graziano.' *Mylai II*, edited by G. Tigano. Messina: Ellegieffe. 23-136.

Lewis, Charlton S., and Charles Short. 1969. *A Latin Dictionary*. Oxford: University Press.

Liddell, Henry George, Robert Scott, Henry Stuart Jones, and Roderick McKenzie. 1996. *A Greek-English Lexicon*. Oxford: Clarendon.

Lienhardt, Ronald G. 1961. *Divinity and Experience; the Religion of the Dinka*. Oxford: Clarendon.

Lilliu, Giovanni. 1945. 'Bronzi figurati esistenti nelle collezioni pubbliche e private non insulari.' *Studi Sardi* VI. Sassari: Istituto per gli Studi Sardi. 23-41.

------. 1982. *La civiltà nuragica*. Sassari: Delfino.

------. 1988. *La civiltà dei sardi dal Paleolitico all'età dei nuraghi.*Torino: Nuova ERI.

------. 1999. *Arte e religione della Sardegna prenuragica. Idoletti, ceramiche, oggetti d'ornamento*. Sassari: Delfino.

------. 2008. *Sculture della Sardegna Nuragica*. Nuoro: Ilisso.

Lipinski, Edward. 2004. *Itineraria Phoenicia.* Leuven: Peeters.

Lippold, Georg. 1922. *Gemmen und kameen des altertums und der neuzeit*. Stuttgart: J. Hoffmann.

Litvinskij, Boris Anatol'evič, and Igor' Rubenovič Pičikjan. 1995. 'River-Deities of Greece Salute the God of the River Oxus-Vakhsh: Achelous and the Hippocampess.' *In the Land of the Gryphons: Papers on Central Asian Archaeology in Antiquity;* edited by Antonio Invernizzi. Firenze: Le Lettere. 129-149.

Liverani, Mario. 2011. *Antico Oriente. Storia società economia*. Bari: Laterza.

Lloyd, Seyton. 1935. 'Architectural Description of the Aqueduct.' *Sennacherib's Aqueduct at Jerwan*; edited by Thorkild Jacobsen and Seton Lloyd. Chicago: University Press. 6-18.

Lo Cascio, Elio. 1975. 'La leggenda SYS delle monete siculo-puniche e il concetto politico di *epikrateia.*' *La Parola del Passato. Rivista di Studi Antichi*, Vol. CLXI. Napoli. 156-161.

Loftus, Ronan T., David E. MacHugh, Daniel G. Bradley, Paul M. Sharp, and Patrick Cunningham. 1994. 'Evidence for Two Independent Domestications of Cattle.' *Proceedings of the National Academy of Sciences of the United States of America*, Vol. 91, No. 7. Washington, D.C.: The Academy. 2757-2761.

Lonis, Raoul. 1979. *Guerre et religion en Grèce à l'époque classique*. Paris: Belles Lettres.

Lo Porto, Felice G. 1986. *La collezione Cipriota del Museo di Antichità di Torino*. Roma: Bretschneider.

Lo Schiavo, Fulvia. 1996. 'Bronzetti di età nuragica dalla Gallura.' *Archeologia del territorio, territorio dell'Archeologia. Un sistema informativo territoriale orientato sull'archeologia della regione ambientale Gallura*; edited by Giovanni Maciocco, Roberto Caprara, and Alberto Luciano. Sassari: Delfino. 65-96.

------, Paola Falchi and Matteo Milletti. 2013. 'Sardegna ed Etruria tirrenica: identità in formazione. Ripostigli e scambi della fase di transizione fra la fine del Bronzo Finale e la prima età del Ferro.' Δόσις δ'ολίγη τε φίλη τε, *Studi per Antonella Romualdi*; edited by Barbara Arbeid. Firenze: Edizioni Polistampa. 371-416.

Loreto, Luigi. 1990. 'Per una 'Quellenforschung' della pax Caudina,' in *Bullettino dell'Istituto di Diritto Romano 'Vittorio Scajola'*. Vol. XCII-XCIII (1989-1990). MIlano: Giuffre. 653-665.

Lucca, Rita. 1995. 'Il culto di παν ακτιος a Sibari e Turi.' *Hesperìa*, Vol. 5. Rome: Bretschneider. 233-7.

Luce, Stephen B. 1923. 'Heracles and Acheloös on a Cylix in Boston.' *American Journal of Archaeology*, 27. New York: Macmillan. 425-37.

Luckenbill, Daniel D. 1927. *Ancient Records of Assyria and Babylonia, Vol 2: Historical Records of Assyria from Sargon to the End.* Chicago: University Press.

Luraghi, Nino. 2006. 'Traders, Pirates, Warriors: The Proto-History of Greek Mercenary Soldiers in the Eastern Mediterranean.' *Phoenix*, Vol. 60, No. 1/2. Toronto: University Press. 21-47.

MacDonald, George. 1899. *Catalogue of Greek coins in the Hunterian Collection, University of Glasgow,* Vol.I. Glasgow.

------. 1905. *Coin Types, Their Origin and Development.* Glasgow: J. Maclehose and Sons.

Mackay, T. S. 1938. 'Metropolis: Thessaly.' *The Princeton Encyclopedia of Classical Sites*. Princeton, N.J.: Princeton University Press.

Mackenzie, Donald A. 1915. *Mythology of the Babylonian People.* London: Braken Books.

Macnamara, Ellen. 1973. *Everyday Life of the Etruscans.* London: Batsford.

Magee, Peter. 2015. 'The chronology and environmental background of Iron Age settlement in southeastern Iran and the question of the origin of the qanat irrigation system.' *Iranica Antiqua*, Vol. XL. Leiden: Brill. 217-231.

Maggiani, Adriano. 1999. 'Culti delle acque e culti in grotta in Etruria.' *Ocnus*, Quaderni della Scuola di Specializzazione in Archeologia, VII. Bologna: C.L.U.E.B. 187-203.

Magini, Leonardo. 2007. *L'etrusco, lingua dall'oriente indoeuropeo*, Studia Philologica, Vol.21. Roma: Bretschneider.

Maiuri, Amedeo. 1978. 'Orizzonti storici della Campania antica.' *Mestiere d'Archeologo*; edited by C. Belli. Milano: Libri Scheiwiller. 43-52.

Malati, N. Shende. 1997. *The Language of the Harappans: From Akkadian to Sanskrit.* New Delhi: Abhinav Publications.

Mallory, James P., and Douglas Q. Adams. 2006. *The Oxford Introduction to Proto-Indo-European and the Proto-Indo-European World.* Oxford: University Press.

Manassero, Niccolò. 2004. 'Il Signore degli animali nella glittica di età accadica. Indagine iconografica ed analisi delle fonti.' *Mesopotamia. Rivista di Archeologia, Epigrafia e Storia orientale antica.* Vol. XXXIX. Firenze: Licosa. 71-92.

Mandolesi, Alessandro, and Daniela De Angelis. 2011. 'Il Tumulo della Regina di Tarquinia fra tradizioni levantine e innovazioni etrusche.' *Archeologia Classica*, Vol. LXII, 1. Roma: Bretschneider. 7-39.

Manfredi, Lorenza Ilia. 2009. 'Iconografia e leggenda. Il linguaggio monetale di Cartagine.' *Mediterranea. Quaderni annuali dell'Istituto di Studi sul Mediterraneo antico.* Vol VI. Pisa-Roma: Fabrizio Serra. 203-218.

Manganaro, Giacomo. 1969. 'Intervento.' *Atti del II Congresso Internazionale di Studi sulla sicilia antica. Kokalos*, Vol. 14-15 (1968-1969). Palermo: Banco di Sicilia. 134.

------. 1984. 'Dai mikrà kermata di argento al chalkokratos kassiteros in Sicilia nel V. sec. a.C.' *Jahrbuch für Numismatik und Geldgeschichte*, XXXIV. München: Im Eigenverlag der Bayerischen Numismatischen Gesellschaft. 11-39.

------. 1996. 'Per una storia della chora katanaia.' *Catania Antica, Atti del Convegno della S.I.S.A.C. Catania 23-24 maggio 1992*; edited by B. Gentili. Pisa. 19-59.

------. 2001. 'Metoikismos dei Danklaioi a Mylai.' *Schweizerische Numismatische Rundschau*, Band 80. Bern: Schweizerische Numismatische Gesellschaft. 83-95.

------. 2003. 'Il paesaggio di Panormos riflesso nei dodici tipi delle serie frazionarie a legenda punica SYS, un nuovo kerma col polipo ed un triemiobolion a legenda SICHAS degli Ichaninoi.' *Quarte Giornate Internazionali di Studi sull'Area Elima. Erice, 1-4 dicembre 2000*, Atti Vol. II. Pisa. 847-860.

Mangani, Elisabetta, and Orazio Paoletti. 1986. *Corpus Vasorum Antiquorum: Italia. Grosseto - Museo archeologico e d'arte della Maremma.* Parte 1. Roma: Bretschneider.

Mangieri, Giuseppe Libero. 1994. 'Problemi di circolazione monetaria a Nuceria Alfaterna dall'età classica a quella imperiale.' *Nuceria Alfaterna e il suo territorio. Dalla fondazione ai Longobardi.* Vol. II, edited by A. Pecoraro. Salerno. 21-35.

Manni, Eugenio. 1976. 'Su alcune recenti proposte di identificazione di centri antichi della Sicilia.' *L'Italie préromaine et la Rome républicaine. I. Mélanges offerts à Jacques Heurgon.* Publications de l'École française de Rome, Vol. 27, No. 1. Roma: École Française de Rome. 605-617.

------. 1981. *Geografia fisica e politica della Sicilia antica.* Testimonia Siciliae Antiqua, I, 1. Roma: Bretschneider.

Māṇi, Veṭṭaṃ. 1975. *Purāṇic Encyclopaedia: a Comprehensive Dictionary with Special Reference to the Epic and Purāṇic Literature.* Delhi: Motilal Banarsidass.

Mansuelli, Guido Achille. 1986. 'Topografia storica della regione Etrusca.' *Rasenna. Storia e Civiltà degli Etruschi.* Milano: Libri Sheiwiller – Credito Italiano. 677-713.

Manunza, Maria Rosaria. 2008. 'La stratigrafia del vano a di Funtana Coberta (Ballao - CA).' *F.O.D.R. The Journal of Fasti Online.* Roma: Associazione internazionale di archeologia classica. http://www.fastionline.org/docs/FOLDER-it-2008-120.pdf (accessed spring 2016).

Maras, Daniele. 2007. 'Le iscrizioni.' *Il museo delle Antichità Etrusche e Italiche, Vol.II, Dall'incontro con il mondo greco alla romanizzazione;* edited by G.M. Benedettini. Roma. 553-560.

------. 2010. 'Suri il nero signore degli inferi.' *Archeo.* Luglio. Novara: Istituto geografico de Agostini. 108-115.

Marcotte, Didier. 1985. 'Le Premier Koinon Acarnanien et la Fin de la Seconde Ligue Délienne.' *L'Antiquité Classique*, Vol. 54, No.1. Bruxelles. 254-258.

Mari, Zaccaria, and Maria Sperandio. 2006. 'L'insediamento dell'età del bronzo presso il lago delle Colonnelle nella piana delle acque albule (Tivoli).' *Atti e Memorie della Societa Tiburtina di Storia e d'Arte.* Volume LXXIX. Tivoli. 81-111.

Maric, Miroslav. 2014. 'Encircled in Water: modelling watercourses of the late Neolithic - early Copper Age Vinca culture sites in the Danube region (c. 5300-4500 BC).' *Quaternary International* XXX. United Kingdom: Elsevier. 1-10. Online publication, http://dx.doi.org/10.1016/j.quaint.2014.06.030 (accessed Spring 2016)

Markoe, Glenn. 1996. 'The emergence of Orientalizing in Greek art: some observations on the interchange between Greeks and Phoenicians in the eight and seventh centuries B.C.' *Bulletin of the American Schools of Oriental Research,* 301. South Hadley, MA: American Schools of Oriental Research. 47-67.

Marshack, Alexander. 1991. *The Roots of Civilization.* Mount Kisco, N.Y.: Moyer Bell.

Martelli, Maria. 1996. 'Bronzi ciprioti dall'Etruria.' *Studi in memoria di Lucia Guerrini*; edited by M.G. Picozzi and F. Carinci. Roma: Bretschneider. 47-60.

Marroni, Elisa. 2012. 'Considerazioni sul santuario di Circei.' *Sacra nominis Latini. I santuari del Lazio arcaico e repubblicano, Atti del Convegno Internazionale, Roma, Palazzo Massimo, 19-21 febbraio 2009; edited by Elisa Marroni.* Ostraka volume speciale, Tomo I Napoli: Loffredo. 619-624.

Masetti, Susanna. 2014. 'Monumenti Nuragici di Culto sulle montagne di Irgoli.' *Archeologia Viva*, XXXIII, n.165. Firenze: Giunti. 66-71.

Massa, Giovanni A. 1709. *La Sicilia in Prospettiva Parte Seconda.* Palermo: Cichè.

Masseria, Concetta. 2001. 'Garaguso. Santuari e culti di un centro Enotrio.' *Il mondo enotrio tra VI e V secolo a.C.: atti dei seminari napoletani (1996-1998),* Quaderni di Ostraka I, 1; edited by M. Bugno and C. Masseria. Napoli: Loffredo. 83-107.

Masson, Oliver. 1968. 'Notes de Numismatique Chypriote.' *Opuscula Atheniensia.* Volume VIII. Lund:
C.W.K. Gleerup. 111-118.

------. 1983. *Les inscriptions chypriotes syllabiques.* Paris: de Boccard.

Mastrocinque, Attilio. 2002. 'Alcuni aspetti degli dei fluviali centro-italici.' *Paesaggi d'acque. Atti del quinto incontro di Studi, Preistoria e Protostoria in Etruria;* edited by Nuccia Negroni Catacchio. Vol. II. Milano: Centro Studi Preistoria e Archeologia. 417-420.

Mastronuzzi, Giovanni. 2005. *Repertorio dei contesti cultuali indigeni in Italia meridionale, 1. Età arcaica.* Beni Archeologici Conoscenza e Tecnologie, Vol. 4. Bari-Lecce: Edipuglia.

Matarazzo, Pasquale. 2008. 'Martorelli, Giacomo.' *Dizionario Biografico degli Italiani,* Vol. LXXI. Roma: Istituto dell'Enciclopedia Italiana. 361-364.

Matthaus, Hartmut. 2001. 'Studies on the Interrelations of Cyprus and Italy During the 11th to 9th Centuries B.C.: A pan-Mediterranean Perspective.' *Italy and Cyprus in Antiquity: 1500 - 450 BC*; edited by L. Bonfante and V. Karageorghis. Nicosia: Costakis and Leto Severis Foundation. 153-214.

Matthews, Donald M. 1997. *The Early Glyptic of Tell Brak: Cylinder Seals of Third Millennium Syria.* Fribourg: University Press.

Matthiae, Paolo. 1989. 'Masterpieces of Early and Old Syrian art: discoveries of the 1988 Ebla excavations in a historical perspective.' *Proceedings of the British Academy*, LXXV. Oxford: University Press. 25-56.

Matz, Friedrich. 1913. *Die Naturpersonifikationen in der griechischen Kunst.* Göttingen, W.F. Kaestner.

Maximova, Maria Ivanova. 1927. *Les Vases Plastiques dans l'Antiquité*. Volume II. Paris: P. Geuthner.

Mazochius, Alexius Symmachus. 1754. *Alexii Symmachi Mazochii Commentariorum in Regii Herculanensis Musei aeneas tabulas Heracleenses: Pars I-II*. Neapoli: Ex Officina Benedicti Gessari.

Mazzorin, Jacopo De Grossi, and Claudia Minniti. 2012. 'L'uso degli astragali nell'antichità tra ludo e divinazione.' *Atti del VI Convegno Nazionale di Archeozoologia. Orecchiella, 2009*. Pisa: Universita di Pisa. 213-220.

Mayhoff, K.F.T. 1870. *C. Plini Secundi naturalis historiae libri XXXVII. Recognovit atque indicibus instruxit Ludovicus Janus*, Vol.1. Lipsiae.

McDonald, Diana K. 1994. 'The Serpent as Healer: Theriac and Ancient Near Eastern Pottery.' *Essays for Dr. Edith Porada. Source. Notes in the History of Art*, Vol. 13, No. 4. New York: Ars Brevis. 21-27.

McHugh, William P. 1974. 'Cattle Pastoralism in Africa—A Model for Interpreting Archaeological Evidence from the Eastern Sahara Desert.' *Arctic Anthropology*, Vol. 11, Supplement: Festschrift Issue in Honor of Chester S. Chard. Madison, WI: University of Wisconsin Press. 236-244.

McNaughton, Sean, Jason Lee, Jane Vessels, Mollie Bates, and Rebecca Hale. 2010. 'Hidden Water.' *National Geographic*, April 2010 Supplement. Washington D.C.: National Geographic Partners.

Mele, Nazarena Valenza. 1993. 'Napoli.' *Bibliografia Topografica della Colonizzazione Greca in Italia e nelle Isole Tirreniche*, Vol.XII. Pisa-Roma: Scuola Normale Superiore. 165-239.

Melis, Maria Grazia. 2008. 'Osservazioni sul ruolo dell'acqua nei rituali della Sardegna preistorica.' *Rivista di Scienze Preistoriche,* Vol. LVIII. Firenze: Istituto Italiano di Preistoria e Protostoria. 111–124.

Melis, Paolo. 2002. 'L'area nuragica di S. Maria di Tergu (Sassari).' *Etruria e Sardegna centro-settentrionale tra l'Età del Bronzo finale e l'Arcaismo, Atti del XXI Convegno di Studi Etruschi e Italici, Sassari 13-17 ottobre 1998*. Pisa-Roma: Istituti Editoriali e Poligrafici Internazionali. 453-461.

Mellaart, James. 1965. *Earliest Civilizations of the Near East*. New York: McGraw-Hill.

Meloni, Giovanna Maria. 2000. 'Le domus de janas del Logudoro-Mejlogu.' *L'ipogeismo nel Mediterraneo: origini, sviluppo, quadri culturali: atti del Congresso internazionale, 23- 28 maggio 1994, Sassari-Oristano.* Università degli studi di Sassari, Facoltà di Lettere e filosofia, Istituto di Antichità, Arte e Discipline Etnodemologiche e Dipartimento di Scienze Umanistiche e dell'Antichità, Vol. II. Sassari: Stampacolor. 789-802.

Menander Comicus, and Theodor Kock. 1888. 'Fragmenta.' *Comicorum Atticorum Fragmenta*. Vol. 3. Lipsiae: Teubner.

Mertens Horn, Madeleine. 1991. 'Una nuova antefissa a testa femminile da Akrai ed alcune considerazioni sulle Ninfe di Sicilia.' *Bollettino d'Arte del Ministero della Pubblica Istruzione*, Vol. 76. Milano: Istituto Poligrafico dello Stato. 9-28.

Mertens, Kenneth N., et al. 2012. 'Quantitative estimation of Holocene surface salinity variation in the Black Sea using dinoflagellate cyst process length.' *Quaternary Science Reviews*, Vol. 39. United Kingdom: Elsevier. 45–59.

Mikov, Vasil. 1958. 'Kul'tura neolita, eneolita i bronzy v Bolgarii.' *Sovetskaia arkheologiia*. No. 1. Moskva: Akademia nauk SSSR. 5-13.

Miller, Harvey F. 1984. 'The Practical and Economic Background to the Greek Mercenary Explosion.' *Greece & Rome*, Second Series, Vol. 31, No. 2. Cambridge: University Press. 153-160.

Milletti, Matteo. 2008. 'Riflessioni sul tema dei contatti tra la Sardegna e l'Etruria tra bronzo finale e prima età del ferro.' *Gli Etruschi e la Sardegna tra la fine dell'età del bronzo e gli inizi dell'età del ferro, Catalogo della mostra, 11 Aprile – 30 Settembre 2008*; edited by F. Lo Schiavo, P. Falchi, and M. Milletti. Cagliari. 17-24.

Millingen, James. 1812. *Recueil de quelques médailles grecques inédites. Roma:* De Romanis.

------. 1834. 'On a Fictile Vase, Representing the Contest Between Hercules and the Achelous.' *Transactions of the Royal Society of Literature of the United Kingdom*, Vol. 2, Part 2. London: Murray. 95-101.

Minervini, Giulio. 1852. 'Osservazioni sulle monete di Napoli colla protome del Sebeto.' *Bullettino Archeologico Napoletano.* Nuova Serie. Anno primo, No. 6, Settembre 1852; edited by Raffaele Garrucci and Giulio Minervini. Napoli: Giuseppe Cataneo. 45-48.

------. 1852. 'Moneta inedita di Napoli, che risolve la questione del toro androprosopo.' *Bullettino Archeologico Napoletano. Nuova Serie. Anno primo,* No. 8, Ottobre 1852; edited by Raffaele Garrucci and Giulio Minervini. Napoli: Giuseppe Cataneo. 57-58.

Minetti, Alessandra. 2004. *L'orientalizzante a Chiusi e nel suo territorio*. Roma: Bretschneider.

Mingazzini, Paolino. 1936. 'Saticula.' entry in *Enciclopedia Italiana Treccani*, Vol. 30. Roma.

Minniti, Claudia, and Luca Peyronel. 2008. 'L'uso degli astragali a Tell Mardikh-Ebla (Siria): oggetti simbolici o funzionali?.' *Uomini, piante e animali nella dimensione del sacro*. Lecce-Bari: Edipuglia. 171-192.

Minoja, Marco Edoardo. 2002. 'Elementi rituali in pozzi per acqua nell'età del bronzo: il caso dell'abitato del C.I.R.A (Capua - Ce).' *Paesaggi d'acque. Atti del quinto incontro di Studi, Preistoria e Protostoria in Etruria;* edited by Nuccia Negroni Catacchio. Vol. II. Milano: Centro Studi Preistoria e Archeologia. 465-469.

Miranda, Elena. 1995. *Iscrizioni greche d'Italia, Napoli,* Vol. II. Roma: Quasar

Mirone, Salvatore. 1918. 'Le monete dell' antica Catana.' *Rivista italiana di Numismatica*. Vol. XXXI. Milano: Società Numismatica Italiana. 9-76.

Möller, Astrid. 2000. *Naukratis – Trade in Archaic Greece*. Oxford: University Press.

Mommsen, Theodor. 1846. 'Sulle desinenze delle epigrafi nelle monete osche.' *Annali di Numismatica*,Vol.I. Roma. 35-44.

------.1865-75. *Histoire de la monnaie romaine*. Paris: Rollin et Feuardent.

Momrak, Kristoffer. 2014. 'Greeks and the East in the Iron Age: interpreting interaction in the Eastern Mediterranean.' Unpublished (pre-print) manuscript, accessed Fall 2014 via academia.edu

Montanari, Franco. 1998. 'Zenodotus, Aristarchus and the *ekdosis* of Homer.' *Editing Texts- Texte edieren*; edited by G.W. Most. Göttingen: Vandenhoeck & Ruprecht. 1-21.

Morandi Alessandro. 1982. *Epigrafia Italica. Guida alle scritture e alle lingue dell'Italia antica preromana*. Roma: Bretschneider.

Moravetti, Alberto. 2012. *Sardegna archeologica dal cielo. Dai circoli megalitici alle torri nuragiche*. Sassari: C. Delfino.

Morcom, John. 2000. 'Some South Italian Questions.' *Pour Denyse. Divertissements Numismatiques*; edited by Silvia Hurter and Carmen Arnold-Biucchi. Bern: Dr. Schüler. 159-163.

Morello, Antonio. 2008. *Prorae, La Prima Prua di Nave sulle Monete della Repubblica Romana, Origine di un simbolo imperituro del potere di Roma, un inno a Caio Duilio*. Cassino: Classica Editrice Diana.

Moretti, Giuseppe. 1913. 'Terrecotte inedite del Museo delle Terme.' *Bollettino d'Arte del Ministero della P. Istruzione,* Anno VII, Fasc.4. Roma: P. Calzone. 125-141.

Mørkholm, Otto, and Günter Neumann. 1978. *Die lykischen Munzlegenden*. Göttingen: Vandehoeck und Ruprecht.

Morgan, Catherine. 2003. *Early Greek States Beyond the Polis*. London: Routledge.

Morris, Desmond. 1985. *The Art of Ancient Cyprus*. Oxford: Phaidon.

Morris, Sarah P. 2001. 'The Towers of Ancient Leukas: Results of a Topographic Survey, 1991-1992.' *Hesperia,* Vol. 70. Cambridge: Harvard University Press. 285-347.

Moscati Castelnuovo, Luisa. 2003. 'Tucidide (VI 3, 3) e gli ecisti di Catane.' *Hommages à Carl Deroux, III-Histoire et épigraphie, Droit*, edited by P. Defosse. Bruxelles. 321-327.

Moskowitz, Clara. 2013. 'Kepler Telescope Finds Plethora of Earth-Size Planets.' *Scientific American* web site. http:// www.scientificamerican.com/article/kepler-telescope-earth-sized-planets (accessed Spring 2016)

Moysey, Robert A. 1986. 'The silver stater issues of Pharnabazos and Datames from the mint of Tarsus in Cilicia.' *Museum Notes*, American Numismatic Society, Vol. 31. New York. 7-61.

Mugione, Eliana. 2000. 'Problemi di trasmissioni iconografiche.' *Miti della ceramica Attica in Occidente.*
Problemi di trasmissioni iconografiche nelle produzioni Italiote. Taranto: Scorpione. 123-152.

Murti, Michelle. 2013. 'Deaths Associated with Hurricane Sandy. October-November 2012.' *Morbidity and Mortality Weekly Report*. Atlanta: Center for Disease Control and Prevention.

Mussini, Elena. 2002. 'La diffusione dell'iconografia di Acheloo in Magna Grecia e Sicilia. Tracce per l'individuazione di un culto.' *Studi Etruschi*, Vol. LXV-LXVIII, Serie III. Roma: Bretschneider. 91-120.

Myres John L. 1914. *Handbook of the Cesnola Collection of Antiquities from Cyprus*. New York.

------. 1933. 'The Amathus Bowl: A Long Lost Engraving.' *Journal of Hellenic Studies*, No. 53. London: The Council for the Society for the Promotion of Hellenic Studies. 25-39.

Nagel, Alexander. 2007. 'Searching for the Gods at Ancient Akarnania: New Evidence From a Ritual Deposit Near Stratos.' *Anodos: Studies of the Ancient World*, 6-7. Trnava, Slovakia: Fakulta humanistiky Trnavskej univerzity. 289-97.

Naso, Alessandro. 1996. *Architetture dipinte: decorazioni parietali non figurate nelle tombe a camera dell'Etruria meridionale: VII-V sec. a.C.* Roma: Bretschneider.

------. 2000. *Piceni. Storia e archeologia delle Marche in epoca preromana*. Milano: Longanesi.

------. 2012. 'Gli influssi del Vicino Oriente sull'Etruria nell'VIII-VII sec. a.C.: un bilancio.' *Origine degli Etruschi. Storia archeologia antropologia*; edited by V. Bellelli. Roma: Bretschneider. 433-453.

Nassa, Mario, and Valentino Nassa. 2010. *Cubulteria. Ragguagli sulla moneta attribuitagli e sul controverso simbolo del toro androprosopo*. Roma: Gruppo Editoriale L'Espresso.

------. 2012. *Teanum Sidicinum, Rilettura sommaria, con raffronti, dei più significativi contributi sulla monetazione antica.* Roma: Gruppo Editoriale L'Espresso.

Naumov, Goce. 2010. 'Neolithic anthropocentrism: the principles of imagery and symbolic manifestation of corporeality in the Balkans.' *Documenta Praehistorica*, Vol. XXXVII. Ljubljana: University Press. 227-238.

Nava, Maria Luisa, and Antonio Salerno (eds.) 2007 *Ambre. Trasparenze dall'antico. Catalogo della mostra. Napoli, Museo Archeologico Nazionale. 26 Marzo – 10 Settembre 2007.* Milano: Mondadori Electa.

Negroni Catacchio, Nuccia, Massimo Cardosa, and Marco Romeo Pitone. 2012. 'Dalla grotta naturale al tempio, tra natura e artificio: forma ed essenza del luogo sacro in etruria durante l'età dei metalli.' *Antropologia e Archeologia a confronto: rappresentazioni e pratiche del sacro. Atti dell'incontro internazionale di studi, Roma, Museo Nazionale Preistorico Etnografico 'Luigi Pigorini' 20-21 maggio 2011*. Roma: E.S.S. 595-607.

Neils, Jenifer. 1987. *The Youthful Deeds of Theseus*. Rome: Bretschnider.

Newell, Edward Theodore. 1938. *The Coinage of the Eastern Seleucid Mints: from Seleucus I to Antiochus III*. New York: American Numismatic Society.

Nicol, Donald M. 1958. 'The Oracle of Dodona.' *Greece and Rome,* Vol. 5, No. 2. 128-43.

Nicoletti, Fabrizio and Sebastiano Tusa 2012. 'L'età del Bronzo nella Sicilia occidentale.' *Dai Ciclopi agli Ecisti. Società e Territorio nella Sicilia Preistorica e Protostorica. Atti della XII Riunione Scientifica. San Cipirello (PA), 16-19 novembre 2006*. Firenze: Istituto Italiano di Preistoria e Protostoria. 105-130.

Nieddu, Fabio. 2008. 'Il 'pozzo sacro' di Riu Sallìu (Guasila-Cagliari). Osservazioni sull'opera isodoma negli edifici cultuali di età nuragica.' *La Civiltà Nuragica. Nuove Acquisizioni, Atti del Convegno (Senorbì, 14-16 Dicembre 2000)*. Vol. II; edited by Soprintendenza per i Beni Archeologici di Cagliari. Dolianova: Grafiche del Parteolla. 379–390.

Nielsen, Thomas Heine. 2002. 'Phourion. A note on the term in Classical Sources and in Diodorus Siculus.' *Even More Studies in the Ancient Greek Polis*, Historia Einzel-schriften 162. Stuttgart. 49-64.

Niemeier, Wolf Dietrich. 2001. 'Archaid Greeks in the Orient: Textual and Archaeological Evidence.' *Bulletin of the American Schools of Oriental Research*, No. 322. South Hadley, MA: American Schools of Oriental Research. 11-32.

Nijboer, Albert J., Johannes Van Der Plicht, Anna Maria Bietti Sestieri, and Anna De Santis. 2000. 'A high chronology for the early Iron Age in central Italy.' *Palaeohistoria*, Vol.41-42. Steenwijk: Balkema. 163-176.

Nikolaou, Kyriakos. 1965-1966. 'Archaeology in Cyprus, 1961-1966.' *Archaeological Reports*, No. 12. London: The Society for the Promotion of Hellenic Studies. 27-43.

Nilsson, Martin P. 1950. 'Lampen und Kerzen im Kult der Antike.' *Opuscula archeologica*, 6. Lund: C.W.K. Gleerup. 96-111.

Ninck, Martin. 1921. *Die Bedeuntung des Wassers im Kult und Leben der Alten. Eine symbolgeschichtliche Untersuchung,* Phylologus. Supplement 14, II, XXXX. Leipzig: Dieterich.

Nissen, Heinrich. 1870. 'Der caudinische Friede.' *Rheinisches Museum für Philologie,* Volume 25. Frankfurt am Main: Sauerländer. 1-65.

Noe, Sydney P., and Ann Johnston. 1984. *The Coinage of Metapontum, Parts 1 and 2. With Additions and Corrections by Ann Johnston.* New York: The American Numismatic Society.

Nys, Karin. 1995. 'The use of Masks in Cyprus during the Late Bronze Age.' *Journal of Prehistoric Religion*, Vol.9. Göteborg: Paul Åström. 19-34.

Oakley, Stephen P. 2005. *A Commentary on Livy Books VI-X*. Vol. III, Book IX. Oxford: Clarendon.

------. 2005. *A Commentary on Livy, Books VI-X*. Vol. IV, Book X. Oxford: Clarendon.

Oates, David, and Joan Oates. 1991. 'Excavations at Tell Brak 1990-91.' *Iraq*, Vol. 53. London: British Institute for the Study of Iraq. 127-145.

Oates, Joan. 2001. 'The Evidence of the Sealings.' *Excavations at Tell Brak Vol. 2: Nagar in the Third Millennium BC*; edited by D. Oates, J. Oates and H. McDonald. Cambridge, McDonald Institute for Archaeological Research. 121-140.

------. 2001. 'Organic Material.' *Excavations at Tell Brak Vol. 2: Nagar in the Third Millennium BC*; edited by D. Oates, J. Oates and H. McDonald. Cambridge, McDonald Institute for Archaeological Research. 295-300.

------, and David Oates. 2001. 'Archaeological Reconstruction and Historical Commentary.' *Excavations at Tell Brak Vol. 2: Nagar in the Third Millennium BC*; edited by D. Oates, J. Oates, and H. McDonald. Cambridge: McDonald Institute for Archaeological Research. 379-396.

Oberhummer, Eugen. 1887. *Akarnanien, Ambrakia, Amphilochien, Leukas im Altertum*. München: Theodor Ackermann.

Oleson, John Peter. 1975. 'Greek Myth and Etruscan Imagery in the Tomb of the Bulls at Tarquinia.' *American Journal of Archaeology*, Vol. 79, No. 3. New York: Macmillan. 189-200.

Oppenheim, A. Leo. 1969. 'Babylonian and Assyrian Historical Texts.' *Ancient Near Eastern Texts Relating to the Old Testament*; edited by J.B. Pritchard. Princeton: University Press. 264-317.

Oren, Eliezer D. 1997. *The Hyksos: New Historical and Archaeological Perspectives. International Seminar on Cultural Interconnections in the Ancient Near East*, Museum Monographs No. 96. Philadelphia: University of Pennsylvania.

Oriani, Eufemia. 1980. '*I candelabri etruschi in bronzo.*' *Materiale fittile architettonico rinvenuto sotto la chiesa di Santa Maria in Camuccia*. Vol. II, 4 Todi. 19-22.

Origlia, Vittorio. 1989. *'Le arule a Locri Epifiziri.' Locri Epifiziri III. Cultura materiale e vita quotidiana;* edited by M. Barra Bagnasco. Firenze: Le Lettere. 135-144.

Orsi, Paolo. 1911. 'Rapporto preliminare sulla quinta campagna di scavi nelle Calabrie durante l'anno 1910. Locri Epizephyrii.' *Notizie degli Scavi di Antichità, 1911, Suppl.* Roma: Tip. Della R. Accademia dei Lincei. 3-76.

------. 1912. 'Scavi di Calabria nel 1911 (relazione provvisoria).' *Notizie degli Scavi di Antichità, 1912,*

Suppl. Roma: Tip. Della R. Accademia dei Lincei. 3-56.

------. 1918. 'Gli scavi intorno a l'Athenaion di Siracusa: negli anni 1912-1917.' *Monumenti Antichi pubblicati per cura della Reale Accademia dei Lincei*, Vol. XXV. Roma: Tip. della R. Accademia dei Lincei. 353-762.

Orville, Jacques-Philippe d', Pieter Burman, Gerrit Tielenburg, and Joseph-Victor Le Clerc. 1764. *Jacobi Philippi d'Orville Sicula, quibus Siciliae veteris rudera, additis antiquitatum tabulis, illustrantur.* Amstelaedami: apud Gerardum Tielenburg.

Osborne, Robin. 1996. *Greece in the Making, 1200-479 BC.* London: Routledge.

Oshima, Takayoshi. 2011 *Babylonian Prayers to Marduk.* Orientalische Religionen in der Antike. Vol.7. Tübingen: Mohr Siebeck.

Ostrowski, Janusz A. 1991. *Personifications of rivers in Greek and roman art.* Studia ad Archaeologiam Mediterraneam Pertinentia, Vol. XII. Warszawa-Krakòw: Sumptibus Universitatis Iagellonicae.

Ovid, B. P. Moore, and Victor Reinganum. 1965. *Ars amatoria.* London: Folio Society.

Pagano, Mario. 2004. 'L'Italia romana delle Regiones. Regio I Latium et Campania: Teano.' *Il mondo dell'Archeologia*, Enciclopedia Archeologica Vol.VI. Roma: Istit. Della Enciclopedia Italiana.

Paleothodoros, Dimitris. 2007. 'Commercial Networks in the Mediterranean and the Diffusion of Early Attic Red-figure Pottery (525-490 BCE).' *Mediterranean Historical Review*, 22.2. London: F. Cass. 165-182.

Palermo, Dario. 1981. 'Polizzello.' *Contributi alla conoscenza dell'età del Ferro in Sicilia. Monte Finocchito e Polizzello.* Cronache di Archeologia, Vol.XX. Catania: Università di Catania, Istituto di Archeologia. 103-150.

------. 1983. 'Askoi ornitomorfi della Sicilia indigena.' *Cronache di Archeologia*, Vol. 22. Catania: Università di Catania, Istituto di Archeologia. 93-97.

------. 2003. 'Il gesto e la maschera. Rappresentazioni umane dal centro indigeno della Montagna di Polizzello.' *Annali della Facoltà di Scienze della Formazione.* Catania: C.U.E.C.M. 145-156.

------, and Davide Tanasi. 2006. 'Diodoro a Polizzello.' *Diodoro Siculo e la Sicilia indigena. Atti del convegno di studi, Caltanissetta 21-22 maggio 2005*; edited by Calogero Miccichè, Simona Modeo, Luigi Santagati. Palermo: Regione siciliana, Assessorato dei Beni Culturali, Ambientali e della Pubblica Istruzione. 89-102.

------. 2008. 'Doni votivi e aspetti del culto nel santuario indigeno della Montagna di Polizzello.' *Doni agli dei. Il sistema dei doni votivi nei santuari. Atti del Seminario di Studi, Napoli 21 Aprile 2006*; edited by Giovanna Greco and Bianca Ferrara. Pozzuoli: Naus. 257-270.

Pallottino, Massimo. 1954. *Testimonia Linguae Etruscae. Biblioteca di Studi Superiori*, Vol. XXIX. Firenze: La Nuova Italia Editrice.

------. 1958. 'Urartu, Greece and Etruria.' *East and West*, Vol. 9, No.1/2. Roma: Istituto italiano per il Medio ed Estremo Oriente. 29-52.

------. 2000. *La Sardegna Nuragica;* edited by Giovanni Lilliu. Nuoro: Ilisso Edizioni.

Palmucci, Alberto 2007. 'Virgilio, Erodoto e il DNA degli Etruschi (Corito Tarquinia),' *Aufidus. No. 66-67 Dipartimento di Scienze dell'Antichità.* Università di Bari: Dipartimento di Studi del Mondo Antico.

------. 2010. *Aruspicina Etrusca: ed Orientale a confronto. Tarquinia e i libri Tagetici, con traduzione dei frammenti greci e latini.* Roma.

Panebianco, Venturino. 1945. *La colonia romana di Salernum. Introduzione allo studio di Salerno romana.* Salerno: Linotipografia Spadafora.

Pantuliano, Silvia. 2005. 'La monetazione della colonia latina di Cales.' *XIII Congreso Internacional de Numismática. Madrid, 2003.* Madrid. 357-368.

Paoletti, Orazio, and Luisa Tamagno Perna (eds.) 2002. *Etruria e Sardegna centro-settentrionale tra l'età del Bronzo finale e l'Arcaismo, Atti del XXI Congresso di Studi Etruschi e Italici (Sassari-Alghero-Oristano-Torralba, 13-17 ottobre 1998).* Pisa-Roma: Istituti Editoriali e Poligrafici Internazionali.

Paoletti, Maurizio. 2010. 'Sibari sul Traente.' *Bibliografia Topografica della Colonizzazione Greca in Italia e nelle Isole Tirreniche*, Vol.XVIII. Pisa-Roma: Scuola Normale Superiore, Edizioni ETS. 787-799.

Parise, Nicola. 1981. 'Unità ponderali orientali in Occidente. Osservazioni e postille intorno alle 'antiche rotte del Mediterraneo'.' *Il Commercio greco nel Tirreno in età arcaica: atti del seminario in memoria di Mario Napoli, Salerno 1977.* Salerno: Università degli Studi. 97-110.

Parisio, Prospero. 1591. *Rariora Magnae Graeciae Numismata.* Roma.

Parker, Robert. 2000. 'Sacrifice and Battle.' *War and Violence in Ancient Greece*; edited by Han van Wees. London: Duckworth. 299-314.

------. 2011. *On Greek Religion.* Ithaca-London: Cornell University Press.

Parpola, Asko. 1984. *New Correspondences between Harappan and Near Eastern Glyptic Art.* Cambridge: University Press.

Parrot, André. 1948. *Tello, vingt campagnes de fouilles (1877- 1933).* Paris: Albin Michel.

------. 1956. *Mission Archeologique de Mari. Volume 1, Le Temple d'Ishtar.* Paris: Librairie orientaliste P. Geuthner.

Passaro, Colonna, and Gabriella Ciaccia. 2000. 'Cales: la necropoli dall'Orientalizzante recente all'eta` ellenistica.' *Studi sull'Italia dei Sanniti.* Catalogo della mostra, Roma 14 gennaio - 19 marzo 2000 Milano: Electa. 20-25.

Pasquali, Giorgio. 1927. 'Acheruns, Acheruntis.' *Studi Etruschi*, Vol I. Firenze: Olschki. 291-301.

Patané, Andrea. 1996. 'Saggi di scavo all'interno del Castello Ursino di Catania.' *Atti del VIII Congresso Internazionale di studi sulla Sicilia antica. Kokalos*, Vol. XXXIX-XL (1993-1994), Tomo II, 1. Roma: Bretschneider. 901-914.

Pautasso, Antonella. 1994. *Il deposito votivo presso la Porta nord a Vulci. Corpus delle stipi votive in Italia*, Vol. 7, Regio VII, 3. Archaeologica 107. Roma: Bretschneider.

Payne, Humfry. 1931. *Necrocorinthia: a study of Corinthian art in the archaic period*. College Park, MD: McGrath.

Payne, William J.A. 1991. 'Domestication: A Forward Step in Civilization.' *Cattle Genetic Resources*; edited by Charles G. Hickman. Amsterdam: Elsevier. 51-72.

Perlman, Paula Jean. 2000. *City and Sanctuary in Ancient Greece: The Theorodokia in the Peloponnese*. Göttingen: Vandenhoeck & Ruprecht.

Pellegrino Carmine. 2008. 'Pontecagnano: la scrittura e l'onomastica in una comunità etrusca di frontiera,' *La colonizzazione etrusca in Italia. Atti del XV Convegno Internazionale di Studi sulla Storia e l'Archeologia dell'Etruria;* edited by G. Della Fina. Annali della Fondazione per il Museo 'Claudio Faina' Vol. XV. Roma: Quasar. 423-463.

------. 2010. 'Pontecagnano: l'uso della scrittura tra Etruschi, Greci e Italici.' *Meetings between cultures in the ancient Mediterranean, 17th International Congress of Classical Archaeology (Rome, 22-26 September 2008).* Bollettino di Archeologia Online, I, 2010, Volume speciale F/F3/2. Roma: Direzione Generale per le Antichità. 1-19

------. 2013. 'La Campania degli Etruschi.' *Vetulonia, Pontecagnano e Capua. Vite parallele de tre città Etrusche, Catalogo della mostra, Vetulonia 14 Luglio – 10 Novembre 2013*; edited by Simona Rafanelli. Monteriggioni: ARA Edizioni. 34-39.

------, and Simona Rafanelli. 2013. 'Vetulonia, Pontecagnano, Capua. Vite parallele di tre città Etrusche.' *Archeologia Viva*, XXXII, No.162. Firenze: Giunti. 26-39.

Perego, Lucio Giuseppe. 2005. *Il territorio tarquiniese. Ricerche di topografia storica*. Milano: LED.

------. 2008. 'Rileggendo vecchi dati. Spunti sull'Orientalizzante Tarquiniese.' *Aspetti nell'orientalizzante nell'Etruria e nel Lazio. Aristonothos*, 3. Milano: CUEM. 171-193.

Perkins, Dexter, Jr. 1969. 'Fauna of Çatal Hüyük: Evidence for Early Cattle Domestication in Anatolia.' *Science*, New Series, Vol. 164, No. 3876. Washington, DC: American Association for the Advancement of Science. 177-179.

Peroni, Renata. 1994 *Introduzione alla protostoria italiana*. Bari: Laterza.

Peterson, Roy M. 1919. *The Cults of Campania*. Rome: American Academy in Rome.

Pezzini, Elena. 2012. 'La scultura funeraria.' *Gli Etruschi a Palermo. Museo Casuccini, Palermo, 17 ottobre 2012-6 gennaio 2013*. Milano: Silvana. 18-19.

Philemo, and Theodor Kock. 1884. 'Fragmenta.' *Comicorum Atticorum Fragmenta*. Vol. 2. Lipsiae: in aedibus B. G. Teubneri.

Phocylides, and Theodor Bergk. 1882. 'Fragmenta.' *Poetae Lyrici Graeci*. Vol. 2. Lipsiae: Teubner.

Pick, Behrendt, and Kurt Regling. 1898-1910. *Die antiken Münzen von Dacien und Moesien. Die antiken Münzen Nord-Griechenlands*, Vol. I, Parts 1 and 2; edited by Friedrich Imhoof-Blumer. Berlin: Georg Reimer.

Pighius, Stephanus Vinandus, Silvester Pardo, and Andreas Schottus. 1615. *Annales Magistratvvm Et Provinciar. S. P. Q. R. Ab Vrbe Condita: Incomparabili Labore Et Indvstria Ex Avctorvm Antiqvitatvmq. Varieis Monimenteis Svppleti Per Stephanvm Vinandvm Pighivm Campensem ; In Qveis Reipvblicae Mvtationes Potestatvm Ac Imperiorvm Svccessiones Acta Leges Bella Clades Victoriae Manibiae Atq. Trivmphi Nec Non Inlvstria Stemmata Familiarvmq. Propagines Ad Annos Et Tempora Sva Redvcvntvr ; Opus non solùm Historiæ Rom. Artiumq[ue] liberalium sed etiam omnis humani Iuris & antiqui Politeumatis studiosis vtilissimum.* Antverpiae: Officina Plantiniana.

Pigorini, Luigi 1908. 'Uso delle acque salutari nell'età del Bronzo.' *Bullettino di Paletnologia Italiana*, Anno XXIV, No. 9-12. Parma: Battei. 169-191.

Pindar, and William H. Race. 1997. *Pindar: Olympian Odes, Pythian Odes*. Cambridge: Harvard University Press.

------. 2006. *Nemean Odes. Isthmian Odes. Fragments*. Carmbridge: Harvard University Press.

Pini, Ingo. 1968. *Beiträge zur minoischen Gräberkunde*. Wiesbaden: Steiner.

Pipili Maria. 1992. 'Nereus.' *Lexicon Iconographicum Mythologiae Classicae* Vol. VI. Zürich: Artemis & Verlag. 824-837.

Pitzalis, Giovanni. 2002. "Un athyrma dal pozzo sacro di Predio Canopoli-Perfugas.' *Etruria e Sardegna centro-settentrionale tra l'età del bronzo finale e l'arcaismo. Atti del XXI Congresso di Studi Etruschi e Italici (Sassari-Alghero-Oristano-Torralba, 13-17 ottobre 1998)*; edited by O. Paoletti and L. Tamagno Perna. Pisa-Roma: Istituti editoriali e poligrafici internazionali. 563–568.

Pizzirani, Chiara. 2014. 'Il mare nell'immaginario funebre degli Etruschi.' *Il viaggio oltre la vita. Gli etruschi e l'aldilà tra capolavori e realtà virtual*; edited by Giuseppe Sassatelli and Alfonsina Russo Tagliente. Bologna: Bononia University Press. 71-79.

Plato, and Harold N. Fowler. 2001. *Plato: Euthyphro, Apology, Crito, Phaedo, Phaedrus*. Cambridge: Harvard University Press.

Plato, and Peter Kalkavage. 2001. *Plato's Timaeus*. Newburyport, MA: Focus Publishing.

Pliny, and Jean Hardouin. 1783. *Historiae naturalis libri xxxvii*. Biponti: Ex typographia Societatis.

------, and H. Rackham. 1938. *Natural History*. Cambridge: Harvard University Press.

Poccetti, Paolo. 1996. 'Culti delle acque e stadi della vita muliebre: dottrine misteriche e fondo religioso italico nella Tavola osca di Agnone.' *La Tavola di Agnone nel contesto italico. Convegno di Studio, Agnone,13-15 aprile 1994*. Firenze: Olschki. 219-241.

Poggesi, Gabriella, Elisabetta Bocci, Lucia Pagnini, and Fulvia Lo Schiavo. 2011. 'Rapporti fra l'Etruria settentrionale interna e il territorio di Capua: i kyathoi con anse a corna tronche e cave.' *Gli Etruschi e la Campania settentrionale: atti del XXVI Convegno di Studi Etruschi ed Italici, Caserta, Santa Maria Capua Vetere, Capua, Teano, 11-15 novembre 2007. Istituto Nazionale di Studi Etruschi ed Italici, Atti di convegni, 26. Pisa*; edited by Orazio Paoletti and Maria Chiara Bettini. Pisa-Roma: Fabrizio Serra. 167-179.

Polish-Syria Expedition to Tell Arbid. 2013. 'Akkadian and Post-Akkadian Periods.' *Sector S- Step Trench*. Online Webpage. University of Warsaw, Polish Centre of Mediterranean Archaeology.

Polybius, and Robin Waterfield. 2010. *The Histories*. Oxford: University Press.

Pomponius Mela, and Piergiorgio Parroni (ed.). 1984. *De Chorographia. Libri tres*. Roma: Ed. di Storia e Letteratura.

Pons Gabriel. 1988. 'Sarcòfagos tauromorfos en la Protohistòria Mallorquina.' *Revista de Arqueologia,* 83. Madrid. 32-39.

Popham, Mervyn, and Elizabeth Milburn. 1971. 'The Late Helladic IIIC pottery of Xeropolis, Lefkandi: a summary.' *Annual of the British School at Athens,* Vol. 66. Cambridge: University Press. 333-352.

Popp, Harald. 1957. *Die Einwirkung von Vorzeichen*. Unpublished Dissertation. Erlangen.

Porada, Edith. 1948. 'The Cylinder Seals of the Late Cypriote Bronze Age.' *American Journal of Archaeology*, Vol. 52, No. 1. New York: Macmillan. 178-198.

Postgate, Carolyn, David Oates and Joan Oates. 1997. *The Excavations at Tell al-Rimah: The Pottery*, Iraq Archaeological Reports, Vol. 4; edited by the British Institute for the Study of Iraq. London: Aris & Phillips.

Posteraro, Luigi. 1916. 'Origine di Alife. Simbolismo delle sue tradizioni e della sua moneta.' *Rivista Italiana di Numismatica e scienze affini*. Vol. XXIX. Milano: Cogliati. 307-320.

Powell, Benjamin. 1904. 'Oeniadae: I. History and Topography.' *American Journal of Archaeology*, Vol. 8, No.2. New York: Macmillan. 137-173.

Prayon, Friedhelm. 1989. 'L'architettura funeraria Etrusca. La situazione attuale delle ricerche e problemi aperti.' *Atti del II Congresso Internazionale Etrusco, Firenze 1985*; edited by G. Maetzke. Roma: Bretschneider. 441-9.

Prestianni Giallombardo, Anna Maria. 1977. 'Per una edizione dei frammenti della Tabula Halaesina.' *Archivio Storico Messinese*, Vol. XXVIII. Messina: Poligrafica della Sicilia. 209-212.

------. 2006. 'Ducezio, l'oracolo e la fondazione di Kala Akte.' *Diodoro Siculo e la Sicilia indigena. Atti del convegno di studi, Caltanissetta 21-22 maggio 2005*; edited by Calogero Miccichè, Simona Modeo, Luigi Santagati. Palermo: Regione siciliana, Assessorato dei Beni Culturali, Ambientali e della Pubblica Istruzione. 135-149.

Price, Martin Jessop. 1969. 'Greek coin hoards in the British Museum.' *Numismatic Chronicle*. Vol. IX. London: Royal Numismatic Society. 1-14.

------. 1983. *Les inscriptions chypriotes syllabiques: recueil critique et commenté*. Paris : De Boccard.

Prisciano, and E. Baehrens, 1883. *Periegesis. Poetae Latini minores*, Vol. V. Lipsiae.

Pritchett, William Kendrick. 1979. *The Greek State at War*, Vol. 3. Berkeley: University of California Press.

Privitera, Santo. 2009 'Lo sviluppo urbano di Catania dalla fondazione *dell'apoikia alla fine del V secolo d.C.' Catania. L'identità urbana dall'antichità al settecento;* edited by L. Scalisi. Catania: Sanfilippo Editore. 37-71.

Procelli, Enrico. 1995. 'Appunti per una topografia di Catania pregreca.' *Kokalos*, Vol. XXXVIII. Roma: Bretschneider. 69-78.

Psôma, Selene. 2007. 'Le monnayage fédéral acarnanien de l'époque classique.' *KLIO. Beiträge zur Alten Geschichte*, Vol. 89, Issue 1. Leipzig. 7-23.

Puglisi, Mariangela. 2005. 'Distribuzione e funzione della moneta bronzea in Sicilia dalla fine del V sec. a.C. all'età ellenistica.' *Actas XIII Congreso Internacional de Numismática, Madrid, 15-18 sieptembre 2003*, Vol. 1; edited by C. Alfaro, C. Marcos, P. Otero. Madrid. 285-294.

Pulleyn, Simon. 1994. 'The Power of Names in Classical Greek Religion.' *Classical Quarterly*, New Series, Vol. 44, No. 1. Oxford: University Press. 17- 25.

Raccuia, Carmela. 1999. 'Presenze e contatti fra le genti nell'area di Gela nelle età preistorica e protostorica.' *Origine e incontri di culture nell'antichità. Magna Grecia e Sicilia. Stato degli studi e prospettive di ricerca*; edited by M. Barra Bagnasco, E. De Miro and A. Pinzone. Messina: Di.Sc.A.M. 321-330.

Radner, Karen. 2011. 'Nineveh, Assyria's capital in the 7th century BC.' *Knowledge and Power in the Neo-Assyrian Empire*. York: Higher Education Academy. (Available online at: http://oracc.org/saao/knpp)

Raduncheva, Ana. 1997. 'Eneolithic craft-manufacturing center of the Sedlare village of Kardzhali.' *Yearbook of the National Archaeological Museum*. Volume X. Sofiia: Bŭlgarska akademiia na naukite, Arkheologicheski Institut s muzeĭ. 162-175.

Rafanelli, Simona. 2010. 'Miti e divinita` del mare, creature simbolo e fantastiche del mare.' *Il mare degli Etruschi*. Atti del Convegno, Piombino – Orbetello, 18-20 Settembre 2009 Firenze: Consiglio regionale della Toscana. 37-61.

------ (ed.) 2013. *Vetulonia, Pontecagnano e Capua. Vita parallele di tre città etrusche. Catalogo della mostra, Vetulonia 14 Luglio – 10 Novembre 2013* Monteriggioni: ARA Edizioni.

Ranieri, Nicola. 2011. *Archeologia della Morte*. Roma: Carocci.

Rasmussen, Tom. 2011. 'Etruscan ritual and religion.' *The Oxford Handbook of the Archaeology of Ritual and Religion*; edited by T. Insoll. Oxford: University Press. 708-719.

Rathje, Annette. 2007. 'Murlo, Images and Archaeology.' *Etruscan Studies*, Vol.10. Berlin: Walter De Gruyter. 175-184.

Ravel, Oscar E. 1928. *The 'Colts' of Ambracia*. New York: American Numismatic Society.

Ravelli, Franco, and Paula J. Howard. 1988. 'I cunicoli etrusco-latini: tunnel per la captazione di acqua pura. Irrigazione e drenaggio.' *Irrigazione e drenaggio*, XXXV, 1, gennaio-marzo, 1988. Bologna: Edagricole. 57-70.

Raviola, Flavio. 1995. *Napoli Origini*. Hesperia Vol. 6. Roma: Bretschneider.

Reade, Julian Edgeworth. 1979. 'Assyrian Architectural Decoration: Techniques and Subject-Matter.' *Baghdader Mitteilungen*. Vol. 10. Berlin: Mann. 17-49.

Rebuffat, René. 1966. 'Les Phéniciens à Rome.' *Mélanges de l'École française de Rome*, Vol. LXXVIII, No. 1. Paris: De Boccard. 7-48.

Reccia, Giovanni. 2014. *Atella/Aderl: Confronti etimologici e riscontri geocartografici. Novissimae Editiones*, Vol.33. Atella: I.S.A.

Redford, Donald (ed.). 2003. *Oxford Guide to Egyptian Mythology*. Oxford: University Press.

Reese, David S. 1985. 'Shells, Ostrich Eggshells and Other Exotic Faunal Remains from Kition.' *Excavation at Kition V. The pre-Phoenician levels*, Part II; edited by V. Karageorghis, and M. Demas. Nicosia: Published for the Republic of Cyprus by the Dept. of Antiquities, Cyprus. 340-416.

Rellini, U. 1918. 'La Caverna di Latronico e il culto delle acque salutari nell'età del bronzo.' *Monumenti Antichi pubblicati per cura della Reale Accademia dei Lincei*, Vol. XXV. Roma: Tip. della R. Accademia dei Lincei. 461-615.

Rendeli, Marco. 2010. 'Monte 'e Prama: 4875 punti interrogativi.' *Meetings between cultures in the ancient Mediterranean, 17th International Congress of Classical Archaeology (Rome, 22-26 September 2008)*. Bollettino di Archeologia Online, I, 2010, Volume speciale D/D2/7. Roma: Direzione Generale per le Antichità. 58-72.

Reyes, Andres T. 2007. 'The Iconography of Deities and Demons in Cyprus.' *Iconography of Deities and Demons in Ancient Near East: An Iconographic Dictionary with Special Emphasis on First-Millenium BCE Palestine/Israel*. Electronic pre-publication available at http://www.religionswissenschaft .uzh. ch/idd/prepublication.php. Zürich: Universitat.

Riccio, Gennaro. 1852. *Repertorio, ossia descrizione e tassa delle monete di città antiche: compresse ne' poerimetri delle province componenti l'attuale regno delle Due Sicilie al di qua del Faro, con la enunciazione delle altre inedite o nuove, venute in luce dopo il decesso del cav. Carelli*. Napoli: Tramater.

Rice, Michael. 1998. *The Power of the Bull*. London: Routledge.

Richardson, Emeline Hill. 1983. *Etruscan Votive Bronzes. Geometric, Orientalizing, Archaic*. Mainz am Rhein: Verlag P. von Zabern.

Richardson, Nicholas. 1993. *The Iliad: A Commentary*. Cambridge: University Press.

Rizza, Giovanni. 1978. 'Attività dell'Istituto di Archeologia dell'Università di Catania. Scavi e ricerche in Sicilia negli anni 1972-1975.' *Atti del IV Congresso Internazionale sulla Sicilia antica. Kokalos* Vol. XXII-XXIII (1976-1977) Tomo II, 1. Roma: Bretschneider. 636-645.

Rizzello, Marcello. 1980. *I santuari della Media Valle del Liri, IV-II sec. a.C.* Sora: Centro di studi sorani Vincenzo Patriarca.

Rizzo, Giulio Emanuele. 1938. *Saggi Preliminari sull'arte della moneta nella Sicilia greca*. Roma: Libreria dello stato.

------. 1946. *Monete greche della Sicilia*. 2 Volumes. Roma: La Libreria dello stato.

Roaf, Michael. 1996. *Cultural Atlas of Mesopotamia and the Ancient Near East*. New York.

Robb, John. 2015. 'Burial and Human Body Representation in the Mediterranean Neolithic.' *The Oxford Handbook of Neolithic Europe*; edited by Chris Fowler, Jan Harding, Daniela Hofmann. Oxford: University Press. 959-985.

Roberts, John M. 1976. *History of the World*. New York: Penguin.

Robertson, Roland. 1995. 'Glocalization: Time-Space and Homogeneity-Heterogeneity.' *Global Modernities;* edited by Mike Featherstone, Scott Lash and Roland Robertson. London: Sage Publications. 25-44.

Robinson, Damian, and Andrew Wilson. 2011. 'Introduction: Maritime archaeology and the ancient economy.' *Maritime Archaeology and Ancient Trade in the Mediterranean*. Vol. 6. Oxford: Oxford Centre for Maritime Archaeology. 1-11.

Robinson, Edward Stanley Gotch. 1973. 'A hoard of Greek coins from Southern Anatolia?.' *Revue Numismatique*, 6e serie, Tome 15. Paris: Blois. 229-237.

Rocco, Giulia. 2006. 'Modelli orientali e rielaborazioni Greche: originali iconografie di creature fantastiche nell'Orientalizzante.' *Varia Iconographica ab Oriente ad Occidentem*; edited by Giovanna Pisano. Studia Punica Vol. 14. Roma. 29-40.

Rogers, Edgar. 1932. *The Copper Coinage of Thessaly*. London: Spink.

Romanelli, Pietro. 1948. 'Tarquinia. Scavi e ricerche nell'area della città.' *Notizie degli Scavi di Antichità*. Vol. II. Roma: Accademia nazionale dei Lincei. 25-270.

Romano, Licia. 2008. 'La corona del dio. Note sull'iconografia divina nel Protodinastico.' *Vicino Oriente XIV. Annuario del Dipartimento di Scienze Storiche Archeologiche e Antropologiche dell'Antichità - Sezione Vicino Oriente.* Rome: University Press. 41-57.

Rossi, Filli. 2005. *La dea sconosciuta e la barca solare. Una placchetta votiva dal santuario protostorico di Breno in Valle Camonica.* Milano: ET.

Rouault, Olivier, Maria Grazia Masetti-Rouault, and Ali Abou-Assaf. 1993. *L'Eufrate e il tempo le civiltà del medio Eufrate e della Gezira siriana*. Milano: Electa.

Roy, Jim. 2000. 'Review: Oliver Dany, *Akarnanien im Hellenismus. Geschichte und Völkerrecht in Nordwestgriechenland. Münchener Beiträge zur Papyrusforschung und antiken Rechtsgeschichte, Heft 89.*' *Bryn Mawr Classical Review*. http://bmcr.brynmawr.edu/2000/2000-02-21.html (Accessed Spring 2016).

Rudhardt, Jean. 1971. *Le thème de l'eau primordiale dans la mythologie grecque*. Berne: Francke.

Ruffo, Fabrizio. 2010. *La Campania antica. Appunti di storia e di topografia. Parte I. Dal Massico-Roccamonfina al Somma-Vesuvio*. Napoli: DiLibri.

Runnels, Curtis. 'Acarnania.' *Perseus Encyclopedia*, available from the Perseus Digital Library at Tufts University.

Rupp, Wayne L., Jr. 2006. *Shape of the Beast: The Theriomorphic and Therianthropic Deities and Demons of Ancient Italy*. Unpublished PhD Dissertation, The Florida State University.

Russell, Nerissa. 2012. *Social Zooarchaeology: Humans and Animals in Prehistory*. Cambridge: University Press.

Russi, Angelo. 1975. *Teanum Apulum: le iscrizioni e la storia del municipio*. Roma: Istituto Italiano per la Storia Antica.

Russo, Roberto. 2009. 'Prima bozza preliminare di uno studio organico sulla monetazione del centro Italia e della Magna Grecia tra il 326 a.C. al 215 a.C..' *Numismatica Sottovoce*. Zürich: Numismatica Ars Classica.

Russo Tagliente, Alfonsina. 1996. 'Il santuario Lucano di Armento-Serra Lustrante.' *I Greci in Occidente. Greci Enotri e Lucani nella Basilicata meridionale.* Napoli: Electa Napoli. 190-93.

Rusten, Jeffrey S. 1982. 'Ovid, Empedocles and the Minotaur.' *The American Journal of Philology*, Vol. 103, No. 3. Baltimore, MD: Johns Hopkins University Press. 332-333.

Rutilio Namaziano, and Étienne Wolff. 2007. *De reditu suo. Rutilius Namatianus: Sur son retour. Collection des Universités de France. With the collaboration of S. Lancel and J. Soler.* Paris: Les Belles Lettres.

Rutter, N. Keith. 1979. 'South Italy and Messana.' *Le origini della monetazione di bronzo in Sicilia e in Magna Grecia. Atti del VI Convegno del Centro Internazionale di Studi Numismatici – Napoli 17-22 Aprile 1977. Annali dell'Istituto Italiano di Numismatica* Vol. 25, Suppl. 6. Roma: Istituto Italiano di Numismatica. 193-218.

------. 1979. *Campanian Coinages 475-380 BC*. Edinburgh: University Press.

------. 1993. 'The myth of the Damareteion.' *Chiron* 22. St. John, KS. 171-188.

------.1997. *Greek Coinages of Southern Italy and Sicily*. London: Spink.

------, (ed.). 2001. *Historia Numorum: Italy*. London: British Museum Press.

------. 2012. 'The Coinage of Italy.' *The Oxford Handbook of Greek and Roman Coinage*; edited by William E. Metcalf. Oxford: University Press. 128-141.

------, John Morcom, and Suzanne Frey-Kupper (eds.) Forthcoming. *Historia Nummorum Sicily and Adjacent Islands*. London: British Museum Press.

Rutter, Jeremy B. 1968. 'The Three Phases of the Taurobolium.' *Phoenix*, Vol. 22, No.3. Toronto: University Press. 226-249.

Ryan, William B. F., and Walter C. Pitman. 1999. *Noah's Flood: the New Scientific Discoveries about the Event that Changed History*. New York: Simon & Schuster.

Sakellarakis, Yannis A. 1971. 'Ἐλεφάντινον πλοίον εκ Μυκηνων.' *Archaiologike Ephemeris*. Athens: Typografeion Estia. 188-233.

Salinas, Antonino. 1867. *Le monete delle antiche città di Sicilia descritte e illustrate*. Palermo: Stabilimento tipografico di Francesco Lao.

Salmon, Edward Togo. 1967. *The Second Samnite War in Samnium and the Samnites*. Cambridge.

------. 1985. *Il Sannio e i Sanniti*. Torino.

Salamone, Grazia. 2013. *'Una' e 'molteplice'. La ninfa eponima di città, Iconografie monetali e semantica. Semata e Signa. Collana di Studi di Iconografia Monetale, Vol. 6* Reggio Calabria: Falzea.

Sambon, Arthur. 1903. *Les monnaies antiques de l'Italie*. Paris: Bureaux du 'Musée'.

Sandars, Nancy Katharine. 1968. *Prehistoric Art in europe*. London: Penguin.

Sanna, Barbara, Emerenziana Usai, and Raimondo Zucca. 2009. 'Il Santuario costiero di Orri (Arborea).' *Naves plenis velis euntes*; edited by Attilio Mastino, Pier Giorgio Spanu, Raimondo Zucca Tharros Felix, Vol.3. Roma: Carocci. 236-257.

Sannibale, Maurizio. 2013. 'Orientalizing Etruria.' *The Etruscan World*; edited by Jean MacIntosh Turfa. London: Routledge. 99-133.

Santangelo, Alberto Ettore. *Radici Scite degli Etruschi.* Sabaini: Milano, 2002

Santelli, Giovanni. 2000. 'Monete d'epoca tardo-repubblicana della zecca siciliana di Segesta: le contromarche ed il motivo dell'aquila.' *Annotazioni Numismatiche*, Suppl. XV, anno 10°, serie III. Milano. 3-24.

------, and Alberto Campana. 2008. 'Le prime contromarche siciliane su bronzo.' *Monete Antiche*, Anno VII, No.38. Cassino: Diana. 11-15.

Santoni, Vincenzo. 2001. Il Nuraghe Su Nuraxi di Barumini.' *Guide e studi*, Volume 2. Cagliari: Soprintendenza per i Beni Archeologici per le province di Cagliari e Oristano.

Sassatelli, Giuseppe. 1993. 'Spina nelle mmagini etrusche: Eracle, Dedalo e il problema dell'acqua.' *Spina.*
Storia di una Città tra Greci ed Etruschi. Ferrara: Ferrara Arte Editore. 114-128.

Sasson, Jack M. 1995. *Civilizations of the Ancient Near East.* New York: Scribner.

Scary, Elaine. 2001. *On Beauty and Being Just.* Princeton: University Press.

Schaeffer, Claude F. A. (ed.) 1971. *Alasia I.* Paris: Klincksieck.

Schrevel, Cornelius, and John Richardson. 1853. *Schrevelius' lexicon, in Greek and English, for the use of colleges and schools: to which is added, a copious English and Greek lexicon.* London: R. Baldwin.

Schwartz, Friedrich L. W. 1860. *Der ursprung der mythologie, dargelegt an griechischer und deutscher sage.* Berlin: W. Hertz.

Schwarz, Shirley J. 1974. *The iconography of the Archaic Etruscan Herakles: a study of three adventures: Nessos, Pholos and Acheloos.* Maryland: University Press.

------. 1990. 'Herakles/Hercle.' *Lexicon Iconographicum Mythologiae Classicae.* Vol. V/1. Zürich: Artemis & Verlag. 196-253.

Sciacca, Ferdinando. 2003. *La tomba Calabresi e la tomba del tripode di Cerveteri.* Città del Vaticano: Musei vaticani, Museo Gregoriano Etrusco.

Seaby, Herbert A., David Sear, and Robert Loosley. 1989. *Roman Silver Coins, Volume I, The Republic to Augustus.* London: Spink.

Seibert, Jakob. 1979. *Die politischen Flüchtlinge und Verbannten in der griechischen Geschichte: von d. Anfängen bis zur Unterwerfung durch d. Römer.* Darmstadt: Wissenschaftliche Buchgesellschaft. 7-26.

Seltmann, Charles Theodore. 1955. *Greek Coins: a History of Metallic Currency and Coinage down to the fall of the Hellenistic Kingdoms.* London: Methuen.

Semerano, Giovanni. 1984. *Le Origini della Cultura Europea. Vol. I Rivelazioni della linguistica storica. Tomi 1 e 2. Biblioteca dell' 'Archivum Romanicum'*, Serie II, Vol. 38. Firenze: Olschki.

------. 1994. *Le Origini della Cultura Europea. Vol. II. Dizionari etimologici. Basi semitiche delle lingue indeuropee. Tomo 1: Dizionario della lingua greca; Tomo 2: Dizionario della lingua latina e di voci moderne. Biblioteca dell' 'Archivum Romanicum'*, Serie II, Vol.43. Firenze: Olschki.

------. 2001. *L'infinito. Un Equivoco Millenario. Le antiche civiltà del Vicino Oriente e le origini del pensiero Greco.* Milano: Mondadori.

------. 2003. *Il popolo che sconfisse la morte. Gli Etruschi e la loro lingua.* Milano: Mondadori.

------. 2005. *La favola dell'indoeuropeo.* Milano: Mondadori.

Sestini, D. 1829. *Descrizione d'alcune medaglie greche del museo del Signore Carlo d'Ottavio Fontana di Trieste, Parte Terza.* Firenze: G. Piatti.

Settis, Salvatore. 1987. *Archeologia in Calabria. Figure e temi.* Roma.

Shanks, Michael. 2003. *The Classical Archaeology of Greece: Experiences of the Discipline.* London: Routledge.

Schlesier, Renate. 2011. *A Different God? Dionysos and Ancient Polytheism.* Berlin: De Gruyter.

Sherratt, Susan, and Andrew Sherratt. 1991. 'From luxuries to commodities: the nature of Mediterranean Bronze Age trading systems.' *Bronze Age trade in the Mediterranean*; edited by N.H. Gale. Jonsered: P. Åström. 351-386.

------.1993. 'The growth of the Mediterranean economy in the Early First Millennium BC.' *World Archaeology, Vol.* 24, No. 3. Ancient Trade: New Perspectives. London: Taylor & Francis. 361-378.

Simantoni Bournia, Eva. 2004. *La céramique grecque à reliefs. Ateliers insulaires du VIII au VI siècle avant J.C.* Hautes Études du monde Gréco-Romain, III, 32. Genève: Droz.

Sirano, Francesco. 2008. 'Identità culturali nella Campania settentrionale: un aggiornamento.' *Dalle sorgenti alla foce Il bacino del Liri-Garigliano nell'antichità: culture, contatti, scambi. Atti del convegno, Frosinone-Formia 10-12 novembre 2005*, edited by Cristina Corsi and Eugenio Polito. Roma: Quasar. 37-59.

Sisci, Nicola. 2008. 'La Candelora a Montevergine, Nuove tradizioni e antichi diritti.' Videodocumentario Prodotto da Univerisità degli Studi di Napoli Federico II, in collaborazione con Sof-Tel. Napoli: Univerisità degli Studi di Napoli Federico II.

Smith, William. 1854. *Dictionary of Greek and Roman Geography.* London.

Snodgrass, Anthony M. 1964. *Early Greek armour and weapons, from the end of the bronze age to 600 B.C.* Edinburgh: University Press.

Sogliano, Antonio. 1925. 'Disegno storico della Campania antica.' *Atti della Società Italiana per il Progresso delle Scienze*, Vol. XIII. Roma. 262-270.

Solin, Heikki.1993. *Le inscrizioni antiche di Trebula, Caiatia e Cubulteria.* Caserta: Associazione storica del Caiatino.

Sommella, Paolo. 1967. *Forche Caudine in Antichi campi di battaglia in Italia: Contributi all'identificazione topografica di alcune battaglie d'età repubblicana.* Roma: De Luca.

Sophocles, and Francis Storr. 1913. *Sophocles: Ajax, Electra, Trachiniae, Philoctetes.* London: Heinemann.

Sophocles, and Alfred C. Pearson. 1963. *The Fragments of Sophocles.* Amsterdam: Hakkert.

Sophocleus, Sophocles. 1985. 'L'Aphrodite en tant qu' androgyne.' *Archaeologia Cypria*, I. Nicosia: Association of Cypriot Archaeologists. 79-96.

------. 1985. *Atlas des représentations chypro-archaïques des divinités. Studies in Mediterranean Archaeology.* Göteborg : P. Åström.

Sørensen, Lone Wriedt. 1997. 'Traveling pottery connections between Cyprus, the Levant and the Greek world in the Iron Age.' *Res Maritimae – Cyprus and the Eastern Mediterranean from Prehistory to Late Antiquity*; edited by S.Swiny, R. L. Hohlfelder, and H. W. Swiny. Atlanta: Scholars Press. 285-299.

------. 2015. 'Here There be Monsters. Hybrids Painted on Cypriot Iron Age Pottery.' *Tradition: Transmission of Culture in the Ancient World*; edited by Jane Feifer, Mette Moltesen, and Annette Rathje. Acta Hyperborea, 14. Copenhagen: Collegium Hyperboreum and Museum Tusculanum Press. 427-450

Sourvinou-Inwood, Christiane. 1996. *'Reading' Greek Death to the End of the Classical Period.* Oxford: University Press.

Spalinger, Anthony. 1976. 'Psametichus, King of Egypt: I.' *Journal of the American Research Center in Egypt*, Vol. 13. Boston, MA: American Research Center in Egypt.133-147.

Spanheim, Ezechiel. 1664. *Dissertatio de praestantia et usu numismatum antiquorum.* Romae: Apud Blasium Deuersin.

Spasić, Miloš. 2012. 'Cattle to settle – bull to rule: on bovine iconography among Late Neolithic Vinca culture communities.' *Documenta Praehistorica*, XXXIX. Ljubljana: Filozofska fakulteta, Oddelek za arheologijo. 295-308.

Spatafora, Francesca. 2000. 'Indigeni, Punici e Greci sulla Montagnola di Marineo e nella valle dell'Eleuterio.' *Atti delle Terze Giornate Internazionali di Studi sull'Area Elima, Gibellina - Erice - Contessa Entellina 1997.* Pisa: Scuola Normale Superiore. 895-918.

------. 2010. 'Indigeni e Greci negli emporia fenici della Sicilia occidentale.' *Meetings between cultures in the ancient Mediterranean, 17th International Congress of Classical Archaeology (Rome, 22-26 September 2008).* Bollettino di Archeologia Online, I, 2010, Volume speciale A/A5/4. Roma: Direzione Generale per le Antichità. 34-46.

------. 2012. 'Le Vie dell'acqua: città e villaggi nelle vallate fluviali della Sicilia centro-occidentale tra Età Arcaica ed Ellenismo.' *Cultura e religione delle acque Atti del Convegno interdisciplinare, Qui fresca l'acqua mormora... (S. Quasimodo, Sapph. fr. 2,5) Messina 29-30 marzo 2012;* edited by A. Calderone. Roma: Bretschneider. 301-313.

Sporn, Katja. 2013. 'Mapping Greek Sacred Caves: Sources, Features, Cults.' *Stable Places and Changing Perceptions: Cave Archaeology in Greece*; edited by F. Mavridis and Jensen J. Tae Jensen. Oxford: Archaeopress. 202-216.

Spycket, Agnès. 1981. *La statuaire du Proche-Orient ancien.* Leiden: Brill.

Staccioli, Romolo Augusto. 1980. 'Le finte porte dipinte nelle tombe arcaiche etrusche.' *Quaderni dell'Istituto di archeologia e storia antica, Università di Chieti*, Vol. 1. Roma: Viella. 1-17.

Statius, P. Papinius, and D. R. Shackleton Bailey. 2003. *Silvae.* Cambridge: Harvard University Press.

Stazio, Attilio. 2011. 'Monete a leggenda Irnthi.' *Scritti di Numismatica.* Taranto-Foggia: C. Grenzi (reprint of the original 1990 essay). 394-401.

Steadman, Sharon R., and Gregory McMahon (eds.) 2011. *The Oxford Handbook of Ancient Anatolia: (10,000-323 BCE.)* Oxford: University Press.

Stein, Gil J. 2010. 'Local Identities and Interaction Spheres: Modeling Regional Variation in the Ubaid Horizon.' *Beyond the Ubaid: Transformation and Integration in the Late Prehistoric Societies of the Middle East*; edited by R.A. Carter and G. Philip. Chicago: The Oriental Institute. 23-44.

Stelluti, Napoleone. 2011. 'Monete della zecca di Frentrum, Larinum e Pallanum.' *Proceedings of the 14th International Numismatic Congress, Glasgow 2009*, Vol.I, edited by Nicholas Holmes. London: Spink. 1056-1064.

------. 2015. *Monete della zecca di Aesernia, Venafrum, Bonavium, Aquilonia e Bellum Sociale.* Campobasso: Tipolitografia Fotolampo.

Sternberg, Henry. R. 1976. 'Die Silberprägung von Laos ca. 510-440 v. Chr.' *Proceedings of the 8th International Congress of Numismatics, New York - Washington September 1973*; edited by Herbert Adolph Cahn and Georges Le Rider. Paris: International Association of Professional Numismatists. 143-162.

Stein-Hölkeskamp, Elka. 1989. *Adelskultur und Polisgesellschaft: Studien zum griechischen Adel in archaischer und klassischer Zeit.* Stuttgart: Steiner.

Stibbe Twist, Annek. 1978. 'Herakles in Etrurien.' *Thiasos. Sieben archäologische Arbeiten*; edited by T. Lorenz. Amsterdam: J.E. Zeylmans van Emmichoven. 80-107.

Stillwell, Richard, et al. 1976. *The Princeton Encyclopedia of Classical Sites*. Princeton, N.J.: Princeton University Press.

Stoll, Heinrich W.1886. 'Acheloos.' *Ausführliches Lexikon der griechischen und römischen Mythologie*; edited by Wilhelm Heinrich Roscher. Leipzig: B.G. Teubner.

Strabo, H.C. Hamilton, and W. Falconer. 1903. *The Geography of Strabo*. London: George Bell & Sons.

Strazzulla, Maria Josè. 2002. 'La tegola con Acheloo.' *Il Santuario della Musica e il Bosco Sacro di Anna Perenna*. Roma: Electa. 79-83.

Strazzullo, Franco. 1984. 'Il carteggio Martorelli-Vargas Macciucca.' *Settecento napoletano: documenti II.* Napoli: Liguori.

Streber, Franz. 1838. 'Über den Stier mit dem Menschengesichte auf den Münzen von Unteritalien und Sicilien.' *K. Akademie der wissenschaften, Munich. Philosophisch-philologische classe. Abhandlung.* München: Verlag der Akademie. 454-555.

Summerer, Latife. 2014. 'Topographies of Worship in Northern Anatolia.' *Space, Place and Identity in Northern Anatolia;* edited by Tonnes Bekker-Nielsen. Geographica Historica, Vol 29. Stuttgart: Steiner. 189-213.

Sutherland, Carol H.V.1984. *The Roman Imperial Coinage, Vol I, From 39 BC to AD 69*. London: Spink.

Szasz, Thomas Stephen. 2001. *Pharmacracy: Medicine and Politics in America*. Westport, Conn: Praeger.

Tagliamonte, Gianluca. 1994. *I figli di Marte: mobilità, mercenari e mercenariato italici in Magna Grecia e Sicilia*. Roma: Bretschneider.

------. 1999. 'Rapporti tra società di immigrazione e mercenari italici nella Sicilia greca del IV secolo a.C.' *Confini e frontiera nella Grecia d'Occidente. Atti del trentasettesimo convegno di studi sulla Magna Grecia, Taranto 3-6 ottobre 1997*. Napoli: Arte Tipografica. 547-572.

Tahberer, Bekircan. 2012. 'Astragaloi on Ancient Coins: Game Pieces or Agents of Prophecy?.' *The Celator*, Vol.26, No.4. Lancaster, PA: Kerry Wetterstrom. 4-20.

Talamo, Pierfrancesco. 1987. *L'area aurunca nel quadro dell'Italia centromeridionale. Testimonianze archeologiche di eta` arcaica*. Oxford: BAR, International Series.

Taliano-Grasso, Armando. 1995. 'La presenza brettia sul Traente attraverso nuovi documenti monetali.' *I Brettii. Cultura, Lingua e Documentazione Storico-Archeologica*. Soveria Mannelli: Rubbettino. 197-205.

------. 1999. 'Riflessioni sull'etnonimo dei Brettii.' *Aitna. Quaderni di topografia antica*, Vol.3. Catania: Greco. 181-190.

Taliercio Mensitieri, Marina. 1987. 'Il bronzo di Neapolis.' *La monetazione di Neapolis nella Campania antica: atti del VII Convegno del Centro internazionale di studi numismatici, Napoli 20-24 aprile 1980*; edited by Attilio Stazio, Marina Taliercio Mensitieri, and Valeria Zagli. Napoli: Arte Tipografica. 219-373.

Tanda, Giuseppa. 1977. *Arte preistorica in Sardegna. Le figurazioni taurine scolpite dell'Algherese nel quadro delle rappresentazioni figurate degli ipogei sardi a 'domus de janas'*. Quaderni della Soprintendenza Archeologica per le province di Sassari e Nuoro, No. 5. Sassari: Soprintendenza ai Beni Archeologici per le province di Sassari e Nuoro.

------. 1983. 'Arte e religione in Sardegna. Rapporti fra i dati monumentali e gli elementi della cultura materiale (Nota preliminare).' *Atti del Valcamonica Symposium 'International Symposium on the Intellectual Expressions of Prehistoric Man: Art and Religion.' Valcamonica, 28 july-3 August 1979, Capo di Ponte*; edited by Antonio Beltrán Martínez. Brescia: Edizioni del Centro. 261-279.

------. 2000. 'L'ipogeismo in Sardegna: Arte, Simbologia, Religione.' *L'ipogeismo nel Mediterraneo: origini, sviluppo, quadri culturali: atti del Congresso internazionale, 23- 28 maggio 1994, Sassari-Oristano.* Università degli studi di Sassari, Facoltà di Lettere e filosofia, Istituto di Antichità, Arte e Discipline Etnodemologiche e Dipartimento di Scienze Umanistiche e dell'Antichità, Vol 1 Sassari: Stampacolor. 399-425.

------. 2012. 'L'Arte del Neolitico recente in Sardegna: origine, sviluppo ed esiti finali.' *Preistoria Alpina*, 46, I. Trento: Edizione del Museo di Scienze Naturali. 133-152.

Taramelli, Antonio. 1915. 'Il tempio nuragico ed i monumenti primitivi di S. Vittoria di Serri (Cagliari).' *Monumenti Antichi pubblicati per cura della Reale Accademia dei Lincei*, Vol. XXIII, No.1 (1915-1916). Roma: tip. Della R. Accademia dei Lincei. 313-440.

------. 1922. 'Nuovi scavi nel santuario nuragico presso la chiesa di Santa Maria della Vittoria sull'altopiano della Giara.' *Notizie degli Scavi di Antichità. 1922, Fasc. 7-8-9*. Roma: Accademia Nazionale dei Lincei. 296-334.

------. 1924. 'Perfugas. Tempietto a pozzo di carattere preromano scoperto nell'abitato.' *Notizie degli Scavi di Antichità*, Fasc. 10-11-12 Roma: Accademia Nazionale dei Lincei. 522–533.

------. 1933. 'Tempietto protosardo nel Camposanto di Olmedo (Sassari).' *Bullettino di Paletnologia Italiana*, Vol. 53. Roma: Museo preistorico etnografico. 110–122.

Tasso, Annalisa. 2013. *Pylai aidao: un percorso iconografico e letterario sulla diffusione del tema delle Porte dell'Ade da oriente a occidente*. Oxford : Archaeopress.

Taylor, John H. 2001. *Death and the Afterlife in Ancient Egypt*. London: The British Museum Press.

Taylor, Rabun. 2009. 'River Raptures: Containment and Control of Water in Greek and Roman Constructions of Identity.' *The Nature and Function of Water, Baths, and Hygiene from Antiquity through the Renaissance*; edited by C. Kosso and A. Scott. Leiden: Brill. 21-42.

------. Forthcoming. 'Chapter Three - The Early Coinage of Neapolis.' *A Documentary History of Naples: Ancient Naples*. University of Texas at Austin, Working Paper Series. Accessed September 2010.

Teissier Beatrice. 1984. *Ancient Near Eastern Cylinder Seals from the Marcopolic Collection*. Berkeley.

Terzani, Cristiana and Maurizio Matteini Chiari. 1997. *Isernia: la necropolis romana in località Quadrelle*. Rome: Gangemi.

Testa, Antonella. 1983. 'Considerazioni sull'uso del candelabro in Etruria nel V e IV sec.' *Melanges de l'Ecole Francaise de Rome. Antiquité*, Vol.95, No.2. Paris: De Boccard. 599-616.

Thucydides, and Steven Lattimore. 1998. *The Peloponesian War*. Indianapolis: Hackett.

Tiné, Santo. 1963. 'L'origine delle tombe a forno della Sicilia.' *Kokalos. Studi pubblicati dall'Istituto di storia antica dell'Università di Palermo,* Vol. IX. Palermo: Banco di Sicilia. 73-92.

Tondo, Luigi. 1991. 'Riflessi numismatici della vittoria di Dionysos.' *Dionysos. Mito e mistero, Atti del convegno internazionale, Comacchio 3-5 novembre 1989*; edited by F. Berti. Ferrara: Liberty House. 209-215.

Torelli, Mario. 1991. 'L'acqua degli Etruschi dalle forme ideologiche alle pratiche sociali.' *Gli Etruschi maestri di idraulica*; edited by M. Bergamini. Perugia: Electa. 19-28.

Tritsch, Franz J. 1943. 'False Doors on Tombs.' *Journal of Hellenic Studies*, No. 63. London: The Council for the Society for the Promotion of Hellenic Studies. 113-115.

Trombi, Caterina. 2003. 'Il materiale indigeno presente nelle colonie Greche di Sicilia. La Sicilia occidentale. Parte I.' *Quaderni di Archeologia. Università di Messina* No. 3. Soveria Mannelli: Rubbettino. 91-111.

Tropea, Giacomo. 1901. 'Numismatica siceliota del Museo Mandralisca in Cefalù (Palermo), classificata e descritta.' *Archivio Storico Messinese,* Vol. I, 3-4. Messina: Tipografia d'Amico. 146-176.

Troxell, Hyla A., and William F. Spengler. 1969. 'A hoard of early Greek coins from Afghanistan.' *American Numismatic Society. Museum Notes*, No.15. New York: American Numismatic Society. 1-19.

Trucco, Flavia, Daniela De Angelis, and Cristiano Iaia. 2001. 'Villa Bruschi Falgari: il sepolcreto villanoviano.' *Tarquinia Etrusca. Una nuova storia. Catalogo della Mostra*; edited by A.M. Moretti Sgubini. Roma: Bretschneider. 81-93.

Tsantsanoglou, Kyriakos. 1997. 'The First Columns of the Derveni Papyrus and their Religious Significance.' *Studies on the Derveni Papyrus*, edited by André Laks and Glenn W. Most. Oxford: Clarendon. 93-128.

Tusa, Vincenzo. 1971. 'Le Necropoli di Selinunte.' *Odeon e altri monumenti archeologici*; edited by V. Tusa. Palermo: Banco di Sicilia. 175-178.

------. 1990. 'Il territorio degli Elimi. Stato attuale degli studi e delle ricerche.' *Gli Elimi e l'area Elima fino all'inizio della I guerra punica. Atti del Seminario di Studi. Palermo - Contessa Entellina 25-28 maggio 1989;* edited by Giuseppe Nenci, Sebastiano Tusa, Vincenzo Tusa. Palermo: Società Siciliana per la Storia Patria. 9-15.

Tykot, Robert H. 1994. 'Radiocarbon Dating and absolute Chronology in Sardinia and Corsica.' *Radiocarbon Dating and Italian Prehistory. Accordia Specialist Studies on Italy*, Vol. 3; edited by R. Skeates and R. D. Whitehouse. London: Accordia. 115-145.

Ugas, Giovanni. 2000. 'Strutture insediative seminterrate e ipogeismo sepolcrale nella Sardegna Preistorica.' *L'ipogeismo nel Mediterraneo: origini, sviluppo, quadri culturali: atti del Congresso internazionale, 23- 28 maggio 1994, Sassari-Oristano*. Università degli studi di Sassari, Facoltà di Lettere e filosofia, Istituto di Antichità, Arte e Discipline Etnodemologiche e Dipartimento di Scienze Umanistiche e dell'Antichità, Vol. II. Sassari: Stampacolor. 887-908.

------. 2005. *L'Alba dei Nuraghi*. Cagliari: Fabula.

Uggeri, Giovanni. 2015. 'Aesernia.' *Brill's New Pauly*. Brill Online.

United States Geological Survey. 2005. 'Magnitude 9.1 – Off the West Coast of Northern Sumatra.' U.S. Dept. of the Interior, Geological Survey. Online Report. Washington, DC: U.S. Dept. of the Interior.

University of Pennsylvania Museum of Archaeology and Anthropology. 2013. *Iraq's Ancient Past: Rediscovering Ur's Royal Cemetery.* Exhibit. Philadelphia: University of Pennsylvania Museum of Archaeology. Online publication: http://www.penn.museum/sites/iraq/?page_id=58 (accessed Spring 2016)

Usai, Luisanna. 2012. 'Il complesso cultuale di Santa Vittoria-Serri.' *Simbolo di un simbolo: i modelli di nuraghe*; edited by F. Campus and V. Leonelli. Monteriggioni: ARA edizioni. 314–322.

Vagi, David. 2013. 'Rome's First Didrachm in Light of the *foedus Neapolitanum* and the *equus October*.' *Essays in Honor of Roberto Russo*, edited by P.G. van Alfen and R.B. Witschonke. Zürich: Numismatica Ars Classica. 73-94.

Vagnetti, Lucia. 1968. 'I bacili di Bronzo di Caldare sono Ciprioti?.' *Studi Micenei ed Egeo-Anatolici*, Vol. 7. Roma: Edizioni dell'Ateneo. 129-138.

Valk, Marchinus van der. 1963. *Researches on the Text and Scholia of the Iliad*. Leiden: Brill.

Valerio, Paolo, Nicola Sisci, and Serena Ferrara. 2009. 'The Myth of Cibele and Attis: New Theoretical Hypothesis about Transsexualism.' *Childhood-Adulthood, Culture and Brain. The World Professional Association for Transgender Health, WPATH XXI Biennial Symposium*. Oslo. 82.

------, Nicola Sisci, Serena Ferrara, and Aurora Cuomo. 2009. 'A Particular Expression of Gender Identity in Italian Southern Culture: The Neapolitan Femminielli.' *Childhood-Adulthood, Culture and Brain. The World Professional Association for Transgender Health, WPATH 2009 XXI Biennial Symposium*. Oslo. 79.

Van Berchem, Denis. 1967. 'Sanctuaires d'Hercule Melqart. Contribution à l'étude de l'expansion phénicienne en Méditerranée.' *Syria: Revue d'art oriental et d'archéologie*, Vol. 44. Paris: P. Geuthner. 73-109.

Van De Mieroop, Marc. 2005. 'The Eastern Mediterranean in early antiquity.' *Rethinking the Mediterranean*; edited by W.V.Harris. Oxford: University Press. 117-140.

Van Dijk, Renate M. 2011. *The Motif of the Bull in the Ancient Near East: An Iconographic Study*. Unpublished MA Thesis, University of South Africa.

Vanschoonwinkel, Jacques. 1982. 'La barque dans le culte et la religion cretomyceniens.' *Revue des archeologues et historiens d'art de Louvain*, No.15. Louvain: Institut Supérieur d'Archéologie et d'Histoire de l'Art. 20-56.

Van Straten, Folkert T. 1981. 'Gifts for the Gods.' *Faith, Hope and Worship: Aspects of Religious Mentality in the Ancient World*; edited by Hendrik S. Versnel. Leiden: Brill. 65-151.

------ (ed.). 1995. *Hiera kala: Images of Animal Sacrifice in Archaic and Classical Greece*. Leiden: Brill.

Vargas Macciucca, Duca Michele. 1764. *Dell'Antiche colonie venute in Napoli, ed i primi si furono i Fenici [ed i secondi furono gli Euboici], opera del duca Michele Vargas Macciucca*. Napoli: Simoni.

Vecchi, Italo. 1997. *Nvmmorvm Avctiones*, 5. London: Italo Vecchi Ltd.

------. 2012. *Etruscan Coinage*. Milano: Ennerre.

Ventriglia, Alessia. 2010. 'L'Osco: un esempio perfetto di integrazione etnica e culturale.' *Seminario Scuola Normale Superiore di Pisa, 22 giugno 2010*. Congress Presentation.

Vermeule, Cornelius C. 1960. 'Greek, Etruscan and Roman Bronzes Acquired by the Museum of Fine Arts, Boston.' *The Classical Journal*, Vol. 55, No. 5. Cambridge: University Press. 193-204.

------, and Jerome M. Eisenberg. 1992. *Catalogue of the Greek, Etruscan, and Roman Bronzes in the Collection of John Kluge*. New York and Boston.

Veronese, Francesca. 2006. *Lo spazio e la dimensione del sacro. Santuari e territorio nella Sicilia arcaica*. Padova: Esedra.

Verzár, Monica. 1980. 'Pyrgi e l'Afrodite di Cipro considerazioni sul programma decorativo del tempio B.' *Mélanges de l'Ecole française de Rome. Antiquité*, T. 92, No.1. Paris: De Boccard. 35-86.

Viggiano, Gregory, and Hans Van Wees. 2013. 'The Arms, Armor, and Iconography of Early Greek Hoplite Warfare.' *Men of Bronze. Hoplite Warfare in Ancient Greece*; edited by Donald Kagan and Gregory Viggiano. Princeton: University Press. 57-73.

Villar, Francisco. 2008. *Gli indoeuropei e le origini dell' Europa: lingua e storia*. Bologna: Il Mulino.

Villaronga, Leandre. 2003. 'La troballa de l'Emporda.' *Acta Numismatica*, 33. Barcelona: Societat Catalana D'Estudis Numismàtics, Institut d'Estudis Catalans. 7-13.

------, and Jaume Benages. 2011. *Ancient Coinage of the Iberian Peninsula = Les monedes de l'edat antiga a la Península Ibèrica: Greek, Punic, Iberian, Roman*. Barcelona: Societat Catalana d'Estudis Numismàtics, Institut d'Estudis Catalans.

Villing, Alexandra, Marianne Bergeron, Giorgos Bourogiannis, and Alan Johnston. 2013. *Naukratis: Greeks in Egypt*. New York: Columbia University and the Metropolitan Museum of Art.

Viollet, Pierre-Louis. 2007. *Water Engineering in Ancient Civilizations: 5,000 Years of History*. International Association of Hydraulic Engineering and Research, Monograph Series. London: CRC Press.

Virgil, and C. Day Lewis. 1947. *The Georgics of Virgil*. Oxford: University Press.

Vitozzi, Giuseppina Capriotti. 2011. 'Elementi di tradizione egizia nella documentazione di Locri.' *Rivista di Studi Fenici*, Vol. XXXVI. Pisa-Roma: Fabrizio Serra. 109-128.

Von Dippe, Roger David. 2008. *The Origin and Development of Continuous Narrative in Roman Art, 300 B.C. - A.D. 200*. University of Southern California: UMI Microfilm 3291874, Doctoral Dissertation.

Von Fritze, Hans. 1912. 'Die Elektronprägung von Kyzikus.' *Nomisma*, VII. Thoune, CH: Chalet Wart.1-38.

Voskos, Iaonnis, and Arthur Bernard Knapp. 2008. 'Cyprus at the end of the Late Bronze Age: Crisis and Colonization or Continuity and Hybridization?.' *American Journal of Archaeology*, 112. New York: Macmillan 659-684.

Vullo, Mariasilvia. 2013. 'Produzioni specializzate di età arcaica a Policoro.' *Amphi Sirios Roas: Nuove ricerche su Eraclea e la Siritide*; edited by Massimo Osanna and Gabriel Zuchtriegel. Osanna: Venosa. 69-87.

Wachter, Johann Georg. 1740. *Archaeologia nummaria, continens praecognita nobilissimae artis, quae nummos antiquos interpretatur*. Lipsiae: Ex Officine Breitkopfiana.

Waggoner, Nancy, and Jonathan Rosen. 1983. *Early Greek Coins from the Collection of Jonathan P. Rosen*. New York: American Numismatic Society.

Waldbaum, Jane C. 1994. 'Early Greek contacts with the Southern Levant, ca. 1000-600 B.C.: the Eastern perspective.' *Bulletin of the American Schools of Oriental Research*, 293. South Hadley, MA: American Schools of Oriental Research. 53-66.

Wallensten, Jenny. 2008. 'Personal protection and tailor-made deities: the use of individual epithets.' *Kernos*, 21. Liège. 81-95.

Ward, William Haynes. 1910. *The seal cylinders of western Asia*. Washington: Carnegie.

Ward, William A. 1982. 'A Sumerian Motif on a Phoenician Seal.' *Archéologie au Levant. Recueil à la mémoire de Roger Saidah. Collection de la Maison de l'Orient méditerranéen. Série archéologique*, Vol. 12, No. 1. Paris: Boccard. 221-224.

Waser, Otto. 1909. 'Flussgotter.' *Real-Encyclopadie der classischen Altertumswissenschaft,* Vol. 6. Stuttgart. 1774-2815.

Webb, Jennifer M. 1999. *Ritual Architecture, Iconography and Practice in the Late Cypriot Bronze Age.* Studies in Mediterranean Archaeology, Vol. 75. Lund: P. Åström.

------, and David Frankel. 2010. 'Social Strategies, Ritual and Cosmology in Early Bronze Age Cyprus: An Investigation of Burial Data from the North Coast.' *Levant*, 42, 2. London: Council for British Research in the Levant. 185-209.

Webster, Maud. 2014. *Water-temples of Sardinia: identification, inventory and interpretation*. Uppsala University. Deparment of Archaeology and Ancient History, Master's Degree Thesis, 2014.

Weege, Fritz. 1909. *Oskische Grabmalerei*. Berlin: Reimer.

Weiss, Carina. 1984. *Griechische Flussgottheiten in vorhellenistischer Zeit: Ikonographie und Bedeutung*. Würzburg: K. Triltsch.

------. 1988. 'Fluvii.' *Lexicon Iconographicum Mythologiae Classicae*. Vol. IV, 1. Zürich: Artemis. 139-148.

Weiss, Harvey. 1985. *Ebla to Damascus: Art and Archaeology of Ancient Syria: an Exhibition from the Directorate-General of Antiquities and Museums, Syrian Arab Republic*. Washington, D.C.: Smithsonian Institution Traveling Exhibition Service.

Wengrow, David. 2001. 'Rethinking 'Cattle Cults' in Early Egypt: Towards a Prehistoric Perspective on the Narmer Palette.' *Cambridge Archaeological Journal*, 11, 1. Cambridge: University Press. 91-104.

Wentzel, Georg. 1893. 'Acheloos.' *Paulys Realencyclopädie der classischen Altertumswissenschaft*. Stuttgart: Alfred Druckenmuller.

Werner, Daniel S. 2012. *Myth and Philosophy in Plato's Phaedrus*. Cambridge: Cambridge University Press.

West, Martin L. 1983. *The Orphic Poems*. Oxford: Clarendon.

------. 1997. 'Hocus-Pocus in East and West.' *Studies on the Derveni Papyrus*; edited by André Laks and Glenn
W. Most. Oxford: Clarendon. 81-90.

------. 1999. *The East Face of Helicon: West Asiatic Elements in Greek Poetry and Myth.* Oxford: Clarendon.

Westenholz, Ulla Koch. 2000. *Babylonian Liver Omens, the Chapters Manzāzu, Padānu and Pān tākalti of the Babylonian Extispicy Series Mainly from Aššurbanipal's Library.* The Carsten Niebuhr Institute of Near Eastern Studies. CNI Publications No. 25. Copenhagen: University Press.

Westerman, Ulla, and Gilbert Kenneth Jenkins. 1980. *The Coinage of Kamarina*. London: Royal Numismatic Society.

Wetterstrom, Wilma. 1993. 'Foraging and farming in Egypt: the transition from hunting and gathering to horticulture in the Nile Valley.' *The Archaeology of Africa: Food, Metals and Towns*; edited by T. Shaw et al. London: Routledge. 165-226.

Whitehouse, Ruth. 1992. *Underground Religion: Cult and Culture in Prehistoric Italy*. London: Accordia Research Centre.

Whittaker, Gordon. 2009. 'Milking the Udder of Heaven: A Note on Mesopotamian and Indo-Iranian Religious Imagery. ' *From Daēnā to Dîn. Religion, Kultur und Sprache in der iranischen Welt: Festschrift für Philip Kreyenbroek zum 60. Geburtstag*; edited by Christine Allison, Anke Joisten-Pruschke, and Antje Wendtland. Wiesbaden: Harrassowitz Verlag. 127-137.

Wiggermann, Frans A. M. 1986. *Babylonian Prophylactic Figures: the Ritual Texts*. Amsterdam: Free University Press.

------. 1992. *Mesopotamian Protective Spirits: the Ritual Texts*. Groningen: STYX & PP Publications.

------. 1992. 'Mythological foundations of Nature.' *Natural Phenomena: their meaning, depiction and description in the ancient Near East*; edited by D. W. J. Meijer. Amsterdam: North Holland. 279-306.

------. 1996 'Scenes from the Shadow Side.' *Mesopotamian Poetic Language: Sumerian and Akkadian*; edited by M. E. Vogelzang and H. L. J. Vanstiphout. Groningen: Styx. 207-230.

Williams, Dyfri. 2005. 'The beginnings of the so-called 'Pontic' Group and other Italian black-figure fabrics.' *Aeimnestos: miscellanea di studi per Mauro Cristofani*; edited by B. Adembri. Firenze: Centro Di. 352-360.

Woodard, Roger D. 2010. 'Phoinikēia grammata: an alphabet for the Greek language.' *A companion to the ancient Greek language*; edited by Egbert J. Bakker. Oxford: Blackwell Publishing. 25-46.

World Health Organization. 1998. '50 Facts: Global health situation and trends 1955-2025.' *World Health Report*. Geneva: World Health Organization. http://www.who.int/whr/1998/media_centre/50facts/en/.

Yon, Marguerite. 1987. *Studia Phoenicia*, Vol. V. Leuven: Peeters.

Young, Philip H. 2005. 'The Cypriot Aphrodite Cult: Paphos, Rantidi, and Saint Barnabas.' *Journal of Near Eastern Studies*, Vol. 64. Chicago: University Press. 23-44

Zaccagnini, Carlo. 1991. 'Nuragic Sardinia: metrological notes.' *Atti del secondo Congresso Internazionale di Studi Fenici e Punici. Roma, 9 - 14 novembre 1987;* edited by Enrico Acquaro. Istituto per la civiltà Fenicia e Punica. Collezione di Studi Fenici, Vol. 30. Roma: Consiglio Nazionale delle Ricerche. 343-347.

Zaccagnino, Cristiana. 2004. 'La ceramica di periodo orientalizzante.' *Science and Technology for Cultural Heritage*, 12. Pisa-Roma: Istituti Editoriali e Poligrafici Internazionali. 47-63.

Zancani Montuoro, Paola. 1949. 'Il fiume Lirino.' *La Parola del Passato*, Vol. IV. Napoli: G. Macchiaroli. 61-68.

------. 1985. 'Συρρεντόν Surrentum-Sorrento.' *Annali dell'Università degli Studi di Napoli 'L'Orientale.'* Rivista del Dipartimento del mondo classico. Sezione Linguistica, N.6. Napoli. 313-320.

------. 1990. 'Riepilogo sui rinvenimenti e sul culto del santuario.' *Punta della Campanella. Epigrafe rupestre osca e reperti vari dell'Athenaion.* Monumenti Antichi, Serie Miscellanea, III, 5. Roma: Accademia Nazionale dei Lincei. 257-259.

Zanini, Alessandro. 2012. 'Contributo alla rilettura della necropoli del Bronzo Finale di Milazzo – ME.' *Dai Ciclopi agli Ecisti. Società e territorio nella Sicilia preistorica e protostorica. Atti della XLI riunione scientifica San Cipirello (PA), 16-19 novembre 2006.* Firenze: Istituto Italiano di Preistoria e Protostoria. 895-904.

Zettler, Richard L., and Lee Horne. 1998. *Treasures from the Royal Tombs of Ur*. Philadelphia: University of Pennsylvania Museum.

Zifferero, Andrea. 1991. 'Forme di possesso della terra e tumuli orientalizzanti nell'Italia centrale tirrenica.' *The Archaeology of Power, Papers of the Fourth Conference of Italian Archaeology. London, January 1990.* Volume 1, 1. London: Accordia Research Centre. 107-134.

Zona, Mattia. 1820. *Calvi antica e moderna o sia memorie istoriche dell'antichissima città di Calvi.* Napoli: Miranda.

Zucca, Raimondo. 1988. *Il santuario nuragico di S. Vittoria di Serri.* Sardegna Archeologica, Guide e Itinerari, 7. Sassari: Delfino.

Numismatic catalog and collection references

Alteri: Alteri, Giancarlo. 2000. *Le antiche monete di Neapolis*. Napoli: Banco di Napoli.

AMNG I: Pick, Behrendt, and Kurt Regling. 1898-1910. *Die antiken Münzen von Dacien und Moesien. Die antiken Münzen Nord-Griechenlands*. Vol. I, Parts 1 and 2; edited by Friedrich Imhoof-Blumer. Berlin: Georg Reimer.

Arnold-Biucchi LIMC: Arnold Biucchi, Carmen. 1981. 'Alaisos.' *Lexicon Iconographicum Mythologiae Classicae*, Vol. I. Zürich: Artemis & Verlag.

Babelon-De Luynes: Babelon, Jean. 1924. *Catalogue de la collection de Luynes: monnaies grecques. Vol.I, Italie et Sicile.* Paris: Florange-Ciani.

BCD Akarnania: Münzen und Medaillen GmbH, Auction 23. *Sammlung BCD: Griechische Münzen Akarnaniens und Aitoliens Akarnanien.* Stuttgart. 18 October 2007.

BMC Italy: Poole, Reginald Stuart. 1873. *Catalogue of the Greek Coins in the British Museum: Italy.* London: Woodfall and Kinder.

BMC Sicily: Gardner, Percy and Barclay Vincent Head. 1876. *Catalogue of the Greek Coins in the British Museum: Sicily; edited by Reginald Stuart Poole. London: The Trustees of the British Museum.*

BMC Thessaly: Gardner, Percy. 1883. *Catalog of the Greek Coins in the British Museum : Thessaly to Aetolia; edited by Reginald Stuart Poole.* London: The Trustees of the British Museum.

BnF: Bibliothèque Nationale de France, Department of Coins, Medals and Antiques. Paris.

Buceti: Buceti, Giuseppe. 2010. *Monete, storia e topografia della Sicilia greca.* Messina: Ellegieffe.

Buceti 'inedite': Buceti, Giuseppe. 2008. *Alcune monete di bronzo inedite della Sicilia Greca.* Cassino: Diana.

Cammarata: Cammarata, Enzo. 1984. *Da Dionisio a Timoleonte. Problemi di Numismatica della Sicilia Antica.* Modica: La Grafica.

Campana: Campana, Alberto. 1992-2003. 'Corpus Nummorum Antiquae Italiae (Zecche minori).' *Panorama numismatico*. Nos. 57-178. Serravalle: Nomisma.

------. 2007. 'Aggiornamento al Corpus Nummorum Antiquae Italiae. Sicilia: Kersini.' *Monete Antiche*, No. 36. Cassino: Diana. 5-9.

------. 2007. 'Aggiornamento al Corpus Nummorum Antiquae Italiae. Samnium: Malies (300-275 a.C.).' *Popoli dell'Italia antica. Gentes Fortissimae Italiae. Samnium, Latium et Campania. Le antiche città scomparse. Atti del II Convegno San Vittore del Lazio, 28 ottobre, 2007.* Quaderni di Studi II dell'Associazione Culturale Italia Numismatica. Cassino. 267-271.

Carelli: Carelli, Francesco. 1850. *Francisci Carellii Nvmorvm Italiae Veteris*. Lipsiae: Wigand.

Castrizio: Castrizio, Daniele. 2000. *La monetazione mercenariale in Sicilia: strategie economiche e territoriali fra Dione e Timoleonte*. Soveria Mannelli: Rubbettino.

CNS: Calciati, Romolo. 1983-1987. *Corpus nummorum siculorum: la monetazione di bronzo. The bronze coinage*. 3 Volumes. Milano: Edizioni G.M.

Fiorelli: Fiorelli, Giuseppe. 1870. *Catalogo del Museo nazionale di Napoli: Medagliere,* Vol 1. Monete Greche. Napoli: Stabilimento tipografico in S.ta Teresa.

Frey-Kupper: Frey Kupper, Susanne. 2001. 'Ein 'neuer' Acheloos der Iaitiner. Ein Beitrag zur Erforschung der frühen Münzprägung von Iaitas.' *Zona Archeologica: Festschrift für Hans Peter Isler zum 60. Geburtstag*. Bonn: Dr. Rudolf Habelt GMBH. 159-173.

Garrucci: Garrucci, Raffaele. 1885. *Le monete della Italia Antica, raccolta generale del P. Raffaele Garrucci. Parte seconda: monete coniate.* Roma: Salviucci.

Graziano: Graziano Luigi. *Campaniae Nummis*. Unpublished Manuscript.

Grose-McClean: Grose, Sidney William. 1923. *Catalogue of the McClean Collection of Greek Coins*. Volume I: Western Europe, Magna Graecia, Sicily. Cambridge: University Press

Head: Head, Barclay Vincent. 1911. *Historia Numorum: A Manual of Greek Numismatics*. Oxford: Clarendon.

HM Frankfurt: Forshner, Gisela. 1986. *Die Münzen der Griechen in Italien und Sizilien. Die Bestande des Munzkabinetts. Historisches Museum Frankfurt am Main*. Melsungen: Gutenberg.

HN Italy: Rutter, N Keith. 2001. *Historia Nummorum: Italy*. London: British Museum Press.

Hoover HGC 2: Hoover, Oliver D. 2012. *Handbook of coins of sicily (including Lipara): civic, royal, Siculo-Punic, and Romano-Sicilian issues, sixth to first centuries BC*. Lancaster, PA: Class Numismatic Group.

Hoover HGC 4: Hoover, Oliver D. 2014. *Handbook of coins of Northern and Central Greece: Achaia Phthiotis, Ainis, Magnesia, Malis, Oita, Perrhaibia, Thessaly, Akarnania, Aitolia, Lokris, Phokis, Boiotia, Euboia, Attica, Megaris and Corinthia, sixth to first centuries BC*. Lancaster, PA: Classical Numismatic Group.

Hunterian: MacDonald, George. 1899. *Catalogue of Greek coins in the Hunterian Collection, University of Glasgow,* Vol.I. Glasgow.

Imhoof-Blumer: Imhoof-Blumer, Friedrich. 1878. *Die Münzen Akarnaniens*. Wien: Manz.

Imhoof-Blumer 'Fluss- und Meergötter': Imhoof-Blumer, Friedrich. 1924. 'Fluß- und Meergötter auf griechischen und römischen Münzen. (Personifikationen der Gewässer).' *Schweizerische Numismatische Rundschau*, Band 23. Bern: Schweizerische Numismatische Gesellschaft. 173-421.

KM Berlin: Dressel, Heinrich. 1894. *Konigliche Museen zu Berlin. Beschreibung der Antiken Münzen. Italien.* Berlin: Spemann.

Lafaille: Strauss, Pierre. 1990. *Collection Maurice Lafaille. Monnaies Grecques en Bronze*. Bâle: Monnaies et Médailles S.A.

Lazzarini: Lazzarini, Lorenzo. 2005. 'La Monetazione e il sito di Halykiai (Alicie).' *Schweizerische numismatische Rundschau,* Band 84. Bern: Schweizerische Numismatische Gesellschaft. 15-24.

Lindgren: Lindgren, Henry Clay. 1989. *Ancient Greek Bronze Coins: European Mints from the Lindgren Collection*. San Mateo, CA: Chrysopylon Publishers.

Minì: Minì, Adolfo. 1979. *Monete di bronzo della Sicilia antica*. Palermo: SicilCassa.

Mionnet I: Mionnet, Théodore Edme. 1806. Description de Médailles antiques Grecques et Romaines, Tome Premiere. Paris.

Mionnet, Suppl. III: Mionnet, Théodore Edme. 1824. *Description de médailles antiques, grecques et romaines, avec leur degré* de rareté et leur estimation*: ouvrage servant de catalogue à une suite de vingt mille empreintes en soufre prises sur les pièces originales*, Supplément, T. 3. Paris: Selbstverl.

Moretti: Cahn, Herbert Adolf., et al. 1988. *Griechischen Münzen aus Grossgriechenland und Sizilien. Antikenmuseum Basel und Sammlung Ludwig*. Basel.

Moustaka: Moustaka, Alikē. 1983. *Kulte und Mythen auf thessalischen Münzen*. Würzburg: Triltsch.

Naster-Hirsch: Naster, Paul. 1959. *La Collection Lucien de Hirsch*. Bruxelles: Cabinet des Médailles.

Pozzi: Boutin, Serge. 1979. *Catalogue des monnaies grecques antiques de l'ancienne collection Pozzi: monnaies frappées en Europe*. Maastricht: A.G. van der Dussen.

RBW: Russo, Roberto, and Alberto de Falco. 2013. *The RBW Collection of Roman Republican Coins*. Zürich: Numismatica Ars Classica AG.

RRC: Crawford, Michael H. 1974. *Roman Republican Coinage*. Cambridge: University Press.

Riccio: Riccio, Gennaro. 1852. *Repertorio, ossia descrizione e tassa delle monete di città antiche: compresse ne' poerimetri delle province componenti l'attuale regno delle Due Sicilie al di qua del Faro, con la enunciazione delle altre inedite o nuove, venute in luce dopo il decesso del cav. Carelli.* Napoli: Tramater.

Rogers: Rogers, Edgar. 1932. *The Copper Coinage of Thessaly*. London: Spink.

Salinas: Salinas, Antonino. 1867. *Le monete delle antiche città di Sicilia descritte e illustrate*. Palermo: Stabilimento tipografico di Francesco Lao.

Sambon: Sambon, Arthur. 1903. *Les monnaies antiques de l'Italie*. Paris: Bureaux du 'Musée'.

Santangelo (also Fiorelli): Fiorelli, Giuseppe. 1866. *Catalogo del Museo nazionale di Napoli: Collezione Santangelo,* Vol 1. Monete Greche. Napoli: Stabilimento tipografico in S.ta Teresa.

Santelli: Santelli, Giovanni. 2000. 'Monete d'epoca tardo-repubblicana della zecca siciliana di Segesta: le contromarche ed il motivo dell'aquila.' *Annotazioni Numismatiche,* Suppl. XV, anno 10°, serie III. Milano. 3-24.

Sestini: Sestini, D. 1829. *Descrizione d'alcune medaglie greche del museo del Signore Carlo d'Ottavio Fontana di Trieste, Parte Terza.* Firenze: G. Piatti.

SC: Bopearachchi, Osmund. 1999. 'The Seleukid Coins of Central Asia and the Bactra Mint.' *Travaux de Numismatique Grecques Offerts à Georges Le Rider*; edited by Michel Amandry and Silvia Hurter. London: Spink. 17-37.

SNG ANS (Panormos): Jaunzems, Eva. 1977. *Sylloge Nummorum Graecorum: the Collection of the American Numismatic Society.* Part 4, Sicily II: Galaria - Stiela. New York: The American Numismatic Society.

SNG ANS (Campanian Mints): Fisher, Joan E. 1969. *Sylloge Nummorum Graecorum: the Collection of the American Numismatic Society.* Part 1, Etruria - Calabria. New York: The American Numismatic Society.

SNG Ashmolean I: Milne, J.G. 1951. *Sylloge Nummorum Graecorum Vol. V, The Ashmolean Museum. Part 1, Evans Collection.* London: Published for the British Academy by Oxford University Press.

SNG Ashmolean Ia.1: 1962. *Sylloge Nummorum Graecorum Vol. V, The Ashmolean Museum. Part 1A, Italy: Etruria - Lucania (Thurium).* London: Published for the British Academy by Oxford University Press.

SNG Budapest: Torbàgyi, Melinda. 1992. *Sylloge Nummorum Graecorum Hungary: Budapest, Magyar Nemzeti Mùzeum, Vol. I : Hispania – Sicilia, Part 1 : Hispania – Apulia.* Milano : Edizioni Ennerre.

SNG Churchill: Churchill, Edward George Spencer, and Edward Stanley Gotch. 1931. *Sylloge Nummorum Graecorum Vol. 1, Part 1. The Collection of Capt. E.G. Spencer-Churchill, M.C., of Northwick Park.* London: Published for the British Academy by Oxford University Press.

SNG Cop: Niels Breitenstein, Willy Schwabacher, et al. 1981. *Sylloge Nummorum Graecorum. The Royal Collection of Coins and Medals, Danish National Museum. Vol. 1: Italy – Sicily.* West Milford: Sunrise Publications.

SNG Dreer: Moro, Gotbert. 1967. *Sylloge Nummorum Graecorum: Sammlung Dreer/Klagenfurt in Landesmuseum für Kärnten. I. Teil: Italien – Sizilien.* Klagenfurt: Geschichtsverein für Kärnten.

SNG Evelpidis: *Bank of Greece. 1970. Sylloge Nummorum Graecorum Grèce. Collection Réna H. Evelpidis. Athènes. Première partie: Italie – Sicilie – Thrace. Louvain: Imprimiere Orientaliste.*

SNG Firenze: Catalli, Fiorenzo. Forthcoming. *Sylloge Nummorum Graecorum Firenze. Arimunum-Terina.*

SNG Fitzwilliam: Heichelheim, Fritz M. 1947. *Sylloge Nummorum Graecorum Vol. IV, The Fitzwilliam Museum. Leake and Genera Collections, Part 2: Sicily - Thrace.* London: Published for the British Academy by Oxford University Press.

SNG France: Parente, Anna Rita, and Bibliothèque Nationale de France. 2003. *Sylloge nummorum Graecorum – France, 6: Département des Monnaies, Médailles et Antiques, Bibliothèque Nationale de France: Italie.* Part 1. Bologna: Editrice Compositori.

SNG Gale: Sheedy, Kenneth. 2008. *Sylloge Nummorum Graecorum Australia, Vol. I: The Gale Collection of South Italian Coins.* Sidney: Australian Centre for Ancient Numismatic Studies.

SNG Levante: Vecchi, Italo, Peter Weiss, and Edoardo Levante. 1986. *Sylloge Nummorum Graecorum: Switzerland.* Berne: Credit Suisse, Numismatic Department.

SNG Lewis: Carradice, Ian. 1972. *Sylloge Nummorum Graecorum, Great Britain, Vol. VI, Corpus Christi College Cambridge, The Lewis Collection Part I: The Greek and Hellenistic Coins.* London: Published for the British Academy by Oxford University Press.

SNG Lloyd: Robinson, Edward Stanley Gotch. 1933. *Sylloge Nummorum Graecorum, Great Britain, Vol. II, Lloyd Collection.* London: Published for the British Academy by Oxford University Press.

SNG Manchester: Healy, John F. 1986. *Sylloge Nummorum Graecorum Vol. VI, Manchester University Museum, The Raby and Güterbock Collections.* London: Published for the British Academy by Oxford University Press.

SNG Milano: Vismara, Novella (ed.) 1988-1998. *Sylloge Nummorum Graecorum: Italia.* Vol. I-IV. Milano: Civiche Raccolte Numismatiche.

SNG Morcom: Morcom, John. 1995. *Sylloge Nummorum Graecorum, Great Britain. Vol. X, The John Morcom Collection of Western Greek Bronze Coins.* London: Oxford University Press and Spink & Son.

SNG München (Campanian mints): Franke, P.R., and H. Küthmann (eds.). 1970. *Sylloge nummorum Graecorum, Deutschland: Staatliche Münzsammlung München.* Part 2. Berlin: Gebr. Mann.

SNG München (Sicilian mints): Franke, P.R., S. Grunauer von Hoerschelmann,et al (eds.). 1977-1980. *Sylloge nummorum Graecorum, Deutschland: Staatliche Münzsammlung München.* Parts 5-6. Berlin: Gebr. Mann.

SNG Sweden II: Westermark, Ulla. 1976. *Sylloge Nummorum Graecorum, SNG Sweden II, The Collection of the Royal Coin Cabinet, National Museum of Monetary History. Stockholm. Part I,*

Gallia - Sicily. Stockholm: The Royal Academy for History and Antiquities.

SNG Tübingen: Mannsperger, Dietrich. 1981. *Sylloge Nummorum Graecorum, Deutschland, Münzsammlung Universität Tübingen. Part 1, Hispania – Sikelia.* Berlin: Mann.

SNG von Aulock: Aulock, Hans von, and Gerhard Kleiner. 1960. *Sylloge Nummorum Graecorum Deutschland: Sammlung v. Aulock. Part 6: Ionia.* Berlin: Mann.

Stazio: Stazio, Attilio. 2011. 'Monete a leggenda Irnthi.' *Scritti di Numismatica.* Taranto-Foggia: C. Grenzi. (reprint of the original 1990 essay). 394-401.

Stelluti: Stelluti, Napoleone. 2015. *Monete della zecca di Aesernia, Venafrum, Bonavium, Aquilonia e Bellum Sociale.* Campobasso: Tipolitografia Fotolampo.

Taliano Grasso (1995): Taliano-Grasso, Armando. 1995. 'La presenza brettia sul Traente attraverso nuovi documenti monetali.' *I Brettii. Cultura, Lingua e Documentazione Storico-Archeologica.* Soveria Mannelli: Rubbettino. 197-205.

Taliercio: Taliercio Mensitieri, Marina. 1987. 'Il bronzo di Neapolis.' *La monetazione di Neapolis nella Campania antica: atti del VII Convegno del Centro internazionale di studi numismatici, Napoli 20-24 aprile 1980*; edited by Attilio Stazio, Marina Taliercio Mensitieri, and Valeria Zagli. Napoli: Arte Tipografica. 219-373.

Torino: *Fabretti,* Ariodante, Francesco *Rossi, and* Ridolfo Vittorio *Lanzone.* 1883. *Regio Museo di Torino. Monete Greche.* Torino: Paravia.

Tropea: Tropea, Giacomo. 1901. 'Numismatica siceliota del Museo Mandralisca in Cefalù (Palermo), classificata e descritta.' *Archivio Storico Messinese,* Vol. I, 3-4. Messina: Tipografia d'Amico. 146-176.

Virzi: Virzi, Thomas. c. 1907. *The Thomas Virzi Collection of Greek Bronzes.* Unpublished Manuscript.

Weber: Weber, Hermann, and Leonard Forrer. 1922. *The Weber Collection: Greek Coins.* London: Spink & Son.

Dealers and auction houses

ACR: ArtCoins Roma, Rome

AH Baldwin: AH Baldwin and Sons, London

Ancient Imports: Ancient Imports, Grand Marais, MN

Ancient Numismatic Enterprise: Ancient Numismatic Enterprise, Toronto

Artemide: Artemide Aste Slr, Dogana – Serravalle

Auctiones : Auctiones GmbH, Bern

Brunetti: London Ancient Coins Ltd, Essex

CNG: Classical Numismatic Group, Lancaster, PA

HJB: Harlan J. Berk, Chicago

Denant: Den of Antiquity, Cambridge

Dix Noonan Webb: Dix, Noonan, & Webb, London

Dr. Busso Peus: Dr. Busso Peus Nachfolger, Frankfurt am Main

Edgar L. Owen: Edgar L. Owen, Lake Hopatcong, NJ

Elsen: Jean Elsen & ses fils, Bruxelles

Forvm: Forvm Ancient Coins, Morehead City, NC

Gemini: Gemini Numismatic Auctions, LLC / Harlan J. Berk, Chicago

Gitbud & Naumann: Gitbud & Naumann, München

HD Rauch: HD Rauch, Vienna

Heritage: Heritage Auctions, Dallas, TX

Hirsch: Gerhard Hirsch Nachfolger, München

HJB: Harlan J. Berk, Chicago

InAsta: Inasta s.p.a., Serravalle

Jeneck H.E.: Jeneck Historical Enterprise, San Mateo, CA

Katane: Numismatica Katane, Catania

Künker: Fritz Rudolf Künker, Osnabrück

LAC: London Ancient Coins Ltd, Essex

Lanz: Numismatik Lanz, München

Leu: Bank Leu and Co., Zürich

LHS Numismatics: LHS Numismatics Ltd., Zürich

M&M GmbH: Munzen & Medaillen GmbH, Weil am Rhein

Münzen Ritter: Münzhandlung Ritter GmbH, Düsseldorf

NAC: Numismatica Ars Classica NAC AG, Zürich

Nomisma: Nomisma s.p.a., Serravalle

Nomos: Nomos AG, Zürich

Numismatica Fiorentina: Numismatica Fiorentina, Firenze

Numismatik Naumann: Numismatik Naumann GmbH, München

Obolos: Nomos AG, Zürich

Pecunem: Pecunem GmbH, München

Pegasi: Pegasi Numismatics, Holicong, PA

Roma: Roma Numismatics, London

Spink: Spink and Son, London

Sternberg: F. Sternberg, Zürich

Tintinna: Numismatica Tintinna, Scandiano, Italy

The New York Sale: Dmitry Markov Coins & Medals, New York

Walter Holt's Old Money: Walter Holt's Old Money, Bondi Junction, Australia

Index

(Including Numismatic Devices)

Normal font indicates terms appearing in the narratives. The main catalog sections for specific locations are in bold font. Italicized entries indicate the use as a numismatic device.